International Handbook
on
Mental Health Policy

International Handbook on Mental Health Policy

EDITED BY
DONNA R. KEMP

Foreword by
Eugene Brody

GREENWOOD PRESS
Westport, Connecticut • London

RA
790
.I55
1993

Library of Congress Cataloging-in-Publication Data

International handbook on mental health policy / edited by Donna R.
   Kemp ; foreword by Eugene Brody.
         p.   cm.
   Includes bibliographical references and index.
   ISBN 0–313–27567–X
   1. Mental health policy.   I. Kemp, Donna R.
   [DNLM: 1. Health Policy.   2. Mental Health Services—organization
& administration.   3. Mental Health Services—trends.   4. World
Health.   WA 540.1 I6345   1993]
   RA790.I55   1993
   362.2—dc20   92–48399
   DNLM/DLC
   for Library of Congress

British Library Cataloguing in Publication Data is available.

Library of Congress Catalog Card Number: 92–48399
ISBN: 0–313–27567–X

First published in 1993

Greenwood Press, 88 Post Road West, Westport, CT 06881
An imprint of Greenwood Publishing Group, Inc.

Printed in the United States of America

The paper used in this book complies with the
Permanent Paper Standard issued by the National
Information Standards Organization (Z39.48–1984).

10 9 8 7 6 5 4 3 2 1

To Gwen Lee and Vince, who awoke my interest in the mentally disabled; to all persons who suffer from mental disabilities; and to all family members, caregivers, and friends who have struggled to help their loved ones with mental disabilities and who have suffered from the consequences of those disabilities.

Contents

Tables and Figures

FIGURES

Preface

The *International Handbook on Mental Health Policy* is a reference book for mental health professionals, scholars, and students. Its focus is on mental health policy, including the extent of the problem; mental health history; policy, organization, and services in the 1980s and 1990s (current policy developments, current organization, current services, and mental health personnel and treatment); public policy process; special policy issues (the mentally ill and the mentally retarded, the mentally ill and substance abuse, the mentally disordered offender, deinstitutionalization, funding issues, and consumer rights); and conclusions and discussion. Its intent is to provide comparable information about mental health policy in a spectrum of countries, developed and developing, around the world.

The book is descriptive and analytical. As there is a lack of theory concerning comparative mental health policy internationally, this book is not theoretically based. Its structured description and analysis may help lead toward theory building. The book has been written by a variety of authors with very diverse backgrounds. Some of the authors are involved as practitioners delivering mental health services, others are involved in government agencies developing mental health policy and/or organizing mental health service delivery, and others are academics studying mental health policy. Some authors have been involved in the mental health field for over thirty years, while others have been specialists in public policy but have researched mental health policy in their country for the first time. Thus the viewpoints vary from a fresh outsider's view of mental health policy to viewpoints based on a high degree of specialty and long-term historical involvement with the area. Likewise, the authors come from diverse fields of study, including political science, psychology, sociology, social work, health sciences, medical sciences, and psychiatry. This means that there is a variety of viewpoints and approaches to discussing and analyzing the topic, and the chapters vary from mostly descriptive to highly analytical and prescriptive.

There have been many limitations for the authors in preparing their chapters. All of the authors have had limitations in respect to data. Even in the most developed countries there are problems with collection and interpretation of mental health data, and in some developing countries the data are virtually nonexistent or too highly inaccurate to be used to draw reasonably good conclusions. These problems will particularly be seen in the sections on the extent of the problem. The lack of accurate data can also clearly be seen in the sections on funding. In addition, some authors have been limited because their governments will not release some data, and in some countries, for political reasons, authors have had to be careful in the presentation of their criticism.

This project was begun in 1989, and because of difficulties in locating and maintaining contacts with authors, the chapters were over the period 1990 to 1992. While every effort has been made to update material prior to publication, as is the nature of edited volumes, there will be some variation in currency. This is also influenced by the fact that in several countries mental health policy is currently in a high degree of flux, with the situation changing rapidly over a period of weeks or months.

While no book can consider, in depth, mental health policy in all the countries of the world, this project originally hoped to cover approximately twenty-three countries. Over time, however, it became obvious that a smaller number of countries would be included. This resulted for two reasons. First, there were many difficulties in locating and maintaining contact with authors around the world, and while chapters had been completed for some countries, authors were unable to complete chapters in other countries, so a growing problem of a time lag began to occur between countries with completed chapters and countries whose chapters were not yet in draft. In order to prevent material from becoming dated and to avoid the need for major rewriting by original authors, it became clear that a final deadline had to be set for completion. This situation was aggravated by the changing world scene. For example, a chapter had been completed for the USSR at the time that that country, through political changes, became the Commonwealth of Independent States. This required modifying comments, but at the same time a complete rewrite was not possible because of the constantly changing nature of that governmental system. Less extreme situations involved countries like New Zealand, where a change in government brought about a change in the focus on mental health policy. Second, and most important, it became obvious that mental health policy was very complicated and diverse in many countries, and in order for authors to adequately describe and explain what was happening in their countries, many of the chapters would have to be longer than originally anticipated. This was true not only for some of the large countries that are highly complex in terms of their governmental systems and multiple provider and interest-group involvement, but also for some of the smaller countries that had experienced considerable change and had extensive sources for analysis available.

Consequently, the handbook covers twenty nations representing a range of political, social, and economic systems. These countries are diverse in terms of their industrialization, wealth, and historical contexts. The countries included are Argentina, Canada, Chile, India, Israel, Italy, Japan, Korea, the Netherlands, New Zealand, Nigeria, Pakistan, People's Republic of China, Romania, Russia and the Commonwealth of Independent States, Saudi Arabia, Turkey, the United Kingdom, the United States, and Zambia. Mental health policy is explored within each of these countries, and the editor and authors hope that their contributions will add to our knowledge about mental health policy around the world.

I wish to thank the Fulbright Foundation and the N.Z.-U.S. Educational Foundation for their sponsorship of my research at the Mental Health Foundation of New Zealand; Irv Schiffman, Chair of the Department of Political Science; and James Haehn, Dean of the College of Behavioral and Social Sciences, California State University, Chico, for assistance with funding for word processing of the manuscript; and Kathie Pendo and the university word-processing staff for the word processing of the manuscript. My special thanks goes to David Rochefort of Northeastern University who suggested this project; the editing staff of Greenwood Press, especially Mildred Vasan and Sasha Kintzler; and to the chapter authors.

Foreword

Mental health policies are diverse. That of any particular country is an aspect of its overall health policy, itself a subfield of its overall social policies and an inevitable reflection of the socially transmitted values at the heart of its culture. Decisions leading to social policy inevitably reflect insufficient data, unexpected events, and unsubstantiated assumptions. Further, no policy can be understood without reference to the political context in which it has developed, and the political process of debate and compromise through which it has been formulated. In short, mental health policies, just as other public policies, reflect the workings of something we might call "the policy process." This is the set of interactions through which individuals with social power are persuaded to support legislative, judicial, and regulatory decisions that will ultimately influence the nature of rational behavior and capacities, in this instance the well-being of its primary resource, its people. The compromises at which power-holders arrive reflect competing political philosophies and allegiances, personal status, values, market forces, perceptions of need, and varying demands upon limited resources.

Even more fundamentally, the national contexts in which policies emerge are continually influenced by demography: population growth and aging are fundamental determinants of social need and, hence, policy. They are influenced by the overall economic status of the nation and its ethnic composition. International influences come from commercial organizations, the intergovernmental system (i.e., the United Nations), and the voluntary, nongovernmental (NGO) sector, as well as world events impinging on various countries such as war and migration. The bulk of the world's migrants, economic as well as political, are moving from the developing to the developed nations, and this imposes additional burdens on health and mental health policy.

The International Handbook on Mental Health Policy represents a much needed effort to understand the nature and determinants of mental health policies throughout the world. Given the viscissitudes of process and context, what constitutes the bedrock of policy? To what end does the process within a particular context lead?

The most fundamental aspect of any health policy is access to care. Does it conceive of health care as a right or a privilege? How is its allocation balanced against the need for other life necessities? Is it justly apportioned, beneficently applied (for the benefit of the patient, not the family, profession, or state), and in a manner which protects individual autonomy? These are fundamental in a stable society, but under the emergency conditions which characterize many parts of the world this question is not central. The stark lack of subsistence resources has led many countries and international agencies, in the face of massive refugee streams, natural disasters, civil war, and famine to focus on policies aimed at simple life maintenance which have no place for other health concerns.

In more fortunate areas where resources are sufficient to permit access to mental health as well as other forms of health care, a leading policy question concerns quality assurance. The allocation of available resources remains crucial since appropriate diagnosis and treatment require facilities, supplies, trained personnel, and the kind of scientific and record-keeping establishment available to relatively few of the world's nations.

Prevention, essential to an enlightened national mental health policy, depends significantly on other facets of health care (e.g., prenatal and obstetrical and well-baby policies), as well as on more distal aspects of social policy (e.g., employment policies and social security for older people).

The policy issue to which most observers attribute at least as much importance as quality assurance concerns the human or civil rights of persons who become patients. The presence of restrictive or non-restrictive legislation and practices regarding persons considered mentally ill reflects tensions between historically reified political philosophies emphasizing individual rights and self-determination versus those emphasizing state (and professional) authority and paternalism. These issues are equally important for other aspects of health-related social policy (e.g., those bearing on reproductive freedom).

At the international level the major institutional influence on health departments and policies in the developing world is the World Health Organization (WHO), the health arm of the United Nations. While its policies are significant models for the less developed countries, which also depend upon it for consultation, they are less so for the industrialized democracies that are able to depend upon their own resources.

Perhaps the most powerful, unregulated, twentieth-century influence on health policy is the development of biomedical technology. This includes psychoactive drugs for treating psychiatric illness. Drug (''psychopharmacological'') treatment, aggressively promoted by commercial interests, has accelerated in the developing world at the expense of indigenous, community-based therapeutic and social-support approaches, and in the industrialized world at the expense of the psychotherapies. This development has been influenced both by the scientific and professional establishments, and the diminished availability of resources for interpersonal care. Thus, it is fostered by a simultaneous intensification of professional research on psychiatric diagnostic classification aiming at diagnosis-specific prescribing, and reduced emphasis on training for time-consuming, labor-intensive psychotherapy and counselling.

The traditional international voluntary health sector is exemplified by international nongovernmental organizations with a direct impact on health policy, such as International Planned Parenthood. In the mental health field, organized psychiatry in the Western industrial democracies has been confronted by a mental health consumerism that, at its core, is a patients' rights movement. This began to acquire international force with the first annual meeting of the European Regional Council (ERC) of the World Federation for Mental Health (WFMH) in Copenhagen in 1984, focused on compulsory hospitalization and treatment of persons defined as mentally ill. The views of that meeting, attended by government officials, lawyers, and jurists, as well as by health-professionals and volunteers, were transmitted to the Council of Europe which is concerned with the mental health legislation of all of its member countries. Since that time the policy influence of ERC/WFMH has been greatly increased and made visible through its designation as the leading nongovernmental organization in mental health in relation to the European Community. Much of its work has been aimed at upgrading mental care facilities in Europe, with particular reference to extending the influence of users (consumers). This fits the activities of WFMH in other parts of the world, often in collaboration with WHO or its agencies (e.g., PAHO, the Pan American Health Organization).

WFMH, established in 1948 soon after the second World War at the suggestion of the then Interim committee for WHO and the still fledgling United Nations Educational Scientific and Cultural Organization (UNESCO), is the oldest and the leading voluntary, nongovernmental, international, and interdisciplinary organization in the mental health field with representation in 106 countries. Accredited as a consultant in mental health to all of the major agencies of the United Nations, its first official recommendation, in 1949, was for the establishment of a mental health unit within the WHO, the precursor of what became its Division of Mental Health. It has continued its intimate consulting relation with United Nation agencies, and in the past decade has been the leading health NGO in ensuring the passage through the United Nations of resolutions affirming the rights of victims of violence, both legally and in the mental health arena, and the human rights of mentally ill persons and "the improvement of mental health care." As a consultant for UNESCO it has participated in a series of conferences on biomedical technology and human rights and the preparation of a volume on the subject.

Independently of the United Nations, WFMH's advocacy, education, and, in some instances, service in nearly every region of the world, have covered such policy issues in relation to mental health as the prevention of mental illness and ill-health, the mental health care of refugees and other migrants, the delivery of mental health care within primary care services, the impact of unemployment on youth, the prenatal period and infancy in relation to preventive health care, drug abuse, paternalism in medical care, adolescent pregnancy, the exploitation of children with special attention to child labor and prostitution, and women's health. Throughout it has continued its efforts to ensure the quality of care in mental health facilities and to protect human rights in relation to mental health.

This volume gives us a comprehensive look at mental health policy in countries throughout the world. Twenty national contexts are described in terms of the geographic, demographic, historical, societal, and cultural frameworks that contribute to their particular mental health policies, and the policy processes through which they were developed. There are clear expositions of major issues that affect mental health policy today including the state of epidemiological studies and adequate national statistics, the organization of mental health services and access to them, the allocation of financial and other resources, the relationships of policies regarding mental health and those concerned with mental retardation, substance abuse, and mentally disordered offenders; and the significance of the consumer (''user'') and civil rights movement within each country.

Professor Kemp and her contributing authors have tackled an important and difficult subject and we are pleased to contribute to the preparation of this volume.

Eugene Brody

International Handbook
on
Mental Health Policy

1

An Overview of Mental Health Policy from an International Perspective

Donna R. Kemp

There is much to be learned about mental health policy by looking at what has happened in the past in various countries and how that has changed over time and by looking at the similarities and differences in mental health policy in various countries today. An overview of the chapters in the *International Handbook on Mental Health Policy* reveals some interesting facts and issues concerning the state of mental health policy in the world.

EXTENT OF THE PROBLEM

Clearly, one of the major problems for the development of mental health policy in countries around the world is the lack of complete and accurate data on mental health on which to base decisions. All countries, even the most developed, have problems with mental health data. In Italy, the world's largest wine producer, reliable statistics on the incidence of alcoholism on a national level have not been available since the passage of Law 180, and estimates must be made from the rates of alcohol-related diseases (Ghirardelli & Lussetti, chap. 7). In Israel there are no current data on the extent of mental health problems because data are limited to hospital-admission data and a few clinical research studies (Yishai, chap. 6). In New Zealand also official data consist of the number of psychiatric patients in hospitals and annual rates of first psychiatric admissions and readmissions. Outpatient visits have not been recorded at the national level, and there is no estimate of what percentage of total mental disorders is represented by the psychiatric utilization rates. Thus, while treatment is increasingly occurring in the community, in many countries no national data reflect mental disorders and treatment in the community. For developing countries, this is a problem of enormous proportions. As the authors of the chapter on Argentina write: ''After all, if the country is currently unable to provide the means for adequate psychiatric care for its population, it should come as little surprise that it also lacks the resources for keeping accurate and verifiable statistics'' (Fiasche, Fiszbein, Gorelick, & Fakiel, chap. 2). Even in countries where supposedly modern studies have been made, questions may be raised about how those studies were actually conducted. For example, a 1976 law required reporting of data on mentally disordered people in Romania, and a longitudinal study was conducted for more than a decade, but methodological problems and lack of concordance with World Health Organization (WHO) and other data throw doubt upon the accuracy of the information (Diacicov, Tudorache, & Cîmpeanu, chap. 15).

However, what is also clear is that mental health problems are one of the major public health problems facing countries. For example, Canadian statistics estimate that one in eight Canadians will be hospitalized for mental illness at least once in their lifetime; mental illness is the second-leading cause of illness among general hospital patients twenty to forty-four years old; and suicide is the second-leading cause of death in Canadians fifteen to nineteen years of age (Lakaski, Wilmot, Lips, & Brown, chap. 3). In the former USSR in 1989, 18.1 cases of mental disorders were reported per 1,000 population, and 16.2 cases per 1,000 population were treated for chronic alcoholism or drug abuse. Mental disorders are the fourth reason for loss of work capability in the former USSR (Vartanyan, Yastrebov, Rotstein, Solokhina, Liberman, & Shevchencko, chap. 16). In the United States 18.7 percent of adult Americans have a diagnosable mental illness at some point during a six-month period; approximately one-third have been mentally ill sometime during their life; and approximately 25 percent of all hospital inpatient days are for diagnosed mental disorders (Hudson, chap. 20). It has been noted in Italy, as in other industrialized countries, that the suicide rate has been increasing over the last several years. Canada, with an aging population, is also expecting the number of cases of dementia, especially Alzheimer's disease, to double over the next twenty-five years. This is also a problem for other countries, such as the United States and Japan.

The data in numerous countries show that there are different mental health issues for men, women, and children and for different socioeconomic levels, urban areas, and rural areas. Such data also raise concerns about rates of overutilization, especially in psychiatric hospitals, by certain groups disadvantaged in societal power bases, such as women and minorities. This question can be raised concerning countries such as the United States, the United Kingdom, and New Zealand, among others. Problems related to mental health issues and socioeconomic concerns are primary for some countries. For example, the authors of the chapter on Argentina (chap. 2) tie over thirty years of socioeconomic deterioration in that country to rising mental health problems. Developing countries such as Pakistan and Korea may have a connection between their rapidly changing psychosocial environment and weakening traditional values and increased rates of mental disability. In India the weakening of the traditional family and social support systems is seen as increasing psychiatric problems in old age, particularly in urban areas (Sharma, chap. 5).

Israel has experienced the impact of societal problems in a different context, involving immigrants to Israel who have been uprooted from their countries of origin and must adjust to a new culture and face economic dislocation. Added to this problem is the fact that Israel has a large number of survivors of the Nazi Holocaust, and they and their children suffer problems related to the parents having undergone that experience (Yishai, chap. 6). Also, mental distress has been caused in some countries through their exposure to wars or other violence. This is a significant problem for a country like Israel, which has faced constant insecurity and frequent wars, and was also recently a problem for Saudia Arabia as a result of Desert Storm (al-Radi, chap. 17).

Underlying some of the issues concerning collection and analysis of data is the issue of what the definition of mental health is. This very definition is changing over time and around the world. Internationally standardized diagnostic categories are found in the *International Classification of Diseases*. In the United States mental illnesses are defined by the American Psychiatric Association's *Diagnostic and Statistical Manual of Mental Disorders*, third edition, revised, which is currently undergoing revision, and the methodologies developed for the Epidemiological Catchment Area surveys of the National Institute of Mental Health.

In the United Kingdom the question of prevalence is complicated by an ongoing debate over "the concepts that explain mental health and the language that best describes people's experience" (Goldie & Sayce, chap. 19). The term *distress* is becoming preferred to *illness*. This terminology is based on a preference for psychosocial over medical approaches, while in the United States there is a growing focus on the biomedical approach, with a heavy orientation to medicalization. For Argentina, the focus on the impact of the declining economy leads to the use of terminologies such as *economic major depression* and *psychiatry of poverty* (Fiasche, Fiszbein, Gorelick, & Fakiel, chap. 2). Thus it is difficult within countries as well as internationally to reach agreement on terms and definitions.

MENTAL HEALTH HISTORY

A look at the history of mental health policy in various countries shows that mental health policy has not been the same for all countries. While trends have swept through some countries, they may have come much later or not at all to other countries. In addition, culture, religion, and politics have clearly played a significant role in the development of mental health policy. Mental health history began hundreds of years ago. Chinese traditional medicine addressed mental function and disorders in ancient classical literature before 400 B.C.

Mental health problems were originally largely left to the family, and this remains the case for many people in some countries, like India, today. In countries like the Netherlands, mental health services developed from individual charity and government aid to the poor. Various asylums and detention homes developed from that framework. Religion has played a key role in some countries; for example, the involvement of the Protestant and Catholic churches in the Netherlands. Religion still plays a key role in mental health treatment in Saudi Arabia, where a religious therapist is involved in treating patients in accordance with Islamic beliefs (al-Radi, chap. 17). Sometimes the role of religion has been benign, as in the establishment of shelter and care, but other times it has been harmful, as when the person was perceived to be possessed of evil spirits that should be purged.

In Europe an institutional structure of asylums was developed, and the medical profession came to dominate mental illness by the mid-1800s, with mental health legislation appearing in France in 1838 and in England in 1844. Colonization by European countries led to establishment of mental asylums in other countries; for example, the British model of mental asylums was copied in India. Frequently, concepts begun in one country have been transferred to other countries. Traditionally in historic Russia the medical disease model served as the major model for mental disorders, and Russian psychiatry was heavily oriented to German and Scandinavian psychiatry. After World War II the viewpoints of the USSR became dominant throughout Eastern Europe. In Argentina asylums were developed in the 1800s, and by the early 1900s diagnoses were made according to the French school of psychiatry. In Turkey mental health policy was influenced particularly by Germany and France and later by neuropsychiatrists educated in the United States. Most of the industrialized nations have followed a pattern of the development and growth of mental hospitals that reached a peak during the mid-twentieth century and led to attempts at reform and development of community alternatives, while many developing countries have been influenced by European models.

Social control was often a major element in mental health policy in industrialized countries like Great Britain, and the philosophy was passed on to developing countries like Nigeria when they were colonies. In Saudi Arabia mentally ill persons were isolated from society and kept in houses known as *bimaristan* where they were treated as prisoners (al-Radi, chap. 17). Over time there has been a movement away from social control and toward developing patients' rights. Italy began a major mental health revolution in the 1960s focused on the development of therapeutic communities and involving a movement that worked inside the institutions, in contrast to British and American antipsychiatric movements that were more focused outside the institutions. Law 180, passed in Italy in 1978, became a model for other countries in the move to limit and eventually end the asylum. A number of countries, such as the Netherlands, the United Kingdom, and the United States, saw the growing antipsychiatry movement increase resistance to biological psychiatry and psychotropic drugs. However, while some countries began seeking to disband psychiatric hospitals, other countries were just beginning to build modern psychiatric hospitals. Saudi Arabia opened its first modern psychiatric hospital in 1962.

It has not been unusual for political philosophy to have a major impact on mental health systems. For example, in the former USSR a specific philosophy underpinned the operation of the mental health system. Psychiatry was seen as a branch of medicine, and priority was given to the view that medical aid was public and free within an exclusively state system with a highly centralized administration. Political theory also dictated the etiology of mental disease and led to the belief that the social reasons for mental disorder would tend to disappear under socialism. Thus it was expected that there would be a reduction of mental illness in the USSR (Vartanyan, Yastrebov, Rotstein, Solokhina, Liberman, & Shevchenko, chap. 16). The establishment of the Communist regime in Romania became a major turning point for that country's psychiatry. A generation of psychiatrists came under attack for their views, which were seen as dangerous to a new social order. This resulted in reeducation, deportation, death in labor camps, and execution. Survival in Romanian psychiatry became based on un-critical acceptance of Soviet psychopathology. The ideology focused on changing man's personality. In Romania this became Nicolae Ceauşescu's idea of the " 'New Man,' the perfect worker, highly productive in his profession, raising a family with many children, lacking any other political perspective than the Communist one—in general, an absolutely appropriate and perfectly performing person" (Diacicov, Tudorache, & Cîmpeanu, chap. 15). Any deviation from the standard was considered pathological, and mental illness was believed to be highly undesirable. This ideology led to ignoring development of the mental health care system, dismantling some of the existing system, missing and in-consistent statistics, and unreliable information. Such views also allowed for psychiatry to be used for political purposes. In such countries, and sometimes in other countries for other reasons, political dissidents have faced action by the mental health system.

In other cases, such as prestate Israel, mental illness has been ignored. Pioneers were listed as suffering from various physical diseases, but mental illness was not included. Those who could not cope often returned to their country of origin, and self-selection focused on the fit. Tolerance of mental problems was low, and mental health was neglected. The mass immigration of the 1950s ruled out self-selection and also brought in individuals suffering from battle stress. This led to greater development of mental health services, but a hospital and medical focus based on professional expertise of refugees from Europe, large numbers of immigrants, and massive demographic and cultural changes made community development difficult. Israel's uncertain security has led to the recognition of the impact of the stress of wars and threats of attacks upon the population and the importance of mental health and illness in relation to defense of the country. This has impacted mental health policy formation in that country (Yishai, chap. 6).

A stigma has been attached to mental illness that has continued in most countries as a significant problem and has a negative impact on policy development and resource allocation. This stigma appears in industrial countries and is also pervasive in developing countries such as Korea and Pakistan. In such developing countries the masses may still perceive mental disorders as caused by demonic influences or possession, and abuse and lack of treatment may be pervasive. In Saudi Arabia the popular view of mental illness is based on Islamic and traditional concepts and includes both modern and ancient views, including organic lesion in the brain, emotional trauma, instinctual inhibition, punishment from Allah for sins, evil eye, magic, and evil spirit or jinn (al-Radi, chap. 17). Over time, terms used to designate mental disorders tend to become pejorative, so periodically new names come into favor. For example, the term *patients* becomes *clients*, then *consumers* or *members*. However, in some places old, changed legislation continues terminology from earlier eras. For example, Pakistan still uses 1912 legislation that uses the term *lunatic*.

POLICY, ORGANIZATION, AND SERVICES IN THE 1980s AND 1990s

Current Policy Developments

In some countries mental health policy is in the process of redefinition. In Canada this means a new definition of mental health much broader than traditional definitions. The 1988 definition that may be read in chapter 3 reflects a number of themes, ''including psychological and social harmony and integration, quality of life and general well-being, self-actualization and growth, effective personal adaptation, and the mutual influences of the individual, the group, and the environment. Furthermore, it emphasizes the social context of mental health by explicitly indicating the importance of social justice and equality to mental well-being. The definition also recognizes that all individuals possess a capacity for mental health, whether or not they have a mental disorder'' (Lakaski, Wilmot, Lips, & Brown, chap. 3). This approach emphasizes the common needs of all and focuses on solidarity among those with mental disorders rather than emphasizing the growing divisions among mental health constituencies. This broad-based approach stresses the importance of social, psychological, and biological issues. Other countries also recognize the need for this broad approach to mental health. Argentina has broadened its definition of mental illness and mental health policy. This has been the result of socioeconomic deterioration and poverty (Fiasche, Fiszbein, Gorelick, & Fakiel, chap. 2). Included in Turkey's mental health policy is the promotion of healthy living conditions (Cifter, chap. 18). In countries like Israel psychiatric care is still defined basically in medical terms, although there is a growing trend toward recognizing a broader spectrum of mental health problems (Yishai, chap. 6).

Some countries, such as New Zealand, have been exploring problems with their piecemeal planning process and describing the problems they have found in their mental health policy and services. The set of criticisms developed in New Zealand could well apply to many other countries: a lack of national coordination; a lack of coordination between government departments; lack of adequate funding; lack of consultation; inappropriate management structures; and a lack of liaison and consultation between hospital and community services (Abbott & Kemp, chap. 11).

Health promotion and prevention of illness are major elements of some countries' approaches to mental health policy. Canada focuses on health promotion through fostering healthy, adaptive behaviors such as parenting practices, social skills development, and lifelong learning, and on the prevention of maladaptive behaviors such as alcohol and drug use, suicide, and child abuse. It also seeks the elimination of discrimination. Creating environments and policies that support these approaches is a high priority in Canada (Lakaski, Wilmot, Lips, & Brown, chap. 3). Since the return of democracy in 1984, Argentina also has focused on primary and secondary prevention (Fiasche, Fiszbein, Gorelick, & Fakiel, chap. 2).

In many countries there is a move to focus policy and services on the seriously and chronically mentally ill. Even in Canada, with its very broad-based mental health definition, there is a broad consensus to give the highest service priority to those with chronic and serious mental disorders. Such prioritization in countries is often driven by funding issues, and in many cases there may be little if any public funding to provide for mental health issues beyond the seriously and chronically mentally ill.

In numerous countries, including Turkey and the People's Republic of China, mental health policy includes the concept of integrating mental health with physical health. Nigeria in 1990 redefined its mental health policy to emphasize primary health care based on the 1978 Alma Ata declaration (Ilechukwu, chap. 12). The development of the new Canadian definition recognized this link and involved an examination from the mental health perspective of the three major health challenges that had been described in a 1986 paper: reducing inequities, increasing prevention, and enhancing coping (Lakaski, Wilmot, Lips, & Brown, chap. 3). In Italy the movement from mental hospitals to the community and general hospitals has brought closer integration of mental health with primary practice and other medical branches. But other countries continue with the isolation of mental health problems. For example, the author of the Korean chapter describes Korean policy as characterized by isolation in mental health facilities, and policy calls for building more mental hospitals (Kim, chap. 9). Of course, this approach could encourage further segregation of physical and mental health. In addition, there are other countries such as India that have a shortage of active treatment beds.

In countries like Canada that have developed extensive hospitalization services, current mental health policy usually calls for development of community alternatives. In Italy the community mental health center is the center of the psychiatric network. However, Italy, even after its major reform, has faced problems because the quality and distribution of services are not homogeneous (Ghirardelli & Lussetti, chap. 7). Application of this approach has been slow in some countries, for example, Japan. In that country the government's welfare policy has not supported the social rehabilitation of those with psychiatric disabilities, but has left it to psychiatric hospitals and family associations. Only in 1987 was Japan's mental health law revised to promote social rehabilitation. Not until 1988 was that legislation operational, and even then, problems with funding remained (Asai, chap. 8). In the People's Republic of China there is also a recent focus on developing community approaches and psychosocial rehabilitation programs that was encouraged by the establishment of the Chinese Mental Health Association in 1985, with a university association of psychological counselling branch and a psychotherapy and psychological counselling branch added in 1990 (Shen, chap. 14). Even where there has been more rapid movement in the direction of community alternatives, the results still are vastly varied.

Another core concept in mental health policy in countries like Turkey is decentralization of services. Such decentralization may or may not be associated with development of community alternatives and integrating mental and physical health. Countries with federal systems of government like Canada and the United States have long had systems that have allowed for different approaches in different parts of the country. Now most of Canada's provinces have identified priorities for their service systems, with priorities including chronically and seriously mentally ill; specialized care for children, youth, and the elderly; and prevention programs for high-risk groups (Lakaski, Wilmot, Lips, & Brown, chap. 3). Of course, along with this decentralization comes the need for coordination. Countries like Canada are striving to achieve coordination of services and service development.

Current Organization

Because of the federal system of government in many countries, jurisdiction over government activities is frequently divided among different levels of government. In Canada major roles are played by the federal, provincial, and territorial governments. The federal role is one of standard setting and regulatory processes. The provinces are responsible for health care delivery, including community mental health services. Even in countries like China with strong central planning, local mental health coordinating committees have been established in many provinces and cities. In many countries like Nigeria the central government's Ministry of Health, various professional health organizations, and medical schools play the major roles, while in other countries like the United States there are many government, voluntary, and profit-making organizations involved.

The definition of mental health plays an important role in the organization of mental health services. For example, in Israel the medical definition of mental health has determined the structure of services. In Turkey and other countries a lack of alternatives has determined the organization, as psychiatric treatment is mostly available in psychiatric hospitals.

Current Services

Mental health services are very diverse, but among the most frequently found services are psychiatric hospitals, psychiatric units in acute-care hospitals, mental health clinics, day hospitals, rehabilitation centers, residential services, consumer-aid projects, recreational programs, educational programs, psychological services in schools, and various office-based psychiatric and counselling services. Also, services may be specialized for various population subgroups such as the elderly, children, and minorities. But the extent, quality, and mix of these services vary widely from country to country, and services may also vary widely within a country. For example, in Argentina a much higher level of services is available in the major cities like Buenos Aires, Córdoba, and Rosario than in the rest of the country. In India also the distribution of psychiatric beds is very uneven among the states. In China occupational rehabilitation units have been established in urban areas and large cities, while in rural areas community home care services are the majority of the delivery system, with local primary health workers being trained to deliver services (Shen, chap. 14).

The quality of care in psychiatric hospitals varies widely. The authors of the chapter on Argentina view the care in asylums as deficient throughout that country (Fiasche, Fiszbein, Gorelick, & Fakiel, chap. 2). Also, there may be a considerable difference in private versus public care. In Israel the level of care in private mental hospitals is believed to be inferior to that in public hospitals; whereas in the United States the public psychiatric hospitals operated by the states are generally viewed as largely for low-income people, while those who can afford private care buy it in private facilities. While in Israel the government has a growing role in psychiatric hospital treatment, in the United States that role is in decline, and there frequently is a two-tier system of care, with those with insurance or able to pay frequently obtaining care in different settings than the poor who rely on public care.

Access to services in some countries such as Israel is an entitlement, while in other countries large parts of the population have no access. In India less than 10 percent of those needing urgent mental health care are able to receive it, and the situation is worse in rural areas (Sharma, chap. 5). In Turkey mental health services are also insufficient to meet the need (Cifter, chap. 18).

Mental Health Personnel and Treatment

There is a growing move away from the traditionally medically focused psychiatric professions such as psychiatrist and psychiatric nurse and toward other mental health professions, including psychologists, counselors, occupational therapists, and social workers. In the Netherlands general practitioners play a major role, as people with mental problems usually go to their general practitioner first. GPs in the Netherlands tend to serve as gatekeepers for mental health care, and they are viewed as quite successful at identifying problems of a psychological origin (Evers, Haveman, Jacobs, & Bijl, chap. 10), while in the United States such physicians are frequently seen as deficient in identifying and managing mental health problems.

Having an adequately trained care staff in psychiatric hospitals remains a problem in many countries. In Argentina psychiatric nursing staffs are composed mostly of unsupervised nurses' aides. Israel has had a major shortage of professional psychiatric staff of all kinds. Japan also has a shortage of labor in medical and other professional fields, and mental hospitals suffer from a shortage of nurses and other professionals. In Turkey an insufficient number of psychiatrists is made worse by their being located primarily in cities.

In Israel there is a cultural and social gap between mental health professionals and much of Israel's population. Most of the professional psychiatrists are of European origin, while more than half of the population is of Asian or African origin (Yishai, chap. 6). The United States has experienced a similar problem with insufficient availability of psychiatrists, leading in some places, and particularly in state psychiatric hospitals, to the use of immigrant psychiatrists with language difficulties and cultural differences. Some countries have lost many of their trained mental health personnel to other countries. Many of Argentina's psychiatrists and psychologists have emigrated to the United States, France, and Italy. The United States, Israel, and some other countries have also had difficulties in recruiting people into working in some mental health professions like psychiatry because the profession has a low status among other medical professions.

PUBLIC POLICY PROCESS

Elaborate formal structures for policy making are in place in some countries. Canada has a Conference of Ministers of Health, a Conference of Deputy Ministers of Health, and a number of advisory committees. The advisory-committee structure assists the Conference of Deputy Ministers by providing a consultative mechanism between the levels of government. There are advisory committees on mental health and alcohol and other drug problems. In China mental health policy is set at the national level as part of five-year plans, while in Saudi Arabia mental health policy also is very centralized in the Ministry of Health. The Council of Ministers is headed by the king himself and his deputy the crown prince.

In countries like Israel there is little involvement in the mental health policy process by nonmedical representatives (Yishai, chap. 6), and in Pakistan the major consumer groups are apathetic and do not attempt to impact the policy process (Niaz, chap. 13). In contrast, in the United States there are powerful

coalitions among bureaucrats, legislators, and special-interest groups that can lead to conflict among competing interests.

The public policy process in many countries has been a long battle. In the public policy process of the Netherlands the biggest problem, as in many other countries, has been the lack of a comprehensive organizational framework. This has meant a constant failure to coordinate new initiatives and to integrate fragmented services. This problem has been addressed in two white papers over a ten-year period, but the problem has yet to be fully resolved (Evers, Haveman, Jacobs, & Bijl, chap. 10). Some countries have operated with outdated mental health laws. This was the case in New Zealand, where a 1969 law became outdated. The growing number of special-interest groups, while increasing useful input to the public policy process, also made it more difficult to reach compromises and establish new policies. New Zealand tried to pass new mental health legislation for some ten years and was only successful in 1992. Much worse yet is the situation of a country like Pakistan, which is still using a 1912 Lunacy Act.

It is not uncommon for the theory and practice of mental health policy to be different. In Argentina the National Administration of Mental Health is theoretically responsible for mental health policy, but in reality psychiatric and psychological associations, private hospitals, and trade-union representatives play a major role (Fiasche, Fiszbein, Gorelick, & Fakiel, chap. 2). In Italy after Law 180, a weak executive has led to the lack of specific national rules and mixed compliance with the law at the regional and local levels (Ghirardelli & Lussetti, chap. 7). Thus implementation has been uneven. In Israel there is a gap between policy and what actually occurs. While there is an emphasis on treatment in the community, resource allocation shows community treatment to be an "underdog" (Yishai, chap. 6). These are problems common to many countries.

SPECIAL POLICY ISSUES

There are a number of policy issues that are particularly important to mental health policy. Among these are issues concerning the mentally ill and the mentally retarded, issues involving the mentally ill and substance abuse, mentally disordered offenders, deinstitutionalization, funding issues, and consumer rights.

The Mentally Ill and the Mentally Retarded

The first issue that needs to be addressed concerning the mentally ill and the mentally retarded is the term *mental retardation* itself. As noted earlier, terminology for the various mental disorders as well as terminology for defining what to call the persons provided with services has changed over time, often because previous terms have been regarded as pejorative. This is the case for people with mental retardation. The term *mentally retarded* was chosen to be used in subheadings throughout this book because it is a widely recognized term. However, it is realized that the term is seen as negative in some countries and that several other terms are used, including *developmentally disabled*, *mentally handicapped*, and *intellectually handicapped*, among others.

Some people may question why mental retardation is being included in this book on mental health policy. At one time this question would not have been raised because persons with mental retardation were treated in psychiatric hospitals and by psychiatrists. However, in many countries mental retardation has become very separated from mental illness and psychiatry, and advocates for people with mental retardation have sought to have them removed from the mental health policy arena and into other policy arenas such as education, social welfare, and physical disability and rehabilitation. But because of the historical significance of the connection between mental illness and mental retardation and because in many countries such as New Zealand and Saudi Arabia, even though the disorders are now clearly recognized as different, the systems still treat many mentally retarded persons in psychiatric hospitals, this issue is still pertinent to mental health policy. In addition, there is a very important and often-unresolved issue regarding who is responsible for dual-diagnosed persons with mental illness and mental retardation.

Many countries like Israel regard mental retardation as a social handicap and have very few persons with mental retardation in psychiatric facilities. In some countries separate government departments deal with mental retardation. It is not unusual for persons with mental retardation to be represented by very powerful interest groups, as is the case in New Zealand, the United Kingdom, the United States, and Israel. This enhances their ability to obtain resources. It has also not been unusual for policy reform for that population to have been earlier and more successful than for persons with mental illness, as has been true in Italy (Ghirardelli & Lussetti, chap. 7).

It also is not unusual for spokespersons for the two groups to deny any relationship between the two and to avoid association with each other, as frequently occurs in Israel and the United States. The fact that people with mental retardation are not seen as dangerous in countries like Korea, where mental illness is seen as threatening and is avoided, also helps supporters of persons with mental retardation to gain support more easily than supporters of persons with mental illness.

Even though many countries such as Argentina recognize the special needs of people with mental retardation, because of economic reasons many of the mentally retarded from poor families are still in psychiatric hospitals. This has been a backward trend for Argentina, which had established a facility for the exclusive treatment of the mentally retarded as early as 1906 (Fiasche, Fiszbein, Gorelick, & Fakiel, chap. 2). In India services cover only 1 percent of mentally handicapped persons and are unevenly distributed, with services for the severely retarded person almost unavailable because only recently has mental handicap been seen as a significant problem that should be addressed in planning services, and public apathy toward the issue has been a major problem (Sharma, chap. 5).

In the case of dual diagnosis, the psychiatric diagnosis prevails in countries such as Italy, where the result has been a greater rejection from school and even mental retardation services (Ghirardelli & Lussetti, chap. 7). In Canada specialized assessments may be made by the Health Department in a special unit of a psychiatric hospital for people with dual diagnosis—developmental delay and behavioral disturbance. In some countries the primary diagnosis determines treatment. However, significant problems remain in that many countries either do not recognize dual diagnosis or find that persons who are dual diagnosed tend to be shuttled between the two areas and have trouble receiving adequate services.

There also is a linkage between substance abuse and mental retardation. In Russia and the Commonwealth of Independent States, where there has been an increase in the number of children with mental retardation, there is a frequent connection with the rise of parental substance abuse, "the incidence of which in the 1980s acquired the character of a national catastrophe" (Vartanyan, Yastrebov, Rotstein, Solokhina, Liberman, & Shevchenko, chap. 16). Some populations in the United States, particularly native Americans, have also seen this linkage through rising rates of fetal alcohol syndrome (FAS), which in many cases includes mental retardation.

The Mentally Ill and Substance Abuse

The situation regarding the mentally ill and substance abuse is similar to the situation involving the mentally ill and the mentally retarded. Historically, in many countries people with substance abuse problems were treated in the mental health system and psychiatric hospitals. However, in many countries substance abuse has become a distinct policy arena and is now treated largely in a separate system. This issue is included here because of the historical linkage and again because in some countries, although there is increasing recognition of the uniqueness of substance abuse issues, substance abuse remains a part of the mental health system. However, in some countries, although substance abuse is still a part of mental health policy and the mental health system, it is in a process of growing distinctness and potential separation. In addition, there is the important issue regarding dual diagnosis of people with mental illness and substance abuse and their treatment.

In some developing countries, like Argentina, the incidence and prevalence of drug abuse has not reached the levels seen in developed countries. However, cocaine and amphetamine abuse are on the rise (Fiasche, Fiszbein, Gorelick, & Fakiel, chap. 2). Even though use may not be high in some countries, it still may receive much attention. For example, in Israel drug abuse receives a prominent place on the political agenda because of its perceived threat to the country's security (Yishai, chap. 6). In other countries, like the United States, drug abuse is a major problem and receives special funding initiatives.

Some countries have problems with controlling prescription drugs. For example, Argentina has a problem with self-medication, particularly with anxiolytics and antidepressants, that is encouraged by illegal street trade and illegal sale at some pharmacies (Fiasche, Fiszbein, Gorelick, & Fakiel, chap. 2). In addition, there is a problem with inappropriate prescribing by physicians, which is also a problem in the United States.

Alcohol abuse remains a major problem in most countries. In Argentina it is facilitated by low cost, in that a bottle of wine is cheaper than a bottle of Coca-Cola, and there is easy availability. Russia and the Commonwealth also have a major problem with alcohol. Though separate entities have been established for the treatment of substance abuse, there are still many patients undergoing compulsory treatment in special medical settings for long-term treatment. This system is criticized for infringing on human rights (Vartanyan, Yastrebov, Rotstein, Solokhina, Liberman, & Shevchenko, chap. 16). The Alcoholics Anonymous approach is quite new in countries like Russia and some of the Eastern European countries. Nonprofit organizations using approaches similar to that of Alcoholics Anonymous are seen as having better long-term outcomes in treatment in Argentina, while private profit-making clinics are seen as having mostly benefitted the professionals and clinic owners who are psychiatrists and addictionologists (Fiasche, Fiszbein, Gorelick, and Fakiel, chap. 2).

In Israel, as in many countries, substance abuse is seen as a social problem, but other countries are moving away from this approach and toward a criminal justice and punitive approach. Italy's 1990 law introduced punishment for the personal use of drugs. It also overturned a previous principle of voluntary cure and moved to cure as a coercive alternative to administrative or criminal sanctions (Ghirardelli & Lussetti, chap. 7). India's policy is also focused heavily on the criminal justice system, although a court may release a person with his or her consent to undergo treatment (Sharma, chap. 5), and in Pakistan drug addicts are feared and face the worst social stigma. Substance abuse has a low priority, with little opportunity for drug or alcohol abusers to receive treatment (Niaz, chap. 13).

In Canada drug or alcohol abuse programs are usually the responsibility of a separate entity, but there is growing recognition of the need to coordinate mental health services with substance abuse services. Dual diagnosis has achieved a high profile in countries like the United States, with much concern about appropriate treatment, but in Italy, where dual diagnosis is not yet perceived as a problem, the primary diagnosis usually determines the choice of treatment.

The Mentally Disordered Offender

In addition to people with dual diagnosis being unique populations within the mental health system, there is also a unique population consisting of people with mental illness who are involved in some way with the criminal justice system. Social control early became one of the philosophies underlying the development and implementation of mental health policy, and social control remains the primary public policy value relating to people who are mentally ill and involved with criminal offending. Issues involving mentally disordered offenders, how the criminal justice and mental health systems should interface, and what the primary focus of forensic psychiatry should be—social control or individual treatment—remain problems with which most countries are struggling.

Argentina has a lawyer routinely incorporated into many mental health services to deal with criminal issues, and the state psychiatric hospitals have a special ward for the criminally insane. But in some countries there are no specialized units. Japan does not have security hospitals or security units. Most mentally disordered offenders are hospitalized in public or private mental hospitals (Asai, chap. 8). In Chile there is only one forensic psychiatric hospital in the country (Vicente & Vielma, chap. 4). Concerns are also raised in countries like New Zealand, where small forensic units are being established, whether civil patients with behavior problems may also be confined to those units. In the United States a court in Montana is reviewing a claim for damages from civil patients confined to a forensic unit.

The qualifications of psychiatric experts in court testimony is another important issue. In Israel any practicing psychiatrist has been able to testify to the legal aspects of mental illness without demonstrating proficiency. Because of concern over this situation the Association for Legal Psychiatry has recently been organized.

Deinstitutionalization

In recent years in many countries deinstitutionalization, the attempt to move mental health care away from the large psychiatric hospitals and to community treatment alternatives, has become an important policy issue. In Italy, which has had probably the most highly publicized reform, there was a significant drop in inpatients in mental hospitals, and some wards were closed and reused for hostels, day centers, or work cooperatives for former patients, given to schools or social centers, turned into public offices, or left empty. Although there are no new admissions, mental hospitals still accommodate patients who were admitted before Law 180. These hospitals have largely been neglected by the reform, rehabilitation is rare, and funds for upkeep of the buildings are lacking (Ghirardelli & Lussetti, chap. 7). The reform focus has moved from an entitlement to life outside the institution to creation of new services capable of empowering the consumers to live in a normal setting. In the Netherlands the differences between de jure and de facto policy are clear regarding deinstitutionalization. Although there has been a policy of deinstitutionalization, no formal steps have been taken to close mental hospitals, and no budgetary or legal actions have been initiated to restrict admissions or length of stay. However, some positive steps have been taken in development of community care, so some modest gains have been made (Evers, Haveman, Jacobs, & Bijl, chap. 10). In other countries, like Pakistan, there has been no deinstitutionalization because they never had a highly institutionalized population and have not developed an interest in moving in the direction of creating more institutions (Niaz, chap. 13). In countries like the United States and the United Kingdom homeless mentally ill living on the streets have been attributed to the failure of deinstitutionalization.

In some countries, such as Argentina and New Zealand, labor unions have successfully resisted proposals for deinstitutionalization. In other countries, like Israel, the development of psychiatric wards in general hospitals has been slow; evidence regarding integration between psychiatric wards and other wards is inconclusive, and the extent to which the staffs maintain reciprocal relationships is still unknown (Yishai, chap. 6). In Japan the number of long-term patients in psychiatric hospitals is still increasing, and more than 50 percent of residential patients have been in the hospital for more than five years (Asai, chap. 8), thus the extent and results of deinstitutionalization are highly variable around the world.

Funding Issues

Central to mental health policy is the question of funding. Fine policy statements may be made, excellent pieces of legislation may be formulated and promulgated, but most mental health policy is not implementable without a solid funding base. This is often the step at which the policy breaks down and the de jure, legally established policy becomes "symbolic politics," wonderful statements of policy, versus de facto policy, the actual policy in existence.

In countries like Israel where mental health care is considered an integral part of general health care, mental health care remains a funding "stepchild," and the proportion of funding allocated to mental health out of the general health expenditures is in decline (Yishai, chap. 6). In Italy the famous reform Law 180 carried with it no budget for implementing the reform. Italy has learned from this negative experience and is now somewhat more sensitive to funding issues, yet while the health services are increasing their share of funding, funding for psychiatry still has remained stagnant or has decreased (Ghirardelli & Lussetti, chap. 7).

Funding is also one of the weakest links in analysis of mental health policy. Most countries lack adequate data bases on how much money is really expended on mental health, and the number of entities expending funds may be so great as to be hard to identify. In the Netherlands nearly 70 percent of funding is financed through national and private health insurance (Evers, Haveman, Jacobs, & Bijl, chap. 10), but funding sources in other countries are often multiple. In Canada funding of provincial health insurance plans, social services, and vocational rehabilitation is shared between the federal government and the provinces. In Argentina funding comes from the federal government, provinces, cities, the Social Security administration, labor unions, and private organizations.

Attempts to integrate these funds have not been successful (Fiasche, Fiszbein, Gorelick, & Fakiel, chap. 2). Also, where there are multiple funding sources, attempts may be made to shift funds from one source to another to reduce the costs of one government or agency, and this may occur with little regard for the impact on the client. This has been a recurring problem in the United States, where state and federal governments have sought ways to shift costs to a different level of government than their own. In countries like Argentina, where there is private health insurance funding, the insurance funds of the unions may reject claims in order to pass the costs off onto the government. In Israel, Kupat Holim, a sick fund, has insisted that mental health care be the responsibility of the state. Funding may also distort goals. For example, the funding system in Israel encourages the government hospitals to keep their beds occupied by increased admissions or increased lengths of stay (Yishai, chap. 6).

Funding is often inadequate, and there may be disastrous consequences. For example, in Argentina the mental health budget is inadequate for the psychiatric hospitals, and the personnel justify stealing food and goods based on their low salaries (Fiasche, Fiszbein, Gorelick, & Fakiel, chap. 2).

Consumer Rights

Last, one of the most important changes in the mental health field is the growing development of consumer rights. This is supported by the increasing formation of special-interest groups involving family members and consumers themselves who are seeking to change mental health policy and to establish protection for the consumers in the mental health systems.

In Canada the protection of rights for mentally ill persons is found at the highest level in the Canadian Charter of Rights and Freedoms, which defines protection for all Canadians. The charter is the measure that is applied by the Supreme Court of Canada to other legislation to determine its legality. Although mental health legislation is constitutionally the responsibility of the provinces, the provinces are examining their legislation for compliance with the charter. In Italy all treatment is voluntary, consent must be actively sought, and legal protections are high, with the judiciary fully involved. In the United States the court system is frequently used to make legal challenges on behalf of the mentally ill, and a whole system of mental health law has developed since the 1970s.

On the opposite end of the continuum was Israel, where consumer rights were "the most vulnerable area in Israel's mental health policy" (Yishai, chap. 6). Israel followed the psychiatric model in its mental health law, which relied heavily upon professional standards of individual physicians, with hospitalization and release procedures exclusively in the medical domain. Only recently has new legislation been passed to remedy this situation. If well implemented, this legislation will bring Israel into the forefront of modern approaches. Other countries, however, continue to have problems in protecting the consumer. In Korea treatment and protection are emphasized, and consumer rights are not reflected in mental health policy (Kim, chap. 9); in Pakistan there are no consumer rights under legislation, no guidelines, and no accountability (Niaz, chap. 13); and in Chile a survey of consumers and relatives found levels of satisfaction amazingly high for the quality of the services, as well as a reluctance to accept reform (Vicente & Vielma, chap. 4). Extensive and modern legislation, however, still may not be a sufficient safeguard. For example, although the United Kingdom has fairly new legislation, there continue to be reports of abuse (Goldie & Sayce, chap. 19).

One of the earlier attempts at protecting rights in psychiatric hospitals was the establishment of hospital visitors (New Zealand) and inspecting officers (India) who could enter facilities at any time, inspect them, and interview patients. Canada has been among a number of countries that have gone on to institute other mechanisms for review and appeal to protect the rights of mental patients. These procedures include review panels and patient advocate/advisory services. The United States also uses Human Rights Committees. Another approach that has been taken is to regulate mental health procedures through licensing. India has a separate system of licensing for psychiatric nursing homes and hospitals from other medical facilities, an approach that is contrary to attempts to integrate mental and general health services. The United States has an extensive regulatory approach which is both integrated and segregated.

The antipsychiatry movement has appeared in many countries around the world. In Argentina in 1972 the instruments of psychiatric "torture" (insulin therapy, hoses for cold-water therapy, and so on) were burnt in a public demonstration (Fiasche, Fiszbein, Gorelick, & Fakiel, chap. 2). This movement has considerable power in Europe and North America in its ability to influence policy.

CONCLUSIONS AND DISCUSSION

Viewpoints vary as to how bright the future of mental health policy may be. A promising future is seen by the authors of the chapter on Argentina, and the Italian authors see an ongoing active and rich experimentation being performed by the staffs of services themselves. However, the summation from New Zealand paints a more questionable future and may well be reflected in many countries: "Major progress has been made in all areas, and service provision today more closely matches consumer needs and preferences. However, these gains are precarious, and there are many uncertainties in New Zealand with regard to future policies and services. . . . There are too many unknowns at this point to be able to make confident predictions about the future" (Abbott & Kemp, chap. 11). In some cases, such as Zambia, it has not been difficult to convince the system to move toward thinking of community care and the Alma Ata concept of primary health care because there was no existing complex system already in place (Haworth, chap. 21). Each country is faced with problems both similar to and different from those of other nations as it moves toward the World Health Organization's goal of Health for All by the Year 2000, but unquestionably, the ability of the world to manage its environmental, social, and economic problems will to a great extent determine the availability of resources for mental health policy in all countries.

2

Argentina

Angel Fiasche, Abraham Fiszbein, Amy Gorelick, and Martin Fakiel

OVERVIEW

Argentina is part of the continent of South America and is located, along with Chile, in its southernmost part. Its geography also includes the Malvinas (Falkland) Islands and a part of Antarctica. It has, in an area of 3,600,000 square kilometers (excluding Antarctica), a population of 32 million inhabitants and, consequently, a very low population density. Argentina is somewhat different from its neighboring countries in the cultural and racial composition of its people, that is, in the relationships between its native and immigrant populations, and in its access to the cultural sources of development.

The European component of the Argentine people is a consequence of the massive immigrations to the country, especially from 1860 to 1920. These immigrants were Europeans from the poorest countries, usually those with Latin-rooted languages, mostly from Spain and Italy, but also from Portugal. The exchange of habits and lifestyles between these immigrants and the native Indian population in the three major cities of the country (Buenos Aires, Córdoba, and Rosario) determined the cultural influence over the minority groups that came from other European countries, such as Poland, Russia, France, and England, and some Arab countries, particularly Syria and Lebanon. During this period, and along with these minority groups, other community groups were formed along religious lines. This was the case with the Jewish community, whose members were unified by their common religious and cultural traditions, regardless of the different countries of their origin.

The native population, the product of the joining of the Spanish conquerors with the indigenous Indian people, was initially concentrated in the provinces. During World War II many moved to the three major cities, accompanying the industrial development that the war stimulated in those countries that supplied raw materials. This produced a large, unplanned migration that induced an immense population growth of the "belt" formed by the three major cities. For example, the city of Buenos Aires alone had three million inhabitants in 1943 and presently has eight million (a 266 percent increase in forty-seven years), while the country as a whole increased its population from eighteen million in 1925 to over thirty-two million at the present time (a 177 percent increase in sixty-five years) (Fiasche, 1985).

The general population growth in Argentina was slower than in the rest of Latin America. This was in part due to the high male/female ratio (2:1 in 1910) (Fiasche, 1985), a consequence of the disproportionately large immigration of young, single men, as well as the efforts of the new immigrants to limit the size of their families. The European influence of certain middle-class values put the country at an advantage with respect to the prevention of unplanned pregnancies. This slow population growth was also related to the people's life projects and their desire to obtain adequate housing, education, and health care for their children. Only in the upper class was it possible to support many children, in contrast to the lower classes who were in a struggle to provide their children with access to the education, social privileges, and cultural patterns of the middle class.

The European immigration to Argentina in the nineteenth century was similar to the one to the United States during that period. Many Spanish and Italians came to the country wishing to leave poverty behind and come to a destiny of prosperity. This cultural, racial, and ethnic influence allowed growth in all areas of development (economic, cultural, and technical). This skilled human "rainbow" made achievements that placed Argentina in a position of cultural and technological leadership in Latin America at that time. In 1910 Buenos Aires was the only city in Latin America to join London, Paris, and New York in having the subway as a means of public transportation.

Argentina had a moderate industrial and metallurgical development that insured its inclusion among the most developed countries of that time. Its agricultural and cattle wealth became integrated with this industrial evolution, making good use of the contributions of the enterprising immigrants. The bulk of them, Spaniards, Italians, and Jews, concentrated in the cities of the provinces of Buenos Aires, Santa Fé, Entre Ríos, and Mendoza, mostly during the 1880–1910 period. The agricultural development of the country was greatly stimulated by this immigration. In contrast to this, the aristocracy enjoyed the benefits of the natural wealth of *la pampa húmeda* (the wet flatland) without contributing much technology, just letting the cattle graze and fatten on their own.

The Patagonia, a large expanse of territory with a small population, received the migratory contribution of the British community, especially the Welsh and Scottish, who dedicated themselves to sheep breeding and wool making. Previously the wool was sent to England to be processed, but presently it is processed and manufactured into finished goods in Argentina as a consequence of the growth of the country's own textile industry.

The native Indian population of the country was decimated, in part by the Desert War carried on at the end of the nineteenth century by the president of that time, General Julio Roca, and in part by the lack of adequate food, shelter, and support to improve or even maintain minimal life conditions. Some of these communities are now extinct; others live without the basic resources of survival.

The country's middle class predominated in the big cities: Buenos Aires, Rosario, and others. In the last few years this class has entered a process of pauperization, which has generated an economic polarization among the social classes. As the middle class loses its primacy, the differences between rich and poor deepen. This phenomenon contributes to sharp increases in the country's illiteracy and child mortality rates.

The structure of the Argentine government is, in general, similar to that of the United States, except that the president stays in office for six years and cannot be reelected for a second consecutive term. By law, only a Roman Catholic can be president. The government's structure is federal. It is ruled by the president, who appoints his own ministers. Each province votes for its own governor, who also appoints his ministers. The Congress is composed of the Senate and the House of Deputies.

There is a multiparty system whose spectrum runs from the most conservative ideologies to the most radical ones (Communist Party, Trotskyist Party, and others). The majority fall within the two biggest parties: the Justicialista Party, also called Peronist, and the Unión Cívica Radical. As is the case in the United States, the two biggest parties are defined not only by their political ideology but also by their programs.

EXTENT OF THE PROBLEM

The problems related to mental health issues in Argentina are bound mainly to its socioeconomic deterioration over the last thirty years. The fall in the quality of life due to the impoverishment of the general population, together with the deterioration in the educational and health systems supported by the government, have increased the number of "clinical depressions due to financial reasons," for example, due to the loss of social status or the loss of child care support. These losses have produced severe sequels that have not been conceptualized globally in spite of a social awareness of the extent and nature of these problems. Certain problems recently seen more and more by Argentine mental health professionals, such as "economic major depression," preventable mental retardation, infant abandonment and abuse, juvenile delinquency, the battering of women, and prostitution, have caused them to include a clinical approach directly related to this "psychiatry of poverty."

Neither private nor government-owned institutions have updated statistics about the increases in these pathologies. Statistics for psychopathology require social and epidemiological studies. Some are done with the support of the Consejo Nacional de Investigaciones Científicas y Técnicas (the National Council of Scientific and Technical Research) or CONICET, but most are incomplete, without well-established validity or reliability as general survey statistics. There is no survey that encompasses all the different areas of assistance, such as national, municipal, state, and private hospitals, mental health centers, and private-office practices. The only valid statistics are those regarding the psychiatric inpatients of the national, state, and municipal jurisdictions.

The incidence and prevalence of mental health problems in the Argentine population are still unknown statistics because in the private area, especially in individual assistance, it is not mandatory to keep records. The same applies to statistics for other mental health problems, such as the prevalence of drug and alcohol abuse, the number of suicides, and even the total number of visits to mental health services. Any attempt to quantify them so far would be subjective. After all, if the country is currently unable to provide the means for adequate psychiatric care for its population, it should come as little surprise that it also lacks the resources for keeping accurate and verifiable statistics.

MENTAL HEALTH HISTORY

At the beginning of the nineteenth century the mentally ill were set aside in asylums where they did not receive any treatment. In 1860 the institutional structure and the basis for the asylum treatments were organized. This system of institutionalization was frequently modified and improved according to the most current theories of the time and reached a peak between 1900 and 1910, thanks to the creative work of Dr. Domingo Cabred and Dr. M. A. Montes de Oca. Soon thereafter, residential treatment facilities with open doors (*colonias*) were created for the mentally ill, and inpatient statistics were organized.

The diagnoses were made according to the French school of psychiatry. Emphasis was placed almost exclusively on the field of psychoses, because the knowledge that Freud had developed about neuroses in Europe was yet to be incorporated into psychiatry in Argentina. A psychiatric admission was done either in the public or private sector, depending on the economic resources of the patient. By custom, the chiefs of service of the hospices would open their own small private sanatoriums. The differences in treatment were (and still are) in the quality of meals and lodging, as well as in a greater staff/patient ratio. The therapeutic models are still the same, but they are more adequately systematized in the private sanatoriums.

In 1903, when Cabred inaugurated the first psychiatric residential treatment facility with open doors, he incorporated the concept of work as an essential therapeutic factor in mental health. About the same time he also introduced the concept of *peculio* (an economic gratuity for the working patient). This system has evolved to such a degree that there are now many protected factories throughout the country managed by the National Administration of Mental Health where inpatients and outpatients work and receive payment for their work. The crystallization of this project, which began in 1972, not only allowed the mentally ill access to jobs, but also gave them the possibilities of learning and training in a wide range of working areas.

As a consequence, nowadays furniture, metal work, pharmaceuticals, clothing, and other textile products, for example, are made in these factories throughout the country and supply clothes for ill people, textile materials for hospitals, furniture for the government itself, and other products. There are currently thirty-four protected factories in the entire country, and their personnel consists of psychologists, workshop teachers, occupational therapists, and consultants of the National Council of Technical Education (Consejo Nacional de Educación Técnica).

This scheme has developed successfully also in the area of the handicapped. There are many nonprofit institutions that have created protected workshops to give jobs to these patients. An agreement was signed many years ago between the Ministry of Transportation and the Ministry of Health and Welfare that allows the mentally ill and the disabled of any kind to travel at no cost.

The concept of *asylum* changed to that of *hospice* and finally to *hospital*. During this process, psychiatric services were created in general hospitals, first for consultation and to treat outpatients, and later on, for the inpatient treatment of psychotic crises. Along with this change, the concept of *psychiatry* evolved to that of *psychopathology* and eventually to that of *mental health*. This new concept of mental health then joined those of *prevention* and primary *assistance* started in the 1950s and helped Argentine psychiatry join other countries in providing psychiatric treatment within general hospitals, which later generalized throughout the country.

The early development of psychoanalysis in the 1930s in Argentina compared with the rest of Latin America, along with the philosophy of social psychiatry started by Cabred in 1900, influenced important changes in mental health policies. They were given a more definitive shape by Dr. José Ingenieros. The influence of psychoanalysis has increased greatly since 1930. Argentine psychiatrists, pediatricians, and general practitioners became interested in Freud's works and organized themselves to learn the psychoanalytic theories. In 1938 the Argentine Psychoanalytic Association was founded by Dr. Angel Garma, a Spanish psychoanalyst trained in the Berlin school, and Dr. Celes Cárcamo, an Argentine professional trained in France, together with a group of Argentine physicians who had already incorporated a sufficient knowledge of psychoanalysis.

The impact of this development influenced the entire Latin American continent. Interested by psychoanalysis, professionals from Brazil, Chile, Colombia, Mexico, Peru, Uruguay, and Venezuela came to Buenos Aires to receive their initial training and then returned to their countries of origin to form new associations. This expansion of psychoanalytic knowledge influenced the understanding of the dynamics of mental conflicts and illness. In addition, the psychoanalytic training became an important complement to the education and training received by clinicians in the medical schools. Concomitantly, the field of clinical, educational, and labor psychology was created in 1955. Since that time, the Universidad de Buenos Aires (University of Buenos Aires) alone has trained approximately 40,000 graduates in this program.

In 1966 the community mental health centers were created and run by the government of the city of Buenos Aires. These centers are still managed with a community orientation, broadening the spectrum of treatment of emotional problems so as to include the impact of poverty and misery on mental health. The general hospitals now include recognition and treatment of the problems of the battered woman, the abused child, and the troubled marriage, as mental health professionals have become aware that these symptomatic expressions of societal ills in the individual must be considered within the field of mental health.

POLICY, ORGANIZATION, AND SERVICES IN THE 1980s AND 1990s

Current Policy Developments

Public assistance to children and poor families was generally available until the arrival of the military government in 1976. This government destroyed an entire system of free assistance in health and education that had been shaped along the lines of the one used in Scandinavia. Until 1955 the country had grown with the praxis of the social-democratic model; thus the quality of its programs and policies reflected that model. Since that time, the services offered to the community have progressively deteriorated.

With the return of democracy in 1983, after the fall by discredit, of the military dictatorship, a new movement was generated to update the policies, programs, and information of mental health systems. It placed the focus on primary and secondary prevention and deemphasized rehabilitation and tertiary assistance. As a first step, the Department of Mental Health was created, replacing the Department of Psychiatry. The university professors became Professors of the Branch of Mental Health, and the Chair of Psychiatry was eliminated. There were openings for the teaching of mental health in the universities in all of the humanistic disciplines: medicine, psychology, social work, nursing, sociology, anthropology, and so on. At the present time, the requirements to become a professor of mental health in the School of Medicine of the University of Buenos Aires encompass all of these disciplines, with the exception of a small number of positions that are for mental health with a psychiatric orientation. This ideological change in the School of Medicine of the university was accompanied by the federal government's creation of the multidisciplinary Residency Training Programs in Mental Health, which began offering certification for specialist in mental health. The School of Psychology also created the Chair of Mental Health and Community Psychology. These programs are still in effect and have done much to erase the traditional limits between psychiatrists and other mental health professionals, even though psychiatrists are still the only ones who can prescribe medication.

Financed by the federal government, these programs have had positive general repercussions in some of the provinces. As a consequence of this influence, for example, the province of Río Negro submitted a project through its Provincial Administration of Mental Health, approved by its local congress, to eliminate the psychiatric hospitals, organize all psychiatric admissions to the general hospitals, and discharge many of the chronic inpatients to their homes. The participation of the Pan-American Office of Mental Health in Washington, D.C., has helped to unify criteria of definitions and to elaborate projects and programs. It has not, unfortunately, contributed to changes of importance in tertiary prevention.

The internal migration that broke up the stability of the big cities through the growth of the slums has aroused professional interest in epidemiology and social psychiatry. These disciplines have the financial support of CONICET (a governmental institution that trains researchers), but not of the National Administration of Mental Health, because it does not have a budget for this purpose.

The socioeconomic deterioration of the working classes and of the retired senior citizens, as well as other disgraces related to extreme poverty, have broadened the spectrum of the definition of mental illness and, consequently, of policies in the field of mental health. Professionals are aware of these effects and actually include them in their treatment plans. Although the socioeconomic situation has affected the quality of treatment, it has not affected the awareness of the need for additions and changes of policies and programs in mental health in Argentina. However, this professional struggle has remained over the last few years just "discussions among intellectuals."

Current Organization

In theory, the major responsibility for mental health policy belongs to the National Administration of Mental Health, a government entity; but the reality is that associated to it is an intersectorial committee formed by (1) psychiatric and psychological associations, (2) private hospitals, and (3) trade-union representatives directly involved in matters of Social Security. This committee acts as a bridge between the demands of the professionals and the requirements of the National Administration of Mental Health. The National Administration of Mental Health can, by itself, advise, recommend, and, on occasion, give some economic help, but it does not have authority over this committee.

Current Services

Argentina's capital, the city of Buenos Aires, has 3 million inhabitants, and 5 million more people live in its surrounding suburbs. Córdoba and Rosario, two other large cities, have 3 million people between them. The rest of the population of the country is spread out over a large expanse of territory whose population density is very low.

The practice of psychiatry in Córdoba and Rosario is not very different from that in Buenos Aires in the system and philosophy of care. The cities have similar professional resources, similar psychiatric treatments in their general hospitals and chronic-care asylums, and similar populations with similar psychiatric needs. The most important advances could potentially happen in the provinces with a low population density, which are currently underserved and have inadequate resources. Neuquén, for example, a city whose population is less than 375,000 inhabitants, has its psychiatric admission needs covered by only a small number of beds in a well-equipped general hospital. Río Negro, a province in this area, has passed a law that allows the dissolution of its big asylums and prevents the possibility of further excesses in these chronic psychiatric inpatient facilities (Legislatura, 1991).

According to the 1988 census, of the 25,000 hospital beds scattered throughout the country, 70 percent belong to the federal and provincial governments. The rest belong to the private sector, which includes both nonprofit and for-profit enterprises (table 2.1).

The care in all of the asylums throughout the country is deficient in almost every aspect. Many times the food is sparse and of poor quality. The wards, which have between 100 and 150 inpatients, are run by one or two psychiatrists and one or two nurses. If they are absent, especially on weekends, a ward may be left without even a single nurse, and the inpatients with a higher level of functioning have to fill this gap. In addition, these asylums have a large number of patients who also have neurologic problems, many of whom do not receive the specific care that their conditions require due to the lack of appropriately trained nursing staff.

Changes are occurring in these institutions, albeit slowly. The administrative structure of the big chronic-care hospitals wisely limits the potential of its directors to abuse their authority. The chiefs of each ward have more autonomy than those in Anglo-Saxon countries. For example, they have the authority to make changes in any rules or regulations of their wards. Often now, one ward chief will approach another with a discussion of new ideas and, after a long process of debate of its benefits and disadvantages, convince him to make a change. Both would then learn from this experience. This is another way in which things change in the psychiatric hospitals. This system of learning has been very helpful, not just to rectify old, useless laws, habits, and regulations, but also to improve the compassion and humane philosophy in the therapeutic approach to the patients.

The development of psychoanalytic ideas over the past years in Argentina provoked a polarization between dynamic (psychoanalytic) psychiatry experts, on the one hand, and, on the other hand, the traditional psychiatric group that accepts more the biological theories and therapies in psychiatry, including the

Table 2.1
Major Psychiatric Institutions in Argentina, 1987

THE MAJOR NINE (Total number of beds available)		
National Health Administration	-National Hospital "Dr. Jose T. Borda"	1,633
	-National Hospital "Dr. Braulio A. Moyano"	1,841
	-National R.T.F. "Manuel A. Montes De Oca"	1,200
Buenos Aires Province	-Hospital "Dr. A. Estevez"	1,240
	-Hospital "Dr. Domingo Cabred"	1,533
	-Hospital "Dr. Alejandro Korn"	2,393
Córdoba Province	-R.T.F. "Dr. Emilio Vidal Abal"	1,680
	-Hospital Santa Maria	800
Santa Fé Province	-Psychiatric R.T.F. "Dr. Alberto Freire"	860
	Total	13,180
THE 32 INSTITUTIONS WITH 100 TO 476 BEDS	Total	5,906

Abbreviation:
R.T.F.: Residential Treatment Facility   Public

Source: Departamento de Estadísticas, Ministerio de Salud y Acción Social, 1987.

isolation of patients in asylums. This confrontation lasted for approximately forty-five years and was won by the dynamic psychiatrists with the general acceptance of a psychodynamic theory of psychopathology.

In 1955 the postgraduate Schools of Clinical, Educational, and Labor Psychology were officially created. They have already trained more than 40,000 psychologists, mostly in clinical areas. The massive predominance of these clinical psychologists, mostly psychoanalytically oriented, has created a disproportionate growth of this way of understanding issues and to some extent has prevented the development of other valuable scientific contributions to the field. In spite of this, the general balance has been beneficial in that, year after year, the number of admissions to the asylums has diminished considerably (by approximately 50 percent over the last ten years), and the average length of stay is now two months. The percentage of all psychiatric inpatients who were admitted more than ten years ago is growing larger in proportion to the percentage of patients recently admitted. The reason is that many of these chronic patients no longer have families who can care for them due to a variety of reasons, including financial difficulties and the dissolution of their family. In some cases it is not possible to locate the family due to its increased geographic and social mobility. Related to these phenomena, a most important problem has been the lack of development of the small hostels (halfway houses) and other dispositions for discharge of patients to the community.

Another area of care that is covered poorly is the treatment of psychiatric patients admitted to the general hospitals, especially those in the city of Buenos Aires. Few general hospitals have psychiatric inpatient units. Of the fifteen city hospitals in Buenos Aires, only four have inpatient psychiatric units, each with fewer than twenty-five beds. The other hospitals have only outpatient clinics, consultation and liaison, and/or community services. They refer their admissions to a modern hospital for the acutely ill that has one hundred beds and a relatively short average length of stay (usually less than two weeks) due to its high turnover. The city also has four mental health clinics that work in collaboration with the hospitals but are administratively and technically autonomous.

The treatment in the general hospitals is managed with a consultation-liaison mentality throughout the country. In the psychiatric hospitals there are medicine and surgery departments that include all of the medical and surgical subspecialties (including dentistry). Unfortunately, the treatment of the chronic psychiatric patients there is generally deficient, many times almost nonexistent, and worsened by the lack of motivation and interest on the part of the physicians in treating these patients.

All the general hospitals of the country, whether state, city, university-affiliated, or private, have a Department of Psychopathology (this term is replacing the former Department of Psychiatry), and the autonomous centers are called mental health clinics. These changes have occurred due to the predominance of numerous educational institutions of psychoanalytic theory over the past years and the influence of the Pan-American Office of Mental Health.

The primary care in the clinics generally does not have a very long waiting list because there are enough professionals for the number of patients who go there. In the outpatient clinics of the hospitals and especially in the mental health centers of the community, people receive free assistance thanks to the large number of professionals, such as psychiatrists, psychologists, psychoanalysts, social workers, and volunteers, who work without being paid. This contribution of the mental health workers is in part a consequence of their generosity with their time, and in part due to their hopes for a future salary and private referrals.

Mental health treatments in the private sector are carried out in several ways:

Private-office practice. This is the most important source of income for the medical and psychological professions in Argentina, because the salaries in the public institutions are often low and sometimes nonexistent. In the private institutions, with rare exceptions, professional services are also provided without remuneration.

There is a great variety of therapeutic modalities in mental health for the treatment of patients in Argentina. The complex variety is due, basically, to the large number of professionals from the different disciplines who are often forced to become competitive in the marketplace and offer a variety of treatment modalities, some advertised as imported, as a way of attracting patients.

In private-office practice there are a huge number and variety of practitioners who do not receive any clinical exposure prior to starting to treat patients (e.g., the clinical psychologists of several graduate schools in Argentina complete their education having acquired a wealth of knowledge, but having had no patient contact). They use multiple theoretical approaches, often incorporated into their practices without formal training or examination, as opposed to other professionals, who undergo lengthy and expensive training in institutions recognized for their formal education and supervision.

In Argentina words such as *psychotherapy* and *psychoanalysis* have been incorporated into the everyday language of all social classes. Offices for psychotherapy are seen even in the slums. Psychoanalysis is part of the regular everyday life and is visible in every order of life. People "think" psychoanalytically. Psychoanalysis is so ingrained and accepted now that some of the country's ministers and even presidents have been in psychoanalytic therapy. In the psychoanalytic community the most recent trend involves the ideas of the French school, placing a capital clinical importance on linguistics.

Prepaid medical system. Only a few of the prepaid systems of health insurance include psychiatric coverage. When it is included, this is often at the cost of imposing restrictions that make its use very cumbersome (for instance, with only partial coverage, a limit on the number of office visits, and so on).

Health maintenance organizations system. The health maintenance organizations (HMOs) that belong to the labor unions have two sources of income: the government and the workers. The contributions of the workers are mandatory, and a certain percentage of their salary is deducted each pay period. The HMOs' medical coverage includes psychiatric care.

Many of these HMOs have economic constraints that often conflict with providing their members with optimum psychiatric care. Some agreements between the HMOs and the private psychiatric hospitals are accomplished through bribes, which often leads to poor quality of care in the treatment. The corruption of some union leaders and government officials who administer the finances of these union HMOs has deteriorated and impoverished a system of health care that used to be an example of efficiency.

On the other hand, some HMOs, like the one of the railroad union, have hospitals that include psychiatric inpatient units whose staff can assist the whole family. Others even have the resources to research certain job-related illnesses.

Private psychiatric hospitals. The for-profit motives and the high costs of the private psychiatric hospitals have prevented them from being efficient and adequate and from developing a therapeutic process in a limited time. The types of treatment are not very different from those used in the developed countries. Currently, the private sanatoriums offer both group and family therapy as part of the routine treatment.

What is relevant is the absolute predominance of the psychological therapies, both individual and group therapies, over any other offer of treatment. The clinical orientation has a marked influence from the British schools of psychoanalysis, for example, those of Melanie Klein and Donald Woods Winnicott. However, in the last few years new orientations of treatment of American influence, especially the systemic theory in family treatments, have become more popular. Some private hospitals even demand that the family members of a patient agree to be involved in a systemic way in the treatment as a condition for the admission of their relative. In some private settings therapeutic community meetings and multifamily group meetings are frequently used as a way of social rehabilitation and family therapy. In general, the average length of stay in the private sanatoriums, like that in the public hospitals, has shortened.

The private clinics charge a sliding-scale fee for the lodging and treatment of the patients. They require a deposit in advance of fifteen days' stay at the time of admission as a fixed honorarium. If the inpatient's stay is shorter than fifteen days, some clinics reimburse the difference; others keep it. (In contrast, the state provides care in the chronic-care facilities for free.)

There is a new proposal of the secretary of health and social action that is being financed by the Inter-American Development Bank. This is a project for designing and building three very modern hospitals of mental health. Originally, nine were proposed to cover the necessities of an underserved area of the Argentine Northeast. Finally, after many discussions and budget negotiations between Argentina and the bank, three hospitals were approved: one in Córdoba (in the center of Argentina), one in Neuquén (in the Southwest), and the third in Mendoza (in the Northwest). These hospitals are scheduled to start functioning by the end of 1993.

Briefly, the model is that they will operate with a unified Department of Social Medicine and Psychiatry. The ideological basis is that there is need for the services that can be provided by one department that combines the traditional services of both a Department of Social Medicine and a Department of Psychiatry, as it can better treat problems such as "depressions due to economic reasons" and conditions commonly found with poverty, namely, substance abuse, marginalization, child abuse, battered women, and others. Three main areas will be included in this new Department of Social Medicine and Psychiatry: Psychiatry, Social Epidemiology, and Social Pathology.

Psychiatry will include acute psychiatric admissions, crisis intervention, outpatient treatment, and consultation-liaison services. Its admission unit will have an unusual arrangement because it will consist of five to ten psychiatric beds on a medical floor.

A contract will be made with each patient's family at the time of admission that the entire hospitalization will not exceed ten days, though, if necessary, the patient will be readmitted. It is expected that these brief admissions will be more efficient because they will force the treatment to focus rapidly on the psychiatric pathology and on the family crisis. The plan will also allow a follow-up intervention in the patient's home by the hospital staff if it is considered necessary. The psychiatric treatment will be integrated into the general medical clinic.

Soon to be decided is which service, Psychiatry or Internal Medicine, will be responsible for doing the initial evaluation and intake of the patient. Within the first twelve hours of every acute psychiatric admission, the patient will routinely get a full medical and psychiatric workup, including laboratory tests, to rule out an organic brain syndrome and to ensure that the patient has proper medical clearance for admission. This joint medical/psychiatric treatment will begin as soon as the patient is admitted. This will help to protect the patients from their families' tendencies, in times of anxiety, to cause conflict over what is desired by relatives and staff, which could worsen their psychiatric prognoses.

The area of Social Epidemiology will be responsible for designing and implementing all of the necessary epidemiological surveys of the hospitals' catchment areas. This will allow more efficient utilization of their resources and will help in the planning of primary prevention and community interventions with a more "participatory" approach. This area of Social Epidemiology, then, will work very closely with the other two areas, Psychiatry and Social Pathology.

The area of Social Pathology will treat all pathologies that have social repercussions, such as AIDS, substance abuse, family violence, juvenile delinquency, child neglect, child abuse, social microsystems impoverishment, families damaged by marginalization, and police brutality. The staff will include social workers, lawyers, and some consultants from the area of labor, who will also be affiliated with this Department of Social Medicine and Psychiatry.

The Outpatient Departments (OPDs) connected with these new hospitals will also cover these areas with social repercussions. These OPDs will work closely with the area of Social Pathology. They will be able to provide their patients with a variety of treatment modalities, including group psychotherapy, group admission, group psychopharmacological evaluation, family therapy, and supportive psychotherapy, to help them better manage conflicts with their community, in their neighborhoods, and with the police.

Mental Health Personnel and Treatment

The socioeconomic deterioration that has progressively increased, especially over the last thirty years, has generated the extreme contradiction of inadequate services provided to the lower and middle classes in the contrasting setting of an overabundance of professionals not seen in most developed countries. Recently, the United States, France, and Italy have been "invaded" by Argentine psychologists, many of whose forced relocations are a consequence of the lack of job opportunities in Argentina and become an irreversible process.

Nowadays all of the institutions related to the area of mental health include clinical psychologists, and the public schools have school psychologists who counsel students and can detect, diagnose, and treat learning difficulties early in childhood. The mental health professionals in the general hospitals are psychiatrists, psychologists, and, in some departments, a small number of social workers. All national, city, and university hospitals have a Department of Social Work whose primary task is to take care of the needs and difficulties of the patients in issues related to family, society, or finances (e.g., completing and filing forms regarding Social Security benefits, pensions, and poverty certificates that grant free medical care, or the search for a job or vocational training). All hospitals have a small number of salaried social workers; but, overall, there are many social workers competing for only a few available positions, so many go on later for additional training in psychology to eventually become dynamic psychotherapists.

The number of other salaried professionals is small and the salaries are very low. Consequently, the thirty-six-hours-per-week hospital schedule is often not filled due to the need to spend more hours in private practice to earn a living. The concurrent staff is the unsalaried (ad honorem) staff that works four hours a day, with only a part of this time spent in patient contact activities. The rest of the time is spent in supervision and seminars, which provide a kind of payment for their work.

The psychiatric nursing staff is composed for the most part of unsupervised nurses' aides. The country's few registered nurses usually do not go into psychiatric nursing, but almost entirely into surgery. When they go into psychiatric nursing, they prefer to work in private hospitals where they are better paid. As a result, there is a big lack of psychiatric nursing personnel in the government-supported hospitals. Frequently, staff who started working in these hospitals as housekeepers later become "empiric nurses" by default, functioning as nurses without having the proper training or qualifications. The National Administration of Mental Health has a plan at the present time to train these people during their work hours to become qualified nurses' aides (see figure 2.1). These nurses' aides could then become registered nurses by the same plan.

It is expected that within five years the number of well-trained nursing staff will increase greatly and the quality of care in these chronic-care facilities will consequently improve. At the present time, there is no specialty of psychiatric nursing in either the university or the School of Public Health. This is a step that will likely be taken into practice very shortly, with the growing awareness of the critical role that good psychiatric nursing plays in improving psychiatric care.

PUBLIC POLICY PROCESS

The mental health programs are implemented under the National Administration of Mental Health (Dirección Nacional de Salud Mental), but the final decisions, especially the economic budgets and the political decisions, require the pertinent ministry approval. For this reason, in the last few years many of the programs in mental health have been only good intentions without corresponding actions.

SPECIAL POLICY ISSUES

The Mentally Ill and the Mentally Retarded

The mentally retarded have a different disposition, depending on whether or not they also have psychotic symptoms. In the government-run institutions, however, the mentally retarded whose relatives do not have economic resources are admitted and live with the other psychiatric inpatients. This is different from the way it was in 1906 when the Montes de Oca Treatment Facility was created for the exclusive treatment of the mentally retarded. This early achievement at the turn of the century was lost along with the boundaries of this distinction.

Poor families are often forced by economic hardships to give away an "unproductive" family member, and they may consider hospitalization of their mentally retarded relative in a chronic psychiatric hospital as a solution to their financial problem. This does not mean that the interest in maintaining the distinction between mental illness and mental retardation has been ignored. To the contrary, many groups of professionals and volunteers organize small nonprofit institutions by creating training workshops, schools for the disabled, and other services. The National Administration of Mental Health has tried to share the management of these institutions with the National Bureau of Special Education, but so far this project has not been successful.

The Mentally Ill and Substance Abuse

The incidence and prevalence of the major addictions have not reached the levels that they have in the developed countries. Argentina is no longer just a place of transit for the drug trafficking, but also a place of consumption, because

Figure 2.1
The National Administration of Mental Health Plan in Argentina

As approved by the National Directorate of Human Resources. Includes plan of education of nurses' aides in psychiatry as a new advance. It is coordinated by both the Ministry of Health and Social Action and the Ministry of Education and Justice.

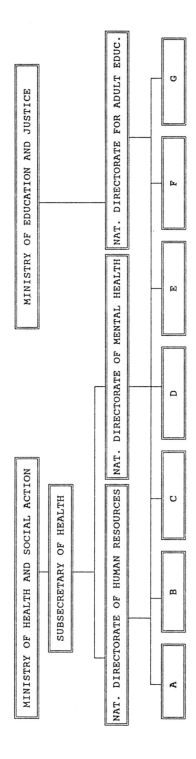

A = Social Skills Training for Patients Who Will Be Discharged Soon
B = Orientation Course in Mental Health for Nurses' Aides
C = Official Career of Professional Nurses
D = Orientation Course in Mental Health for Professional Nurses
E = Full Program of Literacy for Primary School
F = Program of Literacy for Primary School
G = Official Course for Nurses' Aides

Source: Dirección Nacional de Recursos Humanos, Ministerio de Salud y Acción Social, 1991.

the substances are well paid; for example, one gram of cocaine costs ten to fifteen dollars (depending on its purity) ("Segun un documento," 1992).

Cocaine abuse has been increasing gradually over the past three to four years, mostly in the upper and upper-middle classes, though it is found in the poorer classes as well. The middle class has not incorporated fully the culture of abusing cocaine. Its tendency to hold its basic structure preserves it from the addictive regressions of things like expensive and illegal substances. The middle class in Argentina has lately been impoverished economically and, as a consequence, has lost comfort and diminished its consumption of material goods. It continues to keep its cultural links to the intellectual growth of its children, encouraging them to go preferentially into the professional fields. Their primary motivations are participating actively in their family network, reading, motion pictures, arts, theater, and conferences. These interests help to keep them away from addictions to major drugs.

The abuse of amphetamines is also a growing problem; they are now seen as a drug of choice by teenagers of the lower classes. Although their sale without a prescription is illegal, it is not difficult to obtain them from some pharmacies without one or through an underground market.

Marijuana use is common in the intellectual, journalistic, and artistic environments, as opposed to cocaine use, which is more common in corporate staff and business environments. Across all social classes, people abuse anxiolytics (especially teachers), nicotine, alcohol, and caffeine (Sessa, 1992). The general public of Argentina is not as aware as those of some other countries of the adverse health consequences of smoking cigarettes or drinking large amounts of caffeinated beverages.

The practice of self-medication with psychotropics, especially anxiolytics and antidepressants, has achieved a worrisome level because the control of their selling, buying, and using has been practically lost. In spite of the fact that these medications should only be bought in pharmacies with a prescription (and sometimes in triplicate), they can still be obtained in the street or by illegal sale at some pharmacies. This tendency to self-medicate is worsened by the lay impression that all of these medications are harmless. To make matters worse, some physicians have prescription practices that reflect a lack of concern and a knowledge about these medications that seems to have been desired from the literature that the pharmaceutical companies provide, rather than from the established scientific publications. Other drugs, like heroin and methadone, are not part of the general problem, and hence thorough investigations or epidemiologic surveys of their use have not yet been done.

According to Programa Andrés, a nonprofit substance abuse program, it is currently evaluating 40 percent more patients than two years ago, and their age distribution is 35 percent sixteen to nineteen years of age; another 35 percent twenty-five to thirty-five years of age (and these are usually near the collapse of their family); 15 percent twenty to twenty-five years of age; and the remaining

15 percent over forty years of age. Most of its patients are still fully employed (Sessa, 1992).

Currently, very few corporations have employee assistance programs for substance abuse. One of the few exceptions, the oil company Esso S.A.P.A., tests its employees randomly with the breathalyzer for the presence of alcohol or with urine screens for abuse of other substances. If any of these tests are positive, the employee is referred for appropriate treatment ("Prevención en el trabajo," 1992).

Alcohol abuse is a more widespread problem, facilitated in part by the low cost and easily availability of alcoholic beverages. Because the massive production and sale of wine and other alcoholic beverages are very important for the Argentine economy, the prices of these products are kept very low. (As an illustration, either a bottle of wine or of *aguardiente* [thunderbird] is cheaper than a bottle of Coca-Cola.)

The per capita consumption of wine is quite high. The alcoholic habits of Argentina are similar to those of Latin European countries like Spain, Italy, and France: People drink a lot, but most of it with lunch and dinner; there is almost no drinking of alcoholic beverages between meals or any "happy hour" after work or before dinner. Much alcohol is also consumed during the traditional *asado y vino* (barbecue and wine), a typical part of current Argentine cultural and social life that originated in the country's folklore history of the life of its admired and often-glamorized gauchos (cowboys).

As a consequence of the large consumption of alcohol, there is, unfortunately, a high rate of deadly car accidents due to drunken driving. The Ministry of Health, through the National Administration of Mental Health, has a technical council that organizes campaigns and congresses related to this issue, but it has had little significant impact.

The media send irresponsible messages promoting the use of tobacco and alcohol, implying that they make men more macho and women more feminine, and that wine is the beverage of "strong people." They associate their use with attractive lifestyles, sexual successes, and risky but exciting activities, misleading and misinforming the public about their damaging effects, especially on pregnant women and youths, and the dangers of driving while intoxicated. The advertisements are not regulated by any consumer protection agencies, as they are in some other countries. The deputy L. Pepe is working in the House of Deputies of the Nation on a project that would forbid encouragement of this type of advertisement, but so far, powerful economic interests have prevented the formulation of this project.

Recently, adolescents have increased their consumption of beer compared to prior years. Beer is sold without a special license on every street block from small outlets that sell candies and cigarettes as well. Teenagers, as a habit, often buy it illegally to take it with them when they go dancing.

In the area of government-supported substance abuse treatment, the Centro Nacional de Recuperación Social (CENARESO), the National Center for Social

Recovery, is an institution that has the capability to treat both inpatients and outpatients. So far, it has been of dubious efficacy. It does not yet have a good image in the population and is not used efficiently.

The efforts made in the private sector for the treatment of substance abuse, be they through individual outpatient treatment or inpatient treatment in private clinics, have not had satisfactory long-term results either, from both the psychological and medical viewpoints. They have benefitted mostly the professionals and clinic owners who function both as psychiatrists and addictionologists.

This area is covered with a much better long-term outcome by a number of institutions that are nonproft: Programa Andrés, Viaje de Vuelta, and others. The therapeutic treatment and resocializing approach of these programs have been the most efficacious so far and have given the best results. It is for this reason that they function as rehabilitative farms located far away from the main urban centers and include in their contract the commitment of the family's involvement in the treatment of the patient.

In these institutions one can find the same type of methodology that is found in AA (Alcoholics Anonymous), which continues to be the most successful institution in the treatment of alcohol abuse. This methodology allows the creation of a complementary superego and increases the group solidarity. These programs have the support of religious organizations, especially Catholic institutions, and have now become the predominant base of secondary and tertiary prevention in this area.

Primary prevention is addressed by the National Direction of Promotion and Protection of Health and is funded by the Ministry of Health and Social Action. The National Direction of Promotion and Protection of Health promotes educational programs sponsored by the Ministry of Education and by other foundations that contribute funds in exchange for advertising and publicity. Still, there is no single agency that can efficiently coordinate all of these funds, and the monies often become diluted due to their poor administration.

The Mentally Disordered Offender

A lawyer for some years now has been routinely incorporated into many mental health services to deal with certain economic, social, legal, and criminal issues that impact on mental health. In the field of law, the country received the influence of Dr. Jiménez de Asúa, whose psychological theories about crime and delinquency contributed to the change in thinking about the relationship between criminal behavior and psychiatry.

The state psychiatric hospitals have a special ward to which only the criminally insane are admitted. They receive psychiatric treatment and are discharged as per the treating specialist's report.

There is a committee of judges dedicated to the area of minors and incompetents. This committee, together with the National Administration of Mental Health, is instituting new projects, such as activating the legal process and encouraging the direct participation of these professionals in the discharge of patients (particularly those patients who are admitted because they are psychotic, violent, and/or behaving in a way that requires the participation of the police or the law in their admission process).

Deinstitutionalization

Since the turn of the century, Argentina has led the commitment to psychiatric, psychological, and psychosocial developments in Latin America and has been a powerful influence on the rest of South America. The social approach has been a predominant factor of the professional work from the start.

Changing the anachronistic structures of the big asylums has not yet been accomplished. There has been a great deal of resistance from the labor-union leaders who benefit from the perpetuation of these structures. Proposals to dissolve these enormous structures (which have more than a thousand inpatients each) have been presented. They have included the patients' reincorporation into their families with a subsidy, and the creation of small residences and hospitals (for the acutely mentally ill) that would be associated with the general hospitals whose censuses are fewer than one hundred inpatients. This proposal also included the privatization of the care provided in the patients' homes and the small residences, which would limit the government's responsibility to overseeing new institutional structures, each with fewer than one hundred inpatients (Fiasche, 1991).

Had the plan of transferring the care of the chronic mentally ill to the private sector been carried out (including the sale of the big asylums at current real-estate market value), the economic value of the grounds alone where the two big asylums of Buenos Aires are located would have been sufficient to cover the cost of moving all three thousand inpatients into small residences and of providing many of them with domiciliary assistance as well. This project was about to be implemented with the World Bank's support, but the change of authorities, including those in the National Administration of Mental Health, paralyzed this possibility. New legislation has been passed in the province of Río Negro that includes a project to sell all of its old and huge mental health institutions.

Funding Issues

The structure of financial assistance in Argentina is a combination of funds from the federal government, provinces, cities, the Social Security administration, the different labor unions, and private agencies. The efforts to unify all of these have not been successful, due to conflicting economic interests. The psychiatric services in the general hospitals are supported by each province's budget in the maintenance and budgets of the facilities, and in exchange, each provincial government has input into the philosophy and organization of assistance.

Budgets for health and education have been deteriorating, especially in the last few years. As a consequence of these budget reductions, the rates of infant mortality, illiteracy, and preventable mental retardation (due, for instance, to nutritional deficiencies or lack of an early diagnosis) have increased. Each of the areas of assistance supported by the government is in a state of crisis: health, education, housing, and transportation. The social-democratic model, similar to the one in Sweden and in many ways to the one in Great Britain, has been collapsing as the budgets in these areas have been progressively reduced. The present mental health budget is below that which is required for adequate treatment, and to make matters worse, the hospitals' personnel steal food and other goods, justifying this by the low salaries that they receive. The nursing absenteeism goes beyond 50 percent, and this adds enormously to the patients' poor care.

The budgets for mental health services are developed and funded through different sources. The big, old psychiatric hospitals are funded by the Ministry of Health and Social Action through its office of the National Administration of Mental Health. In essence, then, the chronic-care hospitals are supported with government funds in their totality. As a consequence of the constant struggle of the National Administration of Mental Health to increase their funding, they also receive extra subsidies, though infrequently. Another source of extra funding is the Administración Nacional del Selguro de Salud (ANSAL), the National Administration of Health Insurance, an organization that regulates the funds of the public health insurance plans.

This entire system is extremely bureaucratic and allows corruption and mismanagement to exist on a regular basis. For example, in 1990 the government's budget allocated the equivalent of twenty-five dollars per day per patient to the chronic-care hospitals, but the cost of the benefits that these inpatients finally received as food, lodging, and medications was less than the equivalent of five dollars per day. As a consequence, the food was bad (causing massive malnutrition), the clothing was inadequate, and the professional treatments were poor and insufficient (Fiasche, 1991).

A huge number of the inpatients have health insurance from their different employers, but the amount of coverage that they provide is not legally regulated. Consequently, the insurance plans from the unions often reject claims with various arguments (for example, "the lodging capacity of the place is insufficient") to avoid the responsibility of having to pay for their members. In this way they place the economic burden on the government's funds.

Other economic resources are, of course, the patient's own funds. Decisions regarding the money of mentally ill patients who have been declared incompetent are made through the patient's legal guardian, appointed by a judge.

Other funds come from a pool of donations, frequently very generous, run by a voluntary organization called Cooperadora (Auxiliary). This group exists in every single hospital, psychiatric or not, and its mission is to try to cover all the needs that the official budgets, be they national, municipal, or university, cannot provide. The administration of these funds is neither strict nor efficient. They are not regulated by the national budget, and they have a high degree of discretion in their spending. The other national institution that also contributes to the resources of those institutions is the Prestación Asistencial Médico-Integral (PAMI), the Comprehensive Medical Treatment Plan. PAMI is somewhat equivalent to Social Security in the United States. Thus far the meetings between this official institution and the chronic-care hospitals or the National Administration of Mental Health have been unsuccessful.

PAMI is the institution in charge of providing geriatric medical and psychiatric treatments for the nation's senior citizens. In contracts with private services (e.g., hospitals and agencies) to treat patients, sometimes including home visits. Although it centralizes and coordinates all types of treatment, it has no formal protocols or regular revisions of the quality of its care. Consequently, although some institutions that service PAMI are top-level, others are quite inadequate and place patients in overcrowded and dangerous situations.

Surprisingly, both the very top and the poor-quality groups receive the same amount of funding per patient. This happens because the state organizations lack an executive system capable of inspection and revision that would be fair and appropriate. Laws and regulations exist, but usually the inspectors are bribed. At the level of the hospitals in the provinces, one can find the same discrepancies in the quality of care, especially in those that have a massive concentration of patients.

Consumer Rights

Various factors have led to advances in consumer rights in mental health, including the pressure in favor of voluntary admission and the work of a group of judges, who fight to speed up the discharge of patients who are admitted through applications made within the judicial power (e.g., patients who have been admitted because of their dangerousness or violence). The main goal of the legislation passed through the years in the area of mental health is to protect the patients' legal right to refuse treatment and to request a court hearing in order to be discharged, while ensuring their right to receive treatment and society's right to protect itself from patients who are potentially dangerous or violent. Although the two laws that became landmarks in this field, one instituted in 1905 and the other in 1983, vary in form, they share the same spirit.

For example, the law of 1905 requires either a signed application from another person or an order from the police or appropriate mental health authorities to admit anyone who is considered a danger to self or others to a psychiatric facility. It requires that the family be informed within forty-eight hours of any admission, and that within fifteen days the medical director has to examine the patient and give his or her opinion. It further stipulates that the patient be discharged from the facility when he or she is cured or no longer "affected by mental insanity." If the patient is admitted by the application of others, he or she can request to be released by those same persons, even if he or she is not yet completely cured. If the patient is found to be dangerous, the law requires that he or she not be discharged, and that the judge be informed of this. In the case when a person is admitted by the police or the order of the appropriate authorities, he or she must be discharged back to the authorities who applied for the admission. The law stipulates, furthermore, that the person admitted or any other interested party can ask for the immediate release of the patient, and that this should be considered by the judicial authorities. These same judicial authorities are, according to the law, involved in all involuntary admissions.

Under the 1983 law the requirements of the 1905 law remain more or less the same, with the important addition of the creation of the Ministry of Minors and Incapables. This is a progressive step that provides protection to patients by an outside official agency from potential abuses. This agency is to be informed of every step taken in the process of admission or discharge. The law further stipulates that its advisors must visit the hospitals at least every six months to verify the evolution of the patient's mental and physical health, the psychiatric treatment regimen, the housing conditions, the personal care, and the medical treatment that he or she receives, and must inform the judge of all of their findings.

One goal that the law of 1983 affirms more emphatically than its 1905 counterpart is the control that the executive branch should keep over the process of admission. It also introduces the concept of voluntary admission, eliminating the participation of the law in the discharge plans and, consequently, making the discharge easier. This can be considered progress. Again, its ultimate goal is to protect the patients' rights to freedom and adequate treatment.

Trials for malpractice, although moving very slowly, are increasing in number due to a greater awareness in the population of their rights. An anecdote of the public's awareness of the consumer rights of the mentally ill is an incident that occurred in 1972. All of the so-called instruments of psychiatric torture (the instruments for insulin therapy, hoses for cold-water therapy, jail-like seclusion, and other such instruments) were burnt in a public demonstration. These methods of treatment are no longer used in the hospitals and universities in Argentina. If they are still used in any private clinics in violation of the medical recommendations, this is not a matter of public knowledge. They could still be used in some remote regions of the country that are unable to be controlled by the official institutions. Psychosurgery has not been practiced widely for many years and is not currently included in the philosophical approach of the mental health experts in Argentina as "one more therapeutic tool as important as the others" in the treatment of mental illnesses.

CONCLUSIONS AND DISCUSSION

Argentina has been, and in many respects continues to be, a leader in South America in the dynamic and constant transformations in the area of mental health.

Despite serious inadequacies and limited financial resourses, it has been able to address many of its problems, largely due to its commitment to constantly reviewing and updating its developments and treatment strategies in mental health. This capacity for self-reflection and self-criticism is characteristic of the philosophical methodology of thinking in Argentina, derived from its European cultural influence and heritage. One of the factors that has influenced this humanistic motivation is that the country and its provinces have had presidents and governors who came from the medical field.

New contributions to treatment approaches are being offered now as a consequence of the demands of a new and harsh economic reality and of the changes in the quality of life in Argentina, together with the current needs of its population. These approaches include a critical introspection of the lack of basic elements of survival, of outdated ideas, of corruptions, and of discriminations in the professional area, which are believed to be preventing Argentina from maintaining the same high scientific level as other advanced countries of the world.

In the same way that Argentina has been a leader in the opening of the therapeutic community in the 1900s and other progressive clinical decisions, it has also been responsible for the deterioration of many of these advances. Much still needs to be done. It is hoped that the new laws, including the one already approved in Río Negro, will generate a very progressive step in the near future that will allow the definite dissolution of the huge and at times shameful chronic-care psychiatric hospitals.

The country has huge human resources, all invested in a change of politics of mental health. The presence of more than 40,000 psychologists constantly pressures the country to continue the transformations. In addition, the growing movement of social psychology with a clinical orientation has opened a view that promises comprehension and understanding of mental pathology also from a sociological perspective.

Plans to improve nursing training and staffing are currently working at full speed in order to compensate for a background that was inexcusable, and within the next few years the country should be capable of having a system of nursing, general as well as psychiatric, more like those in the developed countries. If the project involving the dissolution of the big chronic-care hospitals of Buenos Aires can be accomplished successfully, this will probably promote positive repercussions in the provinces.

We are convinced that our future is a promising one, not only to rescue all of the innovativeness of the Argentine mentality that has been lost, but also to continue to improve and produce new approaches, not just of deinstititonalization, but also of humanization. We are now finally approaching a degree of stability between the tendencies of massive hospitalizations lasting innumerable years (which were often unjustified) and massive discharges out of the so-called revolutionary psychiatric processes that carelessly sent thousands of homeless mentally ill people into the streets. Finally, it is a pity that Argentina continues to give away its bright brains, not only to other fields, but also within the area of mental health, due to the huge number of mental health professionals who should be encouraged and supported to work in the primary prevention of psychiatry, but who instead get trained as superspecialists who later must emigrate due to economic crisis.

REFERENCES

Fiasche, A. (1985). Estructura social de los países de América Latina y la salud mental. In E. Pavlovsky (Ed.), Buenos Aires: *Lo Grupal*. Editorial Búsqueda.

Fiasche, A. (1991, October 3). Manicomios: La edad de la sinrazón. *Desbordar*, pp. 14–15.

Legislatura de la Provincia de Río Negro. (1991), October 3). Ley de Promoción Sanitaria y Social de las Personas que Padecen Sufrimiento Mental. *Desbordar*, pp. 22–23.

Prevención en el trabajo. (1992, January 26). *Diario La Nación*, p. 12.

Según un documento de la U.N.—Consideran a la Argentina como un país de tránsito de la cocaína. *Diario La Nación*. (1992, January 14).

Sessa, V. (1992, January 26). Los ambientes laborales y el consumo de estupefacientes. *Diario La Nación*, p. 12.

SELECTED BIBLIOGRAPHY

Berman, G. (1964). La psicoterapia en la Argentina. *Acta Psiquiátrica y Psicológica de América Latina, 10*, 4.

Berman, S. (1964). La asistencia psiquiátrica en Latino América. *Acta Psiquiátrica y Piscológica de América Latina, 9*, 1.

Boyers, R. and R. Orrill (Eds.). (1971). *R. D. Laingand anti-psychiatry*. New York: Harper & Row.

Brown, S. (Ed.). (1983). *Psychiatry in developing countries*. London: Royal College of Psychiatry.

Comisión Asesora de Asilos y Hospitales Regionales. (1908); (1909); (1912); (1913); (1914). *Memoria 1906–1907; 1907–1908; 1909–1911; 1911–1912; 1912–1913*. Buenos Aires: Imprenta y Encuadernación del Hospicio de las Mercedes.

Corsico, R. (1960). La actividad psiquiátrica de Alejandro Korn. *Revista de la Universidad Nacional de La Plata, 11*.

Ethchegoyen, H., Fiasche, A., & Arensburg, B. (1965). Dinámica de grupo operativo. *Revista de Psicología y Psicoterapia de Grupo, 4*, 1.

Fernandez Amallo, J., & Ballsells de Ragoza, M. E. (1981). Bases para un Plan Nacional de Salud Mental. *Neuropsiquiatria y Salud Mental, 12*, 3.

Fiasche, A. (1979). Discusión: Tema sobre la perversión: La caracteropatía perversa (Author: Rolla, E.). *Trevista de Psicoanálisis, Asociación Psicoanalítica Argentina, 36*, 6.

Fiasche, A., & Ullman, M. (1971). Intervención en las crisis. *Revista Argentina de Psicología, 3*, 6.

Goldenberg, M. (1984). *Lineamientos generales de un Plan de Salud Mental*. Buenos Aires: Ministerio de Salud Pública.

Holden, N., & Edwards, G. (1989). *Post-graduate training in psychiatry (option for international collaborations)*. Geneva: WHO (Mental Health Division).

Manfredi, M., et al. (1987). *Concepto de salud mental en el currículum de* Enfermería: *Programa de personal de salud*. Geneva: WHO (Mental Health Division).

Meléndez, E. (1984). El alcoholismo en América Latina. *Acta Psiquiátrica y Psicológica de América Latina, 30*, 1.

Meyer, L. (1986). La implantación del sistema "Open Door" en Argentina. *Acta Psiquiátrica y Psicológica de América Latina, 34*, 1.

OMS–UNICEF (1989). *Declaración de ALMA-ATA*. Secretaría de Salud de Entre Ríos, Revista Salud, 3.

Plott, H., Fiasche, A., & Gilbert, A. (1979). Epilepsia y desmistificación de las disrritmias. *Cuadernos de Clínica, Temas de Pisquiatría y Psicopatología, 1*, 1.

Sociedad de Beneficencia de la Capital Federal. (1924). *Reglamento del Hospital Nacional de Alienados*. Buenos Aires: Talleres Graficos del Asilo de Huérfanos.

Tossenberg, A. (1991, October 3). La desmanicomialización en Río Negro. *Desbordar*, pp. 19–21.

3

Canada

Carl M. Lakaski, Valerie Wilmot, Thomas J. Lips, and Monica Brown

OVERVIEW

Canada extends from the Atlantic Ocean in the east to the Pacific Ocean in the west, and north to the Arctic Ocean. As of March 1991, the population occupying its 9.2 million square kilometers was estimated at 27,296,859. There is no permanent settlement on approximately 89 percent of Canada's land. More than half of the nation's people live within 240 kilometers (149 miles) of the Canada-U.S. border, and three-quarters live in an urban environment (Statistics Canada, 1989).

Over the past twenty-five years, Canada has experienced a gradual decline in the rate of population growth, accompanied by major changes in population age structure. The "baby boom" of the 1950s and 1960s, followed by the "baby bust" of the 1970s and 1980s, has had a significant impact on school systems, the labor force, family formation, health care, and many other aspects of society. Currently, the child population is stabilizing, while the youth population (fourteen to twenty-four years) is declining. The Canadian family has an average of only 1.3 children, with notable highs of 2.0 in the Northwest Territories and 1.7 in Newfoundland.

In more than 60 percent of two-parent families, both parents work outside the home. Women now make up approximately 44 percent of the labor force. At the time of the 1986 census, there were over 850,000 single-parent families in Canada, of which four out of five were headed by women.

Single mothers, women, and the elderly make up most of the 4 million individuals defined as having low incomes; in 1988 an estimated 3.3 million Canadians (13.1 percent) spent more than 58.5 percent of their income on food, shelter, and clothing. Not included in this estimate of low- or no-income earners are those individuals who reside in institutions (including jails and penitentiaries, psychiatric hospitals, and homes for the aged) and those who are homeless and/ or shelterless. Generally, unemployment is highest in the Atlantic provinces and lowest in central Canada, and more prolonged periods of unemployment are noted among individuals living in rural areas. Rural areas also tend to lack affordable housing and social services.

Canada is officially bilingual, and the federal government provides services in both English and French. English and French are cited as the mother tongues of 61 percent and 24 percent of the population, respectively.

Canada has over 750,000 individuals (about 2.9 percent of the population) who trace their ancestry to Canada's first inhabitants. Approximately 200,000 native people lived on reserves and settlements in 1986.

One in six Canadians was born outside the country. In the first half of the century, individuals immigrated to Canada mostly from Europe and the United States. However, immigration is now far more diverse with respect to national, linguistic, religious, and racial background (Health and Welfare Canada, 1988a).

Chronic conditions and mental health problems have replaced communicable diseases as the predominant health problems faced by Canadians. These conditions are greatly influenced by environmental and behavioral factors, particularly the stress of modern living.[1]

EXTENT OF THE PROBLEM

Mental illness is one of the major public health problems facing developed countries today. Statistics Canada estimates that one in eight Canadians will be hospitalized for mental illness at least once in a lifetime. Suicide is the second leading cause of death in Canadians aged 15 to 39 years, and mental illness is the second leading category of illness among general hospital patients aged 20 to 44 years. Studies have shown that the life expectancy of those suffering from mental disorder is reduced by as much as one-third. According to Statistics Canada, hospital costs for mental illness in 1978 exceeded one billion dollars, a cost that has since increased, and is at least matched by the costs of unemployment and social support for the mentally ill and their families. Many more individuals with mental illness are treated out of hospital than in hospital, yet most of the funds for treatment are spent for hospital in-patient services. (Bland, 1988)

Schizophrenia is one of the most common mental disorders, affecting about one in every hundred Canadians during the course of their lives (Mills, 1990). Approximately 40 percent of mental and psychiatric hospital beds and 7 percent of general hospital beds are occupied by schizophrenic patients. In addition, there are numerous undiagnosed and borderline cases; some individuals manage on their own in the community, and others are part of the homeless population. Individuals with bipolar affective disorder are another major population requiring mental health services.

Among children, adjustment reaction, conduct and emotional disturbance, acute reaction to stress, depression, and hyperactivity are the most common diagnoses. Many mental health problems are believed to result from sexual, physical, and psychological abuse and neglect.

Among women, neurosis is the most common diagnosis in the hospitalized population, while men are most often admitted for alcoholism. Schizophrenia and affective disorders are the next most common diagnoses among the hospitalized.

As the population ages over the next twenty-five years, we can expect the number of cases of dementia (especially Alzheimer's disease) to double (Canadian Mental Health Association, 1988). Dementia is a major factor contributing to the need for long-term care and support (Health and Welfare Canada, 1990b).

Individuals who are directly affected by mental illness face problems related to housing, finding and holding a job, stigmatization, depression, and social and emotional dependence on family and society. Most mental disorders present in late adolescence and early adulthood, a time when the individual is completing his or her education or entering the work force. Individuals who suffer from mental disorder are also at great risk of being neglected. Consequently, mental disorder is disabling to the individual in both the short and the long term. The financial and emotional strain may be felt by all family members, but potential years of life and income lost and the cost of health care and social support are long-term concerns for society itself.

MENTAL HEALTH HISTORY

In the 1800s many individuals who suffered from mental disorder were either jailed or cared for within the family home. The first mental hospitals were constructed in the latter part of the century to provide greater care and better living conditions for these individuals.

Until 1948 almost all treatment of severely ill psychiatric patients was provided in the provincial institutions, which were often located in very isolated areas. Patients were often admitted by legal process and retained in locked wards. These institutions often operated at more than 100 percent capacity, with the number of patients on the books averaging more than the rated bed capacity. Understaffing, overcrowding, and the lack of effective treatments led to an emphasis on custody rather than therapy. This type of care was primitive and restrictive, and it relied on methods involving seclusion and chemical and physical restraints. During the years from 1948 to 1961 many improvements were made in the treatment of mentally ill Canadians. Increased expenditures on mental health services and advances in mental health research contributed to these improvements. Pharmacological advances dramatically altered the course of some disabling mental conditions, allowing many patients to resume higher levels of functioning in the activities of everyday life without constant supervision and care.

In May 1948 the federal government made funds available to the provinces to assist in the extension and improvement of services in specific health fields, including mental health. The early emphasis was necessarily placed on strengthening both professional and technical training facilities and improving the quality and quantity of staff.

The distribution of funds stabilized in the last years of the Mental Health Grant, with about 53 percent going to institutions, 23 percent to clinics and psychiatric units, and 13 percent toward the training efforts. Research in psychiatry reaped particular benefit, coming to account for about 8 percent of total expenditures. The research funding mechanism of the National Health Grants Program was retained as the still-operating National Health Research and Development Program (NHRDP).

The Hospital Insurance and Diagnostic Services Act of 1958 specifically excluded psychiatric services as well as other services delivered within a psychiatric hospital unless they were deemed medically necessary and were rendered by a medical practitioner. At this time the provinces and territories were already meeting the costs of psychiatric hospitals' services. The federal contributions to provincial health insurance programs were designed to assist in providing active care services; tuberculosis hospitals, nursing homes, and psychiatric hospitals were considered to be custodial care facilities.

In the 1960s several of Canada's larger, more isolated institutions were closed. Long hospitalization was slowly being replaced by shorter, intermittent stays. More and more, treatment was being offered by private practitioners and other staff in clinics and day hospitals in psychiatric units in general hospitals.

In the last three decades, in recognition of the need for a multidisciplinary network of support for the individual at each stage of a mental illness, mental health services have been increasingly oriented toward a community-based model of care. In several cities local mental health centers have teams that address needs in areas of daily living, personal care, finances and financial management, social and recreational contact, and support for individuals and their families. The voluntary work-force and consumer advocacy groups are strong in Canada and have been recognized as an essential component of a comprehensive continuum of care.

POLICY, ORGANIZATION, AND SERVICES IN THE 1980s AND 1990s

Current Policy Developments

The federal mental health discussion paper *Mental Health for Canadians: Striking a Balance* was released in 1988 (Health and Welfare Canada, 1988c). This document advanced an innovative definition of mental health that eclipsed the limitations of traditional definitions. It stated:

Mental Health is the capacity of the individual, the group and the environment to interact with one another in ways that promote subjective well-being, the optimal development and use of mental abilities (cognitive, affective, and relational), the achievement of individual and collective goals consistent with justice and the attainment and preservation of conditions of fundamental equality.

This definition of mental health reflects a number of themes, including psychological and social harmony and integration, quality of life and general well-being, self-actualization and growth, effective personal adaptation, and the mutual influences of the individual, the group, and the environment. Furthermore, it emphasizes the social context of mental health by explicitly indicating the importance of social justice and equality to mental well-being. The definition also recognizes that all individuals possess a capacity for mental health, whether or not they have a mental disorder.

In addition, the paper examines, from a mental health perspective, the three major health challenges described in the 1986 federal discussion paper *Achieving Health for All: A Framework for Health Promotion*, namely, reducing inequities, increasing prevention, and enhancing coping. It offers a set of guiding principles for use in developing, reviewing, and implementing mental-health-related policies and programs. These principles address human rights and citizenship, mutual aid and voluntary service, consumer participation, professional participation, the strengthening of communities, knowledge development, and policy coordination.

There are many advantages to this approach to mental health. It offers hope for people with chronic mental disorders by emphasizing the needs that all Canadians have in common, and it is conducive to solidarity among those with mental disorders. Most important, it invites a broader range of strategies to address mental health needs. A positive vision of mental health as much more than the absence of disease or disorder encourages Canadians to take an active role in determining the full range of conditions that affect their mental health.

Recent provincial policy papers echo *Mental Health for Canadians: Striking a Balance* and have proposed a broader scope for mental health services. For example, British Columbia and Quebec have adopted a focus that recognizes the need for programs to address the biological, psychological and social issues associated with mental disorder (British Columbia, Ministry of Health, 1987; Ministry of Health and Social Services, Government of Quebec, 1989b). It has been widely acknowledged that the needs of individuals go well beyond the treatment and control of symptoms.

Most of the provinces have identified priorities for their respective service systems. There is a broad consensus that the needs of individuals with chronic and serious mental disorders demand the highest service priority (e.g., Ontario's *Building Community Support for People* [Provincial Community Mental Health Committee, 1988]; Manitoba Health, 1988). Other priorities include the provision of specialized care for children, youth, and the elderly, in addition to prevention programs aimed at high-risk groups.

Emerging trends in mental health policy, service development, and administrative reform reflect several critical objectives or themes that have been expressed in federal, provincial, and territorial documents pertaining to mental health. Key themes include the following:

1. A greater emphasis on community care
2. Achieving coordination of services and service developments
3. Protecting human rights and freedoms
4. Working for the promotion of mental health and the prevention of mental disorder

Mental health promotion activities reflect a different set of priorities, including, for example, the fostering of healthy, adaptive behaviors (sound parenting practices, social skills development, lifelong learning), the prevention of maladaptive behaviors (alcohol and drug use, suicide, and child abuse and neglect), and the elimination of discrimination on the basis of age, ethnicity, or disability (Health and Welfare Canada, 1987, 1988b). *Mental health promotion* is a term that is defined differently by different constituencies and jurisdictions. In its broadest sense, mental health promotion can be said to address mental health as a collective goal of society; it can include all measures designed to foster, protect, and improve mental health, ranging from mutual aid to sound urban planning and social policy. More conventionally, mental health promotion can be said to include interventions designed to foster skills, attitudes, and behaviors conducive to mental health. Such interventions typically focus on informing, educating, and persuading a target audience—either a group considered ''at risk'' for mental health problems, or a group whose behavior has implications for the mental health of others (e.g., parents, teachers, caregivers, the general public). Because so many of the factors affecting mental health are beyond the control of the individual, there is a growing tendency to go beyond the conventional responses to mental disorders and mental health problems to consider a wider range of interventions (e.g., reform of social and organizational structures and policies) that could promote mental health.

Although prevention of mental disorder is often an implicit secondary goal, mental health promotion is best considered in positive terms: Its primary objective is to strengthen the positive factors underlying mental health (e.g., skills, knowledge, motivation, relationships, sense of control, and empowerment). These factors can be strengthened even in the presence of a mental disorder that is not, in itself, ''curable.''

Many biological and psychosocial factors have been implicated in triggering and worsening mental disorders, but until more is known about the etiology of such disorders, there can be only limited application of the ''public health model'' of primary prevention. Ongoing research in pharmacological and other modalities has facilitated secondary prevention (i.e., treatment and the prevention of relapse). Now, growing attention is being given to tertiary prevention, which attempts to intervene to prevent or minimize disability associated with a disorder.

The mediating effects of social networks on mental health are increasingly being taken into account. Creating environments and policies that support these processes should be a matter of compelling priority for every community in Canada.

Current Organization

Jurisdiction over governmental activities is divided, and sometimes shared, between the federal and provincial governments in the Constitution Act of 1867. Federal-provincial relations are a central element in Canadian government and policy making and a fundamental characteristic of Canadian federalism.

Although health care is constitutionally assigned to provincial jurisdictions, the Canadian health care system is the result of sustained federal, provincial, and territorial efforts that have achieved a national program based on a set of twelve health insurance plans with common elements. Saskatchewan introduced the first system of universal hospital insurance in 1947 and the first medical care insurance program in 1962.

The federal role has historically been one of standard setting, in order to maintain a system of high-quality care under state-sponsored health insurance. The Hospital Insurance and Diagnostic Services Act (1957) and the Medical Care Act (1966) brought universal health care to Canada. By 1972 all provinces and territories had medical insurance plans that satisfied broad national standards and health care systems that were cost-shared by the federal government.

To prevent extra-billing and user charges from interfering with the principle of reasonable access to a comprehensive health care system, the federal government brought in legislation to reaffirm its commitment to universal, prepaid, public national health insurance. The Canada Health Act (1984) entrenches the basic principles underlying the national network of health insurance programs. It strengthens the program conditions and criteria of public administration, comprehensiveness, universality, portability, and accessibility. All provincial plans cover essential medically necessary services, including inpatient and outpatient services provided in patients' homes, in physicians' offices, or in hospitals.

Services that are beneficial to health, but that are not considered essential medically necessary services under the Canada Health Act (1984), may be added to the basic coverage at the discretion of the provinces and territories. Examples of additional benefits provided by some provinces include subsidized medications for seniors, dental care for children, and the services of certain nonphysician health practitioners. At present, the provinces and territories can charge chronic-care patients, including users of psychiatric hospital services who are permanently resident in a facility, to cover the cost of accommodation and meals. Payments to physicians are negotiated with their respective medical associations, and, with few exceptions, doctors are paid on a fee-for-service basis. Premiums can be levied for coverage under the health care legislation, but have been eliminated in all but two provinces.

The Established Programs Financing Act of 1977 was amended in accordance with the Canada Health Act (1984) and renamed the Federal-Provincial Fiscal Arrangements and Federal Post-Secondary and Health Contributions Act; it subsumes the financing component of the Canada Health Act. At present, although health care costs continue to rise, these financing arrangements have stabilized the federal contribution to these costs.

Specific responsibilities for health care in Canada are divided among the three levels of government. In the health field the federal government has assumed responsibility for the following:

- Fiscal transfers to provincial health programs
- Sustaining grants to national voluntary organizations
- National standards and guidelines
- Health promotion
- Monitoring the quality of food, drugs, and medical devices
- Funding for research and development
- Health services for Indians on reserves, the Royal Canadian Mounted Police and the armed forces, and immigrants and refugees at certain stages of the settlement process
- Funding for special projects
- Facilitation of information sharing and collaboration with provinces and territories

Provincially, specific health care responsibilities include the following:

- All aspects of health care delivery: fee setting; hospital standards and operating budgets; community public and mental health services
- Supporting research and development
- Ownership, funding, and administration of psychiatric hospitals
- Dental and drug services
- Hospital and medical care insurance

Provincial governments delegate certain responsibilities to municipal governments and articulate the interests of these governments. These responsibilities include the following:

- Managing primary-care health services
- Environmental and public health
- Administration of hospitals

Direct federal involvement in issues of mental health and mental illness has been primarily through the Mental Health Division of Health and Welfare Canada. The Mental Health Division strives to promote the mental health of Canadians while encouraging the development of high-quality treatment, rehabilitation, prevention, and community support programs for individuals with mental disorders. It seeks to meet these objectives through

- publishing a multidisciplinary journal, *Canada's Mental Health*;
- providing monographs, guidelines, reports, and pamphlets;
- providing staff consultants from varied professional backgrounds;
- hosting conferences and symposia; and
- supporting the work of the Federal/Provincial Advisory Committee on Mental Health and its substructures.

Other federal departments, working both independently and in collaboration with Health and Welfare Canada, address a number of important mental-health-related issues, including the following:

- Applying regulatory and other measures in order to control neurotoxins in the environment and in manufactured products and to prevent accidents that may result in brain injury. (Environment Canada, Transport Canada, Consumer and Corporate Affairs, Agriculture Canada, Labour Canada, and other federal agencies are all currently involved in these areas.)
- Sponsoring regulatory, research, informational, and other measures related to the protection and advancement of human rights, autonomy, and the personal, cultural, and communal identity of various groups in the Canadian population. Particular attention is focused on groups identified as having special needs, including Indians and Inuit, women, immigrants and refugees, ethnic communities, physically disabled persons, and persons disabled by psychiatric disorders, neurological conditions, or mental retardation. (The Departments of the Secretary of State, Justice, Employment and Immigration, and Indian and Northern Affairs, the Canadian Human Rights Commission, Status of Women Canada, and other federal agencies are all currently involved in these areas.)
- Providing mental health care to inmates in federal penitentiaries and mental-health-related programs to witnesses, victims of crime, the Royal Canadian Mounted Police, and others involved in the administration of criminal justice; preventing crime (Solicitor General).
- Providing mental health services and related programs for members of the armed forces and entitled veterans (National Defence, Veterans Affairs).
- Collecting, analyzing, and publishing statistics concerning diagnoses, hospital admissions and discharges, deaths, and related data (Statistics Canada).
- Consulting and facilitating activities to improve labor relations, with implications for mental health in the workplace (Labour Canada).
- Sponsoring activities and programs to maximize employment and meet the information, training, and income-security needs of the unemployed and immigrants (Employment and Immigration).

Voluntary organizations provide health-related services such as mutual aid, respite care, public education, and advocacy and are responsible for the administration of some hospitals. These organizations also offer social services, including family and child services and support, child care, and meals-on-wheels, as well as operating food banks and legal-aid clinics. Self-help, advocacy, and consumer groups may provide services or make appropriate referrals, as well as contributing practical knowledge to the process of health and social service system development. Some of the services offered by the private sector include home care, homes for the elderly, and residential boarding for children and disabled individuals, as well as pharmaceutical development and distribution.

Responsibility for health care within the two territories has already been transferred from the federal government to the Northwest Territories and is being similarly transferred in the Yukon. The Medical Services Branch of Health and Welfare Canada still provides services to Inuit and Status Indians. The branch maintains nursing and health stations, health centers, and small hospitals. It also trains and employs indigenous health workers and pays for care provided by health workers and institutions outside of Medical Services Branch programs. Also, the Non-Insured Health Benefits Program of the branch makes provision for such costs as travel expenses to obtain treatment, prosthetic appliances, and aids such as eyeglasses and pays fees for services of nonmedical practitioners such as psychologists where these are medically prescribed. The provinces are responsible for health services to native peoples living off-reserve and to individuals who are covered under the provincial medical and hospital insurance programs.

Current Services

Hospital services are currently provided by over 1,200 general, pediatric, teaching, and specialty hospitals, over half of which have fewer than 100 beds each. Approximately 171,000 beds are available for individuals to receive insured standard ward services and all available diagnostic, treatment, and rehabilitation services. At present, about half of all hospital beds in Canada are short-term medical and surgical beds, while one-quarter are extended- and chronic-care beds. Over the past decade there have consistently been approximately 7.0 hospital beds and an additional 9.2 residential beds per 1,000 Canadians. Unique service systems have developed in the different regions of the country, influenced by geography and available resources (Health and Welfare Canada, 1990c).

All provinces and territories provide for psychiatric services under their respective health insurance plans. Acute-care services are usually provided by general hospitals, by a general practitioner, or, upon referral, by a specialist. Providers of longer-term care in psychiatric hospitals can, if they wish, charge users of psychiatric hospital services a per diem rate, although none do so at present. When delivered as part of a general hospital service, nursing, psychological services, occupational therapy, social work, and other clinical services are normally covered by the individual plans. The provinces and territories may choose to extend this basic coverage by funding certain community-based mental health services delivered by nonphysician practitioners. Services in psychiatric hospitals are excluded from the national cost-sharing arrangements and are entirely funded by the provinces and territories.

In most jurisdictions today there is a commitment to deliver services on an outpatient basis to individuals affected by mental disorder. However, psychiatric institutions continue to provide some acute-care and long-term-care services, albeit for shorter periods of time than in past decades. Inpatient care, in some form, will always be needed for assessment, for treatment of recurrent episodes of acute illness, and for problems arising from residual disabilities. A minority of patients with severely disabling chronic conditions will require a residential environment and care that acknowledges the importance of family and friend support systems and quality of life.

Patients in chronic-care facilities may require intermittent access to the acute-care system. Short-term facilities can deal effectively with diagnosis, therapy, and rehabilitation services. Other residential care facilities may include nursing homes, homes for special care, group and foster homes, and sheltered boarding homes.

The development by the general hospital of an array of coordinated services, including outpatient services, partial hospitalization, consultation and liaison, and emergency services, complements inpatient services. Psychiatric services in general hospitals are often provided in a special ward, with associated outpatient and emergency services, and are usually funded from the global hospital budget. Services include crisis intervention, assessment, referral to community support, and specialized services.

Crisis intervention outside the hospital is a key component in preventing admissions and providing more cost-effective alternatives. It is also less disruptive to individual lives. Discharge planning combined with individual case management can contribute to a smoother transition into the individual's community. Local mental health centers, standing placement committees, and community agencies (e.g., community living associations and housing coalitions) can work with hospital staff to ensure that suitable housing is found for discharged patients and that continuity of care is maintained.

Day hospitals are appropriate settings for the assessment and rehabilitation of patients who require more medical and therapeutic intervention and/or clinical observation than would be possible on a strictly outpatient basis. Admission to a day hospital may delay or entirely avert the need for full hospitalization. Patients stay from one to five days per week, five to six hours per day. Day care provides long-term supportive care, supervision, and a range of social and recreational activities.

Community-based services include those provided by private psychiatrists, by a variety of for-profit agencies (e.g., private counselling services), and by non-profit organizations operating many residential and outreach programs. School psychologists, mental health workers, group homes, mental health clinics, consumer advocacy groups, and self-help/mutual-aid groups contribute considerably to the network of mental health services within the community.

Community mental health centers and clinics provide public education, outreach services, and drop-in centers, lending support to those individuals who require assistance in coping with the stresses and problems of everyday life. Early detection and prevention programs aimed at high-risk groups can also be effective in helping individuals to achieve a greater degree of personal control and strength for future crises and may have the effect of preventing further problems.

Action is being taken to ensure that a wide range of mental health services is available in each region of the provinces and territories. Attempts are being made to balance institutional with community care. In several regions large psychiatric hospitals have been or are being closed, with beds being reallocated to smaller facilities (e.g., British Columbia). Generally, the psychiatric hospital can be seen as a specialized component of a comprehensive mental health system.

Community care enables an individual suffering from mental disorder to live near family and friends and may help to prevent social isolation. In practical terms this has meant the following:

• Access to a range of housing alternatives, so people may function with appropriate degrees of professional supervision and personal autonomy

• An emphasis on day programs (e.g., life skills and vocational training, social and recreational opportunities) for individuals who do not require inpatient services

• Recognition of the role of informal and natural support networks with respect to care and rehabilitation efforts, and of the need to support and strengthen these networks

• Recognition that the involvement of service consumers is an essential part of planning and developing services that will meet their needs

An important feature of such a comprehensive community care system is its ability to meet the needs of special populations defined by age, disability, and/ or other characteristics.

Mental health centers can facilitate access to a wide range of services, such as assessment, medical monitoring, crisis intervention, short-term treatment and counselling, long-term treatment and care planning, day and rehabilitation programs, and aftercare services. These centers may collaborate with local mental health programs, service providers, and advocacy groups to develop outreach, education, prevention, and mental health promotion programs, some of which are geared to the general public.

Service systems vary according to provincial size, location of population, and available resources. There is typically a wider range of services and available professionals in or near large urban centers than in places where the population is less concentrated. In rural or northern environments informal helping networks (e.g., voluntary organizations, advocacy groups, and self-help and mutual-aid groups) play a greater role in service delivery.

The movement toward community-level authority for planning, development, and funding of local programs makes it more likely that gaps in service will be identified and appropriate programs developed. Integrating services at the point of delivery makes them more responsive to the needs of the individual and fosters a sense of control on the part of both the consumer and the service providers. This trend should allow greater sensitivity to local cultural, linguistic, and other concerns, which is an expressed goal in several regions.

Mental health services for children and youth are an important portion of the community programs provided by health and/or social services departments. Psychiatric services may be delivered through specialized child and youth clinics and teams and within children's hospitals. Regional guidance centers may provide outpatient services and consult with schools, welfare agencies, the courts, and mental health services throughout the province in order to coordinate and develop programs for children and youth.

For seniors, there are a growing number of special programs. The challenge of coping with dementia and depression among elderly people is increasingly recognized. Specialized geriatric assessment units and day programs are available through many local hospitals. In some regions community teams provide services that may enable individuals with serious cognitive impairment or psychiatric disorder to remain longer in their own homes. Long-range planning for services for the elderly has begun in most regions.

Native people have access to mainstream mental health services. Historically, aboriginal people living on reserves have attended off-reserve provincial facilities and hospitals when they experienced psychiatric problems, with travel expenses covered by the Medical Services Branch of Health and Welfare Canada. However, in recent years the importance of community-based mental health programs and the benefits of addressing mental health problems in the context of family and community have been recognized. Clinics staffed by native mental health workers are currently delivering services in northern Ontario, and community mental health work on reserves has begun in some locations in Manitoba, Alberta, and British Columbia.

Education-based mental health promotion activities are increasingly common across Canada. In some cases a mental health promotion component is built into a general health promotion initiative (e.g., Saskatchewan's Everyone Wins Campaign) (Saskatchewan Commission, 1990); or the primary focus may be on mental health. Collaboration at the community level may include the development of mental health programs provided within schools and recreational settings; these may include programs that are focused on enhancing skills for coping with normal life transitions (e.g., the physical changes associated with puberty on aging) and aimed at making it more acceptable to seek advice concerning mental health matters. Youth suicide information centers (e.g., Albert and Manitoba) and suicide prevention programs are operating in many areas of the country, often

Table 3.1

Estimated Numbers of Health Care Professionals in Canada

General Practitioners & Family Physicians	26,079
Psychiatrists	2,972
Psychologists	8,346
Social Workers	10,002
Occupational Therapists	3,322
Psychiatric Nurses[1]	6,000
All Nurses	268,674

[1] Estimate from the Psychiatric Nurses Association of Canada, 1990.

Data as of December 31, 1988.

Source: Health Personnel in Canada, Policy, Communications and Information, Health and Welfare Canada.

under the auspices of local school boards (Alberta Health, 1988; Manitoba Health, 1988).

Some public education campaigns seek to promote the mental health of former psychiatric patients by changing the behavior of others toward them (i.e., by reducing stigma and promoting understanding and acceptance). The need for such ongoing public education has been expressed by several provincial authorities.

Programs designed to alter or prevent maladaptive behaviors such as substance abuse or wife battering are growing in number; these tend to straddle the boundaries between treatment, prevention of disorders, and promotion of mental health.

Mental Health Personnel and Treatment

Table 3.1 shows the estimated number of health care professionals who often provide mental health services to the population. In a number of regions there is a chronic shortage of specialists, often accompanied by high turnover rates.

PUBLIC POLICY PROCESS

A formal structure has been established to ensure federal/provincial/territorial cooperation on health issues. It includes the Conference of Ministers of Health, the Conference of Deputy Ministers of Health, and a number of advisory committees. The advisory-committee structure was established to assist the Conference of Deputy Ministers responsible for health by providing a mechanism for consultation and collaboration between the federal, provincial, and territorial governments. Each of the following advisory committees provides advice to the conference within a specific broad area of the health field:

- Mental Health
- Environmental and Occupational Health
- Health and Human Resources
- International Health Affairs
- Community Health
- Institutional and Medical Services
- AIDS
- Alcohol and Other Drug Problems

A special working group on women's health is presently also reporting to the conference. Subcommittees and working groups reporting to the appropriate advisory committees are mandated to address specific ongoing issues or processes (e.g., long-term care, guidelines for special services in hospitals).

The Advisory Committee on Mental Health, established in 1986, has been mandated to

- consider issues delegated by the Conference of Deputy Ministers of Health or accepted by a significant number of the provinces as matters where a general consensus of informed opinion would be helpful, and make recommendations, where appropriate;
- advise on the development and implementation of policies and programs for mental health treatment services, with the aim of developing a uniformly high level of quality and effectiveness across Canada;
- provide a forum to assist the provinces and territories in the development, organization, and evaluation of mental health services within each jurisdiction;
- serve as a means for the presentation and exchange of information, relevant data, current research findings, and expert opinion between federal and provincial governments, universities, and treatment settings on problems of jurisdiction, organization, legislation, service delivery, evaluation, and other relevant issues;
- make proposals for federal, federal-provincial, and provincial strategies for mental health promotion to enhance the mental health status of the population at large and particularly that of the child and youth population; and
- receive reports on current mental health activities and programs at the national level and give advice, direction, and support to these as may be appropriate (Committee on Mental Health, 1987).

Currently, the Sub-Committee on Mental Health Research is the only substructure reporting to the Advisory Committee on Mental Health. The subcommittee provides a means for interpreting research findings and advising the Advisory Committee on Mental Health on more economical, effective, and efficient approaches to the management of limited resources and identifies priority areas for research.

National health issues sometimes require the involvement of more than one advisory committee. For example, the Committees for Mental Health and Health and Human Resources are jointly addressing the issue of the shortage of psychiatrists in Canada.

The coordination of mental-health-related policies and services at all levels of government is a priority concern. Provincial Health Departments have made changes to realign mental health services and better coordinate institutional and community care. For example, Ontario now has an interdepartmental coordinator of mental health and addictions, who consults with Institutional Health, Personal Health, and Community Health to ensure communication between, and integration of, programs inside and outside the Health Department.

Most of the provincial authorities for mental health are developing closer links with other departments. For example, Nova Scotia has codirectors of Child and Adolescent Health Services who work to bridge the province's Departments of Health and Fitness and Community Services. Alberta has a mental health coordinating committee, with representation from Education (promotion and prevention activities), Solicitor General (some direct care inside the institutions), Social Services (residential care, welfare, and financial aid), and the Alcohol and Drug Abuse Commission. The Ontario Ministry of Health is working with representatives from Community and Social Services and the Ministry of Housing to implement community mental health plans.

Many provincial plans for mental health services include regional coordinating mechanisms, some of which are already in place. For example, in British Columbia five regional authorities centrally manage mental health centers and suboffices. In Quebec Health and Social Service Councils are the administrative bodies for each of the seven sociohealth regions. They are responsible for planning, programming, financing, and evaluation, and for encouraging local participation in these decisions. Local community service centers are involved in prevention, service provision, and referral. In Ontario District Health Councils are responsible for the coordination of institutional and community care with other direct mental health services, as well as for the application of provincial legislation and policy to the community situation. These councils also make recommendations to the Ministry of Health regarding which local programs should be funded.

Some provinces have established commissions to plan for resource reallocation and to set overall policies and standards for mental health care. The New Brunswick Mental Health Commission provides a good example of the extent to which regional planning has developed, with seven regional boards responsible for the coordination of service delivery. The Saskatchewan Commission on Directions in Health Care has recommended the creation of a similar commission, with a mandate to recommend service initiatives, monitor service development and delivery, and establish related standards for mental health services in the province.

Generally, regional planning bodies are in a strategic position to define what comprehensiveness means to the population in their regions and to implement and monitor change. However, some governments have expressed a need to clearly define the roles of the different components of the mental health system so services will be well coordinated, and proper referral systems can be developed and maintained (e.g., British Columbia, Ministry of Health, 1987; Prince Edward Island Department of Health, 1987).

Some provinces have taken action to increase consumer input into decisions that affect them, especially at the local planning level (e.g., New Brunswick, British Columbia, Quebec). Including service users in the process of needs assessment also helps to ensure that their rights will be acknowledged and protected.

Consumer advocacy groups work to keep consumers informed of their rights and entitlements (e.g., financial) and to put them in touch with available resources. They also lobby and campaign for changes to legislation, policies, and programs and to ensure that the people they represent receive the full benefit of laws and programs that are already in place. They have a vital role in promoting mental health and preventing physical, psychological, or other abuse of consumers.

SPECIAL POLICY ISSUES

The Mentally Ill and the Mentally Retarded

Community-based services for individuals suffering from mental handicap are usually provided by social services departments and may include diagnosis and assessment, preschool services (e.g., infant development programs), residential and day-care programs, and genetic counselling. For individuals with dual diagnoses (e.g., developmental delay and behavioral disturbance), specialized assessments may be made by the Health Department in a dedicated unit of a psychiatric hospital. Although there has been a consistent trend toward living in the community, severe impairment obliges some children and adults to remain in long-term institutional care.

The Mentally Ill and Substance Abuse

Drug or alcohol abuse programs are usually the responsibility of a separate body or commission. There is growing recognition of the need to coordinate mental health services with these more specialized services.

The Mentally Disordered Offender

The federal minister of justice and the attorney general of Canada have introduced new proposals for legislation that will bring the criminal law's approach to mentally disordered accused persons into line with the Canadian Charter of

Rights and Freedoms and contemporary mental health care practices. The new proposals respond to an important Supreme Court of Canada decision and will have two aims: (1) to protect the public from dangerous mentally disordered persons who come into conflict with the law, and (2) to ensure that individuals are not deprived of their charter rights by being confined for mental disorder without a fair hearing and regular review of their cases.

Deinstitutionalization

A combination of psychopharmacological developments and economic factors made it possible and desirable in the 1950s and 1960s for patients suffering from severe and chronic behavioral disorders to leave long-term hospital care. The consequences and processes of deinstitutionalization have been alluded to earlier in our discussion of policy developments and service organization. Nevertheless, it is important to emphasize that the efforts to provide adequate community support and alternatives to institutional treatment are an ongoing process that will require the continued commitment of all levels of government, health care providers, voluntary organizations, consumers and their families, and the communities themselves.

Funding Issues

The federal government contributes to the operation of provincial health insurance plans (insured health services) according to the provisions of the Federal-Provincial Fiscal Arangements and Federal Post-Secondary Education and Health Contributions Act. Expenditures on mental health research in Canada, as reported to the Medical Research Council of Canada by sponsoring agencies during the 1986–87 period, totalled $22.2 million.[2] The National Health Research and Development Program provided $4.1 million in funding for extramural research in 90–91 and $3.9 million in 1991–92. Many projects funded under the Health Promotion Contribution Fund deal with mental health issues exclusively or as one component of a broader health promotion program.

Important linkages between health services and social services are fostered by joint federal-provincial funding programs. The Canada Assistance Plan and the Vocational Rehabilitation of Disabled Persons Act, two formal agreements that link these two levels of government, are discussed here. Other federal programs support research efforts, community initiatives, and mental health promotion programs.

The Canada Assistance Plan (CAP), enacted in 1966, is flexible and comprehensive, involving agreements between the federal and provincial or territorial governments. Through CAP the federal government shares 50 percent of the costs incurred by provinces and territories in providing social assistance and welfare services to persons in need. Under the plan ''assistance'' applies to those in need of food, shelter, clothing, fuel, utilities, household and personal expenses, and specified health and social services. "Persons in need" under the plan include persons who, regardless of the cause of their need, are unable to provide adequately for themselves and/or their dependents or who are likely to be in need if they do not receive such services.

"Welfare services" may include homemaker and home support to assist individuals and families in emergency situations or to facilitate independent living in the community for the elderly and the disabled; casework, counselling, assessment, and referral services; rehabilitation services, including services to the chronically unemployed and services to meet the special needs of persons at risk of being socially isolated, with particular emphasis on the aged and the physically and mentally disabled; and community developed services designed to encourage and assist members of disadvantaged communities to participate in improving the social and economic conditions of their community.

Generally, the Canada Assistance Plan does not share in the costs of educational, recreational, cultural, correctional, police, health care, hospital, and mental hospital social services. Since 1977 the federal arrangements for the funding of long-term adult residential care have been subsumed under the Federal-Provincial Fiscal Arrangements and Federal Post-Secondary Education and Health Contributions Act. Homes for alcoholics, homes for battered women, and halfway houses for individuals who have been previously institutionalized are eligible for funding under CAP. Hospitals and residential treatment homes do not qualify as special care homes. Certain professional fees (e.g., those for psychologists and social service agencies) that are not covered under the Canada Health Act or by provincial health insurance plans may be shared on behalf of "needy" individuals.

The Vocational Rehabilitation of Disabled Persons Act (VRDP) enables the federal government to contribute 50 percent of the costs incurred by the provinces and territories in providing a comprehensive program for the vocational rehabilitation of physically and mentally disabled persons. The act provides for time-limited cost-sharing agreements, and all the provinces and territories have signed an agreement. While the federal government specifies the terms for obtaining cost sharing, provinces and territories are solely responsible for the administration of their programs, including their design, eligibility requirements, and method of delivery.

There are several cost-sharable goods and services provided to individuals with physical and mental disabilities. These are provided either directly by the provinces or territories or through their supported agencies, and vocational rehabilitation services are provided both in the community and in psychiatric hospitals.

Consumer Rights

The issue of human rights and the mentally ill ultimately involves the Canadian Charter of Rights and Freedoms, which defines the standard for government intervention in the lives of Canadians. The Supreme Court of Canada has described the charter as the yardstick against which all other legislation is to be measured. The charter is particularly significant for mental health legislation since this legislation is frequently concerned with involuntary admission, which constitutes a deprivation of liberty to the individual.

Mental health legislation is constitutionally the responsibility of the provinces. In view of the charter, the provinces have proceeded to examine their mental health legislation, and amendments have been made regarding the definition or redefinition of mental disorder (e.g., Alberta, Manitoba); criteria for involuntary admission for psychiatric assessment and procedures for involuntary admission (e.g., Manitoba now has a staggered, two-certificate system in which the first certificate, signed by a general practitioner, allows assessment for up to seventy-two hours, and the second, signed by a psychiatrist, permits admission for up to twenty-one days); and patients' rights (e.g., in Ontario patients have the right to view their clinical records, with few exceptions).

Other related issues that have been or are being discussed include consent to treatment; appointment of decision-making authority for those individuals who are to receive treatment as involuntary patients; and setting clinical standards for assessing mental competence.

Among other new provisions for protecting patients' rights, mechanisms for review and appeal have been put in place. Saskatchewan has instituted a system of automatic appeals to review panels (e.g., with respect to detention and treatment within a facility). Patient advocate/advisory services have also been developed (e.g., in Alberta and Ontario). Patient advisors can offer assistance and advice to involuntary patients in psychiatric facilities and can ensure that these individuals are aware of their rights throughout the treatment process.

CONCLUSIONS AND DISCUSSION

Canada is a vast country with a small population sharing many of the same demographic trends evidenced in other advanced industrial societies. The Canadian mental health system is decentralized into provincial and territorial jurisdictions, producing twelve historically unique systems. Federal government financial assistance and insurance programs have created and sustained national standards in service delivery, ensuring access to quality mental health services for all Canadians.

The recent federal discussion paper *Mental Health for Canadians: Striking a Balance* (Health and Welfare Canada, 1988) offers a democratically inspired vision of mental health. The definition directs our attention to the full range of factors that affect the quality of our everyday lives. The three challenges— reducing inequities, increasing prevention, and enhancing coping—alert us to the essential tasks for improving the lives of all Canadians. The principles provide us with procedural guidelines on moving toward a just, equitable, and more mentally healthy society.

NOTES

1. Much of this chapter was excerpted from *Mental Health Services in Canada 1990*, which was produced by the Mental Health Division of the federal government in co-operation with the provinces and territories of Canada. The document was designed and prepared by Carl M. Lakaski, Valerie Wilmot, Tom Lips, and Monica Brown.

2. All dollar amounts are in Canadian dollars.

REFERENCES

Alberta Health. (1988). *Mental health services in Alberta*. Edmonton: Alberta Health.

Bland, R. (1988). Prevalence of Mental Illness. *Annals of the Royal College of Physicians and Surgeons of Canada, 21*(2), 89–93.

British Columbia, Ministry of Health. (1987). *Mental health consultation report*. Victoria: Queen's Printer for British Columbia.

Canadian Mental Health Association, Committee on Mental Health and Aging. (1988). *Mental health and aging in Canada*. Toronto: Canadian Mental Health Association, National Office.

Committee on Mental Health. (1987). *Proceedings of the sixty-ninth annual meeting of the uniform law conference of Canada: Appendix F—Uniform Mental Health Act*. Victoria: Uniform Law Conference of Canada.

Government of Canada. (1984/86). *Canada health act: Office consolidation, chapter 6*. (Cat. YX 79–1984/6). Ottawa: Minister of Supply and Services Canada.

Health and Welfare Canada. (1986). *Achieving health for all: A framework for health promotion*. Ottawa: Minister of Supply and Services Canada.

Health and Welfare Canada. (1987). *Suicide in Canada: Report of the national task force on suicide in Canada*. Ottawa: Minister of Supply and Services Canada.

Health and Welfare Canada. (1988a). *After the door has been opened: Mental health issues affecting immigrants and refugees*. Ottawa: Minister of Supply and Services Canada.

Health and Welfare Canada. (1988b). *Canada's health promotion survey: Technical report*. J. Rootman, R. Warren, T. Stevens, & L. Peters (Eds.). Ottawa: Minister of Supply and Services Canada.

Health and Welfare Canada. (1988c). *Mental health for Canadians: Striking a balance*. Ottawa: Minister of Supply and Services Canada.

Health and Welfare Canada. (1989). *Health personnel in Canada*. Ottawa: Minister of Supply and Services Canada.

Health and Welfare Canada. (1990a). *Mental Health Services in Canada 1990*. Ottawa: Minister of Supply and Services Canada.

Health and Welfare Canada. (1990b). *Services to elderly residents with mental health problems in long-term care facilities: Guidelines for establishing standards*. Ottawa: Minister of Supply and Services Canada.

Health and Welfare Canada. (1990c). *Trends in utilization of psychiatric services: 1982–83 to 1987–88*. Ottawa: Health Information Directorate.

Manitoba Health. (1988). *A new partnership for mental health in Manitoba*. Winnipeg: Manitoba Health.

Mills, D. (1990). *Research on Schizophrenia in Canada*. Ontario: Schizophrenia Society of Canada.

Ministry of Health and Social Services, Government of Quebec. (1989a). *Improving health and well-being in Quebec: Orientations*. Quebec: National Library of Quebec.

Ministry of Health and Social Services, Government of Quebec. (1989b). *Mental health policy, Quebec/Politique de santé mentale*. Quebec: National Library of Quebec.

Premier's Commission on Future Health Care for Albertans. (1989). *The rainbow report: Our vision for health (Volume III)*. Edmonton: Author.

Prince Edward Island Department of Health. (1987). *Review of the mental health system* (Canadiana: 890823391). Charlottetown: Author.

Provincial Community Mental Health Committee, Robert Graham, Chairman. (1988). *Building community support for people: A plan for mental health in Ontario*. Toronto: Ontario Ministry of Health.

Saskatchewan Commission on Directions in Health Care. (1990). *Directions for health care in Saskatchewan*. Regina: Government of Saskatchewan.

Statistics Canada. (1987). *Profile series: (1986) Census divisions and sub-divisions* (Cat. Nos. 94–101 to 94–124). Ottawa: Minister of Supply and Services Canada.

Statistics Canada. (1989). *Canada yearbook, 1990* (Cat. 11–402E/1990). Ottawa: Minister of Supply and Services Canada.

Statistics Canada, Canadian Centre for Health Information. (1989). [Mental health statistics]. Unpublished information.

4

Chile

Benjamin Vicente and Mabel Vielma

OVERVIEW

Chile is a long, narrow ribbon of land stretching almost 2,700 miles along the west coast of South America. Although it is one of the world's longest countries, its average width is only 100 miles, with a maximum width of only 250 miles.

Chile is wedged between the Andes Mountains on the east and the Pacific Ocean on the west and is bordered by Peru on the north and Bolivia and Argentina on the east. It is larger in area than any European country except the former USSR. Southern Chile is an archipelago with Cape Horn at its tip, where the Atlantic merges with the Pacific. Chile has four distinct and well-defined geographic regions divided into thirteen political regions: the northern desert (one-fourth of the country's land area); the high Andean sector; the central valley; and the southern lake district and archipelago.

Chile's population was about 13.17 million in 1990. Unlike most Latin American countries, Chile is mainly urban (79 percent). More than one-third of its people live in the capital (Santiago) and environs. As in the other developing countries, the population is youthful, with nearly 80 percent of all Chileans under forty years of age and half of the population under twenty-one. Only about 5 percent are sixty-five or over. Chile is one of the more sparsely populated countries of Latin America (about 44 persons per square mile). Its annual population growth rate is slightly over 1.8 percent.

The largest ethnic group is Spanish. Other groups include German, English, Italian, Yugoslav, French, and Arab. The population includes a small number of Indians, but few Asians or blacks. The Indians live mainly south of the Bio-Bio River and in the North. The most important aboriginal group is the Mapuches, also known as Araucanians. Few South American populations are more homogeneous than the Chilean, despite the diversity of its origins. The homogeneity and insularity are due in large part to the isolation resulting from geographic factors: mountains, deserts, a vast ocean, and the distance from world cultural and political centers.

In pre-Columbian times the Incan Empire dominated the northern half of modern Chile. The first Europeans to arrive were Diego de Almagro and a band of conquistadors who came from Peru in 1535, seeking gold. The conquest of Chile was carried out by Pedro de Valdivia in 1550. Until the end of the eighteenth century Chile was ruled by governors-general under the viceroy of Peru. On September 18, 1812, a junta proclaimed Chile an autonomous republic within the Spanish monarchy. A movement for total independence soon won wide support, and on February 12, 1818, Chile was proclaimed an independent republic under Bernardo O'Higgins's leadership.

After years of political strife a new constitution in 1833 established an ''autonomous'' republic headed by a president with wide powers. A long period of prosperity and constitutional government followed. In the War of the Pacific, 1879–83, Chile defeated Peru and Bolivia and acquired its two northern nitrate- and copper-rich provinces. In 1890–91 a revolt by a majority of Congress led to the establishment of a parliamentary-based democracy that limited the powers of the president.

The current century has been one of social and economic transition. The nation has sought to industrialize and to carry out various social reforms. In 1925 a new constitution was adopted, which reestablished a strong executive, mandated separation of church and state, and promulgated social security legislation and a labor code.

On September 4, 1970, Senator Salvador Allende, heading a leftist coalition, won a plurality of votes in a three-way contest and was named president by the Chilean Congress. After almost three years of government, Allende and the Unidad Popular (Popular Unity) coalition, formed mainly by Socialists, Communists, the Christian Left, and Radicals, were overthrown by a military coup on September 11, 1973. During more than sixteen years, the commanders-in-chief of the Army, Navy, Air Force, and National Police made up the junta that held legislative power. A new constitution was approved on September 11, 1980, and Augusto Pinochet, former head of the military junta, was appointed president of the republic for an eight-year term. During that time the country remained under a state of emergency with one or two exceptions until 1987. Under that state various civil liberties were limited, political parties and partisan political activities were banned, many Chileans abroad were denied reentry, and restraints of freedom remained until the end of the military dictatorship.

On December 5, 1989, Patricio Aylwin was elected president by an overwhelming majority and came to power in March 1990. Since then, the nation has been in a transition to a real democracy regarding political and social rights.

Chile's open economic policy remains mainly unchanged. The annual real growth rate is approximately 2.4 percent, the average inflation rate is 25 percent, and the national unemployment varies between 9 and 12 percent. Major social programs for the poor are under way.

EXTENT OF THE PROBLEM

Until very recently in Chile there were no reliable epidemiological data that would help the authorities to estimate the real extent of the mental health problems in the community. The policy making was mainly based on the results of old surveys undertaken in the late 1950s (Horwitz, Munoz, & Marconi, 1958) and on the prevalence of mental disorders among users of the state's general health services and psychiatric services.

Since 1990 a program on epidemiological psychiatry has started trying to produce national community prevalences of specific psychiatric disorders in order to understand as far as possible the factors associated with the illnesses and to know the needs of the users and relatives, including their attitudes to psychiatry and the degree of satisfaction with the services provided. These studies are supported by the Pan-American Health Organization (PAHO), the National Commission for Science and Technology (CONICYT), and the Chilean Ministry of Health.

The combined lifetime prevalence rate of the psychiatric disorders studied in Concepción (one of the four sites in which the epidemiological survey will take place) is 36.5 percent (Vicente et al., 1992). If this is extrapolated to the Chilean population in the fifteen-year and older age range ($n = 9,140,096$) and a standard error of 1.7 is considered, one would estimate that approximately 3,200,000 to 3,450,000 people meet the lifetime criteria for one or more of these disorders and would therefore require psychiatric attention at some point in their life.

Generally, Concepción's lifetime and six-month prevalence rates for most psychiatric disorders do not differ significantly from those reported from three Epidemiological Catchment Area (ECA) sites in the United States (Myers et al., 1984) and from Puerto Rico's epidemiological studies (Canino et al., 1987), with the exception of severe cognitive impairment and affective disorder (dysthymia and major depressive episode), which have higher rates in Concepción. Alcohol abuse and dependence were among the most prevalent disorders, and schizophrenia, panic disorder, and somatization were among the least prevalent in the site studied.

According to the lifetime prevalence found in Concepción, it can also be said that approximately 1 million people living in Chile would be diagnosed as suffering from alcohol abuse or dependence at a given point in their lives, while only between 100,000 to 200,000 would be found dependent on abusing any other psychoactive drug. On the other hand, the 4.6 percent who are severely cognitively impaired may reach the amazing figure of 500,000. Most of these people are not able to look after themselves.

The relationship between demographic characteristics and diagnoses shows that affective and anxiety disorders are more common among women, while alcoholism and antisocial personality disorder are more prevalent among men. There are no significant differences between urban and rural prevalence in this study.

MENTAL HEALTH HISTORY

Chilean psychiatric history can be artificially divided into three overlapping periods. The first is known as the custodial era and goes approximately from the middle of the last century until the 1950s. The general hospital period runs from the 1960s up to the present, and the third, which could be called community psychiatry, starts in the 1970s, more as a theoretical proposal than a concrete reality (Chilean Ministry of Health, 1978).

The first madhouse in the country was built in Santiago in 1852 following the European custodial model of the time. The second one, mainly dedicated to rehabilitation of suitable chronic patients, was set up in 1928, again in Santiago. At the beginning of 1927 the first legislation on mental health was enacted (Chilean Ministry of Health, 1927). The concepts and regulations contained in it have never been amended and are still in use. It sanctioned the organization of two types of psychiatric services, the psychiatric hospitals and the asylum-colonies. The former were to be built in each of the large health areas and would deal with short-term admissions that could not last more than four months. The patients that did not recover in such a period were to be sent to the asylum-colonies, which would only admit "chronic patients."

The structure and organization of the hospitals and asylums would allow for "the security of the patients" and would "control and direct them with the minimum staff possible." Admission could be voluntary or compulsory, the latter needing just an administrative order that anyone considered responsible for the patient could easily get.

The custodial ideology is so obviously embedded in the law that Article 21 explicitly states that "anyone having at home or wanting to care for a demented or mad person needs special permission from the corresponding Health Authority." The law also established that outpatient clinics should be set up near the hospitals and top-security wards should be provided for patients with legal problems. Nothing was said about the numbers of staff or beds needed in each different service except that they should be kept as small as possible.

Only in 1952 was the old madhouse of Santiago officially converted into a psychiatric hospital. It was redecorated, and some new wards were built that finally allowed the separation of acute from chronic patients, as the asylum-colonies were never built throughout the country. This move came around the same time that neuroleptics made a radical change possible in treatment of acute patients, but the so-called chronic patients remained in the same situation without any improvement (Medina, 1990).

In the second period the emphasis was put on the organization of mental health teams that mainly worked within the traditional institutions or in small psychiatric units being set up in some of the major general hospitals in the country. The third period has been recognized only due to a very few, almost-individual efforts to bring out human and material resources from the institutional settings, both psychiatric hospitals and units, to the community. Financial, legal, and ideological problems have made this ideal a very difficult task.

POLICY, ORGANIZATION, AND SERVICES IN THE 1980s AND 1990s

Current Policy

Some attempts have been made by the central authorities to improve or replace the very old legislation still in force. The country has known four such attempts. The first was the Reform Act of 1971, immediately derogated by the next government, followed by the so-called National Mental Health Policy of 1978 and 1981 and the National Plan of Mental Health and Psychiatry of 1990 (Chilean Ministry of Health, 1990). The 1981 document became a bill but was never enacted. Currently, the Mental Health Unit of the Ministry of Health is working on the formulation of a mental health law that would take into consideration the previous documents, a long-term mental health policy, patients' rights, and the community psychiatry models already in progress in a good number of places in Chile.

Current Organization

The 1978 National Mental Health Policy had as a central purpose to set up, expand, and improve psychiatric outpatient facilities in all regions of the country, stating the need of a minimum of one professional team per region. These teams for the first time included occupational therapists and a larger proportion of psychologists. It also made provision for the setting up of a nonspecialized mental health team for each 50,000 inhabitants that would include a doctor, a psychologist, a social worker, a nurse, and four nursing auxiliaries. The team would mainly be dedicated to assisting small communities and handling minor problems. At the same time it gave guidelines for the improvement of the psychiatric units and hospitals throughout the country. There was no official evaluation of the effects of these regulations or even evidence of whether they were implemented at all. At the beginning of 1990, just a month before the democratically elected government took over, the previous authorities enacted the National Plan of Mental Health and Psychiatry, which reemphasizes most of the regional orientation described above but still has a relatively weak emphasis on the enormous potential role of the primary health care level and the community in identifying and solving most mental health problems.

Table 4.1
Psychiatric Resources in the Public Sector in Chile

Resources	1966	1971	1978	1981	1990
Population (Millions)	8.77	9.68	10.82	11.33	12.96
Numbers of Beds	3,984	4,491	4,412	4,427	3,359
Metropolitan Region	3,666	3,939	3,236	2,918	2,262
Percentage	92.0%	88.0%	73.0%	66.0%	67.0%
Beds per 1,000 inhabitants	0.45	0.46	0.41	0.39	0.26
Psychiatrists	139	80	78	88	112
In Metropolitan Regions		60	60	60	71
Percentage		75%	77%	68%	63%
Psychiatrists/10,000 Inhabitants	0.16	0.08	0.07	0.08	0.09

Source: Chilean Ministry of Health, 1990.

Current Services

Compared to the 1960s, human and material resources dedicated to mental health and psychiatry in the public sector have significantly decreased, and despite the efforts made in the last two years they still are very limited and not evenly distributed throughout the country. Most of them are concentrated in the metropolitan region; as table 4.1 shows, approximately two-thirds of the resources are located within or around Santiago, where no more than 35 percent of the Chilean population actually live.

There are four large psychiatric institutions in Chile. Two are in Santiago, the Instituto Psiquiátrico Dr. Jose Horwitz B and the Hospital Sanatorio el Peral, and the other two, Hospital Psiquiátrico de Putaendo and Hospital Salvador de Valparaíso, are in the Fifth Region, which is approximately 200 kilometers west of the capital. These major hospitals have 84 percent of all the psychiatric beds available in the country. Only 843 beds are for acute patients, giving a ratio of 6.50 per 100,000 inhabitants, while the number of beds for chronic patients represents approximately 14.8 per 100,000. Small acute bed units are located in ten of the twenty-six Health Services areas into which the country is divided. Currently, major efforts are being made to establish a mental health unit with or without beds in the largest general hospital of each Health Service.

Mental Health Personnel and Treatment

Mental health professionals are also very limited and tend to work either in Santiago or in large cities such as Concepción or Valparaíso. At the end of 1990 there were 112 psychiatrists, which represented a ratio of 0.86 per 100,000 inhabitants; 63 percent of them lived in Santiago. Fifty-three psychiatric nurses and 55 psychologists at that time were working in the public sector, representing a ratio of 0.41 and 0.42 per 100,000 inhabitants, respectively. Social workers and occupational therapists were at the even lower ratio of 0.30 per 100,000 inhabitants (Medina, Riquelme, & Figueras, 1990). Child psychiatry is even more underdeveloped. It has only one differentiated service, also located in Santiago, with 17 beds and an outpatient clinic that covers almost the entire country.

Mental health teams at the primary health care level of some Health Services are a promising new development. These are working integrated groups of general physicians, psychologists, social workers, nurses, and nursing auxiliaries who are in close collaboration with the community, identifying and taking care of most psychosocial and mental health problems that were previously referred to the psychiatric services, as well as emphasizing a preventive approach that will undoubtedly enhance quality of life.

The private sector has steadily increased its participation in the mental health area since the last decade. It is mainly represented by psychiatrists and psychologists in private practice, as well as psychiatric clinics that serve a minority of wealthy people and a middle-class high-income group that have access to health insurance systems.

PUBLIC POLICY PROCESS

Mental health policies and programs have been rapidly changing in the last two years within the global process of restructuring the entire Chilean society. The Chilean society as a whole and its political authorities are increasingly concerned with the very different aspects of social problems; consequently, psychosocial indicators such as family violence, drug- and alcohol-related problems, pregnancy and sexual risk behavior among adolescents, and lack of opportunities for youngsters are on the daily work agenda of policy makers, as well as in the news and scoring very high in regular public opinion surveys. The parliament discusses violence, social stressors for youngsters and women, and new alcohol and drug laws. The Catholic church asks for a national policy against alcoholism, "one of the most dehumanizing problems of Chilean society." Community members are organizing "committees against drugs" in the northern cities of Arica and Iquique, where the rates of free-base cocaine abuse are rapidly increasing.

Three main objectives were proposed in 1990 relating to the mental health field:

1. To significantly increase public opinion awareness about psychosocial well-being as an area for which the entire society should be responsible

2. To increase, decentralize, and diversify mental health services, conceiving them as a network of facilities fully incorporated into the general health system
3. To provide a scientific basis for modern legislation on mental health issues that will effectively promote and protect Chileans' psychological and psychosocial well-being

Progress has already been made in all these areas. Especially important are the introduction of mental health objectives in primary health care; the incorporation of sixty psychologists at the primary health level; the reorganization of twenty-eight family mental health centers, working mainly in the prevention of mental illness; and the increase in the number of psychiatrists' posts to enlarge the small staffs of various cities. Also, since the beginning of the present government, the health authorities have stated clearly that no new psychiatric hospitals will be built, but small mental health units will be located in large general hospitals.

Four mental-health-related legislative initiatives are currently being considered by the Parliament. Three of them are about control measures in the areas of alcohol, drugs, and tobacco. The other one deals with physical, sensorial, and psychological disability and all of its implications regarding social and educational aspects, workplaces, treatment, rehabilitation, and other issues.

Simultaneously, mental health authorities are designing a new model for a rehabilitation and community reinsertion network that will include halfway houses and/or residential settings located in the community under public, private, or cooperative social services dependency (probably nonprofit associations, family members' associations, and the like). Additionally, regional or local Health Services will provide accessible and comprehensive outpatient and inpatient psychiatric care that will react promptly and effectively to referrals from the primary level. This is expected to decrease in the near future the number of beds occupied by chronic patients (Peajean, 1992).

SPECIAL POLICY ISSUES

The Mentally Ill and the Mentally Retarded

There has never been a difference regarding the mentally ill on one side and the mentally handicapped on the other. Both groups have been treated in the same way. No difference has been made in the academic field, where mental retardation is taught just as any other mental illness, nor is there a specialty devoted to the specific problems that the mentally handicapped might pose. Urgent measures are needed to face the problems of approximately half a million people who are not always properly looked after in an ordinary psychiatric service.

The Mentally Ill and Substance Abuse

In addition to the 11 percent of people that might be diagnosed as alcohol abusers or dependents according to DSM-III-R criteria, there are at least another

10 percent of adults in the community that could be identified as problem drinkers by a seven-item self-report questionnaire that has been regularly utilized with primary-care outpatients since 1990. These two figures represent what is beyond any doubt the most striking public health problem in Chile.

The abuse of other psychoactive substances is still only a problem for a minority of wealthy people in the case of cocaine and a group of very poor youngsters that use solvents. A more widespread use of free-base cocaine is starting in the northern part of the country, and its consequences for the rest of Chile in the near future are predictable.

The Mentally Disordered Offender

Very little has been done in terms of an institutional response to the mentally ill offender. Only one forensic psychiatric unit, located at the largest psychiatric hospital in Santiago, exists in the country. There are two other centers in Chile, in Concepción and Valparaíso, where the judges can send the alleged mentally ill offender to be psychiatrically evaluated on an ambulatory basis. In Chile the plea of diminished responsibility is almost always accepted by the courts, but unfortunately there is no place or institution where these people could be appropriately treated.

Deinstitutionalization

The process of deinstitutionalization has just begun in the four large psychiatric hospitals in Chile. Chronic patients have been slowly transferred to small clinics run by private organizations funded by the state and ethically and technically controlled by the psychiatric authorities. These hospitals are also in the process of differentiating outpatient care for the area in which they are located and inpatient units especially dedicated to treat acute patients from their own catchment areas, while still keeping some units for chronic patients referred from all over the country.

Funding Issues

The lack of resources has always been the main problem of the public health sector in Chile. Fortunately, the present authorities seem to be giving priority to mental health issues and allocating increasing amounts of resources to the prevention and assistance of mental illness.

Consumer Rights

There are no laws to protect the rights of the mentally ill, nor have any kinds of human rights committees ever been established to look after the rights of mental patients. In a survey of attitudes toward psychiatry and mental health services undertaken a few years ago, consumers and their relatives showed a considerable adherence to the more traditional and institutionalized ways of offering services. The levels of satisfaction were incredibly high considering the miserable conditions in which the help was delivered. Practically all of the respondents perceived community facilities as nonexistent, but they did not ask for them as had been expected, and despite a few exceptions, they appeared resistant to the eventual changes being suggested (Vicente, Vielma, & Lliapas, 1990).

Effective action requires the support of the population. The population, however, needs to be informed, and those informing it, especially the media, need to grasp current attitudes and fears and a vision of what is possible. In countries like Chile we feel that the professionals' role in enhancing consumers' rights is central.

CONCLUSIONS AND DISCUSSION

The feasibility of the projects and goals described here seems to be assured in the current political situation. The formalization of a policy for mental health development, which is almost ready, will consolidate the direction of the process. National efforts and innovative developments have been enhanced by guidelines, meetings, and consultation provided by WHO and PAHO. A new mental health policy, modern legislation, and political will to implement plans and programs are key factors in the development of accessible and adequate mental health services where consumer rights are fully respected, but above all it is necessary to involve as much of the community as possible in the debate, a debate that is only meaningful if the population is given visions of possibilities as well as knowledge of what is so.

REFERENCES

Canino, G., Bird, H., Shrout, P., Rubio-Stipec, M., Bravo, M., Martinez, R., Sesman, M., & Guevara, L. (1987). The prevalence of specific psychiatric disorders in Puerto Rico. *Archives of General Psychiatry, 44*, 727–735.

Chilean Ministry of Health. (1927). *Reglamento general para la organización y atención de los servicios de salubridad mental y reclusión de insanos.* Santiago: Ministerio de Salud.

Chilean Ministry of Health. (1978). *Políticas de salud mental del Ministerio de Salud.* Santiago: Ministerio de Salud.

Chilean Ministry of Health (1990). *Plan nacional de salud mental y psiquiatría.* Santiago: Ministerio de Salud.

Horowitz, J., Munoz, L., & Marconi, J. (1958). Investigaciones epidemiologicas acerca de morbilidad en Chile. *Revista del Servicio Nacional de Salud, 3*, 227–310.

Medina, E., (1990). Panorama institucional de la psiquiatría chilena. *Revista de Psiquiatría, 6*, 343–360.

Medina, E., Riquelme, R., & Figueras, T. (1990). Informe sobre recursos de salud mental y psiquiatría del Sistema Nacional de Servicios de Salud, Marzo 1990. *Revista de Psiquiatría, 7,* 595–638.

Myers, J. K., Weissman, M. M., Tischler, G. L., Holzer, C. E., Leaf, P. J., Orvaschel, H., Anthony, J. C., Boyd, J. H., Burke, J. O., Kramer, M., & Stoltzman, R. (1984). Six month prevalence of psychiatric disorders in three communities. *Archives of General Psychiatry, 41,* 959–957.

Peajean, A. (1992). *Current trends in mental health policies in Chile.* Santiago: Ministerio de Salud.

Vicente, B., Rioseco, P., Vielma, M., Uribe, M., Boggiano, G., & Torres, S. (1992). Prevalencia de vida de algunos trastornos psiquiátricos en la provincia de Concepción. *Revista de Psiquiatría, 9,* 36–51.

Vicente, B., Vielma, M., & Lliapas, I. (1990). Tipo y calidad de atención psiquiátrica: La opinión y niveles de satisfacción de los usuarios como una forma de evaluación. *Revista de Psiquiatría, 7,* 509–518.

5

India

Indira Sharma

OVERVIEW

Traditionally, mental health is considered to be of relevance only to affluent societies. There has been very little recognition of the mental health needs of the population in general health programs of developing countries like India. Perhaps this has been because of the misconception that mental illness is less prevalent in developing countries than in the West and that no effective treatment is available.

Psychiatric services in India are woefully inadequate, and there is no prospect in the next ten to twenty years of providing enough specialized personnel to meet even the most basic mental health needs (Neki, 1973). The situation is worse in rural areas due to the heavy concentration of psychiatrists and facilities in the cities. The limited mobility of the rural population is an important delaying factor. Furthermore, ignorance and misconception among the rural folks also lead to delay in mental health care.

September 12, 1978, was a significant day in the progress of mental health care, when several countries including India signed the Alma Ata declaration in the USSR, promising primary mental health care to all citizens of the world by the year 2000. It was hoped that this attainment of a level of health by people would permit them to live a biologically healthy, socially enriching, and economically productive life, irrespective of any national boundaries, racial prejudices, economic deprivations, and political commitments.

India is the seventh-largest and second most populous country in the world. Its population was 843,930,861 in March 1991, following China's 1,160 million people. India's population constitutes 16 percent of the world's population. India is triangular in shape, extending over an area of 3,287,263 square kilometers and lying between 8°N and 37°N latitudes. The tropic of Cancer (23½°N) passes through India. The southern part of India lies in the tropical region.

Uttar Pradesh is the largest state, with 16.44 percent (138,760,417) of the country's people, followed by Bihar (86,338,853) and Maharashtra (78,706,719). Bombay metropolis is the most populated city in the country, Calcutta is second, and Delhi is third, followed by Madras. Population growth during 1981–91 has registered an increase of 23.50 percent but has varied from state to state. Nagaland registered the highest rate (56.86 percent) and Tamil Nadu the lowest (14.94 percent). Outside of Nagaland, the northern zone has had the highest decadal growth and the southern zone the lowest growth. The rates in different zones of the country, as per the 1991 census, are the following: north, 27.6 percent; east, 23.7 percent; central, 25.6 percent; west, 23.7 percent; and south, 19 percent. The density ratio has gone up with the increase in population from 216 persons per square kilometer in 1981 to 267/per square kilometer in 1991.

In India the sex ratio is defined as the number of females per 1,000 males. The ratio as per the 1991 census was 0.929. Kerala, however, represented a different spectrum: 1,040 females for 1,000 males. The number of females in the sex ratio in India's population has been declining since 1901, except for 1981. A five-point decline in the sex ratio in the year 1991, the Year of the Girl Child, is a matter of serious concern. An important finding is that the sex ratio is considerably lower in northern India, roughly about 22°N latitude, while it is substantially above the national average in the southern zone. It is for demographers to explain these trends.

The literacy rate in 1991 of 52.11 percent is higher than the 43.5 percent rate of ten years ago. Kerala has retained its position by being at the top with a 90.59 percent literacy rate. Bihar stands at the bottom, with a literacy rate of 38.54 percent, with Rajasthan standing close to it at a 38.81 percent literacy rate. The literacy rate among women is lower than among males (39.42 percent versus 63.86 percent). Among women, Rajasthan has registered the lowest rate, 20.84 percent for women compared to 55.07 percent for men, while Chandigarh has registered the highest rate (78.73 percent) among females.

The main feature of the Indian Constitution is a democratic government. The people elect their representatives both at the center and at the state level. The Indian Constitution is federal and recognizes separate states. It also has a strong government at the center that maintains the unity of the states. All persons above the age of eighteen years have the right to vote. Laws are passed by a majority of the elected representatives in the legislatures. No tax can be levied and no money can be spent without the sanction of these representatives. Every Indian has the right of citizenship. The constitution guarantees certain fundamental rights to every citizen. The Supreme Court is the protector of these rights. Directive principles are applied by the government while making laws. Constitutionally, India is secular in character. All religions in India are equal. India treats all citizens alike irrespective of their religion, caste, creed, or sex.

The union (central) government consists of the Parliament, the president, the prime minister and his council of Ministers, and the Supreme Court. These together form the three organs of the union government: union legislature, union executive, and union judiciary.

The union legislature (Parliament) is formed by the president, the Lok Sabha, and the Rajya Sabha. The Lok Sabha is called the lower house and consists of 543 members who are elected directly by the people every five years. One member is elected from a constituency having a population of 500,000 to 750,000. The Rajya Sabha has a maximum of 250 members. Twelve members are nominated by the president of India; the remainder are elected by the legislative assemblies of the states every six years. One-third of the members retire every two years, the vacant seats being filled by new members. A bill has to be passed by both houses of Parliament and duly signed by the president before it becomes a law.

In every state there is a state government just like the one at the center. The governor is the head of the state and is appointed by the president for five years.

EXTENT OF THE PROBLEM

Research studies from different parts of the country have shown that mental illness is as common in India as it is elsewhere and is equally common in rural and urban areas. Cheap, effective, and simple methods of treatment are now available for a large number of seriously disabling mental disorders. Furthermore, it has been proven that effective treatment can be delivered for a certain range of disorders without having to rely solely on doctors and psychiatrists. Besides, mental health skills can be used to promote the quality of general health services and reduce the ever-increasing threat of the dehumanization of modern medicine so repeatedly talked about in all countries.

According to most surveys, about 1 to 2 percent of the population are affected by a severe incapacitating mental disorder, and 10 percent suffer from mild mental disorders at any point in time. Thus there are about 85 million citizens with mental disorders in the country (*National Mental Health Programme for India*, 1982–1990). The annual incidence of serious mental disorders has been estimated to be roughly 35 per 100,000 population, or about 250,000 in the country (*National Mental Health Programme for India*, 1982). Several field surveys have shown that mental disorder is nearly as prevalent in rural as in urban areas (Seshadri, 1986). Mental retardation is estimated to affect 2 percent of the population. Reliable separate data on psychiatric disturbances among children, especially learning and behavior problems in schoolchildren, do not seem to be available. However, the number is about in the order of 1 to 2 percent of children (*National Mental Health Programme for India*, 1982). Although the rates of alcohol and drug dependence are in general lower than in the West, there are pockets showing rising trends, for example, use of heroin and cannabis in the urban student population in Varanasi, Delhi, and Bombay and alcohol consumption in Punjab.

Factual data on the loss of productivity and income because of mental illness are not currently available. The weakening of the traditional family structure and social support system are causing increased psychiatric problems in old age, particularly in the urban population.

The main burden of psychiatric morbidity in the adult population consists of the following conditions:

1. Acute mental disorders (schizophrenic, affective, or of unknown etiology), paranoid reactions, psychosis resulting from cerebral involvement in communicable diseases like malaria, typhus, or bacterial meningitis, alcoholic psychosis, and epileptic psychosis.

2. Chronic frequently recurring mental illnesses like some cases of schizophrenia, affective psychosis, epileptic psychosis, and dementias and encephalopathies associated with intoxications.

3. Neurotic illnesses such as anxiety, hysteria, and depression, which may often be associated with physical diseases.

4. Alcohol and drug dependence and alcohol abuse, which are growing problems.

MENTAL HEALTH HISTORY

Although there is reference to some asylums in the period of Mohammed Khilji (1436–1469), there really was no mental health policy in India before 1946. The mental asylums in the Indian subcontinent were entirely a British conception and were designed to protect the community, not to treat the insane. They were constructed with high enclosures, away from cities, and mostly in dilapidated buildings like barracks left by military men. The decade of the 1920s was a period of positive growth in that Dr. O. Berkeley Hill, superintendent of the European Mental Hospital at Ranchi, persuaded the government of India to change the name of all mental asylums to mental hospitals. In addition, social scientists were associated in the diagnosis and management of psychiatric patients. Occupational therapy departments and token economy programs were established along with training of psychiatrists and psychiatric nursing personnel. The Ranchi Mental Hospital was established as a symbol of excellence.

The Health Survey and Development Committee, popularly known as the Bhore Committee (1946), was a landmark in the health planning of the country. It clearly described the situation around the time of independence as follows: "The existing number of mental hospital beds is in the ratio of one bed to about 40,000 population, which is very low compared to one bed to 300 population in England" (*National Mental Health Programme for India*, 1982–1990). The committee made the following recommendations:

1. The creation of a mental health organization as part of the establishment under the director general of health services at the center and the provincial directors of health services

2. Improvement in the existing seventeen mental hospitals and the establishment of two new institutions in the first five years and five more during the next five years

3. The provision of facilities for training in mental health work for medical men in India and abroad and for ancillary personnel in India

4. The establishment of a Department of Mental Health in the proposed All India Medical Institute

A major outcome of the recommendations was the setting up of the All India Institute of Mental Health (AIIMH) in 1954, which twenty years later became the National Institute of Mental Health and Neurosciences (NIMHANS), Bangalore. Similarly, mental hospitals were built in Amritsar (1947), Hyderabad (1953), Srinagar (1958), Jamnagar (1960), and Shadara, Delhi (1966), as part of the committee's recommendations. The Mudaliar Committee (1962) was pleased to note the positive development in the setting up of AIIMH at Bangalore and suggested "arranging such that ultimately each region, if not each state, becomes self-sufficient in the matter of training its total requirements of mental health personnel" (*National Mental Health Programme for India*, 1982–1988).

The last two decades have witnessed a spurt in growth of general hospital psychiatric units (GHPUs), which have produced radical qualitative change in the whole approach to psychiatric treatment. Even though the setting up of such units started as early as 1933, a major spurt occurred in the 1960s, coinciding well with the building of the last mental hospitals in the country. They have provided a big push for the greater acceptance of psychiatric services by the public without the fear of social stigma. Seventy-five percent of the research comes from professionals working in these units. An extension of these units has been the setting up of district hospital psychiatric units. In Kerala and Tamil Nadu, at present, there is a psychiatrist in each district.

Departments of psychiatry are currently available in sixty-seven (60 percent) of the medical colleges. Poor undergraduate training in psychiatry can be attributed to the lag in having full-fledged psychiatry departments in all medical colleges. At present, steps to remedy this problem are receiving attention.

POLICY, ORGANIZATION, AND SERVICES IN THE 1980s AND 1990s

Current Policy Developments

The next phase of development of mental health services, from 1982 onwards, has been the community care approach. The overall goal as observed by the late prime minister of India, Indira Gandhi, while addressing the World Health Assembly in 1981, has been "in India we would like to go to homes instead of large numbers gravitating towards centralized hospitals. Services must begin where people are and where problems arise" (Srinivasa Murthy, 1990). The impetus for the development of the community approach has emerged from various sources:

1. The realization of the magnitude of severe mental disorders in the community and availability of simple interventions for these conditions
2. The Alma Ata declaration, which envisages health for all by the year 2000 as its goal
3. The existence of a large infrastructure for general health services, the primary health care (PHC) system
4. Encouraging experiences of community mental health care at Bangalore and Chandigarh centers
5. The recommendation of the WHO International Conference on Primary Health Care of promotion of mental health as one of the eight components of primary health care

The first center to start rural mental health care was the Central Institute of Psychiatry at Ranchi in 1964. Subsequently, Bangalore and Chandigarh took up community mental health (CMH) work in 1975, followed by various other centers like Baroda, Calcutta, Hyderabad, Lucknow, Jaipur, Patiala, Delhi, and Vellore. These programs have been assisted by the Indian Council of Medical Research in New Delhi and the World Health Organization in Geneva. The feasibility of including mental health care as a part of general health services has been examined, and it has been shown that it is possible to develop simple training materials for primary health care personnel and to train them to carry out a limited range of tasks to benefit the mentally ill in the rural areas. These developments have culminated in the development of the National Mental Health Programme for India (NMHP) (1982). This program was formulated by a group of mental health professionals. The new approach emphasized self-help, community care, and decentralization of services.

The 1980s also witnessed other legislative and policy measures. Notable amongst them were the Narcotic and Psychotropic Substances Act (1985), the Mental Health Act (1987), and the National Policy on Mental Handicap (1986). This period also saw the much-neglected mental hospitals occupying a front position. At the same time public litigation directed at mental hospitals and subsequent court orders resulted in massive improvement. The demand for better services is a reflection of the growing awareness of the general public. Trivandrum, Ranchi, Delhi, and Pune mental hospitals are on the way to modernization. A modern 200-bed hospital has been built at Tezpur.

Current Organization

The Mental Health Act (MHA) (1987) outlines the organization of mental health care in the country. Unlike the Indian Lunacy Act (1912), the new act incorporates recent concepts in the field of mental health. Some of the salient features of the MHA are the following:

1. Establishment of a Mental Health Authority at the center and state levels for regulation, development, and coordination with respect to mental health services (governmental and private) (sections 3 and 4).

2. Separate hospitals for special categories: There is provision under section 5 for establishment of separate hospitals for children, addicts, psychopaths, and other categories of mental patients.

3. In order to ensure minimum facilities for the care of mentally ill persons, there is provision for licensing of private nursing homes under sections 6–9.

Mental health care in India is delivered by private and government sectors. Private practitioners are primarily private psychiatric consultants who provide treatment to psychiatric patients on an outpatient basis. Private nursing homes are managed by private psychiatrists, who in addition to outpatient treatment also provide inpatient care to psychiatric patients. Because of the stigma of psychiatric illness, a large number of patients from the affluent and middle socioeconomic classes seek treatment with private practitioners or in private nursing homes.

Private hospitals are managed by voluntary organizations. There are few voluntary organizations in the area of mental health. The majority of them are general hospitals where psychiatric patients may sometimes be admitted for treatment. There are some private hospitals for special categories of patients such as the mentally retarded, addicts, and schizophrenics. The Schizophrenia Research Foundation (India) (SCARF) is applying a community-based rehabilitation program to schizophrenics that involves substantial community participation. The Richmond Fellowship Society (India) for community health is a registered charitable society concerned with rehabilitation in the field of mental health. Through similar organizations is runs a network of therapeutic communities in America, Australia, Austria, Canada, Hong Kong, Israel, New Zealand, the United Kingdom, and a growing number of other countries. The society has set up two halfway homes in Bangalore and aims to use this experience to develop facilities in other parts of India.

Voluntary organizations (nongovernmental organizations) (NGOs) usually raise their own resources. Some of them are provided financial assistance under regulations by the Ministry of Health and Family Welfare. While many function on a nonprofit basis, there are some NGOs that are primarily profit-making centers. The charitable trusts are registered associations that are broad-based and operate on a nonprofit basis. They can set up permanent structures like a hospital and regular outpatient department and employ salaried staff. They may levy charges for services rendered on a sliding scale, with a percentage of patients also being treated free. In order to raise their resources, the donations to such trusts are given exemption under income tax rules. The Ministry of Health, through the Indian Council of Medical Research and the Department of Science and Technology, has laid down guidelines for tax exemption for such trusts.

The government accepts the vital importance of the voluntary agencies or organizations in the goal of Health for All by the Year 2000. The voluntary organizations (NGOs) have a major role to play in the aftercare rehabilitation of chronic mentally ill (particularly schizophrenics and mentally retarded children), child and school mental health services, services for drug dependence, early detection of psychiatric problems, and mental health education.

The government sector provides health care at the following levels:

Primary Health Care at the Village and Subcenter Level: Under the supervision and support of a medical officer, multipurpose workers and health supervisors undertake the management of psychiatric emergencies; administer and supervise maintenance treatment for chronic psychiatric conditions; recognize and manage grand mal epilepsy; act as liaisons with parents and schoolteachers for management of childhood behavior and developmental problems, including mental retardation; and counsel drug abuse and alcohol patients. A difficulty level is specified for each task beyond which it is to be referred to the next level of health care.

Primary Health Center: The tasks to be carried out by medical officers include supervision of multipurpose workers' (MPWs) performances on specified mental health tasks; elementary diagnostic assessment of cases using diagnostics and management flowcharts; treatment of functional psychosis, mild to moderately severe depressive illness and anxiety syndromes, and uncomplicated cases of psychiatric conditions associated with physical ailments like malaria and typhoid with appropriate drugs; management of psychosocial problems without use of drugs; and counselling regarding principles of rehabilitation. In addition, they make surveillances of mental morbidity in the area for review and planning for future services. The medical officer is all along guided by specified cutoff points for referral of problems to a higher level of health care.

District Hospital: The psychiatric specialist in a district hospital provides medical consultation to the hospital's medical officer with regard to difficult psychiatric cases. The main task is to admit and provide brief hospital treatment for psychiatric patients, particularly those presenting with severe excitement, refusal of food, complicated neurotic problems, and the like. Thirty to fifty beds can be allotted for psychiatric patients in a district hospital. The district hospitals have linkages with state mental hospitals and teaching departments of medical colleges for further referral.

Mental Hospitals and Teaching Psychiatry Departments: These centers have links with the periphery. They are advanced centers of care providing also for treatment of difficult patients and specialized facilities such as occupational therapy, psychotherapeutic help like group therapy, marital counselling, and behavior therapy. In addition, these centers take up the task of mental health education and training psychiatrists, who function later as leaders of mental health care programs and trainers of supervisors of nonspecialist health workers, who in turn provide basic health care to the community.

Current Services

Over a period of forty-five years the number of mental health hospitals has increased from seventeen to forty-five and the total bed strength in them has doubled from 10,148 to 20,674 (*National Mental Health Programme for India*, 1982–1990), but the bed/population ratio has remained the same, as the population has also doubled. Because there has been a tenfold increase in the annual admission rate, presently touching a figure of 55,000, the hospitals have not been able to cater to the growing demands. It is salient to note that currently there are no mental hospitals in Haryana, Himachal Pradesh, Manipur, Meghalaya, Mizoram, Pondicherry, and Lakshadweep. Also, it is important to mention that the bed population is not evenly distributed in the states. The presently available mental health facilities in India include 20,674 beds in 45 mental hospitals and 3,000–5,000 psychiatric beds in general and teaching hospitals. Total health beds in India are less than 0.7 per 1,000 population, out of which psychiatric beds constitute only 0.033, which comes to 1 psychiatric bed per 32,000 population (*National Mental Health Programme for India*, 1982–1990). Besides, almost 50 percent of the beds are occupied by chronic patients, adding to the shortage of active treatment beds.

Outpatient clinics operating in general hospital psychiatric units and mental hospitals are an important source of mental health services in many cities. Specialized inpatient and outpatient facilities for children and old persons are insignificant.

Mental Health Personnel and Treatment

There were only a handful of psychiatrists, with no recognized facility for training of psychiatrists, in the country at the time of independence. In January 1955 the diploma in psychological medicine was started at the All India Institute of Mental Health (AIIMH). At present, about four dozen centers are providing training for D.P.M. and M.D. courses, and almost 250 psychiatrists qualify annually. Currently, there are about 2,500 psychiatrists in the country.

Training facilities for clinical psychologists, psychiatric nurses, and psychiatric social workers are available at two centers: Ranchi and Bangalore. Psychiatric social work training is at present suspended at Ranchi. A two-year M.Sc. course in psychiatric nursing is available at Delhi and Chandigarh. It is estimated that 600–700 clinical psychologists, 600 psychiatric nurses, and about 500–600 psychiatric social workers are working in the country.

The foregoing makes it abundantly clear that the mental health personnel and mental health services in the country are woefully inadequate and cater to not more than 10 percent of those requiring urgent mental health care. The situation is worse in the rural areas because of the heavy concentration of services in the cities.

PUBLIC POLICY PROCESS

The National Mental Health Programme for India (NMHP) was adopted in 1982 by the Central Council of Health, which resolved that it be implemented in the states and union territories of India. The development of this legislation shows the operation of the policy process in India. The program was conceived with the following objectives: to ensure availability and accessibility of minimum mental health care to all in the foreseeable future, particularly to the most vulnerable and underprivileged section of the population; to encourage application of mental health knowledge in general health care and in social development; and to promote community participation in mental health service development and to stimulate efforts toward self-help in the community. It has adopted the following approaches:

1. Diffusion of mental health skills to the periphery of the health service system.
2. Appropriate appointment of tasks in mental health care.
3. Equitable and balanced territorial distribution of resources.
4. Integration of basic mental health care into general health services.
5. Linkage to community development.
6. Mental health care, which includes three subprograms: treatment, rehabilitation, and prevention.
   a. The focus of the treatment subprogram is on the following:
      i. Acute mental disorders—schizophrenia and affective psychosis; paranoid reactions; psychosis resulting from cerebral involvement in communicable diseases like malaria, typhus, or bacterial meningitis; alcoholic psychosis; and epileptic psychosis.
      ii. Chronic or frequently recurring mental illnesses like some cases of schizophrenia and of periodic cyclic affective psychosis; epileptic psychosis and dementias; encephalopathies associated with intoxications or chronic organic diseases; and so on.
      iii. Neurotic illnesses: Specified forms of diagnostic work and treatment are to be implemented at four levels of regional health care systems: Primary health care at the village and subcenter level, primary health center, district hospital, and mental hospitals and teaching psychiatric hospitals.
   b. Rehabilitation of psychiatric patients is to be facilitated largely by maintenance treatment of epileptics and psychotics at the community level. Counselling regarding principles of rehabilitation shall also be provided by the medical officer at the primary health center. Rehabilitation centers are to be developed at the district level as well as at the higher referral centers.

  c. The prevention subprogram is to be community based, mainly concentrating on alcohol-related problems and later on addictions, juvenile delinquency, and acute adjustment problems. The main carriers are to be the medical officer and community leaders.

7. Mental health training to a large number of health personnel of all categories, along with better training of medical undergraduates and inclusion of mental health training in teaching programs of nurses, public health administrators, and health staff.

8. Mental retardation and drug dependence: The health workers, including those of the Integrated Child Development Scheme, are to have the know-how to refer such children to social welfare agencies for rehabilitation.

9. A strong linkage at all levels and also with social welfare agencies is envisaged. The central mechanism of cooperation is to be the National Advisory Council.

10. Very close links are to be maintained with the Indian Council of Medical Research (ICMR) for continuous monitoring through evaluation research.

11. Appropriate legislation for proper implementation of the program shall be looked into.

The NMHP has a plan of action including time lines. An examination of the implementation and progress of the NMHP shows that the NMHP found a place in the seventh plan document with an allotment of ten million rupees. Now the eighth five-year plan is in process. It is beneficial to evaluate the progress made, what the gains and constraints have been, and what issues merit attention.

Developments at the administrative level have been a government order in September 1987 on the pattern of assistance; formation of the National Mental Health Advisory Group (NMHAG) in August 1988; two meetings of the NMHAG, with specific plans for utilizing the NMHP funds; and regular review of NMHP by health administrators and planners.

The important technical developments include the following:

1. Involvement of different groups of mental health professionals. NMHP has been discussed at the annual conferences of the Indian Psychiatric Conference at Varanasi and Jaipur. Separate workshops have been held periodically by psychiatrists, clinical psychologists, psychiatric social workers, and nurses.

2. Development of support materials, including manuals of mental health for doctors, health and development workers, and teachers and parents of the mentally handicapped; case records for use by different health personnel; health education materials for public education; and evaluation tools for training programs.

3. The other major activity has been the training of medical practitioners, primary health doctors, and multipurpose workers. Training programs of variable durations—two days, four days, six weeks, and three months in three sessions—have been developed for training of primary health center personnel and multipurpose workers (Sharma, 1991).

4. Three models have been suggested for delivery of mental health care services (*National Mental Health Programme for India*, 1982–1990):

a. Center-to-periphery model of establishing or strengthening of psychiatric units in district hospitals.

b. Periphery-to-center model (community mental health model) of training an increasing number of different categories of health personnel in basic psychiatric health skills. This model has been propagated at Bangalore and Chandigarh. These two models are not mutually exclusive since the differences between them lie mainly in the emphasis, in the priority assigned to different levels of service development.

c. The Ranchi model of providing three weeks' training to three to four nonspecialist physicians and two medical officers working in the Directorate of Health Services in each northeastern state, so that they can provide the needed mental health care, organize similar programs in their own states with the help of faculty members, and also extend them to the district and PHC levels.

Currently, a first-phase mental health program has been initiated in all the states and union territories. Attempts directed at integrating mental health with the education, welfare, and voluntary sectors are in progress. Also, activities are under way toward developing a model curriculum in mental health for medical undergraduates and enhancing the skills of the staff of mental hospitals. These have provided further impetus and have broadened the scope of NMHP.

Delay in the formation of NMHAG, a limited amount of funds in the seventh plan period, nonformation of the DGHS (Director General of Health Services) unit, variable enthusiasm at the state and union territory levels, and lack of administrative mechanisms for monitoring the programs have hindered the progress of NMHP. Consequently, the targets identified for the first five years of NMHP remain unmet.

There are also a number of limitations to the National Mental Health Program. The lack of clear-cut models of mental health care delivery and the lack of adequate resources have been cited as the two major hurdles in the implementation of NMHP and numerous questions have been raised by psychiatrists regarding the NMHP. Does it attend to the needs of all patients, including those with chronic and acute problems, alcoholics and drug abusers, the children, and the aged? Does it provide prompt evaluation and diagnosis by a competent diagnostician? Is it truly prevention oriented, or does it pretend to do more prevention than it really does? Does it sponsor research on prevention? Does it appropriately utilize qualified psychiatrists?

There are also apprehensions that NMHP would lead to two different systems of care for urban and rural populations with differing degrees of sophistication. This would be undesirable in a democratic country. Finally, the involvement of professionals in the community envisages a change in the role of the psychiatrist from a clinical specialist to a leader and planner of mental health services in his or her territory. Besides, it would mean restriction of the range of therapeutic interventions and require short-term goals for treatment (Sharma, 1991). The approach would require simplification of each of the professional activities and skills from dosages, counselling, and emotional support to behavior modification skills without losing the essence of the intervention so that less trained personnel can provide satisfactory care.

SPECIAL POLICY ISSUES

The Mentally Ill and the Mentally Retarded

At present there are a little over 200 institutions for the mentally retarded with facilities for care of about 10,000 individuals (*National Policy on Mental Handicap*, 1986). The current services cover only 1 percent of mentally handicapped persons. The services are not only meager but also unevenly distributed. Services for severely retarded persons are almost unavailable in the country.

Until recently, mental handicap, that is, arrested or delayed development, was not considered a significant problem in the planning of services. The biggest hurdle was the apathy of the general public toward such persons, as it was widely believed that the mentally handicapped person was a liability to the family and society. With advances in the care of the mentally handicapped and the National Policy on Education (1986) emphasizing universal coverage of education, the mentally handicapped have received increasing attention from teachers and families. The National Policy on Education aims to integrate physically and mentally handicapped individuals with the general community. To achieve this objective, it has outlined the following measures:

1. Integration of education of handicapped children with that of other children

2. Special schools with hostels at district headquarters

3. Vocational training

4. Reorientation of teachers' training programs to deal with handicapped children

5. Encouragement of voluntary efforts

Mentally handicapped persons require the efforts of a number of disciplines: health, welfare, education, law, rehabilitation, and nursing, along with efforts of voluntary agencies. Also, many persons may require lifelong support of one form or another.

Development of treatment approaches for the mentally handicapped have shown a gradual and general shift toward the family as a unit. This change has been happening because comprehensive care by professionals is not only expensive but also difficult to link to all developmental stages. Besides, the capacity of the family to serve as primary care providers with appropriate training, continuous professional help, and administrative support has been demonstrated. Implementation of the National Policy on Mental Handicap began under the administration of Sri Rajiv Gandhi on January 14, 1988.

The Mentally Ill and Substance Abuse

Epidemiological surveys carried out in India reveal that 60.03 to 79 percent of Indians are abstainers (Varma, Singh, Singh, & Malhotra, 1980; Singh & Gupta, 1988), 15 to 45.9 percent of subjects above the age of fifteen years are current users of alcohol (Varma et al., 1980; Ramchandran, 1991) and nearly 10 percent are regular or excessive drinkers (Ramchandran, 1991; Singh & Gupta, 1988). By most of the presently used diagnostic standards, less than half of these (roughly 4 to 5 percent) would be clinically labelled alcoholic (Singh & Gupta, 1988). A recent study, however, of Madras city found that 16.67 percent of males were suffering from alcoholism (Ponnudurai, Jayakar, Raju, & Pattamuthu, 1991). The prevalence of alcoholism in male psychiatric inpatients was reported to be 19 percent (Ray & Chandrasekhar, 1982). Fifteen to 20 percent of admissions in psychiatric facilities are for alcohol dependence in departments of psychiatry, and there are 10 percent or more patients in the same hospital in various other departments receiving treatment for alcohol-related problems such as gastritis, hepatic dysfunction, injuries, organic brain syndrome, and suicide attempts.

Alcoholic consumption patterns differ widely within the country, as there is wide variation between racial, ethnic, religious, and occupational groups. Sex differences also exist, the problem being negligible in females, that is, in less than 1 percent of all females (Singh, 1984). Studies have shown that there is more alcohol use in rural than in urban populations. Among rural men 32.1 to 74.1 percent have been reported to be current users in various parts of the country (Dev & Jindal, 1979; Sethi & Trivedi, 1979; Mohan et al., 1980; Varma et al., 1980). In an epidemiological study of rural and urban Chandigarh and two villages of Jullundur district, 23.7 percent of subjects were current users. Nineteen percent and 31.4 percent of urban and rural samples, respectively, of Chandigarh and 45.9 percent of a Jullundur rural sample were current users (Varma et al., 1980). Age differences are also seen. Young adults drink more than adolescents and older people (Singh & Gupta, 1988).

Alcohol causes psychosocial problems such as disruption in the family and a fall in work efficiency and also contributes to accidents, suicides, crimes, and violence. Although no factual data are available on this, individual, public health, and social problems associated with current use of alcohol are extensive, far-reaching, and grave.

It is customary to use the Lederman equation, which is based on total alcohol consumption of the state, for estimating the number of mild, moderate, and heavy drinkers in a population. In field studies in India a much higher number of heavy drinkers was found (nearly 10 percent) than was predicted by the Lederman equation, which in fact tended to underestimate the number of moderate and heavy drinkers in the Indian setting (Singh, 1984). The reasons for this discrepancy are manifold. First, the Lederman equation was based on samples of drinkers from Western societies in which drinking is socially approved and indulged in by the majority (approximately 70 percent of the population), with the result that only a minority are abstainers, while the majority are moderate drinkers and a few are heavy drinkers. In India drinking is neither socially approved nor widespread. It is estimated that less than 30 percent of the population comprise the drinkers in India, and there are a larger number of abstainers, some moderate drinkers, and few heavy drinkers. Another factor is the marked sex differences in drinking habits. Whereas in Western countries the ratio of male to female drinkers is roughly 3:1, in India it is estimated that roughly 50 percent of the adult males drink, but the number of female drinkers is negligible (less than 1 percent of all females). It is generally believed that only 4 to 5 percent of all drinkers become alcoholics in the West.

Primary prevention is included among the directive principles of the state policy set out in the Constitution of India, article 47. In 1960 the Ministry of Home Affairs, in consultation with the state governments, set up a Central Prohibition Committee to advise the government on a phased introduction of prohibition. Recommendations were given for strengthening the legal framework and involving voluntary agencies in the implementation of prohibition. Parts of only three states implemented the scheme, and one of these became wet after a short time.

From 1973 to 1975 the government approved a series of measures aimed at reducing alcohol consumption and preparing for total prohibition, but they did not have the desired impact. In 1975 the government resolved that from October 1975 a minimum program for prohibition should be pursued by all the states.

The Central Prohibition Committee recommendations for enforcement leading to total prohibition in four years were accepted by the government in 1977. However, the prohibition program was actually followed by an increase in consumption, smuggling of liquor from neighboring states, and illicit distribution. Besides, there was a great loss of revenue to the public and the government. For these reasons, the prohibition program was revoked in most states in 1981.

Prohibition is now in force only in the states of Gujarat and Tamil Nadu and in selected areas of Rajasthan, Uttar Pradesh, Karnataka, and Maharashtra. The political and financial power of the alcohol beverage industry and the societal ambivalence toward drinking versus prohibition led to the lifting of prohibition and the introduction of control measures. There are laws and regulations controlling production, outlets, number of types of alcoholic beverages, pricing, excise duty, and hours of sale of alcoholic beverages. Under the prevention subprogram of the National Mental Health Programme (1982), the medical officers and community leaders at the primary health centers are involved in the prevention and control of alcohol-related problems.

The Indian Council of Medical Research (ICMR), along with All India Radio, has taken up the study of the effects of a drug education program on the listening public. Research on the effect on utilization of services by education through videotapes and personal contacts of community workers with the vulnerable groups of people in the community and places of occupation are being considered by ICMR.

Secondary prevention is achieved by early identification and detection of alcohol-related problems in the community and getting incipient alcoholics into treatment. There are very few specialized treatment and rehabilitation centers for alcoholics. The majority of the patients are treated in psychiatric units of general hospitals or hospitals run by nongovernmental organizations or private psychiatric nursing homes, managed by private psychiatric practitioners, where the patients present directly or are referred from other health facilities. In these centers patients are admitted with other psychiatric patients. Apart from this, a large number of patients with medical complications are treated either by physicians in medical units of general hospitals or by private physicians.

Until 1985 centers for the exclusive treatment of alcoholics and drug addicts did not exist in India. The Expert Committee on Drug Deaddiction was appointed by the government of India to draw up a plan for the implementation of health services in the area of drug and alcohol dependence. On the recommendation of the committee the National Center was started in New Delhi in the All India Institute of Medical Sciences, and state centers are being developed for rapid training and development of various categories of health personnel.

During the Nehru birth centenary (1988–89), the Ministry of Health started creating a number of thirty-bed designated centers (deaddiction units) in the country. These centers undertake detoxification and also carry out early identification and follow-up with the assistance of the dispensaries and voluntary organizations. The medical doctors in primary health centers, aided by multipurpose workers and health supervisors, conduct surveillance of mental morbidity. Some centers conduct special training programs for primary-care physicians for early diagnosis and interview skills of alcoholics (Ramchandran, 1991).

The contribution of voluntary organizations and self-help groups (such as Alcoholics Anonymous) in the management of addicts has been little. There are voluntary organizations that are broad-based (social health) or more focused (All India Prohibition Council). In the field of drug and alcohol dependence only a few NGOs, for example, the All India Prohibition Council, exist with a national framework. However, of late the government has accepted the vital role of voluntary agencies in the early detection, follow-up, and rehabilitation of alcohol addicts in the community when they work in tandem with the designated centers. Also, the role of voluntary agencies in educating the public at different levels and removing the stigma attached to such problems has been appreciated. Increasing efforts are being made to involve voluntary organizations. For this purpose the government is providing financial assistance, tax exemptions, and requisite training to staff. However, despite these endeavors there has been little coordination between the treatment and rehabilitation centers, with the result that finances have been drained without significant changes in the desired direction.

The usual goal of a conventional treatment program is total abstinence and alleviation of associated social and interpersonal problems. Most centers offer a multimodal treatment package of four to six weeks, including drugs, behavior therapy, and psychotherapy, which is invariably carried out in the family setting. The treatment package consists of an initial phase of detoxification that is carried out with tapering doses of benzodiazepines and vitamin supplements. In most centers the spouse, parent, or another close relative must stay with the patient during treatment in the ward. Supportive psychotherapy is given, and the patient and his or her family are educated about the ill effects of alcohol on the person, the family, and the society. Also, attention is focused on specific issues related to work, marriage, and family. After discharge, follow-up of the patient with his or her spouse or parent is maintained on an outpatient basis. The family is given the main responsibility to provide emotional support and to police the patient so that abstinence is maintained.

Only a few centers in the country are using disulfiram therapy regularly for the management of addicts (Bagadia, Dhawale, Shah, Pradhan, 1982; De Sousa & De Sousa, 1984; John & Kuruvilla, 1991). The De Sousas (1984) have been using disulfiram for over fifteen years in their private clinic. Other techniques such as behavior therapy, group therapy sessions, and family therapy are regularly employed in a few centers having full-fledged departments of psychiatry. Behavior therapy techniques include Jacobson's progressive muscular relaxation, assertiveness training by modelling, role playing and behavioral rehearsal, electrical aversion therapy (Bagadia, Mundra, Gopalari, & Pradhan, 1979; John & Kuruvilla, 1991; Dutta, Prasantham, & Kuruvilla, 1991), covert sensitization, and training to develop alternate responses to stimuli in the environment that trigger drinking behavior.

Some centers, such as the Department of Psychiatry of the National Institute of Mental Health and Neurosciences, are regularly running family therapy programs for alcoholics. The psychiatric team, comprising a psychiatrist, a clinical psychologist, resident staff and social workers, sees the patient with one or two significant family members, the group ranging from ten to twenty in size. The family is assessed for leadership, role, communication and reinforcement patterns, cohesiveness, and social support systems. Family interaction and typology scales are also used. The treatment of these families consists of entering the orbit of the family system as a leader, understanding the interactional patterns, and evaluating the family while experientially participating in the actual process and restructuring the family.

Community-based treatment for alcoholics is still in its infancy. Dutta et al. (1991) developed a community-based (village) approach that utilizes the existing health care facilities as well as family involvement, which is essential. Experience has shown that it is a potentially useful tool in the treatment of alcoholism. It was initiated in Christianpet, a village of about 500 families twenty-one kilometers from Velore hospital. After an initial phase lasting for three months in which villagers in general and alcoholics and their families in particular are contacted and motivated for treatment, detoxification of alcoholics is carried out in groups in the health centers. Thereafter, they are put on disulfiram. The twelve steps of Alcoholics Anonymous are explained to them, and they are encouraged to set up Alcoholics Anonymous groups of their own. The aftercare program consists of group sessions at the center and weekly visits by the treatment team, consisting of two psychologists and one psychiatrist. The patients organize their own Alcoholics Anonymous meetings every Sunday evening. Follow-up of patients is maintained for one year.

Agnihotra is being used by some psychiatrists for the treatment of alcoholics (Golecha, Sethi, et al., 1991). Agnihotra is a Vedic ritual of lighting fire in a small rectangular copper pyramid pot using dried cakes of cow dung and offering ghee and rice to the fire at the time of sunrise and sunset with the whisper of two mantras. It is reported to enhance the state of tranquility of the mind and to be of benefit to alcohol addicts. It is found that agnihotra leads to total abstinence without other restraint after two weeks of regular practice. After it is discontinued, the effects lasts for another few weeks. Though relapse may develop on discontinuing agnihotra, a sizeable number of cases (53 percent) continue to remain abstinent for more than eight weeks. Agnihotra is not a total cure for alcoholism, but has been found to serve as a useful adjuvant.

The origin of agnihotra can be traced to the Rigveda, where positive gains of physical and mental health and energy are preached with regular practice of this ritual. Outside India, its popularity has achieved a new height during the last decade in the United States, Germany, Switzerland, France, Spain, Holland, Austria, Italy, Chile, and many other countries, where it is popularly known as "homa therapy."

In conclusion, it may be stated that facilities for the management of alcoholics in the country are meager. There are very few specialized centers for deaddiction, and they lack adequate facilities and personnel. The specialized centers should have an epidemiologist, health educators, social workers, psychologists, psychiatrists, and nurses trained in deaddiction. In particular, laboratory facilities and rehabilitation services also need to be strengthened.

Before 1985 drug-related matters were dealt with under four main pieces of legislation. The Opium Act (1857, 1878) dealt exclusively with matters relating to opium. The Dangerous Drugs Act (1930) dealt with other drugs like cannabis and cocaine. It did not deal with psychotropic drugs, which are partially covered under the Drugs and Cosmetics Act (1940). When the drug situation in the country worsened in the early 1980s due to an influx of heroin, the Narcotic Drugs and Psychotropic Substances Act (NDPSA) (1985) was enacted to cope with the situation.

The NDPSA came into force on November 14, 1985. It is an act to consolidate and amend the laws relating to narcotic drugs, to make stringent provisions for the control and regulation of operations relating to narcotic drugs and psychotropic substances, to provide for the forfeiture of property derived from, or used to carry on, illicit traffic in narcotic drugs and psychotropic substances, to implement the provisions of the International Conventions on Narcotic Drugs and Psychotropic Substances, and to cover matters connected therewith. Under the provisions of the act, possession, production, transports, interstate imports, interstate exports, sale, purchase, consumption, and admission to warehouses of narcotic drugs or psychotropic substances in contravention of any provision of the act are punishable. The act includes the following provisions:

1. The punishment for contravention in relation to "poppy straw," "coca plant and leaves," "prepared opium," "opium poppy," "opium," "cannabis" (except ganja), "manufactured drugs," and "psychotropic substances" is ten to twenty years' rigorous imprisonment (fifteen to thirty years for the second and subsequent offenses) with a fine of 100,000 to 200,000 rupees (150,000 to 300,000 rupees for the second and subsequent convictions) (28.5 rupees = $1.00 in 1992).

2. For contravention in relation to ganja or cultivation of cannabis plants the punishment is up to five years' rigorous imprisonment with a fine of up to 50,000 rupees (for second and subsequent offenses, ten years rigorous imprisonment and a fine of up to 100,000 rupees).

3. Punishment for contravention in relation to any "controlled substance" is rigorous imprisonment up to ten years with a fine of 100,000 rupees.

4. A death penalty may be administered for a person who has been convicted earlier (under section 15–25 or 27a) and who is subsequently convicted in relation to narcotic drugs and psychotropic substances involving quantities equal to or more than the following: hashish, 20 kilograms; opium, 10 kilograms; morphine, heroin, codeine, or thebaine, 1 kilogram; amphetamine or methaqualone, 0.5 kilograms; and LSD or THC, 0.5 kilograms.

5. Possession of small quantities of any narcotic drugs or psychotropic substances constitutes an offense and is punishable with imprisonment for up to six months to one year or a fine or both (section 27). Here the burden of proving that the substance was intended for personal use lies on the person. The small quantities specified are the following: heroin, 250 milligrams; hashish/charas, 5 grams; opium, 5 grams; cocaine, 125 milligrams; and ganja, 500 grams.

The court, however, may, with regard to other factors, instead of punishing the offender at once, with his or her consent release him or her to undergo treatment and require a report to the court within a year. If satisfied, the court may release the offender after due admonition and execution of a bond covering a period of a maximum of three years (sections 27, 39). Where a psychotropic substance is in the possession of an individual for his personal medical use, the quantity thereof shall not exceed 100 dosages at a time (section 66). Under the provision of the NDPSA the government may at its discretion, establish centers, as many as it thinks fit, for the identification, treatment, education, aftercare, rehabilitation, and social reintegration of addicts and for supply of narcotic drugs and psychotropic substances to registered addicts and to others where such a supply is a medical necessity.

However, the health services have been ill equipped to handle the demands arising from the provisions of the act. Strong linkages between the police, the judiciary, and the health services are needed for those who are arrested under the Small Quantities Provision Act. The Expert Committee on Drug Addiction, appointed by the government of India on January 3, 1986, recommended a plan for health services in the area of drug dependence, keeping in view provisions of NDPSA.

Small quantities of drugs: The small quantities of drugs recommended for NDPSA are as follows: raw opium, 25 grams; heroin, 1 gram; cocaine, 50 grams; ganja, 75 grams; and hashish/charas, 25 grams. These quantities were calculated keeping in view the average dose that drug-dependent persons might need for personal consumption. It was suggested that the small quantities be reviewed after eighteen months of enforcement.

Development of drug dependence services: The committee recommended two parallel systems of health care: first, a custodial care system for the treatment of addicts for the purposes of the act, and second, a system for those seeking voluntary treatment. The committee suggested the development of a national network in the long-term perspective, and, in the immediate context, resource mobilization on a priority basis from within the existing system. The national network is to have centers at the national and state/union-territory levels and designated centers; linkages between these centers are to be maintained. The national and state centers have not primarily been visualized as treatment centers, but as consultancy and referral centers for all sources to provide the following services:

- Expert advice to the Ministry of Health and Family Welfare, the Ministry of Welfare, state centers, and designated centers
- Adoption and implementation of curriculum courses for various categories of health professionals and voluntary agencies so as to increase trained person power
- Training to trainers, an opportunity for exchange of personnel that work in different centers, development of evaluation strategies and instruments for uniform data collection, and storage and retrieval of information
- Development of low-cost effective treatment models having sixty beds
- Development of and training in laboratory services related to drug and alcohol abuse problems
- Operational research on a continuing and coordinated basis

Each designated center shall have thirty beds with concomitant staff and equipment. It shall undertake detoxification and follow-up under the act, carry out early identification and follow-up with the assistance of dispensaries, general hospitals, and voluntary organizations, function as a registration center for purposes of the act, and undertake liaison work with community leaders.

Ethical issues: The committee recommended that absolute confidentiality be maintained regarding the identity of the patients seeking assistance either on a voluntary basis or through court referral.

Improvement in existing health services: In particular, emergency services in public hospitals are to be provided with antagonist drugs (naloxone), resuscitation apparatus, and better laboratory facilities.

Voluntary organizations: The committee accepted that nongovernmental organizations (NGOs) have a vital role to play in identification and surveillance in the community. The government provides financial assistance to these NGOs in accordance with specified rules and also exempts them from income tax.

Maintenance programs: In patients in whom drug intake is a medical necessity, maintenance programs—raw opium for opium addicts and tincture opium for heroin users—are recommended to reduce adverse social costs of illicit drugs. The latter programs, however, need to be tested before considering their extension.

Drug abuse monitoring system: Monitoring is to be done at all levels (national and state centers, general hospitals, designated centers, voluntary agencies, and police) to obtain continuing data on drug/alcohol dependence.

The Mentally Disordered Offender

Insanity (mental illness) as a defense is usually used in charges of murder in order to escape capital punishment. The law regarding criminal responsibility in India is based on the M'Naghten rule. Section 84 of the Indian Penal Code (Act 45 of 1960, IPC) states that "nothing is an offense which is done by a person who, at the time of doing it, by reason of unsoundness of mind, is incapable of knowing the nature of the act, or that he is doing what is either wrong or contrary to law." When the defendant is found "not guilty," he or she is kept in safe custody, usually in a mental hospital (asylum), so that society is protected against the "lunatic." It may be noted that for a person to benefit from this section, it must be proved that unsoundness of mind existed at the time of committing the offense. Subsequent unsoundness of mind may affect the trial, but is not accepted as a defense. The burden of proof is on the defense. No reference in this act is made to lack of control, irresistible impulse, or diminished responsibility.

Idiots, imbeciles, and persons who are deprived of all understanding and memory, for example, children below the age of seven years and children between seven and twelve years of immature understanding, are clearly not criminally responsible. In situations of partial insanity, for example, paranoid schizophrenia, where dysfunction is in the delusional area and understanding and memory are intact, it has been suggested that the accused should be placed as regards criminal responsibility in the same situation as if the facts of his delusions were true and real.

The insanity defense is involved in few cases and is upheld in only a fraction of them. It is usually a desperation defense in criminal law when all else fails.

Judges and juries are quite skeptical. If the defendant is acquitted on grounds of insanity, the magistrate orders detention in an asylum (mental hospital) in accordance with the Mental Health Act (1987) or orders him or her to be delivered to any relative or friend, who will provide security that he or she will be properly cared for, will be prevented from injuring himself or herself and others, and will be produced before the court or any officer when required (section 335 Criminal Procedure Code, CPC).

If intoxication is caused by voluntary use of alcohol or some other substance, this is no excuse for the commission of a crime. However, insanity produced by drunkenness, voluntary or otherwise (e.g., delirium tremens), absolves one from criminal responsibility if section 84 inclusive is applicable. Sections 85 and 86 of IPC provide that an accused person is not criminally responsible if the intoxication was administered to him without his knowledge or against his will.

Attempted suicide or commission of any act toward commission of suicide can be punished under section 309 IPC with simple imprisonment for a term that may extend to one year or with a fine or with both. The offense is cognizable, but bailable. However, a mentally ill person is not responsible if at the time of committing the act, by reason of mental illness, he did not know that what he was doing was either wrong or contrary to law. Apart from these provisions, a mentally ill person may be involved in any crime, such as unnatural offenses (e.g., sexual perversions, section 377 IPC); affrays (e.g., in mania, section 159 IPC), and misconduct in public while drunk (e.g., in alcohol dependence, section 510 IPC).

Sections 328 and 339 of the Code of Criminal Procedure 1973 (Act 2 of 1974; CPC) relates to provisions as to accused persons of unsound mind, including fitness to stand trial and subsequent procedures. The law provides the accused the right to consult his lawyer when he feels he is being exposed to a situation not receptive to his viewpoint. A defendant who lacks the capacity to understand the nature and the object of proceedings against him, or to consult his lawyer and to assist in preparing the defense, may not be subjected to a trial. His mental condition at the time of the offense has no bearing on the matter. When initiated by the prosecution, the process is often called "preventive detention," while when it is raised by the defense, it is known as "medical immunity."

When the accused is a "lunatic" and is consequently incapable of making his defense, the magistrate inquires into the fact of unsoundness of mind, including examination of the accused by a medical officer. Further proceedings of the case are postponed if the magistrate is satisfied that the accused is of unsound mind and is incapable of making his defense (section 328, CPC). The accused is then either detained in safe custody or in a mental hospital, in accordance with the Mental Health Act 1987, or released pending investigation or trial if bail can be taken and sufficient security is provided by a relative or friend that he will be properly cared for, will be prevented from injuring himself or

Table 5.1
Mental Hospital Utilization in India

Year	No. of Mental Hospitals	Beds	Admissions	Discharges	Deaths
1951	30	10,148	5,837	5,831	471
1961	35	12,533	21,641	6,292	1,266
1971	38	18,507	32,064	31,975	1,113
1981	45	20,559	49,195	48,353	931
1991	45	20,674	54,759	53,169	922

Source: Sharma, 1990.

others, and will be produced before the court when necessary. If the accused subsequently ceases to be of unsound mind, the trial can be resumed.

Deinstitutionalization

In India there has been over the years since independence a rapid transition in emphasis on mental health services from institutional care in mental hospitals to general hospital psychiatric units (GHPUs) and then to community care. In 1951 there were 30 mental hospitals, all state owned, with a bed strength of 10,148, and the number of patients admitted was only 5,837, with an average stay of more than one year. Over the years from 1944 to 1984, the number of mental hospitals and their bed strength increased, but the bed/population ratio remained the same because of a concurrent increase in population. The statistics of mental hospitals since 1951 (see table 5.1) reveal that though the number of beds has increased only marginally, there has been a significant increase in the number of patients utilizing the hospital service (Sharma, 1990). This is probably partly related to the fact that before 1961 there was more focus on insulin treatment and electroconvulsive therapy (ECT), whereas later, drugs and tranquilizers were used more liberally.

Even though the GHPUs are generally acknowledged to be better, no mental hospital has closed down since independence. The mental hospitals have had to meet the needs of the chronically mentally ill and the criminal and dangerous patients who cannot be attended to in the general hospital setting or be permanently rehabilitated in the community.

The GHPUs have provided a big push for greater acceptance of psychiatric services by the public without fear of social stigma. In these units patients are treated with other medical patients in the same hospital. Most GHPUs have an outpatient section and an inpatient section with thirty to fifty beds. By and large, acutely disturbed patients, patients requiring specialized investigations or treatment, and patients not responding to conventional outpatient treatment are admitted to these inpatient units. All the other patients are managed on an outpatient basis. During inpatient treatment in GHPUs the family is invariably involved in the treatment program, and the emphasis is on short-term management with early discharge and return to the family and community. The average stay of patients in the psychiatry ward is from three to six weeks. In most cases the patient is accepted in the family, which facilitates rehabilitation of the patients in the community. Rehabilitation is hardly a problem for rural patients, who can always resume their original occupation of farming. Follow-up treatment of these patients is maintained on an outpatient basis.

The latest phase in the development of mental health services in India has been the community care approach and the involvement of primary health care physicians. This has occurred because of the commitment of the country to provide primary mental health care to all, realization of the magnitude of severe mental disorders in the community, and the fact that simple interventions are available for these conditions.

Many centers have undertaken community mental health work. The most recent trends have been (a) the training of nonpsychiatric physicians and paramedical personnel in psychiatric know-how skills, (b) provision of three or four essential psychotropic drugs at the primary health center level, (c) integration of basic mental health care into general health services, (d) the setting up of regional centers of community mental health, (e) the involvement of the health, education, and welfare sectors in mental health care programs, and (f) involvement of voluntary agencies.

Funding Issues

Under the Mental Health Act of 1987 the cost of maintenance of a mentally ill person detained in any psychiatric hospital is borne by the government of the state or by the person legally bound to maintain the patient. If the mentally ill person has an estate, the cost of the maintenance can be met out of it (section 28). The government health services are usually managed and funded by either the central government, state governments, or the University Grants Commission, which receives funds from the central government and finances some of the teaching psychiatric units in the country. Ten million rupees were allotted for the launching and implementation of the National Mental Health Programme during the seventh five-year plan (table 5.2).

Consumer Rights

Under the Mental Health Act of 1987 an inspecting officer may at any time enter and inspect any psychiatric nursing home or hospital, require the production

Table 5.2
Mental Health Budget Proposal for India's Seventh Five-Year-Plan (in Lakhs)
(NMHP 1982–1988)

	Item	1986-87	1987-88	1988-89	1989-90	Total
1.	PHC-State Programme*	7.50	12.00	11.00	13.00	43.50
2.	Regional CMH Centres	8.00	8.50	11.00	12.00	39.50
3.	Manuals (Dr/MPW) Eng	10.00	-	-	-	10.00
4.	Records	5.00	-	-	-	5.00
5.	Health Education Materials	5.00	1.00	2.00	2.00	10.00
6.	Evaluation Team	-	1.00	2.00	2.00	5.00
7.	Training of PHC Training School staff	-	5.00	5.00	5.00	15.00
8.	Mental Hospital Task Force	-	1.00	1.00	-	2.00
9.	DGHS Cell	0.25	0.75	0.75	0.75	2.50
10.	NIMHANS, Bangalore	0.25	0.75	0.75	0.75	2.50
11.	C.I.P. Ranchi	0.25	0.75	0.75	0.75	2.50
12.	Institutionalized Children	-	2.00	4.00	4.00	10.00
13.	Voluntary Agencies	0.50	1.00	1.50	2.00	5.00
14.	NAGMH**	0.50	0.50	0.50	0.50	2.00
15.	Undergraduate Medical Education	0.25	0.50	0.75	0.50	2.00
16.	Promotion of Mental Health	0.50	1.50	1.50	1.50	5.00
	Total	38.00	36.25	42.50	44.75	161.50

* 1986-87: 10 Centres; 1987-90: 20 Centres
** National Advisory Group on Mental Health

U.S. $1 = 28.5 Rupees

Source: National Mental Health Programme for India, 1982-1988.

of any records, interview any patient in private, and report to the licensing authority for action (section 13). Admission on a voluntary basis is permitted on the request of a patient or his or her guardian, if he or she is a minor. Discharge of these patients must be made within twenty-four hours after request for the same, except in special circumstances when the admission period can be extended for ninety days on the recommendation of a board comprising two medical officers.

Involuntary admission can be made on an application by a relative or friend supported by two medical certificates from two medical practitioners (one being in government service) to the medical officer in charge of a hospital for a period not exceeding ninety days. Any patient so admitted can apply by himself or herself or through his or her relative or friend to the magistrate for discharge before this period.

A reception order for detention in a psychiatric hospital or psychiatric nursing home may be made by the magistrate for the personal safety of a psychiatric patient, for the safety of others, or for treatment for more than six months on an application made by a medical officer in charge of a psychiatric hospital or by a relative of a mentally ill person (section 22). A reception order can also be made on presentation of a mentally ill person before the magistrate by the officer in charge of a police station (section 23).

Any private person or officer in charge of a police station can report to the magistrate if he learns that a mentally ill person is not under proper care or is being ill treated. The magistrate can then order the relative legally bound to maintain the patient to take proper care of the patient. If the relative willfully neglects to comply with the order, he can be punished with a fine that may extend up to 2,000 rupees (section 25).

Protection of the human rights of mentally ill persons is provided for. No mentally ill person can be subjected to physical or mental cruelty, nor can he or she be used for research, unless it is of direct benefit to him or her for purposes of diagnosis and treatment and written consent has been obtained (section 81). There are relatively severe penalties for maintaining psychiatric nursing homes in contravention of the various clauses under the act (sections 82–86).

A critical appraisal of the Mental Health Act shows the following:

1. The definition of mentally ill person in this act includes all categories of mental disorders. It is felt that the law should be restricted to serious forms of mentally disordered persons (who are incapable of exercising judgment and self-restraint in their behavior), because the provisions of the act do not give psychiatric patients a right to keep their personal problems secret.

2. A system of licensing only psychiatric nursing homes and hospitals has been introduced. This provision separates the practice of psychiatry from the practice of medicine and surgery. This is against the basic spirit of the NMHP, which envisages the integration of basic mental health into general health services at all levels.

3. Inspection of all records by the inspecting officer is an encroachment on the fundamental rights of confidentiality of patients. It would discourage many patients from taking treatment in private nursing homes or hospitals because of a fear of stigma and thus would deprive many of them of skilled psychiatric treatment.

4. The status (psychiatrist or nonmedical person) of the inspector is not mentioned. If he is a nonpsychiatrist, there would always be a danger for the treating psychiatrist to get into difficulties, as the inspecting officer cannot understand the complaints of paranoid patients, who may well have systematized delusions directed at times toward the treating doctors.

5. No provision has been made in the Mental Health Act for treatment of persons who do not have any estate or whose relatives cannot bear the cost of treatment.

6. The law is silent regarding checks on unscientific treatment and cruelty in nonmedical situations.

The objectives of the Mental Health Act are the following:

1. To evolve a policy concerning health, education, social security, and legislative measures for improving the quality of life of the mentally handicapped persons in the country

2. To ensure availability and accessibility of basic care for all mentally handicapped persons in the foreseeable future

3. To promote community participation and stimulate efforts toward self-help in the families of mentally handicapped individuals

Strategies of action include the following:

1. Early identification: Health personnel (health volunteers, bal sevakas, multipurpose workers, health supervisors, medical officers, and pediatricians) are to be oriented to intensify their efforts toward prevention, early identification, and guidance for home care.

2. Care, including rehabilitation, by home training, special schools, and vocational training.

3. A national trust to provide guardianship, foster care, and mobilization of resources to strengthen the family and the community for the mentally handicapped.

4. Special school units with residential facilities at the district level.

5. Pilot programs for examining the feasibility and operational details of services with universal coverage and accessibility.

6. Community participation (individuals and groups, voluntary agencies, and self-help groups).

7. Establishment of a national information and documentation center at the center and later at the state level.

8. Research to be directed at studying

   a. the effectiveness of prevention measures to decrease mental handicap;

   b. the impact of public education and awareness of activities;

   c. the impact of mentally handicapped persons on the family;

   d. comparative evaluation of different models of care;

   e. the effect of school integration on handicapped children;

   f. genetics of the mentally handicapped, especially with regard to community studies of consanguineous marriages;

   g. the utility of Yoga for mentally handicapped persons.

The policy has been receiving encouraging support from the planners and administrators (politicians). The starting of parent training programs at Delhi, Vellore, Chandigarh, and Bangalore and a self-help-group movement are positive developments.

CONCLUSIONS AND DISCUSSION

The NMHP is now in line with other larger developments in the country, and the needs of mental health promotion, prevention of illness, and cure have become well recognized. Because of financial constraints, efforts are now being directed at developing modest and viable programs in each state rather than ambitious plans for a wider coverage (Srinivasa Murthy, 1990). It is hoped that the eighth plan will provide a greater thrust to the NMHP with greater monetary support.

It is a matter of concern that despite the best efforts of the professionals involved in carrying out the program, it has failed to have any significant impact in the majority of the states (Agrawal, 1991). Needless to say, no scheme can be achieved without a strong political will to pursue it. The administrators and politicians often put forward the plea of lack of sufficient funds and claim that health priority areas are family planning and control of infectious diseases and malnutrition. It is intriguing that the decision makers have not yet perceived that the target program and mental health services are of a complementary nature.

Suprisingly, both the layman and experts from other medical disciplines view psychiatrists as doing nothing more than giving tranquilizing pills and indulging in pep talks with patients. The unhealthy image of psychiatry has been a deterrent in the progress of mental health in the country. There should be a greater focus on providing adequate mental health education to the public, encouraging the availability of modern methods of psychiatric treatment, and emphasizing the brighter aspects of recovery. A somewhat widespread apathy toward the plight of mental patients has continued.

Finally, dealing with the stigma of mental disorder must be a goal if success is to be achieved. The future of the NMHP will largely depend on professional support, public support and education, and the political will to give due importance to mental health in the development of the country. Motivation is required at all levels, among the providers as well as the acceptors, so that our cherished goal of Mental Health for All by the Year 2000 may become a reality.

REFERENCES

Agrawal, A. (1991). Mental health programme: Need for redemption. *Indian Journal of Psychiatry*, *33*, 85–86.

Bagadia, V. N., Dhawale, K. M., Shah, L. P., & Pradhan, P. V. (1982). Evaluation of disulfiram in the treatment of alcoholism. *Indian Journal of Psychiatry*, *24*, 242–247.

Bagadia, V. N., Mundra, V. K., Gopalani, J. H., & Pradhan, P. V. (1979). Chronic alcoholism: The responder on electrical aversion therapy. *Indian Journal of Psychiatry*, *21*, 64.

De Sousa, A., & De Sousa, D. A. (1984). Experience with disulfiram therapy in India. In A. De Sousa, & D. A. De Sousa (Eds.), *Psychiatry in India*. Bombay: Bhalani Book Depot.

Dev, P. C., & Jindal, R. B. (1979). *Drinking in rural areas: A study in selected villages of Punjab, Ludhiana.* Ludhiana: Punjab Agricultural University.

Dutta, S., Prasantham, B. J., & Kuruvilla, K. (1991). Community treatment for alcoholism. *Indian Journal of Psychiatry, 33,* 305–306.

Golecha, G. R., Sethi, I. C., et al. (1991). Agnihotra in the treatment of alcoholism. *Indian Journal of Psychiatry, 33,* 44–47.

Government of India. (1986). *Expert committee report on drug dependency services.* India: Ministry of Justice.

Indian Council of Medical Research. (1988). Severe mental morbidity. *Indian Council of Medical Research, 18,* 12.

John, S., & Kuruvilla, K. (1991). A followup study of patients treated for alcohol dependence. *Indian Journal of Psychiatry, 33,* 2, 113–117.

Mental Health Act. (1987). In S. D. Sharma (Ed.) (1990), *Mental hospitals in India* (pp. 99–143). New Delhi: Directorate General of Health Services.

Mohan, D., et al. (1980). Pattern of alcohol consumption of rural Punjab males. *Indian Journal of Medical Research, 72,* 702–711.

Narcotic Drugs and Psychotropic Substances Act. (1985). *Gazette of India, Extra,* part 2, sect. 1, pp. 1–34.

National mental health programme for India (NMHP) (1982). Ministry of Health and Family Welfare. Bangalore: Government of India.

National mental health programme for India (NMHP) (1982–1990.) Progress Report. Ministry of Health and Family Welfare. Bangalore: Government of India.

National mental health programme for India (1982–1988): Progress report. New Delhi: Director General of Health Services and World Health Organisation, SEARO.

National policy on mental handicap (1986): Report on national policy on mental handicap. Hyderabad: Thakur Hariprasad Institute of Rehabilitation for Mentally Handicapped Children.

Neki, J. S. (1973). Psychiatry in South East Asia. *British Journal of Psychiatry, 123,* 257–267.

Ponnudurai, R., Jayakar, J., Raju, B., & Pattamuthu, R. (1991). An epidemiological study of alcoholism. *Indian Journal of Psychiatry, 33,* 176–179.

Ramchandran, V. (1991). The prevention of alcohol related problems. *Indian Journal of Psychiatry, 33,* 3–10.

Ray, R., Chandrasekhar, K. (1982). Detection of alcoholism among psychiatric inpatients. *Indian Journal of Psychiatry, 24,* 389–393.

Seshadri, S. (1986). Prevalence of mental disorders in India—adults. *Community Mental Health News, 2,* 2–3.

Sethi, B. B., & Trivedi, J. K. (1979). Drug abuse in a rural population. *Indian Journal of Psychiatry, 21,* 211–216.

Sharma, I. (1991). Community mental health care in the developing world. *Indian Medical Gazette, 125*(7), 216–220.

Sharma, S. D. (1990). *Mental hospitals in India.* New Delhi: Directorate General of Health Services.

Singh, G. (1984). Alcoholism in India. In A. De Sousa & D. A. De Sousa (Eds.), *Psychiatry in India.* Bombay: Bhalani Book Depot.

Singh, G., & Gupta, V. (1988). *Treatment approaches to alcoholism and problem drinking: Continuing Medical Education Programme.* New Delhi: Indian Psychiatric Society.

Srinivasa Murthy, R. (1990). National Mental Health Programme in India (1982–1989): Mid-point appraisal. *Indian Journal of Psychiatry*, *3* (2), 267–270.

Varma, V. K., Singh, A., Singh, S., & Malhotra, A. (1980). Extent and pattern of alcohol-related problems in North India. *Indian Journal of Psychiatry*, *22*, 331–337.

6

Israel

Yael Yishai

OVERVIEW

Israel is a relatively small country (covering an area of 21,501 square kilometers) with a population in 1989 of 4.5 million. Approximately 83 percent of Israeli citizens are Jews, with the remainder divided between Arabs, Druze, and some other minority communities. The major distinction within the Jewish population is between those who immigrated from countries in Europe or America and their descendants and those who came to Israel from Asia and Africa and their offspring. The Jewish population is divided roughly equally between these two groups. The state, founded in 1948 after thirty years of British rule, adopted a parliamentary unitary regime that provided the government with considerable power. The 120 members of Israel's unicameral legislature (Knesset) are party delegates. The electoral system is extremely proportional, granting each party winning over 1 percent of the total vote parliamentary representation. The country is a party democracy where political parties hold pervasive power over both political and socioeconomic affairs (Arian, 1989, p. 7). The major parties are the right-wing Likud and the Labor Party. Israel is currently an affluent society with a national income in 1989 of $11,540 per capita. To some extent the country shares several problems with the rest of the Western world: the decline in parental authority, the disintegration of the family, the exposure to violence in the media, and the alienation of the individual. In addition, Israel faces three problems that may be unique: immigration, the memories of the Nazi Holocaust, and, most important, the strains of a precarious security. Some 20 percent of the national income is earmarked for defense expenditures.

Israel is one of a handful of "new societies" throughout the world founded by immigrants, in the same company as countries such as the United States, Canada, Australia, and New Zealand. New societies stand in sharp contrast to both traditional societies and those that have undergone modernization (Elazar, 1986). From the outset, the key to their birth as modern societies lies in the migration of their members to new "frontier" environments where they could create a social order with a minimum amount of hindrance by the entrenched ways of the past. Although the country was inhabited by several thousand Arabs, the Jewish settlers initially aimed at establishing a new society alongside the non-Jewish population. Israel is described as a country of immigrants, for immigrants, and led by immigrants (Ben-Porath, 1986). In contemporary Israel 63.3 percent of the Jewish population was born in the country; of these an overwhelming majority (approximately 80 percent) are second-generation natives (*Statistical Abstract of Israel*, 1989, p. 83). Mass immigration has produced social and cultural heterogeneity and stimulated economic development. It has also served as a source of many mental disturbances. The uprooting of people from their countries of origin and the need to adjust to a new environment and acquire a new language caused wide-ranging dislocation. Economic difficulties in the period of adjustment and a scarcity of jobs added stress to the strains of absorption that are evident even when integration into the new society appears smooth and successful. The high mobility encountered by the immigrants and their descendants is likely to cause pressure on the individual and provide a stimulus to mental disorders.

A substantial proportion of Israeli citizens are survivors of the Nazi Holocaust who arrived with recurring anxieties and other mental disorders following the horrors of the Nazi regime. The children of Holocaust survivors have also suffered from the experience undergone by their parents (Danieli, 1982).

Israel's precarious security has also been a source of mental stress. Since its establishment the country has been engaged in six open wars with its Arab neighbors and countless belligerent activities. The stress of security is evident in all walks of life. Recurrent terrorist attacks within Israel and the possibility of the outbreak of yet another war put a heavy strain on Israeli citizens. Moreover, the small size of the country blurs the distinction between the military front and the home front. The compulsory military service brings the threat of war to each and every family. The large number of people handicapped by war and the relatives of war casualties places a heavy burden on mental services. This combination of immigration, the life stories of many Israelis, and the strains caused by problems of defense have an impact on mental illness and on the formation of mental health policy.

EXTENT OF THE PROBLEM

Unfortunately, there are no current data concerning the extent of mental health problems in Israel. Most of the studies conducted on mental health in the country depend on hospital admissions and clinical research (Sanua, 1989). A few existing publications on the subject (Abrahamson, 1966; Litman, 1983) indicate that compared to Britain and the Netherlands, Israel ranks higher in the prevalence of mental disorders (Maoz & Stern, 1985). The rate of psychiatric morbidity, including minor emotional problems and transient mental disorders, per 1,000 inhabitants in the community as measured by health questionnaires was 274 in Israel, compared with 250 in Britain and 175–260 in the Netherlands. Israel also possesses the highest rate of psychiatric cases referred by a general practitioner (GP) to the mental health ambulatory services: in Britain, 17 per 1,000 population; in the Netherlands, 27 per 1,000; and in Israel, 32 per 1,000 (Seligson-Singer, 1983). The distribution of mental illness among the population is uneven. Halevi (1963) found that Jews coming from Middle Eastern countries had higher overall rates of mental illness than European Jews. Miller, in a later study (1979), also found basic personality differences among Jews of Middle Eastern birth as contrasted to those from Western countries. Rahav, Popper, and Nahon (1981) measured the "contribution" of immigrant cohorts to the inpatient population between 1950 and 1980. They cautiously suggested that the immigrants of the late 1940s and the early 1950s had higher rates of admission to mental hospitals than cohorts from other years. Both Abrahamson (1966) and Polliack (1972) found that women are more afflicted by mental illness than men. Rahav, Popper, and Nahon noted, however (1981, p. 262), that the sex distribution among inpatients first admitted is approximately even. Data provided by the Health Ministry on hospitalization (1988) reveal that men constituted 55.6 percent of the first admitted patients (Information System, 1989). The largest age group represented among the mental patients was the cohort aged twenty-five to forty-four, with 34.1 percent of the total. These data, however, pertain only to persons receiving some sort of treatment in psychiatric hospitals. In 1988 the number of Israelis admitted to mental health institutions of all types was 10,795 (*Statistical Abstract of Israel*, 1989, p. 668), that is, approximately 5 percent of the total number of patients. More general epidemiological studies were reportedly faulty because they were based on family practice samples, they were focused on limited geographic regions, and the findings were not corroborated by psychiatrists (Gilboa, 1990).

Data on other forms of mental disturbances are thus largely inaccurate and based only on estimates. An official document presented by health authorities claims that 0.5 percent of the country's total population (some 20,000 to 25,000 people) are drug addicts. The proportion of alcoholics in 1987 was 0.25 percent (*Long-Term Policy Lines*, 1989). Snyder, Palgi, Eldar, and Elian (1982) reviewed the frequency of alcoholism among the various ethnic communities in Israel on the basis of 311 alcoholics who had been admitted to Israel's five rehabilitation centers. The general finding suggests that among the alcoholics there is a higher proportion of Jews of Middle Eastern population than among the Israeli population at large. This may simply be due to selective factors, as rehabilitation centers are used mainly by persons of lower social economic status (Michaeli & Eldar, 1989, p. 434). Data regarding suicides are more accurate. A clear growth tendency is evident. In 1949, when the country was embroiled in a war for its independence, the rate of suicides and attempted suicides was only 32 per 100,000 persons (Jews aged 15 and over); in 1985 the rate had more than doubled to 72 per 100,000 persons. It is worthwhile to note, however, that the rate of actual (as distinct from attempted) suicides decreased from 18 in 1949 to 12 in 1985. The male suicide rate is higher than the female rate (16 compared to 8 in 1985); the proportion of females is considerably higher in attempted suicides (68, compared to 52 for males in 1985) (*Statistical Abstract of Israel*, 1989, p. 681). The meaning of these data is ambivalent. On the one hand, the frequency of mental health problems appears to be high; on the other hand, symptoms of mental difficulties such as alcoholism, drug addiction, and suicide are less prevalent in Israel than in other industrialized countries.

MENTAL HEALTH HISTORY

The mental health and psychiatric needs of Israel, and the services organized to meet them, have been greatly conditioned by the social history of the country. Two major factors have impinged on the development of these services: the dramatic population growth and the pioneering ideology. The mass immigration that flooded the country in the first five years following independence produced an immense population growth. The number of Israelis doubled within three years from some 700,000 in 1948 to 1.4 million in 1951. The rapid population growth and its unusual demographic composition created exceptional demands on psychiatric and other mental health services. Prior to 1948 only a small number of mental hospital beds were available. The British Mandatory government was reluctant to invest public resources in welfare (including health care) services. Jewish welfare institutions did not regard psychiatric care as a top priority. Whereas the pioneers who immigrated to build a homeland for the Jewish people in Palestine before independence may have suffered from malaria and other tropical diseases, mental illness was not included in the list of "pioneer ailments." Many of those who failed to cope with the difficulties of the situation in Palestine returned to their country of origin or emigrated to other countries. Immigration to prestate Israel was selective: Only those deemed fit to overcome the difficulties of pioneering were granted certificates to the Promised Land by Zionist authorities. Tolerance of mental problems was reportedly extremely low (Aviram & Shnit, 1981, p. 32), an attitude that led to a negligence of mental health problems in the prestate era. Psychiatric services in 1948 were rather poor. Toward the end of the Mandate two mental hospitals, one for men and one for women, were established by the British authorities. Two additional mental hospitals had been founded on Jewish initiative—one in 1895 in Jerusalem, and the other in 1942 by the country's largest health insurance fund. A number of small private institutions, mostly substandard, also existed. During the first year of independence, however, hospitalization facilities expanded markedly. In January 1949 the total number of beds was 1,197, which gave a ratio of 1.32 per 1,000 population (Grushka, 1968, p. 142). The reasons for expansion were grounded in societal changes.

The mass immigration of the early 1950s did not comprise young pioneers who deliberately chose to settle in Israel; it consisted of whole communities. The state's commitment to the ingathering of Jews from throughout the world precluded any kind of selection. Israel was flooded with people, including the mentally ill. The war of independence (1948–49) who contributed to the expansion of mental illness by adding those who had suffered from battle stress. To accommodate their needs, two psychiatric wards were set up in general hospitals in the north and south of the country. At the end of the fighting, these institutions were transferred from the army to the Ministry of Health and became the cornerstone of the state psychiatric and mental health services.

From their inception mental health services were biased toward a medical definition of the illness. The hospitalization of patients was clearly preferred to community care. There were three reasons for the preference of hospital treatment. First, the cultural gap between the established population and the newcomers was so great that community treatment based on individual support, understanding of particular problems, and a therapeutic environment was very difficult to provide (Aviram & Shnit, 1981). Second, the country was in the midst of immense demographic change in the early days of statehood. The foundations of "communities" able to support the mentally ill were largely lacking. The high rate of geographical and social mobility excluded the formation of strong community support in Israel (Miller, 1977). Third, professional expertise leaned heavily toward the clinical model. Jewish psychiatrists who fled from Germany established a strong tradition of psychoanalytic activity (Winnik, 1977). The need to provide an immediate solution to thousands of people suffering from mental illness hindered a community approach. Deserted military camps and other public areas were turned into mental institutions. Hospitalization became the hallmark of psychiatric treatment. The priority of this option was manifested both in budgetary allocations and in legislation.

With the social and economic consolidation of the state, the demand for mental health care increased and the variety of services expanded. Psychiatric wards were established in general hospitals, admitting patients with psychoses, especially those of a passing depressive type. Chronic psychotics were hospitalized in "work villages" that were aimed at promoting social contact and cooperation. The problem of geriatric psychiatric services was also high on the mental health agenda. Prestate immigration had been drawn mainly from younger age groups. Consequently, in 1948 the population was relatively young (3.8 percent over the age of 65 years). Subsequent waves of immigration caused a rapid demographic shift in the direction of the older age groups. Adjustment to the new country caused great personal stress on many of the elderly. Villages for mentally ill aged were established by voluntary associations and state authorities. Even though the cause of mental illness in the older age group may have been associated with social dislocation, the problem was nevertheless defined in medical terms.

Other forms of mental disturbances, for example, alcoholism and drug addiction, were treated as social, rather than clinical, problems. Even today, individuals with these problems are tested as social deviants rather than as mentally ill. Mental retardation has also been excluded from the confines of mental health care. It, too, is considered a social problem coming under the aegis of welfare agencies.

POLICY, ORGANIZATION, AND SERVICES IN THE 1980s AND 1990s

Current Policy Developments

Two contrasting trends may be identified in the current definition of mental problems. On the one hand, psychiatric care is still defined basically in medical terms. Rapid progress in pharmacology brought about the inclusion of mental disturbances among the list of curable diseases. Although a clinical definition is still dominant, a change of mood is evident. Physicians refer to psychiatrists not only patients who suffer from psychotic or neurotic illnesses, but also those who have family and marital problems or social and existential conflicts, such as bereavement, loneliness, or old age. Even alcohol and drug abuse are gradually being regarded as belonging to the domain of psychiatry. Several socioeconomic processes have been identified as causing this shift (Neumann, 1982), chief among which are the increasing levels of urbanization and the "Westernization" of Israeli society. Anxieties caused by unfulfilled economic expectations, the disintegration of community, and the growing alienation of the individual have had an impact on the definition of mental illness. These changes have had a marked impact on the organization and distribution of mental health care as they have proliferated; second, there has been a shift toward community psychiatry.

Current Organization

An incomplete list of psychiatric services includes public psychiatric hospitals, privately owned psychiatric hospitals, psychiatric wards in general hospitals, day-care wards, community centers for mental health, clinics for mental health, a mental health section in the Israel Defense Forces (IDF), a mental division in prisons, and private ambulatory psychiatric treatment. Generally speaking, treatment of the mentally ill is distributed between three major institutions: state health authorities, the Histadrut Health Insurance Fund (Kupat Holim), and private mental care.

The medical definition of mental illness determined the structure of its services. Although Israel does not have a national health insurance scheme, health care is nevertheless regarded as a public service for which the Health Ministry is responsible. The ministry is not only responsible for the administration and planning of health services throughout the country, but is also a major provider of these services. The state operates a wide network of general hospitals (thirteen hospitals including 36 percent of all hospital beds in the country) and psychiatric hospitals (10 percent of total hospital beds in 1988). The share of the government in the national expenditure on hospitals for the mentally ill in 1986–87 was 60 percent of the total (*Statistical Abstract of Israel*, 1989, p. 662). Provision of services is highly centralized. The Ministry of Health determines the number of services provided by the hospital. The ministry's autonomy, however, is curbed by the Treasury, an extremely powerful organ in Israel's centralized system of government, and by the State Service Authority, responsible for personnel in the civil service.

The overwhelming majority of Israelis are insured in one of the five sick funds, of which the largest is Kupat Holim, owned and operated by the Labor Federation (Histadrut), an organization controlled by the Labor Party. Provision of health services had already been one of the Histadrut's functions in the prestate era, and it had become a major instrument for commanding resources and furnishing political support. The politicization of health services is not a unique Israeli phenomenon (Altenstetter & Bjorkman, 1981), but it has reached a very high level in Israel. Since 1937 medical insurance has been an inseparable part of the regular Histadrut dues. Most of the public who became members of the Histadrut did so only in order to enjoy the health services it provided (Arian, 1981; Yishai, 1981). Relations between the Ministry of Health and Kupat Holim have been ambiguous, determined by the political composition of the government. Kupat Holim enjoyed immense state support under the Labor government; under Likud measures were taken to curb the sick fund's power, albeit with little success. The fact that Kupat Holim insures some 80 percent of the population gives it strong leverage over state authorities. However, this has little impact on the provision of mental health care for the simple reason that Kupat Holim insists that mental health care be the responsibility of the state. As already noted, psychiatric care does not enjoy a high priority on the health care agenda. The chronic hospitalization of the mentally ill and the lack of medical glamour associated with psychiatric care also act as a barrier to the inclusion of mental health among those services provided by Kupat Holim, which devotes very meager resources to this important medical domain. The major burden of caring for the mentally ill thus falls on the state.

Current Services

In 1978 an agreement was signed between Kupat Holim and the Health Ministry committing the state to finance the provision of all mental health services. These services were to be delivered on a regional bias regardless of the type of medical insurance. It should be noted that all efforts to establish general medical services on a regional basis and to extricate medicine from affiliation with the insurance agent have persistently failed, mainly because Kupat Holim refuses to amalgamate its own facilities with those of the state. Nevertheless, Kupat Holim is eager to "pass the buck" and relieve itself of the responsibility for the mental health of its members. However, owing mainly to budgetary constraints, the agreement between the state authorities and Kupat Holim was in operation for only one year. At present, patients admitted to one of the three Kupat Holim psychiatric hospitals are financed by the sick fund for a period not longer than two years. The demand for mental health care by Kupat Holim members, however, far exceeds resources earmarked for psychiatric services.

A distinction should be drawn between private mental hospitals and private ambulatory psychiatric care. Private hospitals have a low rating on the scale of medical care. There is general agreement that the level of medical are in the private mental hospitals is lower than in public hospitals. Of the ten private mental hospitals, only one is considered to be on a higher level than public institutions. State authorities refer the most serious cases and chronic patients whose chances for recovery are dim to private hospitalization. Most of the private psychiatric institutions are understaffed and their personnel underqualified. Most of the patients are hospitalized for life. Hospitalization is funded by the state, but the cost of a psychiatric patient in a private ward is estimated to be half as much as the cost of a patient in a public institution. Data regarding admissions to psychiatric hospitals indicate that in 1987, 57.3 percent of the patients were admitted to state hospitals; 20.6 percent to Kupat Holim hospitals; and only 3.0 percent to private hospitals (the remaining 19.1 percent were admitted to psychiatric wards in general hospitals) (*Trends in Psychiatric Hospitalization*, 1989, p. 15). Private hospitals are theoretically under state scrutiny and supervision. In practice, the quality of inspection is rather poor, and medical standards are far from adequate.

This is not the case regarding ambulatory psychiatric treatment, which is gradually but continuously expanding. The growing demand for these services has led to a growing supply. A wide network of services for relieving tension is offered to Israelis. These include a variety of psychiatric and psychological services provided by clinical social workers, psychologists, or psychiatrists, or by mental health institutions, eight of which are authorized to train clinical psychologists. It is thus evident that the provision of mental health ambulatory services is guided by the rules of the free competitive market. These services, however, do not cater only to the needs of more affluent segments of the population but also to the general public. In 1986 seventy-six public mental health clinics provided services to the population at large (*Survey of Mental Health Services,* 1986).

Mental hospitalization occurs through three service providers: the state, Kupat Holim, and private hospitals. The data reveal the growing role of the state in psychiatric hospital treatment. While Kupat Holim has retained its share in the general pool, the proportion of psychiatric beds in private institutions declined from 46.3 percent in 1979 to 41.4 percent in 1987. The transfer of patients from state hospitals to private institutions continues to decline.[1]

The distribution of responsibility for the mentally ill has had a positive bearing on access to services. Every Israeli citizen, regardless of nationality, age group, level of income, or length of residence in the country, is entitled to mental health services. This encompasses the Arab minority, new immigrants, and low-income

Table 6.1
Psychiatric Hospitalization and Day Care in Israel: Beds, Day-Care Positions,
Day-Care Patients, and All Patients, 1975–1987

Rates per 1,000 persons at the end of the year	1975	1979	1983	1987
Beds	2.3	2.3	2.0	1.7
Positions of day-care patients	0.2	0.2	0.2	0.2
Patients hospitalized	2.5	2.3	2.0	1.6
All patients	2.7	2.6	2.2	1.9

Source: Trends in Psychiatric Hospitalization, 1989, p. 12.

groups. Interviews with the medical personnel of a psychiatric hospital in the Haifa region revealed that the patients represented all sectors of society. The distinction between private and public mental health institutions is not related to economic differentials but, as noted earlier, to medical indications and the severity of the illness.

Since 1983 there has been a considerable decline in the number of psychiatric beds in the country and a marked movement to community care. The winds that have blown through psychiatry in Western societies have eventually reached Israel. Although mental problems are still defined in medical terms, there has been a growing awareness of the importance of the congenial social environment as a curative method. It was, however, mainly the progress in medicine that spurred a considerable reduction in length of hospitalization. Extensive medication has enabled the early discharge of patients or a change in their status to day patients. These developments have had repercussions on the patterns of mental health care, as presented in table 6.1.

The data clearly reveal how health authorities have been dealing with mental health care. First, a striking decline is evident in the number of hospitalized patients, from 2.7 per 1,000 in 1975 to 1.9 per 1,000 in 1987. This reduced rate of hospitalization does not reflect a decrease of mental problems in the population; rather, it signifies a policy shift. It is a product of the growing awareness of the benefits of community care for the mentally ill. The number of outpatient centers operated by the state and Kupat Holim grew from thirty-seven in 1965 (Popper & Rahav, 1984, p. 4) to fifty-six in 1986 (*Survey of Mental Health Services*, 1986).[2] A major trigger for the growth of community care for the mentally ill was provided by the IDF's military psychiatric services introduced during the war of independence (1948–49). These services constituted the nucleus of the community psychiatric approaches centered on the open-door hospital and the fostering of community life in the institutions, early treatment, rapid discharge with continuity of care, and consultation with other services.

After the cessation of hostilities, the army services were transferred almost completely to the Ministry of Health, providing working models for a community approach.

An early form of community approach may also be found in "work villages" that aimed to provide a shelter for longer-stay patients and those organically impaired. The village had all the elements that were later designated as the basis of a "therapeutic community," such as housing small groups of patients with a more or less continuous relationship to a subgroup and staff; the involvement of patients, especially in social and vocational activities; and the work placement of patients in the general community. During the 1950s the concept and practice of services based on a team in city neighborhoods and in rural areas began to take shape. These trends represent a growing awareness of primary mental health work with individuals and families and service involvement in social action. During the 1960s the community approach expanded. Regional public health liaison nurses were introduced into the mental health system; outpatient services for follow-up care were instituted in most psychiatric hospitals; therapeutic community methods were introduced into shorter-stay psychiatric hospitals; and more nurses were trained both in public health and in psychiatry for ambulatory centers (Miller, 1977, p. 305).

These trends led to an administrative reform. In 1972 a national program for the reorganization of mental health services in Israel was introduced by the mental health services and was ratified by the Ministry of Health (*Proposal for Reorganization*, 1972). The proposal divided the country into nineteen regions that corresponded generally with the administrative subdistricts of the country. Each area was to be allocated, from existing or new services, an independent mental health center set in a subdistrict urban complex with satellite centers according to the distribution of population. A preliminary standard for hospital beds was proposed for adults, youth, and children. A model for a community clinic was also set out. It included, in addition to the interdisciplinary team for adults and children directed by a psychiatrist, specialized staff such as a community liaison, a community organizer, and an anthropologist.

A major indicator of the increasing role of the community approach was the dramatic rise in the rate of day patients among all hospitalized patients. In 1970 day patients were 3.7 percent of all patients; in 1988 this proportion had risen to 17.3 percent (*Statistical Abstract of Israel*, 1989, p. 668). Data on hospital admissions were also striking. In 1975 there were 11,992 admissions to psychiatric hospitals and wards; in 1987, despite population growth, the total number of admissions decreased to 11,647 (*Trends in Psychiatric Hospitalization*, 1989, p. 15). To some extent, the reduction of admissions reflected the alternative models of treatment that take into account the individual's changing psychopathological needs and the varying psychosocial circumstances. Statistical evidence thus confirmed the gradual adoption of a model of community psychiatry. The prospects for a shift from a medical-centered approach toward a social approach were very promising. These data, however, were somewhat misleading since there were major impediments on the road to community care. Community treatment lagged far behind expectations and was thought of as a "stepchild" of the psychiatric service. Evidence for the inferior status of community care was ample.

The Achilles' heel of mental health policy is the gap between the policy as set out and the actual situation. When judged by declarations, the treatment of psychiatric patients ought to be conducted in the community, and the data do indeed indicate that the number of psychiatric beds has continually been decreasing. However, at the same time, when judged by resource allocation, community treatment is and has been an underdog. Budgetary expenditures provide a clear indication for the ministry's order of priorities. In 1976, four years after the initiation of the administrative reform, the share of community services in the total expenditure on mental health was 8 percent. In 1988 this share had decreased to 4.09 percent (*Health System in Israel*, 1989). It is thus evident that the funds saved by the reduction of hospitalization have not been transferred to community treatment, but have been deducted from the total budget for mental health.

Why, then, is Israel not moving rapidly toward community-based mental health services? One of the answers concerns financial constraints. Community treatment is reportedly more expensive than mental hospitalization. The shortage of public funds is allegedly the cause for the paucity of community facilities for treating psychiatric disease. Professional ideology and training are also responsible for the failure of the community approach. Israeli psychiatrists are trained as medical doctors. They usually regard with suspicion, if not with disdain, any form of treatment outside the clinical model. A third, more compelling reason is administrative. The policy network determining the course of mental health policy comprises bureaucrats and professionals who adhere to a medical definition of psychiatry. They have made the first step toward deinstitutionalization of mental care: The development of psychiatric wards in general hospitals is dramatic, and so is the decrease in the number of hospitalized patients. Yet many of these patients have been left without an adequate alternative. The fact is that communities do not participate in mental health programs, a feature due to the patterns of ownership. Mental health community centers are part of other health agencies in which the barriers between staff and clients are seldom, if ever, crossed (Levav, 1981). Mental health is still monopolized by members of the professional psychiatric community. A major break away from the current institutionalized service system is unforeseeable in the near future.

Public attitudes are a fourth major hindrance to change. Zohar, Floro, and Modan (1974) presented a survey of opinions regarding mental illness on the basis of a random sample of residents of a major city. Their findings suggest that there is a marked rejection of the mental patient as well as relative ignorance of the subject of mental disease in Israeli society. The degree of rejection was more marked among immigrants from the Middle East and North Africa as compared with those from Europe and the Israeli-born, but negative attitudes were pervasive among all interviewed. Half the respondents were of the opinion that a psychiatric hospital should be isolated by a fence and protected by guards; 80 percent rejected the notion of marrying a person who had had mental illness; 40 percent were unwilling to associate or maintain social contacts with such a person.

A study conducted on the attitudes of Knesset (Israel's parliament) members reaffirmed the previous findings (Ramon, 1981). An underlying assumption was that the politicians' views are directly linked to their involvement in the legislative process, and that the law constitutes an official expression of social attitudes and norms. Ramon concluded that the approaches of Knesset members to the mentally ill constitute a mixture of fear and rejection. This attitude leads to a wish to protect the public from them, but at the same time there is a desire to provide them with a place of refuge and treatment. Community services are placed very low in the order of priorities. The roots of these attitudes are grounded in national myths and mores. Mental illness is seen as totally incongruent with the image of the brave, robust Israelis. Articles published in the bulletin of the Israel Medical Association (IMA) in the late 1940s reflected a highly negative attitude toward soldiers suffering battle stress. They were described as "hypochondriacs, psychopaths, defectors." It was proposed to demobilize them immediately in order to be rid of them. The Zionist-socialist ideology of the early state era thus stigmatized mental disability. Documentation related to mental hospitalization in the first five years of statehood is reportedly extremely poor owing to the fact that psychiatric problems were considered "inappropriate" in a society that worshiped mental and physical competence. The myth of the "strong man" was reflected in legislation, in funding, and in the administration of mental health policy, all of which will be discussed in detail later.

Mental Health Personnel and Treatment

Israel has had a prolonged period of shortages in professional psychiatric staff of all types. This is the result of an unusual rate of expansion of services and the high standards generally prevailing in medical care. The ratio of physicians to population in Israel is one of the highest in the world (2.9 per 1,000) (Yishai, 1990), but this is not true in the case of psychiatry. The reasons for the paucity of professional personnel are grounded in what has been termed the "crisis in Israeli psychiatry" (Neumann, 1981, 1982). Psychiatry in Israel faces many of the problems reflected in American psychiatric literature. There is no agreement on what should be taught in medical schools and which is the best treatment. There are also three problems unique to Israeli psychiatry. First, although more than half of Israel's population is of Asian and African origin, very few psychiatrists belong to this specific cultural and social milieu. Most of the professional psychiatrists are of European origin. Hence there is a deep cultural gap between patients and doctors, and many of the doctors are unfamiliar with the values and norms of a significant portion of the mentally ill. Second, a similar gap has developed with regard to the large population of Holocaust survivors and their families. For many years there was a process of denial and disregard of the existence of the problem. There was a tacit assumption that it was better to forget the horrid experience and let life heal the wounds. The survivors themselves tried to ignore their suffering and attempted to avoid their traumatic past. In many cases Israeli psychiatry failed to provide an encouraging environment to ''clear the air'' and deal adequately with the suffering population. Finally, as already noted, psychiatric problems were considered highly dysfunctional in a young, pioneering society. This image reflected the status of the psychiatrists. The upshot of these facts was that only a very small percentage of doctors (much smaller than in the United States) chose psychiatry as their career. Most of the psychiatrists in Israel are immigrants from Europe and America. A minority of the graduates of Israeli medical schools specialize in psychiatry. Medical schools in Israel put emphasis on the teaching of basic sciences and the innovations of modern medical research and technology. The human aspect of medicine and a greater involvement of the doctor-to-be in social and psychological problems were neglected until recently. According to Neumann (1982, p. 233), the amount of teaching time, resources, and attention given to behavioral sciences and to psychiatry was relatively small in comparison with the other principal branches of medicine.

In contrast, the picture regarding clinical psychology is different. Here, demand was much greater than supply. Psychology is regarded as one of the most prestigious disciplines in social science. Sharp competition over admission has enabled the Psychologists' Federation to lobby for a law limiting entry to the profession. The legislation (enacted in 1980) restricts the practice of clinical psychology to those who, after completion of extensive academic and field training, have passed a series of difficult examinations. These limiting practices have curtailed the development of surplus personnel in clinical psychology.

The shortage of qualified personnel is also evident in the paramedical labor force. In the early 1950s continuous in-service training of all categories of workers, qualified or not, became the order of the day. The situation created by mass immigration ruled out prolonged formal training for qualified paramedical personnel. The first steps in training ''practical nurses'' were taken when the hospitals were opened. Selected candidates, with a minimum standard of schooling, were put through short theoretical and practical courses lasting eighteen months (Grushka, 1968, p. 152). The number of registered nurses in psychiatric hospitals was small. The shortage was also evident in other branches of mental health care. Psychiatric social workers had graduated from a two-year course of the Ministry of Social Welfare. Academically trained personnel came at first from schools in the United States, gradually followed by graduates of the Hebrew University School of Social Work.

There are mixed trends among professionals in mental health care. The proportion of professionals associated with a community approach, that is, social workers and occupational therapists, has not proportionally increased (in the case of the latter, it even decreased); at the same time there has been a decline in the proportion of nurses, which may reflect the process of dehospitalization. The increased proportion of both psychiatrists and clinical psychologists points to the growing professionalization of mental health care in Israel.

To sum up, a review of policy developments, current organization, patterns of ownership, composition of personnel, and values that guide the provision of psychiatric services reveals that mental health care is dominated by the public sector and is based mainly on patronizing clinical attitudes. Changes are nevertheless discernible, the most significant of which is dehospitalization of psychiatric treatment. The policy process that triggered this change is the subject of the next section.

PUBLIC POLICY PROCESS

The mental health policy process comprises two subsections: organizational and human. The first pertains mainly to the administration of psychiatric services focusing on medical aspects; the second emphasizes consumers' (i.e., the mentally ill patients') rights. The policy universe of organizational mental health policy making mainly comprises bureaucrats in the Ministry of Health and psychiatrists. Obviously, the Knesset and the judicial branch have also contributed to the formulation of policy, but the major actors are to be found in the administrative and professional communities.

As noted earlier, despite the fact that Israel does not have a national health insurance law, health care is regarded as a public good, allocated under the authority of a special ministry for health. The reason for the absence of such a law is grounded in the pervasiveness of Kupat Holim, the Labor movement's sick fund, whose strong political clout has impeded nationalization of health services. The eagerness of Kupat Holim to provide health services to an overwhelming majority of the Israeli population stops short of the psychiatric disorders, which come under the aegis of the state. A special unit for mental health, which enjoyed financial and administrative autonomy, was set up within the ministry. The Department for Mental Health initiated the 1972 reform that was partly implemented a decade later in the form of decreasing hospital admission. It also lobbied for budgetary increases. In the late 1980s, however, an intra-ministerial organizational reform was introduced that resulted in abolishing the Department for Mental Health within the ministry and amalgamating its functions with other ministry departments.

The reform was proposed by a Steering Committee composed of the Health Ministry's senior officials and eight senior psychiatrists, managers of psychiatric hospitals, selected by the Minister of Health on the basis of their opinions regarding the structure of psychiatric treatment. The medical definition of psychiatric problems was the principle underpinning the committee's work. It was believed that mental illness is not significantly different from any other illness.

According to its proponents, the reform was also a result of a growing awareness among physicians of the psychological factor in diseases defined purely on a physiological basis. The interlock of physiological and mental aspects of health instigated the proposed reform. From the organizational perspective, it was therefore deemed superfluous to maintain a special subdivision for psychiatry. The Steering Committee nevertheless continued to provide policy guidelines. Its operation enabled retention of partial autonomy for psychiatric services within the Ministry of Health. One of the members of this committee, a nationally renowned psychiatrist, is a state employee responsible for mental health services. The uniqueness of psychiatry has thus not been totally eroded, although amalgamation with other administrative units is well under way. Priorities are determined on a ministry level with little involvement of the psychiatric community. Although officials evade conflicts with the professional community and try not to antagonize the psychiatrists with whom they have had stable working relations, tensions were reportedly inevitable. These have been evident primarily in fiscal issues rather than in problems of a medical nature.

The involvement of nonmedical representatives in the organizational policy process is almost nil. Potential members include the Union of Social Workers, the Federation of Psychologists, the Federation of Nurses, and the clients or their families. The Union of Social Workers, some of whose members are involved in psychiatric care, is a well-organized trade union operating under the auspices of the Histadrut. By virtue of its monopolistic representation the Union of Social Workers is effective in labor relations. However it is not considered as a partner to policy making (Yishai, 1991). The Federation of Psychologists enjoys more prestige that the Union of Social Workers. It was granted a monopoly over clinical psychology, but this was not translated into influence over the policy-making process. Neither the Steering Committee nor the administrative staff of the Ministry of Health include a single psychologist. The other unions play no role whatsoever in formulation of policy. Although highly organized (under the umbrella organization of the Labor Federation), the paramedical associations have no say in the shaping of authoritative decisions. Nor have the clients any impact on the policy process. Only one association focuses its interests solely on psychiatric issues. Enosh (in Hebrew, human being), founded in 1979, consists mainly of relatives of mental patients. Its major goals are ''to initiate and promote community services for the mentally ill and their families, to develop mutual aid among those inflicted by a mental disease, to increase public awareness of the needs of the mentally ill and to change public attitudes regarding psychiatric problems.'' Enosh's success in expanding the issue and marshaling financial or moral support has been modest. Israeli people still regard mental illness as an aberrant, bizarre, and threatening event and remain reluctant to participate in an activity aimed at alleviating the miseries of psychiatric patients. Policy making regarding the organizational aspects of mental health services is thus dominated not by an iron triangle, comprising members of the administration, the legislative committee, and powerful interest groups (Lowi, 1979), but by an "iron duo" (Yishai, 1992) including senior civil servants and professionals, selected on the basis of their known compliance with administrative opinions.

The policy universe is much different when the human aspect is considered. Here the role of both the state bureaucracy and the professional community is much less conspicuous. The prominent actors are mostly individuals operating outside the confines of their institutions and include several members of the Knesset (MKs) who have submitted various private member's bills on the subject of the rights of the mentally ill and individual psychiatrists, social workers, and members of the academic community who have fought adamantly to promulgate the rights of the mentally ill. The legislators have not acted on behalf of their respective parties, but have shown personal concern for the issue on the basis of humanistic orientations. Members of the academic community, too, do not represent their respective organized interest groups. Two associations, however, may be added to the list: the Israel Medical Association and the Civil Rights Association (CRA). These launched a campaign to alter legislation regarding compulsory hospitalization of the mentally ill. Both associations are powerful, prestigious, and known for their public influence. A third minor association also may be added, the Association for the Protection of Human Rights in Psychiatry. This group, comprising "victims of psychiatric care," attempts to influence legislation. Its public exposure, however, is extremely limited.

All efforts made at rectifying existing laws governing the treatment of the mentally ill have so far been abortive. There is much talk about the need to reformulate legislation that was enacted more than thirty-five years ago, but not much has been accomplished. Policy is still governed by the elitist orientation of Israeli decision makers. The movement toward change is incremental, extremely slow, and gradual.

SPECIAL POLICY ISSUES

The Mentally Ill and the Mentally Retarded

In Israel the mentally ill are considered to be a different category than the mentally retarded. This is apparent in both the administrative and treatment domains. Responsibility for the mentally retarded is vested in the Ministry for Work and Welfare. Whereas mental illness is defined as a medical problem, mental retardation is regarded as a social handicap. Developmentally disabled persons are, by and large (with the exclusion of a few autistic individuals), not hospitalized in psychiatric institutions. The expenses of caring for mentally retarded persons are divided between the Ministry of Education and the National Insurance Institution. The state is committed to providing mentally retarded persons with education and shelter. Their interests are well looked after by a powerful and resourceful interest group, Akim (the Hebrew acronym for Association for Rehabilitation of the Retarded). Admittedly, mental retardation is not any more "prestigious" than mental illness, and the proportion of mentally retarded persons in the population as a whole is no higher than that of the mentally ill. Although several prominent people have been personally involved with the problem of mental retardation, this may also have been the case regarding mental illness. One marked difference between the two problems is that serious mental retardation is relatively hard to hide, while mental illness remains, in many cases, a private issue unexposed to public view. Spokespersons for each category deny any relationship between the two. The representatives of the mentally ill attempt to regard their problem as curable; those who speak for the mentally retarded shy away from any association with the mentally ill.

The Mentally Ill and Substance Abuse

The rules defining the relationship between the mentally ill and the mentally retarded also govern the terms of reference between the former and alcoholics and drug addicts. Abuse is regarded as a social problem caused by unfortunate life circumstances. The laws relating to the treatment and hospitalization of drug addicts have been incorporated in the Criminal Law (1977) rather than in the Mental Treatment Law (1955). The law permits the retention of drug addicts in a "closed institution" for a period of no more than three years upon the recommendation of a psychiatrist. In later regulations it was specified that a psychiatric hospital may be regarded as a "closed institution" for treating drug addicts. In practice, there are only fourteen hospital beds in the country designated for drug treatment. However, in contrast to mental retardation, which is regarded as an individual misfortune that can perhaps be minimized but not totally eliminated by means of modern medical technology, drug and alcohol abuse are perceived as constituting a national problem. Of particular significance is the fear that both types of abuse have a bearing on Israel's defense posture, thus potentially endangering the country's security. Drug abuse has been placed more prominently on the political agenda and has attracted wide public attention. Although the problem exists on a smaller scale than in the United States, it may touch upon a very sensitive chord in Israeli society—the effectiveness of the armed forces. Increased awareness of the problem has led to much administrative activity, especially in regard to drug abuse. An Anti-Drug Authority was established in 1980 comprising representatives of numerous social and political institutions. The authority was mandated to propose an overall plan for prevention and treatment of drug abuse. In practice, its achievements have been rather modest.

Alcohol addiction has been placed lower on the political agenda. In 1982 a hostel for alcohol treatment based on the principle of community care was opened. It is interesting to note that specialists in alcoholism demand the acknowledgment of alcoholism as a disease rather than a social problem, yet hospitalization in psychiatric institutions is not regarded as adequate treatment for alcohol abuse.

According to the Alcohol Prevention Association, resources devoted to its prevention and cure are conspicuously insufficient.

The Mentally Disordered Offender

Mental hospitalization of offenders is regulated by the 1955 law, which makes a distinction between those already sentenced and those who have not stood trial. Regarding the second category, the law differentiates between those who are incompetent to stand trial and those acting under an uncontrolled drive. Those declared insane may be hospitalized by the court if their state of health requires such an act. The court has no discretion regarding offenders found competent to stand trial. They must be hospitalized even though their disease may not necessarily be acute at the time of trial. Detainees that have not been brought to court, and those not sentenced, may be ordered by the court to undergo medical examination. The court may also order that such persons be detained in a psychiatric hospital or in a prison's psychiatric ward. A court's hospitalization decree is sufficient in cases where the offender consents to be hospitalized. Those who do not consent are hospitalized by the order of a district psychiatrist (DP), who is, by law, superior to the judicial authority in determining the need to enforce hospitalization in the absence of voluntary consent. The authority to release a hospitalized offender was granted to a psychiatric committee rather than to the hospital manager.

In 1988, 500 patients were hospitalized by court decree.[3] The mentally disordered offenders are not separated from the other mentally ill identified as dangerous to themselves or the public. Although there are special prison wards for psychiatric patients, the majority of the mentally ill are hospitalized in general psychiatric institutions. It is worth noting that the Association for Legal Psychiatry has recently been organized. Psychiatric opinion is given in court by any practicing psychiatrist, and there is no requirement to demonstrate proficiency in the legal aspects of mental illness.

Deinstitutionalization

The principles guiding the process of deinstitutionalization have been discussed earlier. This section will concentrate on one neglected aspect of deinstitutionalization: the development of psychiatric wards within general hospitals. Shifting the locus of mental health care from mental health hospitals to psychiatric wards marks, in a sense, the erosion of the institutional approach. Hospitalization in wards is generally for a short term and is clinically oriented. It is also purported to destigmatize mental illness and to "normalize" those afflicted by it. The inception of the process took place in the 1950s, when it had already been well established in the United States and the United Kingdom. It was warmly welcomed by the families of the mentally ill. The framework of the general hospital lifted some of the humiliation attached to psychiatric treatment. The underlying principle was to enable close contact between the patient and his or her environment and to shorten the period of hospitalization. New medications decreased the danger posed by the mentally ill to themselves and to others. Hospitalization in general wards was regarded as an optimal compromise between a strict community approach and the specialized psychiatric institutions.

A review of the Israeli data reveals that some progress in this regard has been achieved, but that its pace is nevertheless slow. The first psychiatric ward was opened in a Haifa general hospital in 1954 (Assael & Meter, 1981). In 1982 there were eight psychiatric wards in forty-two general hospitals; in other words, 80 percent of the country's hospitals were without wards for the mentally ill. Psychiatric wards were opened in the large regional medical centers; there was much less activity in rural areas. In total in 1982 there were 5,660 hospital beds. Of these, only 2.6 percent were psychiatric beds (Halevi, 1987, p. 65). The evidence regarding the type and degree of integration between psychiatric wards and other wards in the general hospital is inconclusive; the extent to which staffs in general wards and mental wards maintain reciprocal relationships is unknown. However, this aspect of deinstitutionalization has gained legitimacy and is expanding, albeit slowly.

Funding Issues

Funding of psychiatric services is based on two contradictory principles: On the one hand, mental health care is considered an integral part of general health care. The rules guiding the allocation of resources to health services in general are applicable also to the psychiatric domain. On the other hand, mental health care is the ''stepchild'' of medicine. As such, it suffers from constant deprivation.

The principles for allocating resources earmarked for health care are rather blurred. At present, there is no clear-cut definition in Israel regarding the citizens' entitlement for a ''basket'' of medical services. There are no limitations based on age or other criteria, but at the same time there is no defined obligation to delivery services. The stringency of health resources, moreover, constrains the provision of health services. Thus a kidney transplant is not restricted to people under a certain age, but the long queues and the shortage of organs produce unwritten limitations. Psychiatry also comes under the uncertainties of the budgetary constraints. Although the state in 1978 took upon itself the commitment to provide mental health care to all Israeli citizens, membership in a health insurance scheme does not entitle a person to unlimited psychiatric care. The paucity of mental health services in Kupat Holim accentuates the financial role of the state in funding mental health care.[4]

Patterns of health funding are also applicable to psychiatric care. The allocation of state funds is determined by the number of staff positions based on the previous year's number of beds and occupancy rate. Thus there is a built-in incentive for government hospitals to keep their beds occupied, either through increased admissions or increased lengths of stay of patients, so as to preserve their size and budget allocation. This practice has been a major impediment to efficiency in psychiatric care; it prevented, or at least slowed down, the shift toward community care that does not require hospitalization. It has also been a constraint on curbing expenditures in general health care. The private hospitals, which account for over 40 percent of the inpatients, are funded on a fee-per-day hospitalization basis. This practice has a dual effect: On the one hand, private institutions act under the conventional rules of maximizing their profits by attempting to decrease their expenses, while on the other, they also endeavor to maximize their occupancy rates. As in other medical domains, the mental health sector demonstrates the phenomenon of the supply of services (mental inpatient beds) acting to create or induce its own demand (Ginsberg, 1981).

The marginality of psychiatric services is clearly demonstrated in the makeup of the budget. The proportion of finances allocated to mental health out of the general health expenditure has decreased markedly over time. The following data demonstrate the extent of this decline. In 1980–81 psychiatric services consumed 13.9 percent of the Health Ministry's budget; in 1988–89 that proportion had decreased to 12.2 percent (*Health System in Israel*, 1989). The diminishing share of psychiatry in the general medical budget is a result of its vulnerability. Not having a patron in the Health Ministry, and shunned as an illegitimate child of the medical establishment, the mental health sector is prone to budgetary cuts. A government decision taken after the 1988 elections (under the title of Economic Policy and the 1989 Budget Proposal) included a section regarding the closure of Mazra psychiatric hospital in northern Israel. The expected savings from closure were 2.5 million shekels (approximately $1.25 million). This trend continued in 1989, when the intention to close one of Kupat Holim's three psychiatric hospitals was declared. This proposed closure was aimed at shrinking the enormous financial deficits of Kupat Holim, which had laid its fiscal problems at the doorstep of the state. The proposals to close mental health hospitals were introduced by ministry officials. The medical community has not been involved. Consequently, a senior psychiatrist (who also served as the head of the IMA's Scientific Council) stated: "We shall not allow the adoption of professional medical decisions by non-professional persons who will determine the fate of many individuals by themselves" (*Haaretz*, May 2, 1990). This sharp professional objection, coupled with other political pressures, succeeded in preventing the closure of the psychiatric hospital for the time being.

Consumer Rights

The rights of the consumers of psychiatric services have been the most vulnerable area in Israel's mental health policy. Patients' rights may be analyzed from specific and general viewpoints (Aviram & Shnit, 1981). The law prescribes that the mental patient has rights concerning his or her contacts with the outside world, confidentiality, and privacy. The patient is eligible to receive and deliver mail and to have visitors. Medical confidentiality is also assured by law. Psychiatric patients have limited rights regarding treatment modalities. The use of electroconvulsive therapy (ECT) requires the consent of the patient or his or her guardian. Psychosurgery (lobotomy), like any other surgery, requires the patient's or guardian's consent. The law does not allow refusal of other forms of treatment such as insulin. Restriction of movement requires written authorization by a physician, including the reasons for limitations and the conditions for implementation. The law specifies a limit on restriction of movement—a maximum of four hours. The use of physical restraints above this time limit requires written approval of the ward's director. More general rights regarding admission, release, transfer, and vacations from hospital have been much more problematic.

The most problematic area regards hospitalization in a psychiatric institution. The rules for the hospitalization of mental patients were for many years embodied in the Mental Treatment Law (1955). Two major viewpoints have been identified in mental health legislation in general. The psychiatric model relies heavily upon the integrity and professional standards of the individual physician. The legal steps are considered to be a further source of social stigmatization of the patient, enhancing that which already stems from psychiatric treatment and hospitalization. In contrast, the social viewpoint stresses the need to respect, as far as possible, the rights of patients even where treatment is compulsory, and also when the patient is dangerous. The psychiatrists are not considered to be trained or qualified to protect patients' rights, which should be safeguarded by the judiciary. Israel adopted the first model, expressing the spirit of psychiatric care based on clinical practices rather than custodial care based on attributes of human compassion. Hospitalization and release procedures were regarded as falling exclusively within the medical domain. This was true not only for those hospitalized by consent but also in cases of compulsory hospitalization. The authority to enforce hospitalization was a medical prerogative with minimal judiciary involvement. The absolute supremacy of medical discretion was manifested also in procedures for ratifying medical verdicts and implementing them despite objections by the patient or the family. State patronage was the principle underlying the 1955 legislation. It was believed that the medical system could care for the mentally ill, taking into consideration their needs and well-being. No "outside" interference was deemed necessary. As a result of this attitude, the law regulated the hospitalization of the mentally ill and totally avoided psychiatric services outside hospitals. The emphasis on the admission and discharge of mental patients indicated the limited scope of the law and its disregard for community treatment (Aviram & Shnit, 1981, p. 46).

In part, the 1955 law was obscure and vague. The definition of mental illness was tautological: A mentally ill person was a person suffering from a mental illness. In practice, the medical definition of psychosis was the basis for the law's application. The law established that hospitalization was purported to have one or more of three objectives: examination and diagnosis of mental illness; medical treatment; and supervision and control, especially for incapable patients who posed a danger to themselves or to others. The liberty of the individual to resist hospitalization remained unclear. No rules were laid down specifying and prescribing the nature of the evidence required for imposing hospitalization. In fact, the Supreme Court established the need to take legislative measures in this regard and recommended that the Psychiatric Society precede legislation by offering its members guidelines in order to "alleviate their own and their patients' burdens and anxieties" (Civil Appeal 219/79).

Over the years several major sets of regulations, many of them of a technical nature, were passed. In 1977 a set of regulations for the Treatment of the Mentally Ill—Hospital Care and Supervision, was adopted (in 1981 these regulations were partially amended). This set of regulations specified the provisions necessary for admission and the limitations on freedom of movement within the hospital (including observation, special supervision, and forced measures). These regulations were desperately needed because the 1955 law was too brief and vague on these issues. Since 1977 other legislative changes have been carried out. Several paragraphs of the 1955 law regarding the material interests of the hospitalized patient were changed, and better reporting to the various authorities was required (1978). In 1980 three changes were made: The hospitalized patient was required to be checked every six months by a doctor (but not by an independent doctor outside the hospital); physically restraining the patient for more than four hours had to be explained in writing by the head of the ward; and finally, very detailed procedures for the use of ECT were issued. This amendment resulted from public pressure exerted after the media had disclosed malpractice cases.

In 1983 two additional changes were introduced: The attorney general published directives in which he instructed that an appeal should automatically be made on every order for first compulsory hospitalization. It was reported that this change, too, had the flavor of public pressure, because what it says is that the considered opinion of the district psychiatrist (DP), the person authorized to issue an order of compulsory hospitalization, is not to be trusted automatically when he or she deals with first hospitalization, but is to be trusted when he or she deals with all other hospitalizations (Levy & Davidson, 1986, p. 150). The second change of 1983 was the duty to explain to the newly admitted patient his or her rights and obligations.[5] In the past few years extensive efforts have been made to amend psychiatric legislation. These efforts have been aimed at enhancing and protecting individual rights in psychiatric care.

Admission to a mental hospital or ward was specified in great detail by the 1955 law and the regulations that followed. The general rule was that the patient's consent was the basis of his or her admission to hospital, while withdrawal of the consent should lead to his or her release. Upon admission the patient received a document specifying his or her rights and obligations and was requested to sign, indicating his or her consent to hospitalization. This practice obviously did not apply to involuntary hospitalization. According to Israeli law, a district psychiatrist's order was mandatory for enforcing hospitalization on a person who had initially refused to be hospitalized. Appeals could be presented to the DP's committee.[6] The committee's decision could be revoked by a district court on the basis of an appeal made by the attorney general, the patient, or his or her relative or guardian. The state's attorney general was to be notified of every compulsory hospitalization.

Discharge from a psychiatric hospital took place only if the hospital's director "has examined him/her and found that he/she has recovered or that hospitalization is no longer required in the interests of protecting the public." A patient's hospitalization was therefore almost an irrevocable surrender of his or her rights to the hospital director's full medical discretion. Right of appeal to the District Psychiatric Committee (DPC) was granted in 1981. In a general hospital no such subjugation of rights was evident. A patient's relative or guardian could object to his or her discharge from the psychiatric hospital. Hospital authorities were obliged, however, to release anyone who had withdrawn consent in the absence of a compulsory decree. The enforced hospitalization of a mentally ill person thus contained an element of conflict between the need to protect that person's civil rights and freedom to determine his or her own affairs and the paternalistic interest of society to act on his or her behalf when medical authorities considered the sick person insufficiently aware of his or her own best interests. This dilemma has been described as a "catch–22" (Shnit, 1978). On the one hand, protection of individuals on paternalistic grounds is often unavoidable in both civil and criminal cases; on the other hand, no person should be compelled to act against his or her will solely because society's paternalistic representatives consider it as being in his or her interests. How has the Israeli society coped with this dilemma? According to the spokespersons for the professionals, solutions have proved to be largely inadequate from the perspective of civil rights. In 1985–86 the proportion of enforced hospitalizations was 2.3 percent of the first hospitalizations and 10 percent of repeat hospitalizations, for a total of 621 forced hospitalizations and over 1,000 forced returns to hospital (State Comptroller, 1987, p. 269).

The major flaws in the Israeli system were several. First, the law entrusted the DP with extremely wide authority. The DP was a senior psychiatrist, nominated by the state to deal with enforced psychiatric admission within his or her district. In addition, the DP had many other responsibilities, demanding heavy investment of time and effort. During the 1950s it was assumed that the medicalization of psychiatric hospitalization would humanize the process. It was further predicated that mental doctors were the best judges of mental illness. The notion that only a judicial authority had the right to negate fundamental civil rights was not widely accepted. The results of this attitude were manifested in the 1955 legislation. There was no need to obtain judicial approval of enforced hospitalization. The DP's authority was almost unchallenged. The law did not require that the prospective patient be examined or even seen by the DP. No specification or medical diagnosis was required in order to enforce unlimited hospitalization on an Israeli resident.

Second, the role of the DPC was highly ambiguous. Its supervision over enforced hospitalization was ensured automatically only in cases of first hospitalization. The law did not specify a time limit for its convening. Thus several weeks might pass before the voluntarily hospitalized patient was examined by the committee. The composition of the DPC was also criticized: Its chairperson was a state-employed psychiatrist, the second member was a state-employed physician, and only the third person had legal training.

The Health Ministry, aware of the harsh criticism of the Supreme Court and the professional community, has established since 1977 four committees to propose legislative changes (Levi, 1987). The most recent committee, made up of lawyers and physicians, all of whom are Health Ministry employees, was formed in 1986. Various proposals were introduced to amend existing laws regarding the treatment of the mentally ill. Space limitations enable only a short summary of some of these proposals. The Civil Rights Association proposed changing the composition of the DPC, nominating a judge as its chairperson alongside two physicians, one of whom would not be a state employee. It was further suggested to limit the period of examination by the DPC to ten days and to review conditions for hospitalization every half year. The DPC also was to consider a report written by a social worker regarding the treatment of the patient within a community framework (Civil Rights Association [CRA], 1986).

Three legislative initiatives have also been evident. The first (Treatment of the Mentally Ill Law), submitted to the Knesset agenda in October 1987 by MK Shulamit Aloni (a member of the Civil Rights Movement—Ratz), proposed eliminating enforced hospitalization except in cases in which two physicians, one of them a psychiatrist, have approved the need for hospitalization on grounds of endangering self or others. A time limit of forty-eight hours was set for hospitalization, which could be prolonged only after the DP, after examining the patient, had given written consent. In November 1987 a second private member's bill was submitted by Yair Tzaban, a member of Mapam, a small left-wing party, and twenty-two other MKs focusing on the authority of the DPC. A time limit was set for review of the DP's decision, and a review of the original decision after three months of hospitalization was proposed. It was also proposed to nominate a judge to chair the DPC and to enable the nomination of a physician not employed by the state. A later version of the proposed law was submitted by Shoshana Arbeli-Almoslino of the Labor Alignment, who served as minister of health between 1986 and 1988. The thrust of her proposal was that a person should not be hospitalized unless he or she were thoroughly examined (physically and mentally) by a physician. The proposed law also would require that a mentally ill person hospitalized by consent should be discharged by his or her will unless the DP ordered hospitalization within forty-eight hours. The rights of patients would thus be more carefully considered, compared with the existing law.

On November 12, 1990, the Knesset adopted the Treatment of the Mentally Ill Law, which reflected the principles embodied in the proposed amendments. The 1990 legislation is different from the 1955 bill in five respects. First, the DP's authority regarding enforced hospitalization has been limited considerably. No such act can take place without examination of the patient; a strict time limit for such hospitalization has been set (seven days; then additional seven-day periods, up to a maximum of three months); and enforced hospitalization is justified only on medical grounds and not as a means for protecting the public. Second, enforced treatment is not confined to hospitalization but can take place in a clinic. This provision constitutes a dramatic departure from previous practices because it legitimizes the psychiatric clinic as an effective treatment for the mentally ill. Third, the authority of the DPC has been curtailed and its composition altered. According to the 1990 law, the psychiatric committee includes legal representatives, state-employed psychiatrists, and psychiatrists not employed by the state who are recommended by the Israel Medical Association. State-employed psychiatrists thus no longer monopolize the compulsory care of mental patients. Fourth, the 1990 law puts patients' rights in the foreground. As before, a mentally ill hospitalized person can handle his or her own affairs (depending on his or her medical condition), but the new law explicitly stipulates that the patient has a right to information and should take an active part in the medical treatment. Finally, the 1990 law established the nomination of a head of the Mental Health Services Division in the Ministry of Health whose function is to plan and administer mental health care services and to supervise and coordinate mental health institutions. The head of the Mental Health Services Division has also been vested with the authority to supervise district psychiatrists and to regulate procedures regarding medical secrecy and psychiatric documentation.

The 1990 law thus presents a positive state response to the criticism waged against previous practices. It minimizes (if not eliminates) the faults identified in the 1955 law. In terms of legislative output Israel now stands in the forefront of modern treatment for mental illness. It remains to be seen to what extent the law will be implemented and what effect it portends for the humanization of the care of the mentally ill.

CONCLUSIONS AND DISCUSSION

Israel's mental health policy is marked by the following characteristics that present a considerably incongruent policy picture tinted with many contrasting colors. Several unique phenomena provided fertile soil for the development of mental-health-related problems: mass immigration, devastating life experiences, and persistent security problems that have produced a frequency of mental problems higher than in other Western states. At the same time, deep-rooted national values regard mental illness as an unfortunate aberration, rather than as a normal and legitimate life experience. The juxtaposition of high frequency and low regard has created problems for mental health care.

Mental illness is defined in medical terms. This definition has two implications: First, the medical approach has enhanced the power of physicians as gatekeepers. Physicians were noted to be resistant to allocative thinking or to outside supervision (Stone, 1979). They monopolize the determination of the clinical disposition of a mentally disturbed person. Their judgment remains almost unchallenged by other authorities. However, the medical approach is also advantageous from a public utility perspective. It enables the application of modern medical developments to mental illness. Israeli psychiatric patients enjoy the advantages of the latest developments in medical psychotherapy.

Trends in mental health policy are also equivocal. The deinstitutionalization of mental health services was proposed by the state's administration and endorsed by the psychiatrists, in line with developments in other countries. It was manifested mainly in the diminishing rates of hospitalization. However, the pace of expanding community care did not match the decrease in hospital beds. The psychiatric community welcomed the expansion of psychiatric wards in general hospitals. It did not pressure health authorities to compensate for the decrease in hospitalization by allocating more resources to the alternative—community health ambulatory clinics. The state's bureaucrats were also reluctant to adopt the community model, partly because of bureaucratic conservatism but mainly because of the financial costs entailed. The structure of policy making—a duo comprising civil servants and professionals—decreased the effectiveness of pressures from without.

The most acute problem of Israel's mental health policy has been consumers' rights. Confronted with immense problems of immigration absorption and defense, the state developed a paternalistic attitude regarding citizens' services. The Israeli government is, in fact, one of the strongest and most intrusive in the democratic world in terms of its economic and social powers. The size of the public budget, the economic powers of the state, and the legitimacy of its institutions have turned it into a very powerful organization. This fact is also reflected in mental health policy, which has been defined and controlled by public authorities. Mental health policy thus encapsulates many problems of the unfinished process of nation building in Israel. It reflects fears of ancient demons and desires to ''normalize'' the Jewish people gathered into Israel from the Diaspora. It also demonstrates the state's commitment to protect the public, often at the expense of individual rights.

The protective attitude has many advantages. Mentally ill persons do not roam the streets but are taken care of by health authorities. Involuntary hospitalization has never been used as a means to detain political opponents or to combat subversiveness. Yet the time seems ripe for a change, brought about by both the progress in medical treatment and mounting public pressures. The fact that mental health is perceived more as a health and less as a mental problem is also conducive to change. A policy shift is thus imminent. It remains to be seen whether this change will be followed by a normative transformation legitimizing mental illness and those who treat it.

NOTES

1. In February 1990 private mental hospitals admitted only twenty patients, that is, 1.8 percent of all admissions. The proportion of private beds in the general pool is 39.1

percent. Ministry of Health, *Summary of Patients Transfer in Psychiatric Hospitals and Psychiatric Wards*, February 1990.

2. The lion's share of these medical units for mental health (36) is owned by the state; 20 are operated by Kupat Holim, and a further 20 are distributed between other health insurance schemes, the IDF, and others. Information was provided by Miriam Popper, a senior official in the Ministry of Health.

3. This information was derived from a memorandum sent to the Judicial Committee by Dr. Michael Schneidman, November 27, 1988.

4. Some qualifications are in order. First, Kupat Holim finances mental hospitalization in its own hospitals for a period of up to two years; second, hospitalization in general hospitals' mental wards is financed by sick funds. In a case where the health insurance plan refuses to pay the cost, the patient is transferred to a state psychiatric hospital.

5. Levy and Davidson (1986, p. 150) reported that this step was brought to the psychiatrists by the health minister during a congress of psychiatry and law and through the media. No circulars or other information were provided at all.

6. In 1990 the patients' rights document still specified that appeals should be presented through the head of the psychiatric services in the Ministry of Health, although this position had been abolished two years before.

REFERENCES

Abrahamson, S. H. (1966). Emotional disorders, state inconsistency, and immigration: Health questionnaire in Israel. *Milbank Memorial Fund Quarterly, 44*, 23–48.

Altenstetter, A. C., & Bjorkman, J. W. (1981). Planning and implementation: A comparative perspective on health policy. *International Political Science Review, 2*, 11–42.

Arian, A. (1981). Health care in Israel: Political and administrative aspects. *International Political Science Review 2*, 43–56.

Arian, A. (1989). *Politics in Israel: The second generation*. Chatham, NJ: Chatham House.

Assael, M., & Meter, K. (1981). Psychiatric services in a general hospital framework. *Family Physician, 10*, 5–9 (Hebrew).

Aviram, U., & Shnit, D. (1981). *Psychiatric treatment and individual liberties: Compulsory hospitalization of mental patients in Israel*. Tel Aviv: Zmora-Bitan-Modan (Hebrew).

Ben-Porath, Y. (1986). Patterns and peculiarities of economic growth and structure. *Jerusalem Quarterly 38*, 43–63.

Civil Rights Association (CRA). (1986). *Proposal for a reform in mental health care*. Jerusalem: Author.

Danieli, Y. (1982). Families of survivors of the Nazi Holocaust: Some short- and long-term effects. In C. Spielberger, I. Sarason, & N. Milgram (Eds.), *Stress and anxiety: Vol. 8. Psychological stress and adjustment in time of war and peace* (pp. 405–422). New York: Hemisphere Publication Corporation.

Elazar, D. (1986). *Israel: Building a new society*. Bloomington: Indiana University Press.

Gilboa, S. (1990). Community surveys and a research method in psychiatric epidemiology. *Harefua, 118*, 339–341.

Ginsberg, G. M. (1981). Budgetary influences on psychiatric care. *Israel Journal of Psychiatry and Related Sciences, 18*, 327–330.

Grushka, T. (1968). *Health services in Israel*. Jerusalem: Ministry of Health.

Halevi, H. (1963). Frequency of mental illness among Jews in Israel. *International Journal of Social Psychiatry, 9*, 268–282.

Halevi, H. S. (1987). Psychiatric wards in general hospitals in Israel. *Social Security, 28*, 61–78. (Hebrew).

Health system in Israel: Data and trends. (1989). Presented to the Statutory Committee for the Examination of the Function and Efficiency of the Health Care System in Israel. Jerusalem: Ministry of Health.

Levav, I. (1981). Community psychiatry in Israel: Evaluative reflections. *Israel Journal of Psychiatry and Related Sciences, 18*, 109–118.

Levi, A. (1987). Psychiatry and law: The rights of the mentally ill in Israel, in the 1955 law and its regulations. *A Letter to the Member*, 49/2, 7–8 (Hebrew).

Levy, A., & Davidson, S. (1986). Legislation concerning patients' rights in Israel and in Britain. *Israel Journal of Psychiatry and Related Sciences, 23*, 147–156.

Litman, A. (1983). *Emotional disorders in two Israeli villages*. Unpublished M.P.H. thesis, Hebrew University School of Medicine, Jerusalem.

Long-term policy lines for national health policy in Israel. (1989). Jerusalem: Ministry of Health.

Lowi, T. J. (1979). *The end of liberalism*. New York: Norton.

Maoz, B., & Stern, J. (1985). Psychiatry and primary care practice in Israel and other countries. *Israel Journal of Psychiatry and Related Sciences, 22*, 233–244.

Michaeli, N., & Eldar, P. (1989). Hospitalization home for alcohol treatment. *Harefua, 116*, 432–436.

Miller, L. (1977). Community intervention and the historical background of community mental health in Israel. *Israel Annals of Psychiatry and Related Disciplines, 15*, 300–309.

Miller, L. (1979). Culture and psychopathology of Jews in Israel. *Psychiatric Journal of the University of Ottawa, 4*, 302–306.

Ministry of Health. (1989). Information System Data. Jerusalem: Ministry of Health.

Neumann, M. (1981). Problems of psychiatry in Israel today. *Family Physician, 10*, 131–143 (Hebrew).

Neumann, M. (1982). Psychiatry in Israel today: Problems, objectives, and challenges. *Israel Journal of Psychiatry and Related Sciences, 19*, 227–238.

Polliack, M. R. (1972). Factors affecting Cornell Medical Index scores of married couples. *Journal of the Royal College of General Practitioners, 22*, 471.

Popper, M., & Rahav, M. (1984). *A national information system of ambulatory psychiatric services*. Jerusalem: Ministry of Health.

Proposal for reorganization of the mental health services: A comprehensive integrative scheme. (1972). Jerusalem: Ministry of Health.

Rahav, M., Popper, M., & Nahon, D. (1981). The psychiatric case register of Israel: Initial results. *Israel Journal of Psychiatry and Related Sciences, 18*, 251–267.

Ramon, S. (1981). Politicians' approaches to the mentally ill and mental illness: A comparison between members of the Knesset and members of the British Parliament. *Social Security, 21*, 127–144 (Hebrew).

Sanua, V. D. (1989). Studies in mental illness and other psychiatric deviances among contemporary Jewry: A review of the literature. *Israel Journal of Psychiatry and Related Sciences, 26*, 187–211.

Seligson-Singer, S. (1983). The mental health services of Kupat Holim (general sick fund of the Labor Federation) in the community. *Annual Report, Kupat Holim Publications* (Hebrew).

Shnit, D. (1978). The "catch" in granting consent. *Israel Yearbook on Human Rights, 8,* 343–353.

Snyder, C. R., Palgi, P., Eldar, P., & Elian, B. (1982). Alcoholism among Jews in Israel: A pilot study: Research rationale and a look at the ethnic factor. *Journal of Studies of Alcoholism, 43,* 623–654.

State Comptroller. (1987). *Annual report.* Jerusalem: Government Press.

Statistical Abstract of Israel. (1989). Jerusalem: Central Bureau of Statistics.

Stone, D. A. (1979). Physicians as gatekeepers: Illness certification as a rationing device. *Public Policy, 27,* 227–254.

Survey of mental health services. (1986). Jerusalem: Ministry of Health.

Trends in psychiatric hospitalization, 1975–1987: Patients movement in psychiatric hospitals by ownership and type. (1989). Statistical Publication No. 6 Jersualem: Ministry of Health.

Winnik, H. Z. (1977). Milestones in the development of psychoanalysis in Israel. *Israel Annals of Psychiatry and Related Disciplines, 15,* 85–91.

Yishai, Y. (1981). Politics and medicine: The case of Israel's national health insurance. *Social Science and Medicine, 16,* 285–291.

Yishai, Y. (1990). *The power of expertise: Israel Medical Association.* Jerusalem: Jerusalem Institute of Israel Research.

Yishai, Y. (1991). *Land of paradoxes: Interest politics in Israel.* Albany: State University of New York Press.

Yishai, Y. (1992). From an iron triangle to an iron duet? Health policy making in Israel. *European Journal of Political Research, 21,* 91–108.

Zohar, M., Floro, S., & Modan, B. (1974). The image of mental illness and the mentally ill in the Israeli society. *Harefua, 86,* 8–10.

7

Italy

Roberto Ghirardelli and Marco Lussetti

OVERVIEW

Italy, with its 57 million inhabitants, is, by population, the second-largest country in the European Economic Market. From the Alps in the north to the island of Sicily in the south, the Italian peninsula forms an almost-complete bridge across the Mediterranean Sea. This central position between North and South, East and West, has favored Italy in playing a central role in the development of ancient and modern Western civilizations from the Roman Empire to the fourteenth century. This is demonstrated by its artistic works, which represent, according to UNESCO, 30 percent of the world's treasures.

Despite the more than one hundred years that have passed since the unification of the country in 1861, the differences between the rich and industrialized North and the poor and agricultural South are still marked. In 1987 the North had an income per inhabitant of 874,000 lire (U.S. $700), versus 579,000 lire (U.S. $463) in the South; a lower unemployment rate (6.9 versus 20.6 percent); and a lower birth rate (7.6 versus 12.6 percent) (Centro Studi Investimenti Sociali, 1989).

The Republic, born after the defeat of fascism, succeeded only by the late 1960s in overcoming "the great social problems and social tensions of the postwar period" (Centro Studi Investimenti Sociali, 1989, p. 209) and allowing an open society to progressively replace a relatively closed one. In that period a welfare state was developed out of the "historical compromise" between the strong Communist Party and the Catholic church, which for centuries had controlled and managed schools, hospitals, and charitable organizations.

In the 1980s Italy had reached the level of one of the most advanced countries, competing with Britain "to become the fifth largest industrial nation of the

Western world'' (Ginsborg, 1990, p. 408). The traditional forces (i.e., political parties, the Catholic church, and the trade unions) have progressively lost their drive, allowing a more complex society to develop (Centro Studi Investimenti Sociali, 1989).

The legislative power is held by the government and by a bicameral congress, whose members are elected under an almost perfectly proportional system (Ginsborg, 1990). Among the many parties represented, no one has ever had an absolute majority of votes, and the Christian Democrats have continuously ruled the country since the beginning of the Republic through numerous short-lived coalition governments (fifty in the forty-six years after World War II). To stabilize the executive power, the ruling parties proposed, at the beginning of 1991, to change the constitution and move the country toward a presidential republic. The Communist Party, which in 1990 changed its name to the Democratic Party of the Left (Partito Democratico della Sinistra), is the major opposition party and won, in the 1987 Chamber of Deputies elections, 26.6 percent of the votes, versus 34.3 percent by the Christian Democrats.

The Italian National Health Service, which was created in 1978, went through a crisis of confidence in the 1980s with a shift toward private services. From 1980 to 1987 the spending for private services, where both service production and actual funding are private, increased from 16.7 percent to 21.7 percent and public spending for contracted services, a ''blend of public spending and private enterprise'' (Centro Studi Investimenti Sociali, 1989, p. 99), from 34.6 percent to 40.6 percent (Centro Studi Investimenti Sociali, 1989). Among the new challenges of the 1990s are AIDS and the increasing number of aged people.

EXTENT OF THE PROBLEM

With the Italian reform of 1978, psychiatric care shifted from the hospital to the community. In 1965 the inpatient population of mental hospitals reached a peak of 91,684; it declined to 25,379 persons in 1986 (a rate of 45 inpatients per 100,000 inhabitants) (Istituto Centrale di Statistica, 1989). The new psychiatric wards in the general hospital (Servizio Psichiatrico Diagnosi e Cura [SPDC]), created after 1978, had 5,877 beds in 1987 (a rate of 10 beds per 100,000 inhabitants) and 89,221 admissions (Istituto Centrale di Statistica, 1989). As of 1987 the mean hospitalization period was nineteen days, and compulsory treatment represented about 20 percent of all admissions (Istituto Centrale di Statistica, 1989; De Salvia, 1989).

In a comparative study between two areas in Holland and Italy covered by psychiatric case registers, the treated prevalence was 3 times higher and the incidence 2.5 times higher in Groningen, Holland, than in South Verona, Italy. In the Dutch register aged patients, alcohol-related disorders, and organic brain syndromes were overrepresented in comparison with other categories (Balestrieri, 1990). The prevalence per 1,000 persons at risk in one week, in a study on mental illness in the population of South Verona, was 226.7 for the general population, 34.2 for those treated at the level of general primary care, and 3.7 for those treated by the psychiatric services (Marino, 1990).

In Italy there are six judiciary mental hospitals (JMHs), with 1,344 persons detained in 1985. Between 1980 and 1985 there was an increase of 5.5 percent, compared to a 32 percent increase, in the same period, of people in prison (De Salvia, 1989).

The suicide rate is relatively low (5.7 per 100,000 inhabitants). The number of suicides has increased, as in the other industrialized countries, over the last several years (Biggieri, Ferrara, & Steffanini, 1990). The incremental rate of suicide did not increase after 1978, when mental hospitals were closed to new admissions (Williams, De Salvia, & Tansella, 1986).

Italy is the world's biggest wine producer, with a high cultural tolerance for alcoholism. In 1977 there were 12,783 admissions to psychiatric hospitals for alcoholism, but after Law 180 the only reliable statistics on the incidence of alcoholism on a national level are rates of alcohol-related diseases. The mortality for cirrhosis is heavy, compared with other European countries, with a rate of 34.5 for men and 13.6 for women per 100,000 inhabitants (Cipriani & Allameni, 1990). In 1988 drug addicts treated in 389 public ambulatory services, 454 private residential services, and 134 nonresidential private facilities were estimated to be between 30,000 and 42,000 (Labos, 1989b).

MENTAL HEALTH HISTORY

In Italy before unification in 1861, most of the asylums were not institutions in themselves, but were wards or dependencies of hospitals and hospices. The first national law on asylums, called Disposizioni sui manicomi e sugli alienati (Legal Provisions on Asylums and Lunatics), was passed in 1904 (Law n. 36 of February 14, 1904) and was supplemented five years later with its Regulations (Regolamento per l'esecuzione della legge 14 febbraio 1904, n. 36, Royal Decree n. 615 of August 16, 1909). This specific legislation came later than that of other European countries such as France (1838) and England (1844), where the "medical profession had already taken over lunacy" (Canosa, 1979, p. 100). Law n. 36 (1904) restricted admission to the public asylums to alienated people "dangerous to themselves or to others or causing public scandal" (article 1), with compulsory registration in the criminal records (article 2).

The increase of patients in asylums that began in the last half of the eighteenth century came to an end in the mid-1960s. In this period the treatment of mental illness was "almost exclusively in the field of social control" (Canosa, 1979, pp. 15–16). Organicism was the main school of thought, and little attention was paid to John Conolly's "no-restraint" policy or to the Scottish "open-door" system (Canosa, 1979). The first new treatments to be rapidly introduced were electroconvulsive therapy, developed by Cerletti in Rome (1939), and neuroleptics in the late 1950s (Piro, 1988). In the 1960s informal groups of professionals started to discuss new theories, from psychoanalysis to existentialism, and to criticize the archaic structure of the asylums, still ruled by the old law of 1904.

The French policy of *secteur* was extensively applied in northern Italy, where the catchment area, instead of type of illness, became the criterion of ward assignment and where some extramural work began (Labos, 1989a). In 1968 an amendment, the Law Provvidenze per l'assistenza psichiatrica (Provisions for psychiatric care) (Law n. 431 of March 18, 1968) introduced, for the first time in Italy, the possibility of voluntary admission. Ambulatory services placed outside the hospitals (the *centri di igiene mentale*), but still formally dependent on them, were opened in Milan and other northern cities, with functions often "restricted to drug prescription and hospital readmission" (Labos, 1989a, p. 34).

In 1962 Franco Basaglia changed the remote mental hospital of Gorizia into the first Italian therapeutic community, based on the Maxwell Jones model (Basaglia, 1968). The movement started by Basaglia assumed the asylum to be a symbol of the institution of social control, but contrary to the British antipsychiatric movement, he and his followers decided to work inside the institution that they wanted to "deny." Only when the asylum had been dismantled completely could mental health be "produced" in the normal fabric of society (De Leonardis, 1990).

The law n. 180 on Accertamenti e trattamenti sanitari volontari e obbligatori (Voluntary and compulsory ascertainments and treatments), of March 13, 1978 (popularly known as "Law 180" or "Basaglia's Law"), was passed as a transitional part of the National Health Service reform act to avoid a popular referendum against the 1904 law. It placed an irrevocable sentence on asylums. In the meantime, the new structures that should have taken the place of the hospitals were, by and large, still to be created (Canosa, 1979). The judiciary mental hospitals, opened in 1891 and fully developed under fascism, were "forgotten" by the reform.

POLICY, ORGANIZATION, AND SERVICES IN THE 1980s AND 1990s

Current Policy Developments

During the 1960s and 1970s the old psychiatric system, based on asylums and on seclusion of mental illness from society, collapsed, and a new policy was introduced by Law 180 (1978) that (1) excluded dangerousness as a criterion for commitment, (2) restricted compulsory admission to the general hospital, (3) hindered prolonged hospitalization by setting the duration of compulsory treatment at seven days (renewable) and by establishing a ceiling of fifteen beds for the psychiatric wards in civil hospitals (SPDCs), and (4) sanctioned the abolishment of mental hospitals (Maj, 1985).

Current Organization

Implementation of services is performed, following regional standards and avoiding duplication, by the local health authority (Unità Sanitaria Locale or USL), which is in charge of a catchment area of between 40,000 and 200,000 inhabitants. The access to psychiatric services is direct, with no prior request from primary care, and is free of charge. Drug addicts, alcohol abusers, and children needing psychiatric services are usually dealt with by other services.

When the public sector is not able to answer a proper psychiatric need, as may happen for long-term inpatient care involving mental retardation and old age, it can pay an established rate for a substitute private service. Private hospitals are more numerous in central and southern Italy and are often run by religious bodies.

Current Services

In Italy the hub of the psychiatric network is the *servizio di salute mentale* (SSM) or community mental health center, which can supply nonhospital beds and day-care services. The SPDC is a psychiatric unit of 15 to 20 beds in the general hospital for acute patients and for compulsory treatment. The former mental hospitals accommodate the patients who were admitted before Law 180 and who could not be discharged into the community. The following December 31, 1984, data come from research commissioned by the Department of Health (Labos, 1989a):

The catchment area of the Community Health Centers (SSMs) generally correspond to the U.S.L. In 1984 there were 674 SSMs: an average of one center for every 47,100 inhabitants. Most patient contacts are made at the service (60.2 percent); 28.8 percent at the patient's home, and the rest in different contexts. More than two-thirds of the services are open at least six days a week. The SSMs are in charge of patients even during hospitalization, in order to guarantee continuity of care.

The staff averages fifteen persons: three to four doctors and twice as many nurses, psychologists, and social workers. The work is usually organized through multiprofessional teams that are in charge of a subset of the total catchment area.

The quality and distribution of services are far from homogeneous. Labos (1989a) defines five different service levels:

1. Services poor in resources, with no systematic projects, and not integrated with other services (11.4 percent of the total)

2. Services lacking in projects and not integrated (33.4 percent)

3. Services of insufficient size, with few resources, but efficient in avoiding hospitalization and having good connections with the hospital and other agencies (23.4 percent)

4. Services efficient and endowed with sufficient resources (18 percent)

5. Services highly efficient and rich in the complexity of care they can offer (13.8 percent)

The best services tend to be the oldest, opened before 1978, and located in the North of Italy. One well-known example of the highest level of services is the SSMs of Trieste, with seven centers for 290,000 inhabitants that are open twenty-four hours a day. Each center can offer up to seventy meals, eight beds for night accommodation, day care, home visits, and other services, making the only SPDC (psychiatric ward in a civil hospital) in the city superfluous (Mauri, 1983). These "strong" services are becoming a model for regional and national legislation (Centro Studi Ministero della Sanità, 1989).

At the level of intermediate service facilities, the Labos research found that half of the 245 residential services were in the premises of the former mental hospitals and housed long-term patients. The 50 day centers, mostly in the North, are clearly not sufficient and treat the heaviest pathologies (62 percent of patients are schizophrenics).

The intermediate facilities belong to the community centers, and only 11 percent are private. As they are the fastest-growing structures, the 1984 number of 245 is now an underestimate. Shortages of buildings and staff, particularly nurses, are the main obstacles for further development even with new standards and adequate budgets to provide the necessary resources.

Inpatient services have continued. On December 31, 1984, 28,000 patients were still hospitalized in 91 public mental hospitals, and 6,100 patients were in private mental hospitals under contract to the National Health Service. After the passage of Law 180, the mental hospitals were closed to new admissions and were neglected by the reform. Rehabilitation is rarely practiced, there is no on-the-job training, and even the funds for the most urgent upkeep of the buildings are lacking.

In 1984 there was a rate of 5.4 beds per 100,000 inhabitants in 236 SPDCs (psychiatric wards). The Lazio region, with a bed rate of only 1.4, has to rely heavily on private hospitals. Most SPDCs (85 percent) are located inside a general hospital. They have an average of twenty square meters per bed. The main treatment is pharmacological and the turnover is fast, with a mean hospitalization of 12.4 days for voluntary admission and 12.8 days for compulsory treatment. Contact with families is regular, but usually collaboration with the community centers is poor.

Mental Health Personnel and Treatment

Of the 37,000 persons working for the psychiatric sector in Italy, 64 percent are nurses, 11 percent are doctors, 2 percent are psychologists, and 4 percent are social workers. One-third of the personnel working in the community centers have been employed since 1978, and half of these came from mental hospitals. Half of the staff in the community centers (and higher percentages in the other services) have never had on-the-job training, and most of the nurses who came from the mental hospitals have not even had a proper professional course.

Most of the organization and treatment approaches of the services have been applied out "in the field," with a resulting blurring of roles and a great variety of styles, evident even among services placed in the same city. In the 1980s, with the establishment of the new services, more attention was paid to the professionalizing of staff and the development of specific areas of competence. The transition of psychiatry from closed mental hospitals to the community and civil general hospitals brought a closer integration of this discipline with primary practice and other medical branches and a progressive fading of a stronger political involvement that was based on a separate mental health identity.

PUBLIC POLICY PROCESS

Law 180 (1978) "functioned as a *guideline law*, not as *prescriptive law*, entrusting the regions with the task of drafting and implementing detailed norms" (De Girolamo, 1985, p. 451; italics in original). The lack of specific national rules, due to a weak central executive power, and the different degrees of compliance or noncompliance with the principles of the law at regional and local levels (USLs) have produced an uneven implementation, defined by Labos (1989c) as "pelle di leopardo" (leopard skin). The factors playing a role at the local level are the following:

1. The existence of the mental hospitals before 1978: As no budget was set by Law 180 for the new structures, most of the resources such as staff (article 7 of Law 180) were drawn from the hospitals. Southern Italy, in which the mental hospitals were mainly private (Piro & Oddati, 1983), started out with an unfavorable environment that partly explains their current backward state of development.

2. Previous political involvement in the anti-institutional movement established the basis of community work before Law 180 was issued in 1978 and promoted the concentration of "progressive" doctors and staff that, after 1978, represented important human and experiential resources for the full implementation of the law. With the establishment of the Italian National Health Service in 1978, there was, for several years, a block of new employments and of transfers, hindering formation of new "progressive" groups.

3. The local political environment: In Italy politics have been openly interwoven with psychiatry (Mosher, 1982; Lovell, 1986; Tansella & Williams, 1987). A political struggle was the only means to overcome the inertia of the old psychiatric system and the absence of clear guidelines.

Not even the universities played a significant role in the transforming process of Italian psychiatry. The first two faculties of psychology opened in the 1970s, and the Department of Psychiatry, which was officially separated from Neurology just two years before the reform (1976), trained future psychiatrists on the descriptive and mind-brain–oriented aspects of mental illness with no reference to the social and relational aspects of the disease (De Martis, 1981).

Franco Basaglia formed a movement for the ideological and practical struggle against asylums which took the name, in 1973, of Psichiatria Democratica (democratic psychiatry). It was formally a cultural association, but in practice it was an influential political pressure group aligned with left-wing parties. In the early 1970s most of the persons involved in the process of deinstitutionalization associated themselves, at least in part, with the ideals of the movement. Basaglia and Psichiatria Democratica used mass media to denounce the scandal of the outdated asylums. Some of the members of the movement, with the help of political links, reached key roles in the top management of the psychiatric services.

In the early 1980s, when the closure of mental hospitals shifted the main burden of care from the institutions to the patients' families, the families organized themselves into associations. Some of them were in favor of the law and instigated pressure for fully developing an adequate network of residential and day-care community services. Others saw a solution in the creation of "small or medium sized wards for 'severe' and long-term cases as a guarantee of greater stability in the provision of care" (Giannichedda, 1989, p. 65).

In the 1990s, with the controversy for or against the mental hospital over, a common agreement was reached on the necessity (1) to define the number, features, and functions of the new residential and day-care structures in the community; (2) to implement them on a national level; (3) to capitalize the projects; and (4) to organize a better collection of data for future planning and coordination. A 1990 bill presented by Minister of Health Francesco De Lorenzo moved, in part, away from the spirit of Law 180 by proposing less restrictive rules on compulsory admission (which can also be done by private hospitals) ("Approvato dal Governo," 1990). It was approved by the Cabinet in February 1993, but still must be debated by the Parliament. De Lorenzo has resigned and the bill is not expected to pass soon.

SPECIAL POLICY ISSUES

The Mentally Ill and the Mentally Retarded

The policy of reform for the mentally retarded went more smoothly than that for psychiatry as a result of the age-old tradition of care by orphanages and other charitable foundations such as the Cottolengo in Turin. Also, there was relatively higher family and social acceptance of mental retardation. In the 1960s special schools and classrooms were created for the handicapped. Eventually, criticism against any form of seclusion and discrimination led, in the 1970s, toward the complete integration of these children into ordinary classrooms.

A pioneer experiment was done in Arezzo in 1971, at the time of the first law on integration (Law n. 118/1971), where professionals of the mental health services (psychologists, social workers, physical therapists, and speech therapists) worked in schools and with families (Salvi & Cecchini, 1988). The aim was to help the relatives not to reject their handicapped children, but to develop a more realistic and rewarding attitude; to promote motivated and spontaneous behavior; and to avoid the use of psychotropic drugs through a better understanding of the disturbing behavior at a psychological level. The interventions took place in normal settings: home, classroom, playground, and even on holiday (Martini, Cecchini, Corlito, D'Arco, & Nascimbeni, 1985).

With the second law of 1977 on integration (Law n. 517/1977), this experience became a standard for the country. Support teachers (*insegnanti di sostegno*) were assigned to classrooms, with no more than twenty pupils, to look after the integration of the handicapped. A normal environment was thought to be capable of boosting school performance, helping the recovery from disabilities, lessening social stigma, and improving self-esteem (Guidi, 1985). However, when integration in the school was achieved, the lack of employment and recreational opportunities became more evident (Salvi & Cecchini, 1988).

Franco Tommasini, a former chairman of the Provincial Health Committee of Parma, who worked with Basaglia for the closure of the local mental hospital, promoted the "opening up [of the] communities" (Lovell & Scheper-Hughes, 1987, p. 22) by providing opportunities for adequate housing and work in factories or in cooperatives, even for the very severely mentally retarded. Tommasini's policy offers practical solutions to the problems of social outcasts without committing them to closed institutions and shows how a correct and progressive administration could deeply change the culture of a city (Ongaro Basaglia, 1991).

Law n. 482 (1968) obliges a firm with more than fifty workers to employ handicapped people. In the 1970s and 1980s several projects of work integration for severe disabilities were sponsored by the European Common Market and local entities, even if, on the whole, the statutory provisions were often being "calmly evaded" (Salvi & Cecchini, 1988, p. 144).

Before Law 180 (1978) children with great difficulties in adapting themselves to the community because of psychosis or severe mental handicap were treated in mental hospitals or in charitable foundations. Some of the mentally handicapped children cared for by private institutions, once they became adults, were transferred to asylums "for competence." With the closure of mental hospitals, psychiatry has a limited number of inpatient beds for a new admissions and few day-care facilities. Therefore, mental retardation in both children and adults is treated independently. Even though an improved welfare policy helps families keep their children at home, the Italian National Health Service offers no special services that systematically deal with the problem, leaving the task of organization to single public and private agencies. As with psychiatry, there is a North versus South difference in the degree of implementation of services. Family associations have focused their pressure on political bodies to ensure an adequate provision of resources for the mentally handicapped, and they organized themselves into a nationwide network of organizations (ANFFAS) in 1964.

In the case of a dual diagnosis, the psychiatric diagnosis usually prevails, resulting in a greater rejection from school and sometimes even from services for mentally retarded persons. To avoid this problem, some regional laws (e.g., Regional Law n. 39/1988 of Liguria) and the Objective Project for Psychiatry (Centro Studi Ministero della Sanità, 1989) provide for stronger coordination between services for mentally retarded persons and those for psychiatric patients. Nationwide statistics on mental retardation and dual diagnosis are lacking.

The Mentally Ill and Substance Abuse

The first victims of amphetamines died in the winter of 1972, and a massive introduction of morphine began in the early 1970s (De Santis, 1982). The first organic law for drug addiction (n. 685 of December 22, 1975) barred the admission of drug addicts to mental hospitals, and detoxification was and still is carried out, if needed, in the nonpsychiatric wards of the general hospitals. Therapeutic communities—most of them run by religious bodies and under contract to the National Health Services—accept newly drug-free youngsters for long periods of rehabilitation.

In the 1960s and 1970s drug abuse was connected with student and juvenile dissent. Prevention started in the early 1970s in schools, where a teacher in each institute was in charge of coordinating seminars on drug addiction in association with doctors, magistrates, and journalists. Addiction was seen in the public eye mainly as a social problem, and the motto was "to understand, not to reject." In the 1980s the problems of drug abuse and crime linked to addiction increased. The first case of AIDS dates back to 1982 and was followed by a steep increase (1,984 cases in 1985 and 1,928 in 1989) (Maciocco, 1990). Heroin addicts, due to the poor and late prevention campaign, were the most impacted (in 1989, 67.6 percent of all victims of AIDS were drug users) (Maciocco, 1990).

Public opinion in the last decade has turned toward a punitive attitude. The new law (n. 162 of June 26, 1990) introduced punishment for the personal use of drugs. Furthermore, it provided "cure" (in the public ambulatories and/or in the therapeutic communities) as an alternative to administrative or criminal sanctions, overturning the principle of the 1975 law on voluntary cure.

Alcoholism and addiction represent only 2.9 percent of the users of psychiatric services, 6.4 percent of those in SPDCs (psychiatric units of general hospitals), and 2 percent of those in the former mental hospitals (Labos, 1989a). Alcohol-related problems are mostly dealt with in primary care and in general hospitals; regions with special wards for alcoholics are few. Since the late 1980s there has been a growing interest in self-help groups such as Alcoholics Anonymous and Alcoholics under Treatment, an association funded by the Yugoslavian Hudolin.

Dual diagnosis is not yet perceived as a problem, and it is usually the primary diagnosis that leads to the choice of treatment.

The Mentally Disordered Offender

Articles 88 and 89 of the Civil Code of 1931 state that a person is imputable when capable of understanding and when having a free will, but if the person is judged totally incapable, he or she cannot be punished. Nevertheless, the person will be sent to the judiciary mental hospital (JMH) if he or she is judged to be a "danger to society" (defined by article 203 of the Criminal Code as the probability to repeat other crimes due to mental illness) at the moment of commitment. If he or she is only partially capable, the punishment is reduced. The judge has recourse to the opinion of experts to decide whether a person is mentally ill and dangerous.

A person can be sent to the JMH (1) when he or she is acquitted because he or she is not imputable, that is, he or she is a person who has committed a crime, but is incapable of "understanding and free will" and is a "danger to society." He or she can be hospitalized for two, five, or ten years, proportionate to the crime. The judge can revoke the commitment. A person can also be sent to the JMH (2) during preconviction for observation and reports for treatment; (3) during the post-trial when he or she can be sent from jail for the same reasons as above; or (4) without a conviction, if he or she is incapable of standing trial.

At the census day of December 31, 1987, 1,225 persons were detained in six JMHs, 80 percent of them (975) "acquitted because not imputable" (Fornari, 1989). Mental retardation and personality disorders are considered as mental illnesses if they compromise the ability to "understand and [exercise] free will" (Fornari, 1989).

The commitment to a JMH is based, *de jure condito*, on the presence of "danger oriented" (Segal, 1989). This can bias the selection system of JMH toward residual categories of mental patients and offenders who are rejected by both the psychiatric and judiciary circuits. The Prison Reform Act of 1975 allows alternative sentences to prison when outside factors, such as a suitable job, are present. If a person is convicted and not sent to the JMH, the community centers can mobilize alternatives to prison, as is done in an experiment performed in Trieste and described by Reali and Shapland (1986). Some suggestions to overcome the contradictions of the JMH as a place of conviction and cure are the implementation of psychiatric wards in jails or, following the lines of Trieste, the abolishing of the judicial notion of imputability and "danger to society" and entrusting to the psychiatric services the cure of the convicted mentally ill.

Deinstitutionalization

The Italian reform was born in a highly ideological era when the mental hospitals, with other "total institutions," were considered, to quote one of the books of Basaglia (1975), a "peace crime." In the 1970s all the institutions were challenged with protests, and new laws were passed for the integration of the disabled into the workplace; to integrate handicapped children into normal classrooms; to improve adoption; and to open up alternatives to prison conviction. To help integration of disadvantaged citizens into society, the municipalities created new welfare and health services.

The number of inpatients in the mental hospitals dropped by one-fifth between 1966 and 1974 (Canosa, 1979). The space left empty by the closure of mental hospital wards was often reused for hostels, day-care centers, and work cooperatives for ex-patients. Other empty wards were allotted to public services such as schools, social centers, or public offices. Some were just left empty, as the Italian National Health Service does not allow the budget from hospitals to be directly used for other sectors. The work of deinstitutionalization differs from the simple closing down of wards in mental hospitals ("dehospitalization"). The functions of the asylum (lodging, catering, laundry, people to speak with, and so on) are "dismantled" and "reassembled" in the context of normal life (Rotelli, 1988). In this way the needs for a house, food, company, and other necessities that keep many "chronic" patients segregated from the world in institutions, even if their doors are open, are used instead to promote a new social life.

An example is the work cooperatives. These were created in the 1970s to change the "black" jobs, performed by the patients for nurses (e.g., cleaning) or disguised as "work therapy," into normal employment that could support life outside the hospital and improve self-esteem. They started with cleaning jobs inside the hospital, growing in some cities like Turin, Trieste, or Prodenone into real enterprises that employ hundreds of users in different sectors, from keeping a hotel to porterage and from catering to the secretarial services of congress. These cooperatives are formally private firms, but in some cases the staff of the psychiatric services support the members in their work or promote new initiatives. Each user has the status of a member who is, under the articles of the cooperative, a worker and "shareholder" of the "company."

The "integrated" cooperatives pay special attention to the specific work problems of people with psychiatric disabilities, though in a normal context, where the members are expected to perform and to behave normally as they are confronted with productivity and with face-to-face interactions with the public and customers of the cooperative. In a way, the cooperatives create richness in wealth and human relationships for very disabled users, instead of dependence and institutionalization.

After the "entitlements" (Dahrendorf, 1988) to a life outside the asylum, the second phase of Italian deinstitutionalization is to create new services capable of empowering the users to live in a normal social context. For Rotelli (1988), such "institutions" cannot be given, but must be continuously "invented" with, and for, their clients.

Funding Issues

In Law 180 (1978) no budget was set aside for implementing the reform psychiatry, but in the first ten years ideology prevailed over cost and efficiency in the debate. Among the few sources available on funding issues, the bill presented on the September 25, 1987, by Senator Franca Ongaro Basaglia (wife of Franco Basaglia), quoting "reliable sources," stated that the 30,000 inpatients still present in the mental hospitals absorbed up to 80 percent of the total expenditures for psychiatry (Ongaro Basaglia et al., 1988). Similar data come from an unpublished paper by Centro Studi Investimenti Sociali (1985): In 1984 the Liguria region (1.7 million inhabitants) spent 55.75 billion lire (U.S. $44.6 million) on psychiatry, 63 percent of which went to the two former regional mental hospitals with an overall population of 1,300 inpatients.

A more qualitative analysis comes from Toresini and Trebinciani (1985), who studied the cost of the public psychiatric services in the Friuli–Venezia Giulia region for the years 1970–80. In the province of Trieste the total expenditure during the decade increased by 359 percent against a rise in the cost of living, in the same period, of 376 percent. After ten years the expenses for drugs were reduced (adjusted for inflation) to about one-third. Benefits were the only items to increase more than the cost of living. In another two provinces, with more conservative psychiatric policies, the expenses were higher than inflation. There is little control, except for inscription to a regional register, of the private hospitals under contract to the National Health Service.

Under a cabinet decree of August 8, 1985, any "social expenditures" such as living benefits, or even the provision of nonmedical lodgings, cannot be supplied by the National Health Service, and mental patients have to compete with other categories of the poor for the meager resources provided by local authorities. New bills are now sensitive to monetary costs. The bill presented by Senator Franca Ongaro Basaglia proposed, in article 9, that at least 8 percent of the budget for health should be spent on the psychiatric sector in the years 1988–90. The European mean was 15 percent (Ongaro Basaglia et al., 1988). The Objective Project for Psychiatry (Centro Studi Ministero della Sanità, 1989) set a three-year budget of 1,085 billion lire (U.S. $868 million) for the implementation of a detailed list of new facilities.

In Italy the Health Service is gradually increasing its share of expenditures. From 1985 to 1988 it increased from 4.5 to 5.2 percent of the GNP (Istituto Centrale di Statistica, 1989), while the cost of psychiatry in the more advanced services did not increase or actually decreased. This happened in Liguria, where the total regional psychiatry budget diminished (adjusted for inflation) by 15 percent between 1977 and 1984 (Centro Studi Investimenti Sociali, 1985).

"Rich" community mental health services, such as the one in Trieste, cost, with drugs included, "only" 2 billion lire (U.S. $1.6 million) per year (Centro Studi Ministero della Sanità, 1989). This means that there is no actual increase compared with the money paid for the old asylum (Toresini & Trebinciani, 1985). In the community the resources are used in a more flexible manner, are closer to individual needs, and, above all, are integrated with the human and economic assets of the users and of their families. Integration empowers the users with more control for the disposal of resources and helps them move out of passive assistance.

Consumer Rights

The National Health Service Act (Law n. 833/1988) specified that all treatments should be voluntary and that consent must be actively sought. Compulsory hospitalization (the *trattamento sanitario obbligatorio*, TSO) "can be applied to people affected by mental illness" only if (1) "there is such a mental disorder that urgent therapeutic measures are needed"; (2) "such measures are not accepted by the patient"; and (3) "a timely and suitable nonhospital therapeutic intervention cannot be implemented." The proposal is made by one physician and confirmed by a second physician. The mayor, as the highest local health authority, prescribes the admission. Notification of the TSO must be made within forty-eight hours to the tutelary judge, who, in the subsequent forty-eight hours, ratifies or does not ratify the compulsory treatment. Anyone, including the patient himself or herself, can appeal against the treatment, with no legal expenses and with a minimum of bureaucracy in order to make the appeal feasible. The TSO lasts for seven days and can be renewed using the same procedure.

The protection offered by the law against abuse is high. The compulsory treatment order is signed by doctors (at least one of whom works for the National Health Service). It is also subject to the control of the mayor and a judge. The police have no role in the decision making. The patient maintains, even during compulsory treatment, his or her social rights, such as the right to "communicate with whom he thinks it preferable to do so" (article 33, Law n. 833/1988) and the right to vote. Some civil limitations (e.g., signing contracts) are limited only due to the incapacity "to understand and [exercise] free will."

To judicially protect the possessions of mentally ill persons, the Italian Civil Code provides for two cases: the *interdizione* (interdiction), with a tutor responsible for all civil acts, and the *inabilitazione* (disqualification) for less serious cases. Both are viewed as cumbersome by some, and more flexible measures for temporary and partial tutorship have been proposed (Cendon, 1987).

The safeguarding of the rights of psychiatrically disturbed persons is clear from the first article of the Health Reform Act (Law n. 833/1988): "The protection of physical and psychic health must be fulfilled with respect for the dignity and freedom of the human person." Regarding compulsory treatments, article 33 adds that they "must be associated with initiatives aimed at assuring consensus and participation of the person obliged to comply." "The Unità Sanitaria Locale [the local health authority] acts to reduce recourse to compulsory treatments by implementing initiatives of prevention and health education and organic links between the services and the community.''

The protection of rights and dignities of the people affected by mental diseases should include the development of service alternatives to hospitalization and a regard for the quality of care (Rubenstein, 1986). This problem is felt by the families, which often sue public authorities for not keeping the few standards of care prescribed by regional laws. In 1990 Psichiatria Democratica filed a complaint against a regional authority for financing private hospitals instead of developing public services (''Contro la privatizzazione,'' 1990).

Electroconvulsive therapy (ECT), widely used in the mental hospitals, is a practice limited in the community to some private hospitals and neurological departments. With most of the care based on voluntary treatment in community centers, abuse of drugs or of other physical treatments is kept to a minimum.

Law 685 (1975) was very tolerant of drug abuse: Addiction and even the possession of ''small amounts'' of drugs for ''personal use'' were not punishable. During treatment the addict had the right to anonymity and could, by law, be hospitalized in mental hospitals or psychiatric wards. The new international climate against addiction, the rising problems of AIDS and criminal acts, and some political propaganda helped to pass a long-debated bill (Law 685/1990) that made any possession of drugs punishable. The punishments (up to three years in jail) are withheld if the person agrees to be treated for his or her addiction. During the cure his or her job is retained.

CONCLUSIONS AND DISCUSSION

The new services have taken root in the community and have worked incisively against social exclusion, warding off old and new trends for institutionalization. The heated national and international debate on the 1978 reform highlighted two important phenomena: (1) a technical and cultural growth into traditional fields such as psychoanalysis and psychopharmacology and into new approaches such as the systemic Milan school (Selvini Palazzoli, Cecchin, Prata, & Boscolo, 1978) or psychiatric epidemiology; and (2) a ''silent,'' but lively and rich experimentation, performed by the staffs of the services themselves, in meeting the needs of new patients without turning to long hospitalization or to mental hospitals. Both these low-profile aspects of the ''Italian experiment'' should now lead to cooperation in building new organizational models capable of spreading, if adequately funded, the standards already reached by the pilot services.

Even if it is still too early to give a definitive judgment on the reform, it has reached its target to close the asylums to new patients without increasing the homeless or prison populations. Above all, the 1978 act has given people suffering from mental diseases the right to live with dignity outside institutions. A renewed effort should be made to help them assert themselves further by improving other opportunities, such as housing, work, schooling, and social relationships; that is, to help them become real citizens.

REFERENCES

Approvato dal governo un ddl: Dalle ceneri della "180" nuove norme sulla tutela della salute mentale [The government has approved a Parliamentary bill: From the ashes of "180" to new regulations on mental health care]. (1990, December 12). *Il medico d'Italia*, pp. 4–5.

Balestrieri, M. (1990). Il registro dei casi per il monitorraggio e la valutazione dei servizi psichiatrici [The case register for the monitoring and evaluation of the psychiatric services]. [Special issue] *Revista sperimentale di freniatria, 114,* 205–350.

Basaglia, F. (Ed.). (1968). *L'istituzione negata* [The institution denied]. Turin: Einaudi.

Basaglia, F., & Ongaro Basaglia, F. (Eds.). (1975). *Crimini di pace* [Peace crimes]. Turin: Einaudi.

Biggieri, A., Ferrara, M., & Steffanini, P. (1990). Epidemiologia descrittiva del suicidio in Italia [Descriptive epidemiology of suicide in Italy]. In M. Gedes (Ed.), *La salute degli Italiani: Rapporto 1990* [The health of Italians: Report 1990] (pp. 81–93). Rome: La Nuova Italia.

Canosa, R. (1979). *Storia del manicomio dall'Unità ad Oggi* [History of the asylums from unification to today]. Milan: Feltrinelli.

Cendon, P. (1987). Una teoria per il diritto [A theory for the law]. In *Atti del convegno di Trieste, 22–23–24 settembre 1986* (pp. 50–63). Pistoia: Centro di Documentazione di Pistoia Editrice.

Centro Studi Investimenti Sociali (CENSIS). (1985). *L'attuazione della riforma psichiatrica nel quadro delle politiche regionali e dell'offerta quantitativa e qualitativa dei servizi: Liguria* [The implementation of psychiatric reform through a picture of the regional qualitative and quantitative services offered: Liguria]. Rome: Mimeo.

Centro Studi Investimenti Sociali (CENSIS). (1989). *Italy today: Social picture and trends, 1988.* Rome: Franco Angeli.

Centro Studi Ministero della Sanità. (1989). *Progetto-obiettivo: "Tutela della salute mentale"* [Project-object: "Tutelage of mental health"]. Rome: Editrice ISIS Società per Azion [stock company].

Cipriani, F., & Allameni, A. (1990). I fattori di rischio: L'alcool [Risk factors: Alcohol]. In M. Gedes (Ed.), *La salute degli Italiani: Rapporto 1990* [The Health of Italians: Report 1990] (pp. 137–170). Rome: La Nuova Italia.

Contro la privatizzazione [Against privatization]. (1990). *Fogli di informazione, 147,* 17–25.

Dahrendorf, R. (1988). *The modern social conflict: An essay on the politics of liberty.* New York: Weidenfeld & Nicolson.

De Girolamo, G. (1985). Misunderstanding the Italian experience. *British Journal of Psychiatry, 147,* 451–452.

De Leonardis, O. (1990). *Il terzo escluso: Le istituzioni come vincoli e come risorse* [The third exclusion: Institutions as bonds and as resources]. Milan: Feltrinelli.

De Martis, D. (1981). La nouvelle loi psychiatrique à la lumière des problèmes de formation et de transmission culturelle [The new psychiatric law in the light of problems of training and cultural transmission]. *L'information psychiatrique, 57,* 581–588.

De Salvia, D. (1989). Évolution de l'assistance psychiatrique après la réforme de 1978

[The evolution of psychiatric assistance after the reform of 1978]. L'information psychiatrique, 7, 677–689.

De Santis, S. (1982). Tossicomanie: Parte storica e psico-sociale [Drug addiction: Historical and psychosocial aspects]. In C. G. Reda (Ed.), Trattato di psichiatria [Psychiatry textbook] (pp. 424–440). Firenze: USES Edizioni Scientifiche.

Fornari, U. (1989). Psicopatologia e psichiatria forense [Forensic psychopathology and psychiatry]. Turin: UTET.

Giannichedda, M. G. (1989). A normality for us without confinement for them: Notes on the associations of families of the mentally ill. International Journal of Social Psychiatry, 35, 62–70.

Ginsborg, P. (1990). A history of contemporary Italy: Society and politics, 1943–1988. London: Penguin.

Guidi, A. (1985). Servizi di assistenza agli handicappati [Assistence services for the handicapped]. In R. Zerbetto (Ed.), Realtà e prospettive della riforma dell'assistenza psichiatrica (pp. 807–818). Rome: Instituto Poligrafico dello Stato.

Istituto Centrale di Statistica (ISTAT). (1989). Annuario Statistico Italiano: Edizione 1989 [Statistical Italian Yearbook: 1989 edition]. Rome: Author.

Labos (Foundation), Laboratorio per le Politiche Sociali. (1989a). Il dopo 180: Primo bilancio di una riforma: Ricerca promossa dalla Direzione Generale Ospedali del Ministero della Sanità [After 1980: The first assessment of a reform: Research promoted by the General Hospital Authority of the Ministry of Health]. Rome: Edizioni T.E.R.

Labos (Foundation), Laboratorio per le Politiche Sociali. (1989b). I servizi per la tossicodipendenza in Italia [Services for drug addiction in Italy]. Rome: Edizioni T.E.R.

Labos (Foundation), Laboratorio per le Politiche Sociali. (1989c). Utenza psichiatrica e servizi: Ricerca promossa dalla Direzione Generale Ospedali del Ministero della Sanità [Psychiatric users and services: Research promoted by the General Hospital Authority of the Ministry of Health]. Rome: Edizioni T.E.R.

Lovell, A. M. (1986). The paradoxes of reform: Reevaluating Italy's Mental Health Law of 1978. Hospital and Community Psychiatry, 37, 802–808.

Lovell, A. M, & Scheper-Hughes, N. (1987). The Utopia of reality: Franco Basaglia and the practice of a Democratic Psychiatry. In N. Scheper-Hughes & A. M. Lovell (Eds.), Psychiatry inside out: Selected writings of Franco Basaglia (pp. 1–58). New York: Columbia University Press.

Maciocco, G. (1990). AIDS. In M. Gedes (Ed.), La salute degli Italiani: Rapporto 1990 [The health of Italians: Report 1990] (pp. 129–136). Rome: La Nuova Italia Scientifica.

Maj, M. (1985). Brief history of Italian psychiatric legislation from 1904 to the 1978 Reform Act. Acta Psychiatrica Scandinavica, Suppl. 316, 15–25.

Marino, S. (1990). L'epidemiologia dei disturbi psichiatrici nella medicina di base [The epidemiology of psychiatric diseases in primary care]. Epidemiologia e Prevenzione, 43, 32–37.

Martini, P., Cecchini, M., Corlito, G., D'Arco, A., & Nascimbeni, P. (1985). A model of a single comprehensive mental health service for a catchment area: A community alternative to hospitalization. Acta Psychiatrica Scandinavica, Suppl. 316, 95–120.

Mauri, D. (Ed.). (1983). *La libertà à terapeutica?* [Is freedom therapeutic?]. Milan: Feltrinelli.

Mosher, L. R. (1982). Italy's revolutionary mental health law: An assessment. *American Journal of Psychiatry, 139*, 199–203.

Ongaro Basaglia, F. (1991). *Vita e carriera di Franco Tommasini burocrate proprio scomodo narrate da lui medesimo* [Life and career of Franco Tommasini, a very troublesome bureaucrat, told by himself]. Rome: Editori Riuniti.

Ongaro Basaglia, F., et al. (1988). Disegno di legge per l'attuazione della 180 (bozza). [Bill for the implementation of 180 (draft)]. *Fogli di informazione, 134*, 1–12.

Piro, S. (1988). *Appunti per una storia della psichiatria italiana dal 1945* [Notes for a history of Italian psychiatry since 1945]. Naples: Edizioni Scientifiche Italiane.

Piro, S., & Oddati, A. (Eds.). (1983). *La riforma psichiatrica e il Meridione d'Italia* [Psychiatric reform and the South of Italy]. Rome: Il Pensiero Scientifico.

Reali, M., & Shapland, J. (1986). Breaking down barriers: The works of the community mental health service of Trieste in the prison and judicial setting. *International Journal of Law and Psychiatry, 8*, 395–412.

Rotelli, F. (1988). The invented institution. *Per la salute mentale/For Mental Health, 1/88*, 196–198.

Rubenstein, L. S. (1986). Treatment of the mentally ill: Legal advocacy enters the second generation. *American Journal of Psychiatry, 143*, 1264–1269.

Salvi, E., & Cecchini, M. (1988). Children with handicaps in ordinary schools. In S. Ramon & M. G. Giannichedda (Eds.), *Psychiatry in transition: The British and Italian experiences* (pp. 138–146). London: Pluto Press.

Segal, S. P. (1989). Civil commitment standards and patient mix in England/Wales, Italy, and the United States. *American Journal of Psychiatry, 146*, 187–193.

Selvini Palazzoli, M., Cecchin, G., Prata, G., & Boscolo, L. (1978). *Paradox and Counter-Paradox*. New York: Aronson.

Tansella, M., & Williams P. (1987). The Italian experience and its implications [Editorial]. *Psychological Medicine, 17*, 283–289.

Toresini, L., & Trebinciani, M. (1985). I servizi territoriali costano meno del manicomio: Ricerca comparata sulla spesa psichiatrica delle quattro provincie del Friuli-Venezia Giulia [Community services are less expensive than the asylum: Comparative research on the psychiatric costs of the four provinces of Friuli-Venezia Giulia]. *Fogli di informazione 111/112/113*, 1–13.

Williams, P., De Salvia, D., & Tansella, M. (1986). Suicide, psychiatric reform, and the provision of psychiatric services in Italy. *Social Psychiatry, 21*, 89–95.

SELECTED BIBLIOGRAPHY

On the history of Italian psychiatry up to the reform, see the referenced article by Canosa (1979). On the experience of Basaglia and his team in Gorizia see the referenced book by Basaglia (1968) and his coworkers. Some of Basaglia's works are translated into English in the book edited by N. Scheper-Hughes and A. M. Lovell, (1987), *Psychiatry inside out: Selected writings of Franco Basaglia* (New York: Columbia University Press).

The most interesting experiences of Italian psychiatry after 1978 are in the collection of twenty-one books edited by the Centro Nazionale delle Ricerche (CNR) [The National Center for Research] between 1981 and 1987: CNR, *Quaderni di documentazione prevenzione malattie mentali* (Rome: Il Pensiero Scientifico). For a picture of psychiatry in the 1980s, see the referenced research by Labos (1989a, 1989b, 1989c), and, in English, section 5 of the book by L. R. Moser and L. Burti, (1989), *Community Mental Health* (New York: W. W. Norton & Company); S. Ramon and M. G. Giannichedda (Eds.), (1988), *Psychiatry in transition: The British and Italian experiences* (London: Pluto Press); and two monograph issues: C. Perris and D. Kemali, (1985), Focus on the Italian psychiatric reform, *Acta Psychiatrica Scandinavica*, *71*(suppl. 316); and S. Mangen (Ed.), (1989), The Italian psychiatric experience: The first ten years, *International Journal of Social Psychiatry*, *35* (special issue).

8

Japan

Kunihiko Asai

OVERVIEW

Japan is an island country stretching along the northeastern coast of the Asian continent. It consists of 4 main islands—Hokkaido, Honshu, Shikoku, and Kyushu, from north to south—and more than 6,800 smaller islands. With a total land area of 377,719 square kilometers, Japan accounts for less than 0.3 percent of the total land area of the world. Of its entire land area, 73 percent is mountainous and the remaining 27 percent is relatively flat. Thus the arable and habitable land is extremely limited.

The population of Japan as of October 1989 was 123 million, ranking seventh in the world with about 2.4 percent of the world population. The average annual rate of population increase from 1986 to 1989 was a little more than 1 percent. In 1989 the rate was as low as 0.38 percent. The population growth of Japan is caused mainly by natural increase, for net international migration is negligible. The birth rate declined sharply from its high level during the postwar baby-boom period of 1947–49 and became 10.1 per 1,000 population in 1989. In the same year the death rate was 6.5 per 1,000 population, the same as in the previous year. As a result, the rate of natural increase recorded was 3.7 per 1,000 population. The infant mortality rate improved to 4.7 per 1,000 live births in 1989. Except for the death rate, these ratios have been declining every year for several years.

The life expectancy at birth of the Japanese has shown a remarkable improvement and has been among the highest in the world. It declined slightly in 1988, when it was 75.54 years for males and 81.30 years for females.

The age structure of the Japanese changed markedly from the typical pyramid form with a broad base in the 1930s as a result of the decrease of the birth rate and the death rate. In 1989 the proportion of the productive-age population (15–64 years of age) was 69.6 percent, the highest level among major industrial countries. However, the aged population (65 years old and over) is projected to attain the significant share of 23.4 percent in 2025. Besides, the age dependency ratio (ratio of children and aged to the productive-age population) is predicted to rise from 43.7 percent in 1989 to 72.8 percent in 2042, when the aged population will reach its peak of 24.2 percent. These estimates demonstrate the remarkable speed and extent of the aging of the population structure in Japan.

The real economic growth rate in fiscal 1988 was 5.3 percent, the second consecutive year of a rise exceeding 5 percent. The Japanese economy has continued its high rate of growth; its GNP now ranks second in the free world. On a per capita basis, GDP of Japan amounted to U.S. $23,270 in 1988, meaning that Japan was ranked third among OECD members, an improvement from the rank of eighth (U.S. $11,144) in 1985. The rapid rise in rank of GDP per capita, however, has been mainly due to the rapid appreciation of the yen.

EXTENT OF THE PROBLEM

The number of long-term patients in psychiatric hospitals is increasing every year. Currently, more than 50 percent of residential patients have been in the hospital for more than five years. The age of the hospitalized patients, becoming older every year, has reached a peak of between 45 and 55 years old. Patients over 65 years old accounted for 22 percent of all the psychiatric patients in 1989. According to the statistics of the Ministry of Health and Welfare in 1990, out of 349,000 hospitalized patients, schizophrenic psychoses were the leading diagnosis (61 percent). Other diagnoses included affective psychoses (4.6 percent), senile and presenile organic psychotic conditions (9.3 percent), alcoholic and drug psychoses (6.0 percent), neurosis (6.2 percent), epilepsy (3.5 percent), and mental retardation (4.4 percent).

Estimates of mentally disordered persons by the Ministry of Health and Welfare in 1990 were approximately 1,600,000 psychotic persons; about 400,000 mentally retarded persons; and about 2 million persons drinking more than 150 milliliters of alcohol per day (Ministry of Health and Welfare, 1990). In Japan there are now 1 million persons with senile dementia, and it is estimated that in twenty years their number will double. Among them, 25 percent of patients are treated in hospitals or other facilities.

MENTAL HEALTH HISTORY

In Japan before World War II there were two pieces of legislation concerned with mentally ill people. The Confinement and Protection for Lunatics Act of 1900 provided procedures to confine the mentally ill patient at his or her own home, and the Mental Hospital Act of 1919 laid down administrative procedures to detain him or her compulsorily in an asylum. These two statutes were designed specifically to permit relatives or local authorities to exert their protective powers for safeguarding the public. After World War II, under the constitution newly promulgated in 1946, the fundamental human rights of the Japanese nation were held in maximum respect, but unfortunately, the Mental Hygiene Law of 1950 was not in line with the philosophies and principles of the constitution.

Through this law the government dictated a policy that psychiatric patients should be institutionalized in psychiatric hospitals. Private custody was prohibited so that the mentally ill could receive adequate medical treatment. This law decreed the principle of compulsory admission by administrative order under the standard of "dangerous to self and others" or involuntary admission by the proxy consent of a legally responsible person. Essentially, both channels were of a compulsory nature for the prospective patients, and over 90 percent of the population in mental hospitals in Japan in 1987 were involuntary patients.

Psychiatric care in Japan has stressed hospitalization. When the Mental Hygiene Law was enacted in 1950, in the aftermath of World War II, the number of beds occupied by "mentally ill" people was low (2 per 10,000 population). Following Japan's rapid industrial development beginning in 1951, a nationwide compulsory health insurance system was instituted in 1958. The government then decided to increase the number of psychiatric hospitals. Despite that move, the number of doctors per patient at these hospitals was only one-third the number of doctors per patient at general hospitals. In 1961 the government started to restrict the number of public hospital beds and to promote private hospitals. As of 1988 there were 345,000 psychiatric beds, a record high of 28 per 10,000 general population (Asai, Takahashi & Tsung-yi, 1991).

In 1965 the Mental Hygiene Law was partially revised, and the Ministry of Health and Welfare started to partially subsidize outpatients and pointed out the necessity of transforming hospital psychiatric treatment to community-based psychiatric care. In accordance with this revised law and its measures, outpatient psychiatric services were increased and gradually became more widespread. Day-care services and rehabilitation programs also were set up. Since then, the total number of outpatients has been increasing every year. However, neither a plan nor a budget were provided for community psychiatric care. Although a system of outpatient care has been developed, the expenditure for outpatient care as a percentage of the total psychiatric care expenditure has remained almost the same since 1965. This means that the basic pattern of psychiatric care delivery has not changed and that the main site of mental health care is still psychiatric hospitals.

POLICY, ORGANIZATION, AND SERVICES IN THE 1980s AND 1990s

Current Policy Developments

Until recently, Japanese psychiatry emphasized hospitalization, where "treating and protecting mental patients" was regarded as the overriding objective.

However, now the philosophy of community psychiatry has become as important as hospitalization.

Although the importance of community psychiatry has been long acknowledged in Japan, application has been relatively slow. For one thing, even today, the social rehabilitation of those with psychiatric disabilities is not supported by the government's welfare policy; this is still left to the goodwill of psychiatric hospitals or the patient's family associations. While many nongovernmental psychiatric hospitals have begun rehabilitation services, their goodwill and efforts alone are not sufficient.

After some improper management of inpatients in Utsunomiya Hospital was reported in 1984, there were many protests domestically and internationally that mentally ill persons in Japan were being subjected to violations of human rights. The government of Japan then declared an amendment of the Mental Hygiene Law in August 1985. There were some confrontations in the course of the investigation between psychiatrists and jurists in reference to the best way to assure patients' rights. After two years of investigations and discussions, the newly revised law, called the Mental Health Law, was legislated in 1987 and has been in operation since July 1988. The basic concepts in the amended Mental Health Law were (1) the protection of the human rights of patients and (2) the promotion of social rehabilitation for mentally disordered persons.

The elongation of mean life expectancy represents a human triumph, but at the same time, the explosion in the absolute number and relative proportion of the older population increases the number of patients with dementia. It is also believed that these changes in demography affect the appropriate operation of the social security system. The Ministry of Health and Welfare established the Task Panel for the Demented Elderly in 1986, and the panel emphasized in its report in 1987 (Ministry of Health and Welfare, 1988a) that the following policies should be executed immediately:

- To enforce health promotion activities that are intended to prevent geriatric diseases, so as to reduce the incidence of cerebrovascular diseases, the most frequent cause of dementia in Japan.
- To improve the availability and accessibility of home care and institutional care.
- To form the basis of needed services, staff must be attracted, retained, and trained, and a network for a continuous care system must be formed.

Mental disorders of childhood or adolescence with social and behavioral symptoms are also of great interest, although the number of institutions with health personnel that are specialized in these fields is insufficient. The need for policy improvement regarding these disorders can not be overemphasized.

Current Organization

Japan has 45 prefectural community mental health centers and 852 public health centers. The activities of the community mental health services of the public health centers are neither well organized nor cooperative with psychiatric hospitals in the community.

According to a 1983 fact-finding survey of mental health by the Ministry of Health and Welfare, more than 30 percent of hospitalized patients could leave the hospitals immediately if there were enough social support systems in the community. However, 60 percent of the patients' families said that they could not look after discharged patients (Asai et al., 1991).

The Mental Health Law is under the jurisdiction of the Mental Health Division of the Health Service Bureau of the Ministry of Health and Welfare. In each prefectural government departments or bureaus of public health are in charge of mental health services, and most prefectures have mental health centers, which have responsibility for promoting public mental health services and for information dissemination at the prefectural level through consultation services, training, education, research, and surveys.

In local districts consultations, visiting guidance, and other mental health activities are carried out mainly by mental health counselors or public health nurses who belong to the health centers. The relationship between these departments and institutions is shown in figure 8.1.

As of the end of June 1990 the institutional care statistics were as follows:

Number of institutions	1,648
Number of psychiatric beds	358,128
Number of inpatients	349,010
Percentage of beds occupied (average per year)	90.0%
Psychiatric beds per 10,000 population	28.4

Only 18.3 percent of total psychiatric hospitals are public, and only 11.7 percent of psychiatric beds are public. Most of the private psychiatric hospitals are incorporated and nonprofit. Two years after implementation of the new Mental Health Law, the types of admission were as follows:

Number of voluntary admissions	184,503	52.9%
Number of admissions for medical protection	139,123	39.8%
Number of involuntary admissions by the prefectural governor	12,566	3.6%
Free admission	12,818	3.7%

There are 1,765 outpatient facilities and clinics, taking care of 700,000 patients. They deliver medical services, including case management and counselling for recovering patients. There are 45 prefectural mental health centers and 852 health centers that coordinate the delivery of public mental health services,

Figure 8.1
The Relationship between Administrative Departments and Institutions in Japan

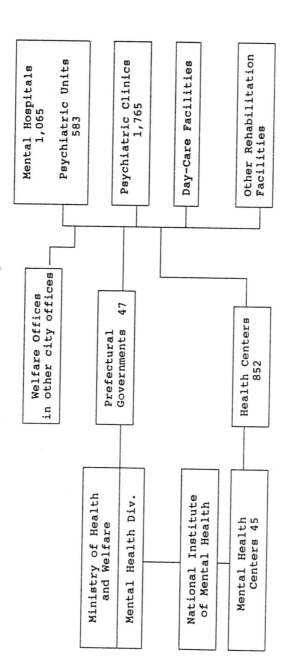

Source: Ministry of Health and Welfare, 1990

including counselling, day-care programs, information dissemination, and other services.

Theoretically speaking, mental health facilities and services fall into the public domain. The Mental Health Law, amended in 1988, refers to the social rehabilitation needs of the mentally ill, but states that only "municipalities and medical juridical persons may establish social rehabilitation facilities for persons with mental disorders." Consequently, though nongovernmental hospitals are aware of the importance of community psychiatry, many of them find it extremely difficult to start loss-producing rehabilitation services without subsidies.

Current Services

In Japan since 1970 community care programs have gradually developed for psychiatric patients (figure 8.2). However, they have not developed enough to become major sites of treatment.

Social resources for activities for the mentally disabled in 1990 (table 8.1) included sheltered workshops, which began in the 1960s, for the physically handicapped, the mentally retarded, and the mentally disordered. As of October 1, 1990, there were 2,231 such workshops, of which 554 served mainly those with mental disorders. These sheltered workshops are run by families or voluntary mental health personnel. There are only 25 sheltered workshops subsidized under the Mental Health Law. There are 186 approved day-care facilities, but only 42 percent of them are public. Among 852 public health centers, 665 centers have community care programs. There are 209 patient clubs in the community.

In 1982 the Ministry of Health and Welfare launched a Rehabilitation Program for Outpatients in close collaboration with prefectural governments. The central government allocates funds to prefectural governments to contract with companies designated and registered as vocational parents. There are now 1,438 companies that are vocational parents, but only 2,300 patients are working.

In Japan there is not yet a protected employment system for mentally disabled persons. In the near future there should be well-organized vocational rehabilitation systems for mentally disabled persons that will be nearly the same as for physically handicapped or mentally retarded persons.

Social resources for living were limited as of 1991. There are poor community residential facilities in Japan (see table 8.2). The amended Mental Health Law in 1988 set forth the legal framework for two types of residential facilities, which may be established and operated by prefectural governments, municipal governments, social welfare juridical persons, and others. As of June 1990 there were only 33 hostel–mental health facilities for social adjustment and 32 care homes. The number of such residential facilities has not grown much. Most of these social rehabilitation facilities were established by juridical persons, and they have been unable to raise funds to build or operate facilities without sufficient subsidies. The number of users will not increase unless the charges for using these facilities change. There are now 95 group homes established by private

Figure 8.2
Rehabilitation System for the Mentally Ill in Community Mental Health in Japan, 1991

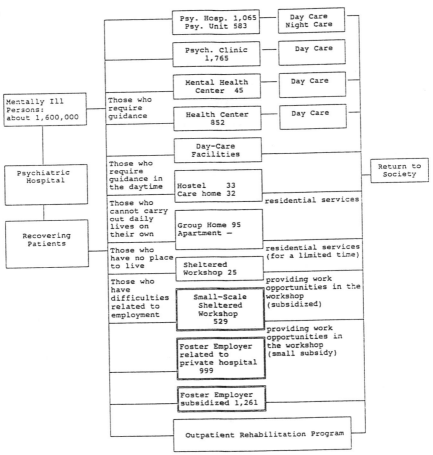

Source: Ministry of Health and Welfare, 1991.

Table 8.1
Social Resources for Activities in Japan, 1990

		Facilities	Clients	Notes
1.	Sheltered workshops with subsidies	25	500	By Mental Health Law
2.	Small-scale sheltered workshops	529 *(209)	9,500	Not by Mental Health Law *Subsidized by the local government and other sources.
	Subtotal	554	10,000	
3.	Day-care facilities (in hospitals & clinics)	186	4,000	
4.	Day-care services community care program (in public health centers)	20	—	
		665	21,885	
5.	Patient clubs and social programs	209	—	
	Subtotal	1,080	25,885	
6.	System for foster employers of ex-mental patients	1,438	2,300	By government subsidy for employers
7.	Foster employer system (for inpatients and outpatients)	999 (related to 280 mental hospitals)	about 2,000	Nonsubsidized by hospital.

Source: Ministry of Health and Welfare, 1990.

Table 8.2
Social Resources for Living in Japan: Residential Facilities, 1990

	Facilities	Patients	Notes
1. Hostels Mental health facilities for social adjustment	33 ↓ [4,000]	995 ↓ [8,000]	With government subsidy by Mental Health Law Capacity: 20
2. Care homes	32 ↓ [500]	320 ↓ [5,000]	Subsidized by Mental Health Law Capacity: 10
3. Group homes	95 ↓ [2,000]	916 ↓ [9,000]	By private hospital & self-help group
4. Independent apartments		[10,000]	
5. Urgent care institutions	171	15,428 *(6,171)	Subsidized by welfare law *40% of them are for the mentally disordered
6. Institutions for rehabilitation	18	1,768	
7. Geriatric nursing homes	—	[13,000]	Under welfare law
Subtotal	189	[20,939]	
Total	3,000 <	50,000 <	

Note: [ ] = the number of facilities needed and patients estimated in future.
Source: Ministry of Health and Welfare, 1990.

hospitals and self-help groups without subsidy. The number of facilities needed and the estimated patients to be served in the future are shown in table 8.2, but there exists a very big gap.

Facilities needed for social rehabilitation of the mentally disordered in Japan still face many problems. Yet Japan has obviously started making serious efforts to expand its resources in this regard. In order to solve problems in the future, the national government, municipal governments, and other parties involved in psychiatric care must work closely together and exert greater efforts to develop social rehabilitation strategies based on the new Mental Health Law.

In Japan deinstitutionalization has not yet progressed. Psychiatric hospitals in Japan play a role that intermediate facilities should play. Therefore, psychiatric hospitals provide hospital functions such as security, emergency services, and acute, subacute, and chronic services, to which the same base charge is applied. Simultaneously, psychiatric hospitals, again for the same base charge, have to serve as nursing homes or sometimes as board-and-care facilities as well. Consequently, there are not street people in the community.

Mental Health Personnel and Treatment

As of the end of June 1988, medical personnel in mental hospitals were the following:

Psychiatrists	8,725
(Designated physicians of mental health)	(7,815)
Nurses	37,087
Assistant nurses	36,402
Nurse's aides	20,342
Qualified occupational therapists	469
Psychiatric social workers	1,235
Clinical psychologists	about 1,000
Mental health workers (in public health centers)	1,656
Public health nurses	8,749

Among paramedical staffs, only occupational therapists meet national qualifications. There is a nationwide shortage of labor both in medical and other professional fields. Mental hospitals also suffer because of a shortage of nurses and other professionals.

Instead of the psychiatric judgment doctor system used under the former law, the new 1988 law specifies a designated physician of mental health. In this system psychiatrists are required to have practiced psychiatry for more than five years and to have proved their experience with eight case reports for registration.

The designated physicians are responsible for daily activities such as decisions on all admissions and discharges, except for voluntary ones, and they are responsible for many kinds of reports. Any restrictions on actions of patients specified by the minister of health and welfare are justified by a designated physician. Thus the treatment in psychiatric hospitals, in general, cannot be executed without a designated physician. The number of designated physicians at the end of 1988 was about 7,815.

SPECIAL POLICY ISSUES

The Mentally Ill and the Mentally Retarded

The estimated number of mentally retarded persons by the Ministry of Health and Welfare in 1990 was about 400,000. Of this number, 14,386 were hospitalized as patients in facilities for the mentally ill. Out of total hospitalized patients, mental retardation accounted for 4.4 percent.

As of October 1, 1988, there were 313 homes and 216 day-care facilities for mentally retarded children. For adult mentally retarded persons, there were 794 rehabilitation facilities, 105 day-care facilities, 167 residential facilities with sheltered workshops, 343 sheltered workshops, and 133 group homes. In 1960 a new Welfare Law for Mentally Retarded Persons was enacted. Under this legislation many kinds of social resources for activities and community residential facilities for mentally retarded persons have been developed.

The Mentally Ill and Substance Abuse

According to the statistics of the Ministry of Health and Welfare in 1990, out of 349,000 hospitalized patients, alcoholic and drug psychoses accounted for 6.0 percent. The number with alcoholism accounted for 19,259, amphetamine addiction for 587, and other drug addiction for 948.

The drinking population and estimated heavy drinkers in Japan have increased annually in proportion to alcohol consumption per capita, doubling from 1965 to 1987. While present alcohol consumption is not as high as in some of the Western countries, the rate of increase may be considered one of the highest. There is a concurrent increase in alcohol-related disabilities, and the mortality in males for liver cirrhosis nearly doubled from 1950 to 1980, while the rate of alcoholism as a whole also doubled.

The Japanese drinking culture is well known as very permissive. More than 50 million people, almost two-thirds of the adult population, are drinkers. Although only a small proportion of those drinking have need of medical care, the increase in the drinking population has definitely led to an increase in the number of clinical cases.

Danshukai is an alcohol self-help group spread widely throughout Japan. Established in 1963, it has 500 local Danshukai and over 45,000 members. More than 70 percent of these members have abstained from drinking for over one year and have succeeded in social rehabilitation.

The Mentally Disordered Offender

The Japanese criminal code provides for pleas of not guilty by reason of insanity and sentence mitigation by reason of mental distress. It does not provide, however, for committing criminals with psychiatric disorders to mental institutions for medical care and custody. Persons with mental disorders who have committed criminal actions come under the jurisdiction of the Mental Health Law and are committed under either "admission for medical protection" or "involuntary admission by the prefectural governor." In Japan there are neither security hospitals nor security units for mentally disordered offenders and refractory patients. Most of them have been hospitalized in some of the public and private mental hospitals. With the progress of community care and open-door treatment for hospitalized persons, forensic psychiatric problems have become more important. The government has decided to establish policies to address that problem.

Funding Issues

Japan has a national medical insurance system where every citizen is covered and accorded equal access to medical services. Under this system the Japanese government determines the charge for each medical service category and thus regulates how much hospitals can claim for reimbursement for their services. One of the claimable categories is for basic inpatient services, which include doctors' fees, medication, and basic nursing. This charge, which is partly borne by the patient and paid mostly through reimbursement from the government is ¥7,200 or U.S. $55 per day per patient.

In 1988 gross national medical expenditures were 5.15 percent of GNP—almost ¥19 trillion or U.S. $146,000,000,000. The problem, however, is that medical resources are not evenly distributed. For example, medical expenditures reimbursed to psychiatric hospitals make up 6.2 percent of total disbursements, although psychiatry has a 22 percent share in terms of number of beds. Monthly medical expenditures per psychiatric patient are approximately half of the average medical expenditures for patients in other medical specialities. It should be added that these expenditures are already much lower than in other countries.

Among the total expenditures of psychiatry—¥1.14 trillion—87 percent were medical expenditures for hospitalization. Medical expenditures for promoting psychiatric rehabilitation in 1989 accounted for ¥101 million or U.S. $7,700,000. From 1984 to 1989 these expenditures increased three times. But Japan needs more funding for psychiatric rehabilitation.

Consumer Rights

Concerning human rights, the main points of the 1987 amendment of the Mental Health Law providing for protection of patients' rights are the following:

1. In case of a need for admission to a mental hospital, the superintendent of the mental hospital shall endeavor to admit the mentally disordered person based on his or her consent (voluntary admission).
2. To guarantee to every involuntarily admitted inpatient the right to appeal to the prefectural governor for his or her discharge or regarding inappropriateness of treatment.
3. To establish a Psychiatric Review Board to review the necessity of involuntary hospitalization and the propriety of treatment through notice on admission and by regular report.
4. To prohibit restrictions on actions, such as correspondence, telephone use, and interviews.
5. To give written notice of the patient's rights at admission.

The principal reforms involved voluntary admission, admission for medical care and custody, involuntary admission by the prefectural governor, and emergency admission.

Voluntary admission was legislated into law for the first time. When the superintendent of a mental hospital intends to admit a mentally disordered person, the superintendent must endeavor to admit the person based on his or her consent, and the patient must be informed in writing of his or her rights. In the case where a voluntarily admitted mentally disordered person has requested to be discharged, the superintendent of the mental hospital must discharge him or her. But when the designated physician deems it necessary to continue the admission of the voluntarily admitted person for medical protection, the superintendent may refrain from discharging him or her for a period not longer than seventy-two hours. This voluntary admission was not provided for in the former Mental Hygiene Law. However, there were a few voluntary admissions (5 to 10 percent of total admissions). These were done through another type of voluntary admission (so-called free admission) that was not included in the Mental Hygiene Law. When a person has been deemed by the superintendent of a mental hospital, as a result of the medical examination of a designated physician, to be mentally disordered and thus to be in need of admission to a hospital for medical protection, and when a person responsible for his or her protection has consented to the admission, the superintendent may admit the person to the hospital without his or her own voluntary consent as an admission for medical protection.

Admission by consent of a legal guardian (referred to hereafter as consent admission) in the former law was changed more radically. This consent admission was unique in Japan. This type of admission was given a priority for admission, even if a person was willing to agree to a voluntary admission. Therefore, this type of admission had been used for both involuntary and voluntary admissions. More than 80 percent of inpatients were admitted with consent admissions, which resulted in the criticism that more than 90 percent of inpatients were either consent admissions or involuntary admissions by governor's order and were detained involuntarily in Japan. This criticism was partially correct and partially incorrect, as many voluntary admissions chose admission by consent of legal guardian to expedite admission. This consent admission was changed to an admission for medical protection that was clearly defined as involuntary admission under the newly revised law.

Under another type of involuntary admission, admission occurs only after medical examinations, made by two or more designated physicians selected by the prefectural governor, lead to agreement on the fact that the examined person is mentally disordered and is liable to injure himself or herself or others because of his or her mental disorder unless he or she is admitted to a hospital. Then the prefectural governor can order admittance to a mental hospital established by the national or prefectural government, or to a designated hospital.

In addition, in cases where the superintendent of a mental hospital designated by a prefectural governor as a facility in compliance with the criteria specified by the minister of health and welfare is required to take urgent action with regard to a person for whom the superintendent has been requested to provide medical care and custody, and for whom he has been unable to obtain the consent of a person responsible for custody, the superintendent may admit the person under an emergency admission to the hospital for a period not longer than seventy-two hours without the consent of the mentally disordered person himself or herself. This may be done only after the superintendent has concluded, as a result of the medical examination conducted by a designated physician, that the person in question is mentally disordered, and there would be extreme interference with his or her medical care and custody unless he or she was admitted to the hospital without delay.

Temporary admission has not changed. Free admission, which was not included in the Mental Hygiene Law, has become general admission with certain diagnostic limitations, for example, neurosis.

Two years after the enforcement of the new law, the percentage of newly prescribed voluntary admissions was 52.9 percent, and that of free admissions was 3.7 percent. This shows that many inpatients moved from consent admission to voluntary admission (Ministry of Health and Welfare, 1988a, 1990).

The law also provides for a Psychiatric Review Board. The number of members of a Psychiatric Review Board shall not be less than five nor more than fifteen. The board includes a lawyer, a specialist of social welfare, and three designated physicians of mental health. This board is expected to review the necessity of involuntary hospitalization and the propriety of the treatment. There are forty-seven Psychiatric Review Boards all over Japan.

CONCLUSIONS AND DISCUSSION

To further develop community psychiatry in Japan, there first needs to be an ability to generate an appreciation about mental health among the general public and to obtain the support of society. Second, strong networks need to be established among public health centers, welfare bureaus, and consultation offices for children, and crisis intervention needs to be provided. Third, a good working relationship must be developed with public health nurses, who regularly visit homes where there are potential health problems, and they must be helped to remedy those problems. Fourth, and most important, psychiatric hospitals should not isolate themselves from the rest of society. Psychiatric hospitals must be open, so that residents in the community will feel comfortable about admission to one.

While public education and public understanding about mental illness are fostered, the country also needs to develop a variety of facilities: day-care and night-care services, supported dormitories, other halfway houses, sheltered workshops for vocational opportunities, and other appropriate programs. With a variety of facilities and services, people with mental disabilities will be able to try, according to their ability, to adapt to a new environment and eventually participate in society as independent individuals. However, psychiatric hospitals should continue to offer prompt medical intervention, if necessary, so as not to arouse unnecessary misgivings in the community.

Given their far-reaching value, rehabilitation services of the mentally ill should not be at the sole expense of psychiatric hospitals. Today, Japan needs a community psychiatry system suitable for its culture and its social needs. Japan also needs a policy that does not impose a financial burden on those willing to undertake community psychiatry. Without registration for financial support to cover almost-inevitable deficits incurred by rehabilitation services for former patients, and with the social stigma still remaining in this society, hospitals have been forced to withdraw from rehabilitation services in some cases.

The Mental Health Law provides that the national, prefectural, and local governments shall endeavor to enable mentally disordered persons to adapt themselves to social life by expanding and improving the facilities needed for medical care, social rehabilitation, and other welfare purposes and education. But there is still no remarkable change to be found in the social rehabilitation of mentally disordered persons. Requests need to be made for more subsidies and legal support to promote the rehabilitation and community care of mentally ill people in Japan.

REFERENCES

Asai, K., Takahashi, T., & Tsung-yi, L. (1991). *The mental hospital as a base for community mental health in Asian cultures.* Tokyo: Keimei Publishing.
Ministry of Health and Welfare. (1988a). *The mental health law.* Tokyo: Koken Shuppan.

Ministry of Health and Welfare. (1988b). *National health administration in Japan*. Vol. 2. Tokyo: Koken Shuppan.

Ministry of Health and Welfare, Mental Health Division of Health Services Bureau. (1991). *Rehabilitation System for the Mentally Ill in Community Health in Japan*. Tokyo: Koken Shuppan.

9

Korea

Cheon Bong Kim

OVERVIEW

The Korean peninsula extends due south of Manchuria. It stands like a rabbit between the Yellow Sea and the East Sea. It is located between China, Japan, and the Soviet Union (C. B. Kim, 1989, p. 3). It is approximately 1,000 kilometers long, north to south, and 216 kilometers wide at its narrowest point. It is separated from China's Shantung Peninsula to the west by a 190-kilometer expanse of the Yellow Sea. The shortest distance between Korea and Japan is 206 kilometers. To the east is the East Sea and to the south is the Pacific Ocean. The Amnokkang (Yalu) and the Tumangang (Tumen) rivers separate the peninsula from Manchuria and Siberia to the north. The peninsula and all of its associated islands lie between 124°11′E and 131°53′E, and between 33°06′N and 43°01′N. The peninsula's area is 221,487 square kilometers, or about 86,500 square miles. The land is presently divided into two parts—Communist North Korea and free South Korea (the Republic of Korea). The Republic of Korea's administrative control covers 99,177 square kilometers, or about 45 percent of the total (H. E. Kim, 1985, p. 14).

Korea is characterized by hills and mountains, which account for nearly 80 percent of its territory. Low hills are predominant in the south and west and gradually yield to higher mountains in the east and north. Thus the western and southern slopes are gradual and meet with plains, low hills, and winding river basins, while the eastern slopes plunge directly into the nearby East Sea.

The population of the Republic of Korea in 1988 was about 42,593,000 (males, 21,476,000; females, 21,117,000), and the population of North Korea in 1987 was about 21,390,000. The rate of population growth has been declining in recent years from a high in 1961 of 2.9 percent to 1.53 percent in 1985 and

1.19 percent in 1988 (National Bureau of Statistics, 1988, p. 39). This decrease is due to a successful family planning program, increased urbanization, a higher standard of living, and a trend toward later marriage. The population of Korea is very young, with 61.17 percent under twenty-nine years of age (National Bureau of Statistics, 1988, p. 44). The population of the country is becoming increasingly urban, with the farm population in 1984 accounting for 22.2 percent of the total. This urbanization is characterized by the dominance of Seoul over the life of the nation. Nearly 20 percent of the population lives in the capital city, which is the center of government, industry, education, and culture. Impressive gains in rural development and the designation of industrial estates outside of the capital area, however, have helped to balance the attractiveness of Seoul, as will a number of satellite cities being built on its outskirts (H. E. Kim, 1985, p. 30).

Since 1948 government structure has been changed many times. In that year the Korean government of the First Republic had eleven ministries, four bureaus, and three committees. In 1961 the Korean government had two boards, two offices, and four bureaus and established an Economic Planning Board under a deputy premier. In early 1991 the Sixth Republic of the Korean Government changed some government organization. For example, a Board of Unification under a deputy premier was established with two boards, twenty ministries, two offices, and fourteen bureaus. The executive consists of a president, a premier, two deputy premiers (minister of the Economic Planning Board and minister of the Unification Board), and the Ministries of Foreign Affairs, Home Affairs, Finance, Justice, National Defense, Education, Agriculture and Fisheries, Commerce and Industries, Health and Social Affairs, Construction, Energy and Resources, Culture, Public Information, Science and Technology, Communication, Transportation, Government Administration, Environment, Labor, and Sports (*Dong-A Ilbo*, 1990, December 17, p. 3). There also are an Office of Legislation and an Office of Patriots and Veterans Affairs. Congress consists of one National Assembly, and the judiciary consists of a Supreme Court, three High Courts, District Courts, and Local Courts.

The beginning of Korean history is often dated to 2333 B.C. when Tan-gun, a legendary figure born of the Son of God and a woman from a bear-totem tribe, established the first kingdom, named Chosun, or the "Land of the Morning Calm." While the history of the Tan-gun myth is a source of argument among scholars, it is known that ancient Korea was characterized by clan communities that combined to form small city-states. They rose and fell until by the first century B.C. three kingdoms, Koguryo (37 B.C.–A.D. 668), Packche (18 B.C.–A.D. 660), and Shilla (57 B.C.–A.D. 935), had emerged on the peninsula (*Facts about Korea*, 1988, p. 23). After Shilla unified the peninsula in 668, the Korean Parhae Kingdom (A.D. 699–A.D. 926) was established by Daejoyung in the northern part of the Korean peninsula to near Manchuria, China. Both the Koryo (A.D. 918–A.D. 1392) and Chosun (A.D. 1392–A.D. 1910) kingdoms consolidated dynastic power and flourished culturally while repelling intruders like the Khitans, Mongols, Manchus, and Japanese. Korea became the focus of intense imperialist competition among China, Russia, and Japan in the late nineteenth century. In 1910 Japan annexed Korea and instituted colonial rule, bringing to an end the Yi Dynasty, and with it, traditional Korea. National liberation in 1945 was soon followed by territorial division. The Republic of Korea in the south has a democratic government, while North Korea is under a Communist regime (*Facts about Korea*, 1988). Since liberation Korea has had a series of governments: the First Republic, the Second Republic, the Third Republic, the Fourth Republic, the Fifth Republic, and currently the Sixth Republic, which was established in 1988.

Korea progressed through the combined efforts of Koreans, including administrators, political elites, entrepreneurs, and students who committed themselves to the development of economic, social, and administrative policies. But Korea is developing several social illnesses. There are increasing numbers of unreasonable and violent acts by students, labor unionists, and other interest groups, riding on the current wind blowing for increased democratization (C. B. Kim, 1989, p. 13; *Korea Times*, 1989, March 8). Among the changes stirring conflict are the effects of the Uruguay round of bargaining on imports, the election of local councils for self-government, and the effects of the Persian Gulf War.

EXTENT OF THE PROBLEM

Korean society is moving toward urbanization and industrialization while experiencing rapid population increases. The rate of mental disability increased from 1.03 percent (male, 0.87 percent; female, 1.19 percent) in 1980 (Moon, 1981, p. 1) to 1.45 percent (male, 1.02 percent; female, 1.88 percent) in 1986 (J. S. Kim, 1988; Moon, 1989, p. 1). In 1991 the Korean government estimated that there were 907,000 people (2.16 percent) suffering from mental illness, of whom 105,000 people were considered to be in need of hospitalization. It is difficult to estimate the numbers or the percentages of people with mental retardation and mental illness because of the widely accepted Korean culture of privacy and dignity. In 1989 there were 5,346 mentally retarded people who had been admitted to institutions for the handicapped (Ministry of Health and Social Affairs, 1990). Since the government does not provide reasonable benefits to the mentally retarded and the benefits of the institutions are limited, those who are rich or who can manage to sustain a basic living hesitate to send a family member to the welfare facilities for the handicapped. Therefore, it can be said that the mentally retarded persons who are admitted to the institutions for the handicapped are only people who have no guardian and are unable to maintain their livelihood.

MENTAL HEALTH HISTORY

From the Yi Dynasty Korea was an agrarian society that depended mostly on agriculture. This continued through the Japanese colonial period to the mid-

1960s, the Third Republic. There were people who suffered mental problems even in agrarian society, but their numbers were few. They were embarrassed by derogatory treatment when they appeared in the community, rather than being treated under mental health policy or services. It can be said that it was a fact that they were dying while living with the ravens at the stack of rice straw or moaning with poverty and exposure to cold weather.

In Korean society, while there were rare cases of mentally deranged people in the earlier agrarian society, these diseases are now increasing because of the population increase, urbanization, industrialization, the conflict of feudalism and the free economy, and the seriousness of social conflict. Also, medical facilities and the numbers of doctors and beds have been increasing. Private organizations have established mental sanatoriums accommodating mental patients and receiving governmental benefits. But in Korean society many mentally deranged people tend to be treated with contempt and are left alone.

In the 1970s and 1980s the social shifts were rapid because of industrialization and urbanization, and Korea experienced increasing mental illness problems due to both psychological conflict and a phenomenon of anomie. Therefore, the Korean government established three national mental hospitals and eight city and provincial mental hospitals and supported seventy-seven mental sanatoriums. In those facilities fifty-eight medical doctors were employed in national facilities, and forty-eight doctors were employed in public facilities. The Korean government provided treatment to patients through 1,950 beds in national mental hospitals and 1,758 beds in public mental hospitals.

Generally, Koreans treat mentally disordered people as abnormal men or women and tend to keep them at a distance. Up to the 1960s Korea had been an agricultural society with fewer people with mental disorders. Therefore, governmental policy had not been conspicuous. Since the 1970s, however, because of accelerated industrialization and urbanization in Korea, the number of patients in the mental health field has increased. Also, the Korean government has taken an interest in social welfare and mental health as the GNP per capita has risen from $82 in 1961 (Economic Planning Board, 1988, p. 397) to reach $2,826 in 1987 (Ministry of Health and Social Affairs, 1987, p. 11). Hence the government built the facilities and placed the personnel, having developed an interest in that policy area. Also, private organizations established mental sanatoriums for mental patients and operated them, receiving governmental supports, and private organizations and religious organizations established a private institute where mental health patients were accommodated and treated. Because Korean society is becoming much more complex and mental patients are increasing, there is another social problem. In 1983 human rights became an issue for patients in the private institutes and brought about recognition of problems related to treatment concerns for mental illness.

Policy considerations arose in the field of mental health through the processes of Korean economic development and national financial growth. Therefore, a more positive mental health policy seems to have developed. In effect, Korea has a greater concern for mental health policy than ever before. Also, Korea began to believe that mental health and physical health were different. Mental health is being treated by establishing private comprehensive hospital psychopathology departments and national and local public mental hospitals and private mental hospitals.

POLICY, ORGANIZATION, AND SERVICES IN THE 1980s AND 1990s

Current Policy Developments

The definition of mental health policy in Korea can be broadly interpreted as including a concern for treatment and rehabilitation and having the characteristic of isolation in mental health facilities. First, the policy for treatment and rehabilitation in the 1990s calls for implementation of a plan that increases the number of national mental hospitals from three (1991) to six and increases the number of doctors and beds from the current fifty-eight doctors and 1,950 beds. Also, the Korean government is implementing a policy to increase the number of public mental hospitals in city and provincial areas from the current eight to fifteen, and to increase the number of doctors to more than the current forty-eight and the number of beds to more than the current 1,758. The Korean government now supports seventy-seven mental sanatoriums that are being turned into formal medical facilities. This policy intent can be seen in articles 6 and 10 of the Mental Health Act, which allows a person who receives a license for establishment of corporate mental health care to establish and operate mental sanatoriums (*Dong-A Ilbo*, 1990, November 13, p. 19).

Second, Korean policy has the characteristic of isolation in mental health facilities. The Korean government and ruling party have prepared a bill and tried to enact it as article 21 concerning legal hospitalization. These articles have been opposed by Korean human rights organizations and mental health science organizations. The articles will be heard in a public hearing. The proposed legal hospitalization article provides that in cases where someone who can be acknowledged as harmful to self or others rejects hospitalization and for whom an agreement of a guardian can not be received, a governor or city mayor, after receiving the diagnosis of two psychiatric specialists, can ask for mental health care facility protection and treatment. The emergency hospitalization article prescribes that in cases where someone is highly likely to injure self or others and the situation is very urgent, after being seen by medical doctors and policemen, he or she can be hospitalized in an emergency.

Of course the younger members of the Korean Association for Neuropsychology, the Medical Doctors' Association for the Practice of Humanism, and the human rights organizations are against these changes, especially the members of the Medical Doctors' Association for the Practice of Humanism. Dr. Byunghoo Kim of Chongno, a neuropsychologist in Seoul, questions whether any legislative members have been in the mental sanatoriums that they intend to acknowledge as medical psychiatric facilities. He opposes the legislative intention of the government, arguing that a mental sanatorium accommodates forty to fifty patients without even one doctor and that patients admitted suffer from violence, surveillance, and animal-like living conditions, like a prison (*Dong-A Ilbo*, 1990, November 13, p. 19). As of 1993 this bill had not been enacted. The future will determine the passage of the bill and its content. However, the Ministry of Health and Social Affairs, which is a major agency in the Korean government, seems to be implementing the policy to increase medical facilities related to mental health. Also, the government and ruling party seem to promote legalization of the use of mental health facilities by enlarging the function of treatment, rehabilitation, and isolation. This policy was enacted after collecting views from the human rights organizations and the Korean Association for Mental Sciences with a tacit understanding that the guidelines of the Korean government will strive to be those of a forward-thinking developed country.

After making this point, we can discuss freely the actions and intentions of the ruling party and why the ruling power has not yet passed the bill that it has tried to enact since the Fifth Republic. It seems that the government now understands that it is a yardstick for the development of Korean democracy. We can see advancement in the level of the Korean people and government by noting the increased attitude toward deliberation and collection of public opinion, without forced passage like that by a totalitarian political power. The author believes that Korea must develop a framework for mental health administration like that of advanced countries through serious review and discussion in enacting a future bill.

It seems difficult for current services to accommodate and treat enough patients. Therefore, it is expected that the Korean government will secure enough financial resources so that mental patients can be treated to return to society as normal persons, more mental hospitals can be established, the number of doctors can be increased and their working conditions can be improved, and the number of beds can be increased as the budget of the Korean government increases (it rose from $32.9 billion [24 trillion, 669.9 billion won] in 1990 to $36.2 billion [27 trillion, 182.5 billion won] in 1991). Also, it is expected that the Mental Health Act currently being promoted will be enacted as law and that the act that passes will promote public health and treat mental diseases with a humanitarian attitude.

Current Organization

The Ministry of Health and Social Affairs provides most of the policy direction, especially through the Hospital Division for mental disabilities, the Management Division for mentally ill persons, the Narcotic Control Division for control of drug addicts, and the Rehabilitation Division for support of mentally ill persons. The medical treatment and management system is supposed to provide for pri-

Table 9.1
**State of the Medical Care System for Mental Patients in Korea as of December
31, 1989**

Division			No. of facilities	No. of beds	%
S p e c i a l	Special mental hospitals	National	3	1,950	
		Public	2	500	
		Private	16	3,920	
B e d s	Dept. of psychiatry in general hospitals		118	4,205	
	Hospitals		229	1,230	
	Public sanatoriums		5	1,058	
	Subtotal		373	12,863	43
	Private sanatoriums		73	17,047	57
	Total		446	29,910	

Source: Division of Hospital Management, Ministry of Health and
Social Affairs, 1989, official document.

mary and secondary treatment. Health centers, consultation offices, and a psychiatrist's office are in charge of the identification of patients, consultation, treatment, and management of outpatients. There are three national mental hospitals, plus national, public, and private special mental hospitals and mental sanatoriums, that provide secondary treatment and are supposed to take charge of rehabilitation, training, and rejoining of patients to society based on respective functions (Ministry of Health and Social Affairs, 1987, p. 167). According to statistics prepared by the Ministry of Health and Social Affairs, there are 10,803 beds for mental patients, and the number of inpatients is 37,698 (Ministry of Health and Social Affairs, 1990, p. 130). Thus there is a great shortage of beds, and conditions are very poor.

Table 9.1 shows that as late as 1989 there were 373 special hospitals that had 12,863 beds and 77 sanatoriums that had 17,047 beds. Approximately 105,000 people were believed to need medical care; therefore, it is difficult to cope with this situation with the current number of beds.

Current Services

In 1989 there were 37,698 inpatients for the 10,803 beds: 5,942 in national hospitals, 4,041 in public hospitals, 19,584 in corporate hospitals, and 8,131 in private mental clinics (hospitals). The total number of mental outpatients was 1,904,703 persons: 235,378 persons served by national hospitals, 209,915 persons by public hospitals, 997,209 persons by corporation hospitals, and 462,201 persons by private clinics (table 9.2).

Among persons who can be treated as mentally disabled are the mentally disordered, the mentally retarded, alcoholics, and drug addicts. Many of these people lead a concentration-camp-like life that is near to maltreatment. The number of inmates at the end of 1989 who were accommodated in concentration camps, not in treatment organizations, was 3,659. Data indicate that 10,000 mentally disabled are in the concentration camp for juvenile vagrants (*Dong-A Ilbo*, 1990, November 13, p. 19). These cases can be seen as maltreatment rather than humanistic treatment for cure. Also, there are approximately 18,000 mentally disabled people who are accommodated in the sanatoriums. In the sanatoriums it is common to accommodate forty to fifty people in a large room without even one doctor. They say that they survive in prisonlike circumstances, enduring animal-like living with cruel violence and surveillance (*Dong-A Ilbo*, 1990, November 13, p. 19).

The mentally ill are dealt with by the Department of Health Administration in the Ministry of Health and Social Affairs and in the various levels of mental hospitals under the following laws and ordinances for regulation and services for mental diseases:

The Law of the Korean Institute of Health and Social Affairs (enacted December 31, 1975) to do research on public health, medical and social welfare, and population problems.

The Narcotics Control Law (enacted April 23, 1957) to control narcotics, and the Hemp Management Act (enacted April 7, 1976) to contribute to the promotion of public health with proper management to prevent the outflow of hemp.

The Positive Psychiatric Medicine Management Act (enacted December 28, 1979) to prevent, through proper management, health and mental health harm from the misuse and overuse of positive psychiatric medicine, and the Positive Psychiatric Medicine Management Act, Ordinances (order of the Ministry of Health and Social Affairs, 654) (enacted August 28, 1980).

The Society Protection Act (enacted December 18, 1980), for people who need to have special education and treatment or have the danger of a recurring disease such as mental handicap, drug addiction, and alcoholism, and also those who commit a crime. This act is for the purpose of returning them to society and protecting society. The Society Protection Ordinances (enacted December 31, 1980) provide treatment and protection in the treatment and protection center (Kongju City) for people who cannot be punished by Criminal Law, article 10, paragraph 1, or who commit a crime that is subject to more than imprisonment,

Table 9.2
Activities of Hospitals with Mental Health Services in Korea, 1989

	No. of Beds	Inpatients		Daily Average No. of Inpatients	Average Length of Stay	Outpatient		Bed Utilization Rate (%)
		No. of Inpatients	No. of Bed days			No. of Outpatient Visits	Average/Day	
Mental	10,803	37,698	3,541,139	9,702	94	1,904,703	5,218	89.8
National	2,246	5,942	581,462	1,593	98	235,378	645	70.9
Public	731	4,041	242,564	665	60	209,915	575	91.0
Corporation	4,599	19,584	2,088,221	5,721	107	997,209	2,732	124.4
Private	3,227	8,131	628,892	1,723	77	462,201	1,266	53.4

Source: Ministry of Health and Social Affairs, 1990, pp. 130-131.

Table 9.3
Plan to Secure Professional Staffs in Korea

				Above: required Below: being secured	
Division/year	1987	1988	1989	1990	1991
Psychiatrist	695	800	906	1,012	1,120
	656	776	896	1,016	1,136
Mental nurse	284	341	386	417	443
	178	248	318	388	458
Mental nurse assistant	284	341	386	417	443
	178	248	318	388	458
Mental social worker	119	140	159	171	182
	30	60	90	130	180
Rehabilitating therapist	119	140	159	171	182
	30	60	90	130	180
Mental sanitary staff	89	103	115	120	125
	20	40	70	100	130

Source: Ministry of Health and Social Affairs, 1987, pp. 169-170.

or who, by the regulation of article 10, paragraph 2, can have a reduced sentence, or who have the habit of overusing a positive psychiatric medicine or hemp, or who eat, inhale, smoke, or inject drugs, or who, when addicted to them, commit a crime and are subject to more than imprisonment.

Last, in terms of Korean mental health services, there are few private organizations for the mentally ill, the mentally retarded, mentally disordered offenders, alcoholics, and drug addicts.

Mental Health Personnel and Treatment

The sixth five-year plan (Ministry of Health and Social Affairs, 1986) not only calls for establishing more mental health institutions, but for creating supportive professional staffs and studying mental diseases. The process of securing professional staffs is shown in table 9.3. The 1991 target called for 1,136 psychiatrists of a required 1,120; 458 mental nurses of a required 443; 458 mental nurse assistants of a required 443; 180 mental social workers of a required 182; 180 rehabilitation therapists of a required 182; and 130 mental sanitary staff of a required 125 (Ministry of Health and Social Affairs, 1987, pp. 169–170). As of March 1993 there were 941 psychiatrists and 644 neurologists. The standards for personnel call for 1 mental nurse assistant per 100 persons in the medical care facilities, 1 mental nurse assistant per 70 persons in the hospitals, 1 social worker and 1 rehabilitation therapist per 200 persons in medical care facilities, and 1 mental sanitary staff person per patient in medical care facilities and hospitals.

Besides reinforcing the management of mental diseases, drug support should be made available for registered patients, and aftercare should be made available for discharged patients. Also, in the case of medical care facilities, public health psychiatrists will have to be forced to go to community treatment facilities, and inhumane actions will have to be actively rooted out by administrative direction. Worn-out medical care facilities should be repaired continuously, and patients should be moved to areas with good healing environments (Ministry of Health and Social Affairs, 1987, p. 170). At the same time, to improve private mental health care facilities, labor expenses and operational expenses for the seventy-four mental care facilities that are working as social welfare corporations should be supported. To accomplish this, the government is planning to protect the treatment of mental patients by supporting the reinforcement of regulations requiring repair of worn-out facilities. In addition, mental sanatoriums should work jointly with mental hospitals for establishing rehabilitation training to increase the social adaptability of patients. This will be required for public sanatoriums, which are going to be built in each city and province.

PUBLIC POLICY PROCESS

In countries with federal systems there is a national or federal government and state governments and local governments, and each government operates its own administration. But the Korean government has a unitary system with a central government at the national level. There also are local governments: a metropolitan government (a direct-control city), provincial governments, city governments, and county governments, which are self-governing bodies that exist nominally. The foundation of self-government lies with the process of proper election procedures, and the head of a self-governing body and local assembly persons are elected by that procedure (Rhee, 1989, p. 14).

Although the head of the central government and members of the National Assembly are elected in Korea by the people, there is no assembly for a metropolitan government (a direct-control city) or the provincial governments. The heads of these governments are not elected by the people, but are appointed by the president of the central government. The administrative activities are conducted by receiving directions and mandates from the central government. Therefore, there are not many independent policies or administrations at the metropolitan and provincial government levels. There are cases where the plans of the metropolitan government and the provincial governments can be implemented after receiving the central government's approval. There are limits to the policies at the provincial and city levels. Mental health policies can only be implemented under the direction of the central government.

Under the current conditions the policy criteria set by the central government do not consider provincial uniqueness in program plans and implementation (Rhee, 1989, p. 291). Rhee believes that the administrative function of the central government should primarily focus on concerns relating to poverty, housing, education, and medical policy, which are policy problems for social welfare. The administrative function of provincial governments should be concerned with child welfare, welfare for the aged, welfare for women and girls, and the welfare of the handicapped (Rhee, 1989, p. 289). But local governments have difficulty in planning and implementation for the future due to dependence on the directions of the central government. They only concentrate their efforts on authoritative control and surveillance of residents.

In the area of mental health policy, the central government establishes and operates the national mental hospitals and sanatoriums and establishes policies regarding general problems of mental diseases. Long-term care causes the family economy to worsen and more often than not leads to bankruptcy and loss of the family's home. Professional care is often avoided because of social morals and biases, and incidents of abandonment of mental patients sometimes occur (Ministry of Health and Social Affairs, 1986, p. 166).

There are only about 16,950 secure beds. The number of beds needed in 1990 was 36,000, so the number of beds is insufficient. This current condition may be the cause of the existence of nonlicensed facilities. There also is a need for a professional research organization that can be responsible for comprehensive research, investigation, and educational training of professionals. Basic programs for the rehabilitation of mental patients and their return to society are insufficient. Also, medical treatment is poor, and there are many cases where there are insufficient skills among facility workers and where rehabilitation facilities are dilapidated (Ministry of Health and Social Affairs, 1987, p. 167). To improve these conditions, the actions of nonprofit organizations should be increased and the support from the private sector should be enhanced.

The judiciary has very little involvement in mental health issues. Regarding questions of mental illness in adjudication, the judiciary only takes mental disability into account based on the evaluation of a psychiatrist. But the executive department is very involved in mental health. The Hospital Management Division in the Korean Ministry of Health and Social Affairs prepares policies about mental illness and operates and manages national and public mental hospitals. The Rehabilitation Division provides a livelihood and medical protection for targeted mentally retarded persons, while the Narcotic Control Division manages and treats drug abuse. The Ministry of Health and Social Affairs in the Korean government has major responsibility for the management of mental patients and prepares various policies regarding them. It is trying to build a management system so that it can smoothly achieve all needed measures from early identification of patients to cure, rehabilitation training, and further management after return to society.

As discussed in the section on services, Korea has many more mental patients

Table 9.4
Numbers of Patients and Plans to Expand Facilities in Korea

Division/year		1987	1988	1989	1990	1991
Total population (thousands)		42,383	42,965	43,541	44,117	44,690
Mental patients (thousands)		424	431	436	443	449
Patients entering the hospital (thousands)		69	70	71	72	73
Required beds		34,500	35,000	35,500	36,000	36,500
Plan to secure:	Total beds	23,960	28,240	32,020	34,450	36,500
	Special beds	10,460	13,740	15,520	16,950	18,300
	Sanitorium beds	13,500	14,500	16,500	17,500	18,200

Source: Ministry of Health and Social Affairs, 1987, p. 169.

than psychiatric beds. To solve this problem, the government plans to add 36,500 beds, which are enough beds for about half the 73,000 patients entering the hospitals in 1991.

Korea approaches mental health policy through centralized planning. A plan calls for 18,300 beds to be secured as special beds and 18,200 beds to be expanded in medical care welfare facilities (see table 9.4). The necessary budget will be allotted to both the public and private sectors. National mental hospitals have been constructed in Seoul, Jeonla, Youngnam, and Kangwon provinces, and one should be completed in Kyungki province by the end of 1993. The plan calls for 2,907 beds in public mental hospitals, 2,380 beds in public sanatoriums, 3,500 beds in private hospitals subsidized by the government, 3,045 beds in private mental hospitals, and 4,055 beds in departments of psychiatry in general hospitals. In the case of the private sector, this will be accomplished by induced voluntary participation, which makes it a duty to establish a department of psychiatry in a general hospital that has more than 300 beds, and by loan support (Ministry of Health and Social Affairs, 1987, p. 166).

SPECIAL POLICY ISSUES

The Mentally Ill and the Mentally Retarded

In Korea the mentally ill and the mentally retarded are perceived differently. Mental retardation is considered to be less serious than mental illness. Mental retardation is seen not as dangerous but as a state of mental deficiency. This is generally accepted in Korea, whereas mental illness is avoided and felt to be very threatening. But mental retardation, while not considered dangerous, is ridiculed. Programs for mental retardation are administered through the Department of Rehabilitation in the Ministry of Health and Social Affairs in the Korean national government. The Korean government defined 907,000 people (2.16 percent of the total population), as of the end of December 1989, as the target for inpatient treatment for mental retardation. Korea is trying to develop 3,090 beds, for a total of 33,000 beds which would still be short of the goal of 33,500 beds by 1991, the end of the sixth five-year plan for economic and social development. For this, it is trying to construct or enlarge the buildings at six sites of mental hospitals, to push the construction program for public mental sanatoriums of one for each city and province, and to make efforts to get comprehensive hospitals that have more than 300 beds to establish psychiatry departments.

Some 5,346 mentally retarded persons are accommodated in 39 institutions, and 1,727 mentally retarded persons are accommodated in the institutions for homeless people (Ministry of Health and Social Affairs, 1990, pp. 130–131, 184–185). It is thought that the actual number of mentally retarded is higher than reported cases, because it is customary to hide a problem of mental retardation rather than to make it public. Korean cultural tradition and social perception encourage this. Therefore, improvement and participation in the management of mental disabilities should be approached gradually, step by step, and continuously. This requires the production and distribution of public information media, education, and consultation projects to enlighten the public (Moon, 1989, p. 90).

Since December 1988 the Korean government has received registrations for mentally retarded persons to receive welfare benefits for the handicapped. They are classified into three categories for registration: IQ 30–49 for the first class, IQ 50–70 for the second class, and IQ 70 or more for the third class. But many cases were missed, and people who were wealthy did not register in order to avoid public exposure. It was estimated in 1985 that there were 79,000 cases of mental retardation.

The Korean government established the Korean Research Institute of Health and Social Affairs at Bulkwang-dong, Seoul, in 1985 and gave it funding for research projects to investigate the actual conditions of mental retardation. It classified mentally retarded persons into two target groups: one for livelihood protection and one for medical assistance. Those in the first class (IQ 30–49) were targeted for livelihood protection and medical assistance and were given the living assistance payment, a monthly payment of $30 regardless of age. Under the medical assistance policy the government provided free medical care for the first class with expenses to be defrayed out of the National Treasury. The government also assisted the second class (IQ 50–70), which is supposed to be self-supporting, with medical assistance to be defrayed out of the National Treasury.

The mentally retarded receive benefits under the Medical Protection Act, the Livelihood Protection Act, and the Welfare Law for the Handicapped. The

Welfare Law for the Handicapped was enacted December 30, 1989, to contribute to the security of living for the handicapped. It supplies 79,000 (1985) mentally retarded people with an IQ of less than 70 and other physically handicapped people with medical care, training, protection, education, promotion of employment, and payment of a money allowance. The Promotion Law of Employment for the Handicapped (enacted January 13, 1990) and its Ordinance (enacted December 8, 1990) assign an obligation to companies who have more than 300 workers to employ handicapped employees as 1 percent of their employees in 1991, 1.6 percent in 1992, and 2 percent in 1993. The Medical Protection Act (enacted December 31, 1977), its Ordinances (enacted May 23, 1978), and its rules (enacted September 1, 1978) promote social welfare and public health by implementing a full payment or a partial payment for people such as the mentally retarded who have no ability to maintain a livelihood. The Livelihood Protection Act (enacted December 31, 1982) and its Ordinances (enacted December 30, 1983) provide payments to people who have no working ability because of mental and physical handicap, that is, a livelihood protection allowance for their maintenance.

The Mentally Ill and Substance Abuse

Drinking alcohol is not a major problem in Korea. In extreme cases people who drink heavily are isolated from the public as alcoholics, and if they commit a crime, they are punished in criminal cases. Illegal drug use is forbidden. The Narcotics Control Law was established in 1957 (Jo, 1991, pp. 3241–3256). The production and distribution of drugs is prohibited, and the treatment of people with a drug addiction is limited to professionals who have licenses.

Alcoholics and drug addicts are regulated by the Narcotics Control Law, the Hemp Management Act, and the Positive Psychiatric Medicine Management Act. People who commit a crime who are mentally and physically handicapped, drug addicts, or alcoholics are supposed to receive a disposition of treatment and protection and are accommodated in the treatment and protection center.

The Mentally Disordered Offender

Even in Korea there are criminally mentally deranged people. As an example, on January 13, 1991, in the living room of a business center apartment in Dangsan-dong, Youngdeungpo-Ku, in Seoul, Mr. Choi (eighteen years old, a senior in high school) stabbed his father in the stomach to death with a dagger thirty centimeters long with the intention of killing an evil spirit in his father's body. He also stabbed the neighbors, Mrs. Aeja Lee (thirty years old) and Mrs. Sookhee Lee (thirty-one years old) in the ribs and knee (*Dong-A Ilbo*, 1991, January 14, p. 15).

In another case, Ms. Bunam Kim (thirty years old), who suffered from symptoms of delusions of persecution due to a rape twenty years previously by Mr.

Backwan Song (fifty-five years old), stabbed Mr. Song to death. A psychiatric evaluation was requested (*Dong-A Ilbo*, 1991, January 31, p. 14). In that case, if the result of the psychiatric evaluation proves to be mental illness, it will fall under the circumstances covered by Criminal Law, article 10, paragraphs 1 and 2. A pleading for using this article of the law is supposed to be taken by the attorney. It is known that the human rights organizations and the Academy of Psychiatrists also are interested in this affair and may make defense efforts.

In Korea forensic problems for mentally disordered offenders are covered under the Korean Criminal Law, article 10. Paragraphs 1 and 2 stipulate that "those who are mentally and physically handicapped are regarded as persons without legal capacity, and, therefore, are not punished. Those who have a weak mind and body are sentenced to a less severe sentence than a normal person and have limited legal liability" (Jo, 1991, pp. 1801–1802). Accordingly, those who have lost their mental and physical health due to a mental disorder are not punished when they commit crimes, but those who are weak in mind and body, decreased remarkably in their decision-making ability and actions (Jin, 1985), but who have a less severe mental handicap, receive a lower sentence for the crime they committed. That is the intent of the law expressed in the text (Japanese Supreme Court's Judicial Precedent, 1931).

Korea has a system of treatment and protection for maintenance of public security and protection against crimes that serves as a substitute for and complement to punishment by accommodating those who are mentally disabled by not punishing them even though they can be dangerous to society. This law also covers those who have a weak mind and body, for whom enlightenment and improvement cannot be accomplished by punishment alone, for example, the drug addicts and alcoholics, who must get treatment, correction, and enlightenment simultaneously. This system was designed to isolate these people, to protect society from them, and to return them to society after training and social rehabilitation (*Bulletin of Treatment and Protection*, 1990, p. 1; *Collection of Criminal Law*, 1990, Articles 8–9, p. 2047). It is impossible to treat and enlighten these people by punishment or correctional theory alone, in spite of increasing crime rates and brutality.

The number of those who had been treated and protected from the end of 1980, when the Social Protection Law was enacted, to 1989 was 866 persons. In 1989 the number of inmates under the Social Protection Law was 506. Also, the number of persons under executors was 105. Those under executors are almost always persons with more severe psychiatric disorders. As can be seen in table 9.5, the number of inmates is increasing yearly.

Deinstitutionalization

Korea is in the process of building more hospitals and has not experienced deinstitutionalization.

Table 9.5
Numbers of Persons under Treatment and Protection in Korea

Year	1981	1982	1983	1984	1985	1986	1987	1988	1989
Inmates	51	122	203	253	305	357	410	472	506
Executors	55	88	115	106	110	78	85	113	105

Source: Ministry of Justice, 1990, p. 133.

Table 9.6
Investment Plan for Mentally Ill Management in Korea

Program		(In thousands of dollars)					
		Total budget	1987 budget	1988 budget	1989 budget	1990 budget	1991 budget
Mentally Ill Management	Total	235,937	50,585	65,502	43,011	38,475	38,359
	National	116,045	21,292	23,766	24,721	24,134	22,132
	Local	33,846	5,745	6,238	7,857	6,200	7,806
	Private	86,041	23,548	35,498	10,433	8,141	8,421

Source: Ministry of Health and Social Affairs, 1987, pp. 250-251.

Funding Issues

The Korean government's budget has been increasing every year. In 1987 the government's budget was $21,059,333,000. In 1991 the government's budget was $36,243,333,000, and in 1992, the government's budget was about $44,000,000,000. But the investment budget for management of the mentally ill, which includes the mentally ill beds plan, the mental sanatoriums facilities plan, the mental sanatoriums management support plan, and the National Mental Health Institute, is not enough. In the Sixth Socio-economic Development 5 Year Plan: Health and Social Affairs, 1987–1991, the Korean government allocated a total of $235,930,000: from the National Treasury, $116,040,000; from the local treasuries, $33,848,000; and from the private sector, $86,042,000. For example, in 1991 the government budget was $36,243,333,000, but the budget for management of the mentally ill from the National Treasury was $38,360,000, that is, about 0.1 percent (table 9.6).

Consumer Rights

Consumer rights are not reflected in mental health policy. Treatment and protection are emphasized, but there are not enough laws for the protection of rights for the mentally ill, the mentally retarded, mentally disordered offenders, alcoholics, and drug addicts. However, doctors and professors who belong to the Association for Psychiatry make extensive efforts for them and make recommendations to the government and the National Assembly regarding medical treatment and protective measures for psychiatric surgery, electroconvulsive methods, psychiatric pharmacology, physical restrictions, and behavior modification.

Mentally disabled people are involved in labor activities under conditions of slavish subordination. Sexual rights and communication rights are not generally restricted, but there are some aspects of restriction in order to receive treatment under a restricted environment based on protection. Mentally ill persons have the right to vote until they are sentenced by a court, after medical certification by a psychiatrist. The Korean Neuropsychological Association has submitted recommendations to the National Assembly to strengthen protections.

CONCLUSIONS AND DISCUSSION

Although Korean mental health policy falls short of that of advanced countries, Korean bureaucrats who are in charge of mental health policy say that Korea has a fairly good system compared to those of other developing countries. In professional mental hospitals Korea has 12,863 beds in 373 organizations that are national hospitals, public hospitals, private hospitals, departments of psychiatry in comprehensive corporate hospitals, public sanatoriums, and the like. The number of hospitals was not enough in 1989, but they were well equipped. There also are 17,047 beds in 73 sites of private sanatoriums, where the conditions are poor. There are also some problems due to a shortage of doctors and the methods of management and operation.

Since the control of alcohol and drugs began in the 1950s and the law regarding their regulation was enacted, there is no possibility of having the dangerous phenomenon of more widespread drugs, as in some Latin American countries. However, even now, with regard to the overuse of drugs, the police and public prosecutors are enforcing the regulation and controlling to prevent this. Also, there are some concerns for mentally disordered offenders under the Criminal Law, since the government accommodates them in the treatment and protection centers for medical treatment. There are also problems in that mentally disordered and mentally retarded persons are accommodated in the juvenile vagrant concentration camp, and that they are detained and accommodated in private sanatoriums without any doctors who can treat them. These facilities should be improved.

Even though government payment of the living allowances for mentally retarded persons is symbolic, it is the foundation for the development of future policy and administration. The author hopes to promote measures for treatment and a guaranteed livelihood for these people, and hopes that cultural and economic development will contribute to a policy of treatment and protection of livelihood for those with mental disorders.

What is hoped for the future is that there will be public enlightenment enhancing the recognition of the need for treatment and management of mental disorders. To summarize the policy statements of professor Ho Young Lee, a psychiatrist at the Medical School of Yonsei University, and the investigation report done by professor Ik Lyun Moon, of the School of Public Health, Seoul National University, we can infer that there should be enactment of a new Mental Health Law, reconsideration of the low priority of mental health programs, integration of mental health programs and general health programs, construction of health management information systems for local communities, and strengthening of mental health education (Moon, 1989, p. 105). Especially, the health management information system should be used as a means to manage effectively and handle efficiently patients with mental disorders by dividing and coordinating the series of activities that include early identification of mentally disordered patients, consultation, treatment, rehabilitation training, and further management after return to society based on the competency level of each administrative unity and the technical level of medical organizations (Moon, 1989, pp. 105–106).

The author believes that before Korea adopts the construction of a major health program, it needs to search for a realistic management system and implement a model program for mental health. The framework of the program, the implementation unit, should be categorized according to the level of government (city and county), but the patient treatment system should be categorized according to the level and area of medical treatment. Also, withdrawal of mentally handicapped from the concentration camp should be pursued steadily, the mental health program should be included in the primary health program, and health centers should be the main body for primary service provision in such a program. A person in charge of mental health should be stationed in mental health centers, and by making this the main treatment point, localization of the mental health program should be enhanced. Many medical facilities should be changed so that a patient system based on level of care can be established. An effective patient system should be established with primary treatments by public health doctors, mental health workers, health treatment workers, and private psychiatrists; secondary treatment by the hospitalized health centers, the sanatoriums, the hospitals of local corporations, and the departments of psychiatry in the comprehensive hospitals; and tertiary treatment by the national mental hospitals, the university hospitals, and the large-sized mental hospitals.

REFERENCES

Bulletin of treatment and protection. (1990). Seoul, Korea: Office of Treatment and Protection, Ministry of Justice.

Collection of criminal law. (1990). "Social Protection Law," Articles 8–9. Seoul, Korea: Ministry of Justice.

Dong-A Ilbo [Newspaper]. (1990, November 13). Seoul, Korea, p. 19.

Dong-A Ilbo [Newspaper]. (1990, December 17). Seoul, Korea, p. 3.

Dong-A Ilbo [Newspaper]. (1991, January 14). Seoul, Korea, p. 15.

Dong-A Ilbo [Newspaper]. (1991, January 31). Seoul, Korea, p. 14.

Economic Planning Board. (1988). *Korean economics 1988.* Seoul, Korea: Economic Planning Board.

Facts about Korea (Revised and condensed edition). (1988). Seoul, Korea: Hollym Corporation.

HankyuRae Shinmun [Newspaper]. (1990, December 21). Seoul, Korea, p. 3.

Japanese Supreme Court's Judicial Precedent. (1931, December 3). *Collection of Criminal Laws, 10*(12), Japanese year Sowha 6, p. 682.

Jin, G. H. (1985). A study on the protest of mentally ill. *Journal of Industrial Management, 3,* 55–58.

Jo, S. W. (1991). *1991 code of laws.* Seoul, Korea: Hyunamsa Publisher.

Kim, C. B. (1989, July). *Administrative modernization in Korea: Institutions, strategies of socio-economic progress, its problems and alternatives.* Paper presented at the Twenty-First International Congress of Administrative Sciences. Marrakech, Morocco.

Kim, H. E. (1985). *Facts about Korea.* Seoul: Hollym Corporation.

Kim, J. S. (1988). *Basic research for management of mental illness and adult's disease.* Seoul, Korea: Ministry of Health and Social Affairs.

Korea Times. (1989, March 8). Seoul, Korea.

Ministry of Justice. (1990). *Yearbook of justice 1990.* Seoul, Korea: Ministry of Justice.

Ministry of Health and Social Affairs. (1987). *The sixth socio-economic development 5 year plan: Plan of health and social affairs, 1987–1991.* Seoul, Korea: Ministry of Health and Social Affairs.

Ministry of Health and Social Affairs. (1990). *Yearbook of health and social statistics 1990, 36.* Seoul, Korea: Ministry of Health and Social Affairs.

Moon, O. L. (1981). *Research of Korean adult's disease.* Seoul, Korea: Ministry of Health and Social Affairs.

Moon, O. L. (Ed.). (1989). *Research on management of state of contracting a mental disease.* Seoul, Korea: Ministry of Health and Social Affairs.

National Bureau of Statistics. (1988). *Korea statistical yearbook 1988, 35.* Seoul, Korea: Economic Planning Board.

Organization chart of government 1991. Seoul, Korea: Ministry of Government Administration.

Park, Y. H. (1990). *Financial administration.* Seoul, Korea: Dasan Publishing Co.

Rhee, C. I. (1989). *Korean local self-government.* Seoul, Korea: Barkyoungsa Publishing Co.

10

The Netherlands

Silvia Evers, Meindert J. Haveman, Curd M.V.W. Jacobs, and Rob V. Bijl

OVERVIEW

The Netherlands is a relatively small (41,574 square kilometers) and densely populated country (nearly 15 million inhabitants in 1989) situated in Western Europe. In the north and west it borders on the North Sea and in the east and south on Germany and Belgium. In the Netherlands 26 percent of all inhabitants are nineteen or younger and 13 percent are sixty-five or older. Of the total population, 4 percent are nonnative, with Turkish and Moroccan people as the largest groups. In addition, a substantial part of this population consists of former inhabitants of the former Dutch colonies, such as Surinam (Dutch Guiana) and the Dutch Antilles.

The Kingdom of the Netherlands is a constitutional and hereditary monarchy with a parliament and a democratically chosen government. The executive power lies in the Crown, while the legislative power is exercised by the Crown and both houses of parliament. The Staten-Generaal consists of the First Chamber and the Second Chamber. The members of the First Chamber are elected indirectly, the members of the Second Chamber directly. The government and the members of the Second Chamber can introduce a bill. The Second Chamber also has the right of amendment. The members of the First Chamber can only pass or refuse a bill without the right of amendment. In the Netherlands there are about ten political parties that have a delegation in the First and Second Chambers. The three main parties are the Christian Democratic Appeal, the Labor Party, and the Liberal Party.

Table 10.1
Patients/Clients in Mental Health Care in the Netherlands

Institution	Admissions[1]	Clients, 31-12-1989
General psychiatric hospitals	30,050	21,680
Psychiatric hospitals for children and adolescents	370	570
Residential institutions for addicts	5,910	650
Forensic psychiatric institutions	200	370
Total psychiatric hospitals	36,530	23,270
Psychiatric departments of general hospitals	16,960	1,920
Psychosocial treatment centers	3,076	338
Psychogeriatric nursing homes	12,000	23,620
Medical children's homes	540	630
Total inpatient care	68,106	49,778
Sheltered homes	780	3,250
Psychiatric day-care centers	7,520	4,610
Psychogeriatric day-care centers	4,260	2,940
Medical children's day-care centers	1,240	2,010
Total semiresidential care	13,800	12,810
Regional Institutes for Outpatient Mental Health Care	216,800	203,540
Outpatient centers for addicts	19,000	29,550
Outpatient centers of psychiatric hospitals	41,490	unknown
Outpatient psychiatric centers of general hospitals	35,050	unknown
Total outpatient care	312,340	

[1] Number of patients who applied for care during 1989.
Source: Jacobs & Bijl, 1991.

EXTENT OF THE PROBLEM

As can be seen in table 10.1, as of January 1, 1990, the Netherlands had about 49,800 patients in inpatient mental health services (about 33.3 permillage of the total population). In semiresidential mental health care there were about 12,800. In outpatient settings there were over 203,500 persons in care with the Regional Institutes for Outpatient Mental Health Care (Regionaal Instelling voor de Ambulante Geestelijke Gezondheidsorg, or RIAGG); about 29,600 patients were in the care of the Outpatient Centers for Addicts (Consultatiebureau voor Alcohol en Drugs). During 1989, 41,500 patients were referred to the outpatient centers of psychiatric hospitals and 35,100 patients to outpatient psychiatric centers of general hospitals (Jacobs & Bijl, 1991).

Since the 1980s there has been a stabilization in the number of patients staying

Table 10.2
Numbers of Patients with a First Psychiatric Diagnosis under Treatment in General Psychiatric Hospitals in the Netherlands, 1989

Diagnosis[1]	Total Number of Patients	Percentage
Dementias	692	3.2
Other organic conditions	1,034	4.8
Schizophrenias	6,563	30.4
Affective psychoses	3,029	14.0
Other psychoses	2,458	11.4
Neurotic conditions	2,423	11.2
Personality disorders	1,939	9.0
Alcohol psychoses/alcohol dependency syndrome	1,106	5.1
Drug psychoses/drug dependence	188	0.9
Nondependent abuse of drugs	127	0.6
Special syndromes	624	2.9
Conditions of childhood and adolescence	173	0.8
Mental retardation	876	4.1
Others	365	1.6
Total	21,597	100.0

[1] The data may vary from other figures because of the differences in definitions used.
Source: *National Inpatient Case-register for Mental Health (PIGG)*, 1990.

in general psychiatric hospitals. Since 1980 both admission and discharge rates have increased about 30 percent. Whereas the number of short-stay patients has increased in the last decade, the number of long-stay patients (more than one year) has slowly decreased. In 1989, 30 percent of the patients under treatment in general psychiatric hospitals were diagnosed as schizophrenics, 14 percent had affective psychoses, 11 percent had other psychoses, and 11 percent had neurotic conditions (see table 10.2).

In 1988, 1,670 suicides were registered (Central Bureau of Statistics [CBS], 1989). Divorced men and widowers were the most likely to commit suicide. In 37 percent of the cases, suicide was committed by the means of hanging or strangling.

MENTAL HEALTH HISTORY

Mental health services in the Netherlands originated with individual charity and governmental aid to the poor (Breemer ter Steege, 1983). Under this framework the forerunners of the psychiatric institutions came into being: the lunatic asylums, detention homes for lunatics and vagrants, and other facilities. During this development the key organization was in the hands of the Protestant and Catholic churches, although later other charitable bodies became involved (Van der Grinten, 1985). In the latter half of the last century more and more lunatics came to be regarded as ill persons with possibilities for treatment.

The Insanity Act (Krankzinnigenwet) of 1884 regulated the governmental supervision of the existing institutions and the care of mentally disordered persons outside these institutions. The purpose of this act was to consider insane people as patients for whom hospital care had to be created. The conviction that psychiatric patients benefit from medical treatment played an important role in the creation of this act. The provincial governments were made responsible for the provision of sufficient nursing capacity, while the municipal governments were charged with the obligation of meeting the costs of institutionalization. In those days psychiatric patients, as well as other mentally handicapped and mentally ill offenders who are nowadays put under hospital restriction, were treated in the same psychiatric hospitals (Romme, 1984). These institutions were situated far away from the urban areas. Later, different institutions were established for these three groups of patients. In 1879 the first institutions for the mentally ill were founded, and after World War II (1945) the first patients were admitted to forensic psychiatric institutions.

Nonresidential mental health services for psychiatric patients outside the hospitals were started in the beginning of this century. This nonresidential care was a matter of charity and had little to do with a medical approach. At the end of the 1920s a start was made when nonresidential services of psychiatric institutions were replaced by facilities for psychiatric pre- and postinstitutional care (Breemer ter Steege, 1983). Before World War II the large cities had set up social psychiatric services, with a staff consisting of social psychiatrists and nurses who had received social psychiatric training.

Organized aid for alcoholism commenced in the 1930s through private initiative (Breemer ter Steege, 1983). This type of aid immediately acquired an additional function in the area of rehabilitation as a result of the fact that alcoholics often tend to infringe upon the law. The outpatient centers for addicts further developed after World War II. These bureaus focused on both the physical phenomena that go hand in hand with addiction to certain drugs and the psychic problems that constitute part of the addictive behavior and underlying social problems. The staff mainly consisted of social workers and nurses, with the cooperation of psychologists, physicians, and psychiatrists.

An examination of history makes it obvious that one should not expect the services for the mentally ill in the Netherlands to be very structured and to be coordinated with one another. The Dutch mental health system is often seen as a patchwork quilt. Over the last twenty to twenty-five years there has been a gradual organization of the different mental health services. Because of the diversity of mental health services, the accessibility and the monitoring of these services were very minimal for both patients and financial investors. In the 1970s several acts were introduced by means of which the government tried to put a check on the proliferation of mental health care facilities. The Hospital Facilities Act (Wet Ziekenhuisvoorzieningen, or WZV) demands a provincial plan that includes the number of beds that are approved by the government. The health care structure paper (*Structuurnota Gezondheidszorg*, 1974) stimulated coherence and the planning of mental health care facilities.

The ideas of the 1970s (Schnabel, 1985) have changed the concept of mental health. The antipsychiatry and deinstitutionalization movements have pleaded for better mental health aid. Better help is mostly understood to mean no involuntary admission, reduction of the length of stay inside the hospital to a period as short as possible, use of small institutions near the patient's home (regionalization), the use of psychotropic drugs as little as possible, a division between residential and treatment functions, more emphasis on training than on treatment, and democratic social relationships with mature and independent patients.

Since the 1970s there has also been a strong increase in the attention that society, politics, and the government pay to mental health (Schnabel, 1985). The legal position of the psychiatric patient and the reorganization of psychiatry have played a major part in this change. Psychiatry has also been influenced by the antipsychiatry and the deinstitutionalization movements. In this period the ideas that "everyone is a little bit mad" and that "nobody should be put away in institutions" became much stronger. There was a growing dislike of biologic psychiatry and psychotropic drugs. In mental health care there was a strong differentiation between the different kinds of care for psychiatric, mentally retarded, and forensic patients. The patients' movement and patients' associations became much stronger, and psychiatric patients were considered as serious partners in negotiations. Before the 1970s patients were powerless and vulnerable. This period led to the installation of patients' councils in general mental hospitals and the assignment of mediators for patients.

POLICY, ORGANIZATION, AND SERVICES IN THE 1980s AND 1990s

Current Policy Developments

The Netherlands has been faced with two major problems. The health care facilities were not attuned to one another, and the diversity of services made it difficult for patients and caregivers to decide what kind of care was best. The second problem involved the continuously growing size of mental health care.

In the 1970s and the 1980s the government tried to restructure mental health care. Various governmental principles played a role in the creation of new mental health services. Through regionalization and small-scale facilities an attempt was made to make mental health care accessible for everyone. By means of coordination and integration an attempt was made to concentrate all knowledge available at one place. A new development is case management, where the individual patient has his or her own social worker. On the individual level, the patient is more frequently seen as a serious partner, with his or her own rights. Through reallocation of budgets, simplification of legislation, and decentralization, the government is trying to reform mental health care.

Current Organization

There are numerous acts pertaining directly or indirectly to mental health care in the Netherlands. It can be said that they refer to four parties: the client or patient, professionals and other service providers, mental health care facilities, and financing (health insurance) (Bauduin, 1988). The most important act dealing with the patient is the Insanity Act of 1884, which, with some modifications, is still in force. The act deals with two main subjects: (1) governmental supervision of mental health care and (2) involuntary admission and inpatient stay.

The most important acts dealing with the availability of facilities are the Hospital Facilities Act (Wet Ziekenhuisvoorzieningen, or WZV) and the Health Care Charges Act (Wet Tarieven Gezondheidszorg, or WTG). The hospital Facilities Act is of major importance for residential health care, as it regulates, among other things, the construction of psychiatric hospitals. The Health Care Charges Act regulates the salaries of nurses, budgets, and other tariffs. This act covers not only residential but also semiresidential and nonresidential care.

By far the greater part of the mental health services (nearly 70 percent) is financed through national and private health insurance. In the Netherlands there are various forms of medical insurance: the Health Insurance Act (Ziekenfondswet, or ZFW) and the Exceptional Medical Expenses Act (Algemene Wet Bijzondere Ziektekosten, or AWBZ). People who are not covered by the Health Insurance Act can take private health care insurance.

There are a number of other acts dealing with social insurance, such as the Industrial Disability Act (Wet op de Arbeidsongeschiktheidsverzekering, or WAO), which provides people who are unfit to work with an income. In addition to these statutory regulations, various kinds of care are also financed by nonstatutory subsidies (about 5 percent) granted by national, provincial, or municipal authorities. Another source of health care funding in the Netherlands is the contribution of the insured persons themselves.

One of the main government agencies involved in mental health care is the Medical Inspectorate for Mental Health (Geneeskundige Inspectie voor de Geestelijke Volksgezondheid, or GIGV), which supervises the quality of mental health care. It is sometimes very difficult for the inspectorate to accomplish this task, mainly because there is a shortage of regional inspectors and other staff. Another obstacle is the absence of standardized methods of supervision and clear norms for medical/psychiatric practice (Brook, 1987). In general, the role of the central and local administrations is seen in the light of the "subsidiary principle" (Van der Grinten, 1985): The Institutions themselves are in the first place responsible for their services.

Current Services

Children with psychological or psychiatric problems are usually referred to a youth care team affiliated with one of the fifty-eight Regional Institutes for Outpatient Mental Health Care. In 1989, 63,960 young patients were admitted to these teams (Jacobs & Bijl, 1991). There are various kinds of care available for children. A Boddaert Center provides day treatment for children and their families who have psychosocial problems. This aid is merely given after school. At the end of 1989, 1,350 youngsters received aid at the Boddaert Centers. In addition to these services, there are a large number of other ambulatory services, such as outpatient care by the psychiatric department of a general hospital (2,390 intakes in 1989), part-time care in an inpatient psychiatric setting (150 youngsters received aid on December 31, 1989), and the crisis centers for the young (1,470 intakes in 1989) (Jacobs & Bijl, 1991).

When ambulatory treatment fails to produce results, and when semiresidential or residential psychiatric care is indicated, children and adolescents may be referred to one of the medical day-care centers, medical children's homes, or psychiatric hospitals for children and adolescents. The thirty-five Medical Day-Care Centers (Medische Kleuterdagverblijven, or MKDs) mainly treat children (birth to seven years old) with developmental, emotional, and behavioral problems. On December 31, 1989, a total of 2,000 infants remained in treatment in these centers, and 1,240 infants were registered during the year. The twelve Medical Children's Homes (Medische Kindertehuizen, or MKTs) mostly deal with psychological disturbances; 630 children were staying at medical children's homes at the end of 1989, and 540 children were admitted during that year (Jacobs & Bijl, 1991). On December 31, 1989, 570 patients stayed at Psychiatric Hospitals for Children and Adolescents, while during that year 370 children were admitted.

The Confidential Physicians Offices for Child Abuse and Neglect (Bureaus Vertrouwensarts) have the task of registering cases of child abuse and neglect (both mental and physical), starting and accompanying aid, evaluating the help given to the child and family, and guaranteeing that aftercare is given. In 1989 physicians at the advice services received 7,200 reports of child abuse and neglect (Jacobs & Bijl, 1991).

The largest part of the mental health care system consists of services to adults, in which most clients aged eighteen to sixty-five years are treated. In this care system relatively more emphasis is put on inpatients and semiresidential care, although outpatient care also is very extensive. In 1989, 68,910 clients (see table 10.3) were admitted to the adult departments of the Regional Institutes for Outpatient Mental Health Care. The number of adult patients treated in the psychiatric departments of general hospitals and in the outpatient centers of psychiatric hospitals is not precisely known, as the available figures include the consultations with children, youth, and elderly people. The majority

Table 10.3
Mental Health Care for Adults in the Netherlands

Institution	Admissions during 1989[1]	Clients, 31-12-1989
Regional Institutes for Outpatient Mental Health Care	68,910	unknown
Outpatient centers of psychiatric hospitals	35,050	unknown
Outpatient centers of general hospitals	39,090	unknown
Part-time care	6,640	4,070
Crisis centers	9,480	860
Psychosocial treatment centers	1,760	300
Psychiatric departments of general hospitals	13,980	1,460
General psychiatric hospitals	18,940	13,010
Sheltered residences	630	2,600

[1] Number of patients who applied for care during the year 1989.
Source: Jacobs & Bijl, 1991.

of the clients treated in psychiatric daytime care are adults. In 1989, 6,640 clients consulted the psychiatric day-care centers, and on December 31 of that year a total of 4,070 people were registered as clients in these centers.

For adult care, crisis centers and women's centers are important. In 1988, 620 women were admitted to a women's center. The majority (62 percent) of these women were admitted together with their children (670 children in total). The crisis centers originated from the need for shelter for those people who due to their mental disease could not remain (at least temporarily) in their own home. At the end of 1989 (31 December) both these kinds of centers had 860 clients in treatment. During that year the number of clients staying in these centers was 9,480.

Three-quarters of the population in psychosocial treatment centers are in the age group of eighteen to sixty-five years. Of this population, 75 percent is female. The psychosocial treatment centers give intensive treatment of short duration to those clients who have a psychological disturbance but who cannot be treated properly in their own environment. Half of these disturbances can be diagnosed

Table 10.4
Mental Health Care for the Elderly in the Netherlands

Institution	Admissions during 1989[1]	Clients, 31-12-1989
Regional Institutes for Outpatient Mental Health Care	28,950	unknown
Part-time care	4,600	3,210
Psychosocial treatment centers	240	40
Psychiatric departments of general hospitals	2,280	350
General psychiatric hospitals	3,800	6,870
Psychiatric nursing homes	12,180	23,800
Sheltered homes	150	650

[1] Number of patients who applied for care during the year 1989.
Source: Jacobs & Bijl, 1991.

as psychiatric. On December 31, 1989, 300 clients were staying in psychosocial treatment centers, while during that year 1,760 clients were admitted.

During 1989, 13,980 clients applied for care at a psychiatric department of a general hospital. On December 31 of that year 1,460 clients were still registered as being under treatment of a psychiatric department of a general hospital. On December 31, 1989, 13,010 clients were staying at a general psychiatric hospital, while during that year 18,940 clients were admitted.

The number of elderly people in Dutch society is growing. In 1980, 11.5 percent of the Dutch population was sixty-five or older, and in the year 2000 this will increase to 13.8 percent. Table 10.4 shows the mental health care that is available for elderly people in the Netherlands, the number of people registered throughout the year, and the number of patients registered on December 31, 1989.

Mental Health Personnel and Treatment

In 1989 there were 66,400 labor places (full-time equivalence) in mental health care. This is about 17 percent of the total labor places in the health care sector. For the greater part (85 percent), these personnel work in inpatient mental health care. In recent years there has been a slight shift of personnel from inpatient to semimural and outpatient care. In 1989 about 9 percent of personnel were working in outpatient mental health care.

General practitioners (GPs) and social workers play an important role in serving

Table 10.5
**Division in Terms of Percentages of the Staff of the Netherlands Regional
Institutes for Outpatient Mental Health Care in Full-Time Equivalents on
December 31, 1989**

Function	Percentage
Psychiatrist	7.3
Pediatrician	0.2
Geriatrician	1.4
Psychotherapist	10.0
Psychologist	11.3
Educationalist	3.2
Other academic professions	1.3
Prevention worker	2.9
Physician resident	1.3
Social psychiatric nurse	18.8
Welfare worker	12.0
Other social workers	2.4
Total mental health care professionals	72.1
Management and staff	4.3
Clerical staff	23.6
total	100.0

Source: Werkgeversvereniging Ambulante Geestelijke Gezondheidszong
              (WAGG), 1990.

people with mental health care problems. In the Netherlands general practitioners
are often confronted with psychological and psychosocial problems (30 percent
to 50 percent), and they spend a great deal of their time on these clients (17
percent) (Abraham, 1985). People with mental problems in general apply for
help to their general practitioner, and quite often the (psychological) origin of
the problem is recognized by the GP. The general practitioner is often a gate-
keeper for mental health care. According to Bensing and Beerendonk (1990),
the general practitioner has some advantages in carrying out this function: He
is well known to the patient, and the relationship continues over time; the service
is available for everyone; and he has a holistic way of giving assistance. Only
a small proportion of these patients are referred to specialized mental health
care, such as the Regional Institutes for Outpatient Mental Health Care. Table
10.5 presents an overview of the staff of the Regional Institutes for Outpatient
Mental Health Care.

Only a modest position is occupied by the medical disciplines (less than 10
percent of the total personnel). Behavioral science and socially oriented therapies

have a more important place: 25 percent of the personnel are either psycho-therapists, psychologists, or educational specialists, and 31 percent are either social psychiatric nurses or welfare workers. The latter group constitutes the largest professional category in nonresidential mental health care. Almost a quarter of the personnel (23.6 percent) in the Regional Institutes for Outpatient Mental Health Care is clerical staff.

The average work force in the psychiatric hospitals per 100 beds is divided as follows: 7 medical and social staff, 14 medical and paramedical social workers, 63 nurses (either qualified or in training), and usually 34 general professionals (Nationaal Ziekenhuis Instituut, 1990). In 1986 a bill was introduced pertaining to professional practice in individual health care (Wet Beroepenuitoefening in de Individuele Gezondheidszorg, or BIG), which in the future will register a large number of professionals and provide protection for accompanying titles. In anticipation of the legal registration of psychotherapists, the Medical Chief Inspectorate for Mental Health (GHIGV) keeps a register for this professional group.

PUBLIC POLICY PROCESS

Since the 1970s the public has become increasingly aware of the position of psychiatric patients. Public interest has been stimulated by campaigns carried out by the patients' organizations. In mental health care there are about twenty-five patients' organizations (Bauduin, 1988). Their emphasis is on the exchange of information and experiences and on influencing mental health policy. The expertise that can be found in the patients' own experience is the point of departure for these new developments. It is difficult to indicate how large the influence of citizens on mental health care is, but through the ages they have played a major part.

The Dutch system of mental health care is widely divided. In the Netherlands mental health care has always been part of the general health care system. Somatic and mental health care are more or less covered by the same legislation and the same system of financing. Thus mental health care is greatly affected by any changes in the health care sector.

The major problem in Dutch mental health care has always been the lack of a comprehensive organizational framework and, as a consequence, the failure to coordinate new initiatives. The integration of fragmented services has been a major concern for the local and the central governments. However, for a long time little attention has been paid to the development of an operational model of an integrated mental health care system (Van der Grinten, 1985).

The growing size of the unorganized network of mental health care in the Netherlands was fundamentally discussed for the first time in a white paper called *Structuurnota Gezondheidszorg* (health care structure) published by the Dutch government in 1974. Three main principles were stated for restructuring mental health care, namely, coordinating in echelons, planning in geographic regions, and integration of services. The principle of creating echelons refers to the concept that the care facilities should be structured in such a way that the patient meets primary health care providers first. Only problems that cannot be dealt with effectively should be referred to the secondary (and more expensive) care of specialists. The second principle refers to the planning of health care facilities within the health care regions; each geographical area should have a comprehensive network of health care facilities at its disposal. The third principle aims at multidisciplinary cooperation within each subsystem of the health care system. In ambulatory mental health care this principle was reached in 1982 by integrating the different institutions of mental health care in the Regional Institutes for Outpatient Mental Health Care. An initiative on this point at the end of the 1980s resulted in the creation of Regional Institutes for Mental Health Care (Regionale Instellingen voor Geestelijke Gezondheidszorg, or RIGG), whose aim is to stimulate and consolidate the collaboration between all existing mental health care facilities within each region.

Ten years after the first white paper, a new mental health white paper (*Ministerie van Welzijn Volksgezondheiden Cultuur*, 1984) noted that mental health care needed strong incentives to improve quality and to increase client and patient participation. The support of a coherent health care delivery system still remained an important issue, as did the concern for the growing number of people receiving mental health care. The government in the 1990s is trying to reform mental health care by reallocation of budgets, by decreasing too-rigid legislation, and by substitution in relation with decentralization. Case management is being used by institutions to try to counteract service fragmentation.

SPECIAL POLICY ISSUES

The Mentally Ill and the Mentally Retarded

The service system for the mentally handicapped has developed its own identity since the 1960s, and since that time it has been separated from the psychiatric service system. The service system for the mentally handicapped in the Netherlands is organized at a regional level. In each region there are a large number of various comprehensive services available for the mentally handicapped and their parents. The cooperation between the various facilities is formalized with regional corporations, but these are often dominated by large residential institutions.

Apart from the general services of social work, district nursing, general practitioners, and home help facilities, there are specialized ambulatory facilities for mentally handicapped persons and their parents, the social psychopedagogic services (Sociaal Pedagogische Diensten, or SPD). In its own region each of the fifty-five SPDs is responsible for providing services to mentally handicapped patients and the persons looking after them. The task of consultation, information, support, and referral of patients is done by more than 500 social workers. In 1986 about 3,400 mentally handicapped patients got help from the SPDs.

A necessary condition for entering day-care programs is that the patients must be handicapped to such a measure that they cannot function well, for example, in adapted work settings. The patients live with their parents, with other family members, or in group homes. The main goals of the day-care programs are maintaining or improving skills as well as the level of social integration. In the programs attention is given to household activities, manual skills, musical training, and training in body motion; furthermore, speech development and self-care of the patients are stimulated. The programs at the 285 day-care facilities are attended by some 12,300 mentally handicapped.

Many of the group homes (Gezinsvervangende Tehuizen) for mentally handicapped were built in the 1960s. About fifteen to twenty-five persons eighteen years of age or older live in such facilities, divided into groups of six to eight persons. Long-term sheltered housing and support are offered to the residents of group homes. The group homes are built like other houses in the street. The residents are stimulated to participate as much as possible in their immediate environment. During the daytime people leave their home for work in sheltered workshops or adapted jobs in industry, trade, or local government. The younger residents go to school for students with learning disabilities or attend day-care facilities. There are some 12,500 mentally handicapped persons living in about 520 group homes.

Like group homes, most institutes for the mentally handicapped started in 1969–70 with many new residents. Nowadays about 27,000 mentally handicapped people live in eighty-five institutes. With an average of 320 residents, they are much bigger than the group homes. The target group of the institutes has changed over the past twenty years. The development of more alternative facilities had consequences for admission and discharge. Only the more seriously handicapped, both mentally and physically, were admitted. The residents live in groups of eight to fifteen persons. Each group has its own housing unit, the pavilion. Most of the institutes in the Netherlands are built as a complex of decentralized pavilions. Some of the residents attend sheltered workshops, but most of them have activities on the grounds of the facility. The institutes have their own group homes located within the local community. The groups in such facilities are small, with four to ten members. About 1,500 residents of institutes are actually staying in such group homes.

The Mentally Ill and Substance Abuse

The Netherlands has a specific network of ambulatory, semiresidential, and residential institutions for the care of alcoholics and drug addicts. At the end of 1989 (December 31) the seventeen Outpatient Centers for Addicts had 29,552 patients in treatment. During that year the number of clients who had contact with the Outpatient Centers for Addicts was 48,560. Four residential institutions for alcoholics and drug addicts have an outpatient function, but it is not known how many patients are treated there. There is a capacity of forty-eight places for partial hospitalization, usually day programs. It is estimated that in 1989, 290 patients were treated in partial hospitalization and that approximately 120 patients were still in treatment at the end of that year. In the psychiatric departments of the general hospitals more than 980 patients admitted were diagnosed as dependent on alcohol or drugs in 1989. In addition to this, it is known that for more than 10,000 patients the dependency on alcohol and drugs played an important role (secondary diagnosis). There are eleven general psychiatric hospitals with a department for the treatment of addicts, but all psychiatric hospitals admit patients with addiction problems (3,810 in 1989). During 1989, 5,910 patients were admitted to the nine independent residential institutions for the care and treatment of alcoholics and drug addicts (Jacobs & Bijl, 1991).

The Mentally Disordered Offender

In the Netherlands there are several groups who receive specific care, including mentally disordered offenders, to whom their offenses have not been (fully) imputed by the criminal court. These people are admitted to forensic psychiatric institutions when the criminal court has imposed an order of detention at the government's pleasure. In 1989, 197 persons were admitted to forensic psychiatric institutions (Inrichtingen voor Terbeschikkingstelling van de Regering, or TBSs) (Jacobs & Bijl, 1991). On December 31, 1989, 368 mentally disordered offenders were staying in these institutions.

For the forensic psychiatric institutions the Ministry of Justice bears responsibility. The TBS order is imposed on persons to whom, due to their mental illness or handicap at the time of committing the crime, their offense has not (fully) been imputed. Furthermore, the dangerousness of the patient toward others or the general safety of persons or goods must require the order. In addition to these offenders, TBS institutions are also intended for persons who have been given a prison sentence, but whose mental state is such that treatment in a TBS clinic is indicated (Bauduin, 1988). A TBS order lasts two years, but it can be extended by one or two years.

There are six TBS institutions in the Netherlands; three of them, including a psychiatric observation clinic, are administered by the Ministry of Justice and three by private organizations. The TBS clinics range from more or less open to maximum-security institutions. In all cases treatment is aimed at providing a therapeutic social environment, but the specific type of treatment varies from one institution to another. They may emphasize social therapy, relational therapy, psychotherapy, occupational therapy, or a combination of these. Where indicated, this treatment is supplemented by creative therapy, physical therapy, and in certain cases pharmacotherapy (Bauduin, 1988).

Deinstitutionalization

In recent years many issues have become important. Deinstitutionalization, the attempt to move mental health care away from the psychiatric hospital to small-scale institutions, is an important policy. Deinstitutionalization policy could briefly be described as governmental policy aimed at reducing mental hospitalization. In the Netherlands this policy is especially aimed at the forty-three general mental hospitals that contain 83 percent of the beds for psychiatric patients.

Most of the psychiatric beds are located in so-called general psychiatric hospitals. The majority of these institutions date back to the end of the nineteenth century and are situated in rural areas. In 1975, twenty-five of forty mental hospitals had over 500 inpatients, with an average number of 727 patients and a maximum of 1,100. Eight years later, in 1983, the average number of inpatients in these large mental hospitals was reduced to 655 patients, but the size of the largest hospital remained the same. On the whole, there was a slight decrease in the overall capacity of the large mental hospitals. More important is the tendency to deconcentrate functions and buildings. Many beds, most of them for long-stay patients, have been rehoused in smaller units just inside or outside the grounds of these hospitals. Nowadays 11 percent of all patients are treated in sociohomes, halfway homes, and family foster care (Haveman & Maaskant, 1990).

The difference between de jure policy (governmental ideas and conceptions) and de facto policy (real governmental action) is clear in the policy of deinstitutionalization (Haveman, 1986). Despite the policy of deinstitutionalization, no formal steps were taken to close mental hospitals, and no legal and budgetary action was initiated to restrict admissions and the length of stay of patients. On the other hand, the policy has been innovative with regard to extramuralization by integrating the facilities for ambulatory mental health care with the Regional Institutes for Outpatient Mental Health Care and incorporating them in the social sickness insurance. The Regional Institutes for Outpatient Mental Health Care are seen as specialized ambulatory facilities (without beds) available and accessible free of charge after referral by a general practitioner for all Dutch inhabitants. Each region of the Netherlands is more or less served by one of the fifty-eight Regional Institutes for Outpatient Mental Health Care. A Regional Institute for Outpatient Mental Health Care is in fact a compulsory joint venture of several facilities with different historical roots, including social psychiatric services with outreach services for acute and chronic patients, institutes for multidisciplinary psychotherapy, institutes for child guidance, and other facilities. Apart from the Regional Institutes for Outpatient Mental Health Care, there are Outpatient Centers for Addicts in some regions.

In spite of the expansion and enlargement of nonresidential mental health care in the last decade, the clinical sector is still dominant. In 1989, 81 percent of the total expenditure and 85 percent of staff were allocated to residential mental health care, such as mental hospitals, psychiatric wards of general hospitals, and psychogeriatric nursing homes. The gap between the de jure policy and the de facto situation is still large.

The internal reorganization of mental hospitals had, of course, negative side effects on dehospitalization. Large amounts of money were spent on making housing conditions more adequate to standards of modern treatment and a suitable way of life. However, in a time of frozen budgets, these costly investments seriously limit the growth of nonresidential mental health facilities.

Despite a significant increase in the number of admissions, the annual number of inpatient days has declined (Haveman, 1986). The explanation for this development must first of all be sought in the discharge and mortality of the old long-stay patients, and second in the fewer new long-stay patients. In fact, the proportion of the new long-stay patients (two to five years) in psychiatric hospitals remained remarkably stable during the period 1970 to 1988. The number of long-stay patients declined from 18,420 in 1970 to 12,114 in 1988. Fifty-six percent of the patients stay longer than two years in a psychiatric hospital, 41 percent stay longer than five years, and 29 percent have a hospital stay of ten years or longer. The relatively dense network of outpatient and day services should have enabled the Netherlands to gain a lead in the development of community-based care of chronic mental patients; however, various surveys of outpatient care have demonstrated that outpatient care does not automatically lead to a reduction in the use of mental hospital care.

In relation to deinstitutionalization, mental health care in the Netherlands is slowly moving away from the large-scale psychiatric hospital to small-scale institutions (Romme, 1984). The small-scale care has some advantages: It is approachable and surveyable, and, most important, there is a greater involvement from both patient and mental health professionals.

Funding Issues

Financial issues have become more important as the Netherlands has spent every year about 10 percent of the GNP on health care and public welfare. With regard to the funding of mental health care, five sources can be distinguished: compulsory health insurance, private health insurance, governmental subsidies, contributions from insured people, and grants from private trusts and foundations.

The largest part of health care is financed by various types of compulsory health insurance: the Health Insurance Act (Ziekenfondswet, or ZFW), which insures people for normal medical care, and the Exceptional Medical Expenses Act (Algemene Wet Bijzondere Ziektekosten, or AWBZ), which covers special and long-lasting medical care, for instance long-stay care (more than one year) in a psychiatric hospital, all services in group homes and institutes for the mentally handicapped, and assistance given by Regional Institutes for Outpatient Mental Health Care.

Private health insurance is open to persons who cannot be insured by the

Health Insurance Act because of their high income or their profession (e.g., public servants). The care for addicts by the Outpatient Centers for Addicts is subsidized by the government.

The costs involved in mental health care are described in the Financial Overview of Health Care (Financieel Overzicht Zorg, or FOZ). From the 9.6 percent of the GNP that is spent on health care and public welfare, approximately 1 percent of the GNP is spent on mental health care. This part (1 percent) is divided as follows: 81 percent on inpatient care; 7 percent on semimural care; and 12 percent on outpatient mental health care (Jacobs & Bijl, 1991).

Consumer Rights

Finally, there is increasing attention being paid to patients' rights and their position in mental health care. In most cases admission to psychiatric hospitals is voluntary. A patient who is admitted is free (in legal terms) to terminate treatment and leave the hospital unless grounds for a committal to custody or a judicial authorization are present. Only a small proportion (15 percent) of the patients stay in psychiatric hospitals by virtue of a committal to custody or a judicial authorization. The Insanity Act of 1884 defines two procedures for involuntary admission, namely, admission by judicial authorization (about 5 percent) and by committal to custody (about 10 percent) (Bauduin, 1988). It is only in emergency situations that patients are committed to custody. An authorization to institutionalize someone is initiated by a relative (either by blood or marriage). He or she must apply to the cantonal judge for permission to have the person placed in a psychiatric hospital. In some cases the public prosecutor can apply to the president of the court for authorization, and in certain cases he is required to do so. A request for commitment must be accompanied by the written declaration of a physician or psychiatrist not presently treating the patient. As a rule, the person against whom this authorization procedure is initiated is awarded legal counsel. No appeal is possible against the decision of the judge to grant the authorization. Once granted, an authorization is valid for six months, after which the court must decide whether or not to extend it, taking into consideration the advice of the physician treating the patient.

In addition to the judicial authorization, the Insanity Act also allows commitment by means of committal to custody (Inbewaringstelling, or IBS). This is a procedure that is used only in emergency situations. The IBS, which is ordered by the mayor, is intended for those cases where there is reason to believe that due to his or her mental disorder a person presents such an immediate danger to himself or herself, to others, or to the public order that it would not be advisable to wait for an authorization. The certificate of a physician or psychiatrist—preferably one who is not treating the patient—must be presented, and wherever possible a GP is also consulted. If due to circumstances a written certificate cannot be obtained, then an oral statement either in person or by telephone will suffice, in which case a written confirmation must be sent to the mayor as soon as possible. He will then see to it that the necessary documents are forwarded to the public prosecutor. Within twenty-four hours the public prosecutor must send them on to the president of the court, together with a requisition for continuation of the committal to custody. Within three days the judge makes his decision, after having heard the patient. Custody can continue for a maximum of three weeks after the decision of the judge.

Since 1971 there has been a Bill on Exceptional Admissions to Psychiatric Hospitals (Bijzondere Opnemingen Psychiatrische Ziekenhuizen [BOPZ]), intended to replace the Insanity Act. Several procedures have been considerably improved in the BOPZ. In this act the legal status of the patient after admission is accurately regulated.

Other proposed pieces of legislation that formulate patients' rights are the bill Democratic Functioning of Care Facilities and the Act on the Treatment Contract. The first-mentioned legislation would give the statutory basis for setting up patients' councils and would define their tasks and powers.

CONCLUSIONS AND DISCUSSION

The mental health services in the Netherlands started on the basis of individual charity and governmental aid to the poor. In the last part of the nineteenth century and throughout the twentieth century the Netherlands developed a complex and differentiated system of mental health care for both psychiatric and mentally handicapped patients. However, the health care facilities were not attuned to one another. Because of the diversity of services it was difficult for both patients and caregivers to decide what kind of care best answered to the needs of the patient. Another problem was the continuously growing size of mental health care. At the end of 1989, 49,800 patients were treated in inpatient mental health services and 12,800 patients in semiresidential mental health services. In outpatient settings there were about 203,500 patients in the care of the Regional Institutes for Outpatient Mental Health Care; 29,600 patients were in the care of the Outpatient Centers for Addicts.

In the 1970s and the 1980s the government tried to restructure mental health care. Various governmental principles played a role in the creation of new mental health services. Through regionalization and small-scale facilities, an attempt was made to make mental health care accessible for everyone. By means of coordination and integration an attempt was made to concentrate all knowledge available at one place. A new development is case management, where the individual patient has his or her own social worker (for a longer period). On the individual level, the patient is more frequently seen as a serious partner with his own rights. Through reallocation of budgets, simplification of legislation, and substitution together with decentralization, the government is trying to reform mental health care so that in the future Dutch mental health care does not remain a patchwork quilt.

REFERENCES

Abraham, R. E. (1985). De toekomst van de psychiatrie [The future of psychiatry]. *Medisch Contact, 10,* 287–291.

Bauduin, D. (1988). *A guide to the mental health care in the Netherlands.* Utrecht: Netherlands Institute of Mental Health (NcGv).

Bensing, J., & Beerendonk, P. (1990). Psychosociale problemen in de huisartspraktijk: Weten en meten [Psychosocial problems in the GP practice]. *Maandblad Geestelijke Volksgezondheid, 6,* 595–618.

Breemer ter Steege, C.P.C., e.a. (1983). *Mental Health Care in the Netherlands.* Utrecht: Netherlands Institute of Mental Health (NcGv).

Brook, O. H. (1987). Supervision of mental health care in the Netherlands. *European Archives of Psychiatric and Neurological Sciences, 236,* 364–368.

Central Bureau of Statistics (CBS). (1989). Zelfdoding [Suicide]. *Kwartaalbericht Rechtsbescherming en Veiligheid, 4,* 80–82. 's Gravenhage: SDU/uitgeverij/cbs-publikaties.

Central Bureau of Statistics (CBS). (1900). *Statistisch jaarboek 1990* [Statistical yearbook]. 's Gravenhage: SDU/uitgeverij.

Haveman, M. J. (1986). Dehospitalization of psychiatric care in the Netherlands. *Acta Psychiatrica Scandinavica, 73,* 456–463.

Haveman, M. J., & Maaskant, M. A. (1990). Psychiatric foster care for adult patients: Results of a study in the Netherlands. *International Journal of Social Psychiatry, 36,* 58–67.

Jacobs, C.M.V.W., & Bijl, R. V. (1991). *GGZ in getallen 1991* [Mental health care in figures]. In *Kwantitatief overzicht van de geestelijke gezondheidszorg: Instellingen, zorgcircuits* [Trends 1980–2000]. Utrecht: Netherlands Institute of Mental Health (NcGv).

Ministerie van Welzijn, Volksgezondheid en Cultuur (1984). *Nota geestelijke volksgezondheid* [Mental health white paper]. Tweede kamer, vergaderjaar 1983–1984, 18463, nrs. 1–2. Rijswijk: Author.

Nationaal Ziekenhuis Instituut. (1990). *Statistiek personeelssterkte 1989* [Personnel statistics 1989], inclusief ziekteverzuim en personeelverloop. Psychiatrische Ziekenhuizen: landelijke tabellen. Utrecht: Nationaal Ziekenhuis Instituut.

National Inpatient Case-register for Mental Health, 1971–1989 (PIGG): (1990). *Patiëntenregister intramurale geestelijke gezondheidszorg* [Inpatient case register for mental health]. Utrecht: NZI/NZR.

Romme, M.A.J. (1984). *Geestelijke gezondheidszorg* [Mental health care]. voorzieningen, werkwijzen, doelgroepen, medewerkers, ontwikkelingen, financiering, omvang. Alphen aan de Rijn: Stafleu.

Schnabel, P. (1985). De zin van de zorg voor ziel en zaligheid, de geestelijke gezondheidszorg in verandering [The Meaning of care for soul and blessing, mental health care in change]. *Gezondheid en Samenleving, 3,* 152–160.

Van der Grinten, T.E.D. (1985). In S. P. Mangen (Ed.), *Mental health care in the European community.* London: Croom Helm.

Werkgeversvereniging Ambulante Geestelijke Gezondheidszorg (WAGG). (1990). *Personeel in de AGGZ '85–89* [Personnel in the outpatient mental health care]. Utrecht: Author.

11

New Zealand

Max W. Abbott and Donna R. Kemp

OVERVIEW

New Zealand is a country of 103,866 square miles, about the size of the state of Colorado, located in the southwest Pacific approximately 1,200 miles southeast of Australia. It consists of two main islands, the North Island and the South Island, separated by the Cook Strait, and numerous small coastal islands.

There are approximately 3.4 million New Zealanders. Most are of British descent. The indigenous Maori of Polynesian origin comprise approximately 10 percent of the total, and Polynesians from other Pacific Islands, 3 percent. In addition, there are a small number of Asians, including Indochinese refugees. Over 75 percent of New Zealand's population lives in urban areas, where manufacturing and service industries are established (Bureau of Public Affairs, 1987). Population growth is slow because of low fertility levels and net migration losses.

New Zealand has a parliamentary system of government patterned after the United Kingdom, and it is a fully independent member of the Commonwealth. There is no written constitution. The governmental system is unitary. Executive authority is vested in a cabinet led by a prime minister, who is the leader of the political party or coalition of parties that holds the majority of seats in Parliament. Cabinet members must be members of Parliament and are collectively responsible to it. The unicameral Parliament (House of Representatives) has ninety-five members, four of whom must be Maori, elected on a separate roll. Representatives are normally elected for a three-year term, but elections can be called sooner. The judiciary consists of the Court of Appeals, the Supreme Court, and the Magistrate's Courts. The major political parties are the National Party and the Labour Party. As a result of the 1990 elections, the former gained control of the government. Both parties stand for free enterprise.

New Zealand was populated by a people of East Polynesian ancestry at least 800 years before the arrival of Europeans. In 1840 the United Kingdom annexed New Zealand and through the Treaty of Waitangi, signed with Maori tribes, established British sovereignty. By 1890 parliamentary democratic government was well established, and at the turn of the century there were major social reforms that established a version of a welfare state. The country became a dominion in 1907 and achieved full autonomy by the Statute of Westminster Adoption Act in 1947, which formalized an independent situation that had existed for many years.

Since 1984 successive governments have embarked on a major economic reform program to reverse the country's economic decline and open the economy to greater competition. The country has experienced drastic fiscal, governmental-structure, and public policy change, with policy focused on deregulation, devolution, private enterprise, and curtailment of long-standing social welfare policies.

EXTENT OF THE PROBLEM

New Zealand has two kinds of official data available regarding the extent of mental illness: first, the number of psychiatric patients in hospital at one time, and second, annual rates of first psychiatric admissions and readmissions (*Mental Health Data*, 1988). However, with increased deinstitutionalization and the development of community services, more people are being treated in the community and will not appear in psychiatric hospital data. Psychiatric utilization rates are thus largely a reflection of severe mental illness. American and British studies indicate that these patients represent only about 5 percent of the total mental disorders in the community (Strole, Langer, and Michael, 1962; Shepherd, Cooper, Brown, & Kalton, 1966). New Zealand has no estimates of what percentage of total mental disorders is represented by the psychiatric utilization rates, and outpatient visits have not been recorded at the national level.

On December 31, 1988, the most recent date for which official data are available, there were 5,654 New Zealanders (170.0 per 100,000 of the total population) resident in psychiatric, mental handicap, and alcohol/drug treatment institutions. During 1988 an average of 308 additional patients were resident in psychiatric units of general hospitals. Of the 5,654 people resident in specialist institutions, 2,629, almost half, had a mental handicap diagnosis, and the majority of these people had been in hospital for more than ten years; 3,393 residents were males, 2,261 females.

During 1988 there were 5,564 first admissions (137.2 per 100,000); 2,370 were males, 2,194 females. During the same period there were 10,424 readmissions (313.4 per 100,000), 5,512 males and 4,912 females. Only 51 people entering hospital for the first time in 1988 had a mental retardation diagnosis, and of this group only 20 were admitted to an intellectual handicap hospital.

Forensic patients are those who both have a psychiatric condition and are involved in the criminal justice system. This includes people referred for assessment, people ordered by the courts to be detained in a psychiatric hospital rather than a prison, and prisoners transferred for treatment from a prison to a psychiatric institution. During 1988, 87 first admissions and 181 readmissions to psychiatric institutions were forensic patients, approximately 2 percent of the total in both cases. Most remand patients are assessed on bail or in prison and are not included in these figures. The large majority are males, and the most frequent diagnoses are substance abuse or dependence, major affective disorder, and antisocial personality disorder (Mason, Ryan, & Bennett, 1988). It is not known what percentage of prison inmates suffer from psychiatric disorder or are mentally retarded.

In 1988 alcoholism accounted for 27 percent of male first admissions and 21 percent of male readmissions to psychiatric institutions. The corresponding figures for women were 8 percent and 6 percent. Nine to ten times as many people again received outpatient treatment for alcohol abuse and dependence (Orchard, 1987). Drug abuse and dependence accounted for 11 percent of total first admissions and 6 percent of readmissions.

The suicide rate for 1987 was 22.2 per 100,000 for men and 6.0 for women. The corresponding figures for suicide attempts were 77.6 and 111.1 (*Mental Health Data*, 1987).

It is estimated that approximately one person in five has sought advice from a health or mental health professional at some time (Haines, 1982). Approximately one practitioner consultation in ten is believed to be for psychiatric problems (Downey & Werry, 1978), and about one-eighth of prescriptions from general practitioners are for psychiatric symptoms (Ferguson & Mailing, 1990). Official records are, at best, a crude estimate of the actual extent of problems in the community and are a poor substitute for epidemiological surveys. While no nationally representative surveys have been undertaken other than in very specialized areas (Abbott & Volberg, 1991, 1992), there are studies of particular communities, the most extensive being the Christchurch Epidemiology Study. The Christchurch study, conducted during 1986, used the Diagnostic Interview Schedule (DIS). Christchurch is the largest city in the South Island. This study indicated that for individual diagnoses the highest lifetime prevalences were sexual dysfunction (33 percent), generalized anxiety (31 percent), alcohol abuse/dependence (19 percent), major depressive episode (13 percent), phobias (11 percent), dysthymia (6 percent), drug abuse (6 percent), antisocial personality (3 percent), panic (2 percent), and obsessive-compulsive disorder (2 percent). Schizophrenia, schizophreniform disorders, mania, somatization, anorexia, and bulimia were rare, all less than 2 percent. There was an estimated prevalence of 51 percent of the population who had at some point in their lives met criteria for at least one disorder. The 25–44 age group had the highest prevalence for most disorders, but age differences were generally small. Only drug disorders and antisocial personality declined with age, and only dysthymia increased with age. For women, the most prevalent disorders were sexual dysfunction (44 percent), generalized anxiety (35 percent), depression (16 percent), and phobia (15 percent). For men, the most prevalent disorders were alcohol abuse/dependence (32 percent), generalized anxiety (27 percent), sexual dysfunction (22 percent), and depression (9 percent). The study found no sex differences for the less common disorders such as schizophrenia, mania, or somatization. When all diagnoses in the study were included, there was no gender difference in the prevalence of having at least one disorder during a lifetime. When comparisons were made with the four American Epidemiological Catchment Area (ECA) Program Sites of Baltimore, New Haven, St. Louis, and Piedmont (Eaton & Kessler, 1985) and other studies in Puerto Rico (Canino et al., 1987) and Edmonton, Canada (Bland, Orn, & Newman, 1988), the Christchurch prevalence figures appear markedly different for affective disorders and to a lesser extent for alcohol abuse/dependence and schizophrenia. The Christchurch rate for affective disorder (14.7 percent) was significantly higher than the rates for Puerto Rico (7.9 percent), Edmonton (10.2 percent), and any of the four ECA sites. The differences were largely due to major depressive disorders, with some differences in dysthymia. Christchurch (18.9 percent) and Edmonton (18 percent) had the highest lifetime prevalences for alcohol abuse/dependence. Consistent with other international studies, the Christchurch study found that the cumulative lifetime risk of depression was changing with birth cohort. Rates of depression were increasing, the onset was occurring at a younger age, and in subjects born after 1960 the six-month prevalence was greater in men than in women. This was consistent with international trends in suicide (Joyce, 1989).

Hospitalization rates are very low for children and adolescents. However, a recent study in Dunedin, the second-largest South Island city, using DSM diagnostic criteria, found high prevalence rates of psychiatric disorder—18.2 percent for males and 25.9 percent for females aged fifteen years. The girls had significantly higher rates of anxiety, phobia, and depression; the boys, much higher rates of aggressive conduct or attention deficit disorders. Six percent of girls and 1 percent of boys reported using nonprescription drugs or alcohol to "help them feel better" (McGee et al., 1990).

Department of Health statistics show that since the postwar years psychiatric service utilization by the Maori has been gradually increasing. By 1986 the first-admission rate was 219.7 per 100,000, compared to 128.7 for non-Maori (National Mental Health Consortium, 1989a). Since 1969 Maori have been increasingly overrepresented in admissions, and they now exceed the first-admission rates for non-Maori for all age groups below age fifty. The overall rates of Maori in psychiatric hospitals are now slightly higher than for non-Maori (Craig & Mills, 1987).

Using the 1983 rates of first psychiatric admission by diagnosis based on the International Classification of Diseases, ninth edition, Maori are overrepresented for schizophrenia and alcohol dependence and abuse and underrepresented for neurotic depression and dementia. Increased psychiatric hospital utilization rates by Maori were largely accounted for by admissions for alcohol abuse, alcohol dependence, and personality disorders. Psychotic disorders and neuroses, except for depressive neuroses, remained essentially the same.

The highest proportion of involuntary admissions (45 percent) occurs in the Pacific Island Polynesian population. This compares to 36 percent of Maori and 24 percent of non-Maori. In 1984, 28 percent of Maori patients over the age of fifteen years were committed under the Mental Health Act 1969, compared with 20 percent of non-Maori (Dawson, Abbott, & Henning, 1987). The Maori, in addition, are admitted more frequently under the Criminal Justice Act 1954 (Sachder, 1989). Although the self-referral rate was similar, Maori were referred more often by law enforcement agencies (18.3 percent of first-time admissions, compared to 8.1 percent for non-Maori and 29 percent for Pacific Islanders; *Mental Health Data*, 1988, p. 50) and less often by general practitioners.

MENTAL HEALTH HISTORY

New Zealand has predominately used a medical model in mental health policy, and traditionally, mental health services have been largely separated from physical health. In the early years of colonization mental illness usually was seen as a law-and-order problem, with ''lunatics'' placed in local gaols (Brunton, 1986). The first asylums in 1844 were for paupers and were gaol hospitals in Wellington and Auckland. As asylums were established on a provincial basis in the 1840s and 1850s, they were largely financed by public subscription. As a result of a negative public attitude toward ''lunatics,'' funding declined. In 1876, when the central government took charge of the eight asylums, as provincial governments were abolished, there were 748 patients, a rate of 190 per 100,000 population (*Mental Health Data*, 1982). Growth of the institutions was encouraged by a financial policy that allowed persons placed in asylums to be paid for by general taxation of the central government rather than local taxes (Blake-Palmer, 1963). Another factor in the increase was the number of alcohol-related committals (Abbott, 1989b). Having begun as small sanctuaries based on ''moral treatment'' with short-term stays, the hospitals during the nineteenth century quickly became more medicalized, with physicians and nurses replacing lay superintendents and attendants. As they became more overcrowded and underfinanced, they became large institutions with their focus primarily custodial and control oriented rather than treatment oriented. Some local hospitals, like Christchurch Hospital in 1885, made it a policy not to admit ''lunatics,'' so mental health cases remained with the national government. Institutionalization increased rapidly during the first half of the twentieth century and peaked in 1944, when 500 persons per 100,000 (about 8,000 patients) were hospitalized and more patients died in hospital than were discharged.

The egalitarian tradition was strong in New Zealand institutions, with patients of all socioeconomic classes being treated the same. It was not until 1882 that alternative and superior facilities to state institutions were made available at Ashburn Hall, Dunedin. Subclassification was gradually recognized; demands for different institutional services were first met for the alcoholic, but not until after World War II were demands for mentally retarded persons met to any real extent (Brunton, 1986). In 1947 the Mental Hospitals Department was amalgamated with the Health Department to increase cooperation between mental and physical health (Blake-Palmer, 1963).

Although hospitalization rates began to fall gradually from the mid-1940s, by the 1950s New Zealand had begun several decades of more active forms of treatment in psychiatric hospitals, including the introduction of psychotropic drugs and physical therapies such as electroconvulsive therapy (ECT) and insulin coma therapy, increased psychotherapies, milieu therapy, and social therapies. In addition, there was a slow but continued growth in outpatient and community services from the peripheral services of institutions of the 1960s. The Mental Health Act Amendment of 1954 allowed for the licensing of short-stay homes, and a rest-home subsidy scheme was introduced in 1960. That year also saw the publishing of a report encouraging psychiatric services in public general hospitals. But the actual total number of psychiatric hospital residents did not start to decrease until the late 1960s, and by 1961 only 12 percent of the patients were in hospitals for less than a year (*Mental Health Data*, 1982). However, the 1961 amendment to the Mental Health Act brought about the possibility of informal admissions that cleared the way for general hospital care. The levelling off of inpatient populations by 1968 allowed for greater movement of resources to nonresident support services, and domiciliary psychiatric nursing services were introduced, allowing for medication provision in the community by visiting nurses. In 1969 section 66 of the Mental Health Act allowed for committed patients to be placed on trial leave in the community for up to two years with the possibility of indefinite yearly renewals.

In 1972 psychiatric hospitals were transferred from the National Health Department to twenty-nine local hospital boards responsible for general hospitals and clinical specialties. National policy initiatives were developed through planning guidelines, a plan to build three large psychopaedic hospitals for mentally retarded persons was abandoned, and a moratorium on psychiatric hospital beds was established. A nationwide survey of hospital patients concluded that only 64 percent of residents required inpatient care and revealed large numbers of mentally retarded persons in psychiatric hospitals. Development of community services was left to hospital boards. With mental health budgets in direct competition with other health specialties, mental health community services were slow to develop, and by 1975 there were only 260 sheltered residential beds in the community in the form of supervised boarding homes, group homes, and aftercare hostels. As a result, in 1977 the Health Department made available additional funding for developing community services. These special funds were quickly committed and were eventually merged into general health allocations in 1982. However, they helped establish Christchurch's Community Mental Health Service, which focused on prevention, Carrington Hospital's Community

Area Outreach services in Auckland, and some family health counselling centers with greater emphasis on prevention and community development.

New Zealand has had a gradual movement away from reliance on psychiatric hospitals as the main source of psychiatric care and toward more resources being directed toward community care and treatment. Policy developments encouraging psychiatric care in public hospitals and limiting growth of psychiatric hospitals were encouraged by anti-institutional attitudes of health professionals and the public in the 1960s and 1970s (Haines & Abbott, 1985). Also, clear divisions have been made in care of the mentally retarded, substance abusers, and, to a lesser extent, the mentally infirm elderly, and different policies are being developed for them.

POLICY, ORGANIZATION, AND SERVICES IN THE 1980s AND 1990s

Current Policy Developments

New Zealand has not had, until very recently, an explicit, formally stated set of principles and objectives to guide mental health service developments. Existing services have been the result of piecemeal planning, described by the Mason inquiry (Mason et al., 1988) as being characterized by

1. a lack of national coordination;
2. a lack of coordination between government departments;
3. lack of adequate funding;
4. lack of consultation;
5. inappropriate management structures; and
6. a lack of liaison and consultation between hospital and community services.

All of these factors contributed to major shortcomings in the country's mental health services, which were highlighted throughout the 1980s by a succession of official inquiries and reports. These reports eventually had an impact on government policy. The most influential were the Mason report (1988) and the National Mental Health Consortium report (1989b).

The Mason inquiry was set up by the government to examine the practices of hospitals with respect to the admission, discharge, and supervision of forensic patients and others considered a risk to the community. The committee extended its brief and investigated all aspects of psychiatric services, with particular attention to community care. The National Mental Health Consortium report arose out of a request from the Cabinet Social Equity Committee for information on the development of community services for people with psychiatric disabilities. These two reports and the Mental Health Foundation's earlier 1987–88 national survey of community services involved wide-ranging consultation with professional, consumer, and community organizations. They provided an information and values base for the Labour government's August 1990 policy statement "Community-based Services for People with Mental Health Disabilities." Prior to this, earlier in that year, the government had already announced that it would follow the Mason Committee's more specific recommendations with respect to forensic services. This included the building of seven medium-secure "safe care" units throughout the country, with additional money to be added to the normal Area Health Board allocations to establish them. It had also released mental health service development guidelines (Department of Health, 1989b) and child, adolescent, and family mental health service guidelines (Department of Health, 1989a) for Area Health Boards. These guidelines, while not binding on the boards, did provide a framework for service development and guidance that was not previously available. Furthermore, the department began to use them in establishing contracts with Area Health Boards.

The National Mental Health Consortium (1989b) indicated the future direction for mental health in New Zealand as reduction in the use of institutional care; development of new services and particularly of integrated community services; improved services for individuals involved in both the mental health and criminal justice systems; passage of a new mental health bill; empowerment of consumers, development of advocacy services, and protection of consumer rights; improved planning, participation, and service development by and for Maori and other ethnic/cultural minorities, with a recognition of the role of the Treaty of Waitangi; prioritization of service development, with first priority given to people with severe or chronic psychiatric illness; holistic care developed on a continuum of care and providing continuity of care; and improved needs assessment, information systems, and evaluation. This report provided the framework for the August 1990 policy statement. The August 1990 policy did not cover all facets of mental health. It did not include mental health promotion or primary prevention, for example. Its purpose was to speed up improvements in the provision of community-based services for people experiencing serious forms of psychiatric disability. To this end, it stated the principles upon which the policy was based and a set of national objectives. The objectives were the following:

1. To have policies and services that provide opportunities for people with mental disabilities to sustain lifestyles within normal community living and achieve maximum possible integration into community life

2. To provide the community-based care of people with mental health disabilities through a comprehensive and coordinated network of services with clearly established responsibilities and lines of accountability

3. To empower consumers and consumer groups to participate in service planning, delivery, and evaluation

4. To have services that are culturally sensitive and policies and services that recognize

the wishes of Maoridom to respond to the care and related needs of Maori people with mental health disabilities

5. To develop and maintain standards of services and apply performance measures and quality-assurance systems to service delivery by both statutory and nonstatutory service providers

6. To have available a means of coordinating and evaluating policy and services

7. To develop and deliver services that incorporate and exemplify the stated principles of community-based mental health services

To assist in bringing these objectives to fruition, the Department of Health began refining its service guidelines, performance indicators, and output measures with the aim of taking a more active role in promoting and monitoring service development. The government also established a $50-million fund to boost community services and help bridge the transition point where funds have to be spent on new services before savings can be made from reducing or closing down old ones. A further fund of $340,000 was set up to assist national voluntary-sector organizations for activities that would further the policy objectives. Finally, a National Mental Health Consultative Group made up of representatives of government departments, service providers, and consumers was planned to improve communication and coordinate policy development and implementation on the part of those organizations and interest groups. Area Health Boards were encouraged to set up similar consultative groups.

The timing of the new policy and special tagged (dedicated) funding was good. In addition to coming shortly after the more wide-ranging departmental service guidelines, it happened at a time when many boards were recognizing that mental health had been the poor relation and that this required redressing, particularly with regard to community services. Changes already occurring in some other agencies, like the Housing Corporation, which was adjusting its allocation system to favor, rather than discriminate against, applicants with a history of psychiatric hospitalization, helped open the way for the goal of providing comprehensive mental health and social services for people most in need.

The special fund was to be allocated during 1991 and 1992 on a per capita basis. However, to qualify, boards were required to specify how they intended to use the money, how the projects related to the national policy, how the new community developments fitted into their overall mental health plan, and how they would be sustained after the special fund had been allocated. Although some administrators complained about how they would cope after 1992, all boards submitted proposals that met the rigorous criteria set and were aimed at helping to fill service gaps. The previous special funding for community-based forensic services; progress on new mental health legislation more in line with community care, the multidisciplinary team, and current thinking with respect to consumer rights and advocacy; and plans to shift responsibility for administering benefits for mentally disabled people to the Department of Health from

Social Welfare were other developments that contributed to a sense of optimism for significant improvements in mental health services during the 1990s.

Shortly after the August 1990 policy announcement there was a change of government. This resulted in an initial freezing of the $50-million fund, but later just under half of the sum was allocated in accordance with the new policy and procedures set in place prior to the general elections. A grant larger than that originally intended by the previous government was also made to voluntary organizations. Given the new government's commitment to cut public expenditure and other budget decisions made at the time, the decision to proceed did indicate an appreciation of, and commitment to, mental health. However, the second year of funding was not forthcoming in 1992, reducing the ''kick-start'' and bridging function originally intended.

Although not vigorously pursued by present ministers or Department of Health officials, the 1990 policy still stands and appears to be supported by most, if not all, Area Health Boards throughout the country. However, this remains a pivotal time. Progress has been made, and most boards have plans to further develop comprehensive services. In some instances this includes plans to close large psychiatric and mental handicap hospitals that now serve small numbers of patients yet continue to consume the majority of mental health expenditure. However, hard-won gains could very easily be lost, and there are now major uncertainties with regard to the future of mental health and health services generally.

The 1991 National Government Budget brought with it plans to restructure the entire health system. Specific details have yet to be determined. Although mental health is not mentioned in the policy papers, the changes will dramatically alter the way mental health services will be delivered. Area Health Boards have been abolished, and commissioners have been appointed to head those areas until a new structure is established in mid-1992. The fourteen Area Health Boards will be replaced by four Regional Health Authorities (RHAs) that will manage the purchasing and contracting for health services, including mental health services, throughout the country. The RHAs, unlike the Area Health Boards, will not own or run any services but will contract with public, private, and voluntary-sector provider organizations. Most bigger hospitals will become Crown Health Enterprises. Smaller hospitals and some other services will be offered to local communities to run as trusts. People will also be given the option of obtaining their health care from sources other than those contracted by RHAs, mainly from health care plans, probably run by private health insurance organizations. Partial user charges have already been introduced for some aspects of hospital and outpatient services, although they have not yet been extended to mental health.

In 1992 the new Mental Health Bill was passed, along with a supplementary order paper. It is still too early to fully appreciate the implications of the new health system for mental health service policy and service development and delivery. However, a major concern is whether or not the recent and long-overdue national policy developments and improved planning and coordination of services at the regional and local levels will survive the transition.

Current Organization

The role of government in mental health can be funding, planning, providing, or regulating. In New Zealand the government has been involved in all four areas. Public-sector mental health policy and services are the responsibility primarily of the national Department of Health and of local-area health boards, which are being replaced by Regional Health Authorities. There are, however, other involvements by government such as the national Department of Social Welfare, the Housing Corporation, and even the universities and technical institutes that provide professional training. The major role of the national government departments has been funding, but none has assumed or been given direct responsibility for overall organization of services. In 1990 government restructuring called for programs involving the mentally ill and elderly to be handled by the Department of Health and programs involving the intellectually handicapped and physically disabled to be handled by the Department of Social Welfare. However, the present government is favoring the status quo. A failure of past government organization has been problems of coordination and overlapping responsibilities. It remains to be seen if the new restructuring will reduce these problems. The major role of the Area Health Boards was service provision either directly or through contracts with the private, primarily voluntary-sector, associations, trusts providing services for those with mental disability, and private profit-making hospitals or residential care. The voluntary agencies are key providers of services, but they are mostly poorly resourced, have problems with low-paid and undertrained staff, fail to provide for long-term planning or coordination, and tend to be focused on short-term funding tied to specific services (National Mental Health Consortium, 1989b). In New Zealand the public sector continues to play a dominant role in mental health. However, the involvement of voluntary associations has been growing rapidly.

Current Services

On December 31, 1988, there were 5,654 New Zealanders (170.0 per 100,000 of the total population) resident in psychiatric, mental handicap, and licensed alcohol/drug treatment institutions. Of the total 5,654 persons, 3,025 had mental illness diagnoses and 2,629 mental handicap diagnoses. Approximately two-thirds (3,771) were resident in the country's ten psychiatric hospitals. This means that over 1,000 mentally handicapped people remain resident in psychiatric hospitals. New Zealand has around 3,000 people with mental retardation in hospitals. Approximately two-thirds are in four specialized facilities called psychopaedic hospitals, but the remainder (approximately 1,000) are in psychiatric hospitals. New Zealand, by international standards, has a high number of people with mental retardation in hospitals.

During the past twenty-five years small psychiatric wards and units have been established in general public hospitals throughout the country. While there were only a total of 308 people resident in these seventeen units, on average, throughout 1988, they took 35 percent of total first admissions and 34 percent of readmissions that year. However, the majority of acute, inpatient treatment of people with severe mental disorders is still provided by psychiatric hospitals.

Auckland, with an urban-area population of approximately 900,000, is the largest city in New Zealand. The Auckland region has provided health services through four districts. Auckland's local mental health data show that the two regional psychiatric hospitals, Carrington and Kingseat, had a fiscal-year (FY) 1987–88 total admissions figure of 4,548. The total outpatient attendance for that year at a range of community health centers throughout the region was 59,524 patient contacts, including 6,644 new contacts. It was estimated that approximately 20 percent of contacts were for psychiatric disorders and 80 percent were for psychological distress (McGeorge & Stacey, 1989). (See the sections on deinstitutionalization and funding issues for further information on services.)

Mental Health Personnel and Treatment

New Zealand has a growing number of different types of professions involved in mental health services, including psychiatrists, nurses, social workers, psychologists, counselors, and psychotherapists. Traditionally, the government has not regulated or licensed most of these professions. There has been a growth of professional associations for groups such as psychotherapists who are interested in professional standards and training. There are an increasing number of these professionals providing services in the community, many of them in private practices.

A separate, specialized segment of professionals is developing around alcoholism. In the early 1980s the Alcoholic Liquor Advisory Council (ALAC) and a higher-education institution established a certificated alcohol counselling course, and in 1985 a National Federation of Alcohol and Drug Workers was formed. The New Zealand Society for the Intellectually Handicapped is also working to develop specialized training for community residential workers who work with the mentally handicapped in the community.

Treatment involves both psychotherapy and psychopharmacology as well as development of community activities and support. ECT and psychosurgery are allowed but regulated.

PUBLIC POLICY PROCESS

Pressure groups play a major role in the development of policies in New Zealand. With political power highly concentrated in a cabinet, the prime minister and cabinet become targets of a great deal of pressure-group activity (Cleveland, 1972). As the majority party in Parliament controls the government and the selection of the prime minister, it is important to maintain support in both parties to be able to influence policy when party control changes. There is no effective way to change political agendas if the executive prime minister and cabinet are not receptive, as the Parliament and the bureaucracy follow the lead of the government (the prime minister and the cabinet), and the judiciary does not play a significant role in policy making in New Zealand.

Development of mental health interest groups was slow in New Zealand. The Mental Health Foundation of New Zealand, Psychiatric Survivors, the Consumer Advisory Network, Mental Health Associations, the Schizophrenia Fellowship, and others interested in mental health lack sufficient political power to have a consistent impact in making mental health policy a major priority. However, they did play a significant role in the development of the Labour government's August 1990 policy and funding initiative.

Increasingly, mental health interest groups are becoming more and more specialized and focused on a particular mental health subgroup such as the intellectually handicapped, alcohol abusers, narcotics abusers, psychogeriatrics, schizophrenics, the eating disordered, and others. Some groups, such as the intellectually handicapped, have defined themselves as outside the mental health arena and have attempted to establish a coalition base with disability groups rather than health groups. The operation of a subgovernment, or cozy-triangle policy making, is probably best exemplified by government bureaucrats, parliamentarians, and the New Zealand Society for the Intellectually Handicapped (IHC) representing intellectually handicapped persons. Parent and consumer groups for the intellectually handicapped have been more successful in their policy arena than other mental health subgroups.

Although the bureaucracy and the government adopted deinstitutionalization as a stated policy, in the absence of a coordinated national policy, deinstitutionalization has proceeded at different rates in different parts of the country (Haines & Abbott, 1984). Thus the de facto, actual policy tends to be irregular and incremental. Unions have sometimes played a role at psychiatric hospitals by resisting community residential facilities. The media have frequently focused on mental health issues and have a mixed record, sometimes supporting the case for community mental health developments, but on other occasions dramatizing violent incidents and reinforcing negative attitudes. The legal profession and the courts have not played a significant role in influencing policy, and only recently have lawyers begun to be involved on a regular basis with committals in some parts of the country.

Until recently, there has been little national planning regarding mental health (Cree & Curson, 1986). A funding formula for national funds dispersed to the Area Health Boards was developed from 1980 to 1983. An overall framework for service planning guidelines was established in 1982. The development of these guidelines is an example of how New Zealand uses a consultative process.

The Department of Health submitted drafts for consideration and revision to a small working party of specialists. Then the revised guidelines were reviewed and commented on by the Area Health Boards. Private and voluntary agencies were encouraged to comment to Area Health Boards, and professional organizations were encouraged to comment to the Department of Health. Final revision was made by the department steering group and the working party before submission to the minister of health, who issued the guidelines. This type of consultative process is common to development of other administrative policies, mental health laws, investigations, and reviews.

The greatest problem in accomplishing mental health policy has been an insufficient political base of interest groups to establish mental health as a major priority with entitlement to major resources. This is reflected in the many years required to pass a modern mental health law, insufficient development and coordination of a broad range of community mental health services, and a continuance of an excessive number of people in institutional settings. A significant accomplishment to date is the recognition that there needs to be a wide range of community services for people with mental disabilities. The greatest accomplishment was persuading the Labour government in 1990 to produce a national mental health policy statement with tagged (dedicated) funding to stimulate the development of comprehensive, community-based mental health services.

SPECIAL POLICY ISSUES

The Mentally Ill and the Mentally Retarded

In the institutions that were built in the nineteenth century, the mentally retarded were included with the mentally ill. Although later, four hospitals were designated psychopaedic hospitals for the mentally retarded, nearly half of the hospitalized mentally retarded population remained in psychiatric hospitals. Over time they were increasingly segregated into separate living units, which were often the least focused-upon back wards. The Mental Health Act 1969 included the intellectually handicapped in the definition of ''mentally disordered.'' In 1971 almost 40 percent of New Zealand's intellectually handicapped persons were in psychiatric or psychopaedic hospitals (Morrison, Beasley, & Williamson, 1976). In 1973 the Royal Commission on Hospital and Related Services rejected the existing policy of confusion of mental illness and mental handicap and the emphasis on large institutions. Community care became the focus, and a recommendation was made to transfer facilities for the mentally retarded from the Department of Health to the Department of Social Welfare based on the view that people with mental retardation are handicapped, not ill, and in need of care, not medical treatment (New Zealand Royal Commission, 1973).

In 1975 a survey of psychiatric hospitals revealed that half of the intellectually handicapped persons in psychiatric hospitals could be placed in homes for the mentally handicapped and independent units (Jeffrey & Booth, 1975). But by

1981 the mentally handicapped still represented 47.8 percent of the psychiatric hospital population (around 3,850 people), which, as a proportion of the psychiatric population, was actually an increase over the 1961 figure of 33.1 percent. There were actually more mentally retarded people in hospitals than twenty years before (National Health Statistics Centre, 1979). However, by 1981 there were proportionately more intellectually handicapped living in community facilities such as group homes and hostels. The increased residence in community facilities was accounted for by a decrease in the percentage living in their family home rather than a decrease in the proportion living in hospitals (Prentice & Barnett, 1983). In the 1970s and 1980s there was a decrease in the number and rate of admissions, and the number of intellectually handicapped in institutions decreased by 39 percent between 1971 (4,329) and 1988 (2,629) even though the resident proportion showed little change (*Mental Health Data*, 1988).

The number of children admitted to and resident in hospitals was reduced markedly. Therefore, the hospital population was increasingly an aging one reflecting both past policies of admitting most intellectually handicapped to hospitals and the inability of aging parents to care for adult intellectually handicapped offspring. The percentage of hospital patients who were males in hospitals increased from 54 percent in 1976 (Morrison et al., 1976) to 62 percent in 1988 (*Mental Health Data*, 1991). Also, increasingly, those in hospitals were the more severely disabled as mildly and moderately handicapped were sent from the hospitals to community placements and new populations of the less handicapped were not admitted (Craig & Mills, 1987). Those who remained in hospitals were generally long-term, with 28 percent having been in hospital twenty or more years and 75 percent five or more years (Watson, Singh, & Woods, 1985). The hospitals increasingly cared for long-term profoundly handicapped people and provided short-term respite care for less handicapped people.

Policy for the intellectually handicapped has increasingly been separated from that for the mentally ill. One marked area of difference for the intellectually handicapped has been the long-term presence of a large and powerful interest group. The New Zealand Society for the Intellectually Handicapped (IHC) was formed by parents of intellectually handicapped people in 1949 as the Intellectually Handicapped Children Parents Association (IHCPA). It received its current name in 1975. The IHC has been very influential in changing philosophy, laws, and services for the intellectually handicapped, and it has become the primary provider of community services for the intellectually handicapped (Caseley, 1985). For the year 1988–89, the IHC had 50 branches providing day and support services to 4,500 people in the community. It provided 3,000 beds in residential homes and assisted over 400 intellectually disabled people in employment. It employed 2,800 full- and part-time staff with an $80-million operating budget. The primary aim of the IHC is "to promote the welfare of all persons with an intellectual handicap" (New Zealand Society for the Intellectually Handicapped [IHC], 1989b). The society's interests include citizens' advocacy, standards and monitoring of services, parental support, and encouragement of special-interest groups. The society has been the primary provider of community services for the intellectually handicapped and in some communities has a monopoly. In the early 1990s it was moving from a standard of six-bed residential facilities to a standard of four-bed residences and was trying to eliminate larger hostels and group homes.

The IHC is increasingly criticized for its service provision role, and staff took nationwide industrial action recently when IHC management announced cuts in wages and conditions of employment. The society has expressed a willingness to reduce direct service provision and concentrate on other issues. However, the reality is that few other service providers have appeared, although there is a growing body of other interest groups for the intellectually handicapped, such as Parent to Parent, People First, and support groups for Down's syndrome, mucopolysaccharidosis, autism, Rett's syndrome, and Praeder Willi syndrome. IHC has assisted the development of some of these groups. To address issues of conflict of interest, IHC has separated service delivery functions from its advocacy and standards and monitoring processes.

IHC has been among the first of the service providers to experience a growing interest by government departments to engage in contract management. The IHC has had contracts with Area Health Boards for moving mentally handicapped people into the community. There has been nothing on a comparable scale for the mentally ill. IHC also played a role in the development of the Department of Health's 1988 *Guidelines for Standards of Services for People with Intellectual Handicaps* and has sought to separate the mentally retarded from mental health legislation. The new Mental Health Act does not include mentally retarded persons.

In 1969 IHC was involved in the establishment of the Trust for Intellectually Handicapped People. The trust provides guardianship and advocacy services. Parents or another contributor can enroll a handicapped person for a fee to ensure that that person will receive appropriate guidance and services upon death or disability of the parents. The trust is managed by a board of trustees. When the parent or guardian is no longer able, the trust appoints a personal visitor, who visits the handicapped member at least monthly and is responsible for overseeing that person's quality of life (Trust for Intellectually Handicapped People, n.d.). Only recently have trusts begun to be established for the mentally ill.

In 1982 the New Zealand Institute of Mental Retardation submitted a working paper, *Guardianship for Mentally Retarded Adults*, which recommended a Guardianship of Adults Act to be administered in family courts. In 1988 the Protection of Personal and Property Rights Act, which established guardianship provisions, became law. This may become an important act for the intellectually handicapped and may also be used for the mentally ill. As of 1992 implementation was limited, so the effectiveness of the act is still unknown.

Another recent law that significantly impacts the intellectually handicapped is an amendment of the Education Act that went into effect January 1, 1990. The law puts the emphasis on schools for all, thus legally obligating the government to provide education for all children. The government did not provide education for some children in the community or for many institutionalized children (Capie, 1986). Under a new policy, Tomorrow's Schools, a charter must be established between the minister of education and the Board of Trustees. The charter framework of national guidelines has several provisions regarding children with special needs. As funding will be allowed to reflect priorities, the IHC has encouraged parents to influence school charters to meet the needs of handicapped children, encourage mainstreaming, and establish the education of special-needs children as a priority.

There is limited legislation in New Zealand regarding employment of the intellectually handicapped. The Disabled Persons Employment Promotion Act of 1960 facilitates the operation of sheltered workshops, and the Industrial Relations Act of 1973 allows for adjustment of the wage rate so that handicapped workers who produce less than normal can receive a lower wage. The IHC has proposed changes in the law to enhance compensation for disabled workers. It operates some of the limited number of sheltered workshops in the country, but currently it is interested in developing and expanding supported employment programs.

The mentally retarded as a group have been more successful than the mentally ill as a group in establishing policy and obtaining resources. The intellectually handicapped have more community residential care and services, and they are now perceived as a separate group, with substantial resources being channeled to them through IHC. Its philosophy is appearing in standards, contracts, and laws. However, how successfully some of these new policies will be implemented is yet to be seen, and large numbers of mentally retarded persons are still in institutions. Although the two groups now see each other as separate, at times they have supported each other, for example, in the passage of the Protection of Personal and Property Rights Act and in efforts to defeat community resistance to residential care homes. Unfortunately, discrimination also appears between the groups, with some members, families, and professionals of one group being adamant about wanting no contact with the other group in service provision. Although there is talk about integrated services with the "normal" community, the reality is often segregated services for each group.

There is yet little attention given to people with a dual diagnosis of mental retardation and mental illness. In Christchurch through Sunnyside Hospital there is a small program to establish special residential care for mentally retarded persons with significant emotional behavioral problems, and the IHC provides teams trained to work with behavioral problems to help residential care workers to try to retain people in group homes. However, members of this population are often not wanted by service providers for the mentally ill or mentally retarded and may be neglected until they appear through the criminal justice system in the forensic services (McGeorge, 1990).

The Mentally Ill and Substance Abuse

During the colonial period alcoholics were handled through the justice system. Legislation allowed for voluntary, family, or court committals to treatment upon application to a magistrate. The greatest number of custodial patients in New Zealand institutions were alcohol related. Referral by the criminal justice system has been suggested as a partial explanation for the large number of young Maori males with alcohol dependence in psychiatric institutions (Stewart & Casswell, 1990). Chronic alcoholics were sent to psychiatric hospitals where, as for psychiatric patients, the care was largely custodial. In 1902 an experimental home for alcoholics was established, but within two years it was closed. In 1909 the Salvation Army, in response to a government request, opened homes for alcoholics. The Inebriates Reformatory Act of 1909 made the Department of Justice responsible for alcoholics. In the 1940s Salvation Army personnel brought back from the United States the biomedical disease model definition of alcoholism, and a greater emphasis was put on treatment and cure. Alcoholics Anonymous was introduced in 1945. A National Society on Alcohol and Drugs (NSAD) was established in 1955, and more counselling facilities and inpatient and outpatient programs were developed by voluntary organizations.

With the growth of the medical model, policy shifted from the justice to the health system, and in tandem with mental health policy, interest turned increasingly to treatment, cure, and community approaches. In 1963 a ministerial directive required health boards to establish alcohol treatment units in general hospitals. The Alcoholism and Drug Addiction Act of 1966 moved responsibility for custodial care and cure to the Health Department. Voluntary and involuntary committals were allowed under the act, and in 1983, 11 percent of all alcohol-related admissions to psychiatric hospitals and special treatment centers were under the act (*Mental Health Data*, 1984).

It was not until 1982 that public drunkenness was decriminalized through an amendment to the 1966 act. Police still retain the power to take drunks into custody and then take them home, to a detoxification center, or to a police cell for sobering up. The main focus for law enforcement has become drinking and driving and alcohol-related violent offending (Stewart & Casswell, 1990).

In 1973 a Royal Commission into the Sale of Liquor recommended the establishment of a specialist advisory organization. This was a reflection of the continued specialization and separation of alcohol abuse from mental health. In 1977 the government formed such an agency under the Justice Department, the Alcoholic Liquor Advisory Council (ALAC). The ALAC Act of 1976 states that the purpose of the council is to "encourage, promote, sponsor, and co-operate in the treatment, care and rehabilitation of those adversely affected by the use of liquor, whether by themselves or others." ALAC conducts research, provides information, funds treatment and research through establishment grants or ongoing funding, and provides a regional and national advisory and coordination service. ALAC's first priorities were to set up treatment in areas outside the main population centers and to encourage hospital boards to establish special outpatient centers for assessment, referrals, and counselling.

There is only one specialist state hospital for the treatment of alcohol and drug dependence, which, in recent years, has at any given time had approximately 100 inpatients. In addition, there are five institutions that are licensed under the Alcoholism and Drug Addiction Act. An average of 217 people were resident in these institutions during 1988. Accurate official records are not kept, but there are approximately 700 additional beds in a further twenty-five inpatient units or therapeutic communities—some in psychiatric hospitals and others run as free-standing units by voluntary organizations (Abbott, Arvell, Varley, Whiteside, & Williams, 1991).

In 1985 approximately 10,000 new clients were admitted for inpatient or outpatient treatment, and by 1989 that figure had risen to 13,000. Eighty-nine percent of clients were outpatients, and hospital boards provided 75 percent of the services, making them the major outpatient service provider. The justice system remained involved through referral of clients from courts, probation services, and prisons. In 1986 it was the largest outpatient referral source, referring 31 percent of new outpatient clients (Orchard, 1987). Alcohol treatment and law enforcement agencies both indicated dissatisfaction with their relationships (Stewart & Casswell, 1990). Inherent conflicts appear to exist between punishment and treatment systems.

Self-help groups such as Alcoholics Anonymous, Women for Sobriety, and Narcotics Anonymous have been developed. Most services now operate from the holistic model, with goals of abstinence or controlled drinking, improved self-esteem and coping skills, and an understanding of the abuse problem from personal and social perspectives. This approach is closely tied to mental health developments in psychotherapy, psychology, and social work. Treatment has moved away from focusing on white males to developing services for adolescents, women, and ethnic groups. As with the mental health system, there has been a tendency to move toward treating a wider range of problems and away from treating severe and chronic patients. The more severely disabled tend to receive treatment through the Salvation Army and psychiatric hospitals (Smith & Tatchell, 1979). Also, as in the mental health system, there has been a recognition of the dissatisfaction by many Maori, which has led to a commitment to biculturalism and a self-help approach in Maori programs. As in the systems for the mentally ill and mentally retarded, there is a growing interest in accountability. There are moves to introduce a voluntary-agency accreditation and review system; to establish standards of care guidelines, a code of ethics, and supervision and peer-review mechanisms; and to increase emphasis on the establishment of data-collection/management-information systems.

Although alcohol is the major misused drug, the 1970s saw an increase in other drug use and abuse and the passage of the Misuse of Drugs Act 1977. A Drug Advisory Committee was established in 1980. The area of drug abuse has been splintered and has not had the focus or resources that the alcohol field has had. The Department of Social Welfare operates a Solvent Abuse Program with a coordinator that focuses on those under seventeen and uses a social model approach. The Department of Health has tightened up on the use of amphetamines and barbiturates. Marijuana is the number one drug used outside of alcohol. The handling of marijuana policy has generated considerable controversy (Abbott, 1985). Marijuana production, supply, and use are criminal offenses, and there has been an increase in marijuana seizures and prosecutions.

There have been problems with overuse of prescription drugs, particularly the use of 40–50 million tranquilizers per year. There has also been misuse and diversion of prescription drugs such as benzotheapines and codeine tablets. Morphine sulfate tablets (MST) used in cancer treatment have also been diverted to drug addicts. Break-ins at warehouses and physicians' offices account for many of the illegally used drugs. There is some small-scale drug manufacturing. Morphine is extracted from codeine in backyard labs. There is good border control, which limits importation of drugs. The National Drug Intelligence Bureau coordinates with the Department of Health, police, and customs. But occasionally drugs are found coming into New Zealand. In 1990 "ice," a derivative of speed (methamphetamine), appeared in New Zealand for the first time. The drug was seized by customs officers in a parcel mailed to Auckland from California along with a second parcel of LSD (" 'Ice' Import Discovery Alarms Drug Squad," 1990). Hard drug use is limited, with no cocaine or crack of significance. There is a methadone maintenance program for heroin addicts. The Misuse of Drugs Act was amended in 1987 to allow for a clean-needles exchange program to reduce risk of AIDS. However, the program is not allowed in prisons, and the criminal justice system is also resistant to methadone maintenance while a person is awaiting trial (Miller, 1989). In 1989 the Royal Australian and New Zealand College of Psychiatrists called for urgent consideration of decriminalization of heroin and other illegally injected drugs to slow down the spread of AIDS ("Make Heroin Legal Say Doctors," 1989).

The Department of Health has held discussions with NSAD, ALAC, the Drugs Advisory Committee, and the minister of health over possible options for a coordinating body. Currently, there is no national policy for substance abuse, and there are problems with coordination and accountability. Over 700 drug abusers are treated each year, and there has been an increase in people presenting with polydrug abuse (Orchard, 1987). A continuing problem is treatment of people with dual diagnosis of substance abuse and mental illness. Psychiatric patients deinstitutionalized into the community may have or develop substance abuse problems. Alcohol treatment personnel may refuse referrals because they believe that psychiatric problems are beyond their scope, while psychiatric services may regard the psychiatric symptoms as insufficiently severe for hospitalization and believe that the alcohol abuse is primary. This is a similar situation to that of dual-diagnosed mental retardation/mental illness clients, and like them, dual-diagnosed substance abuse/mentally ill may appear via the criminal justice system in the forensic psychiatric services (McGeorge, 1990).

The Mentally Disordered Offender

Murray Cree (1986) commented that the history of mental health services suggests that as a system of social inequality, it is hard to distinguish the criminal justice system from the mental health system. In terms of living conditions, there is little difference between Lake Alice, a high-security psychiatric hospital, and the maximum-security prison at Paremoremo. The difference is in the philosophy, as psychiatric facilities under the medical model tend to treat their inmates as patients and to have a more humanitarian service. Community placement of offenders has been resisted, as has community placement of the mentally ill or mentally retarded.

The actual incidence of prisoners with mental disorder is not known, and the incidence of mental disorder depends on how wide the definition is, for example, whether personality disorders or psychopathic disorders are included. Based on other countries' studies, it is estimated that 20 percent to 60 percent of prisoners have some mental disorder. Of those accused of homicide, the estimate is 30 percent to 60 percent. Mental health and drug and alcohol issues have not been adequately addressed in the prisons, although there have recently been some positive initiatives in this regard, and suicides have begun to decline (Mason et al., 1988).

A study of patients released from Lake Alice, a high-security psychiatric hospital, revealed that 72 percent reappeared before courts over a five-year period, with 25 percent being charged with violent offenses (Young, 1983). Clinical prediction of violent offending by mentally disordered persons has proven to be inadequate. The single most important predictor for reoffending is the extent and type of previous convictions (Gibbens & Robertson, 1983).

New Zealand has two laws that deal with mentally disordered offenders: the Mental Health Act 1992 and the Criminal Justice Act 1985. Under section 121(2)(b)(ii) of the Criminal Justice Act 1985, a court may remand a person to a psychiatric hospital for a psychiatric report. Most such reports can be done while the person is on bail as an outpatient or at the prison. However, in a few cases the person can be certified for up to one month for evaluation if he or she is charged with an offense punishable by imprisonment; is held in custody; is not able to be practicably assessed while on bail or in prison; and if a psychiatrist or another medical practitioner certifies that it is desirable to assess the person at a psychiatric hospital. Such a person would be deemed a ''special patient,'' and there is no authorization for his or her treatment without consent.

A person may be acquitted on the grounds of insanity or may be found to be under disability (unable to plead, understand the proceedings, or confer adequately with a lawyer for defense). In that event, section 115 of the Criminal Justice Act 1985 can be applied, under which the court orders the person to be committed as a special patient under the Mental Health Act. Under the Mental Health Act 1992 a person who is mentally disordered, as defined by the act, and under an assessment or treatment order can be detained and treated without consent until discharge.

Section 118 of the Criminal Justice Act 1985 allows the court to make a committal order rather than passing sentence on someone convicted. Two medical practitioners must certify that the person is mentally disordered and needs to be detained in a hospital for his or her own interest or for the safety of the public. The hospital superintendent is required to discharge the person when it is no longer necessary to detain him or her for his or her own good or the good of the public. Section 118 patients are not defined as special patients.

Section 33 of the Mental Health Act 1992 allows a superintendent of a prison to apply for a psychiatric assessment under section 5 of the act. This application is required to be accompanied by a certificate from a medical practitioner stating that there are grounds for believing that the detainee is mentally disordered. He or she will be admitted to and detained in a specified hospital for further assessment and treatment for a maximum of five days. If further examination confirms the presence of mental disorder as defined in the act, the clinician responsible for the patient is required to apply to a family or district court for a compulsory treatment order. The court has the authority to grant six-month orders to be carried out in a hospital (inpatient order) or in prison (community treatment order). These orders can be extended by the court. Section 34 allows any prisoner who would benefit from psychiatric treatment not available in prison to be transferred, with the individual's consent, to a hospital. Both section 33 and 34 detainees become special patients. Prison sentences continue to run during committal.

In 1986 the director of mental health issued guidelines to all Area Health Boards on establishment of safe care units (specialized secure treatment units for special or committed patients) and declared their responsibility to provide that type of care. After a series of suicides, a Committee of Inquiry was established in 1987. That committee's report, known as the Mason report, found that forensic psychiatry was "poorly disciplined, under-funded, and under-staffed; and that the role conflict between the justice and health systems over care of the mentally disordered offender was unresolved; and that while facilities to examine patients under the Criminal Justice Act were good, facilities for non-remand forensic patients were not good." The report recommended allowing psychiatric assessment by any person approved by the director of forensic services without requiring a psychiatrist or other medical doctor, and it recommended establishment of a National Review Panel and Regional Review Panels to review all patients in forensic services. It recommended at the regional level establishment of medium-secure and minimum-secure units with no separation of civilly committed and forensic patients. Maximum security was to remain at the National Maximum Security Unit at Lake Alice. The report also recommended forensic services at prisons on an outpatient basis, hostels for community placement, and aftercare community multidisciplinary teams. In addition, a recommendation was made for a direct allocation from the government for three years to fund the establishment of the services (Mason et al., 1988).

The regional forensic services are now in the process of development in six regions with a government allocation of NZ$24 million for three years for capital expenses and NZ$15.5 million annually for operation of medium-secure units. In addition, there is NZ$3.6 million to establish community multidisciplinary forensic teams.

In South Auckland in 1987 a Court Liaison Nursing Service to the Justice Department and Mental Health Services was established. It is part of the Auckland Regional Forensic Service and is funded by the Auckland Area Health Board. It is a mental health resource and advisory service to the justice system, including police, counsel, defendants, probation, families, and victims. The nurse coordinators can assess referred persons and, if necessary, help locate further resources for them (Wade, 1989).

Deinstitutionalization

Deinstitutionalization, in the sense of a reduction in the percentage of people resident in psychiatric and mental handicap institutions, relative to the total population, has been under way in New Zealand for more than forty years. It seems that hospitalization rates began to fall somewhat earlier in New Zealand than in other countries such as England, Australia, and the United States. In 1944 there were 10,000 people living in psychiatric and mental handicap hospitals. Inpatient rates reached a high point of 500 per 10,000 in that year. From then on they began to decline, gradually during the mid-1940s to mid-1960s and more steadily thereafter. Although rates started to fall in the 1940s, it was not until the late 1960s that the total number of people living in these institutions also began to decline.

Numbers resident and rates have continued to fall steadily in recent years. There were 7,067 residents in specialist institutions (197.1 per 100,000) on December 31, 1985. Just three years later, in 1988, the corresponding figures were 5,654 (170.0 per 100,000)—a 20 percent reduction in numbers resident.

Three state psychiatric hospitals have closed in recent years, and there are plans to close a further three within the next two to three years. Most institutions have reduced bed numbers by closing wards and villas. On average, the bed numbers in each institution are one-half to one-third what they were twenty years ago.

Although numbers resident and bed numbers have dropped substantially in the case of the mentally ill, this has not come about by fewer admissions. Total admissions in fact rose from just over 200 per 100,000 in 1960 to approximately 450 per 100,000 by the mid-1970s. They have remained at this level. First admissions also increased during the 1960s, albeit less dramatically, and levelled off at 130 to 140 per 100,000 during the 1970s and 1980s. During the past twenty years there has not been a significant drop in the number of patients who have been resident for long periods of time. Twenty-eight percent of residents with a mental illness diagnosis in 1988 (845 people) had lived in hospital for more than ten years. This means that the large reduction in occupancy numbers has largely been the consequence of a considerable increase in the number of inpatients who stay for short periods of time. During 1988, 65 percent of patients leaving hospital had a stay of less than thirty days.

The large minority of mental health funding, probably in the vicinity of 85 percent, goes to psychiatric and mental handicap institutions. Adequate cost data are not recorded, although this is likely to be remedied shortly. It is widely believed that very little funding has been transferred by most Area Health Boards to provide community-based services. National surveys and government inquiries have concluded that adequate resources have not anywhere followed, let alone preceded, the movement of psychiatric patients from hospitals. Mental handicap has fared better but still has deficiencies.

A Mental Health Foundation survey concluded:

This research shows that community mental health services for psychiatric patients are, in the opinion of those concerned with such services, severely under-resourced, despite the fact that deinstitutionalisation is well under way. Some Boards appear to have fewer resources in relation to their needs than others. The lack of sheltered housing, daytime activities and employment schemes is particularly marked. The barriers to good community care are not only financial. Though the majority of respondents had quite positive attitudes to community care, they reported "outmoded" attitudes on the part of some colleagues and some hospital boards as a problem. Poor planning and lack of coordination of resources was also a barrier, sometimes stemming from lack of cooperation between various groups concerned. A particular problem was the difficulty of getting resources where it was not clear where responsibility lay, for example, the various government departments, local bodies and hospital boards in relation to the provision of sheltered housing.

While New Zealand appears to have avoided, so far, the more severe adverse effects of deinstitutionalisation that have been documented in some other countries, this survey and other sources of information indicate that significant problems do exist, especially in Auckland. (Abbott, 1989a, p. 2)

This assessment was shared by two subsequent government inquiries (Mason et al., 1988; *National Mental Health Consortium Report*, 1989b). Collectively, the conclusions reached by these wide-ranging investigations contributed to the development of new policy and funding initiatives by the Labour government in 1990, specifically aimed at accelerating the development of comprehensive, community-based mental health services. Although some of the funding was subsequently withdrawn in 1991 by the new national government, and this government's radical reforms to health organization generally have since overtaken the 1990 initiatives, they were instrumental in boosting community services and led to the establishment of specialist forensic units throughout the country.

Although fears remain that community care policies may yet prove to be a cruel euphemism for community neglect, on balance they have the support of the present national government and the large majority of people most closely involved with mental health and handicap issues. There is no strong lobby for a reversal of deinstitutionalization and community care developments.

Funding Issues

Funding insecurity is a significant part of the mental health scene in New Zealand, as most funding comes from the national level, and that funding is subject to annual appropriation by parliamentary vote. Funding has gone to Area Health Boards, but under reorganization will be going to Regional Health Authorities. Funds are not specifically designated for mental health, and the elected members of Area Health Boards have determined mental health expenditure for their region in a competitive arena involving expenditure for all health services. The Department of Health has provided grants from the Work Force Development Fund to Area Health Boards and to community organizations to establish training programs, to research work-force issues, to develop work-force skills, and for human resource management. In FY 1988–89 NZ$5.4 million was expended, NZ$240,000 (4.4 percent) for mental health. Service development and bridging loans can be provided. There was NZ$19.3 million in FY 1988–89 for these loans, of which NZ$2.3 million (11.9 percent) was in the area of mental health (National Mental Health Consortium, 1989b). As previously indicated, an additional NZ$25 million was allocated to Area Health Boards for specific community mental health projects in 1991. By FY 1988–89, out of a total budget of NZ$2,267.2 million for the Area Health Boards, it was estimated that NZ$181.4 million (8 percent) was allocated to psychiatric services (National Mental Health Consortium, 1989b), which was a decrease from the 1970s. The upper level of budget spent on mental health care by an Area Health Board is estimated to be 20 percent of health dollars, yet mental health accounts for 42 percent of patient bed days in hospital. It is estimated that 15 percent of mental health expenditures are for community services. In 1988 a community mental health survey found inadequate funding rated as the number one barrier to the provision of sufficient community services (Mental Health Foundation, 1988).

Most Area Health Boards have not had good cost figures for mental health services. In the late 1980s the Area Health Boards were in the midst of organizational change. Several boards, including Auckland, had greatly overspent budgets and went through a process of cutback management to balance budgets. Also, Auckland and other boards changed management systems by removing the old triumvirate management system of medical superintendent, principal nurse, and administrator, using a consultative decision-making process, which was condemned by the Gibbs report (Gibbs, Fraser, & Scott, 1988), and establishing in most hospitals one general administrator with a management background for final decision making. Attempts were also made to establish accounting systems to be able to track costs effectively. Auckland was establishing population-based budgets for each of the four districts within the region. Each district was then responsible for tying planning to budgeting through establishing prioritized needs in a strategic plan. Contracting for services was also becoming more popular, and as contracting increased, more private companies were encouraged to operate alcohol treatment or mental health services under public-sector guidelines.

There has been no nationally agreed proportion of funding for mental health or substance abuse services. Mental health and substance abuse services must compete against each other and other health services for funding. When competing with other health services, they have not usually received a high priority. There is no clear responsibility in regard to funding of services. This has resulted in a lack of funding for some services, duplication of others, and poor coordination. There are gaps in funding, as funding is not provided for some types of services. The National Mental Health Consortium has recommended a system of funding linked to the assessed needs of individuals and specified budgets for community mental health services (National Mental Health Consortium, 1989b).

Historically, the boards have primarily funded hospital-based services. If the bias toward institutional care continues, by the year 2000 there will be a need for a massive increase in funding for elderly, mentally ill, and handicapped people (Gibbs et al., 1988). One of the major difficulties with deinstitutionalization has been the problem of shifting funds. There has been no transportability of funding. Funding does not follow individuals as they are deinstitutionalized. Few economies can be gained in reducing the number of patients in institutions. It would take large increases in funding to retain the institutions and create comprehensive community services (Abbott, 1989b). Two alternatives are closure of some hospitals, with their funding rebudgeted to community services and an upgrading of the remaining hospitals, or closure of all hospitals, with all resources shifted to community services. Most people currently in psychiatric or psychopaedic hospitals do not receive Social Welfare benefits, and by placing people in the community, Social Welfare and Housing Corporation funds can be obtained, thus shifting some of the costs from health.

An anomaly in the national system is that highly structured services and residential placement in the health system for mentally handicapped or mentally ill persons are free to the family, even for a lifetime, at a public cost of NZ$30,000 to $35,000 annually, but for people remaining at home, services are often not available or are means tested (Regional Planning Project, 1989). The publicly funded system also absorbs most costs for treatment of people with substance abuse problems, providing most of their treatment free. Most nonhospital board residential services can get a substantial part of their funding from means-tested sickness benefits. The one small private alcohol treatment hospital receives sickness benefits and charges fees. Sickness benefits are paid on the basis of patients, not beds, which creates pressure not to have empty beds. Most outpatient services have no fees or have flexible, sliding-scale fees. Some programs charge the

Justice Department for probation assessments. ALAC is funded through a levy on alcohol sales. Since 1980 the agency has received less growth in funding, as annual budget increases have been based on a government-designated inflation rate. In the past ALAC has taken over funding for services faced with closure, but the percentage of funds spent on treatment has been decreasing. Although ALAC expends a budget of over NZ$5 million, recently government grants for substance abuse have tended to be for seed or demonstration projects rather than ongoing funding. Innovative community-based programs have been more favored. Treatment services also receive funds from the Lottery Board, the Department of Social Welfare, the Ministry of Health, Area Health Boards, and voluntary agencies.

There is a small but growing involvement in mental health by the private, profit-making sector in the form of private boarding houses, rest homes, and private mental health practitioners. There are also a number of voluntary organizations providing services for the mentally disabled. The Department of Social Welfare provides the major funding for social welfare services such as various types of workshops, rehabilitation programs, capital subsidies, and salary subsidies for private agencies that provide sheltered workshops or rehabilitation programs. People with mental disabilities make up 27 percent of sheltered workshop clients and 19 percent of social rehabilitation program clients. Sheltered workshops can also charge tuition. The Social Rehabilitation Subsidy program provides benefits and program-deficit funding for prescribed residential social rehabilitation programs. Approximately 25 percent of the FY 1988–89 budget of NZ$1.4 million for this program went to the psychiatrically disabled. The Home Help and Family Support Disabled Persons Services Programme provides salary subsidies for field care workers for home help services. People with mental disabilities are seldom means tested to receive services, and NZ$300,000 of a NZ$2.35 million FY 1988–89 budget went to psychiatric disability groups (National Mental Health Consortium, 1989b).

The Rest Home Subsidy Scheme may be used for people sixty-five or over or for people close in age and lifestyle. It has been used for Alzheimer's patients, and an agreement has been made in Christchurch to use it to fund some psychiatric patients. Organizations are contracted with on a fee-for-service basis, and standards of service are required. The Department of Health handles the monitoring and licensing. This funding was shifted from the Department of Social Welfare to the Department of Health in July 1990.

The Department of Social Welfare has also provided directly about $37 million to the IHC for intellectually handicapped (Wilson & Newlove, 1989). The IHC in FY 1988–89 received NZ$33,690,399 from government subsidies and capitation, NZ$858,392 in Area Health Board funds, NZ$18,276,136 in fees for IHC services and facilities, NZ$6,158,630 for aid to families, state wards, and disability allowances, NZ$3,887,322 from fund-raising, NZ$4,382,930 from workshop and other income, NZ$1,542,673 from interest, and NZ$210,680 from the Education Department's transport subsidy (IHC, 1989a). The IHC has negotiated with Area Health Boards to move intellectually handicapped persons from institutions to the community. Contracting has involved a payment of NZ$25,000 per client for providing community services (Grey, 1989).

Voluntary organizations receive some funding through donations and community fund-raising. Tax exemptions are available to individuals making charitable donations. Local body rates are also used by some local authorities to fund some services they have established.

The Housing Corporation provides funding directly to people with psychiatric disability or intellectual handicap through the rental housing program, and indirectly to the private sector through the special tenancies program and a program for the provision of residential supported housing. In FY 1988–89 NZ$3.3 million for twenty-two special tenancies, NZ$5 million in loans to community agencies for supported accommodation, and 100 houses allocated to people discharged from psychiatric institutions were provided (National Mental Health Consortium, 1989b). IHC and some small trusts have made use of these funds. However, currently these arrangements are threatened.

Private therapy has been partially paid for by the Accident Compensation Corporation (ACC) and private insurance (Southern Cross). Mental health is not covered under the National Health Insurance even with a general practitioner referral. The Department of Social Welfare has taken over funding counselling for sexual abuse. The Area Health Boards pay some consultancy fees to private practitioners.

People with a psychiatric disability are often unable to find work and are poor. They usually qualify for sickness or invalid benefits, but if they do, they may have only minimal employment benefit entitlements. The lack of money contributes to the reduction in meaningful activity and restricts housing options (Kearns, 1990). Families often subsidize a family member with a mental disability by paying for clothing, meals, transport, rent, phone bills, doctor's bills, or vacations.

The Department of Social Welfare provides funding for people with psychiatric disabilities through the income-maintenance system and provides services under the Disabled Persons Community Welfare Act. Services are often add-on services to those developed for physical or intellectual disabilities and may result in inappropriate services (National Mental Health Consortium, 1989b). The income-maintenance benefits that can be used by psychiatrically disabled persons are Sickness Benefit, Invalids Benefit, Special Benefit, Accommodation Benefit, Disability Allowance, and Residual Care Supplement. Intellectually handicapped receive Invalids Benefits, about NZ$30 million (Wilson & Newlove, 1989), and about 20 percent of Invalids Benefits go to people with mental illness. Seventeen percent of Sickness Benefits, plus probably a majority of those categorized as "signs, symptoms, and ill-defined conditions," are for mental illness. In special residential rehabilitation programs benefits may be maximized and paid to the service provider. For example, additions to the Invalids Benefit (NZ$155.48) may be for accommodation allowance (NZ$40), residential care supplement (NZ$20), disability allowance (NZ$34), and special benefit (NZ$50), for a total of NZ$299.48 a week.

In 1988 the Gibbs report recommended that all health services be put on a payments-related-to-outputs approach under a case-based payment system like the diagnosis-related group (DRG) used in the United States. The International Classification of Disease (ICD) Code used in New Zealand for patients' diagnoses is compatible with overseas DRG systems. Work on DRGs has begun as a part of a study on cross-boundary flows (Gibbs et al., 1988). In the United States DRGs are also being developed for payment of mental health services.

Consumer Rights

With a unitary system of government, New Zealand has no written constitution, so there is no constitutional bill of rights. A statutory bill of rights has recently been enacted by Parliament. The act provides a measure of protection for fundamental rights and freedoms, a limit on powers of government, and a minimum set of standards for public decision making. Although originally proposed as a form of supreme law requiring amendment by a majority of 75 percent of all members of the House of Representatives, or in an election by a majority of the votes cast in a referendum by the voters for the House of Representatives, it was enacted as a nonsupreme law with the same status as other legislation.

New Zealand has had six major mental health statutes (1846, 1868, 1882, 1911, 1969, and 1992). The law has been revised, on the average, about every twenty-nine years. The first law, the Lunatics Ordinance 1846, focused on the recognition of the mentally ill as a separate problem group needing social control. The act was focused on law and order and aimed at custody and prevention of offenses of dangerously insane people. Over time several safeguards were developed, including certification; documentation involving registers of admissions, discharges, transfers, escapes, and deaths and a system of notification of patient movements to a central authority; inspection by district inspectors, the director of mental health, and official visitors; and sections of law dealing with neglect or ill treatment (Brunton, 1985).

Committal means loss of freedom and possibly of other rights. New Zealand has recently had considerable focus on the rights of patients. An inquiry into cervical cancer treatment at National Women's Hospital found that the system for protecting patients' rights in research and/or treatment had failed in significant areas (Cartwright, Goddard, & Paul, 1988). As a result, the Department of Health looked at the status and functions of all ethics committees and in October 1988 released a national standard. Each Area Health Board is required to have an ethics committee with a membership representative of the community at large, with no single profession or group in control. The committee is to approve all proposed health research involving humans by unanimous consent; the maximum approved research time is twelve months. All subjects of research must give informed consent. Any concerns regarding unethical behavior may be reported to the committee (Horswill, 1990).

Under the Mental Health Act 1969 district inspectors and official visitors were appointed by the minister of health and required to visit the hospital for which they were responsible at least every three months. They were empowered to inspect any part of the hospital, to see any detained person, and to inspect any records. The district inspector, always a legal practitioner, had special powers to conduct inquiries under the direction of the director of mental health.

Professional, paid patient advocacy programs are new to New Zealand. In late 1988 Kingseat Hospital in Auckland made an agreement with the Mental Health Foundation for establishment of an advocacy program at the hospital. The Area Health Board funds the program, and the Mental Health Foundation manages it. In 1989, a year after its inception, an evaluation of the program was made. Changes were made in the program, and a policy and procedures manual for the Kingseat program and a guide for the development and establishment of advocacy programs nationwide was completed in 1990. In 1988 an advocacy program was also established at Carrington Hospital, Auckland, by Psychiatric Survivors, a consumer group. In 1989 part-time advocacy programs were also begun by the Waikato Trust, Hamilton, for developmentally disabled persons, and by Cherry Farm Psychiatric Hospital, Dunedin. Three psychiatric hospitals have legal advocacy available to patients through a panel of lawyers provided by Legal Aid.

In 1983 New Zealand began the process of developing a new mental health act. This legislation, the Mental Health (Compulsory Assessment and Treatment) Act was passed in 1992. The legislation basically is compulsory treatment legislation and involves several major areas of change from current legislation (James, 1988). All references to gazetted psychiatric hospitals are eliminated. This means that no mental health legislation applies only to psychiatric hospitals, but all legislation applies to all hospitals. This eliminates the need for travelling long distances to psychiatric hospitals and allows short-term treatment in hospitals in the community.

The definition of mental disorder is changed. The new definition has a qualitative orientation focused on psychosis involving abnormal state of mind whether of a continuous or an intermittent nature characterized by delusions or disorders of mood, volition, cognition, or perception. It also has a quantitative aspect, namely, that the psychosis is present to such a degree as to endanger the health, welfare, and safety of the person or others, or that it seriously diminishes the capacity of the person to take care of himself or herself. There also is an exclusionary aspect forbidding commitment based only on religious or political beliefs, sexual preference, criminal or delinquent behavior, substance abuse, or intellectual handicap.

The committal process is changed to allow any person over eighteen to apply to the director of Area Mental Health Services for the psychiatric assessment of another person if the request is accompanied by a medical certificate from any doctor. The person can then be ordered to have a psychiatric examination at a convenient place such as his or her home or an outpatient clinic. A medical practitioner can require further assessment and/or treatment of up to five days, which may be in a specified hospital. At that point the person involved, any welfare guardian for that person, and the applicant for assessment will be provided a certificate of preliminary assessment, information on the legal consequences of the finding, and information on the recipient's right to apply for a review. If further assessment and/or treatment is sought, a copy of the certificate of further assessment is provided to the medical practitioner, a district inspector, an official visitor, and other specified persons. The district inspector, after talking to the patient, determines whether or not a review should be applied. The second assessment and treatment period continues for an additional fourteen days. Before expiration of the second period, the responsible clinician can apply to the court for a compulsory treatment order. Pending determination of the application, the person can be held and treated. Also, the judge can add on fourteen days and then an additional one month before a hearing. When the judge, preferably from a family court, holds the hearing, the patient can be present unless the judge examines the patient and excludes him or her based on the patient's "best interest." A compulsory treatment order can be issued at the hearing for six months. Provisions of the act also allow for community treatment orders, for leave from the hospital for a maximum of three months while the compulsory committal order is still in effect, and for the establishment of regional Review Tribunals of at least three people, including a lawyer and a psychiatrist. The tribunal could for any particular case add a person with special knowledge or expertise, or a person of the patient's ethnic identity or gender. Patients have the right to apply to review periodically, and the tribunal has the right to discharge the patient from any order. The right to also apply to a high court judge for a review remains.

Every patient under a compulsory treatment order is required during the first month to accept treatment. After the first month, if the patient refuses treatment, a second opinion must be sought from an independent psychiatrist appointed by the Review Tribunal. ECT can be administered only with consent or the determination by a psychiatrist appointed by the Review Tribunal that it is in the patient's "best interest." Psychosurgery can only be performed with consent, review as to the appropriateness by a Review Tribunal psychiatrist, and review by the Review Tribunal as to whether informed consent was freely given.

In addition, the section on rights is considerably expanded after submissions and review. That section requires a written statement of rights to be given to every person upon becoming a patient. Patients are entitled to be kept informed of their rights, including legal status, right of judicial review, right of Review Tribunal review, and right to seek a judicial inquiry on all orders made by the court or Review Tribunal respecting their case. Every patient has a right to be dealt with in a manner that is in accord with his or her cultural and ethnic identity. There is a right to treatment and to be informed about treatment, including the right to be informed of any visual recording being made. Each patient has the right to independent psychiatric advice and to legal advice. Restrictions are placed on the use of seclusion. There is a right to receive visitors, make phone calls, and receive and send letters and postal articles. However, provisions are made to allow restriction of all of these rights. Complaints can be made to the district inspector, the official visitor, or, if the patient is not satisfied with the result of those complaints, to the Review Tribunal.

One of the most controversial aspects of the proposed law is that police can apprehend a person appearing to be mentally disordered in a public place and take the person to a police station, hospital, or surgery for a medical practitioner to examine (*Mental Health [Compulsory Assessment and Treatment] Act*, 1992). The question of patients' advocates was not addressed in the bill, as the minister of health was developing a separate package involving advocacy for the health services in general, including a health commissioner (Keall, 1989).

CONCLUSIONS AND DISCUSSION

Mental health, alcohol and drug dependence, and mental handicap services in New Zealand have undergone major changes during the past few decades. They have to varying degrees separated from each other and developed their own particular policies and patterns of service delivery. However, there are parallels. All have shown a trend away from reliance on long hospital stays in large institutions toward community-based services provided by a wide variety of providers—public, private, and voluntary. Major progress has been made in all areas, and service provision today more closely matches consumer needs and preferences. However, these gains are precarious, and there are many uncertainties in New Zealand with regard to future policies and services as a consequence of recently announced radical changes to the way health and some other social services are to be organized and funded. There are too many unknowns at this point to be able to make confident predictions about the future.

REFERENCES

Abbott, M. W. (Ed.). (1985). *The great marijuana debate*. Auckland: Mental Health Foundation of New Zealand.

Abbott, M. W. (1989a). Community treatment and support of the mentally disabled in New Zealand. In Japanese Association for Mental Health (Ed.), *Proceedings of the International Forum*. Tokyo: Author.

Abbott, M. W. (1989b). Current issues in mental health and developmental disabilities: Challenges for health professionals. *Mental Health in Australia, 20*, 19–32.

Abbott, M. W., Arvell, G., Varley, E., Whiteside, E., & Williams, R. (1991). *Queen Mary Hospital review*. Wellington: Alcoholic Liquor Advisory Council.

Abbott, M. W., & Volberg, R. (1991). *Gambling and problem gambling in New Zealand*. Wellington: Department of Internal Affairs.

Abbott, M. W., & Volberg, R. (1992). *Frequent gamblers and problem gamblers in New Zealand*. Wellington: Department of Internal Affairs.

Blake-Palmer, G. (1963). Trends in mental health services in New Zealand. In P. J. Lawrence (Ed.), *Mental health and the community*. Christchurch: Canterbury Mental Health Council.

Bland, R. C., Orn, H., & Newman, S. C. (1988). Lifetime prevalence of psychiatric disorders in Edmonton. *Acta Psychiatrica Scandinavica, 77*(Suppl. 338), 24–32.

Brunton, W. (1985). Mental health law in New Zealand: Some sources and traditions. *Community Mental Health in New Zealand, 2*, 170–183.

Brunton, W. (1986). Deinstitutionalization: A romance for all seasons. In H. Haines & M. Abbott (Eds.), *The future of mental health services in New Zealand* (pp. 44–63). Auckland: Mental Health Foundation of New Zealand.

Bureau of Public Affairs. (1987, March). *Background notes: New Zealand*. Washington, DC: United States Department of State.

Canino, G. J., Bird, H. R., Shrout, P. E., Rubio-Stipec, M., Bravo, M., Martinez, R., Sesman, M., & Guevara, L. M. (1987). The prevalence of specific psychiatric disorders in Puerto Rico. *Archives of General Psychiatry, 44*, 727–735.

Capie, A. (1986). Deinstitutionalization Action: An IHC perspective. In H. Haines & M. Abbott (Eds.), *The future of mental health services in New Zealand: Deinstitutionalization* (pp. 118–120). Auckland: Mental Health Foundation of New Zealand.

Cartwright, S. R., Goddard, L. P., & Paul, C. E. (1988). *The report of the committee of inquiry into allegations concerning the treatment of cervical cancer at National Women's Hospital and into other related matters*. Auckland: Government Printing Office.

Caseley, T. (1985). The New Zealand Society for the Intellectually Handicapped. In J. E. Singh & J. Wilton (Eds.), *Mental retardation in New Zealand*. Wellington: Research Foundation of New Zealand Society for the Intellectually Handicapped, Inc.

Cleveland, L. (1972). *The anatomy of influence: Pressure groups and politics in New Zealand*. Wellington: Hicks, Smith & Sons.

Craig, T., & Mills, M. (1987). *Care and control: The role of institutions in New Zealand* (Social Monitoring Group Report No. 2). Wellington: New Zealand Planning Council.

Cree, M. (1986). Prison aftercare: A community myth. In H. Haines & M. Abbott (Eds.), *The future of mental health services in New Zealand: Deinstitutionalization* (pp. 121–122). Auckland: Mental Health Foundation of New Zealand.

Cree, M., & Curson, B. (1986). Health, wealth, or stealth: The future politics of mental illness in New Zealand. In H. Haines & M. Abbott (Eds.), *The future of mental health services in New Zealand: Deinstitutionalization* (pp. 16–38). Auckland: Mental Health Foundation of New Zealand.

Dawson, J., Abbott, M. W., & Henning, M. A. (1987). Who gets committed: Demographics and diagnostic data. *New Zealand Medical Journal, 100*, 142–145.

Department of Health. (1988). *Guidelines for standards of services for people with intellectual handicaps*. Wellington: Government Printing Office.

Department of Health. (1989a). *Child, adolescent, and family mental health services: Area Health Board service planning guidelines*. Wellington: Government Printing Office.

Department of Health. (1989b). *Outline of service development for mental health for Area Health Boards.* Wellington: Government Printing Office.

Downey, P. G. & Werry, J. S. (1980). "Psychiatric Care in General Practice." *New Zealand Medical Journal, 87,* 305–308.

Eaton, W. W. & Kessler, L. G. (Eds.). (1985). *Epidemiological Field Methods in Psychiatry.* Orlando, Florida: Academic Press.

Fergusson, R., & Mailing, T. (1990). The Nelson general practitioner prescribing project, part 1. *New Zealand Medical Journal, 103,* 58–60.

Gibbens, T. C., & Robertson, G. (1983). A survey of the criminal careers of hospital order patients. *British Journal of Psychiatry, 143,* 362–369.

Gibbs, A., Fraser, D., & Scott, J. (1988). *Unshackling the hospitals: Report of the hospital and related services taskforce.* Wellington: Government Printing Office.

Grey, J. (1989, October 20). [Interview, Department of Health, Wellington].

Haines, H. (1982, August). *What we know about the epidemiology of psychological disorders in New Zealand?* Paper presented at the Prevention of Psychological Disorders Symposium, New Zealand Psychological Society annual conference.

Haines, H., & Abbott, M. (1984). *Social policy, deinstitutionalization, and the development of community mental health services in New Zealand.* Paper presented at the Social Policy Conference, Victoria University, November 20–December 2.

Haines, H., & Abbott, M. (1985). Deinstitutionalization and social policy in New Zealand: Historical trends. *Community Mental Health in New Zealand, 1,* 44–56.

Horswill, Ian. (1990, February 7). Board wants to vary ethics committees. *Auckland Star,* p. A3.

"Ice" import discovery alarms drug squad. (1990, January 31). *Auckland Star,* p. A3.

James, B. (1988). The new Mental Health Act. In S. Bell (Ed.), *Legal and consumer issues in mental health law.* Auckland: Mental Health Foundation of New Zealand.

Jeffrey, S. J., & Booth, J. M. (1975). *Survey of patients in psychiatric hospitals* (Special Report Series No. 47). Wellington: Department of Health.

Joyce, P. R., Oakley-Browne, M. A., Wells, J. E., Bushnell, J. A. & Hornblower, A. R. (1989). Birth cohort trends in major depression. *Journal of Affective Disorders, 23,* 541–547.

Justice Department. (1988). *The protection of personal and property rights act 1988: A reference guide.* Wellington: Department of Justice.

Keall, J., M. P. (1989, November 16). *Mental health bill: Report back speech.* Wellington: Social Services Select Committee.

Kearns, R. A. (1990). *Coping and community life for people with chronic mental disabilities in Auckland* (Occasional Publication No. 26). Auckland: Department of Geography, University of Auckland.

Make heroin legal say doctors. (1989, September 18). *New Zealand Herald,* sec. 1, p. 10.

Mason, K. H., Ryan, A. B., & Bennett, H. R. (1988). *Report of the committee of inquiry into procedures used in certain psychiatric hospitals in relation to admission, discharge, or release on leave of certain classes of patients.* Wellington: Department of Health.

McGee, R., Freeham, M., Williams, G., Partridge, F., Silva, P., & Kelly, J. (1990). DSM-III disorders in a large sample of adolescents. *American Academy of Child and Adolescent Psychiatry, 29,* 4–9.

McGeorge, P. (1990). [Interview, Auckland Area Health Board, Auckland].

McGeorge, P., & Stacey, F. (1989). *Mental health services development plan.* Auckland: Auckland Area Health Board.

Mental Health Act 1969, No. 16, Wellington: Government Printer.

Mental Health (Compulsory Assessment and Treatment) Act, 1992. Wellington: Government Printer.

Mental health data. (1970 to 1991, annually). Wellington: National Health Statistics Centre, Department of Health.

Mental Health Foundation. (1988, September). *Community mental health services in New Zealand and the role of the voluntary sector: Report of the Mental Health Foundation to the Department of Social Welfare.* Auckland: Mental Health Foundation.

Miller, L. (1989, October). [Interview, Department of Health, Wellington].

Morrison, A. A., Beasley, D.M.G., & Williamson, K. I. (1976). *The intellectually handicapped and their families: A New Zealand survey.* Wellington: Research Foundation of New Zealand Society for the Intellectually Handicapped, Inc.

National Health Statistics Centre. (1979). *Survey of occupied psychiatric hospital beds and psychiatric day and outpatients, 1976.* Auckland: Author.

National Mental Health Consortium. (1989a, June). *The Tangata Whenua report: The Consumer report.* Wellington: Departments of Health and Social Welfare.

National Mental Health Consortium. (1989b). *National mental health consortium report.* Wellington: Department of Health.

New Zealand Institute of Mental Retardation. (1982). *Guardianship for mentally retarded adults.* Dunedin: Author.

New Zealand Royal Commission of Inquiry into Hospital and Related Services. (1973). *Services for the mentally handicapped.* Wellington: Author.

New Zealand Society for the Intellectually Handicapped (IHC). (1989a). *Annual Report, 1988–89.* Wellington: IHC.

New Zealand Society for the Intellectually Handicapped. (1989b). *Philosophy and policy.* Wellington: Author.

Orchard, H. (1987). *New Zealand alcohol/drug outpatient statistics 1986.* Wellington: Alcoholic Liquor Advisory Council.

Prentice, G., & Barnett, P. (1983). *Census and Service of the Intellectually Handicapped in North Canterbury.* Planning and Research Series no. 10. Christchurch: Health Planning and Research Unit.

Regional Planning Project. (1989, October). *Services and advocacy centre: A proposal for a new system of services in Otago/Southland for people who have an intellectual disability.* Dunedin: Author.

Sachder, P. S. (1989). Psychiatric illness in the New Zealand Maori. *Australian and New Zealand Journal of Psychiatry, 23,* 529–541.

Shepherd, M., Cooper, B., Brown, A. C., & Kalton, G. (1966). *Psychiatric illness in general practice.* London: Oxford University Press.

Smith, A. G., & Tatchell, P. M. (1979). *Health expenditure in New Zealand: Trends and Growth Patterns* (Special Report No. 53). Wellington: Management Services & Research Unit, Department of Health.

Strole, L., Langer, T. S., & Michael, S. T. (1962). *Mental health in the metropolis: Vol. 1. The midtown Manhattan study.* New York: McGraw-Hill.

Stewart, L., & Casswell, S. (1990). Treating alcohol problems in New Zealand: Changes in policies, practices, and perspectives. In G. Hunt, H. Klingemann, & J. Takala

(Eds.), *Cure, care, or control: Alcoholism treatment in sixteen countries.* Albany: State University of New York Press.

Task Force. (1976). *New Zealand at the turning point: Social and economic planning in New Zealand.* Wellington: Government Printer.

Trust for Intellectually Handicapped People. (n.d.). *Services and other benefits.* Wellington: Author.

Wade, J. (1989, July). *Court liaison nursing service to Justice Department and Mental Health Services.* Auckland: Auckland Regional Forensic Service.

Watson, J. E., Singh, N. N., & Woods, D. J. (1985). Institutional services. In J. E. Singh & J. Wilton (Eds.), *Mental Retardation in New Zealand.* Wellington: Research Foundation of New Zealand Society for the Intellectually Handicapped, Inc.

Wilson, L., & Newlove, D. (1989, October 18). [Services for older people and people with disabilities, Interview, Department of Social Welfare, Wellington].

Young, W. A. (1983). *Submission to the Commission of Inquiry into the case of Ian Donaldson. Report of the Commission of Inquiry.* Wellington: Government Stationery Office.

12

Nigeria

S.T.C. Ilechukwu

OVERVIEW

Nigeria is located on the Atlantic coast of West Africa and has a land area of 356,669 square miles (923,768 square kilometers). Nigeria is bordered by Benin on the west, Niger and Chad on the north, and Cameroon on the east. The capital city of Lagos is now being replaced by Abuja as the administrative capital. The climate is determined primarily by distance from the ocean and secondarily by elevation and varies from tropical to arid.

The 1992 census indicated a population of 88.5 million. Annual population growth is 3.3 percent. The rural/urban population ratio is estimated at 80/20. About 250 different ethnic groups live in Nigeria. The four largest ethnic groups, which together account for more than 60 percent of the total population, are Fulani and Hausa of the north, the Ibo, who are predominant in the southeast, and the Yoruba, who are in the southwest. The Edo, Ibibio, Kanuri, Nupe, Tiv, Chamba, Ekoi, and Ijaw are smaller but still politically important groups. Other groups are quite small.

Life expectancy is forty-eight years, and the infant mortality rate is 135 per 1,000. The physician/population ratio is 1 per 12,550.

English is the official and most widely spoken language, but outside the south and the cities is little understood. Each ethnic group has its own language, and the language of larger ethnic groups may have up to 200 dialects.

Islam, introduced from the north during the fourteenth century, claims 47 percent of all Nigerians and is the dominant religion in the north. Christianity, claiming about one-third of the population, is dominant in the south, and the remaining 18 percent hold traditional religious beliefs.

There is an adult literacy rate of 42 percent. Six years of primary education are free and compulsory. Secondary school (six years) is also free in the majority of states, but enrollments are limited. More than 120,000 students were enrolled in universities in 1986.

Nigeria has about 1 percent of the world's proven petroleum reserves. By 1985 petroleum provided more than 95 percent of all foreign exchange earnings. The traditional cash crops of cocoa, rubber, cotton, palm oil, and palm kernel have become less important as foreign exchange earners. Nonetheless, agriculture still employs more than half the total population. Also, Nigeria remains one of the world's largest producers of tin and columbite.

Present-day Nigeria came into existence in 1914 by the establishment of the Colony and Protectorate of Nigeria by the British government under Sir Frederick Lugard as governor-general. In 1960 Nigeria gained independence from Britain and became a federation composed of three regions—northern, western, and eastern. The regions have been broken up, and instead there are now twenty-nine states. Presently, the federal republic is under a united military and civilian rule under President Ibrahim Babangida. Since political independence from Britain in 1960, the military has been in control for more than two-thirds of the period. Civilian governments were initially of the British parliamentary type, but after the first spell of military governments (1966–79) a bicameral legislature (as in the United States) was adopted in the central government. A unicameral legislature operated in the states. The government as it currently exists is in a transitional phase, progressing toward complete civilian rule. There is a strong emphasis on local government aimed at encouraging grass-roots participation. The power of local government is bolstered by direct budgetary allocations from the central government. This grass-roots philosophy is expected to influence all aspects of the public policy process.

The diversity of Nigerian arts, both ancient and contemporary, is magnificent. Nigeria has a tradition of wood sculpture, elaborate textile design and weaving, and bronze and metal work. Archaeologists have illuminated an artistic heritage that includes ivory and bronze works of the fifteenth-century court of Benin; the thousand-year-old sculpted heads associated with the culture of Ife; terra-cotta figurines of the ancient Nok culture, dating to the time of Christ; and the elaborate bronze head and copper works found at Igbo-Ukw in eastern Nigeria. Today, Nigerian artists work in traditional modes, while also carving church doors and creating theater pieces, poetry, and music.

Most Nigerians in cities and rural areas have adopted the monogamous marriage pattern recognized by state statutes and the Christian church. However, Islam recognizes up to four wives, and native practices impose no numerical restrictions, so polygamous marriages are still quite common. Some people have argued that this practice has kept down divorce rates and the attendant psychosocial complications.

Extended family relationships are still very much intact even though the system's much-touted supportive implications have been much weakened by internal migration, urbanization, and individual income patterns. The extended family is still the major social insurance system. There is still much respect for the elderly. Parents invest in the upbringing of the young, and the young in turn look after their elderly parents. By proportion, however, the elderly population is still small. The population is still predominantly young, under fifty years of age.

The vicissitudes of mental health care delivery in Nigeria are directly related to overall budgetary allocations to health care and the attitude of health care planners to mental health. The low priority of health care is shown by the frequent allocation of less than 2 percent of the annual budget to health. This is far short of the minimum 5 percent recommended by the World Health Organization (WHO). The low rating of mental health by health planners was perhaps best shown recently by the belated inclusion of mental health components into a National Health Policy that was already in place.

EXTENT OF THE PROBLEM

The Cornell-Aro study (Leighton et al., 1963) remains the only community-based estimate of the prevalence of psychiatric symptomatology in Nigeria. This study attempted to replicate the Stirling County study done by the same research group in Nova Scotia, Canada, with the assistance of local psychiatrists. Clear psychiatric cases were elicited in 21 to 31 percent of the population and probable cases in another 14 to 19 percent. This may be compared to figures obtained in the Stirling County study: 24 percent "notable impairment" and 20 percent in need of psychiatric attention. Considering specific disorders, there is no reason to believe that the WHO (1979) estimates of 3.3 to 5.6 per 1,000 of the adult population for schizophrenia do not apply to Nigeria. There is also evidence that the prevalence of depression (contrary to previous beliefs) may in fact be higher among Africans. Ranges of between 25.3 percent (Orley & Wing, 1979) and 28.5 percent (Leighton et al., 1963) have been suggested, compared to a mean of 18.5 percent in a southeast London sample (Orley & Wing, 1979). Estimates for the prevalence of bipolar illness in Africa reported from mental hospital samples have varied from 5.1 percent (Vanycke, 1957) to 21.4 percent (Shelley & Watson, 1936).

Prevalence studies of neurotic disorders are hard to come by. Nevertheless, descriptions of various somatic distress syndromes, most notably "brain-fag syndrome" (Prince, 1989), have indicated that they are quite common and make up the bulk of psychiatric morbidity (PM) cases that are quite prominent in hospital and community studies. For an overview, including the problem of brief psychotic disorders, see Ilechukwu (1991).

Substance abuse has been an ever-present problem, but newer challenges are emerging with the entry of newer drugs (cocaine and heroin) into the drug scene (Odejide, 1991, as reviewed by Ilechukwu & Prince, 1992). A study of drug-related admissions into twenty-eight psychiatric facilities in Nigeria in 1989, for example, showed the following admission pattern: Out of 10,396 admissions, 10.5 percent (1,096) were for drug-related problems. Of these, 52.6 percent were related to cannabis, 16.4 percent to heroin, 14.4 percent to alcohol, 9.3 percent to cocaine, 2.4 percent to amphetamines, and 5.3 percent to other drugs (Odejide & Ohaeri, 1991, cited in Odejide, 1991). In previous decades the sole substance abuse problem associated with hospitalization was attributable to cannabis (Ilechukwu, 1991).

Problems relating to mental subnormality are widely recognized clinically, educationally, and socially. However, the prevalence of mental subnormality has not been formally evaluated in Nigeria. In the Sudan, a comparable African country, a community-based study of children's problems in a rural setting showed 12.5 percent of children repeating grades in school. This might indicate some degree of mental subnormality (Baasher & Ibrahim, 1976). Some states in Nigeria have set up outpatient and/or custodial care. For example, Lagos State has set up a psycho-educational center for evaluation and special education of the educationally subnormal, while Imo State has a boarding primary-school facility. Both centers are run by the Ministry of Education of the respective states.

There is no recent study of suicide in Nigeria. Asuni's study (1961), in which the rate of 1 per 100,000 was estimated, is still very much quoted. More recent work in another African country (Zambia) suggests that the figure may be much higher (Rwegellera, 1979). This study reported 7.4 percent per 100,000 (9.4 if doubtful cases were included). When only black Africans were considered, a lower figure of 6.9 was obtained. A rate of 20.9 was obtained when only white Africans were considered.

The distinction between nonpsychotic psychiatric illness and physical illness may be quite hazy among Nigerian patients. Psychological distress presenting as somatic symptoms is often taken to the general practitioner, internist, surgeon, or gynecologist. Mbanefo (1971), in a general practice study ($N = 1,460$) in Nigeria, found that equal proportions (15 percent) were diagnosed as suffering psychiatric illness and malaria. Experience elsewhere in Africa (Kenya) suggests that psychiatric morbidity (PM) in the outpatient department may be close to 30 percent (Dhadphale, Ellison, & Griffin, 1983). With regard to children, studies in the Sudan have shown that 10 percent of the total outpatient population may be children with psychiatric problems. A non-hospital-based study in rural Sudan showed that 12 percent of such children had ''severe symptoms'' (Basher & Ibrahim, 1976). Symptoms most often presented by parents (regarding their children) were fear of the dark, 16.2 percent; quarrelsomeness, 13.3 percent; overactivity, 13.3 percent; repeating grades, 12.5 percent; and temper tantrums, 10.3 percent.

Despite the prevalence of child psychiatric problems, there were only two child guidance clinics to serve much of English-speaking West Africa by 1970—one in Enugu, the other in Lagos (Izuora, 1976). The situation has improved only marginally.

MENTAL HEALTH HISTORY

The term *traditional medicine* is used to designate the health care system that existed in Africa before the advent of Western medicine with colonization by

Europeans. Traditional healers specializing in aspects of healing such as fractures or mental illness are recognized. Prince (1965) has described the practice of mental health within Yoruba traditional medicine. Presently, traditional and modern medicine exist side by side in Nigeria. Indeed, patients often change from one mode to the other or use them concurrently. Many Nigerians perceive traditional medicine as more effective in managing mental illness as a whole. More surprisingly, many Nigerian psychiatrists (e.g., Lambo, 1965) have asserted the frequent superiority of traditional treatment methods in neurotic mental disorders. However, modern medicine has enjoyed an almost total monopoly of government funding and regulation.

The first modern psychiatric hospitals in Nigeria (lunatic asylums) were built by the British colonial government in the early twentieth century. Before then, the mentally ill in Nigeria who were under direct colonial government supervision were sent to Sierra Leone, another West African British colony (Anumonye, 1976). The following historical milestones in the development of mental health in Nigeria may be noted:

1907	Building of asylums in Yaba (Lagos), Lantoro, and Calabar.
1928	Druce Dome report.
1936	Cunnyngham-Brown Report III on the care and treatment of "lunatics" in British West Africa colonies: Nigeria. The first report was said to have been suppressed because it was unduly critical.
1952	Arrival of Dr. A. Lambo in Nigeria.
1955	J. C. Carothers's report on the psychiatric services of Nigeria commissioned by the British government.
1938–1960	Bed strength at Yaba Psychiatric Hospital increased from 218 to 246 (13 percent). By comparison, Lagos General Hospital beds increased from 230 to 1,537 (570 percent) over the same period (Anumonye, 1976).

The methods of operation of traditional healers have attracted much attention. Emphasis is often placed on the social and psychological influences embodied in magic and ritual. Physical measures such as abusive restraints and flagellation have been appropriately condemned. However, effective pharmacological and dietary measures are often overlooked (Prince, 1960, 1965). Raymond Prince (1960) has stressed that rauwolfia alkaloids (such as *Rauwolfia vomitoria*) have been used for centuries in the parts of Nigeria studied. Extracts of rauwolfia and other active or enhancing ingredients yet to be clearly defined are used by traditional healers to induce prolonged sleep. Mental conditions associated with certain improper dietary practices are also treated (albeit in blunderbuss fashion) by dietary prescriptions and prohibitions (Prince, 1966).

Mental illness is still largely equated with the severe psychoses in the minds of the majority of Nigerians. The notion that mental illness is caused by supernatural agencies is also quite deep rooted even among the educated. There are signs of change, however. The major agents of change are education and exposure to modern medicine (Ilechukwu, 1988). One of the most important medical events was the establishment of Aro Psychiatric Hospital (Nervous Diseases Hospital) in Abeokuta in 1952. This hospital (at a time when electroshock therapy was one of the most potent therapeutic modes) quickly established that modern medical methods could be more effective than traditional methods. This educative precedent was consolidated by other psychiatric treatment centers. Later, of course, the profusion of neuroleptics that became available in the 1960s improved the effectiveness of modern psychiatry even more. Also, even those who believe in supernatural causation of mental illness use modern services (Ilechukwu, 1988). Also important in changing popular attitudes is the referral pattern of physicians to psychiatric services. In a very real sense, mental illness came to be any illness deemed worthy of referral by a doctor to a psychiatrist. Heads of educational institutions (primary, secondary, or university) have also, at times, served this defining role.

Mental health policy has been influenced by political factors and social perceptions of mental illness. Since the psychiatric services were initially organized to serve the economic and administrative interests of colonizing Britain, it followed that a utilitarian slant was unavoidable. The asylums served the end of maintaining public order. When the psychiatric services were perceived as being excessively out of phase with mental institutions in the mother country (Britain), experts were commissioned to report on the mental health services. This is how the Cunnyngham-Brown (1936) and Carothers (1955) reports were brought about. It is interesting that the Christian churches (especially the Anglican, Baptist, Catholic, and Presbyterian), who had taken pioneering roles in the health services by providing alternative and frequently better health facilities than the government, showed absolutely no interest in the provision of mental health services. However, the sporadic colonial-government-sponsored expert reports and the abiding interest of the World Health Organization (WHO) led to the establishment of model mental hospitals such as the Nervous Diseases Hospital at Aro, Abeokuta (most frequently referred to as Aro Hospital). Other mental hospitals (twelve in all) have been established in other states of Nigeria. Only the mental hospitals in Benin and Yaba (Lagos) in addition to Aro (the "big three") are directly funded and managed by the federal government through a Psychiatric Hospital Management Board.

Psychiatric hospitals, just like other health institutions (state or federal), are managed by the ministries of health, often through a management board. Where psychiatric departments are part of a teaching or specialist hospital, they are funded like other medical specialties. In cases where such departments or units are aligned to a medical school, they also have the benefit of cross-staffing from the academic unit. There are eleven such departments in the country. The burden of salaries and benefits of such staff are mostly borne by the medical schools, which are funded through the Ministry of Education.

There are some conditions that are traditionally classified as psychiatric disorders that are perceived differently in Nigeria. At times it is not a matter of perception, but rather that management of such conditions has evolved separate from the psychiatric hospitals. Most often in such cases the involvement of the Ministry of Health becomes peripheral. For example, the mentally ill in the penal system are often placed in "prison hospitals" funded and supervised by the Ministry of Internal Affairs. Similarly, the educationally subnormal are often supervised by the Ministry of Education, and the conduct-disordered juveniles are placed in "approved schools" funded and supervised by the Ministry of Youth, Sports, and Social Welfare. Another borderline area is the care of persons abusing illegal substances such as cannabis and, more recently, heroin and cocaine. The laws differentiate rather poorly between users and pushers of such substances, and both often end up in the penal system. However, substance abusers who admit themselves into public or private hospitals are treated just like other patients. This reflects a legal ambiguity that makes it a crime to use any prohibited substances, but allows users to seek treatment for health conditions resulting from such abuse without risking prosecution. Owing to legal and social tolerance, use and abuse of alcohol are increasing, but the health problems associated still attract little specific medical attention in Nigeria (Odejide, 1979). There are no special clinics or services for substance- and alcohol-dependent persons.

POLICY, ORGANIZATION, AND SERVICES IN THE 1980s AND 1990s

Current Policy Developments

Mental health policy was redefined in 1990 within the Nigerian National Health Policy. This policy is based on the principle of primary health care (PHC) as enunciated in the Alma Ata declaration of 1978. For the first time in the history of independent Nigeria, mental health was defined and methods of achieving it were outlined. Mental health was defined as the capacity of an individual, a group, and the environment to interact with one another in ways that promote subjective well-being, the achievement of individual and collective goals consistent with justice, and the attainment and preservation of conditions of fundamental equality. Mental illness could therefore result from a disruption of the balance between the individual, the group, and the environment and becomes manifest when there is sufficient cognitive and/or affective impairment.

The underlying philosophy of PHC is health for all. Using this orientation, the Nigerian mental health policy prescribes ways in which this ideal may be achieved. The essential elements are identification of the needs of the people; decentralization of services; active participation of individuals, families, and communities; and the use of nonspecialized personnel as care providers. PHC is seen as a way out of fiscal restraints, inadequate personnel, and communication difficulties, among many other constraints. However, PHC is seen not just as a framework of organization, but as an instrument of mental health. By this is meant that, like all group activity encouraging people or communities to get together and solve their own problems, PHC promotes the balance between the individual, the group, and the environment irrespective of the stated objectives of the group deliberations.

The laws regulating aspects of mental illness were inherited from the British legal system and were retained as such long after the British laws were reviewed. They deal with procedures for compulsory admissions and rights of the mentally ill. For example, section 20 deals with procedures that may be adopted by relatives or physicians by invoking the principle of dangerousness. These laws have been reviewed recently. The main thrust of change is to remove the rather nebulous group of individuals referred to as "psychopaths" from psychiatric responsibility. This recognizes the fact that psychiatry has been able to do very little for these perpetual offenders and thus leaves room open for society to take decisions regarding their disposal.

Current Organization

The major governmental agencies and nongovernmental organizations involved in mental health policy formulation are the Ministry of Health (MOH) and the various health professional organizations, especially the Nigeria Medical Association (NMA). The ministry participates directly and indirectly through representatives of parastatal institutions that it oversees. The Ministry of Internal Affairs and the Ministry of Youth, Sports, and Social Welfare are also involved in ways already indicated previously.

The MOH is usually directly represented by the Planning and Research Division. Representatives of the Association of Psychiatrists in Nigeria, NMA, the Association of Registered Nurses and Midwives, the Nigeria Psychological Association, and the Association of Social Workers in Nigeria present the views of mental and general health professionals. Parastatals are represented by their chief executives or their proxies. The chief executives of the "big three" and heads of departments of representative medical schools are also on such policy committees. There is also a representative of the public—often a political appointee or a respected retired public servant.

Current Services

Before the enunciation of PHC as the vehicle for the delivery of mental health service, services were provided through twelve mental hospitals, eleven university hospital departments, eight psychiatric units in state general hospitals, five units in the armed forces' hospitals, ten community health outposts of some hospitals, and seven private hospitals specializing in psychiatric care. These facilities are unevenly spread, with some concentration in urban centers. With the exception of the armed forces' hospitals, the private hospitals, and the community health centers, all the others function like all federal or state government hospitals—charging minimal fees and dispensing both inpatient and outpatient care. It is important to emphasize that while some may provide long-term care (up to six to nine months), they are not custodial. The teaching hospital psychiatric departments offer consultant, outpatient, emergency, and short-term (up to three months) admission services. The largest of them have up to 30 beds. On the whole, it is estimated that there are only 3,000 psychiatric beds in Nigeria.

Current mental health policy seeks to give individuals with mental, neurological, and psychosocial disorders the same rights to treatment and support as those with physical illness. It proposes to integrate mental health services into general health services at all levels. The major thrust, as repeatedly emphasized, is to increase accessibility and availability. Services therefore are to be spread from the pinnacle of political organization to the grass roots—federal, state, and local government areas and wards. Each ward is to be served by a community health center; each local government is to be served by a community hospital. Interrelationships with tertiary services are yet to be clearly defined. The community health centers provide immunization services, well-baby clinics, maternity services, rehydration services, family planning, emergency first-aid services, and the like. Now they are to be staffed additionally by a mental health aide who will be able to offer a rough diagnostic service and referral. The mental health aide also has access to and will be allowed to prescribe drugs for major mental health disturbances, such as chlorpromazine for psychoses; Akineton or benztropine for reaction to chlorpromazine and related drugs; diazepam for acute anxiety attacks; phenobarbital for convulsive episodes; and paraldehyde for convulsive episodes or acute psychiatric disturbances. The aide will also have stock to give depot neuroleptics (e.g., Modecate) to relieve the burden and disruptive pressure to travel to tertiary centers or mental hospitals just to receive such depot injections. The follow-up visits to see specialists can thus be spaced out and lengthy waiting times for visits reduced. The PHC network has already been tested and is in place in demonstration state, local government, and ward centers. The networks are being established in other places now.

It is often assumed that traditional healing services fill the gaps left by the organized modern health services funded by the government (Ademuwagun, Ayoade, Harrison, & Warren, 1979). The current national mental health policy vaguely espouses and recommends collaboration with traditional healers. In actual fact, nobody is sure of the extent or effectiveness of these services except to say that they have always been there and must, it is thought, have "proven" functions. Hopefully, a committee on traditional healing that has been convened will be able to answer many of these questions. Presently, it seems more reasonable to concentrate on evaluating the deficits in government and registered nongovernmental services as they are known to exist. Identified deficits will be discussed here.

None of the "big three," the state mental hospitals, or university departments of psychiatry are provided with inpatient child services. Older children and adolescents are occasionally admitted into adult facilities. Children admitted into general pediatric wards are often seen on consultation. Otherwise, most hospital-based child services are rendered on an outpatient basis. When children with severe conduct disorder come into conflict with the law, they are taken into the penal system from the courts and may be sent to juvenile homes that serve as a halfway system between the police and prison. Depending on the nature of the "crime" committed, parental involvement or concerned social-worker intervention, and age, such juveniles may be sent to "approved schools" that run a more or less normal curriculum under tight security and supervision by the Social Welfare Ministry. In the absence of any of these mitigating factors, the children may be sent to prison. Again within the prison network, those who have appropriate social networks may be sent to borstals where they may receive vocational training with their peers. Those lacking such networks may end up in regular adult prisons, where they are exposed to various forms of abuse and thus often deteriorate socially. To the best of our knowledge, only one borstal system (in Kaduna) exists in the whole of Nigeria. However, informal surveys of Christian healing homes (e.g., Ilechukwu, 1990/1991) have revealed a high proportion of older children and adolescents of both sexes on "restrictive" admission. We are not aware of the existence of foster, group, or boarding houses outside the settings mentioned here.

There are no special facilities for the elderly in the scheme of public health services. Because Nigeria is made up of a relatively young population (life expectancy less than fifty), it is often erroneously assumed that there is no need for geriatric services. Also, in the rural areas the extended family system still meets the needs of most elderly people. In the urban areas, however, the seams are beginning to show. Charitable organizations run the occasional old people's home. Available examples are poorly supported, and only the most desperate use them.

Rehabilitation services are poorly developed in Nigeria. Two of the "big three" run rehabilitation centers. These are in Lagos and Benin. These centers are located in the outskirts of town where they have access to farm lands and/ or skills training facilities. Sometimes (as in Lagos) there is collaboration with some other service unit such as the armed forces that has a greater commitment to rehabilitation. On the whole, however, these services are small and have shrunk down in recent years, further minimizing any possible impact. The third of the "big three" at Aro took a very innovative approach to rehabilitation right from its inception. In the "Aro village" system a grass-roots community system was stimulated, and relatives voluntarily relocated to the treatment setting during the treatment period. With this approach "dehabilitation" does not occur, and so the question of rehabilitation does not arise. Following a somewhat similar principle, the national mental health policy within the PHC aims at obviating the need for rehabilitation by taking the treatment to the home setting. Inevitably, though, some psychotics become vagrant and need rehabilitation. Some state governments, especially those with large urban populations such as Lagos, have "rehabilitation homes" where destitutes (both poor and insane) are gathered, restricted, housed, and fed. Very soon, however, many of the subjects get back to walking and working the streets. Thus, while it has been shown that the less industrialized settings of third-world countries such as Nigeria seem to have a positive impact on the outcome of chronic psychosis (WHO, 1979), proper provision should be made for rehabilitation of the mentally disabled.

Mental Health Personnel and Treatment

The available personnel for the practice of modern psychiatry include about 80 registered psychiatrists, 3,500 psychiatric nurses, 20 clinical psychologists, 20 medical social workers, and 30 occupational therapists. The ratios of these personnel to the population are as follows: psychiatrists, 1:1.1 million; nurses, 1:25,000; clinical psychologists, 1:4.5 million; medical social workers, 1:4.5 million; and occupational therapists, 1:3 million. There is one psychiatric bed for every 295,000 Nigerians.

Before 1983, when Nigeria produced its first home-trained psychiatrist, most Nigerian psychiatrists were trained in the United Kingdom, the United States, or Canada (Binitie, 1988). Since then, home training has supplemented overseas training. Certification is done by two postgraduate medical colleges, the National and West African Medical Colleges. These colleges have certified two psychiatrists per year on the average. In spite of this effort, there has actually been a decrease in the total number of psychiatrists in Nigeria, since many of those trained abroad have left for better remuneration elsewhere.

Psychiatric nurses are trained in the psychiatric hospitals in Aro (direct and postbasic), Enugu (postbasic), and Benin (direct). "Direct" refers to training of fresh high-school graduates, while postbasic" refers to candidates with prior general nursing (with or without midwifery) training. The output from these centers has enormously enhanced the available nursing personnel.

Clinical psychologists are trained collaboratively by the university departments and the psychiatric hospitals or departments of psychiatry in teaching hospitals. A master's degree is usually acceptable, even though a doctorate degree is considered desirable. There are no licensing or registration bodies for psychologists at the moment. Membership in the Nigeria Association of Clinical Psychologists is considered desirable.

Medical social workers receive basic training in social work from university or other college departments. Medical social-work skills are refined through supervised employment in a teaching hospital social-work department. Eventually, full membership in the Association of Medical Social Workers is required. There are no legal registration bodies.

PUBLIC POLICY PROCESS

As has been observed by social scientists who have worked in colonial and postcolonial Africa (e.g., Bohannan, 1960), the colonial process often generated two parallel systems of government that had interaction points. The colonial power was often based in urban and semiurban areas where the instruments of government (civil service, police, army, prisons, judiciary, and so on) are placed. At the same time there was a native government that operated by its own system of laws and codes within a well-established and accepted hierarchy of authority. The colonial governments often appointed native overseers (chiefs) or recognized preexisting leaders of this indigenous government. They often facilitated the tax collection process. From these beginnings the city-based governments, even indigenous ones, have retained an alien quality. The rural populace often has no feeling of entitlement to participate in government process or national policy. This has contributed to the present state in which most public policy or changes in policy are generated by elitist interest groups such as academics, journalists and mass media, professional associations, university students, and the civil service. The irony of the situation is that even though PHC is aimed at the grass roots (health for all), the conceptualization and formulation of the policy have been done by these elitist interest groups and bureaucrats. This has been unavoidable and with appropriate social engineering may not operate negatively. Fortunately, PHC has built-in evaluative and corrective mechanisms.

SPECIAL POLICY ISSUES

The Mentally Ill and the Mentally Retarded

With some exceptions, mental health service units in Nigeria do not routinely care for the mentally retarded. The exceptions are in three service areas: (1) initial diagnosis, especially following referral from schools; (2) coexisting mental illness; and (3) the occasional research and demonstration projects in the university hospital departments, such as the day-care center of Lagos University Teaching Hospital. Otherwise, the mentally subnormal are generally treated like other patients, that is, they return to their care providers (parents, relatives, educational institutes). As mentioned before, where it exists, organized service is supervised by the Ministry of Education in the various states. For example, there is the psycho-educational center in Lagos. The focus is on the educable subnormal. Nongovernmental bodies such as the Girl Guides also provide much-needed organized day-care and educational services. In a case like this, only subnormals are taken care of. In the Nigerian setting there is usually no competition for resources between the mentally ill and the mentally retarded.

The Mentally Ill and Substance Abuse

For a long time a specific illegal drug, cannabis, was held to be a precipitant or even a cause of schizophrenia illness in Nigeria and other parts of Africa (Asuni, 1964). This was discordant with observations elsewhere, especially in the United States. In fact, in the 1960s and 1970s there was a powerful lobby to legalize cannabis for recreational use in the United States (Ilechukwu, 1991). This was before there was further evidence linking cannabis to potentiation of the neurotoxic effects of alcohol, especially as a causative factor of traffic accidents (Schwartz, 1987). Relapse of otherwise remitted schizophrenia following use of cannabis is well documented outside Africa. It is thus easy to understand how it did not seem necessary to differentiate between substance abuse (most commonly cannabis abuse) and other mental illness. At one time cannabis abuse was associated with 15 percent of all admissions to Aro Psychiatric Hospital; 20 percent of patients seen at the University College Hospital at Ibadan (Lambo, 1965); and 21 percent of admissions to the Yaba Psychiatric Hospital (Boroffka, 1966).

With the advent of cocaine and heroin abuse in Nigeria in the 1980s, new dimensions have emerged. First, many cocaine and heroin abusers are from a higher social class than the average psychiatric patient. Second, most of them are not psychotic. Such nonpsychotic patients, though primarily in need of detoxification and initiation of rehabilitation, are also admitted to psychiatric hospitals. Recently, many of them (and their relatives) have objected to sharing facilities with mentally ill patients. Presently, only in the "big three" is there an attempt to provide separate wards for the care of drug abusers. Clinical experience in some settings has shown that in mixed-admission wards the substance abusers are more disruptive. It has become common practice to restrict the admission of substance abusers into general wards. Competition for resources is implied, but at the present moment there is no other medical specialty willing or equipped to manage substance-dependent patients in Nigeria.

The Mentally Disordered Offender

The laws guiding the compulsory admission or committal of the mentally ill are hardly invoked in Nigeria. Relatives usually find other ways of taking their wards to a mental hospital. It is not unusual to find patients bound and carried struggling into emergency rooms. Most of the time, therefore, the only patients admitted under any part of the legal code are those that are already in the criminal justice system or where the family has become fragmented and there is no trust. A prescribed document signed by a judge is usually required and may be extended by the attending physician depending on his initial findings and the need for further observation. The period of hospitalization may also be extended by the judge. Such persons are usually placed in "secure" wards that are found only in mental hospitals. Those who have already been sentenced are most often kept in the medical wing in prisons—so-called prison hospitals.

The court, when it sees fit, may also order psychiatric evaluation of an offender to establish fitness to stand trial. Defense lawyers may seek discharge of their clients on grounds of mental illness. Evidence of previous mental illness and psychiatric testimony related to that may also be presented. However, the luxury of partisan psychiatric testimony has not yet arrived in Nigeria.

Sometimes a judge may request treatments for an offender, but ethical questions have arisen when this treatment could render the patients fit to stand trial or face punishment (e.g., execution) as eventually determined by the judge. It is usually demanded that there be clear evidence that the criminal acts are clearly a product of mental illness.

Many patients who have been found unfit to stand trial or face punishment (guilty but insane) have nevertheless been remanded to prison custody. Also, many cases in which a person is found "guilty but insane" and subsequently discharged but has remained in prison for several years even after he or she has become well have been reported.

Deinstitutionalization

Institutionalization never occurred in Nigeria and most other African countries. This might have been expected to result in large numbers of vagrant psychotics. On the contrary, most early travellers in Africa reported the rarity of such sights and must have contributed to the discredited notion that schizophrenia was non-existent among Africans, or all "uncivilized people" for that matter. The absence of large-scale institutionalization probably reflected the nature of indigenous societies. Prolonged incarceration in the homes of traditional healers was known to occur, but this seemed to last for the duration of the active illness. At the end of the active illness episode, the patients could return to their homes or relatives. Residual symptoms were not incompatible with functioning within extended families. Families organized treatment and follow-up and undertook rehabilitation as well.

There was also the alternative of staying and working with the traditional healer in exchange for treatment, board, and food. Much has also been written about the existence of roles (as priests, healers, or even clowns) for the mentally ill within many traditional cultures (Abel & Metraux, 1974).

Funding Issues

In Nigeria health services are often perceived as consumers rather than generators of national wealth. In this hierarchy the Internal Revenue Service, for example, is rated much higher than the Ministry of Health. This perception has led to the underfunding of health services as a whole. Health services have always received less than the minimum 5 percent recommended by WHO, and since the crash of the oil market in the 1980s, which sharply reduced Nigeria's external earnings, the situation has become even worse. This has left the various sectors within the health services struggling for preeminence. Until recently, the mental health service sector lost frequently. Some evidence for the low priority accorded mental health has already been presented, including the following: (1) In Lagos, while available general hospital beds increased by 570 percent, beds in the Yaba (Lagos) psychiatric hospital increased by 13 percent over a twenty-two year period (Anumonye, 1976); (2) the first department of psychiatry (with neurology and neurosurgery) at the University College Hospital, Ibadan, was created about fifteen years after the hospital had become fully functional (Anumonye, 1976); and (3) the Nigerian national health policy was formulated and launched in 1987 without a mental health component. This has now been amended.

Presently, two funding options are being explored. The first is a fee for service for all health services offered in government hospitals, whether general or psychiatric. Fees charged are still much below those in profit-oriented private hospitals, but it is hoped that enough financial returns will be made to reduce the burden on government. The plan also aims to reduce waste. The second is organization of a national health insurance scheme. This would initially involve government and corporate employees and others in paid employment for whom deductions can be made at the work site and contributions of employers easily calculated. It is not yet clear how this would affect mental illness, but it is hoped that experience gained in the fee-for-service practice of government and private health institutions will offer some guidance.

Consumer Rights

The so-called Lunacy Laws inherited from the British colonial government have been revised by the same committee that drafted the Mental Health Policy. They will become law after due process through the Ministry of Justice and the executive arms of the government. In general, they will continue to provide guidelines in the following areas:

1. The procedure for confining a citizen to psychiatric service against his or her will
2. Duration of compulsory admission and limits to extension of such compulsory admission
3. Ways of seeking relief from compulsory admission and protection against malicious use of this provision
4. Protection of property rights of the mentally ill
5. Assurance of fitness to stand trial
6. Protection against penalties for crimes that are clearly a result of mental illness

Also, proposals for deletion of certain provisions have been made:

1. Decriminalization of suicide attempts, making such attempts a purely medical/mental health issue
2. Protection of substance abusers from criminal proceedings
3. Removal of provisions for recidivists often labelled "psychopaths" from the referral lists of forensic psychiatry

With regard to protection against treatment modalities in which ethical issues may arise, the following guarantees exist:

1. The need for informed consent before electroconvulsive therapy (ECT). In this regard ECT is regarded the same as surgical procedures for which informed consent must be sought, witnessed, and documented. Psychosurgery is not practiced in Nigeria.
2. The use of physical restraints within hospitals only on prescription (i.e., "when necessary").

However, rights to refuse treatment are not guaranteed to those patients perceived as requiring drug treatment for their own good or for the protection of the family and society. Where patients refuse treatment and are not perceived as dangerous to themselves or others, negotiation is usually done with relatives. As long as relatives are in agreement with the treatment, patients may be persuaded to receive treatment. When the family disagrees, however, it may exercise the option to take the patient away from the hospital by "signing against medical advice."

Doctors may be sued by patients for improper or harmful treatment. By and large this is a rare event, and malpractice insurance premiums are still quite low. More frequently, doctors are arraigned before the Nigeria Medical and Dental Council (NMDC) for unethical conduct even without a malpractice suit. It needs to be emphasized that the NMDC is a statutory body, not a professional association. It has judicial powers and has remained the most effective watchdog of patients' interests. It has members appointed by the government who are not doctors, and defendants may appear with counsel during hearings.

CONCLUSIONS AND DISCUSSION

The Nigerian mental health policy has in the past been focused on building mental hospitals that offered both direct and referral service. The "big three" hospitals were the central models of this policy. The university hospital centers and the two postgraduate medical colleges (Nigerian and West African) have served to train high-level mental health professionals. Their efforts have remained inadequate.

There has always been an officially unrecognized but widely acknowledged traditional mental health service. Many people think that these traditional grassroots services are used by more people than the modern services. The social and possibly health promotive and restorative functions of the traditional services are now being shared by the Christian and Muslim healing practitioners. In fact, there is an amazing proliferation of syncretism, that is, an amalgamation of traditional practices, and these non-Christian/Muslim healing services, aided by religious liturgy, are directed against traditional villains like witches, sorcerers, or malevolent ancestors as much as against sin and the devil. They deserve the kind of detailed study that explores the relationship between participation in such services and health that has been done elsewhere (Peltzer, 1987).

With the adoption of PHC as the instrument for dispensing health in Nigeria, there is an attempt to rethink mental health. The idea of functional balance between the person, the group, and the environment as the ideal of mental health is quite useful. It encourages cooperation between mental health workers, educators, and environmental planners. In this way, sensitivity to mental health needs is built into all community activity from inception rather than added on. Hopefully, the mental health worker may take his or her place among community leaders. Also, location of mental health services within the mainstream of health care at primary, secondary, and tertiary levels will do much to destigmatize mental illness.

Again, the focus of activity of the university and mental hospital centers has been redefined. They now must train and retrain primary-care workers and mount continuing education courses. They will now have to offer consultancy in evaluation of programs and researching new approaches. By the time the PHC has become well rooted, the interlinkages with the existing tertiary services will have to be worked out more thoroughly.

Funding of mental health has followed the pattern of general health care even though it enjoys a lower order of priority. If ongoing efforts to establish a health insurance scheme succeed, the pattern of coverage for mental health will become an issue. It seems likely that the government and parastatal organizations may have no choice but to cover mental health services in the same way as physical health. Private employers may hesitate to cover an illness that they misperceive as leading to inevitable and irreversible loss of productivity or endangerment of the workplace. Fortunately, the labor organizations have considerable clout and experience in negotiating worker welfare in Nigeria. Leaders in the mental health field and professional associations will have to awaken to their responsibility to mount mental health educative and promotive (primary prevention) programs. Early diagnosis and treatment (secondary prevention) will also be emphasized to cut costs and preserve functions.

REFERENCES

Abel, T. M., & Metraux, R. (1974). *Culture and psychotherapy*. New Haven, CT: College & University Press.

Ademuwagun, Z. A., Ayoade, J.A.A., Harrison, I. E., & Warren, D. M. (1979). *African therapeutic systems*. Waltham, MA: Crossroads Press.

Anumonye, A. (1976). *Nigerian mental health directory, Lagos*. Nigeria: Lagos University Teaching Hospital/College of Medicine of the University of Lagos Printing Department.

Asuni, T. (1961). Suicide in Western Nigeria. In T. A. Lambo (Ed.), *First Pan African psychiatric conference report* (pp. 164–175). Ibadan, Nigeria: Government Printers.

Asuni, T. (1964). Sociopsychiatric problems of cannabis in Nigeria. *Bulletin on Narcotics* *16*, 2.

Baasher, T. M., & Ibrahim, H.H.A. (1976). Childhood psychiatric disorders in the Sudan. *African Journal of Psychiatry 2*, 67–78.

Binitie, A. O. (1988). Outstanding contributions to Nigerian psychiatry. *Nigerian Journal of Psychiatry, 1*, 36–44.

Bohannan, P. (Ed.). (1960). *African homicide and suicide.* Princeton, NJ: Princeton University Press.

Boroffka, A. (1966). Mental illness and Indian hemp in Lagos. *East African Medical Journal, 43*, 377–384.

Carothers, J. C. (1955). *A report on the psychiatric services of Nigeria.* London: Crown Standard Agents.

Cunnyngham-Brown, R. (1938). *A report on the care and treatment of lunatics in the British West African Colonies.* Lagos, Nigeria, and London: Crown Standard Agents.

Dhadphale, M., Ellison, R. H., & Griffin, L. (1983). The frequency of psychiatric disorders among patients attending semi-urban and rural general hospital outpatient clinics in Kenya. *British Journal of Psychiatry, 142*, 379–383.

Ilechukwu, S.T.C. (1988). Inter-relationships of beliefs about mental illness, psychiatric diagnosis, and mental health care among Africans. *International Journal of Social Psychiatry, 34*, 200–206.

Ilechukwu, S.T.C. (1990/1991). Ogbanje/Abiku: A culture-bound construct of childhood and family psychopathology in West Africa. *Psychopathologie Africaine, 23*, 19–60.

Ilechukwu, S.T.C. (1991). Psychiatry in Africa: Special problems and unique features. *Transcultural Psychiatric Research Review (TPRR), 28*, 169–218.

Ilechukwu, S.T.C., & Prince, R. H. (1992). Substance abuse in Nigeria [Abstract and Reviews]. *Transcultural Psychiatric Research Review (TPRR), 29*, 45–50.

Izuora, G.E.A. (1976). The Enugu child guidance clinic. *African Journal of Psychiatry, 2*, 131–135.

Lambo, T. A. (1965). Medical and social problems of drug addiction in West Africa with special emphasis on psychiatric aspects. *West African Medical Journal, 14*, 236–254.

Leighton, A. M., Lambo, T. A., Hughes, C. C., Leighton, D. C., Murphy, J. M., & Macklin, D. P. (1963). *Psychiatric disorder among the Yoruba.* Ithaca: Cornell University Press.

Mbanefo, S. E. (1971). The general practitioner and psychiatry. In *Psychiatry and Mental Health Care in General Practice.* Ibadan: University of Ibadan.

Odejide, A. O. (1979). Alcohol use in a subgroup of literate Nigerians. *African Journal of Psychiatry, 5*, 15–20.

Odejide, A. O. (1991, September). *Demand reduction activities of the National Drug Law Enforcement Agency (Nigeria).* Paper presented in a conference organized by the International Council on Alcohol and Drug Addiction in Montreal, Canada. [Abstract in *Transcultural Psychiatric Research Review (TPRR), 29*, 45–50].

Odejide, A. O., & Ohaeri, J. V. (1991). *Alcohol and drug-related admissions into mental health institutions in Nigeria.* Unpublished manuscript, Ministry of Health, Nigeria. Cited in Odejide, A. O. (1991).

Orley, J., & Wing, J. K. (1979). Psychiatric disorders in two African villages. *Archives of General Psychiatry, 36*, 513–520.

Peltzer, K. (1987). *Some contributions of traditional healing practices towards psycho-social health care in Malawi.* Frankfurt: Fachbuchhandlung für Psychologie Verlags-Abteilung.

Prince, R. H. (1960). The use of rauwolfia for the treatment of psychoses by Nigerian native doctors. *American Journal of Psychiatry, 117,* 147–149.

Prince, R. H. (1965). Indigenous Yoruba Psychiatry. In Ari Kiev (Ed.), *Magic, faith, and healing.* New York: Free Press of Glencoe.

Prince, R. H. (1968). Pellagra: Its recognition and treatment by the Yoruba healers of West Africa. In H. Goerke, H. Muller-Dietz, & G. Kolb (Eds.), *Verhandlungen des XX. Internationalen Kongresses für Geschichte der Medizin, Berlin, 22–27. August 1966.*

Prince, R. H. (1989). The brain-fag syndrome. In K. Peltzer and P. O. Ebigbo (Eds.), *Clinical psychology in Africa* (pp. 276–287). Enugu, Nigeria: Working Group for African Psychology.

Rwegellera, G.G.G. (1979). Suicide rates in Lusaka, Zambia: Preliminary observations. *Psychological Medicine, 8,* 423–432.

Schwartz, R. H. (1987). Marihuana: An overview. *Pediatric Clinics of North America, 34,* 305–317.

Shelley, H., & Watson, W. H. (1936). An investigation concerning mental disorder in the Nyasaland natives. *Journal of Mental Science, 82,* 701–730.

Sullivan, J., & Martin, J. (1989). *Global Studies: Africa* (2nd ed.). Sluice Dock, Guilford, CT: Dushkin Publishing Group.

Vanycke, J. C. (1957). *Psychoses et névroses en Afrique Centrale.* Brussels: Academie Royale des Sciences Coloniales.

World Health Organization. (1979). *International Pilot Study of Schizophrenia.* Geneva: Author.

13

Pakistan

Unaiza Niaz

OVERVIEW

As a result of the partition of British India into two sovereign Hindu and Muslim states, Pakistan emerged on the map of the world on August 14, 1947. The eastern wing of the country, now called Bangladesh, seceded in 1971. Pakistan stretches over 1,600 kilometers north to south and about 885 kilometers east to west, covering a total area of 796,095 square kilometers. It comprises four provinces: Baluchistan, North West Frontier Province, Punjab, and Sindh.

Pakistan is a land of diversified relief. In the north it is bounded by the Himalayan ranges, the Karakoram ranges, and the Hindu Kush beyond it. The Himalayas have an average elevation of 6,100 meters, with some of the highest peaks in the world. K2, at 8,611 meters, is the highest peak of the Karakoram range and the second-highest in the world.

Pakistan inherited an old and rich civilization. The areas now constituting Pakistan had a historical individuality of their own before the advent of Islam. Pakistan was constituted as a dominion under the provisions of the Indian Independence Act, 1947.

Pakistan has one of the most rapidly growing populations of the world. Since the inception of Pakistan, four censuses have been conducted. The fourth census was conducted in 1981, and the fifth is being carried out now. According to a report by the Population Census Organization, the total population in 1981 was 84,253,000, and the estimated population for the year 1988 was 105,400,000, which makes Pakistan the world's ninth most populous country. The total male population in 1981 was 44,232,000 (52.5 percent), and the female population was 40,021,000 (47.5 percent), with a sex ratio of 100 females to 111 males. The distribution of population by sex and urban/rural regions was 23,840,000 urban (male 12,766,000, and female 11,074,000) and 60,413,000 rural (31,466,000 male and 28,947,000 female). Population distribution by religion in the 1981 census was 81,450,057 Muslims, 1,310,426 Christians, and 1,276,116 Hindus. Other religions include Ahmedis, Buddhists, Parsis, and Sikhs (Federal Bureau of Statistics, 1989).

The system of Pakistani government is parliamentary. The prime minister is the head of the government. The major political parties are IJI (Islami Jamhoori Itehad), which is a collaboration of nine like-minded political parties, for instance, the historic Pakistan Muslim League and the Jamate-Islami, and the new Mohajir Qomi Movement (MQM). The main opposition party at present is the PPP (Pakistan People's Party) headed by Benazir Bhutto. At present the military is purely concerned with the defense of the country.

Politically the country has undergone tremendous turmoil, leading to several revolutions since its independence. Political disturbances and military interventions have failed to develop a successful democratic system. In elections held in October 1990, Nawaz Sharif became the new prime minister (leader of Islami Jamhoori Itehad). He announced several liberal policies, in particular, increased industrialization and privatization of the national institutions. A new health policy also was being prepared.

EXTENT OF THE PROBLEM

Some epidemiological studies have demonstrated that mental illness is as common in Pakistan as elsewhere. It has been demonstrated that nearly 15 to 20 percent of people who seek medical help in general health care facilities, both in developed and developing countries, have mental health problems (Basher, 1982). According to the statistics of the World Health Organization (WHO), in developing countries, like Pakistan, 1 percent of the population suffers from severely incapacitating mental disorders. Studies carried out in Pakistan substantiate these figures (Sartorius et al., 1983). Roughly 1 million people are severely mentally ill, and about 10 million are mildly mentally ill. If psychosomatic disorders are included, then about 15 million to 20 million people would require psychiatric attention (Ahmed, 1988).

There are 1,300,000 regular drug abusers living in Pakistan according to the National Survey on Drug Abuse (Pakistan Narcotics Control Board [PNCB], 1984). The majority, 820,000 (63 percent), reside in rural areas, and the remainder, 480,000 (37 percent), are in urban communities. Thus it might be concluded that at least 1.55 percent of the total population of Pakistan are regular drug abusers (2.03 percent of the urban population and 1.36 percent of the rural population) (PNCB, 1984). According to a 1986 survey, the figure has jumped to 1.9 million drug abusers. Heroin is responsible for 31.8 percent of the total abuse. Alcohol problems are proportionally fewer in Pakistan compared to the West, as its use is banned in the country for Muslims. Exact figures are not available at present (PNCB, 1986).

Pakistan's rapidly changing psychosocial environment, with the weakening of traditional values, has led to increased emotional morbidity. In the population of children, adolescents, and elderly, emotional morbidity has increased, though exact statistics are not available (Khan, 1986). Reliable studies of the International Labor Organization and the World Health Organization indicate that two-fifths (40 percent) of total disabilities are due to mental illness, though no statistics are available about loss of income, loss of productivity, and social dysfunction (Neki, 1979). Clearly these would be enormous. The concept of a comprehensive mental health policy has not yet materialized in Pakistan, though a new Mental Health Act has been promised to replace the old Lunacy Act.

MENTAL HEALTH HISTORY

The stigma attached to mental illness is also pervasive in Pakistan. Mental disorders are considered by the masses to be caused by demonic influence or possession. Patients are still kept in bondage—chained, beaten, parts of their bodies burnt. People have sought relief from religious leaders and traditional healers, from shrines, and from quacks. In large cities, such as Karachi, Lahore, and Rawalpindi, the educated population has developed awareness regarding psychiatric illness through discussion of the problem, television plays, new media, and promotion of psychiatry by the Pakistan Psychiatric Society during its annual and biennial conferences, which are covered by print and audiovisual media.

Modern methods of treatment are not available to the general masses. The new drugs and treatment methods can bring about substantial recovery and prevent chronic mental disability in 60 to 80 percent of patients, but it is estimated that only 10 percent of the patients who need psychiatric care receive adequate treatment. One of the reasons is the extreme shortage of trained psychiatrists in the country (one psychiatrist for every one million people) (Ahmed, 1988).

The Lunacy Act was inherited by India and Pakistan in 1947. In India it was called Lunacy Act, 1912, and was replaced in 1987 when a Mental Health Act was enacted by the Indian Parliament and came into effect May 22, 1987. In Pakistan the Lunacy Act was adopted and in the early 1990s was still in force. Part 1 deals with preliminary matters, part 2 covers reception, care and treatment of lunatics, part 3 provides for judicial inquisition as to lunacy, and part 4 deals with miscellaneous matters in establishment of asylums and expenses of lunatics.

There are interesting differences in the Lunacy Act, 1912, compared to modern acts of other countries such as the United Kingdom. For example, in part 1, chapter 1, only two terms are of interest to mental health professionals: *asylum* and *lunatic*. Asylum means an asylum for the lunatics established or licensed by the government. This was amended by Act 6 of 1922, and now an asylum means an asylum or mental hospital for lunatics established or licensed by the government. In modern acts the words *asylum* or *mental hospital* are replaced by the word *psychiatric hospital*. In Pakistan it is generally believed that the Lunacy Act does not apply to psychiatric units and is only applicable to asylums and mental hospitals. Under this argument most of the chronic patients are sent to mental hospitals.

The word *lunatic* was derived from the former belief that some people were influenced by the moon or were moonstruck; lunatic is equivalent to what we now call mentally disordered. The term *lunatic* is defined in section 123 of Act 35 of 1858 as ''a person of unsound mind and incapable of managing his affairs.'' It would appear, therefore, that unsoundness of mind alone is insufficient to label a person as a lunatic, but that the person must also be incapacitated from managing his or her affairs. Nor would a person who is unable to manage his or her affairs be a lunatic unless that incapacity was produced by an unsound mind.

This state of affairs is still valid in Pakistan since we still follow the act of 1912. The Mental Health Act, 1987 (India), replaced the word *lunatic* by a new term, *mentally ill person*, meaning a person who is in need of treatment by reason of mental disorder other than mental retardation. In the English Mental Health Act 1959, the word *lunatic* is replaced by the word *mentally disordered*, which is defined as ''mental illness, arrested or incomplete development of mind, psychopathic disorder and any other disorder or disability of mind.''

POLICY, ORGANIZATION, AND SERVICES IN THE 1980s AND 1990s

Current Policy Developments

The Lunacy Act of 1912 that presently governs the custody and care of the mentally ill or handicapped in Pakistan is archaic. It is based on seventeenth- and eighteenth-century concepts of mental illness—a legacy of British colonial rule. The Lunacy Act was designed to protect the society from the nuisance of the ''lunatic'' and to prevent wrongful confinement of the ''sane,'' rather than emphasizing proper care and treatment of the mentally ill. At the time of enactment, emphasis was placed on segregation and custodial care of the mentally ill or mentally handicapped and the management of their assets and property. Clearly, there was neglect of the importance of expert medical opinion in diagnosing the mental illness and neglect of the need for appropriate treatment. The focus was disproportionately on legal and administrative considerations.

Tremendous progress has taken place since the passage of the Lunacy Act, 1912, particularly regarding the understanding of the nature of mental illness and its treatment. It is now well established that most psychiatric problems can be adequately treated and that early diagnosis and intervention in the prognosis is vital. Often it is possible to rehabilitate the patient as a useful and productive member of the society.

The Lunacy Act is outdated and often misused and at times has resulted in incarceration of the mentally ill in jails. As there is no provision for compulsory treatment of disturbed patients, the law is a great hindrance to the delivery of a more humane and modern mental health care system. Hence it is imperative that the obsolete Lunacy Act of 1912 be repealed and replaced by a new mental health act that delivers proper treatment, care, facilities, and safeguards against violations of fundamental rights of patients. In this context greater consideration should be given to expert medical psychiatric opinion.

In 1986 two major developments took place. The Ministry of Health in collaboration with the World Health Organization finalized a National Program of Mental Health, thereby making Pakistan the first country in the Eastern Mediterranean region to formulate such a program. This is now being included in the seventh five-year plan.

A preliminary draft of the national mental health plan was prepared in March 1986. This was the first time the Ministry of Health collaborated with the World Health Organization. With the assistance of various sectors related to mental health, a national program of mental health was finalized in December 1986 in Islamabad. The general aims of the program included prevention and treatment of mental disorders and their subsequent disabilities and the application of mental health techniques and behavioral sciences to improve general health services and the quality of life. Special emphasis was paid to the encouragement of community participation in the development of mental health services (Ahmed, 1988).

This document included such topics as community mental health care guiding principles, social security institution for psychiatric hospitals, mental health legislation, psychiatric education, child psychiatry, forensic psychiatry, and psychogeriatrics. Drug abuse/dependence was included as an integral part of general psychiatric services. Mental health education for the public and social services sector was also emphasized.

The Pakistan Psychiatric Society submitted a proposed document, "Comprehensive Mental Health Care in Pakistan," for the health policy advisory meetings and consultations between various departments of the government and the multidisciplinary health professionals. Since 1986 the Pakistan Psychiatric Society has been unsuccessfully campaigning for the Lunacy Act to be replaced by a new mental health act (Ahmed, 1988). The draft of a new law was still under review in 1991. In late 1992, a draft of the Mental Health Act 1992 was circulated to a selected few individuals by the Ministry of Health. The Pakistan Medical Association, Pakistan Psychiatric Society, Pakistan Mental Health Association, and others strenuously objected to this limited review. The draft is believed to have gross omissions, especially concerning human rights. It is vital that the draft of the mental health act be widely circulated and that expert opinion be sought from not only the psychiatric and legal community before its enactment, but also a wide sector of citizens.

Ironically, there also was no general health policy until 1990, when Prime Minister Benazir Bhutto for the first time announced a national health policy. She promised to double the health allocation, making it up to 10 percent of the total budgeted revenue. But in current health policy there is no mention of this, and multiple issues have been raised. The new government of Nawaz Sharif in 1991 promised a better, more comprehensive health delivery system.

Current Organization

Treatment of mental patients in Pakistan is carried out at the following places:

1. Three mental hospitals—Lahore, Peshawar, and Dhudial
2. Institute of Psychiatry—Hyderabad
3. Teaching units of psychiatry attached to various medical colleges (seventeen medical colleges, one with the status of a university, namely, Agha Khan University Hospital)
4. Nonteaching government and semigovernment hospitals with psychiatric units
5. Private hospitals and nursing homes run on a profit basis
6. Poor houses run by social workers
7. Patients treated at shrines by quacks and charlatans and at private houses

At independence in 1947 only three government mental hospitals existed. Now there are psychiatric teaching departments in each of the seventeen medical colleges with relatively better facilities than the traditional mental hospitals. Still, the departments of psychiatry are understaffed, and some lack inpatient facilities. Child and family psychiatry is still not an essential part of the general psychiatric services, even in the university teaching hospitals (except in Karachi and Lahore). There is yet no provision for a forensic psychiatrist to take care of mentally abnormal offenders or for psychogeriatric services for the elderly.

The private nonprofit/voluntary sector and private profit makers play a fairly significant role in mental health in Pakistan. In Sindh Province, where Karachi is the port city, Edhi Welfare Organization, a purely nonprofit organization, has the famous Apna Ghar for destitutes, disabled, and the mentally ill. In addition, it runs several poor houses and orphanages. In Lahore, Fountain House is the only rehabilitation center for the mentally ill. Several private hospitals have private psychiatric units. In Karachi, for instance, eight such hospitals have inpatient facilities, including the Agha Khan Hospital and Baqai Hospital, which also has an undergraduate medical school.

Current Services

The application of principles of mental health and behavioral sciences can contribute immensely to general health care, can help put to right faulty behavior such as drug dependence and criminal behavior, and can enhance the quality of life. The professional services of psychiatry need to be realigned toward mental health by moving away from facility-based curative care and acquiring community-based approaches that integrate preventive, curative, and rehabilitative services. It is upon this philosophy that the Pakistan Psychiatric Society's Eighth International Psychiatric Conference, held in Islamabad from December 11 to 14, 1990, was based. The theme of the conference was "Mental Health for All, and All for Mental Health." Table 13.1 shows psychiatric services in Pakistan, while table 13.2 shows psychiatric facilities in Karachi, the largest city of Pakistan.

Mental Health Personnel and Treatment

The professional makeup of those providing mental health services consists of psychiatrists, psychologists, psychiatric nurses, psychiatric social workers, special education teachers, and occupational therapists. There are about 100 psychiatrists, of whom about 60 percent are local diploma holders. There are a handful of foreign qualified psychiatrists such as MRCP Psych. (United Kingdom) or State Board in Psychiatry (United States). Most of the senior foreign-trained psychiatrists are in academic units or are heads of semigovernment psychiatric units.

There also are general practitioners who have been trained in mental health through special courses given periodically by the Pakistan Medical and Dental Council. The College of Physicians and Surgeons in Pakistan deals with the two local postgraduate degrees, MCPS (diploma) and FCPS (a higher graduation, equivalent to MRCP Psych. of the United Kingdom). The Pakistan Medical and Dental Council recognizes these two postgraduate qualifications.

PUBLIC POLICY PROCESS

The provincial and federal governments are involved in mental health policy. The major role of the federal government is to finance federal hospitals and projects. The provincial governments finance their own hospitals and projects. Total development, maintenance, and other expenses for the Health Ministry are approximately 3 percent of the GNP, although the government figure is 5 percent and professionals think that it is 1 percent of GNP.

As stated earlier, there is no mental health policy especially designed for Pakistan. The government of Pakistan has several priorities to consider since Pakistan is a fairly young developing country that has had two wars and many political upheavals. Health, of course, is the last priority, and in the Health Department mental health is at the bottom. As there is no modern mental health policy designed specifically for Pakistan, the old 1912 Lunacy Act is still the functioning policy.

The greatest problem in accomplishing mental health policy is primarily at the bureaucratic level. A proposed mental health policy draft prepared by the Pakistan Psychiatric Society has been in review in the ministries for six years, and still no decision has been taken for acceptance or rejection of the policy. Of course, proper, organized lobbying by mental health professionals is needed,

Table 13.1
Psychiatric Services in Pakistan

Name of Institution	Year of Establishment	Number of Beds	Number of New Patients Attending Outpatient Department	Training Facilities for Under- graduates and Postgraduates	Number of Doctors
1. Government Mental Hospital, Lahore	1840	1,400	12,400	——	34
2. Sir. C.J. Institute of Psychiatry, Liaquat Medical College, Hyderabad	1865	500	3,434	Present	16
3. Government Mental Hospital, Peshawar	1942	140	——	——	——
4. Department of Psychiatry, Military Hospital, Army Medical College, Rawalpindi	1950	90	——	Present	6
5. Nerve Health Center, Nazimabad, Karachi	1964	22	2,000	Postgraduates Only	3
6. Government Mental Hospital, Dhudial, Mansehra	1964	80	15,000	Postgraduates Only	3
7. Department of Psychiatry, Jinnah Postgraduate Medical Centre, Karachi	1965	50	12,340	Present	6
8. Department of Psychiatry, Pakistan International Airlines Corporation, Karachi	1974	5	——	Postgraduates Only	2
9. Department of Psychiatry, Dow Medical College, Civil Hospital, Karachi	1975	30	——	Present	——
10. Department of Psychiatry, K. V. Siet Hospital, Karachi	——	——	——	——	——
11. Karachi Psychiatric Hospital, Nazimabad, Karachi	1970	80	2,684	Postgraduates Only	1
12. Department of Psychological Medicine and Neuro- psychiatry, Rawalpindi General Hospital, Rawalpindi Medical College	1973	50	5,964	Present	1
13. Fountain House, Lahore	1971	100	——	Present	1

Table 13.1 Continued

Name of Institution	Year of Establishment	Number of Beds	Number of New Patients Attending Outpatient Department	Training Facilities for Under- graduates and Postgraduates	Number of Doctors
14. Yaseen Psychiatric Hospital, Nazimabad, Karachi	1973	18	—	—	—
15. Child and Family Psychiatry Department, King Edward Medical College, Mayo Hospital, Lahore	1975	6	6,000	Present	6
16. Department of Psychiatry, Khyber Teaching Hospital, Peshawar	1977	45	7,582	Present	6
17. Department of Psychiatry, Bolan Medical College, Quetta	1977	15	10,000	Present	6
18. Department of Psychiatry, Liaqual National Hospital, Karachi	1978	27	15,000	Undergraduates Only	3
19. Department of Psychiatry, Services Hospital, Allama Iqbal Medical College, Lahore	1979	30	2,080	Present	7
20. Rehan Psychiatric Hospital, Nazimabad, Karachi	1983	20	5,200	—	1
21. Psychiatric Unit, Baqai Hospital, Nazimabad, Karachi	1985	16	1,208	Postgraduates Only	3
22. Department of Psychiatry, Agha Khan Hospital and Medical College, Karachi	1985	15	400	Undergraduates Only	4
23. Sheikh Zaid Postgraduate Institute, Lahore	1989	—	—	—	—
24. Asghar Hospital Nazimabad, Karachi	1970	50	—	—	—
25. Edhi Trust "Apra Ghar," Karachi	—	—	—	—	—

Source: Federal Bureau of Statistics, Government of Pakistan, 1990.

Table 13.2

Psychiatric Facilities Available at Karachi in the Public and Private Sectors

Institution	Year	Beds
1.	Department of Psychiatry, Jinnah Postgraduate Medical Centre, Karachi	1965	50
2.	Department of Psychiatry, Dow Medical College, Karachi	1975	30
3.	Department of Psychiatry, Pakistan International Airlines Corporation, Karachi	1974	5
4.	Nerve Health Center, Nazimabad Karachi	1964	22
5.	Department of Psychiatry, K.V. Siet Hospital, Karachi	-----	-----
6.	Asghar Hospital, Nazimabad, Karachi	1970	50
7.	Karachi Psychiatric Hospital, Nazimabad, Karachi	1970	80
8.	Yaseen Psychiatric Hospital, Nazimabad, Karachi	1973	18
9.	Rehan Psychiatric Hospital, Nazimabad, Karachi	1983	20
10.	Baqai Hospital (Psychiatry Unit), Nazimabad, Karachi	1985	16
11.	Agha Khan Medical College Hospital, Karachi	1985	15
12.	Edhi Trust "Apna Ghar," Karachi	-----	-----
13.	Department of Psychiatry, Liaquat National Hospital, Karachi	1978	27

Source: Statistics Bureau, Government of Pakistan, 1990.

and they have so far failed to pursue the cause by lobbying the ministries and legislators.

The Pakistan Psychiatric Society on its own has made several contributions to mental health. These include (1) creating awareness in the general public through the mass media and (2) holding annual and biennial international conferences involving professionals for allied fields like social services, psychology, education, nursing, and general practitioners and lately scientists, journalists, and the judiciary.

SPECIAL POLICY ISSUES

The Mentally Ill and the Mentally Retarded

The problem of mental handicap has been estimated to affect 0.5 to 1 percent of all children in Pakistan. No comprehensive survey has been done to get a prevalence rate of mental disabilities in Pakistan. Scattered attempts at the city or provincial levels give varied figures. The WHO estimate that 3 percent of the world's population is mentally handicapped would make about 3 million mentally handicapped in Pakistan. In this category there are 1.35 million in the age group of zero to fourteen years of age. Existing services provide for the needs of only 2.5 percent of the children who need this help (Neki, 1984).

According to available information, there are twelve special education centers operated by the federal government and about as many by the provincial governments for the education and rehabilitation of the mentally handicapped. Most of these centers are in big cities; 31 special schools being run by social welfare agencies are also mostly in the big cities. Approximately 300 mentally handicapped persons attend these special schools.

There is no policy yet concerning the mentally ill and the mentally retarded, but there is a general understanding that there is a clear-cut distinction between the mentally ill and the mentally handicapped or mentally retarded. Lately, because of growing awareness regarding disabilities in general, mental retardation is no longer a new term to the government or public sector. In fact, the clear differences between the mentally retarded and the physically disabled are a positive factor in enabling the public sector and voluntary organizations such as the Association for Children with Education and Learning Problems (ACELP) to set up special schools, including SAHARA, a school for training and educating the mentally retarded in Karachi.

The Ministry of Health also has a subministry of special education. This step at the government level has led to further identification and clarity of the concept of mental retardation and multiple disabilities. There is a special training center set up in Islamabad, the federal capital, for the training of those with special disabilities, including the deaf, dumb, blind, and physically and mentally handicapped. The government scheme is to set up one such center in each province. There are also special training programs for teachers in special education run regularly by the government. As a group, both the mentally ill and the mentally retarded have worked side by side, except at the federal government level, where there was a special interest in mental retardation by the late President Zia's government. There also has been a greater awareness of multiple disabilities, particularly mental retardation. Both these groups have been supportive to each other.

Fortunately, institutionalization of the mentally retarded in mental hospitals has not been the practice, at least in the last two decades. In the case of dual diagnosis of mental retardation and mental illness the care continues to be at home in the community with follow-up at mental retardation clinics with supportive psychiatric treatment.

The Mentally Ill and Substance Abuse

There is a clear-cut division between the mentally ill and alcohol and drug abuse in both the public and private sectors. The drug menace, especially heroin abuse, has escalated meteorically in the last decade. In 1982, 1.3 million people abused drugs. According to a 1986 survey, this figure was 31.8 percent of total abuse (PNCB, 1986). Initially, the drug abusers were kept along with the mentally ill, but now they have separated drug abuse clinics, hospital beds, and centers for rehabilitation. The problem of alcohol is not as obvious in Pakistan, and whenever such cases are identified, they are treated by psychiatrists and are admitted to psychiatric units.

There is no policy as such laid down for substance abuse, but projects are launched by the government for eradication of poppy cultivation and crop substitution. A large amount of money, mainly from foreign aid, is spent periodically on these projects. During the years 1977 to 1979 three years were spent founding treatment and rehabilitation projects by both the Pakistan government and foreign aid. These projects were extended until 1986, when the central government was to take them over. Apart from the efforts of the government, there are 50 nongovernmental organizations (NGOs) engaged in controlling the narcotics problem.

There are very few drug detoxification centers set up by the government. In 1977 six treatment and rehabilitation centers were set up with the help of the United Nations Federation of Drug Addiction Centers under a tripartite agreement (Khan, 1986). Also, a few private drug detoxification centers have cropped up. Clearly, more efforts at the community level involving drug education programs for the public, inclusion of narcotics education programs in school syllabi, counselling and rehabilitation facilities, and other services are needed to combat this menace.

The policy for the mentally ill is in the doldrums, and there also is still no definite plan of action in practice to treat and rehabilitate drug addicts on a long-term basis. There is a clear-cut distinction between drug addicts and the mentally ill. The drug addicts are feared and constitute the worst of social stigmas. People with dual diagnosis at times are treated for initial withdrawal of drugs at detoxification centers.

The Mentally Disordered Offender

The Lunacy Act of 1912 has no provision for mentally disordered offenders. The law is being misused especially in those cases where patients because of the severity of their mental illness and handicap fail to seek treatment voluntarily. This has at times resulted in such patients being incarcerated in jails. In other cases patients needing psychiatric treatment have been denied admission to a hospital because technical and bureaucratic requirements that have been laid down in law could not be fulfilled.

In the criminal justice system the plea of insanity or a psychiatric defense is allowed. Generally, the mentally ill or mentally retarded person standing trial is assessed by government psychiatrists for competence to stand trial. The facilities for assessment before trial are limited to a few government psychiatric units.

The mentally disordered offender was in the worst case being incarcerated in prisons for years without proper psychiatric care. That trend is changing. Prison authorities now recognize such offenders, and they are transferred to government-based psychiatric units with an appropriate police guard.

Deinstitutionalization

The issue of deinstitutionalization is the only silver lining in Pakistani mental health history. Lack of awareness, extended family systems, and improper facilities for the care of the mentally ill, the mentally retarded, and alcohol and drug abuses led to the community taking over responsibility. Primarily, the families have taken care of their disabled relations. There is a small proportion of mentally ill who lack family support or have no living relatives; they are in the long-stay mental hospitals, of which there are only two, one in Lahore and the other in Hyderabad. Hence in Pakistan the concept of deinstitutionalization does not apply, as Pakistan was never highly institutionalized.

Funding Issues

According to the Pakistani government, 5 percent of GNP is spent on health care, and hence a proportion comes to mental health (Zaidi, 1988). There is no private health insurance, but large organizations like the armed forces, Pakistan Airlines, the Pakistan Steel Mills, banks, and other government and semigovernment organizations provide mental health care as part of their health care facilities.

Consumer Rights

There are so many priorities in the health sector for both the government and private organizations that there is no awareness of consumer rights in mental health law or policy. No statistics are available in this area.

Recently human rights activists, like the Ansar Burney Welfare projects, have taken up some issues like the right to legal representation, hospital visitors, and others. The human rights activists, in particular a young advocate, have started a voluntary group to protect the rights of the mentally ill and to provide adequate treatment facilities and other services. As regards protection against treatment modalities such as psychosurgery and electroconvulsive therapy, which are invasive procedures, a written consent of the relatives is always required.

As there are no consumer rights developed through legislation, there are no guidelines and no accountability. The major consumer groups are rural populations, low-income groups of laborers, students, and the public in general. At present, they are apathetic and indifferent toward development of their own rights, including consumer rights.

CONCLUSIONS AND DISCUSSION

In the last two decades there has been a dramatic increase in private psychiatric facilities, as a general awareness of psychological problems is growing among the public. Many companies and semigovernment organizations have provided employee assistance programs in which the employer directly or by contract provides assessment, referral, and counselling services to employees to improve productivity.

There is no modern mental health policy, though awareness has reached both the government and the public sector. The legislators and the professionals in the field of mental health need to formulate an effective, comprehensive mental health policy. The most distinct change in the attitude of the Health Ministry is the trend to focus on the development of community psychiatry services rather than institutions. This definite shift in the thinking of health planners is a positive step. Hopefully, the long-awaited mental health policy will be delivered soon.

REFERENCES

Ahmed, S. H. (Ed.). (1988). *Psychiatry in Pakistan*. Karachi: Pakistan Psychiatric Society.

Basher, T. A. (1982). Epidemiologic surveys in developing countries: Potential constraints. *Acta Psychiatrica Scandinavica, 65*(Suppl. 296), 45–51.

Federal Bureau of Statistics. (1989). *Pakistan Statistical Year Book*. Islamabad: Statistics Division, Government of Pakistan.

Khan, M. Z. (1986). *Introduction of addictive drugs*. Workshop on Prevention of Drug Abuse, The Agha Khan Health Services, Pakistan.

Neki, J. S. (1979). *Problems old and new*. Geneva: World Health Organization.

Neki, J. S. (1984). Incorporation of mental health into primary health care: Problems of cross-cultural adaptation of technology. *International Journal of Mental Health, 12*, 1–15.

Pakistan Narcotics Control Board (PNCB). (1984). *National survey on drug abuse in Pakistan*. Islamabad: Author.

Pakistan Narcotics Control Board (PNCB). (1986). *The living dead takes its toll*. Islamabad: Author.

Sartorius, N., et al. (1983). *Depressive disorders in different cultures*. Geneva: World Health Organization.

Zaidi, S. A. (1988). *The political economy of health care in Pakistan*. Lahore: Vanguard Books.

14

People's Republic of China

Yu-cun Shen

OVERVIEW

The People's Republic of China is situated in the southeastern part of the Eurasian continent, on the west coast of the Pacific Ocean. By territory the world's second-largest country, China has a land area of about 9.6 million square kilometers, making up 6.5 percent of the earth's land mass.

China is a multinational country with the most people in the world. According to the results of the fourth national census carried out in July 1990, the population of the country was 1,160,017,381 ("The 1990 Census," 1990). The Han nationality made up approximately 94 percent of the total population. The agricultural population constituted around 80 percent. In the mainland's thirty provinces, autonomous regions, and municipalities, each family had an average of 3.96 persons, and the sex ratio (female taken as 100) was 106.6 percent. The age distribution, based on the sampled sum of 10.01 percent from the 1990 census, was 27.70 percent children aged 0–14 years, 63.71 percent adolescents and adults aged 15–59 years, and 8.59 percent people 60 years and over (65 years and over, 5.58 percent).

China is one of the oldest countries with one of the world's earliest civilizations. It has a rich and ancient culture with about five thousand years of history. Yet it is quite young in experiencing the developments of modern industrialization and agriculture. The founding of the People's Republic of China in 1949 ended the history of colonialism that had existed for more than ten decades. Through the work of more than thirty years, the Chinese people have made great progress in the development of industry, agriculture, science, and culture. The living standard of the people has also increased. The average yearly income per person increased from Renminbi (RMB) 57 yuan in 1952 to 601.5 yuan in 1989 for peasants in rural areas, and from 445 yuan to 1,935 yuan for employed in urban areas (National Statistical Bureau, 1990).

China has been a socialist country since 1949. It has a people's congress system and a multiparty political consultation system of nine political parties in which the Chinese Communist Party plays a leading role.

It is well known that since the late 1970s China has been undergoing rapid reforms of its economic system and has been challenged with a series of social changes, such as changes in family and population structures, the social environments in which people live, and value systems. The disease pattern has been changed along with the process of industrialization. A series of psychological and behavioral problems and social adjustment issues is occurring currently in China. The demands for mental health services have been increasing in the community. All these changes encourage the formulation of a new mental health policy involving developing mental health services to cover a wide range of psychological and behavioral problems, in addition to the treatment and prevention of psychiatric disorders (Shen, 1987a, 1987c).

EXTENT OF THE PROBLEM

In light of the results of the first national epidemiological survey on mental disorders among the population aged fifteen to fifty-nine in twelve areas of China, each area covering 500 urban households and 500 rural households, totalling 12,000 households surveyed door-to-door and interviewed with Present State Examination (PSE) in 1982, the time-point prevalence rate of psychiatric disorders was 10.54 per 1,000. Among them, the rate of schizophrenia was 4.75 per 1,000 and that of moderate and severe mental retardation was 2.88 per 1,000, both together making a figure of 7.63 per 1,000. Among children aged seven to fourteen the prevalence rate of moderate and severe mental retardation was 5.8 per 1,000 (Chen et al., 1986).

In another survey of children aged fourteen and under in Beijing the prevalence rate of mental retardation, including mild, was 14 per 1,000 (Zhang et al., 1984). The prevalence rate of mental retardation in an iodine-deficiency area (in Jilin Province, for example) was as high as 86 per 1,000 (Huang et al., 1990). This figure was close to what was found in the first national sampling survey on five kinds of handicapped, conducted in April of 1987 in 28 provinces (396,816 families; 1,579,314 population) except Taiwan Province. The prevalence rate of mentally retarded and psychiatric disabled was around 10 per 1,000 (Committee of the National Sampling Survey, 1987). The majority of them were cared for by family members who resided in the community. Thus there is an urgent need to develop community mental health services and programs for social rehabilitation of the mentally disabled. The need for special education for mentally retarded children also will become more significant as time goes on.

Changes in the family, the population structure, the lifestyle, and the value identification could not but have an impact on the Chinese traditional way to raise children. A tendency for increasing rates of behavior problems in children and increasing juvenile delinquency has been observed in China.

Data from the epidemiological study on behavior problems in 2,432 school children among six primary schools (using Rutter's behavior questionnaire for children) in Beijing in 1986 found that the rate of behavior problems was 8.3 percent, and this was found to be closely related to the children's family and social milieu. Higher rates were found in quarrelling families (17.5 percent), divorced families (17.65 percent), and those whose parents showed few expectations for or concerns about their children's school achievement (19.4 percent) (Wang et al., 1989). There is also a tendency toward increasing psychological disturbances and behavior problems in the students of middle schools and universities.

The proportion of elderly in the general population is increasing nationwide, especially in some major cities. It is estimated that in the next century the process of aging in China will be accelerated to such an extent that the proportion of those aged sixty and over in the general population will become 15 percent in 2025 ("Geriatric Sociology," 1991). A series of financial, social, and medical issues need to be coped with. Among the medical issues, dementia would be one of top priority. According to an epidemiological survey on dementia using Mini-Mental State Examination (MMSE) as a screening instrument and the diagnostic criteria for dementia in DSM-III, the prevalence rate of moderate and severe dementia was 1.82 percent among an urban population aged sixty-five and over in Beijing in 1984. If this Chinese population is standardized with that of an American population in 1984, this prevalence rate would become 3.2 percent (Li et al., 1989). Traditionally, all the demented were kept at home and cared for by family members. With the increase in nuclear families, there is a decrease in the capability to care for aged dementia in the family. Thus there is a need to develop community mental health care services and social support systems for the care of demented elderly in families. With the implementation of a retirement system in China, among elderly people adjustment distress, loneliness, uselessness, hypochondria, and depressive feelings are increasing (Shen, 1987a).

According to the data from some major cities in 1987, cerebrovascular disease, cardiovascular disease, and cancer were the first three causes of death in northern China, while cardiovascular disease, cerebrovascular disease, and cancer were the first three causes of death in southern China, instead of infectious diseases as in the 1950s. Psychosocial variables and stress play a significant role in the occurrence of these three important diseases. Thus knowledge of the role of psychosocial factors and behavior in health and skills to manage mental health problems have to be handled not only by mental health workers, but also by medical professionals and other disciplines.

MENTAL HEALTH HISTORY

Chinese traditional medicine did address mental functioning and disorders. In an ancient classic work of traditional medicine, *'Canon of Internal Medicine,'* written during the Warring States (475–221 B.C.), the author summarized the experience and achievement of traditional medicine and proposed a unique and comprehensive theory to explain the etiology of human diseases and treatment approaches, including those for mental functioning and disorders. The most common clinical features were described; for example, "the severely disturbed mental patient may walk undressed or sing a song at the top of a hill, even refuse to take any food for many days"; "high fever and red face, running and crying without sleep, dilusional vision and speech." Special theories to explain the relationship between functions of visceral organs and mental phenomena were stated as follows: "There were five kinds of mental activities; their function was closely correlated to five important visceral organs: heart, lung, liver, spleen, and kidney." The role of emotion in the occurrence of physical illness was clearly stated: "Anger impairs the liver; agitation impairs the heart; grief impairs the spleen; sadness impairs the lungs; terrible feelings impair the kidney." Various herbal medicines, prescriptions, and different acupuncture points were indicated in the treatment and management of mental disorders according to their symptomatology. Chinese traditional experts treated mental patients at their residence as they did for physical disorders. Many prescriptions have been inherited and are still used by Chinese traditional experts nowadays, and research on these approaches using modern scientific methods was encouraged by the government after the founding of the People's Republic of China.

Psychiatry, as a discipline of Western medicine, was developed much later than other disciplines in China. There were only a few psychiatric hospitals before 1949. The first psychiatric hospital was set up in Guongzhou in 1898, followed by Beijing (1906), Shuzhou (1929), Shanghai (1935), and Nanjing (1947). The medical education of psychiatry was initiated in Beijing Union Hospital in 1922 and then developed in a few medical colleges in Shanghai, Changsha, Nanjing, and Shenyang. This situation began to change when China became an independent country in 1949 (Luo & Shen, 1986).

At the founding of the People's Republic of China, the psychiatric services were faced with a serious shortage of professional staff and technical facilities. There were no more than 100 neuropsychiatrists and no more than 1,000 psychiatric beds in a huge country with a population of more than 400 million (Luo & Shen, 1986). Under the guidance of the public health policy of the People's Republic of China, at the early stage of development the main efforts were directed toward setting up new hospitals and sanatoriums for mental patients, mostly in the big cities. They were meant for the homeless, for those who might cause trouble to the community. These institutions were organized by the Ministries of Civil Administration, Public Security, and Public Health. An intense advanced training course in psychiatry took place in such big cities as Nanjing, Shanghai, and others. By 1958, sixty-two psychiatric hospitals had been built, covering twenty-one provinces.

Inpatient hospital psychiatric services were necessary, but they could hardly meet the requirements of the community, as many patients had relapses after being discharged from the hospitals, and only a limited number of mental patients could get treatment. So in the late 1950s medical workers went out to the community to try to find new forms of services suited for the social and economic features of the country and to develop community services for mental patients with the hospital as a center (Shen, 1981).

The Chinese Neuropsychiatric Association was established as a branch of the Chinese Medical Association in 1954 in Beijing. Its official publication, the *Chinese Neuropsychiatric Journal*, was issued in the same year. Psychiatry as a clinical discipline was taught in the majority of medical schools by 1958 (Luo & Shen, 1986).

Some of the more common mental health problems in the 1950s were psychiatric disorders caused by neurosyphilis, infectious and parasitic diseases, and malnutrition. These were remarkably decreased by the end of the 1950s through effective public health approaches in prophylaxis and treatment of all these diseases, prohibition of prostitution, elimination of starvation, and social reform (Luo & Shen, 1986).

Field surveys of mental disorders were considered to be the basis for formulating programs for treatment and prevention. According to incomplete statistics, in the late 1950s psychiatric field surveys were made in cities and provinces such as Shanghai, Nanjing, Beijing, Hunan, and Sichuan, covering a total of around 18 million inhabitants. In the late 1970s around 30 million inhabitants were surveyed in these cities and some other provinces and cities, according to data collected for the Second Academic Meeting of the Chinese Neuropsychiatric Association, held in Nanjing in 1978 (Luo & Shen, 1986). Since that late 1950s schizophrenia has been prominent in its prevalence rate, and its percentage has been higher than that of all other psychoses. Second has been mental retardation, mainly found in some rural areas. The prevalence rate of schizophrenia in the late 1970s (3.2 to 7.3 per 1,000) was found to be higher than in the 1950s (1.3 to 2.8 per 1,000). This is probably due to the decrease in the death rate of the general population and in infant mortality with the lengthening of average life expectancy of the population (35 years in 1949, 66.95 years for males and 69.55 years for females in 1978) and the improvement of medical care and social welfare for those with chronic disabilities (Shen, 1981).

POLICY, ORGANIZATION, AND SERVICES IN THE 1980s AND 1990s

Current Policy Developments

In the People's Republic of China there is now an urgent need to develop community approaches and psychosocial rehabilitation programs for the chronically mentally disabled. Though the advance of medical treatment has enabled China to control many acute symptoms of psychiatric disorder, there is still no effective approach available to cure chronic mentally disabled or mentally retarded persons. The number of chronic mentally disabled will continue to accumulate as life expectancy is prolonged, so psychosocial rehabilitation programs are needed for the improvement of social adjustment and the quality of daily life of those with mental disabilities.

Some tendencies of increasing rates of behavior and emotional problems in children and adolescents, psychological disturbances and psychosomatic disorders among young people, and adjustment disorders among elderly after their retirement have been observed in recent years (Shen et al., 1990). To meet these urgent demands, the Chinese Mental Health Association was reset up in 1985, and the branches University Association of Psychological Counselling and Psychotherapy and Psychological Counselling were organized in 1990.

Mental health policy was addressed in the Seventh Five-Year Program (1986–90). China still suffers from shortages of qualified professionals and facilities for mental health services. Big achievements have been made in psychiatric education, services, and research in recent years. By 1990 psychiatric hospitals had been increased to 444, psychiatric beds had been increased to 86,000, and qualified psychiatrists to 11,570 (Gu, 1991). Yet the country was still lagging far behind in socioeconomic development and in meeting the demand of the community. Based on the socioeconomic background and health system of China, the mental health program was first formulated in 1986 for 1986–90 (Shen, 1987c). The main components of this program are discussed in following sections.

Current Organization

Besides increasing the number of hospital beds for psychiatric patients, developing community-based mental health services was one of the major tasks under the National Mental Health Program. Social support and community involvement were essential for this task, as it can best be performed and promoted through joint efforts of different social organizations. The National Coordinating Meeting on Mental Health was organized in 1986. In recent years local mental health coordinating committees have been set up in many provinces and cities. These committees consist of several departments, such as public health, the welfare agency, public security, the education committee, and others. They are responsible for mental health services in the cities, counties, or regions and for offering community services on a large scale.

Mental health facilities were much underdeveloped in the northwestern and southwestern parts of China and in minority regions. Large universities on the east coast of China were assigned the responsibility to support mental health programs in these regions. For instance, it was agreed that Beijing Medical University was responsible for minorities in Yunnan Province, while Shanghai Medical University was responsible for Xinjiang Autonomous Region, mainly in the form of regular short-term visits of psychiatrists (two to three months per year) to these regions for teaching and medicine.

Current Services

In China there are two major types of community mental health services, urban and rural. In urban areas and big cities occupational rehabilitation stations were gradually adopted and popularized. For instance, in Shanghai rehabilitation stations or welfare workshops were set up for 90 percent of the streets, and more than 3,900 chronic mentally ill participated (the majority were mentally retarded persons and schizophrenics) (He, 1987). In Suzhou City eighteen out of twenty-two streets organized such workshops. Experience from Shenyang community mental health stations in Liaoning Province in the north of China involved the rehabilitation of chronic mentally disabled in close coordination with a factory. Through well-organized collective rehabilitation activities and vocational training, relapse rates were reduced and social functions of the mentally disabled were recovered to such an extent that they could return to the community, adjust to social life, engage in some simple job, or work in a welfare factory. In the last ten years 114 chronic psychiatric disabled have joined in the program. Of this number, 67 were rehabilitated and employed by the factory (Zhengyang Psychiatry Center, 1987).

In the rural areas community home care mental health services were the major way in which the mental health services net was organized, through the professional training of local primary health workers. Based on the well-developed primary physical health system and the oriental Chinese cultural tradition that family members take responsibility to care for sick members, including mental patients, it was possible to train primary health workers to develop community mental health services and provide home care to those mentally ill. The majority of the chronically mentally ill received drug treatment at their homes, where the primary health workers paid regular home visits under the supervision of medical professionals at higher levels. Psychiatric patients were encouraged to participate in family or farm work as early as possible. For instance, in Haidian District, a suburb of Beijing, the community home care system for psychiatric patients was established from 1974 to 1977. More than 230 schizophrenic patients were treated in this way, and the effects were evaluated annually over fourteen years. It was found that 64.8 percent of schizophrenic patients were kept in clinical remission or had remarkable improvement. The recovery of social function was satisfactory; 60 percent of the schizophrenic patients enjoyed full-time collective farm work or household work (Shen, 1985; Shen et al., 1990). In Yantai City, covering a rural population of 6 million, there were only 328 psychiatric beds, distributed in seven psychiatric hospitals and one psychiatric department. Through ten years' endeavor, more than 7,000 primary health workers received short-term professional training, and 3,385 home beds (up to June 1989) were set up (Yao, 1992). These types of care are much less expensive, more easily reached by the farmer, and better for rehabilitation (Shen, 1985).

The organization of coordinating committees at different levels and the program of community-based mental health service have made definite progress in the last five years even though they have been restricted to several cities, areas, and provinces. However, the program will again be reemphasized in the mental health program for 1991–95.

Mental Health Personnel and Treatment

Enhancing teaching of psychiatry and developing behavioral science teaching programs in the curriculum of medical universities and colleges was called for in the mental health program (Chen et al., 1987). According to the statistical data for 1986, the teaching of psychiatry in three-fourths of the medical colleges was in departments of internal medicine or neurology; only in one-fourth was it in an independent psychiatric department (Shen, 1987c). A few medical universities have been approved by the Education Committee of the State Council, People's Republic of China, to set up mental health facilities, recruiting students in 1989 for a five-year course. The development of these new facilities for mental health would accelerate the provision of more qualified psychiatrists and mental professionals in the country. A textbook of psychiatry for undergraduates was compiled in 1984, with a second edition in 1989, by experts appointed by the Teaching Material Committee, Ministry of Public Health.

To meet the changes of disease patterns in the country, the medical curriculum for undergraduates and postgraduates has to be changed to address the broader mental health concepts and to give them higher priority. Psychological counseling, brief psychotherapy, family therapy, and behavior modification have been rather quickly developed at some general hospitals, universities, and schools in big cities in recent years. This was emphasized in the mental health program for 1986–90 and has been reemphasized in the mental health program for 1991–95 (Shen et al., 1990).

PUBLIC POLICY PROCESS

In the early stages after the founding of the People's Republic of China, public health work was facing serious problems: the prevalence of severe diseases and the shortage of medical personnel and drug resources. The main health problems at that time were acute and chronic infectious diseases and parasitic and endemic diseases, such as plague, cholera, smallpox, and malaria. It was estimated that more than 11 million people suffered from schistosomiasis and 530,000 from Karaya, and tuberculosis had a prevalence rate as high as 4 percent. Before the founding of the People's Republic of China, the death rate of the general population was 25 per 1,000, with an infant death rate of 200 per 1,000 and an average life span of thirty-five years. The majority of sick people could not get medical care, especially in rural areas, where 80 percent of the population lived. The public health policy, initially formulated in 1951 by the government of the People's Republic of China, was ''to meet the health needs of the masses, especially workers, peasants, and soldiers; to provide prevention first; to develop cooperation between Chinese traditional and Western medicine; to combine the health professionals and a mass movement.'' This public health policy has guided the public health work of the People's Republic of China over the last forty years, with a few modifications over time, the most recent revision being in 1991.

The most recent revision of public health policy was stated in the ''Outline of the 10-Year (1991–2000) Program for National Economic and Social Development,'' which was endorsed by the Seventh National People's Congress in April 1991. It states: ''Prevention first; Dependence on advanced science and technology; Encouragement of community involvement; Equal attention to both Chinese traditional medicine and western medicine; Serve for people's health'' (*Guangming Daily*, 1991).

In China psychiatric patients as well as chronic psychiatric disabled enjoy the same public medical care service as patients suffering from physical disease as long as the disease course lasts, and if the patients were staff working in government systems or organizations, even after their retirement. If the patients work in the collective economic system, such as farmers in the rural community, they enjoy full or partial public medical care according to the level of economic development of their commune.

After the 1950s all psychiatric hospitals or clinics were run by the government and received subsidies from the Ministry of Public Health or from provincial or municipal bureaus of health according to the size of the service (number of hospital beds and number of patients in outpatient clinics). Private mental health services were encouraged after the economic reform in the 1980s, but government mental health services are still dominant in resources, facilities, and qualifications of staff.

SPECIAL POLICY ISSUES

The Mentally Ill and the Mentally Retarded

A special education program for mentally handicapped for 1986–92 was developed by the National Education Committee in 1986. The main topics directed toward mental retardation were to popularize the special education classes for mentally retarded children in large and middle-sized cities and to develop schools of occupational training courses for handicapped young people.

Welfare factories for different kinds of handicapped were developed as early as the 1950s. Special regulations providing the opportunity of employment for five kinds of handicapped persons including the mentally handicapped or mentally retarded were developed in August 1980 by the Ministry of Finance and the Ministry of Civil Administration and were reemphasized in October 1984. A series of priorities was given to welfare factories to encourage the employment of the handicapped. For instance, if more than 35 percent of workers employed in a welfare factory are handicapped persons, the factory will be allowed to be exempt from taxation by the government, and all profits will be owned by the factory to be used for the welfare of the workers or for reinvestment. It was reported that 70 percent of handicapped people with a working capacity got a job in large or middle-sized cities (*Handbook for Chinese Handicapped*, 1988).

Special education for mentally retarded children has been developed in some major cities. In Beijing, as an example, there were 126 special education classes set up in normal primary schools, and six special schools were set up; 1,196 mentally retarded with IQs ranging from 50 to 70 and aged under fourteen receive this kind of training (Yang et al., 1988). In an education and behavior program they were taught how to manage their daily life and to be polite in their communication with others. After three years of special education courses some of them received further occupational training and were even employed by welfare factories when they graduated from these special schools. This kind of rehabilitation helped the heavy burden on the family and was highly supported by the families and communities.

The Mentally Ill and Substance Abuse

Opium addiction was a serious social problem in China that had remained rampant for about 200 years before the founding of the People's Republic of China. It was estimated that there were around 10 million opium smokers in 1949 (Institute of Modern History, 1987). A nationwide campaign against opium addiction was launched as early as February 1950 by the administrative council of the central government under the leadership of Premier Zhou En-lai. A circular order on "strictly prohibiting opium trade, use, and cultivation" was signed by Premier Zhou personally. This severe health problem was eradicated within a period of three years (1950–53). This great success was attributed to the tremendous efforts of different departments from the central, provincial, municipal, and county governments; active participation of different social organizations in combination with a mass movement nationwide; and health education together with effective government intervention. With the help of government, opium dens were transformed and shifted into other trades. Food crops replaced opium poppy cultivation on lands formerly used as opium plantations. All opium smokers received compulsory treatment to withdraw from the addiction under the support of the health services, the community, and the family. Smoking, planting, trading, smuggling, and transporting opium were strictly prohibited except for medical purposes (Institute of Modern History, 1987; Shen, 1984). The abolition of the unequal treaties forced on China since the Opium War (1842) and restoration of trade autonomy after the founding of the People's Republic of China provided the opportunity to halt the entry of opium from abroad.

Unfortunately, in recent years this evil practice has been reappearing in some parts of China, especially in those remote provinces such as Yunnan that are near the area called the "golden triangle." Illegal trade and the use of heroin threaten the people's health and the security of society. The Chinese government attaches great importance to drug control, and recently the National People's Congress passed a new antidrug law, sparing no effort in fighting against illegal drug use and traffic. Compulsory withdrawal therapy in special institutions is offered to drug abusers, wherever they are observed ("NPC Enacts Laws," 1991). Treatment and rehabilitation centers as well as research centers have been established.

Alcohol was not a problem in China until the 1980s. The prevalence rate of alcoholism was as low as 0.19 per 1,000 during the first epidemiological study on psychiatric disorders in 1982 (Chen et al., 1986). With the improvement of people's living conditions, alcohol consumption also increased, and the risk for alcoholism has been increasing very rapidly in the last ten years, particularly in some minority areas where people keep a positive attitude toward drinking, believing that "people can make friends through drinking" and "to drink until drunk shows sincere friendship." It was reported that the prevalence rate of alcohol dependence was 35 per 1,000 in the Dai minority (Lu et al., 1987) and 30 per 1,000 in the Bei minority in Yunnan Province (Shen, 1987b). In Yanbian Autonomous District in Jiling Province, where the majority are Korean, the proportion of inpatients with a diagnosis of alcohol-related problems in psychiatric hospitals ranged from 0 to 4 percent in the period 1964 to 1974, but increased to 8 to 23.46 percent by 1980 (Shen, 1987b). Data from a 1991 collaborative study on prevalence rates of alcohol dependence in different professions of ten urban areas (supported by the Western Pacific Regional Office of WHO WPRO), using Diagnostic Interview Schedule (DIS) Screening Interview Schedules and ICD-10 diagnostic criteria among 44,920 people aged fifteen to sixty-five in four occupations (scientific, technical, and professional; administrative staff; light-industry workers; and heavy-industry workers), showed a large increase in prevalency rates. The highest rate was found in heavy-industry workers and minority ethnic populations (Korean). Prevalence rates in heavy-industry workers constituted 58.58 per 1,000 for Han ethnics and 147.52 per 1,000 for Koreans. The lowest rate was found in the scientific, technical, and professional workers, 9.72 per 1,000 for Han ethnics, while for Koreans it reached 72.28 per 1,000 (Zhang et al., 1991). Among 1,674 cases of alcohol-dependent persons, 1,671 cases were male, and only 3 cases of females were found. The highest rate of alcohol dependence was found in two Korean communities (68.75 per 1,000 and 79.61 per 1,000), yet not one female case was found (Shen, 1987b). This research indicated that health education to control alcohol consumption and prevention of alcohol dependence, especially in high-risk populations, must receive more attention in the National Mental Health Program.

The Mentally Disordered Offender

To protect the rights of mental patients was one of the major concerns in the National Mental Health Program for 1986–90. Two major tasks were scheduled:

formulation of a Psychiatric Expert Testimony Regulation and a Mental Health Act.

The first task was initiated in 1985 and successfully completed in 1989 after intensive academic exchanges among psychiatric professionals at the domestic and international levels along with joint meetings among representatives from different government departments, such as the Supervisory Ministry and the Ministry of Justice. The Ministry of Public Health headed the study. The exchange of a wide range of views among different professionals and discussions with foreign experts at the international level efficiently promoted the progress of this task. Through these joint efforts, the provision of "psychiatric expert testimony" was approved July 11, 1989, by the Supreme People's Court, the Supervisory Ministry, and the Ministry of Public Health. In this document it is stated that in order to protect the rights of mental patients the department of forensic psychiatry should be organized in mental hospitals at their different levels: provincial, municipal, and county. The document defines the formal procedure to organize the forensic psychiatric testimony process and the qualifications of the experts participating in the testimony. The main purpose of the forensic psychiatric testimony is to indicate the psychiatric state of the offenders during their performance of dangerous behavior whether they were responsible for their behavior or not, and also to indicate their psychiatric state during the court process. If the mentally disturbed offender is not responsible for his or her behavior, he or she will not be punished; if he or she had diminished responsibility, the punishment will be reduced. Compulsory hospital treatment will be given to those mentally disturbed offenders whose behavior is identified by the forensic psychiatric testimony to be dangerous to the security of surrounding people in the community or to themselves (Document of Health Medicine, November 17, 1989).

Deinstitutionalization

In China the majority of psychiatric hospitals were established after the 1950s. Under the influence of the old European tradition, they were built in the countryside with several hundred beds. There are very few psychiatric hospitals with more than one thousand hospital beds. There has not been a process of deinstitutionalization like that in the West, but there has been a change in approach. To avoid long stays of large numbers of chronic psychiatric patients in institutions, the seventh five-year program for mental health (1985) recommended that psychiatric hospitals be built near the residences of inhabitants and with no more than two hundred to three hundred beds, and acute psychiatric beds or wards were recommended to be set up in general hospitals.

Funding Issues

Resources for the development of psychiatric hospitals in China came from three systems: the Ministry of Public Health, the Ministry of Civil Administration, and the Ministry of Public Security. The Ministry of Civil Administration as a government welfare organization was responsible for building psychiatric institutions for those patients without family members or relatives and for veterans, usually long-stay. Such psychiatric institutions covered a wide range, totaling 191 by the year 1990 in almost every province and many large cities (Huaxi Medical University, 1990). A limited number of psychiatric hospitals, totaling 20, were built by the budget from the Ministry of Public Security to receive the psychiatrically disordered with violent behavior (Huaxi Medical University, 1990).

The majority of mental hospitals were built by the funds from health bureaus, totaling 427 at the different levels (provinces, municipalities, and counties), and health bureaus were taking responsibility to provide funds for maintenance and renewal of the facilities (Huaxi Medical University, 1990). The budget for the development of mental health services after the economic reform of 1980 was usually decided by the local health bureaus; sometimes it was proposed by the bureau of health and finally got approval by the People's Congress at the same government level. The percentage of the health budget used for psychiatric services varied from province to province and city to city according to the level of economic development and the awareness of the leadership of the related government departments in respect to the importance of developing psychiatric services in that area.

Since 1980 special foundations for medical research have been established by the Academy of Science, Education Committee, the Ministry of Public Health, the Academy of Chinese Traditional Medicine, and other organizations at the national and provincial levels. Applications for funds for mental health research, like those for other medical disciplines, can be submitted by the individual researcher or research group to the committee of the foundation of the National Sciences Fund, the Scientific Research Fund for Special Disciplinary Doctoral Programs in Universities, and the Ministry of Public Health's Medical Research Fund and are evaluated by a group of appointed qualified academic experts or scientists, who usually serve for two or three years.

Consumer Rights

The task of formulating a mental health law was initiated in 1985. A series of activities has been undertaken, such as translating mental health law from other countries and organizing group discussions among mental health professionals. As this law was to be more comprehensive in nature, it included the laws to develop mental health services; to establish a multidepartment committee responsible for mental health services; to protect rights of mental patients to get an education and a job, to marry, and to be free of abuse; to protect the right of mental patients to receive treatment; and to regulate involuntary admission of psychiatric patients, among other issues. Up to now the law already has been revised nine times. To complete the mental health law, continuing efforts for discussion between representatives from different government departments and professionals and experts from related departments will be very important. This task is emphasized in the National Mental Health Program for 1991–95 and is expected to be completed during that period (Shen, 1990a, 1990b).

The Law of Safeguarding the Legal Rights of the Disabled People of the People's Republic of China, after being revised eighteen times, was formally adopted by the National People's Congress in December 1990 and was finally put into effect in May 1991. It is designed to guarantee the equal rights of the disabled, including the mentally retarded and mentally handicapped ("Law for the Handicapped," 1991). The implementation of this law will accelerate the formulation of the Mental Health Act in China.

CONCLUSIONS AND DISCUSSION

The national mental health program for 1991–95 was drafted recently. The main approach and policies stated in the program for 1985–90 were continued: a community approach for mental health service; development of mental health coordinating groups at different government levels; development of child mental health programs as well as mental health programs for the elderly, especially care and treatment for Alzheimer's disease and cerebrovascular dementia; and giving higher priority to the task of formulating the mental health law that has been worked on for the last five years and is expected to be completed within the next few years. All these policies are directed toward improvement of treatment and care for mental patients, improving their quality of life and bettering their social adjustment function so that they can return to the community and participate in the social life like other citizens without being abused or neglected, and protecting their right to get treatment, care, schooling, jobs, and other benefits.

The plan also calls for continuing the existing relationships and developing new international academic exchanges and cooperation with foreign counterpart bodies and individuals. In the last six to seven years international academic exchanges and mutual visits have significantly enhanced mental health learning. These activities stimulate and promote the development of mental health programs in China.

In addition, the plan calls for popularizing mental health knowledge through the mass media to eliminate the stigma toward psychiatric illness and to mobilize social bodies in support of mental health programs. It seems very important also to popularize mental health knowledge to the medical professionals, other than psychiatrists; community leaders; and leaders of related government departments.

REFERENCES

Chen, C. H., Zhang, W. X., & Shen, Y. C. (1986). Data analysis of an epidemiological study on psychiatric disorders, drug and alcohol dependences, and personality disorders. *Chinese Journal of Neurological Psychiatry, 19*(2), 70–72.

Chen, C. H., & Shen, Y. C. (1987). Some thoughts on setting up specialties of psychiatry and mental health sciences. *Chinese Higher Medical Education, 2*, 15–17.

Committee of the National Sampling Survey of the Handicapped and State Statistical Bureau of the People's Republic of China. (1987, November 7). *Principal data of the national sampling survey of handicapped in China.* Press Communique. Beijing.

Geriatric sociology. (1991, April 16). *Guangming Daily.*

Gu, W. D. (1991, July 18). [Opening Speech at the Fourth National Coordinating Meeting on Mental Health, Beijing].

Handbook for Chinese handicapped. (1988). Beijing. National Sampling Committee for Handicapped and Earthquake Publishing House.

He, J. S. (1987). Creating a new perspective of mental health programs in China. *Chinese Mental Health Journal, 1*(2), 54–58.

Huang, Y. Q., et al. (1990). Epidemiological survey on mentally retarded children in an epidemic goiter and cretinism area in Jilin city. *Chinese Mental Health Journal, 4*(2), 62–64.

Huaxi Medical University. (1990). *An overview of the national psychiatric hospitals.* Huaxi: Author.

Institute of Modern History and Social Science. (1987). *Chinese modern history* (Vol. 1). Beijing: People's Publishing House.

The law for the handicapped put into effect. (1991, May 12). *Renmin Daily.*

Li, G., Shen, Y. C., Chen, C. H., Zhao, Y. W., Li, S. R., & Liu, M. (1989). An epidemiological survey of age-related dementia in an urban area of Beijing. *Acta Psychiatrica Scandinavica, 79*, 557–563 (in English).

Lu, Q. Y., Wang, Y. F., & Shen, Y. C. (1987). Epidemiological investigation of alcoholism in the minority area of Yunnan Province. *Chinese Mental Health Journal, 1*(16), 253–256.

Luo, H. C., & Shen, Y. C. (Eds.). (1986). *Psychiatry* (2nd ed.) (pp. 3–5, 13). Beijing: People's Health Publishing.

National Statistical Bureau. (1990). *Statistical yearbook of China.* Beijing: Chinese Statistical Publishing House.

The 1990 census. (1990). *Beijing Review, 46*(33), 17–19.

NPC enacts laws on drugs, pornography. (1991). *Beijing Review, 34*(2), 4.

Public health in current China. (1986). Shanghai: Chinese Social Science Publishing House.

Shen, Y. C. (1981). The psychiatric services in the urban and rural areas of People's Republic of China. *Bulletin of Neuroinformation Lab, Nagasaki University, 8*, 131–137 (in English).

Shen, Y. C. (1984). How China ended drug addiction. *China Construction, 33*(3), 27–29 (in English).

Shen, Y. C. (1985). Community mental health home-care programme, Haidan district in the suburbs of Beijing. *Chinese Journal of Neurology and Psychiatry, 18*(2), 65–68.

Shen, Y. C. (1987a). Mental health care in China: A time of transition. *World Health Forum, 8*(3), 379–382 (in English).

Shen, Y. C. (1987b). Recent epidemiological data of alcoholism in China. *Chinese Mental Health Journal, 1*(6), 251–252, 256.

Shen, Y. C. (1987c). Some explanations of the draft of the seventy five-year plan for the mental health program. *Chinese Mental Health Journal, 1*(2), 59–62.

Shen, Y. C. (1990a). *Mental health policy planning for the future: The PRC scene*. Paper presented at the WPA Regional Symposium on Mental Health Services, May 22–25, Hong Kong (in English).

Shen, Y. C. (1990b). Some suggestions for the eighth-five year planning of the mental health program. *Chinese Mental Health Journal, 4*(4), 193–196.

Shen, Y. C., Zhang, W. X., & Chen, C. H. (1990). Psychosocial rehabilitation of the mentally ill in a community mental health home care program: Beijing rural Haidan District. *Archives of Psychiatry, 2*(3), 108–111.

Wang, Y. F., Shen, Y. C., Gu, B. H., Jia, M. X., & Zhang, A. L. (1989). An epidemiological study of behavior problems in school-children in the urban area of Beijing. *Journal of Child Psychology and Psychiatry, 30*(6), 907–912 (in English).

Yang, X. L., Gia, M. X., & Gu, B. M. (1988, November). *Try the best to better the rehabilitation of handicapped children*. Unpublished report.

Yao, J. Y. (1992). Prevention, treatment, and rehabilitation of psychiatric patients in Yentai rural area. *Archives of Psychiatry, 2*(3), 127–129.

Zhang, W. X., Shen, Y. C., & Huang, Y. O. (1991). Epidemiological survey on alcohol dependence in populations of four occupations in nine cities of China: methodology and prevalence. *Chinese Mental Health Journal, 6*(3), 112–115.

Zhang, Z. X., Li, Z., Qian, Y. P., Zue, Q. H., Wu, X. R., Lin, Q., & Xu, G. Z. (1984). Epidemiological study on mental retardation among children in Changqiao Area, Western District of Beijing City. *Chinese Journal of Pediatrics, 22*(6), 336–340.

Zhengyang Psychiatry Center. (1987). Rehabilitation of chronic schizophrenics. *Chinese Mental Health Journal, 1*(3), 129–131.

15

Romania

Sergiu Diacicov, Bogdana Tudorache, and Cezar I. Cîmpeanu

OVERVIEW

Romania has a population of 22,477,703 and an area of 91,699 square miles (237,500 square kilometers). It is located in the southeast of Europe. Romania borders Hungary to the northwest, former Yugoslavia to the southwest, Bulgaria to the south, the Black Sea to the southeast, and the former USSR to the east and north. Bucharest is the capital and the largest city.

Romania includes eight historic and geographic regions: Walachia, Moldavia, and Transylvania and parts of Bukovina, Crisana, Maramures, Dobruja, and Banat. Romania is divided into forty districts and the municipality of Bucharest. The Danube River, which forms part of the border with former Yugoslavia and almost all of the frontier with Bulgaria, traverses Romania in the southeast; its tributary, the Prut, constitutes most of the border with the former USSR. The Carpathian Mountains, of which the Transylvania Alps are a part, cut through Romania in a wide arc from north to southwest; the highest peaks are Moldoveanu (8,343 feet/2,543 meters) and Negoiu (8,317 feet/2,535 meters). The country's climate is continental, with hot, dry summers and cold winters; severe droughts are common during the summer.

The great majority of the inhabitants speak Romanian, although there are sizeable minorities that speak Hungarian and German. By far the largest religious body is the Romanian Orthodox Church (*International Geographic Encyclopedia and Atlas*, 1990).

Romania consists primarily of ancient Dacia, which was a Roman province in the second and third centuries A.D. After the Romans left the region, the area was overrun successively by the Goths, the Huns, the Avars, the Bulgars, and the Magyars. After a period of Mongol rule (thirteenth century), the history of the Romanian people became, in essence, that of the two Romanian principalities—Moldavia and Walachia—and of Transylvania, which, for much of its history, was a Hungarian dependency. The princes of Walachia (in 1417) and of Moldavia (in the mid-sixteenth century) became vassals of the Ottoman Empire, but they retained considerable independence. Michael the Brave of Walachia defied both the Ottoman Empire and the Holy Roman Empire and at the time of his death (1601) controlled Moldavia, Walachia, and Transylvania, but his empire soon reverted to Turkish domination. Although the two principalities technically remained within the Ottoman Empire, after the Russo-Turkish War (1828–29) they actually became Russian protectorates. The Russians and Turks combined to suppress the Romanian revolution in 1848. The election (1859) of Alexandru Ioan Cuza as the prince of both Moldavia and Walachia prepared the way for the official union (1861–62) of the two principalities of Romania.

Prince Karl of the house of Hohenzollern-Sigmaringen was chosen as Cuza's successor in 1866. Romania gained full independence in 1878, but was obliged to renounce southern Bessarabia, which became a part of Russia, and to accept northern Dobruja in its place. In 1881 Romania was proclaimed a monarchy, and Prince Karl was crowned King Carol I.

After World War I, which Romania entered in 1916 on the Allied side, the Romanian provinces of Bessarabia (from Russia), Bukovina (from Austria), and Transylvania and Banat (from Hungary) joined the Kingdom of Romania. The constitution adopted in 1923 claimed to be one of the most liberal in modern Romanian history and in Europe at that time as well. A series of agrarian laws, beginning in 1917, did much to break up the large estates and to redistribute the land to the peasants. The large Magyar populations and other minority groups were a constant source of friction, however, and Romanian politics in the 1920s became violent and unsettled. Fascist groups emerged, and in 1938 Carol II assumed dictatorial powers.

In 1939 the Ribbentrop-Molotov Pact was signed, resulting in Romania's loss of northern Transylvania and of Bessarabia, which became part of Hungary and the USSR. In 1940 Romania became a partner of the Axis, and the same year Marshal Ion Antonescu became dictator. King Carol was forced to abdicate in favor of his son, Michael I. The Soviet army invaded in 1944, and a Communist-led coalition government was set up in 1945. After the war Romania recovered all its territories except Bessarabia, Herta, North Bukovina, and South Dobruja.

In December 1947 Michael I was forced to abdicate, and Romania was proclaimed a people's republic. Nationalization of industry and natural resources was completed by a law of 1948, and there was also a forced collectivization of agriculture. Beginning in 1963, Romania's foreign policy became increasingly independent of that of the USSR. In 1965 Nicolae Ceauşescu became general secretary of the Romanian Communist Party. In 1969 Ceauşescu and President Tito of Yugoslavia affirmed the sovereignty and equality of socialist nations. Romania maintained close economic ties with the USSR in the 1970s but strengthened relations with the West, signing, for instance, a trade agreement with the United States in 1975 (*International Geographic Encyclopedia and Atlas*, 1990).

Under the constitution adopted in 1965, the Grand National Assembly, consisting of 465 elected members, was the chief legislative body. In May 1974 the government was organized, and the authority was concentrated in the new office of the president of the republic. In practice, power in Romania was always controlled by the Romanian Communist party, whose leading members were also the country's chief officials. Practically, in order to occupy any important position, one had to become a member of the Party. In the late 1970s the financial support offered by the Western world to Romania was withdrawn because of the increasing number of human rights violations, which led to a dramatic drop in the standard of living. The Communist regimes imposed by force on the eastern part of Europe after World War II were able to survive only by the maintenance of the laws of terror, and they broke apart at the end of the 1980s.

In December 1989 a Romanian popular revolution overthrew Ceauşescu and his clique, officially marking the end of communism in Romania. On May 20, 1990, a general election brought to power President Ion Iliescu, a former high-ranking Communist official, and the National Salvation Front Party. At the same time, a transitional National Assembly was elected that had to formulate a constitution and to organize the next elections. The new constitution was passed in November 1991, specifying a republican, semipresidential power structure.

EXTENT OF THE PROBLEM

Ministry of Health order number 525/1975 mandated the reporting of data on mentally disordered people starting January 1, 1976, in several major cities: Cluj, Craiova, Iasi, Timisoara, Tîngu, Mureş, Bucharest, and Sibiu (Centrul de Calcul şi statistică medicală al Ministerului Sănătatii, 1982, 1983, 1984, 1986, 1988). This study, which extended longitudinally for more than a decade, is subject to justified questions about its validity and reliability. There were many methodological problems concerning the introduction and standardization of a national research program, a lack of concordance of the obtained data with those published by the World Health Organization (WHO) and in the specialized literature, and a lack of concordance in the incidence and prevalence of mental diseases among different cities and as compared to the national data. The data therefore fail to reflect true differences between cities because of methodological biases and failure to observe rules concerning sampling in order to obtain statistical significance. Important differences among the seven centers appear in the Evidence Index (number of cases recorded until the end of the year multiplied by 100/number of cases recorded at the end of the year 1976). This might be an important source of error; for example, in 1981 Cluj had an index for adults of 611.2 percent, while Bucharest had an index of only 172.7 percent, a difference that reflects mainly subjective factors like the willingness to cooperate among regional mental health professionals. Nevertheless, this study can give an idea about the presence and the trends of psychiatric disorders in the Romanian population.

In this study the mental health laboratories had to report new cases to the center for medical statistics each trimester, and they also had to make annual reports of any clinical changes produced in the previously reported patients. The registration of patients was made on a record card for evidence on psychiatric patients. The study took into consideration the following diagnoses for adults: senile and presenile organic psychotic disorders, other organic psychotic disorders, alcoholic psychoses, transitory organic psychotic disorders, schizophrenia, manic-depressive psychoses, delusional disorders, other functional psychoses, personality disorders, sexual disorders, mental retardation, and epilepsy. For children, the diagnoses were specific psychoses of childhood, other functional psychoses, specific affective disorders of childhood and adolescence, adjustment disorders, mental retardation, and epilepsy. After thirteen years of this research, in 1988, the number of persons included in the study represented 19.3 percent of the entire population of the country. The conclusions are presented in table 15.1. In addition, these details are of interest:

1. Sex differences appear only when diagnostic groups are taken into account: The prevalence of alcoholic psychoses is six times greater for men, delusional states are three times greater for women, affective disorders are two times greater in women, and borderline intelligence is two times greater in men. For epilepsy and schizophrenia, there are no significant differences.

2. Among age groups, the most prevalent is the 40–59 group with affective disorders, personality disorders, and schizophrenia, followed by the 10–14 group with borderline intelligence and epilepsy.

3. Regarding marital status, schizophrenia and epilepsy are clearly more frequent among unmarried persons; for other disorders, this tendency does not appear.

4. Concerning seasonal influence, the clinical evolution of cases has been computed with the labels ameliorated, aggravated, and stationary during each month of the year. The highest values for aggravation were found in January and the lowest in December. The major part of these values, for all the months, is represented by schizophrenia and affective psychoses, with one exception: There is an important cluster for personality disorders in the aggravated group, these disorders being in second place as to their frequency.

5. The most frequent antisocial acts proved to be suicide, homicide, armed attack, violation of property, threats of violence, blackmail, rape, homosexuality, sexual perversions, sexual corruption, incest, slander and defamation, theft, and breach of confidence. Diagnoses most frequently associated with antisocial acts were: personality disorders, schizophrenia, affective disorders, epilepsy, and alcoholic psychoses.

The following are the significant statistical data from the *Study Concerning Mental Diseases, Mental Health Care, and the National Program for Defending and Promoting the Mental Health of the Population* (1976): Exogenous psychoses (syphilis, pellagra, and confusive, alcoholic, and puerperal psychoses) rose sig-

Table 15.1
Mental Disorders in Romania

	1982	1983	1984	1986	1988
Incidence	0.126% (between 0.28% in Cluj and 0.033% in Craiova)	0.097% (between 0.211% in Cluj and 0.025% in Craiova)	0.071% (between 0.021% in Bucharest and 0.207% in Cluj)	0.117%	0.085%
Prevalence	for 7 years, 0.71%	for 8 years, 0.77%	0.73%	0.84%	0.88%
Morbidity structure (the most frequent)	•schizophrenia •personality disorders •affective psychoses •epilepsy •borderline intelligence •delusional disorders	•borderline intelligence •schizophrenia •personality disorders •affective disorders •epilepsy	same as 1983	•schizophrenia •borderline intelligence •personality disorders •affective psychoses •epilepsy	•schizophrenia •personality disorders •affective disorders •borderline intelligence •epilepsy
Sex differences	None for the entire sample	same	same	same	same
Age groups	•most affected 10-14 years group 40-59 years group	•maximum prevalence •females 40-59 years gr. •males 15-19 years gr.	•most affected 10-14 years gr. followed by 40-59 years gr. (females, 40-59 years; males, 10-19 years)	•global: 1. 40-59 years 2. 10-19 years	same as 1986
Working capacity	47.46% normal 22.63% state-paid pension 18.31% others (not working)	•47.86% •21.19% •17.8%	•49.35% •20.19% •16.76%	•49.94% •20.53% •15.10%	•51.23% •21.11% •11.36%
Antisocial acts	Frequence 5.29% (most important: suicide 28.08%)	diagnoses: suicide 33.38% with 1. personal disorders 2. schizophrenia	37.87% suicide	suicide 42.24% (cumulative percentile for all antisocial acts commited in the last 11 years; the same computation for the previous figures)	suicide 44.94%

Table 15.1 Continued

	1982	1983	1984	1986	1988
Level of education	•41.41% for primary school •27.93% for secondary school •20.43% for primary school not graduated •9.99% for high school and academic training •0.23% no schooling	•41.1% •28.3% •20.4% •10.1% •0.3%	•40.3% •29.4% •19.8% •10.2% •0.3%	•42.0% •29.5% •17.6% •10.4% •0.5%	•42.9% •29.7% •16.4% •10.0% •0.5%
Marital status	1. Married 2. Unmarried	same (no difference in marital status)	same	same	same
Sick leaves	—	•89.68% without sick leaves •4.17% of 1-7 day duration	—	•from 18,501 7,892 (42.66%) hospitalized; from these persons only 784 had sick leaves, and out of them 269 had 1-7 days of sick leaves.	from 1,984, hospitalized 9,946 (49.8%), and from the last ones 263 had 1-7 days of sick leaves.
Hospitalization	—	•60.79% outpatient •24.42% (1-30 days) •9.45% (31-60 days) •3.19% (91- days) •2.15% (61-90 days)	•62.50% •23.04% •8.97% •3.36% •2.13%		
Seasonal influence	see in text	see in text	see in text	see in text	see in text
Depression	•most frequent in females of 40-59 years and in those 15-39 years dysthymic personality disorder •40-59 years bipolar disorder depressive episodes.				

Source: Centrul de Calcul si Statistică Medicală al Ministerului Sănătății, 1982; 1983; 1984, 1986, 1988.

nificantly until the 1960s as a direct expression of the low economic, cultural, and medical standards of the great majority of the population. Afterwards, exogenous cases (especially pellagra) declined significantly. Endogenous psychoses (affective disorder, schizophrenia, and epileptic disease) rose in the first decade following World War II, but after 1955 they reached a stable plateau. At the same time, the number of neuroses, personality disorders, and organic brain syndromes rose in the old population, and behavior disorders rose in children.

In a retrospective study (between 1959 and 1965) made by the Ministry of Health, there was an apparent rise from 1.9 to 2.5 percent in psychiatric morbidity. In 1965 there were in Romania 460,000 psychiatric patients, of whom 79,000 (18 percent) suffered from psychoses, dementia, and severe mental retardation, requiring hospitalization; the other 381,000 (82 percent) had neuroses, personality disorders, alcoholism, organic brain syndromes of the elderly, and behavioral and developmental disorders in children and adolescents.

The epidemiologic studies made were insufficient, lacking in many respects the standards of a reliable statistical outlook. Nevertheless, in the 1960s they established clearly a significant rise in psychiatric disorders in Romania. From a 1974 study made by the Institute of Neurology and Psychiatry with the Clinic of Psychiatry of the Bucharest Medical School, we have selected the following statistics: neuroses, 38.89 percent; neurotic states in those with personality disorders, 36 percent; adjustment disorders in those having a personality disorder, 6.87 percent; and chronic alcoholism, 5.52 percent. The Global Gravity Index (number of sick-leave days per 100 employees per year) doubled from 1964 to 1974 and was higher in the coal extractive industry, the publishing industry, the soap and cosmetics industry, and the textile industry. The GGI varied greatly between different districts, being low in Constanta and high in Hunedoara.

In 1974 psychiatric diseases and especially neuroses ranked fourth after respiratory disorders, digestive disorders, and accidents as a cause for sick leaves and absenteeism. After 1967 psychiatric disorders became the third most common cause of disability after cardiovascular diseases and tuberculosis. The number of mentally disordered persons rose proportionally with the development of industry.

An epidemiologic study made in 1974 by the Institute of Neurology and Psychiatry with the Institute of Forensic Medicine revealed among the cases of suicide in Bucharest the present of mental disorders in up to 100 percent of the cases (80 to 90 percent, reactive depression; 10 to 20 percent, endogenous depressive psychoses, organic brain disorders, and behavioral disorders in youth). The study revealed a suicide frequency of 14.7 percent of the population of Bucharest.

Finally, we would like to mention a study that chronologically comes before the two just summarized. It is the Complex Medical Inquiry made in 1964–65. In that study the prevalence of psychoses, psychoneuroses, and behavioral and intelligence disorders showed a global index of 2.3 percent; the rate in urban areas was 3.5 percent, versus 1.5 percent in rural areas. The global frequency for the 20–34 age group was 2.4 percent; for the 35–39 age group, 6.1 percent; for the 40–44 age group, 6.5 percent; and for the 50–54 age group, 5.6 percent.

MENTAL HEALTH HISTORY

In Romania the first phase of mental health history can be called pagan. It prominently featured the primitive conception that mental disease was produced by malevolent unnatural forces. Not much is known about this period, but it may be supposed that there were several resemblances with the ancient views that the insane were ministers of the gods. They were killed by lapidation (stoning) or kept at home and mocked (Predescu, 1976, 1989).

A second period developed under the impact of the Christian religion, when the mentally ill person was conceived as being possessed by evil spirits (Diacicov, u.d.c.; Predescu, 1976, 1989). This is the phase one could define as a religious or sacerdotal one. In accordance with an old tradition, the cloisters provided shelter and food to all travellers. This form of Christian kindness was gradually extended to those who were disordered, and this was the beginning of psychiatric care. The first institution organized within the monasteries or in their vicinity was the so-called *bolnita*. In those kinds of establishments the therapy consisted mostly of beverages prepared of plants and, of course, praying. The agitated "patients" were held in chains; nevertheless, in the Romanian provinces people with mental diseases were never tortured or burned at the stake (Diacicov, u.d.c.). These *bolnitas* became hospices, which later, as their number and importance increased, became specialized. Two kinds of hospices emerged: one for the mentally incompetent and the other for old people (asylums). The medical assistance received within these establishments was provided by skilled monks who possessed the knowledge of popular medicine, especially regarding the curing properties of plants.

During the eighteenth century a law was passed in Moldavia and Walachia regarding the principle of abolished incompetence for alienated people, which specified: "The 5th reason for which the judge is expected to diminish the punishment of the persons found to be liable is the condition of those persons being out of touch with reality or being insane; in accordance with this law the madmen are not to be punished, no matter what deeds they have carried out." The first laws to make specific references to alienated persons were passed during the period 1646–52 in Moldavia, and the principles formulated were maintained in the legislation of the eighteenth and nineteenth centuries. The Pravilniciasca Condica (Code of Orders) was passed in 1780 by Alexandru Ipsilanti, and in 1817 the Caragea and the Calimachi codes were added, which also made specific provisions regarding the mentally disordered. The Organic Regulations, brought out by Pavel Dimitrievici Kisseleff in 1832, caused many changes concerning the organization of medical services and made some significant contributions to the later takeover of hospices and asylums from the authority of the Church.

There are many documents proving the role of monasteries in the care of the mentally disordered at the request of family members, by the decision of the Divan (a sort of local parliament) or directly by the reigning prince, or, later, by the Departamental trebilor dinlăuntru (a king's Home Office); these "hospitalizations" were viewed as a sort of exile and could be ended by an order issued by these officials.

The main hospices for mentally ill persons in Moldavia were Golia, for women in Iasi, and Neamt Monastery for men; in Walachia, the monks' rooms of the Sfînta Vineri Church for nonagitated mentally disordered persons and the Sarindar Monastery for the agitated ones. In Oltenia County the monks' rooms of the Madonna Dudu Church gathered tramps, beggars, and mentally alienated individuals. There were many other such establishments, like the Malamuci or Balamuci Institution, near Bucharest, which later gave its name to one of the Romanian terms for hospice (*ballamuc*); another one was Marcuta, the hospice for beggars and "fools," which later became the Institute for Alienated People, a very important psychiatric center after 1869.

With these developments, a third phase in the history of Romanian psychiatry began, a scientific or humanistic one (Predescu, 1976, 1989). In 1857, under the supervision of Carol Davila, the National School of Medicine and Pharmacy was created. Its Project of Rules, published in 1862, included a course of psychiatry. In 1864 a law was passed transforming the School of Medicine into the Faculty of Medicine, which included the Department of Mental Diseases. In the same year (1864) the hospices and asylums were taken over by the Health Department of the Ministry of Internal Affairs. In 1867 the first law providing protections for alienated people was passed, which stated that any person suffering from a mental disease could not be hospitalized other than on the basis of a medical act or of a court decision. The certificate issued had to explain "the kind and the degree of the alienation and all its details"; the discharging of the patient was left entirely to the decision of the treating physicians.

Another very important event during this time was the concentration of psychiatric assistance. In Moldavia the Golia and Neamt hospices were replaced at the beginning of the twentieth century by the Socola Hospital in Iasi; the Marcuta Hospice or Institute and the Madonna Dudu Hospital or Sanitarium maintained their importance. In 1923, in Bucharest, the Gheorghe Marinescu Central Hospital for Nervous and Psychiatric Diseases was created.

Among the pioneers of Romanian scientific psychiatry are N. Stănescu, I. Protici (from Marcuta), N. Hanselman, I. Fabricius, S. Mileticiu (from Madonna Dudu), and I. Lucaszevschi (from Golia). Also, from the beginning of psychiatric teaching, great professors included Alexandru Sutzu, trained in France, professor of forensic medicine, who succeeded after thirty years of efforts in founding the Department of Psychiatry and Mental Disorders of the Bucharest Medical School and who held the first course of psychiatry in the years 1867–68; he was also the author of the first Romanian textbook of psychiatry, *Alienatul în fata societătii si stiintei* (Alienated persons before society and science), published in 1877. Another important figure was Alexandru Obregia, the so-called Romanian Pinel, trained in Germany and France under the supervision of Wirchow, Westphall, Charcot, and Magnan, who succeeded in founding the greatest psychiatric center of that time in the Balkans, the Bucharest Central Hospital. Also deserving mention are Alexandru Brăscu, trained in Paris, disciple of Charcot and Dejerine, founder of the first modern Romanian hospital of psychiatry, and Professor C. I. Parhon, the pupil of the neurologist Gheorghe Marinescu.

In Moldavia, in 1879, the Faculty of Medicine was founded, the Golia Hospice being organized as a clinical center in 1881. Here the first professors were Alexandru Brăescu and George Pastia.

After World War I and the reunion of Transylvania with the Kingdom of Romania, the Psychiatric Center of Cluj was added to the available mental health care services. In 1918 the Society of Neurology, Psychiatry, Psychology, and Endocrinology was founded, its first president being C. I. Parhon. In 1919 a journal of neurology and psychiatry was begun by the Socola Hospital in Iasi. In 1930 a Sanitary Act was passed, conferring on the hospitals for mental diseases the same status as every public hospital, the patients being received there when they needed care and being discharged when the care was considered not to be necessary any more. In 1938 a nervous and mental diseases bulletin was begun at Cernauti (the hospital was founded in 1866) and a professional association of physicians' bulletin was begun at Chisinau.

In 1938 Romania had 16 psychiatric hospitals with 5,695 beds, 85 physicians, and 3 institutions for mentally retarded people in Cluj, Tîngu Mureş, and Inau. For chronic disabled patients, specialized establishments were founded in Plevna, Balaceanca, Raducaneni, Bohotin, Sipote, Rîul Vadului, and Boita. In this period the main features of Romanian psychiatry were a biological orientation with biochemical research and the addition of social and psychological dimensions with strong philanthropic financial support.

What has to be emphasized at this point is the fact that after World War II and the events that led to the establishment of the Communist regime, there has been one major turning point in Romanian psychiatry, which remained practically unchanged until the upheaval of December 1989. Unfortunately, after a long "treatment" strongly resembling a nationwide "brainwashing," psychiatrists who have been freed from the burden of an oppressive ideology are not at ease in giving up old reflexes and in acknowledging facts that are quite evident. This is one reason why we can speak about two main periods following World War II, one lasting until December 1989 and a second one thereafter. These periods display many common features but also several differences.

The first phase of sharp political delineation, that is, the Russian occupation and the "free" elections of November 1946 that brought to power the almost-nonexistent Romanian Communist Party, brought about gradual and by no means clear-cut changes in the scientific field in general and the medical profession in particular. There was a whole generation of eminent scholars trained in the greatest medical centers of the world whose names were well known and respected. They gathered a new generation of young and talented disciples who should have spread further the ideas of their teachers. Unfortunately, the very core of this alliance was attacked and undermined directly because of its potential danger to those trying to impose the "new socialist order." Deportations, executions, death in hard-labor camps and "reeducation" prisons, and the belittling of intellectual performance as opposed to productive physical work occurred. All the great economic plans, inspired mainly by Marxist and Leninist ideas and especially by the Soviet view of "convincing" people what to do or to think (for instance, the deadly digging of the Danube–Black Sea Channel where thousands of opponents met their end), were only a few of the arguments offered by the new regime. We are not in a position to discuss in detail these matters, but mentioning them from the beginning is very important because of their enormous impact on social activity in Romania, including the practice of psychiatry. Gradually, those who could not live in accordance with the new rules disappeared or were outnumbered by those trying to survive; and surviving in the Romanian psychiatry of the early 1950s meant an uncritical acceptance of Soviet psychopathology.

Psychiatry and psychiatrists at large had and have to fight against many misconceptions originating from laypersons and even other health care practitioners, misconceptions that probably stem from uneasiness in thinking about and handling the mentally disordered. The "shrink" is regarded as something "special"; the accountability and the efficacy of his or her activity have often been questioned; even the right of psychiatry to be considered a medical science has been brought under scrutiny more than once. These are only a few of the problems that confront psychiatrists all over the world.

These introductory notes are necessary to emphasize that the general problems of psychiatry became even more important in a Communist society, which for so long was subjected to an omnipotent ideology that tried to change man's personality. According to Marxist-Leninist ideology, it was necessary to change or even deny many, if not all, of the negative aspects of the human mind and behavior. These characteristics applied exactly to what happened after World War II in Romanian society and psychiatry. The most structured form of the perfectionist delusion of being able to bring man's happiness in "one dimension," as Herbert Marcuse would put it, was Ceauşescu's idea of the "New Man," the perfect worker, highly productive in his profession, raising a family with many children, lacking any other political perspective than the Communist one—in general, an absolutely appropriate and perfectly performing person. This model could be regarded as exceedingly abstract, but in fact it was not. As mechanical and absurd as it might seem to an external observer, its significance was very precise; every deviation from the standard was considered unfit or pathological or was ignored altogether. In this setting mental illness was highly undesirable. This is why the mental health care system was not developed and to a certain extent was even dismantled. This is why we are missing constant and consistent statistical evidence and surveillance of the mentally disabled. While some data exist, they are unreliable and underreported (for instance, the number of institutionalized mentally retarded children before December 1989 was largely unknown or missing from the official reports). An undeniable fact is that after 1944 no new psychiatric hospital was built. Several specialized institutions were created by changing the use of the building, but in general, the number of hospital beds for psychiatric inpatients remained far behind the needs. This is why we can find, even today, hospital rooms with ten, twenty, or thirty beds, and even two patients in a bed. These figures have become worse in the last ten to fifteen years.

When considering an overview of Romanian psychiatry in the Communist era, one has to underline the strong Soviet influence. In the 1950s the only accepted model of psychopathology was the Soviet one. For the sake of scientific rigor, we have to understand the terms of this statement in a very precise manner. We do not deny the merits of the Russian school of psychiatry, which contributed significantly to explaining and understanding, for instance, reactive states and personality disorders; we are also quite aware of the importance of Pavlov and his school to the development of the psychiatric profession. We agree that establishing the value and the real stature of Soviet psychiatry before the *glasnost* era is a contribution to the years to come, but we have to emphasize several negative aspects that provoked major drawbacks in Romanian psychiatry (Ghiliarovski, 1956; Predescu, 1976, 1989).

First, the vast majority of psychopathological issues were explained according to Pavlovian theories and concepts, the so-called nervist school; everything was conditioning, excitation, pathological inertia, ultraparadoxal phase. For instance, hallucinations were considered to be exclusively an expression of pathological inertia of the excitation. If this inertia was present in the first signaling system, it resulted in visual hallucinations, and if it was produced in the second system, there were verbal hallucinations. The same pathological inertia was conceived of as being at the origin of delusions and obsessions. Disorders of motor activity were also considered to originate in impaired equilibria of excitation and inhibition. For example, the hyperactivity of the manic state would be the result of a prominent excitation coupled with a diminished inhibition, or in schizophrenia there would be an inhibition of cortical activity with a concomitant release of subcortical functions that would lead to the chaotic motor excitement of this disease.

Of course, one major area of interest was the conscience and everything related to it. Held in high regard was its definition as the highest form of nature's reflection performed by man, an outcome of superior organized matter. Again, Pavlov and his school were establishing "final" explanations; let us follow him in a carefully quoted paragraph taken from his complete works, cited from Ghiliarovski's *Textbook of Psychiatry*, which was translated into Romanian and published in 1956: "The conscience looks to me like the nervous activity of a certain region of the cerebral hemispheres which finds itself at that given moment and in those certain conditions in a state of optimal excitation, probably of a medium intensity. In this very moment all the rest of the cerebral hemispheres are under—or not—stimulated" (Ghiliarovski, 1956). This statement explains briefly Pavlov's concept of the "lighted spot of the conscience."

Second, one had to try to explain everything in accordance with what was termed by Marxist and Leninist thinkers *materialism* as opposed to *idealism*, with absolute statements concerning the superiority of matter over conscience. This is why nervist theories, which programmatically deny or do not take into account subjective options, were promoted so constantly. Let us see the way in which disorders of the consciousness are introduced in the eleventh chapter of Ghiliarovski's textbook, to understand how far a not-very-refined form of materialism was used as a structural framework for conceiving such an encompassing problem as that of conscience: "Conscience makes its appearance in man during labor, social and productive activity. In the process of labor and of transforming nature, man becomes acquainted with the qualities of objects, discovers these objects, and establishes relationships between phenomena. During labor, he realizes his own attitude toward everything that surrounds him including his fellow-people with whom he is carrying on common activity" (Ghiliarovski, 1956). Along the same line, Lenin's work *Materialism and Empiriocriticism* was frequently quoted: "Acting upon our sensory organs, matter engenders sensation. The latter depends on the brain, nerves, retina a.s.o., i.e. matter structured a special way. The latter's existence doesn't depend, on the other hand, on sensation. The prime factor is that matter, sensations, thoughts, conscience are, at best, nothing more than a superior outcome of matter organized in a special way" (Ghiliarovski, 1956). In the work *Social Psychology*, published in 1974, we find the same basic ideas practically unchanged: "V. I. Lenin brought to life the model of analysis conceived by Marx and Engels, elaborating strategies of action in accordance to which one can obtain the fusion of consciousness with life, of theoretical ideas with real behavior, of ideology and psychology" (Golu, 1974).

A third feature, more aggressive than the previous two, with an evident educational purpose, was concerned with other theories and points of view. Everything except Soviet theory was minimized, denied, or directly attacked with the logical apparatus borrowed from a shallow philosophical scheme combined with a nontolerant and dogmatic range of logical thinking. A classic example of ideological interference that had a disastrous influence on psychiatric practice is the way of understanding Freud, psychoanalysis, and all the psychodynamically oriented theories. Once again we find in the same Soviet textbook very suggestive explanatory statements:

The Freudian theory so widespread in the bourgeois countries remains far behind the scientific understanding of psychological phenomena; the source of Freudianism is idealist philosophy. The Freudians confer a central role in mental activity on unconscious processes, emotions, and inferior drives, especially the sexual ones. According to Freud, between conscience and unconsciousness takes place an unremitting struggle during which unconsciousness overcomes perpetually. In the fight between the satisfaction and reality principles, the inferior drives are always winning, an outcome that dictates every man's behavior and the behavior of the entire society at large. Freud's followers, losing scientific knowledge of nature's and society's laws, became the propagators of bourgeois ideology, which serves aggressive and invasive purposes. (Ghiliarovski, 1956)

Because of this radical point of view, construing Freud and his followers as reactionary thinkers, if not real enemies, psychoanalysis was banned for a long time from the practice of Communist psychiatry. Alteration of views has occurred only gradually, taking the form of an intellectual outlook always critical and never followed by practical consequences in everyday psychotherapy. For example, in the *Romanian Textbook of Psychiatry*, published in 1976 under the supervision of Professor Vasile Predescu, psychoanalysis is given a short overview emphasizing many of its relative shortcomings. "The limits of psychoanalysis are mainly the ignorance of the material neurophysiological background of mental illness. And the fact that is practically unacceptable is the theoretical dogmatism that was adopted by Freud's orthodox followers, which runs counter to any movement of renewal and questions the true scientific character of psychoanalysis" (Predescu, 1976). Or, "Highly objectionable is also the confusion between social and cultural aspects on the one hand, and the field of psychopathology on the other, which blurs the distinction, very important, socially speaking, between normality and illness, a major drawback that limits significantly the practical utility of psychoanalysis. This is why this theory was criticized not only by Marxism, but also by other bourgeois conceptions such as existentialism" (Predescu, 1976). This time we are faced with a more refined and articulate position, but the essence remains the same: The theoretical attitude was to maintain a critical distance, and, as can be easily inferred, clinical practice was kept away from any psychoanalytically inspired influence.

Finally, it is interesting to note a peculiar trend that was a more or less constant feature of many psychiatric and nonpsychiatric books published in the socialist period. To express the fact that the Communist Party and its decisions were, or considered themselves to be, the vital core of the nation, every writing, no matter what the content was, but especially when it had social significance or educational value, had to contain implicit or explicit references to the major lines of the political and economic plans made by the Communist leaders. Over time this obligation led to a mechanical and empty phraseology having the same words repeated again and again until an advanced lack of meaning was reached. We quote again from the 1976 official *Romanian Textbook of Psychiatry*: "In the present phase of social, political, economic, and cultural development beside the glorious aims of raising our country to the heights of culture and civilization, there is, as a very important feature, a continuing preoccupation with multilateral development and balanced fulfillment of the human personality. This is the present framework used by the network of medical assistance for giving a practical shape to the policy of our Party and government concerning health care" (Predescu, 1976). These empty and meaningless lines became a constant presence in every publication, reducing to a minimum personal independence.

Until now, we have tried to present in a concise manner the general features of Romanian psychiatry in the Communist years. In addition, there are several historical facts that have to be mentioned. After World War II the Society of Medical Sciences was founded. In 1956 the publication of the specialized journal *Neurology, Psychiatry, and Neurosurgery* began. The Society of Psychiatry was founded in 1961. In 1970 the Psychiatric Laboratory was organized as a separate department of the Institute of Neurology and Psychiatry, the first and only center carrying on psychiatric research. In December 1972 Consiliul Sanitar Superior (the Supreme Medical Council) passed the Program Concerning the Protection and Promotion of Mental Health, establishing a scheme of psychiatric assistance that included ambulatory facilities, called mental health laboratories, and inpatient treatment in psychiatric hospitals. The program called for the establishment in each district capital and the six sections of Bucharest of a mental health laboratory and a day hospital for adults and children by the end of 1975; it also provided for an increase in the number of psychiatric beds in every district, predicting by the end of 1980 approximately 100 to 150 beds for acute adults, 300 to 400 beds for chronic patients, and 50 beds for the neuropsychiatric health care of children. Unfortunately, this program, which was not regarded as a top priority, was not applied uniformly all over the country; the greatest success was obtained in the districts of Buzău, Brasov, Dolj, Iasi, and Prahova, with modest to poor results in the districts of Braila, Constanta, Timis, Tulcea, and Bucharest. The coordination of psychiatric activity came under the auspices of the Institute of Neurology and Psychiatry, which issued a monthly publication, *Neurology and Psychiatry*, and also under the Ministry of Health and the Academy of Medical Sciences.

POLICY, ORGANIZATION, AND SERVICES IN THE 1980s AND 1990s

Current Policy Developments

The events of December 1989 came suddenly and unexpectedly, taking by surprise the vast majority of the Romanian people, including psychiatrists. This is not the place to try to give an overall explanation of the Romanian revolution phenomenon; nevertheless, one may sketch a psychological overview that is relevant to the present discussion. After the fall of the Communist regime, psychiatrists felt suddenly freed of the burden of imposed silence, general suspicion, and lack of hope; they acquired overnight an enormous need to fill up the numerous gaps in their personal and professional lives, gaps gathered over a lifetime. The psychiatric field was faced with a wide range of reactions, from despair and an irrational and stubborn grip on the old structures to an absolute denial of all values, reaching at times a very concrete antipsychiatric intensity. Old conflicts, buried for a long time under a rigid social and professional climate, reappeared; centrifugal forces developed abruptly in the psychiatric community;

every authority was denied; conflict and recrimination came to the fore again and again; the sense of guilt and shame seemed almost to disappear or to be projected on the Other.

This picture might seem a rather literary and impressionistic account of the complex phenomena that arose in Romania after December 1989, but this profile tries to underline the anarchic, unstructured, and rebounding reactions that broke the already-fragile unity of the psychiatric community. Perhaps the most edifying example would be the controversy related to the appearance of two official psychiatric associations and to the alleged psychiatric abuses so widely and unfavorably exploited by the Romanian and international media.

Shortly after December, some two dozen of the approximately 900 active members of the Romanian Psychiatric Association (RPA) decided to quit and to found another organization, the Association of Free Romanian Psychiatrists (ARFP). It should also be mentioned that a considerable number of psychiatrists decided to remain neutral (Diacicov, n.d., c). At the beginning, this split was thought to be beneficial, offering at least two options, which seemed an important advance from the former unquestioned unity of points of view. This was reinforced by the very functional structure of the ARFP, by its active stance directed toward practical goals, by the writing proficiency of its members, which brought to the public's awareness many problems of the Romanian mental health care system, and by its willingness to establish contacts with foreign psychiatric associations. The prominence of the ARFP was even more important in comparison to the rather amorphous structure and the passive attitude of the RPA. Unfortunately, the ARFP soon started a violent campaign in the media pointing out facts, more or less demonstrated, intermingled with personal attacks. Inconsistencies in its official points of view and the presentation of everything in a very aggressive and intolerant way made the ARFP lose much of its support and even the credibility it had been granted at the beginning. It started a sort of purifying work with a great destructive potential, making statements in many respects difficult to substantiate. For instance, in the June 15, 1990, issue of the magazine *22*, important accusations were made concerning the activity of the RPA, which would be unrepresentative of Romanian psychiatry, which would be the follower of an entirely wrong theoretical orientation, and which would alter very badly the training of a new generation of psychiatrists because of retrograde points of view and a self-imposed scientific and pragmatic solitude.

The Romanian Psychiatric Association at present is, in many respects, the successor of the former organization, which, during the Communist regime, gathered all the psychiatrists of the country. It has over 350 members, who represent one-third of the total number of practicing psychiatrists. It also succeeds the earlier organization in terms of structure and function.

The new RPA was founded at a convention held on March 31, 1990, which adopted a final draft of the Platform and Statutes detailing the aims and responsibilities of the association along with the rights and responsibilities of its members. The RPA was legally registered under Decision 1092 on May 31, 1990.

Its official address is P.O. Box 1-41, Bucharest. Among the regulations included in the official statutes are principles governing the democratic election of the president, the representatives of the leading council, and the specialized commissions and committees through a secret ballot during the General Assemblies for terms of no less than two and no more than four years; the RPA can accept honorary memberships of great Romanian or international personalities. The program adopted at the first General Assembly states:

The Romanian Psychiatric Association is a scientific, nonpolitical and professional association with the aim of promoting and defending activities related to psychiatric teaching, research, and health care. The association is bound in all its activities to the absolute observation of the principle of "The Universal Declaration of Human Rights" and of the Final Papers of the Helsinki and Vienna Conferences. At the same time, the Association respects the widely recognized principles concerning medical ethics and deontology, the Hippocratic Oath, and the principles formulated in the 1977 Hawaii Declaration. (Statute of RPA, 1990)

This declaration program emphasizes professional autonomy in diagnostic and therapeutic matters for every psychiatrist. Another principle explicitly expressed concerns the right to equal and nonsegregated treatment for medical and psychiatric patients and, for the latter, the right to health care in the least restrictive therapeutic setting, which means strictly correlating the severity of the behavioral disturbances with the number of restrictive measures.

Concerning the very controversial psychiatric abuses during the Communist dictatorship, we have tried to describe, at the beginning of this section, the psychological and social changes that took place immediately after December 1989, and that constituted the framework of the first debates upon this subject (Diacicov, n.d., a). The *primum movens* of this affair was a declaration made in the press by a group of psychiatrists from the Gheorghe Marinescu Hospital, who publicly denounced the psychiatric abuses. From this point, events developed in an explosive manner, especially because of the official split of Romanian psychiatrists into two associations.

Questions have been raised about philosophical and concrete subjects. Highly scientific positions, even inconsistent and vulgar ones, have been adopted: Psychiatry as science, psychiatrists as men, the laws of a totalitarian regime and its oppressive organs, or even the entire society have been found guilty (Diacicov, n.d., a).

The problems are not settled yet. A special commission for investigating psychiatric abuses has been appointed. The commission is made up of psychiatrists from both associations. The inquiry is under way and final conclusions have not been formulated. During the hearings more than 100 cases have been reviewed. The preliminary results, without being definitive, are nevertheless suggestive. Among these cases have been found real psychiatric patients, but also persons healthy from the psychiatric point of view. Also, without a precise quantification (we are speaking only about preliminary results), the commission found that abuses, contrary to the principles stated in the Human Rights Charter, existed in Communist Romania. Psychiatry was used for oppressive purposes by the Communist regime, and there was a submissive attitude in several psychiatrists, or, if you like, a nonresistance. When considering every aspect of this vast subject, one has to be aware of what the law means in a totalitarian country: only a meaningless institution, well ordered theoretically, but in practice distorted to serve the interests of the moment, or a legal screen for illegal deeds (Diacicov, n.d., a).

For instance, Decree 313 which regulates involuntary commitment, does not differ in principle from other legislation regulating the same point: obligatory commitment of dangerous psychiatric patients (the differences are concerned with the details and take into consideration the many clinical possibilities). But in Communist Romania this decree easily became an instrument for settling conflicts, especially those involving high-ranking officials or the leader: Hospitalization was imposed as punishment. On the other hand, for those coming into conflict with the authorities, it seemed preferable to become a patient than to be imprisoned. All those examined by the commission were hospitalized by the Militie or Securitate with the participation of a prosecutor (as a legal cover).

The lack of specificity of the legal term *danger* that allowed the police and security forces to give various interpretations to the law was also problematic. Decree 313 had and still has among its provisions obligatory ambulatory treatment, which provides the possibility, after the discharge of patients, for a continuing surveillance. These persons were gathered and rehospitalized as possible troublemakers during important political events (conferences, conventions, summit visits). For the same purpose, that is, a very accurate overview of all the "political patients," every medical hospital and facility had a security man among its personnel. When the commission reaches its final conclusions, they will be published and widely distributed.

Many of the submissive psychiatrists of the old regime have now lost their decision-making power through natural selection, voluntarily, or under pressure from the mass media. There is now under way the preparation of a new law concerning the obligatory commitment of psychiatric patients that will replace Decree 313.

In conclusion, we have learned to accept the inconsistencies and drawbacks of the past and to have a critical and enriching perspective of these events. It is as wrong and detrimental to hide the negative side of one's experience as to blame the entire psychiatric world in the hope of escaping the consequences of one's own guilt (Diacicov, n.d., a).

Current Organization

We have tried to describe the place assigned to psychiatry in Communist Romania. In what follows we will give a concise account of the structure of the Romanian mental health care system.

For the time being in Romania, all medical and psychiatric assistance is offered in state-owned facilities. During the Communist years private property in medicine did not exist; after December 1989 the law created the framework for a free-market economy. Privatization in the medical field has taken its first steps, but we are still far from the desired standards of efficiency and care. Taking all this into account, medical activity is funded for the most part directly from the national budget; in recent years 3 to 5 percent has been allocated for the health field (the top priorities, from a financial point of view, have been the army and security forces).

Current Services

With regard to the structure of the mental health care system, we can describe generally five kinds of facilities: mental health laboratories, day hospitals, psychiatric hospitals, psychiatric consulting rooms in the ambulatory care institutions, and Jilava Jail Hospital (*Studiul privind bobile psihice*, 1976).

The mental health laboratory is an extension of the activity of the psychiatric consulting rooms. Ministry of Health Order 87 from 1974 established sixteen such laboratories. By the end of 1975 they were only in Bucharest, Oradea, Buzău, Cluj, Craiova, Iasi, Sibiu, and Tîrgu Mureş for adults, and Timisoara, Alba Julia, Cluj, and Craiova for children. These laboratories are organized separately for adults and children, either in psychiatric hospitals or in institutions for ambulatory care ("polyclinics"), or in separate, independent buildings. They have or should have rooms for the following activities: medical and psychological consulting; the follow-up of patients; psychohygiene, psychoprophylaxis, and genetic counseling; motor reeducation of children; the surveillance of children at play; legal counseling; sociological and ergonomic research; individual and group psychotherapy; biological treatments; and registration and secretarial work.

The mental health laboratory functions include: discovering and studying the risk factors of psychiatric disorders; active and early diagnosis and treatment of these disorders; follow-up of the patients; offering support for the professional, family, legal, and social problems of the patients; and medical education of the population. These facilities do not have the necessary personnel and financial support to become really efficient (for instance, they have only 15 to 20 percent of the necessary personnel, and they do not have social workers).

The first day hospital was organized in 1964 in Bucharest and was followed by several similar institutions in major urban areas. Their activity was and still is unsatisfactory because of the lack of personnel and funds. Despite their proven efficiency, Romania currently has such institutions only in seven district capitals: Bucharest, Iasi, Cluj, Buzău, Tîrgu Mureş, Craiova, and Brasov.

Psychiatric hospitals, for a long time the only institutions treating psychiatric patients, are still organized in accordance with the old conception of big facilities that gather all mentally disordered persons of a certain geographic area. Other inconveniences of these large hospitals are old buildings, unfit for a warm and rewarding environment; concentration of the hospitals on small pieces of land; location of the hospitals, by and large, far from population centers; very often, exaggerated measures of security; and maintenance of the patients in total passivity, without organizing their program in a pleasurable or useful way.

Psychiatric consulting rooms in the ambulatory care institutions (polyclinics), although obsolete, remain very important in psychiatric care because of the insufficient number of mental health laboratories. In 1975 Romania had 104 such consulting rooms in the polyclinics of the district capitals and the important urban areas. There are many regions without a sufficient number of psychiatrists, their function being supplemented by neurologists, endocrinologists, internists, and even general practitioners. The situation is even worse in the psychiatric health care system for children because the number of specialists in this field is even smaller (there are only 67 consulting rooms for pediatric neuropsychiatry). This is why the activity in the consulting rooms of ambulatory facilities is too intensive to be really efficient: between forty and sixty consultations daily, which reduces the time allotted to a patient to three to five minutes.

Jilava Jail Hospital, a penitentiary hospital, is a special institution with all the medical departments of an ordinary hospital, including psychiatry. Persons under arrest who show signs of mental disturbance are brought here.

As a general feature, all psychiatric facilities are below the needed standards of medical technology, diversity of mental health professionals, and even sanitation. Besides the ideological reasons mentioned previously, this critical situation is the result of a financial policy that failed to give top priority to medical assistance. The situation of the medical field worsened especially in the last decade in accordance with the steep downward trend of the general standard of living in Romania. This is the setting in which hospitals now are fighting every day for the basic needs of water, cleaning products, and heating, not to mention drugs or more sophisticated supplies.

Mental Health Personnel and Treatment

In Romania mental health care is provided mainly by board-certified psychiatrists helped by a medical assistant whose responsibilities lie somewhere between those of a nurse and a physician's assistant. Contributions made by psychologists are minor because of their insufficient number (the Faculty of Psychology was suppressed in 1977 and was reorganized only after December 1989), and also because of the general lack in psychotherapy training. The complete lack of social workers must also be mentioned (some of their duties, such as family and professional inquiry concerning the patients for diagnostic and possibly therapeutic purposes, are performed by the *asistentă medicală*), as well as the absence of the many types of therapists (occupational, art, dance, and others) that should comprise a complete psychiatric team. Until 1969 in Romania the medical services had social assistants, who had the functions of social workers. Unfortunately, that category of worker later disappeared. They were later replaced by the so-called social care assistants, whose number remained below the needs and who lacked specialized training. Later, even this category disappeared.

Another aspect that has to be mentioned here is the training of psychiatrists. In order to enter a residency, medical graduates have to pass a nationally administered admission exam. After passing it, they are supposed to attend a one-year course in one of the six Romanian medical university centers; the remaining two years can be spent either in the medical center where the course took place or in some other psychiatric hospital under the direct supervision of an experienced psychiatrist. Unfortunately, for almost a decade (from 1982 to 1990), no residency admission exam was administered, which led to a significant decrease in the already-insufficient number of psychiatrists (taking into consideration the constant rate of retirement in the population of psychiatrists).

Concerning the evolution of the number of psychiatrists in Romania, we have the following data: From 50 psychiatrists in 1939, the number rose in 1975 to 391 for adults (which means 1 for every 53,488 inhabitants) and 117 for children (which means 1 for every 181,582 inhabitants). Relating these figures to the total number of physicians, we find 1.2 physicians for adults and 0.3 psychiatrists for children for every 100 physicians. These data mean that in 1975 Romania was the worst European country in terms of psychiatric assistance, being far from the WHO standard, which is 1 psychiatrist for every 20,000 inhabitants. This situation was the result of, among other things, the small number of positions that could be occupied through the residency admission exam (before 1982 training positions for psychiatrists represented only 4 to 6 percent of all the available positions).

Data from 1990 showed that the total number of psychiatrists was 900. For every 100,000 inhabitants there were 3.8 psychiatrists, 5.7 psychiatric *asistentă medicală*, 0.87 psychologists, and 0.53 social assistants.

Representative of psychiatric assistance is the number of beds in the mental health care facilities. In 1969 the number of beds in relation to the population was 0.2 to 0.3 percent, and in relation to the total number of medical care beds, 8 to 16 percent. Hospitalization capacity (expressed by the number of beds) rose from 135 in 1948 to 5,272 in 1972, with a slight decline to 5,049 in 1975.

PUBLIC POLICY PROCESS

The public policy process in health care, including psychiatric assistance, is highly centralized in Romania. It is organized and supervised by the government through the Ministry of Health (headed by a physician with cabinet rank) and its regional and local administrative divisions. The regional division is called Directia Sanitara and is headed by a director, who supervises the activity of hospitals and ambulatory institutions. In university centers there are clinics and hospitals engaged in teaching and research; their activity is supervised by the Ministry of Education. A third ministry having an important impact, particularly on the mental health care system, is the Ministry of Labor, which has under its jurisdiction the facilities for mentally retarded and elderly patients. Currently, all the medical assistance is state owned; the health care policy is government derived, and its funding is included in the national budget. Nonprofit charitable and profit-making sectors were introduced after December 1989 and there are important developments concerning them, but they are not at the present time making an important contribution. This also applies to psychiatric assistance.

As concerns the role of professional groups and consumers in influencing health care policy in general and mental health policy in particular, it has to be said that things are moving slowly, partly because of the rigid administrative structure that opposes all changes and partly because professional and consumer groups (for instance, associations, unions, or patients' organizations) are weak and inefficient. The situation to date regarding mental health policy is limited at the individual level by the lack of responsible initiative and improper adherence to positive group interventions and at high administrative levels by the poor managerial outlook. The most striking supporting evidence for these statements is the small financial budget provided for health care assistance, always below 3 to 5 percent of the national budget. An illustrative example is that medical assistance by the government is considered unimportant, and pressure groups among medical professionals are weak. This results in a situation where hospitals and other medical facilities are in need of complete refurbishing for decent hospitalization conditions. Problems include a lack of modern medical technology, an uneven distribution of medical care that lowers accessibility of the population to health care services, and many other deficiencies. In every area, in order to satisfy international standards of care, many improvements have to be made regarding the infrastructure and, to the same extent, the human factor.

SPECIAL POLICY ISSUES

The Mentally Ill and the Mentally Retarded

The institutions for the mentally retarded are owned by the Ministry of Labor and are medically supervised by professionals of different specialties, including psychiatry. Because during the present study the collaboration with the Ministry of Labor could not be considered a success, the authors cannot give very many details about these state-owned facilities, but in general those individuals who have parents and relatives willing and able to support them psychologically and financially are being taken care of in family settings.

Another issue concerns mentally retarded persons having emotional and behavioral problems that require psychiatric intervention. They are hospitalized and treated like any other patient in institutions for adults or children according to their age. As is true for the entire psychiatric system, this particular area is lacking a sophisticated and diversified health care structure that would give these children and adults the chance of a truly independent and productive life. Although there are some institutions specially conceived for the mentally handicapped that try to supplement their lives with stable incomes and social support, specific information concerning the numbers and functions of these centers is not available. Decree 770/1966 allowed therapeutic abortion for mentally retarded persons with very low IQs.

The Mentally Ill and Substance Abuse

The problem of substance abuse in Romania involves primarily alcohol, with drug abuse playing a minor role. Romania does not have addictions to illegal drugs such as morphine or morphine derivatives, cocaine, PCP, LSD, or other major analgesic-narcotic and psychodysleptic drugs. The cases of abuse and/or dependence in this area are quite rare. But alcoholism is a very important problem. The psychotic disturbances associated with alcohol intoxication and withdrawal, as well as psychiatric problems related to the neurologic and nonneurologic consequences of long-term alcohol abuse, are treated within mental care facilities, either in wards of general psychiatry or in special wards for alcoholics. In general, psychiatric emergencies are hospitalized and treated in wards of general psychiatry or, depending on the case, in intensive care units, and chronic problems, including detoxification treatments, are handled either in hospitals of general psychiatry or in special units for alcoholics.

Concerning the association of mental illness and substance abuse, the problem is dealt with using a medical and psychiatric approach. The mental illness can be preexistent or concomitant with the substance abuse or can be a direct consequence of it. Consequently, these disorders are approached and treated taking into account their possible physio- and psychopathological relatedness.

The Mentally Disordered Offender

Obligatory commitment and treatment through a judicial sentence can be decided for two kinds of dangerousness: the prepenal one, in conformity with Law 12 of 1965, and the penal one, in conformity with article 114 of the Penal Code, which is used after an antisocial act has been committed. The aim of the treatment in legal terms is to cure or to ameliorate the disease. The person committed under Law 12 can be treated in a regular regional psychiatric facility. Those fulfilling the criteria of article 114 of the Penal Code are hospitalized in several national centers with high-grade security: the hospitals of Poiana Mare, Săpoca, Dr. Petru Groza, Jebel, and Răducăneni.

For a variety of reasons, bringing together all the mentally ill offenders results in an important additive dangerousness. There is a risk of increasing the alienation of the patients in a huge institution, developing a feeling of isolation and all sorts of adverse effects through imitation and a growing sense of separateness and segregation. Therefore, an attempt has been made to replace the national facilities with small, more secure wards located in every psychiatric hospital, so every case can be handled at a regional level.

Decree 466/1966 established the composition of the Commission for Psychiatric Forensic Examination of offenders. It has specialists in psychiatry and forensic medicine and also legal representatives of the court. This commission is instituted when, in accordance with article 117 of the Penal Code, the court "has doubts as to the mental integrity of the defendant." An arrested person can be hospitalized for a psychiatric evaluation in the Jilava Hospital Jail (near Bucharest), or even in a regular psychiatric hospital with adequate security measures. As to the place of the psychiatric and forensic examination of the offender, article 129 of the Code of Criminal Procedure specifies a laboratory of forensic medicine.

Article 48 of the Penal Code states that a person is not liable for his or her acts if, during the performance of the act, he or she was suffering from a mental disorder. When a defendant is found to be mentally incompetent, he or she cannot be found liable, but he or she can be made to seek medical correction through articles 112, 113, and 114 of the so-called security measures. The provisions of these articles are as follows: Article 112 establishes in general the security measures; it requires medical treatment and/or medical hospitalization and/or forbids the person to occupy a position, to practice a profession, and to be in certain localities. Article 113 provides that if the offender, because of a disease or a chronic intoxication with alcohol, drugs, or any substances related to them, represents a danger to society, he or she is required to come to the hospital on an outpatient basis and receive medical treatment until he or she recovers from his or her condition. If the person does not come voluntarily for treatment, he or she can be involuntarily hospitalized. The same obligatory treatment can be applied to a person during his or her imprisonment for other reasons in the circumstance of a mental disorder. Article 113 applies to those offenders with diminished competency during an antisocial act and provides obligatory treatment; Law 12 of 1965 applies to those mentally disturbed individuals who represent a major threat to society but have not performed an antisocial act. Article 114 of the Penal Code is used for mentally disordered offenders who committed antisocial acts (and thus in cases of mental incompetency).

The Penal Code holds that children below the age of fourteen are not responsible for their acts; after the age of fourteen the person has to be examined by a commission that can recommend special educational measures or, in the case of recurrent and serious antisocial acts, can commit the youth to a special reeducation center.

Law 12 of 1965 indicated the possible use of police forces (Militia) for the involuntary commitment of psychiatric patients proven to be dangerous. In 1980 that law was replaced by Decree 313, which excluded the use of policemen for obligatory hospitalizations. This decree established, as a first step in a rather complicated scheme, a complaint made "by members of the family who live with a person from whose behaviour it can be inferred that he is a dangerous mentally disordered individual; by those who are in frequent contact with this person, at home or at work; or by any other person who is aware of this problem."

A complaint may be addressed to the Territorial Medical Dispensary. The doctor of this dispensary has to examine the person, to offer whatever assistance is necessary, and to report to the Executive Committee of the Popular Council (during Ceauşescu's time) or the Territorial Services of the State Administration, that is, the City Hall (after December 1989). Also, at the primary-care level the doctor has to refer the patient to the polyclinic's psychiatrist (a polyclinic is an outpatient facility). The latter must examine the person referred to him or her and decide whether the person is to be presented to a special medical commission that can determine whether an obligatory hospitalization is called for; the decision has to indicate the diagnosis, the motivations, and all the different options of the commission's members (whenever possible). Dangerous mentally disordered persons are those who "through their behavior endanger their own lives or the lives of others, their health and physical well-being, or repeatedly and seriously disturb the normal conditions of work and living in the family or in society." The commission that mandates obligatory treatment in a medical setting must reexamine the person periodically (at least every two months or whenever needed) and, in accordance with his or her medical status, decide either to continue the treatment or to discharge the patient.

Deinstitutionalization

As has been mentioned in the section on current services, in Romania psychiatric assistance is based upon big hospitals serving large areas along with several types of ambulatory care centers. As large as these hospitals might appear, the number of beds per capita of the population is rather small, and the ambulatory facilities are particularly inefficient in covering the outpatient population. Only in 1989 was the idea of a community-oriented psychiatry started. With the rigid bureaucratic structure at the present date, true accomplishments will probably have to wait until more flexible, operant, and client-centered feedback administration is implemented in the mental health care system.

Funding Issues

As has previously been noted, in recent years 3 to 5 percent of the national budget has been allocated for health care. Further details on specific expenditures for mental health care are not available, but insufficient funding is a severe problem in the Romanian mental health care system.

Consumer Rights

Until 1965 every psychiatric hospitalization had to be reported to the legal institutions in order to protect the patient's rights and to avoid errors or the obtaining of advantages on another person. In 1965 Law 12 was passed limiting the intervention of enforcement organs to patients who were judged to be dangerous in order to submit them to mandatory treatment in accordance with the sentence issued by a trial court. Other psychiatric patients were to be treated as any other person diseased.

Many problems were raised by the concept of *dangerousness*. This term was and still is viewed differently by medical professionals, families, the general population, and institutions. Families are often especially interested in exaggerating the danger posed by a patient in order to obtain hospitalization. On the other hand, there was and still is a common belief in the potential and a priori dangerousness of a patient labelled as having a psychiatric disturbance. We do not intend here to settle, once and for all, the various and difficult problems raised when mental disease comes close to the applicability of laws. There is no universally satisfactory solution. What we want to emphasize is the fact that Romanian psychiatrists have been faced with the same problems as exist elsewhere, but in the rather uneasy environment of a Communist dictatorship. Finally, we have to add that now a commission of experts has been appointed to reformulate and modernize the present legislation concerning the mentally disordered patients in every respect and especially the rights of the mentally ill persons in every situation, including the obligatory commitments. Decision 1210 of the Council of Ministers from 1970 guarantees to a mentally disordered person the constitutional right to work in accordance with his or her capacity without any discriminations.

CONCLUSIONS AND DISCUSSION

The last forty-five years in Romania's history have been a hideous social experiment in which a utopian, inflexible, and man-despising model of society was introduced regardless of historical traditions, geography, and individual aspirations. Proclaiming the messianic goal of "universal brotherhood and happiness," this type of society proved to be one of the most cruel and perfect dictatorships on earth. Its destructive nature was overwhelming and all-encompassing. Psychiatry was not an exception; in fact, it was a target of choice. It was attacked everywhere, from its practice as a medical science to the very core of its theoretical background. Psychiatry shared with other medical specialties and the society at large limitations regarding standards of care. This was a direct consequence of the low standard of living, but psychiatry also had its specific setbacks derived partly from the same politically oriented selection of human values that was so prevalent in Communist Romania. This was also a consequence of the passivity and compliance of psychiatrists who in the face of a threatening outer world became exceedingly self- and family centered, forgetting or neglecting their roles in the community. The real proportions of damages provoked at the societal level and at the individual one are hard to evaluate, and we will only be able to get a full picture over time when life resumes its natural course.

The same outlook is valid when speaking about Romanian psychiatry and psychiatrists.

NOTE

The authors take all responsibility for the statements they are making, which represent their own points of view.

REFERENCES

Centre for Human Rights. (1988). *Human Rights: A compilation of international instruments*. Geneva: United Nations.

Centrul de Calcul si Statistică Medicală al Ministerului Sănătății. (1982). *Aspecte privind statistica bolilor psihice in RSR, esantion 1982*. Bucharest: Author.

Centrul de Calcul si Statistică Medicală al Ministerului Sănătății. (1983). *Aspecte privind statistica bolilor psihice in RSR, esantion 1983*. Bucharest: Author.

Centrul de Calcul si Statistică Medicală al Ministerului Sănătății. (1984). *Aspecte privind statistica bolilor psihice in RSR, esantion 1984*. Bucharest: Author.

Centrul de Calcul si Statistică Medicală al Ministerului Sănătății. (1986). *Aspecte privind statistica bolilor psihice in RSR, esantion 1986*. Bucharest: Author.

Centrul de Calcul si Statistică Medicală al Ministerului Sănătății. (1988). *Aspecte privind statistica bolilor psihice in RSR, esantion 1988*. Bucharest: Author.

Diacicov, Sergiu. (n.d., a). *Abuzurile psihiatrice*. Unpublished paper.

Diacicov, Sergiu. (n.d., b). *Citeva aspecte din evolutia psihiatriei romanesti*. Unpublished paper.

Diacicov, Sergiu. (n.d., c). *Psihiatria romană azi: Orientări si dezorientări*. Unpublished paper.

Ghiliarovski, V. A. (1956). *Psihiatria*. Bucharest: Editura Medicală.

Golu, Pantelimon. (1974). *Psihilogie socială*. Bucharest: Editura didactică si pedagogă.

The International Geographic Encyclopedia and Atlas. (1990). London: Macmillan.

Predescu, Vasile. (1976). *Psihiatrie*. Bucharest: Editura Medicală.

Predescu, Vasile. (1989). *Psihiatrie* (Vol. 1). Bucharest: Editura Medicală.

Studiul privind bolile psihice, asistenta bolnavilor mintali si programul national de apărare si promovare a sănătății mintale a populatiei. (1976). Unpublished paper. Bucharest.

16

Russia and the Commonwealth of Independent States

M. E. Vartanyan, V. S. Yastrebov,
V. G. Rotstein, T. A. Solokhina,
Yu. I. Liberman, and L. S. Shevchenko

OVERVIEW

Current events in the former USSR are so dynamic that any publication will inevitably lag behind. The leading role of the Communist Party of the Soviet Union was eliminated in August 1991, after a failed attempted coup d'état by people from the former Communist structures. The President and the Supreme Soviet took leadership into their own hands, at the same time active work on the Soviet Treaty, which was supposed to define new relations between Union republics, was being carried out. However, complex relations between republics failed to result in the signing of the Union Treaty on federal unification. That is why in December 1991 the presidents of Russia, Ukraine, and Belorussia declared the creation of a new political structure, the Commonwealth of Independent States, which does not have a common administration. In line with this, all the all-union agencies ceased their activities, including the USSR Ministry of Health. The ex-republics of the USSR, having become independent states now solve their problems independently, including problems of health services. Obviously, all these changes may lead to serious differences between the various states in services and in the legal status of the mentally ill. It may happen that the statistical data concerning the number of mental patients and the clinical structure of the contingent known to the mental health services will tend to differ more significantly than at the present time. These differences may affect the provision of mental health services by professional personnel, agencies, and institutions and the use of medication and medical equipment.

However, at present it is hard to judge what is happening. The countries of the Commonwealth of Independent States and the ex-Soviet republics who did not join it are involved in very difficult political and economic processes. To our knowledge, at present in all these states mental health services are accomplished by the old structures, which are experiencing difficult times due to the economic situation. The medication and food supplies in hospitals are insufficient; there is a deficit in the supply of equipment. The number of patients referred for outpatient and inpatient services has fallen drastically, which is quite typical for periods of political destabilization. This situation was characteristic for the period of the 1917 revolution and civil war, as well as during World War II. In both cases the number of patients seeking mental health services dropped by one-third in the country compared to the postwar period, when the number of patients doubled. It can be assumed that in the future there will also be a wave of increased referrals. We are doing everything possible to be ready for such conditions.

The reader may well understand that at the climax of such events it is difficult to receive any statistical material from the former states and remote points. Therefore, what is available, the 1990–92 data, is not sufficient. Having this in view, we have used material that was obtained earlier and that reflected the state of health services in the USSR during the past years of its existence.

The territory of the former Union of Soviet Socialist Republics (the USSR) is located in the eastern part of Europe and in North and Central Asia. It spans 5,000 kilometers from north to south and nearly twice that distance from east to west, occupying an area of 22.4 million square kilometers. In 1989 the population was 286.7 million people, including 135.5 million males (47.3 percent) and 151.2 million females (52.7 percent), with 188.8 million people (65.8 percent) in urban areas and 97.9 million people (34.2 percent) in rural areas. Children under the age of sixteen years were 27 percent of the population, ablebodied adults (males in the age range of sixteen to sixty years and females in the range of sixteen to fifty-five years) were 56.2 percent, and elderly people (males over the age of sixty years and females over the age of fifty-five years) were 16.9 percent of the population.

The former USSR is home to more than one hundred nationalities. Each region of this vast territory reveals significant differences in terms of economy, culture, and the density of population, which fluctuates from 334 inhabitants per square kilometer (Andijan region of Uzbekistan) to one inhabitant per two and one-half square kilometers (Magadan region of the RSFSR).

In the USSR the president was the head of state. The Congress of People's Deputies was the supreme legislative body. It was convened on a regular basis to solve the most important problems. The Supreme Soviet of the USSR, which comprised two houses, exercised legislative power between Congresses. Executive power belonged to the USSR Council of Ministers. The Soviet Union was made up of several constituent republics, and each of them had corresponding bodies of legislative and executive power. But one of the results of *perestroika* was the beginning of a change of power structures, which were to be reorganized and improved.

The history of the USSR is rich in dramatic events that for many decades affected the fates of all its people along with tens of millions living in other countries. In 1991 the USSR was going through one of those major events, known worldwide as *perestroika*. Its starting point goes back to the year 1985. The country was facing the formation of a new society, based on all-out development and extension of democracy, as a result of fundamental changes that were taking place in the economy, policy, and social structures of the Soviet Union.

Under the new Commonwealth of Independent States the leading body was to be a Council of Heads of State (presidents) that would meet at least twice a year. Each member would have one vote, and the chair would rotate among the membership. Under it would be a Council of Government Heads (prime ministers) that would meet every three months. The largest member, Russia, comprises 6.6 million square miles with a population of 148.5 million, mostly Russians. The other countries, besides Russia, that currently constitute the Commonwealth of Independent States are Ukraine (51.9 million), Uzbekistan (20.7 million), Kazakhstan (16.8 million), Belorussia (10.3 million), Tajikistan (5.4 million), Kyrgyzstan (4.4 million), Turkmenistan (3.7 million), and Armenia (3.4 million). Latvia, Lithuania, Estonia, Moldova, Azerbaijan, and Georgia are not members of the Commonwealth of Independent States.

EXTENT OF THE PROBLEM

By January 1, 1989, some 5.2 million people with mental disorders in need of regular treatment or observation by a psychiatrist (18.1 cases per 1,000 population) were identified by the Soviet psychiatric services. That same year 4.2 million people (16.2 cases per 1,000 population) were treated for chronic alcoholism or drug abuse (the latter of these two categories of patients constituted only 0.25 cases per 1,000 population). Thus the total number of those who received regular treatment by a psychiatrist or drug-related therapist made up 10 million people (34.3 cases per 1,000 population).[1]

The results of epidemiological studies carried out at the National Mental Health Research Center indicated that there were another 10 million people in the USSR who needed regular psychiatric assistance, but who have not applied for it due to various reasons (Rotstein, 1977). In addition, about 25 million to 30 million people from time to time need consultation or short-term treatment by a psychiatrist. To calculate the precise number of those suffering from chronic alcoholism or drug addictions is extremely difficult, but it is increasingly obvious that this number is several times as high as those who have already applied for psychiatric assistance.

Approximately one-quarter of the mentally ill receiving systematic psychiatric assistance are children and adolescents. Children constituted 21.8 percent of all psychiatric patients who were treated in 1989 in outpatient psychiatric centers (dispensaries), and adolescents made up 6.1 percent. The organization of psychiatric assistance for elderly people poses a separate problem to be resolved by mental health services. The data obtained from special studies conducted in Moscow show that people over the age of sixty years make up about 15 percent of patients (Trifonov, 1990). Out of the total number of all middle-aged psychiatric patients, the number of males is roughly identical to the number of females. However, this situation changes with the age of the patients; that is, the older the patients, the more female patients are encountered (Gavrilova, 1984). This phenomenon has long been believed to be linked with the difference in life duration between males and females. Among patients with chronic alcohol addiction, the percentage of males to females notably prevails, though it has been steadily decreasing. Previously, in the early 1970s, the rate of female patients treated for chronic alcoholism was at a ratio of one to ten; in the late 1980s the rate of female alcoholic patients increased and reached a ratio of one to five (Lisitsin & Sidorov, 1990).

One of the most acute problems of special concern is suicidal behavior. In 1986–89 the number of suicides fluctuated from 19 to 21 cases per 1,000 population. The frequency of suicides among males is much higher than among females, being six to seven times as high in certain age groups (particularly in the age range of thirty to thirty-nine) ("Vopros—Otvet," 1990). This is generally explained by a higher incidence of alcoholism among males, though this explanation is hardly exhaustive. Alcoholism is more frequently observed between the ages of thirty and fifty years, and in older ages the frequency steadily increases with age and reaches its maximum after the age of seventy years (75.5 cases per 100,000 males and 27.7 cases per 100,000 females; between the ages of thirty and fifty years this index is approximately 1.5 times lower) ("Vopros—Otvet," 1990b).

One of the most important tasks of mental health services in the former USSR is the prevention of socially dangerous acts by the mentally ill. Persons who have committed such acts undergo special observation by a physician in charge, who is provided with additional information on their condition by local militia officials. Much attention is paid to job placement of this category of patients. It should be noted that the mentally ill do not often commit criminal offenses. In the year 1989 that category of patients constituted only 1.69 percent of all patients under treatment in outpatient psychiatric centers (dispensaries). Criminal offenses committed by the mentally ill made up 0.15 percent of all criminal offenses committed in 1989 in the USSR ("Vopros—Otvet," 1990b).

Mental disorders occupy fourth place in reasons for loss of work capability. Of all disabled people living in the former USSR, the mentally handicapped make up 15 percent, and this number is steadily increasing. During the years 1978–89 the number of people handicapped with mental diseases and mental retardation increased from 778,574 to 1,034,620 (from 2.7 to 3.6 cases per 1,000 population). This situation is sharply aggravated by the fact that the loss of work capability in psychiatric patients occurs in the overwhelming majority of cases at a young age, when rehabilitation is rather problematic, thus creating a very complicated task. Naturally, this leads to grave social and economic damage for the country.

The vast territory of the former USSR, consisting of separate regions (different in social, economic, demographic, and cultural structures), accounts for regional peculiarities relating to both the number of identified patients and the possibility of rendering them psychiatric assistance. Thus in Estonia the incidence of mental disease (not including the cases of alcoholism or drug abuse) makes up 25.1 cases per 1,000 population, while in Tajikistan there are only 7.53 cases per 1,000 population. To overcome this discrepancy (to the extent of its dependence upon the organization of psychiatric services) remains a task of high priority to be carried out by the psychiatric services of the former Soviet states.

MENTAL HEALTH HISTORY

Traditionally in historic Russia (and later in the Soviet state) the medical disease model served as the fundamental model for mental disorders. The concept of mental disorders as an expression of disease remained dominant from the moment psychiatry was developed into a medical specialty. In this view the main features of Russian and Soviet psychiatry were oriented more to German and Scandinavian psychiatry.

In scientific research on the nature of mental diseases carried out on the basis of the medical model, primary attention was focused on brain pathology as well as on other somatic functions. In Russia and later in the USSR biological bases of mental diseases were always a principal direction of scientific research in the field of psychiatry. That circumstance could not but exert influence on the structure and the contents of mental health services in the country.

The modern organizational model of psychiatric assistance in the USSR started taking shape in the year 1918. At that time the situation for Soviet psychiatry was defined by two main factors. On the one hand, the country had a number of highly qualified specialists, recognized for their ability both to synthesize the experience of world psychiatry and to enrich it with new competent ideas (P. B. Gannushkin, Yu. V. Kannabich, V. A. Gilyarovsky, T. I. Yudin, and others), while on the other hand, the possibility of rendering practical aid to the majority of the mentally ill living within the vast territory of the USSR was very slim. The most severe cases were treated in eighty psychiatric inpatient hospitals, among which were the six psychiatric hospitals built not long before the revolution (1891–1908), which had met the requirements of that time. The assistance provided for patients who could stay outside the inpatient hospitals in community care was poor in terms of organization. Moscow had only four psychiatrists conducting outpatient hours, while in the provinces care was confined to hospitalization.

To get a better insight into the system of psychiatric assistance and to understand the peculiarities of its subsequent development in the USSR, one should examine the major ideas that formed the basis of psychiatric assistance. Some of these ideas concerned psychiatry as a branch of medicine. Common social concepts that underlay the organization of medical aid in the USSR were applied to psychiatry. A third group of ideas elaborated the subject of psychiatry within the context of social and political situations.

Within the first group of ideas, those concerning psychiatry as a branch of medicine, priority was given first to the concept that medical aid was public and free of charge, and second to the concept of its being an exclusively state system with strictly centralized administration. The second group of ideas, pertaining to those developed specifically for psychiatry, appeared mainly in the first ten to fifteen years after the revolution. These were characterized by considerable progress in the organization of psychiatric assistance. At the Second All-Russia Conference on Psychiatry, held in 1923, the concept of organizing psychiatric assistance on territorial/regional principles was adopted and the necessity to organize a network of outpatient psychiatric centers (dispensaries) was approved. An outpatient psychiatric center (dispensary) as a form of specialized outpatient assistance was established within a number of leading branches of public health, including phthisiology (tuberculosis), oncology, and skin diseases. At that time the top authorities of the public health system considered psychiatry to be one of the core and most significant parts of medicine. The first outpatient psychiatric center (dispensary) was opened in 1924 (Prozorov, 1924). The great achievement of that time was the setting up of daytime inpatient hospitals as a new form of psychiatric assistance. The first inpatient hospital of that kind was opened by Dr. M. A. Djagarov at the First Moscow Preobrazhensky Hospital in 1933 (Djagarov, 1937).

Among the third group of ideas, psychiatry within the concept of social and political situations, one thesis formulated in the mid-1930s was based on a political-sociological view about the etiology of mental diseases. According to that thesis, the social reasons for mental disorders have a tendency to disappear under socialism, thus leading to a steady reduction in mental diseases under a socialist system. All these ideas have led to some contradictory developments in psychiatric assistance and to the occurrence of unique benefits and defects, which are at the root of a number of complicated problems that require addressing.

In 1929 there were already 15 outpatient psychiatric centers (dispensaries) in the USSR, in 1931 there were 23, and in 1941 there were 54. By that time the country had 94 inpatient hospitals available for 35,000 patients. There were separate inpatient hospitals for chronic patients from those who had just experienced the initial, acute form of their condition. Patients with slowly progressive mental disorders (borderline states) filled as many as 3,230 beds in sanatorium-type psychiatric hospitals. For those patients who needed only aftercare, disability homes under the social security system were set up.

During World War II Soviet psychiatry suffered great losses. About 20,000 patients were exterminated by the fascists within the occupied territory of the country (Rokhlin, 1967, p. 378). Funds ran out for 25 percent of hospital beds. During the first decade after the war every effort had to be made to restore the destroyed system of psychiatric service (especially in the western part of the country that had been exposed to fascist occupation). By the year 1945, 111 outpatient psychiatric centers (dispensaries) and some 200 psychiatric inpatient hospitals that accommodated 116,000 beds were functioning in the USSR.

In the following ten years the number of outpatient psychiatric centers (dispensaries) rose to 225, and inpatient psychiatric hospitals numbered 393 with 230,000 beds. Though by that time the main characteristic features of the present organizational model of psychiatric assistance had taken shape, the number of psychiatric institutions and beds continued to grow.

POLICY, ORGANIZATION, AND SERVICES IN THE 1980s AND 1990s

Current Policy Developments

The medical pattern of mental diseases, adopted in the USSR, has significantly fostered the integration and interaction of psychiatric and general somatic services within the system of public health. Psychiatric units (fifty to eighty beds) including psychosomatic patients have been opened in a number of urban general hospitals and clinics. At present this trend to integrate psychiatric and general somatic services is being further developed in Russia, and the expediency of enlarging this sort of practice has been confirmed by a series of clinical and epidemiological studies. The results obtained from studies on the frequency of mental diseases and disorders among patients undergoing treatment in Moscow outpatient general somatic clinics serve as examples of this trend. The specialists of that center have found that some 20 to 25 percent of those attending general somatic outpatient clinics need psychiatric consultation and assistance (Liberman, Ostroglazor, Lisina, & Eliava, 1990). These are persons who earlier never applied for psychiatric aid. The identification of these new patients poses a number of new complicated problems to be resolved by psychiatrists in Russia and the Commonwealth. It has been revealed that these categories of patients represent a rather heterogenous group ranging in diagnostic terms from marked depressions to mild borderline personality disorders. The treatment provided for this group of patients has been insufficiently studied. However, internists with little familiarity with the problems of diagnosis and treatment of this group of patients can hardly provide them with adequate assistance. This poses a number of policy and organizational problems for psychiatrists, including the necessity to teach internists the elements of psychiatry (such experience does already exist in the former USSR) and to expand the participation of psychiatrists in the existing general somatic network of extraclinical services. Psychiatrists are also faced with a major job of extending psychiatric influences to the practical work of other medical professionals (internists, surgeons, pediatricians, and so on) not only in the network of extraclinical services, but in appropriate inpatient hospitals as well. During the next few years this will be a task of high priority for psychiatrists in Russia and the Commonwealth.

Current Organization

In 1988 the system of the USSR Health Ministry embraced 278 outpatient psychiatric centers (dispensaries) of which 183 included beds for inpatients, inpatient hospitals, with outpatient units available in most of them. The total number of beds in inpatient hospitals and outpatient psychiatric centers was 339,167 ("Vopros—Otvet," 1990b).

In 1991 the majority of patients received aid in psychiatric institutions under the authority of the USSR (and the Republican) Health Ministries. Some categories of patients, principally those in need of medical, social, and pedagogical assistance, received it in other agencies (Republican Ministries of Social Security and Public Education). Though the main organization for psychiatric services remained territorial/regional, many of the government departments and even some big enterprises organized services on their own to be provided for their employees.

Typical regional psychiatric services as a part of the USSR Health Ministry systems included inpatient mental institutions, halfway inpatient hospitals, day hospitals, and rehabilitation facilities. In areas with high density and a prevalence of urban population, inpatient institutions were represented mainly by beds in outpatient psychiatric centers (dispensaries). In rural areas, where the density of population is many times lower, inpatient institutions were represented in most cases by psychiatric departments functioning within the framework of local general hospitals. In addition, when necessity occurred, a patient was admitted to a psychiatric inpatient hospital with 600 to 800 beds, which provided for a population of 400,000 to 500,000. In the 1980s that type of hospital was considered to be the best. The hospital's psychiatric unit was not differentiated by the severity of its patients' conditions and provided services for the inhabitants of adjacent districts.

Many psychiatrists now are trying to place their patients in halfway day or night hospitals (rather than inpatient hospitals), which are similar to inpatient hospitals in terms of the scope and intensity of treatment provided but have a considerable advantage because the patient does not break his or her social contacts and in some cases even continues to work. He or she also does not develop hospitalization syndrome, which is almost inevitable with a prolonged period of stay in a hospital. Also, treatment in a day hospital costs less.

Of major importance are specialized units and departments that function within the structure of regional psychiatric services. Almost every hospital includes child, adolescent, and geriatric units along with units for borderline patients and units requiring various types of expertise (labor, military, forensic). Specialized departments are being set up within outpatient psychiatric centers (dispensaries) for special treatment of patients suffering from such illnesses as epilepsy. Departments for child and adolescent treatment are open in most general child polyclinics. The period of the late 1980s was characterized by establishing in some outpatient psychiatric centers specialized gerontopsychiatric departments. These have proved to be quite effective.

A source of special concern to psychiatrists is the organization of psychiatric assistance for borderline patients who might be characterized by sufficient social activity, heightened sensitivity to how their condition is viewed by other people, and striving to avoid social and psychological repercussions caused by their treatment in outpatient psychiatric centers (dispensaries). In the late 1980s that category of patients was provided with psychiatric assistance "beyond the grounds of an outpatient center" as an alternative form to outdated, traditional forms (Kovalev & Gurovich, 1986).

The period of the late 1980s was a significant period of Soviet history. *Perestroika* has concerned all aspects of social life and forced people to revise most of their values. These changes could not but influence the organization of mental health services in the country.

Current Services

Some of the achievements in the organization of psychiatric services are obvious. The former USSR has a sufficient number of qualified specialists (22,763 psychiatrists in 1988) to render adequate psychiatric assistance to any individual in need of psychiatric treatment. Any patient who needs hospitalization can be placed in an inpatient hospital, where he or she can be provided with necessary care and treatment. Patients are guaranteed free medical aid, and in some cases medical drugs are also free of charge. Some categories of patients are entitled to receive a state-owned flat. Due to the integrated state system of psychiatric assistance for the mentally ill, unique statistical data on mental cases have been obtained.

At the same time many problems arise within the psychiatric services system. The fact that medicine is recognized as a sphere of "nonmaterial production" led to the situation where the public health system, including mental health, did not receive priority funding. This situation had a serious impact on psychiatry. First, most subsidies were allocated to "more important" areas of medicine (therapeutics, surgery, protection of mother and child). Second it was assumed (according to a concept mentioned earlier) that the number of mentally ill should decrease. Statistical data, however, were not available for decades. For these reasons, psychiatry was minimally financed, and the situation in this field of medicine was characterized by actual poverty. There were insufficient numbers of hospitals, beds, staff positions, drug and food supplies, medical equipment, and other resources. That is why, when hospitals and outpatient centers (dispensaries) were opened or an increase in the amount of psychiatrists was obtained, it was considered to be a big success (as, incidentally, it still is by many people). As a result, in 1991 there were sufficient numbers of hospitals and psychiatrists, but there was a tremendous gap between the central and peripheral settings. This situation concerned both the management and maintenance of patients, as well as the condition of the resource base (buildings, equipment, and supplies) and a level of diagnosis, treatment, and rehabilitation. In addition, many psychiatrists do not have a sufficiently high level of qualification. All these problems make it necessary to reconsider the concept of organizing mental health services in the country.

Mental Health Personnel and Treatment

The main figure in the curative process for patients with mental disorders is a psychiatrist. In dispensaries one doctor usually controls 700 to 1,000 outpatients, and one medical nurse helps him or her in this work. In hospitals one doctor looks after 20–40 inpatients, and he or she has two or three medical nurses at his or her disposal. The number of medical psychiologists in the former USSR is absolutely insufficient. Before the early 1980s psychologists had rarely been engaged in psychiatric settings. They began to appear in large hospitals in the mid–1980s; even now only one or two psychologists work at major psychiatric hospitals. Because of this deficit, the question of increasing the student body at psychological departments in colleges has become exceedingly important in the former Soviet Union. Besides medical psychologists, the psychiatric services include specialists engaged in the rehabilitation of patients in work activity.

As regards types of treatment, the psychopharmacological method is the most preferred. Shock therapy is applied more rarely. Since the early 1980s psychotherapy has been developing into one of the most important methods of treatment of mental disorders. In the early 1920s psychoanalysis was widely applied in the USSR, but it was considered "a reactionary method of treatment" at the time. Since the late 1980s it has again been used in the former Soviet Union.

PUBLIC POLICY PROCESS

The strategy for organizing mental health services on the national level was determined by the USSR Ministry of Health, within which there was a unit of psychiatric aid and a principal specialist in psychiatry. Recently a decision was made to introduce the position of principal psychiatrist in all the large cities and regions. Thus the directorship of mental health services assumed a multilevel character. Due to the changes of political and executive structures occurring in the country, the local public health (including mental health) authorities achieved more independence as a result of wide decentralization. Therefore, the requirements in different regions of the country concerning the number of beds, drugs, and the training of psychiatrists, psychologists, and other professionals were determined by the constituent and local authorities' (republic, region, and city) mental health services.

The process of decentralization of mental health services, although it is making them more flexible and available to the population, at the same time creates some difficulties as well. First, there are problems related to the coordination of activities in the different agencies connected with problems of mental health: the Ministry of Public Health, the Ministry of Social Welfare, the Ministry of Education, and so on. Obviously, this situation can lead to some conflicts in the determination of priorities in mental health services. In addition, the major differences between the regions, characterized by specific cultural and social traits of the population, can result in differences. The training of highly qualified professionals in local psychiatric settings also may be difficult due to an insufficient amount of training personnel.

The rapidly changing political, social, and economic life in the former USSR has clearly demonstrated the necessity to establish new professional societies (besides state societies and organizations) that are capable of supporting the development of psychiatric services that promote the maintenance and improvement of conditions for the mentally ill. The process of creating such organizations and new forms of support for the mentally ill is only in its initial stage, and, hopefully, in the coming years they will play a positive role in the development of psychiatry in Russia and the Commonwealth of Independent States.

SPECIAL POLICY ISSUES

The Mentally Ill and the Mentally Retarded

In the official annual reports of medical agencies mental retardation is incorporated with mental disorders and includes all individuals with congenital intellectual defect, without a differentiation in regard to severity. Obviously, not all these people, especially those with mild forms of mental retardation, seek aid from psychiatrists. The number of people with mental retardation registered in outpatient psychiatric centers (dispensaries) in 1988 was 1,485,000. This number included 370,000 people with severe forms of mental retardation. Thus the prevalence of mental retardation (according to official reports) amounted to 5.2 cases per 1,000 population, including severe forms, which made up 1.3 cases per 1,000 population.

Since 1970 a significant increase in such patients can be observed. In 1970 the number of registered patients with mental retardation was only 2.4 per 1,000, in 1980 it was 4.5, and in 1985 it was 5.1.[2] It is impossible to definitely claim that this increase could be explained by the fact that more people sought help in outpatient psychiatric centers. During the 1970s and especially in the second half of the 1980s the population tended to avoid such agencies because the fact of registration at a psychiatric setting evoked social discrimination. If this tendency influenced the patients with mental retardation to a lesser degree (which obviously could be understood), their ratio in the psychiatric-center population should have increased over the years. This actually happened (21.6 percent in 1970; 26.6 percent in 1985; 28.6 percent in 1988; during the same time the proportion of patients with borderline states dropped from 38.7 percent to 35.8 percent). Nevertheless, it cannot be claimed that there has been no increase of patients with mental retardation. The problem is complicated by the fact that the concept of mental retardation is not sufficiently well defined. It is not unusual for those who undoubtedly have organic brain lesions to sometimes be diagnosed according to social criteria (Marincheva & Gavrilov, 1988, p. 256). These criteria may change over time (for instance, higher requirements in school programs or for army service).

Incidentally, it should be added that the increase in the number of children with mental retardation is frequently connected with the rise of parental cases of chronic alcoholism and drug-related problems, the incidence of which in the 1980s acquired the character of a national catastrophe. No one can name definitely the exact number of alcoholic patients and drug addicts. However, according to estimates of some experts, it may be 5 percent of the country's population (Krasik & Moskvitin, 1988).

The aid that should be rendered to these groups of patients (people with mental retardation and cases of chronic alcoholism) is so specific that it requires the organization of special services. The main goal of rendering services to the mentally retarded is social rehabilitation and education. The services should be comprehensive and provided continuously, step by step. A characteristic of these services is that treatment, education, and social assistance as well as professional guidance and employment are accomplished by different agencies (public health, social welfare, education and professional training). Services and treatment are provided by multiple types of facilities: through special hospitals, day hospitals, outpatient psychiatric centers, occupational workshops, special workshops within industrial enterprises, day-care centers, and schools for mentally retarded children. For the most severe forms of mental retardation there are special nursing homes run by the Ministry of Social Welfare.

A comprehensive program of social and occupational rehabilitation of patients with different degrees of mental retardation was proposed by the psychiatric services in one of the central regions of the USSR, the Kaluga Region (Lifshits, 1983). This program provides education of patients with borderline and mild forms of mental retardation in special schools with training in different types of physical work for eventual employment in production or service facilities. The results of work in this program over the past ten years have demonstrated that by the age of twenty-five to thirty these patients acquire a relatively stable social and occupational adaptation. Special programs have been adopted for patients with more severe forms of mental retardation. Social rehabilitation in such cases is provided in occupational workshops at industrial enterprises and in many cases also leads to satisfactory results.

The legal situation for mentally retarded persons is much more complicated than for substance abusers. As mental retardation may be expressed in diverse forms, the law cannot regard all the patients in the same way, and for that reason the approach may be determined only by the diagnosis. In any particular case, when issues of social privileges or restrictions are involved or in the case of a criminal offense involving a mentally retarded person, a psychiatrist expert is obliged to participate in the inquiry in order to determine the degree of intellectual deficiency. In case of concomitance of mental retardation with mental illness, a psychiatrist expert is obliged to take into consideration both diagnoses, but the conclusion is to be individual. There are no rules compelling the expert to come to one or another decision. If the court brings in a verdict of guilty for a person with mental retardation, intellectual deficiency is a mitigating circumstance. The conclusion is thus completely within the competence of the court.

The Mentally Ill and Substance Abuse

Substance dependency services became independent entities in 1975. This measure did not have the unanimous support of psychiatrists and would not seem as useful. Drug-related problems and chronic alcoholism are registered by state statistics separately from the mentally ill.

Aid to this category of patients is being rendered both in outpatient and inpatient settings. In 1988 there were 36 special hospitals for patients with substance dependency with 15,865 beds, plus a large number of beds in other agencies (73,538 beds in special outpatient chemical dependency clinics, 17,565 in general hospitals, and 20,308 in psychiatric hospitals). Outpatient services were rendered in 540 outpatient chemical dependency centers and in 3,525 care units opened within different treatment settings (rural hospitals, outpatient clinics, and so on). In addition, there are still many patients undergoing compulsory treatment in special medical settings where they are referred for long-term treatment when voluntary treatment is not possible or when they bring suffering to their families. This system has been criticized because it is seen as an infringement on human rights. Apparently, such facilities in the near future will be nonexistent. Special units for the treatment of alcoholism and drug-related problems have been opened recently at large industrial enterprises. This makes it possible to promote the occupational therapy of these patients.

Alcoholic patients, from the legislative point of view, are not considered to be mentally ill and do not have any special social privileges. For instance, chronic alcoholism or drug addiction provides no release from responsibility for the patient if he or she commits an offense. This pertains to alcoholic intoxication as well. In some cases the court may consider this an aggravating circumstance, and the sentence may be more severe. Sometimes the court may recommend treatment of the chronic alcoholic patient or may sentence him or her to compulsory treatment. The question of special social privileges for patients diagnosed with both substance abuse and mental illness (in particular, releasing a patient from responsibility for committing an offense) should be solved in relationship with the nosology and severeness of the mental disorder. Chronic alcoholism is considered as a concomitant disease and is taken into account in determining the type of treatment.

The Mentally Disordered Offender

From the few works by Soviet researchers containing statistical data on mental patients who have committed socially dangerous acts, it is known that they number 1.7 to 14 percent of all mental patients registered in psychiatric facilities. Only half of them are being brought to trial. These patients undergo forensic psychiatric examination under the law and procedures of various legislative acts of constituent republics. A detailed regulation by intra- and interagency documents (USSR Ministry of Health, USSR Procurator's Office) established guidelines for expert commissions in the USSR. A forensic psychiatric expert commission is set up by departments of internal affairs, inquests, or courts in those cases when there is doubt as to the mental capacity of the patient under investigation, the accused, or the convicted. The accused, his or her relatives, and his or her lawyer have the right to ask for a forensic psychiatric commission.

The most common process is the use of a forensic psychiatric commission for the accused. The main goal of the commission is to determine the mental state of the examinee. Such examinations may be provided in outpatient or inpatient facilities, in the court, or in the office of the investigator.

In order to conduct outpatient examinations, which are used for 75 percent of the total number of referred patients, special outpatient forensic psychiatric expert commissions are located in regional bodies of public health. The commissions consist of at least three psychiatrists. If the outpatient commission has any difficulties in determining the mental state of the examinee, it can decide to conduct an inpatient forensic psychiatric expert commission.

The duty of the expert commission is not only to determine the mental state of the examinee, but to give recommendations to the court as to the competency of the patient in question. This is the most difficult task. The concept of competency includes two criteria—a medical one and a judicial one. The medical criterion of incompetency is determined by the clinical state of the examinee and should be in line with the four groups of disorders defined in the former USSR: (1) chronic mental disease; (2) temporary mental disorder; (3) mental retardation; and (4) other states. The judicial criterion of incompetency (marked by some authors as psychological as well) assumes the existence of two conditions: intellectual, where the individual cannot be aware of the committed actions, and volitional, where the person under question cannot direct his or her activities.

In accordance with USSR criminal legislation, a socially dangerous act committed by a person in an incompetent state could not be attributed to the category of infringement of the law. For these reasons the person could not be punished, but was put under measures of social protection of a medical character. These measures could be diverse, from the observation of a district psychiatrist to compulsory treatment in a mental hospital.

The recognition that a person committing a legal offense is incompetent and the determination of measures of social protection are under the jurisdiction of the court. If the court determines that compulsory treatment is necessary, then the question of its discontinuation is also the prerogative of the court. Such questions are based on the outcome of forensic psychiatric examinations of the patient. In this way the problem of protecting society from socially dangerous acts by mentally ill patients is solved by joint efforts of legislative bodies and psychiatric services.

Deinstitutionalization

The essence of the process called "deinstitutionalization" is the change in maintenance of the mentally ill and their "release" from excessive care in psychiatric facilities. Deinstitutionalization has been a major movement in the United States, Canada, England, Germany, and especially Italy. It has led to many important aftereffects, which are broadly discussed by clinicians, public health organizers, lawyers, and representatives of social organizations and movements. It should be stressed that the concept of deinstitutionalization in most of the countries was related mainly to inpatients (Tansella, 1986). That is why two aspects of this issue are being discussed: the interrelationship of society and severely mentally ill patients discharged from hospitals and the fate of mental hospitals that are left without patients.

It should be noted that up to 1991 the problem of deinstitutionalization in this particular sense did not exist in the USSR. However, due to a gradual change in views on patients' referral to hospitals and especially in the light of new legislation on psychiatry (details are given later in this chapter), national statistics from 1985–1989 indicate a drop in the frequency index of hospitalization (from 446.8 to 427.3 per 100,000). Absolute numbers decreased from 1,238,433 in 1985 to 1,237,187 in 1989. But in the interrelationship between society and patients no tangible effect was seen. Regarding the hospitals, as some of the beds were vacated, some units were reorganized for geriatric patients and patients with borderline states. Some of the hospital authorities used these beds to introduce additional payments and extra services (improved diet, better care, more comfortable conditions in the wards, and so on). However, no significant reduction in the number of beds in psychiatric hospitals could be seen.

A much more tense situation in the USSR was created by the problem of "psychiatric registration" of outpatients. In order to understand this problem, one must examine the history of the issue. The main objective of outpatient psychiatric centers (dispensaries), which were created in the 1920s and 1930s in the USSR, was the principle of active interest in the fate of patients, including participation in their lives even when the patients did not refer for aid. Under conditions of that time (a small number of outpatient psychiatric centers, highly qualified professional psychiatrists, and the low educational and cultural levels of most of the patients) this undoubtedly was of benefit to the patients. However, with time the situation changed dramatically. A flexible and individually developed care program that existed at the beginning of the system was transformed into a rigid bureaucratic structure that led to social stigmatization (and sometimes even discrimination) of the patients under a formal and frequently stereotyped psychiatric surveillance. Grounds for psychiatric registration could be any mental disorder, even if it was not severe or of long duration.

In 1988–89 in the territory of five large regions (Moscow, Leningrad, Latvia, Altai Area, and the Ivanovo Region) the rules of outpatient observation and registration were changed. In accordance with the new rules, the previous forms of registration (the so-called dynamic outpatient observation) were retained only for patients with severe mental diseases, those with profound mental retardation to a degree that they were in need of active rehabilitation measures, or those who recently had committed a socially dangerous act. All the remaining patients were released from psychiatric registration and could of their own accord refer to the outpatient psychiatric center. As a result, almost one-fourth of the previously registered patients who had personally experienced the rigid system of social and other forms of restrictions were removed from that system. Although these rules were introduced only in several regions, many outpatient psychiatric centers followed this example on their own accord. At the end of 1989 the proportion of patients released from registration in the USSR amounted to 18.6 percent of the total registered.

Thus, in discussing issues of deinstitutionalization, it should be mentioned that this process was implemented most actively in the outpatient link of psychiatric services, where the greatest number of mentally ill patients are observed. For instance, according to our data, the outpatient contingent of schizophrenic patients equals 86.1 percent of all patients (Yastrebov, 1983). This may be considered a distinctive trait of deinstitutionalization in the USSR. Unlike other countries, in the USSR the patients of psychiatric facilities experienced the most perceptible change on behalf of outpatient services and not in the inpatient institutions. To what extent deinstitutionalization will influence a reduction in the scope of activity in mental hospitals remains to be seen.

Funding Issues

Expenditures allocated to public health from all sources of financing (centralized and decentralized) in 1988 amounted to 28.9 billion rubles (4.6 percent of the national income or 3.3 percent of the gross revenue). Mental health facilities were mainly financed by the national budget. In 1988 the expenditures for public health in the national budget were 21.9 billion rubles (75.8 percent).

An important instrument in distributing budget allocations for the upkeep of public health facilities is the normative method. This means that the estimate of expenditures for a medical institution includes obligatory calculated norms for acquiring drugs and dressings and for meals, as well as expenditures for upholstered stock (doctor's smocks, bedclothes, towels, and so on). Wages make up the largest proportion (more than 50 percent) of all estimates.

All expenditures for financing treatment and facilities were grouped into the public health part of the national budget. This was then distributed to the constituent republics, regions, districts, and local budgets in accordance with the cost of treatment of one patient per one day in local hospitals and the amount of visits and physicians' positions in outpatient facilities. In other words, financing public health in the USSR was characterized by a hierarchical distribution of monetary resources.

The established method of financing public health institutions in the country did not allow for precisely estimating expenditures from the national budget just for psychiatric services. The authors attempted to do so, using the mean indices in the country (the cost of treatment of one patient per one day, the cost of one visit to outpatient psychiatric facilities, and so on). Moreover, they elicited direct expenditures, which comprised patient treatment (financed by the national budget for public health); benefit payments for temporary disability pension payments (financed by social insurance); maintenance of nursing homes for the chronically ill (financed by social welfare); and boardingschools for mentally retarded children (financed by education). Besides these direct expenditures they included sums from budget allocations for the training of physicians and for research studies. According to their estimates, the summation of direct expenditures by the government related to mental disorders in 1988 amounted to 4.5 billion rubles, or 1 percent of the national budget. The highest expenditures were for hospitalization of the mentally ill (29 percent) and expenditures related to teaching mentally retarded children (24 percent).

The situation at present in Russia and the Commonwealth of Independent States requires a conversion of public health to new principles of financing that would renovate all the structures of the economic process: the budget formulation phase and the phase of distribution and utilization. New principles of financing public health presuppose that the dependence of the budget formulation for a given region is based on its population, as well as the amount of nosological items and the degree of complexity in the therapy of treated patients.

It is more likely that in the near future the main source of resources for public health development will be the national budget. However, that does not mean that the attraction of developing other sources will be impeded by the government. As one option, public health funding could be increased through an insurance fund. Another option is to expand paid services. In 1988 paid services in the USSR amounted to 1 percent of medical services. It is quite possible that medical insurance and paid forms of services will develop as organic parts of the national system of public health and will be included into the general strategy of its development.

Consumer Rights

Legislative acts related to psychiatric aid pursue several goals. First, they guarantee medical and social aid to people with mental disorders, as well as provide the grounds for the procedure for rendering psychiatric aid. Also, they define the protection of rights and lawful interests of mental patients. Finally, they provide protection of people and society from dangerous acts by mentally disturbed patients.

The regulation of social and legal aid to the mentally ill in past years was accomplished by narrow departmental regulations and not by legislative acts (the latter were present only in a general way in the laws of public health in the constituent republics). These regulations were oriented to the mentally ill in general, without dividing them into nosological groups and classes (psychosis, mental retardation, and so on). These regulations did not cover all the previously mentioned goals, but were related only to part of them. Several governmental acts provided social protection for patients. For instance, the Decree of the Soviet People's Commissars of 1928 established that mentally ill patients with certain diseases have the right to receive supplementary housing space free of charge. That list of diseases was endorsed in that decree and in acts up to 1991. A governmental decision in 1965 provided the right to receive free medical drugs for schizophrenic and epileptic patients. From 1973 on the Decree of the Council of Ministers obligated authorities of institutions to employ mentally disabled patients of invalidism, third group.

Quite a number of legislative acts, decrees, and departmental documents were dedicated to the problem of protection against dangerous acts committed by the mentally disturbed. The responsibilities of psychiatrists in preventing socially dangerous actions by mentally disturbed patients were listed in the Instructions for Urgent Hospitalization of Mental Patients Presenting Social Danger, which was endorsed by the USSR Ministry of Internal Affairs and the USSR Procurator's Office.

Clause 51 of the Basic Legislation of the USSR on Public Health established forensic psychiatric expert commissions and attached them to organs of public health. The orders and laws for convening such expert commissions were determined by corresponding clauses of the Criminal, Criminal-Legal, Civil, and Civil-Legal Codes of the constituent republics. In addition, there was a detailed regulation on conducting expert commissions envisaged by documents (including departmental) of the USSR Ministry of Public Health and the USSR Supreme Court. Corresponding clauses of the Criminal and Criminal-Legal Codes of the constituent republics provided for a measure of social protection, while the temporary Instruction of the USSR Ministry of Public Health since March 21, 1988, regulated the implementation of compulsory or other medical measures in respect to patients with mental disorders who committed socially dangerous acts.

Compulsory treatment of alcoholic patients and drug addicts presenting a social danger was accomplished through court decisions, which were made based on the conclusions of forensic and drug addiction expert commissions. Compulsory treatment of such patients was conducted in occupational prophylactic institutions.

On January 5, 1988, a decree of the Presidium of the USSR Supreme Soviet, The State of Conditions and Order of Rendering Psychiatric Aid in the USSR, was confirmed. This was the first attempt to bring legal aid and protection of the mentally ill within international norms. The decree was immediately subjected to acute criticism by judicial and psychiatric public opinion as well as the mass media. That is why in the last months of 1989 a working group was established within the USSR Ministry of Public Health in order to compile a new bill on psychiatric aid. The group included representatives of eminent psychiatrists, public health organizers, legal professionals, and agencies (the Ministry of Defense, the Supreme Court, the Ministry of Education, the Ministry of Social Welfare, and others).

In April 1991 the members of this committee compiled a draft law concerning ''mental health services and guarantees of human rights'' for accomplishing such services. After the draft law had been discussed in psychiatric research institutions, regional psychiatric mental health agencies, and the mass media, it was submitted to the Supreme Soviet of the Russian Federation. The draft law was listened to by both houses of the Supreme Soviet and affirmed at the session of the Supreme Soviet on July 2, 1992.

Along with legal regulation of psychiatric aid, which is envisaged by legislative acts, it is extremely important to establish moral and ethical norms of behavior by the personnel of psychiatric services or people connected with rendering psychiatric aid. To address this issue, the Moral-Ethical Code of Professionals Working in the Field of Psychiatry was developed. This draft code was discussed in regional psychiatric services of the country and was approved as a working document in 1991.

In 1989–90 different public organizations free from the impact of party and government organs were organized in the USSR. For instance, the Association for Protecting Mental Health and Aid to the Mentally Ill embodied prominent cultural and religious figures, deputies of the USSR Supreme Soviet, representatives of public organizations, and leading clinicians and public health organizers. In addition, five other independent psychiatric organizations have been set up, the activities of which are directed toward the protection of the rights of mental patients.

For purposes of promoting legal protection of patients, the utilization of some methods of treatment was changed. For instance, by order of the USSR Ministry of Public Health in 1989 the use of sulfosin was banned. Atropine shock and other methods of electric shock therapy (EST) in mental diseases cannot be used without written consent of the patient or his or her legal representatives. An exclusion is made in cases of febrile schizophrenia and other states where the use of EST is indicated to be necessary (''Prikaz,'' 1990). The use of lobotomy (prefrontal leucotomy) was forbidden in the USSR by an order of the Ministry of Health (no. 1003 of December 9, 1950).

CONCLUSIONS AND DISCUSSION

In summation, it should be noted that a specific and to a certain extent unique system of psychiatric aid took shape in the USSR. Its main feature was its governmental character, where the governmental system was the only one in the country. In some respects it created undoubted advantages, such as the rapidity with which psychiatric aid was provided practically all over the country. The general principles of the Soviet public health system (availability, medical aid, free of charge continuity, and stages in rendering aid) were implemented in psychiatry as well. It was possible to achieve quite extensive data on the prevalence of mental diseases on a wide scale over a large country during several decades. An enormous amount of scientific information from this data awaits analysis.

However, this system from the very beginning had serious shortcomings, which have become especially evident during recent years. This pertains first of all to the absence of legal protections for mentally ill; a rigid system of "psychiatric registration," which led to social discrimination against patients; and the dependence of psychiatric institutions and their personnel on government directives, which hampered any initiative and either led to stereotyped formal work or facilitated a lowering in the qualifications of psychiatric staff. The situation was aggravated by a very low level of financing for a broad network of outpatient and inpatient facilities. As a result, there are very unsatisfactory, almost-disastrous conditions in most of the outpatient psychiatric centers and psychiatric hospitals.

Fortunately, these problems have recently been discussed, not only by physicians, but by the society in general, which gives hope that these issues will be solved. A nationwide program establishing the basic prerequisites for the organization of psychiatric aid was under development. The main participants of this program were the staff of the Department of Mental Health Services Organization in the Institute of Preventive Psychiatry, National Mental Health Research center of the USSR Academy of Medical Sciences. It remains to be seen if this work will continue under the new governments.

NOTES

The authors are very grateful to Mrs. M. Shchirina, Mrs. N. Sofonova, Mrs. N. Morgounova, and Mrs. J. Langbord, who contributed to the translation and printing of this chapter.

1. Most of the data in this chapter are provided by official statistics from government departments. Data obtained from special studies are referenced.

2. This period also was characterized by a major rise in the number of mental disorders registered by outpatient psychiatric centers: In 1970 it was 11.4 cases per 1,000, while in 1988 it was 18.1. It is assumed that this increase was due to the creation of new psychiatric centers and a better screening of patients (Jarikov, 1977).

REFERENCES

Djagarov, M. A. (1937). Opyt organizatsii polustatsionara dl'a dushevnobolnykh [Experience of the organization of a half-day center for the mentally ill]. *Journal of Neuropathology and Psychiatry*, 6–8, 137–147.

Gavrilova, S. I. (1984). *Psikhicheskie rasstroistva v naselenii pojilogo i starcheskogo vozrasta* [Mental disorders in middle- and old-aged population]. Unpublished thesis for a medical doctor's degree, National Mental Health Research Center, Moscow.

Jarikov, N. M. (1977). *Epidemiologicheskie issledovania v psikhiatrii* [Epidemiological studies in psychiatry]. Moscow: Medicina.

Kovalev, V. V., and Gurovich, I. Ya. (1986). O vnedispansernom razdele psikhiatricheskoi pomoshchi [On the nondispensary sector of psychiatric care]. *Journal of Neuropathology and Psychiatry*, 9, 1410–1416.

Krasik, E. D., & Moskvitin, I. N. (1988). Sravnitelnaia rasprostranionnost' p'asntva i alkogolizma sredi naselenia krupnogo promyshlennogo goroda Zapadnoi Sibiri [Comparative prevalence of alcoholism in a large industrial city in Western Siberia]. *Questions of Narcology*, 4, 21–24.

Liberman, Yu. I., Ostroglazov, V. G., Lisina, M. A., & Eliava, V. N. (1990). Kliniko-epidemiologicheskaia kharakteristika psikhicheski bolnykh, vyiavlennykh na terapevticheskom uchastke [Clinical and epidemiological characteristics of mental patients, identified at the therapeutic department]. *Journal of Neuropathology and Psychiatry*, 1, 92–98.

Lifshits, A. E. (1983). *Reabilitatsia psikhicheski bolnykh s t'ajelmi formami patologii* [Rehabilitation of patients with acute pathologies]. Unpublished thesis for a medical doctor's degree, National Mental Health Research Center, Moscow.

Lisitsin, Yu. P., & Sidorov, P. I. (1990). *Alkogolizm* [Alcoholism]. Moscow: Medicina.

Marincheva, I. S., & Gavrilov, V. I. (1988). *Umstvennaia otstalost' pri nasledstvennykh bolezn'akh* [Mental retardation and hereditary diseases]. Moscow: Medicina.

Prikaz o soglasii na primenenie sulphazina i shokovyh metodov lechenia [Order to agree on applying sulphazin and methods of shock therapy]. (1990). *Jurnal Psikhiatria v SSSR* [Journal of psychiatry in the USSR], 1, 27–28.

Prozorov, L. A. (1924). *Problema sovetskoi psikhiatrii v sv'azi s nervno-psikhiatricheskim ozdorovleniem naselenia* [Soviet psychiatry and neuropsychiatric health improvement in the population]. Paper presented at the Second All-Russia Meeting on Issues of Psychiatry and Neuropathology, Moscow.

Rokhlin, L. L. (1967). *Ocherki o psikhiatrii* [Essays on Psychiatry]. Moscow: Medicina.

Rotstein, V. G. (1977). Materialy osmotra psikhiatrom vyborochnykh grupp vzroslogo naselenia v r'ade raionov strany [Results of a psychiatric examination of the adult population in several regions of the USSR]. *Journal of Neuropathology and Psychiatry*, 4, 569–574.

Tansella, M. (1986). A psychiatric community without mental hospitals: The Italian experience: A review. *Journal of the Royal Society of Medicine*, 79(11), 664–669.

Trifonov, Ye. G. (1990). *Kliniko-sotsialnaia struktura dispansernogo kontingenta psikhicheski bolnykh pojilogo i starcheskogo vozrasta* [Clinical and social structures of a middle- and old-aged outpatient contingent]. Unpublished thesis for a degree of medical sciences, National Mental Health Research Center, Moscow.

Vopros-Otvet [Question-answer]. (1990a). *Argumenty i facty* (Newspaper), 24, 8.

Vopros-Otvet [Question-answer]. (1990b). *Argumenty i facty* (Newspaper), 27, 8.

Yastrebov, V. S. (1983). *Vnebolinichnaia shizofrenia: Kliniko-epidemiologicheskoe issledovanie* [Outpatient schizophrenia: Clinical and epidemiological study]. Unpublished thesis for a medical doctor's degree, National Mental Health Research Center, Moscow.

17

Saudi Arabia

Osama M. al-Radi

OVERVIEW

Saudi Arabia is an independent kingdom lying in southwestern Asia. It is bordered on the north by Jordan, Iraq, and Kuwait as well as the Saudi-Iraqi neutral zone, on the west by the Gulf of Arabia and the Red Sea, on the south by Yemen, on the southwest by Oman, and on the east by the Persian Gulf, Qatar, and the United Arab Emirates.

The area of Saudi Arabia is 2,149,000 square kilometers. The Arabian peninsula is like a great block of rock, highest in the west and sloping gradually eastward. This pattern is broken in the southeast by the highlands of Oman. Saudi Arabia can be divided into the following land regions: western highlands, Najd plateau, the two main sand areas of Nufud and al-Ruba al-Khali, and the gulf lands. Fauna and flora in Saudi Arabia are limited.

The population is about 13 million according to the 1988 census. Bedouin make up about 20 percent of the population. All of the population speak the Arabic language with slightly different dialects, and all are Muslims, with the majority of the Sunnah sect and a minority of the Shiah sect, living mainly in the eastern region. Arabs are primarily Semitic. Tribal life values are prevalent, though much less so in large population centers like the capital, Riyadh, and the main seaport, Jeddah.

The ruling system in Saudi Arabia is kingship. The law is Islamic Shariah. There is a consultative council and a council of ministers headed by the king. No political parties are allowed.

The oil economy is the most important part of the modern Saudi economy. Agriculture and industry have smaller shares in the present economy, but plans for their development are being executed.

The modern history of Saudi Arabia is closely related to the history of an Islamic reformation movement founded by Imam Muhammad bin Abdul Wahhab (1703–1793) that was supported by Muhammad bin Saud, a chieftain of the Anaizah tribe of Najd in a religious-political confederacy that aimed to spread Wahhabi doctrine and to reduce the rest of Arabia to the rule of the al-Saud family. After the initial spread of the movement the al-Saud were suppressed by Muhammad Ali Pasha in 1818. After a few years the al-Saud reemerged under the leadership of Imam Truki bin Abdullah, who established a new capital at Riyadh near Diraiyyah. The al-Saud were suppressed again by Egypt's ruler and reemerged again under Faisal bin Turki.

Later a quarrel over the succession within the al-Saud family enabled occupation of al-Hassa (in the northeast) by the Turks in 1871. A few years after that the rival Wahhabi dynasty of al-Rashid of Jabal Shammar gradually took power from al-Saud and actually attacked Riyadh in 1890. The al-Saud were forced to flee to remote corners of Najd and beyond. In 1902 the young Abdul Aziz bin Abdul Rahman emerged from Kuwait to recover Riyadh and to expel al-Rashid from Najd. With the help of his army, called Akhwan (the brothers), he ruled Najd, Hassa, Jabal Shammar, and later Hejaz, the two holy cities and their surroundings, and Asir ("Saudi Arabia," 1989). The establishment of the kingdom of Saudi Arabia was announced by King Abdul Aziz in September 1932, and it was internationally recognized as an independent country.

The government of Saudi Arabia shows great interest in expanding health and educational services to different sectors of Saudi society. This has been facilitated by the huge income from oil that led to remarkably rapid development of the country.

Modern Saudi culture is based on three different traditions: Islamic culture, traditional pre-Islamic Arab cultural elements, and modern Euro-American cultural elements. The presence of these three different and in many ways incompatible elements cause a high level of intrapsychic personal conflict that may impact on different aspects of family and social life with a fair degree of intergenerational conflict. Saudi society is a male-dominated society, with women playing a subordinate role. Economically, women have freedom in business dealings and private ownership, separate even from their husbands. However, in accordance with Islam, the relationship between the sexes in general follows the prevalent culture of separation. According to Islam, a man is allowed to marry more than one wife up to a maximum of four, but most husbands have only one wife. Like any pattern of human relationships, as one wife may be the cause of misery, so multiple wives in a family may be, but are not necessarily, related to a family's interpersonal problems. Saudi society in a number of big cities is currently mixing with a large number of foreigners from different countries and religions who come to Saudi Arabia for work, and this is gradually softening the traditional Saudi tribal prejudices.

One of the most important events in the area that is liable to have long-term consequences is the 1991 Persian Gulf War. Budget cutbacks due to huge war expenses are liable to have different long-term effects on future development plans and consequently on individual and family life. Long-term adverse social and psychological consequences are liable to occur due to the threat to Islamic as well as Arab solidarity resulting from the Gulf crisis itself and from the apparent weak Islamic and Arab response that led to widespread feelings of incompetence among Muslims and Arabs. This still causes a great deal of mental unrest among Muslim and Arab scholars who are trying to assimilate the meaning of what happened within the framework of their own respective ideologies. Other masses of noneducated Muslims and Arabs are liable to respond with more despair and loss of identity and morals, while the slogan "Let's follow the West" is liable to increase in loudness and pitch.

EXTENT OF THE PROBLEM

The widely held popular view, based on Islamic and traditional concepts, is that mental illness is probably caused by one of the following: organic lesion in the brain; emotional trauma; instinctual inhibition; punishment from Allah (God) for sins; evil eye; magic; or Evil spirit or jinn.

Recently, there has been an enhancement in the role of religion in the treatment of mental illness all over the Islamic world. This has resulted in the following religious methods of treatment: recitation from the Holy Quran, Rogia; getting the evil spirit out of the body through recitation of the Holy Quran and other methods; religious group psychotherapy; and antimagic methods.

Information about the extent of the problem of mental illness in Saudi Arabia is derived from psychiatric hospitals' and psychiatric units' statistics. In A.H. 1410 (1989–90) the number of all patients attending governmental psychiatric facilities was 360,256. The number of new cases was 60,288 (16.7 percent). The number of admitted cases was 12,369 (3.4 percent). The number of new admissions was 3,676 (29.7 percent of admitted cases). These statistics were derived from thirty-seven psychiatric facilities, hospitals, psychiatric departments, and clinics. Included in these facilities were 1,624 beds for inpatients in eighteen psychiatric hospitals and departments attached to general hospitals.

According to the Ministry of Health (1989–90), the most common diagnoses for patients attending government psychiatric clinics in the kingdom in A.H. 1410 (1989–90) were the following:

Anxiety	14.81%
Depressive disorders	10.06%
Schizophrenic disorder	7.34%
Epilepsy	7.22%
Psychotic depression	3.59%
Hysteria	3.45%
Obsessive-compulsive neurosis	2.81%

Mental retardation	2.77%
Senile dementia	1.96%
Psychosomatic disorder	1.80%
Manic-depressive psychosis (Manic type)	1.70%
Manic-depressive psychosis (circular type)	1.66%
Personality disorder	1.48%
Alcoholism	1.19%
Reactive psychosis	1.18%
Paranoid psychosis	1.16%
Conduct disorder	0.89%
Organic mental disorder other than senile dementia	0.45%

MENTAL HEALTH HISTORY

Before 1950 there was no proper arrangement for mentally sick patients. They were isolated from society and kept in houses. These houses were known to the public as *bimaristan*. In these houses patients were kept tied and were dealt with as prisoners. One such house used to be in Mecca and had about 100 patients. Then it was shifted to Taif because of the better climate. In Taif the house was placed in Mathnah and accommodated about 150 patients. Then it was shifted to Haweyyah, a suburb of Taif, and later to Qarwah, also a suburb of Taif. Only in 1962 was the first modern-style psychiatric hospital built in Taif, and it is still there. Previously it was a signal-story building, and in the beginning it held only 240 beds, but the number of patients was 600. By the time second and third stories were built the number of patients had increased to 1,500.

When the hospital was established, it had 2 psychiatrists, 4 general practitioners, about 50 nurses, and 50 servants. Then, through the efforts of the administration, by 1980 it had about 24 psychiatrists, 33 general practitioners, 280 nurses, and 641 servants. Also, by 1980 twelve psychiatric units were functioning in different parts of Saudi Arabia; these were psychiatric outpatient clinics or psychiatric short-stay units (Ministry of Health, 1982).

From this brief history it can be seen that before 1962 mental patients were dealt with as prisoners with no proper care and were held just for isolation in a separate house from the rest of the society. All sorts of mental illnesses were believed to be dominations by an evil spirit, the result of an exposure to an evil eye, or due to magic. After 1962 the outlook changed, and mental illness was looked at as some sort of disease affecting the individual's mind. This led to the belief that it could be treated by mental health staff like psychologists and social workers while they remained under the leadership of medically trained psychiatrists.

This change in outlook was mainly caused by wider social changes in the society as a result of modernization under the influence of the economic movement in the oil economy. Also, this change was encouraged by widespread educational and cultural development that was taking place in the society and by changing views on the early Muslim and Arab schools of medical thought such as those of al-Razi and Avicenna (Ibn Sina). They recognized mental illness as some sort of medical illness. This school of thought was established in the old mental health hospital in Baghdad under Abbasid rule and in similar hospitals in Cairo and Andalus (Islamic Spain). Thus after 1962 mental illness was seen as medical due to these influences.

Mental retardation was included with other types of mental illness. Thus the people with mental retardation were originally, and for a short time, dealt with together with those with mental illness. Later, mild and moderate cases of mental retardation were seen as an educational problem. With increased progress, severe cases of mental retardation started to be dealt with in special institutes for care and protection that also included medical supervision for associated problems like epilepsy.

Mentally disordered offenders were dealt with according to Islamic law, which considered them not responsible and not punishable due to their mental illness. Therefore, the suspected offenders were referred to a psychiatric medical legal committee, and if the committee judged that they were mentally ill and their crime was related to their mental illness, they were not punished.

Alcohol and drug addicts, if they sought medical and psychiatric help themselves, were considered as patients and treated secretly in the hospital or psychiatric clinic. First they were treated in the psychiatric hospital, but later specialized units for drug and alcohol addicts were established.

The most significant development in the period between 1962 and 1982 was the very rapid change in the availability of mental health services. In 1962 the first mental hospital was built in Taif as a 240-bed hospital. A few years later two more stories were added to the hospital and twelve more psychiatric units were built all around the kingdom in the cities of Dammam, al-Hafoof, Riyadh, Buraidah, Jeddah, Mecca, Medina, Hail, al-Joaf, Abha, and Jizan. And at Taif's mental hospital the following facilities became available:

- Outpatient department
- Inpatient department
- EEG department
- Physiotherapy department
- Dental clinic
- Chemical laboratory
- X-ray department

- Psychological laboratory
- Library
- Patients' canteen
- Rehabilitation center
- Addiction unit
- Separate pharmacies for inpatients and outpatients

In addition, educational and training programs at the psychiatric hospital in Taif were started in 1976 to deal with the problem of a shortage of psychiatrists and well-trained psychologists. The following educational and training courses were being held in the hospital:

- Diploma in psychological medicine
- Training of assistant psychiatric nurses
- Training of general practitioners to work in psychiatric units
- Training of nurses to work in psychiatric units
- Training of social workers to work in psychiatric units
- Training of psychologists
- Educational training for medical students
- Educational training for general nursing students
- Education of in-service personnel
- Religious lectures

By 1981 this institute had produced sixteen psychiatrists working successfully in mental health services. Thus in Taif a psychiatric hospital became a training center as well as a treatment center for psychiatric patients (Ministry of Health, 1982).

POLICY, ORGANIZATION, AND SERVICES IN THE 1980s AND 1990s

Current Policy Developments

Mental health policy in Saudi Arabia aims at making all mental health and psychiatric facilities available for citizens in all different regions of the country. Also, it aims to concentrate on preventive measures as well as treatment facilities, to involve different sections of society besides psychiatric and health professionals in issues related to mental health, and to involve relatives of the patients in taking responsibility and caring for their mentally ill relatives in a way that will help patients to cope more readily with society after the treatment of the acute episode.

This policy is being carried out through the building of several new psychiatric hospitals and psychiatric units in different cities of the kingdom, by giving more time to the media for general public mental health education, and by participation of psychiatric hospitals in health exhibitions. Also, relatives of the patients are encouraged to receive their relatives once they have passed the acute episode and to facilitate and encourage their adaptation in order to avoid a relapse. This policy is exemplified by using social work development concepts to give practical aid to relatives of psychiatric patients that encourages acceptance of their non-productive relatives. This policy also supports placement of chronic cases, not accepted by their relatives, in social care houses instead of overcrowding the hospitals with chronic cases. This leaves the hospital beds for needy acute cases and rehabilitation cases. Also, psychiatric hospitals have joined other government sections, like the traffic police, in public education about the hazards of drug abuse. Psychiatrists, together with religious men, have started religious psycho-therapy and public education.

The mental health policy is reinforced by the government's attitude toward the development of the kingdom in general. This policy is hindered by a negative attitude of the public. But in spite of that, the general interest of the religious men in the issue gives hope to overcome this hindrance. Economically speaking, the huge oil income was a great help in developing mental health facilities quickly. But the negative economic effect of the Persian Gulf War is looked upon as a factor slowing down the rapidity of future development.

Current Organization

The Ministry of Health is the main government authority involved in mental health policy through its Department of Psychological and Social Health. In addition, there are the psychiatric departments in the medical colleges, mainly the one in King Saud University. As for the private sector, there are private clinics, polyclinics, and hospitals with psychiatric units. Even though there is no special organization for them, they meet each other in conferences and public education sessions.

The Ministry of Health through its various specialized departments administers its health services, including health planning, carrying out health plans, super-vising their implementation, and evaluating the outcome for feedback and further planning. Regarding mental health, the Department of Psychological and Social Health is responsible for planning mental health policy and supervising its ap-plication throughout the kingdom.

The Ministry of Health itself is represented locally in every region in the kingdom by the Government of Health Affairs. The general policy for new units for the mentally ill and for the supervision of existing units is that they are under the control of the Department of Psychological and Social Health of the Ministry of Health, with administration of these services by special direct control under the Government of Health Affairs in each region.

Psychiatrists in psychiatric hospitals are called to general hospitals in the region for consultation and management of psychologically ill patients with some other clinical problems. Also, other medical specialists are called to manage mentally ill patients with physical problems. As mentioned before, mild and moderate cases of mental retardation are considered as educational problems unless they suffer from other superimposed problems such as epilepsy or hyperactivity. Severely mentally retarded cases were accepted in psychiatric hospitals before, but now they are referred to special institutes to keep more hospital beds available for acute psychiatric patients.

Clinical evaluation, investigation, and treatment are all supplied in government hospitals without charge for all patients regardless of sex, socioeconomic levels, or nationality. Private facilities require payment. Social care houses are available for elderly and handicapped people for no charge.

Current Services

The following facilities and services are available:

Governmental

1. Psychiatric clinics in general hospitals
2. Psychiatric short-stay units in general hospitals
3. Psychiatric hospitals, including inpatient and outpatient departments
4. Rehabilitation centers
5. Convalescent homes
6. Drug dependence units in psychiatric hospitals
7. Drug dependence hospitals in Riyadh, Jeddah, and Dammam

Private

1. Psychiatric clinics
2. Psychiatric polyclinics including separate male and female units, having psychiatrists, social workers, psychologists, an EEG unit, and observation rooms
3. Psychiatric units in hospitals
4. Psychiatric hospitals

More recently, since about 1987 or 1988, the implementation of psychiatric primary health care within the domain of the primary physical health care system has been carried out through dispensaries. In order to start this system, the general practitioners working in the dispensaries were given special courses in psychiatry in psychiatric hospitals in different regions; also, some psychiatric drugs were supplied to the pharmacies of these dispensaries. General practitioners were made aware of the problem of differentiation between physical illness and psychiatric illness presenting with physical symptoms. They were allowed to give emergency treatment for acute cases that had already consulted a psychiatrist.

Mental Health Personnel and Treatment

A hospital psychiatric unit is made up of consultants, psychiatrists, general practitioners, nursing staff, associated nurses, and servants. In addition, psychologists, social workers, and other medical specialists may be present, such as a neurologist, a dentist, and a laboratory technician. General practitioners can treat emergency psychiatric cases in the absence of a psychiatrist, and they may do follow-up treatment for chronic cases. Licensing is the responsibility of the government health agency in the region.

Psychologists are important for diagnostic and treatment purposes. They carry out personality tests, IQ tests, tests for organicity, and other evaluations and conduct psychological interviews for psychotherapy and behavioral therapy. They establish the general milieu of the hospital.

Social workers investigate the social background of the patients and the possible social causes or exacerbating factors. Special educators are of great help in special schools and training centers for mentally retarded patients with mild and moderate degrees of retardation. Occupational therapists work in psychiatric units and in convalescent homes. They play an important role in rehabilitating patients after the elimination of acute psychotic symptoms to adapt to social life and to live in society as active members. Nursing staff observe, give medicines to, and join recreational activities of the patients and arrange and take care of a good treatment modality.

In addition, a religious therapist is involved in treating patients in accordance with Islamic principles and beliefs. This method is called Islamic group psychotherapy. It differs from other types of psychotherapy not only by giving more attention to the relationship of the individual to society, but in strengthening the relationship of the individual to Allah (God), both horizontal and vertical coordination. At the same time, it uses other methods of group therapy like games, abreaction, and psychodrama. The main concentration is on the here and now, considering that the Holy Quran and the Prophet's sayings and deeds (Hadeeth) are present here and now. Identification, rationalization of emotions, abreaction, and strengthening of Islamic values and principles are allowed. The aims of this type of psychotherapy are to remove the symptoms of psychiatric illness, to defeat the feelings of loneliness, to change behaviors by means of the conscious efforts by the patients with the help of the group, to help adaptation of the patient in the society, and to encourage personality growth. The final aim is to form a central group of systematized ideas based on Islamic rules and principles for each individual. This group of ideas is intended to become a strong attitude force so that the rest of the individual's activities will revolve around it.

PUBLIC POLICY PROCESS

As was mentioned before, the ruling system in Saudi Arabia is a a kingship. There is also a consultation council. No political parties are allowed. The political power is in the hands of the king and a council of ministers headed by the king himself and his deputy, the crown prince. The different regional rulers (princes) are under direct control of the central authority in Riyadh. Local high governmental offices in some regions are considered as branches of the central ministry, with no separate legislative powers allowed. Thus the actual mental health policy is centrally determined in Saudi Arabia. Local authorities are executors of this policy under supervision of the central authority. The private facilities are allowed to do their work of treatment of patients within limits set by the Ministry of Health. They also share in scientific conferences, join exhibitions, and make suggestions for the development of mental health policy to the Ministry of Health.

Any changes in mental health policy can occur only through changes in policy by the Ministry of Health based on the studies of current institutions and consideration of opinions of different public and private sectors. The opinions of local authorities are always considered, although the Ministry of Health is not obliged to do so.

The main obstacle to carrying out mental health policy that has been proposed by the government in Saudi Arabia is the attitude of the people and their lack of purpose at times. For example, some patients who are badly in need of psychiatric help will be prevented from this help by their own close relatives, whose approval is a must for admission of the patient or for starting emergency treatment. So in spite of the free and easy availability of psychiatric services, they will not always reach some of the needy because their relatives prefer to take them to traditional healers and exclude them from proper psychiatric care in time of need. This is a problem of lack of proper education, and now the media are making a great effort, which we hope will be successful in the future, to overcome this obstacle. Also, it is noticed that some people take their mentally ill patients to a far-away region for treatment in spite of the ready availability of mental health services in their own region. This is due to the fear of the stigma of mental illness. This problem may be partially overcome by increasing psychiatric outpatient clinics and inpatient short-stay units in general hospitals, rather than separate psychiatric hospitals, as patients of separate psychiatric hospitals are more likely to be stigmatized than patients of a psychiatric unit of a general hospital. Also, public education through the media is important in overcoming this difficulty by changing public attitudes.

SPECIAL POLICY ISSUES

The Mentally Ill and the Mentally Retarded

Mental illness and mental retardation were in the beginning dealt with on the same basis, but with the passage of time this policy has undergone gradual change toward separating the group of mentally retarded persons from the group of mentally ill persons. In the beginning, mentally retarded patients were accepted as inpatients in psychiatric hospitals like those patients suffering from other chronic mental illness. Later on, those with uncomplicated mild and moderate mental retardation were viewed as educational rather than mental problems, and special schools and training centers were constructed for educating and training them. Those with complicated mild and moderate mental abnormalities, whether complicated with dysphasia, speech disorder, motor paralysis, epilepsy, or behavioral disorders, were looked upon as medical and educational problems and were exposed to medical, psychiatric, and education interference as favorable for the particular case. Cases with severe mental retardation were dealt with as psychiatric problems like other mental illnesses. After some additional time special institutes were made available for their care and protection. In spite of that, there are still psychiatric hospitals with appreciable numbers of mentally subnormal patients remaining because their relatives refuse to receive them and accept them at home and because the special facilities for mentally retarded cases cannot accept them all. For example, in Taif Psychiatric Hospital we found that cases of mental retardation and behavior disorders amounted to 29.8 percent of the inpatients, and cases of schizophrenia amounted to 56.8 percent (less than the widely accepted 70 percent figure) (al-Rayes, 1988–1989).

The Mentally Ill and Substance Abuse

The policy was to accept patients with alcohol and drug abuse problems in psychiatric hospitals if they suffered from acute mental disturbances secondary to drugs or if they came voluntarily seeking medical and psychiatric help to relinquish their habits. Later, special drug addiction units were established in connection with psychiatric hospitals and units. There are three special hospitals for drug dependence, in Riyadh, Jeddah, and Dammam. These hospitals are called al-Amal (the hope) Hospitals. Patients with drug dependence or alcohol abuse who come voluntarily for treatment or who are brought under compulsion by their own relatives for treatment are treated secretly without any obligation to inform the authorities.

The Mentally Disordered Offender

Regarding mentally disordered offenders, if they are suspected by police authorities or by judges in courts during trial or, if after being arrested for a crime, their relatives claim that they are mentally ill, they are sent by the police to a special medicolegal committee for an opinion. This committee is present in Taif Psychiatric Hospital. Cases are assessed as outpatients or admitted in a special prisoners' ward. It is administered by the hospital's administration, except for the guards, who are supplied by the prisoner's police.

There is an indication if there is a need either for observation or for treatment in cases of those actually sick. When the medicolegal report is issued by the committee, it is sent to the referring authority. If the patient is diagnosed as suffering from a mental illness of a psychotic nature and a judgment is made by the committee that his or her crime was related to his or her mental illness, the patient is exempted from punishment because of mental illness. After the decision by the referring authority, the patient is then dealt with as any other patient in the hospital by being shifted away from the prisoner's ward to a noncriminal ward.

Deinstitutionalization

With the advent of modern psychiatric services in Saudi Arabia, the modern wave of deinstitutionalization was also introduced. Shortly after the building of Taif Psychiatric Hospital, which is the first, largest, and a model psychiatric hospital in Saudi Arabia, a convalescent home with occupational therapy facilities was started attached to it. In the hospital itself recreational therapy and occupational therapy on a smaller scale were given strong emphasis. Religious group psychotherapy was introduced, especially for treating addicts. The policy of treatment was directed toward helping patients to readjust to the outside world after their discharge. Also, rapid discharge after disappearance of acute psychotic symptoms was encouraged. The role of Islamic culture in facilitating the deinstitutionalization policy was impressive, as the strong Islamic family institution could absorb and integrate the discharged patients into the family social system with many fewer complications compared to what happened in Western countries.

Funding Issues

Funding of civilian mental health facilities in Saudi Arabia is mainly through the Ministry of Health and can be considered a part of the Ministry of Health's funds. In A.H. 1410 (1989–90) the Ministry of Health fund was equal to 8,597,000 Saudi riyals, or 6 percent of the general fund of the country. The number of beds for psychiatric services is about 6 percent of the total number of beds for all health services related to the Ministry of Health. The mental health fund for A.H. 1410 was about 6 percent of the Ministry of Health fund, equal to about 515,820 Saudi riyals. Military mental health services are separate, and their budget is nearly equal to the civilian budget, as they have services distributed all over the kingdom for military people and their families.

Consumer Rights

There is no mental health act in Saudi Arabia yet, but a proposal is under discussion. The rights of the mentally ill are protected by Islamic Shariah (law). If the patient is judged by a psychiatrist to be mentally ill and unable to take care of his or her property and to take responsibility for his or her actions, he or she is exempted from punishment for his or her crimes, and a guardian may be assigned by the court to take care of his or her property. The guardian is usually his or her nearest relative (male adult, Muslim, and seared). The guardian is responsible in front of the court if he misuses his guardianship. Psychiatric treatment for the patient, regardless of treatment method, is to be started only after approval in writing by the patient's guardian, whether it is psychopharmacological, involuntary admission, electroconvulsive therapy (ECT), psychosurgery, or other methods.

CONCLUSIONS AND DISCUSSION

Mental health policy has had a very significant and rapid development from 1962 onward that started with the establishment of the first psychiatric hospital in Taif. The rapid development was due to the flourishing oil economy and the positive attitude of the government toward development of the society. There have been gradual changes in the form of mental health services as they have spread over the vast area of Saudi Arabia to all its different regions. Also, there has been a separation of facilities for the mentally retarded and drug and alcohol abusers from other mental patients.

As a result of the strong central government in Saudi Arabia, mental health policy is centrally determined by the Ministry of Health, but with proper programming and good attention to the needs of the society. Due to the large Bedouin population and many uneducated people in the society, there is a lack of proper response from the public at times to the available services, but the media are doing well in trying to overcome this obstacle.

Pellgram is used to resolve mental illness through support, enforcement of religious treatment by recitation of the Holy Quran, and Islamic group psychotherapy. This is reinforced by the research and the resources of modern services and psychiatry.

REFERENCES

Ministry of Health. (1982). *Mental health services in the kingdom*, pp. 1–2, 8–39. Saudi Arabia: Author.

Ministry of Health. (A.H. 1410; 1989–1990). *Yearly Health Report*, pp. 5–7, 179, 676 (Arabic).

al-Rayes. (A.H. 1409; 1988–1989). New trends in anti psychotic treatment. In *Research and Studies in Mental Health* (pp. 221–239). Saudia Arabia: Taif Mental Hospital (Arabic).

Saudi Arabia. (1989). *Collier's encyclopedia*, 20, 450–456.

18

Turkey

Ismail Cifter

OVERVIEW

Turkey is situated between Europe and Asia. In the north, Turkey has a 610-kilometer border with the former Soviet Union, including Georgia, Armenia, and Azerbaijan, and is further bounded by the Black Sea; in the east, it has a 454-kilometer border with the Islamic Republic of Iran; in the south, it has a 331-kilometer border with Iraq and an 877-kilometer border with Syria, plus the northeastern shores of the Mediterranean Sea; in the west it is bounded by the Aegean Sea.

Turkey has an area of 814,578 square kilometers. It occupies the whole of Asia Minor (Anatolia), which has an area of 790,200 square kilometers, and a relatively small portion of Thrace in southeastern Europe (24,378 square kilometers). In Europe, Turkey has a 269-kilometer border with Bulgaria and a 212-kilometer border with Greece. The shores of Anatolia total 6,480 kilometers, whereas the shores of Thrace are only 786 kilometers. The Turkish Islands, on the other hand, have a total of 1,067 kilometers of seashores. The Bosphorus, the Marmara Sea, and the Dardanelles separate the two continents upon which Turkey is located.

The population of Turkey has increased greatly since 1980, when it was 44,737,000. By 1990 it had reached 56,969,000 (State Institute of Statistics, 1991). According to the census taken in 1985, 23,798,701 people (46.97 percent) were rural, and 26,865,757 people (53.03 percent) were urban (State Institute of Statistics, 1989b).

As table 18.1 indicates, Turkey has a rather young population, with almost half of the population under age twenty-five. According to 1985 statistics, the male population made up 50.57 percent of the general population, leaving the

Table 18.1
Distribution of the Population in Turkey by Age Group and Sex

Age Group	Total	Male	Female
0-4	6,078,000	3,113,000	2,965,000
5-9	6,739,000	3,457,000	3,282,000
10-14	6,193,000	3,210,000	2,983,000
15-19	5,407,000	2,744,000	2,663,000
20-24	4,784,000	2,434,000	2,350,000
25-29	4,041,000	2,056,000	1,985,000
30-34	3,374,000	1,724,000	1,650,000
35-39	2,787,000	1,414,000	1,373,000
40-44	2,208,000	1,098,000	1,110,000
45-49	2,009,000	992,000	1,017,000
50-54	2,043,000	1,040,000	1,003,000
55-59	1,649,000	824,000	825,000
60-64	1,130,000	556,000	574,000
65+	2,126,000	955,000	1,171,000
Unknown	96,000	55,000	41,000

Source: State Institute of Statistics, Prime Ministry, Republic of Turkey, 1991.

female population as the remaining 49.43 percent. Of the population over six years of age 23 percent are illiterate, and 77 percent are literate (State Institute of Statistics, 1989b).

The official language spoken is Turkish, but Turkish citizens are free to speak the language they wish. The great majority of the people living within the boundaries of the Turkish Republic today are Turkish. The dominant religion is Islam. This religion played an important role in the governing of the nation until the beginning of the twentieth century. Before that time, not only was the administrative system based on Islamic rules, but also the principles of the Koran were considered as the basic rules of social conduct. The educational system was under the influence of Islam as well, as the Arabic alphabet was used. However, since 1923, when the new Turkish Republic was established, the social structure of the country has changed immensely, acquiring a totally modern nature. The previous religious educational systems and the caliphate were banned; the Roman alphabet was accepted; the educational system was reformed by the establishment of the Turkish medium schools and universities; polygamy was abolished; and women were given equal rights with men.

The first section of the 1982 constitution states that Turkey has a republican form of government. The second section indicates other aspects of the government, such as that the Turkish Republic functions as a democratic, secular state in line with Atatürk nationalism and under the major principles of considering the rights of all humans and serving the public welfare. Ankara is the capital of the Turkish Republic. The constitution states that the Turkish Republic is unquestionably ruled by the nation. The Turkish people have a voice in the ruling of the government through authorized branches established according to the principles of the constitution. The legislative power belongs to the National Assembly. The executive power is exercised by the president of the Turkish Republic and the government in accordance with the principles stated in the constitution. The Turkish Grand National Assembly is made up of 450 members selected by Turkish citizens (*Turkish Republic's Constitution*, 1982). The founder and the first president of the Turkish Republic was Mustafa Kemal Atatürk.

According to the 1982 constitution and the April 22, 1983, Political Parties Law, political parties are inseparable features of the democratic political system. Nowadays, the Motherland Party, the Social Democratic Populist Party, the True Path party, the Democratic Left Party, the Prosperity Party, the Nationalist Labor Party, and the Reformist Democracy Party are among the leading political parties.

In line with great economic development, Turkey is gradually becoming an industrial country, agriculture no longer having a dominant role in the nation's economy. Nevertheless, agricultural resources such a wheat, barley, corn, potatoes, and sugar beets, along with tobacco and cotton, are still considered important commercial crops. Besides the rich coal, iron, chromium, and copper mines, petroleum reserves, as well, seem to promise a good future. In order to maintain electric power and to irrigate the vast farmlands, hydroelectric installations and dams have been built, and many more are still being constructed. Cement, rugs, textiles, electrical appliances, cigarettes, and processed food and fruits are among the chief manufactured items. In 1985, 60 percent of the population was engaged in agriculture, 13.8 percent in industry, and 26.2 percent in the service sector (State Institute of Statistics, 1991).

Although a rapid change can be witnessed in Turkey, the traditional family structure remains very much the same in rural areas, where a few generations live within a large paternalistic family. Traditions are very strong, and the members of the family respect and love each other and are closely united. In contrast, the concept of the family has changed in cities, and large paternalistic families are replaced by nuclear families. Members of the nuclear family have equal rights, and working outside the home enables them to become independent and free in many aspects. The members of the younger generation leave their parents' home after they get married and establish new independent families. This sometimes has a negative psychological effect on the people migrating from the rural areas who are trying to adopt the traditions of the cities. For instance, their elders who are still traditional do not have much tolerance for the younger generation that wishes to adapt to city life, and this causes disagreements and sometimes serious problems within the family. As a result, young people may decide to leave the house, and the elders suffer feelings of depression.

The economic and social change has some negative effects not only on the family, but also on the society as a whole. The rapid growth of the population in cities has created certain problems like lack of accommodation, unemployment, and the lack of sufficient health organizations.

During the fifty-eight years between 1927 and 1985, the population increased at a rate of 354 percent in Turkey. This overpopulation has led to many difficulties in bringing health services to the individuals of the country. The Ministry of Health and Social Services had only 3 hospitals with a 950-bed capacity during the first few years that followed the establishment of the Turkish Republic. Today, however, the number of hospitals has reached 798, and the bed capacity is 127,035. Similarly, in 1985, 137.4 million Turkish lira (TL) of the total 5,412 billion Turkish lira state budget was devoted to the Ministry of Health and Social Services, but in 1989, 898.9 million TL of the total 32,733,400 billion TL budget was devoted to the same ministry. The amount devoted for health has increased from 2.5 percent to 2.7 percent.

Overpopulation and urbanization led to economic pressures that caused a great rise in the rate of psychological disorders. The inability of the government to maintain sufficient financial resources for the physical and psychological welfare of the society has resulted in the establishment of health organizations where patients have to pay in order to be examined and treated. The socialization of health services is now being considered very important in the solution of this problem. Meanwhile, a revolving fund system has been introduced for health organizations, and modern, private hospitals have been established (State Institute of Statistics, 1991).

EXTENT OF THE PROBLEM

In Turkey, as in all countries, the problems of dealing with physical and mental health have reached serious dimensions, and what is being done to overcome this situation is not sufficient. The number of people suffering from mental disorders who were treated in hospitals from 1984 to 1988 and the ratio of mentally disabled patients to the number of general patients are indicated in table 18.2. The distribution according to the diagnosis and sexes of the psychiatric patients being treated in hospitals and other institutions of health is shown in table 18.3.

As can be seen in tables 18.2 and 18.3, there was not much change in the rates of psychiatric patients being treated in hospitals during these five years. The number of psychiatric patients being treated in hospitals is much more than those in other diagnostic groups. Some of the people suffering from mental retardation are still under control and treatment in certain special wards of psy-

Table 18.2
The Number of People in Turkey Suffering from Mental Disorders Treated in Hospitals, and the Ratio of the Number of Mentally Disordered Patients to the Number of General Inpatients

Year	Number of Inpatients	Ratio to General Inpatients
1984	49,253	2.1
1985	50,133	2.0
1986	56,158	2.1
1987	58,227	2.1
1988	56,993	2.0

Source: Ministry of Health, 1990.

Table 18.3
Distribution According to Diagnosis and Sex of Psychiatric Patients Being Treated in Turkey in 1988

Diagnosis	Discharged from Hospital		Average Stay in Hospital (in Days)
	Male	Female	
Psychosis	15,249	9,888	35.8
Alcoholism	4,903	1,473	17.9
Drug abuse	1,331	731	13.4
Neurosis and disorders of personality	9,648	11,719	10.5
Mental retardation	1,015	642	85.9
Convulsive disorders	5,557	3,821	7.8
Geriatric cases	3,104	2,656	9.0

Source: Ministry of Health, 1990.

chiatric hospitals, and their average stay in hospital is much longer than for other groups of patients. The number of psychiatric patients treated in ambulatory or outpatient psychiatric services was more or less the same over the five years from 1985 to 1989 (Ministry of Health, 1989, 1990).

When the figures in table 18.4 are examined, it can be seen that the number

Table 18.4
Suicides in Turkey by Year, Age Groups, and Rates

				Age						
Year	Total	0-15	15-24	25-34	35-44	45-54	55-64	65-74	75+	Unknown
1985 A	1,187	47	376	214	149	140	91	80	53	37
B	100	3.9	31.7	18.0	12.6	11.8	7.7	6.7	4.5	3.1
1986 A	1,068	42	305	233	143	113	87	47	64	34
B	100	3.9	28.6	21.8	13.4	10.6	8.1	4.4	6.0	3.2
1987 A	1,098	39	327	220	133	123	115	55	44	42
B	100	3.6	29.8	20.0	12.1	11.2	10.5	5.0	4.0	3.8
1988 A	1,099	44	316	234	139	130	104	59	39	34
B	100	4.0	28.8	21.3	12.6	11.8	9.5	5.4	3.5	3.1
1989 A	1,172	48	329	231	143	137	126	58	64	36
B	100	4.1	28.1	19.7	12.2	11.7	10.7	4.9	5.5	3.1

A. Number B. Rate (%)

Source: State Institute of Statistics, Prime Ministry, Republic of Turkey, 1990.

Table 18.5
Distribution of Mentally Retarded People in Turkey According to Their Retardation Level and Age Group, 1985

Age Group	Total	Teachable	Trainable
0-4	139,773	18,231	121,542
5-18	539,663	70,566	469,097
19-44	417,616	54,479	363,137
45-59	131,107	17,101	114,006
60+	74,890	9,768	65,122

Source: Ustunoğlu, 1991.

of suicides during the last five years has not changed. Another easily witnessed fact is that a great majority of the incidences of suicide fall in the 15–24 age group. The most frequent mode of death is hanging oneself (50 percent). This figure is followed by taking chemicals (14–15 percent).

The distribution of people with mental retardation according to their age groups and retardation levels is indicated in table 18.5. In Turkey in 1985 there was a total number of 139,773 mentally retarded children in the 0–4 age group, 18,231 of these being teachable and 121,542 being trainable. The table indicates that in almost all age groups the number of trainable mental retardation cases is much higher than that of the teachable group.

The 1989 statistics about children who have committed crimes and have been punished make it clear that children above the age of fifteen are more apt to commit crimes. These children are sent to reformatories where they enroll in special programs to be trained in certain handicrafts. In 1987 there were four reformatories in different cities in Turkey for children under the age of eighteen. A total of 698 young people were in juvenile reformatories (State Institute of Statistics, 1989a). According to 1987 judicial statistics (State Institute of Statistics, 1989a), the total number of people found guilty due to various offenses was 40,254. The offenses due to narcotics (either selling or purchasing) were 1,012.

MENTAL HEALTH HISTORY

Mental health principles and services in Turkey display a progress parallel to that of other medical sciences with a long and interesting history. In the Middle Ages the great Turkish physician Ibn Sina (Avicenna) (980–1037) engaged in science and examined patients with nervous breakdowns and scrutinized their anamnesis, dreams, behaviors, and diets. He could define and diagnose acute meningitis, paralysis, and apoplectic cerebral diseases. He claimed that each of these illnesses was caused by a certain tiny worm, and that cleanliness could be a way of overcoming them. Ibn Sina stated in his book *Canon Medicine* that the soul is created as a function of the brain, and that any dysfunction of the brain would indicate a cerebral illness. He further stated that the "sense commune" serving mental functions through the five senses was located in the frontal lobe of the brain. He voiced his principal belief in the following words: "Wisdom is in the body and mainly in the brain, the brain being an organ of wisdom." It is known that Ibn Sina was in favor of relaxing patients, never using tight bonds, making use of the free association method, and using suggestion techniques.

The Great Seljuk Empire established in Asia and the later-established Anatolian Seljuk State can be associated with a prosperous period in the field of medicine and mental health. A large number of medical institutions and medical training centers were founded in Anatolia during that period. The treatment of mentally ill patients and the training of medical personnel were carried out in the best way possible under their circumstances. Many other hospitals, medical training centers, and pharmacies were added to those founded before and during the Ottoman Empire era. These institutions were named *marussifa*, *darüssifa*, and *bimarhane*, "lunatic asylums." Among these, an outstanding one was the Toptasi Bimarhane (asylum), founded in 1583 to treat psychiatric patients. In the Suleymaniye Darüssifa (asylum) and Darültip Medical School, founded in 1555, there were special wards for mentally ill patients. Richard Krafft-Ebing's book stated that Europe borrowed the idea of establishing special hospitals for mentally ill patients and treatment methods from Turks (Gokay, 1975). In Edirne Darüssifa, founded by Yildirim Beyazit, mentally ill patients were treated in baths and with music. Ali Suuri, a well-known Turkish physician, explained the methods of treatment through music in detail in his book *Tadil-i Emzice* (Changing of moods). The widely travelled Evliya Celebi stated in his famous journal *Seyahatname* that music was a means of treatment in the *bimarhane*. The *darüssifa* in Manisa was founded by Kanuni Sultan Suleyman in 1539. This institution is still functional and enables the treatment of many mentally ill patients (Bayat, 1979).

Nurbanu Hatun, Sultan Murat III's mother, founded the Toptasi Mental Hospital in 1583 in Usküdar-Istanbul. This mental hospital continued treating mentally ill patients until they were removed to Bakirkoy in 1927, which still functions under the name of Bakirkoy Mental Hospital. The first French physician of the Toptasi Hospital, Mongeri Pere, was the first chief physician of this hospital.

The history of modern psychiatry in Turkey dates back to the establishment of the neuropsychiatric clinic of the Gulhane Military Medical Academy, founded by Professor Rasit Tahsin in 1898. Tahsin was a student of Emil Kraepelin (the father of descriptive psychiatry) and helped in the establishment of the Mental Health Association in the years after the 1908 revolution. He was also a member of the International Association of Mental and Neurological Diseases. After his death his assistant, Professor Mazhar Osman, was assigned to the center and was later sent to Europe, where he took courses in psychiatry and neurology in Berlin and Munich. He returned to Turkey in 1911. In 1933 he started teaching in the medical school of Istanbul University. Before that, in 1920 he had founded the society of Green Crescent, which is still functional as a valuable organization struggling to prevent people from alcohol and drug abuse in Turkey. After Osman was assigned as chief physician at Toptasi Mental Hospital, he stopped those types of treatment that were painful for the patients and advised his colleagues to adopt humanistic techniques such as explaining to people their problems, giving positive suggestions, and counselling. He sent many neuropsychiatrists to Germany to be further educated to serve the improvement and development of psychiatry in Turkey. Osman was the author of many books, a few of which are *Psychiatry*, *Intoxicating Drugs*, and *Alcoholism from the Clinical Point of View*. Later his students Sukru Hazim, Ihsan Sukru, Ahmet Sukru, and Fahrettin Kerim started teaching at the Faculty of Medicine, Istanbul University, and Nazim Sakir at the Psychiatry Department of the Gulhane Military Medical Academy. Sukru Hazim was educated at the Eppendorf Hospital, Hamburg, and was Professor Nonnen's student; Ahmet Sukru had been in Munich and had worked with Professor Plaut; and Fahrettin Kerim had been to Professor Emil Kraepelin's clinic and to Dr. Ottograf's Experimental Psychology Laboratory. These industrious people worked at Istanbul University and Gulhane Military Medical Academy upon their return to Turkey and have made great contributions to the development of psychiatry as a modern science.

Later on, other academicians were sent to medical institutions in the United States to keep up with new trends and techniques in psychiatry (Cifter, 1990). Today, in most of the twenty-nine universities in Turkey, scientific studies are being carried out to provide the best treatment for the mentally ill patients. The treatment of psychiatric patients is being conducted efficiently and effectively not only in university hospitals but also in hospitals of the Ministry of Health and Social Services and insurance institutions. In Turkey university hospitals and the hospitals of the Ministry of Health and Social Services and insurance institutions treat patients suffering from mental disorders and conduct first-, second-, and third-degree programs for the prevention of mental disorders. Both governmental and nongovernmental organizations serve to maintain the mental health of the people.

As can be seen from the history of mental health and the development of psychiatry, many mental health policies in the Turkish Republic were initially influenced by European countries, especially Germany and France. Later, in the beginning of the twentieth century, the experiences of the Turkish physicians, especially neuropsychiatrists who were educated in the United States of America, had a great impact on medical and mental policies. The importance of educational exchanges is seen, and through these exchanges Turkish mental health policies have adopted approaches that consider humans as social, biological, and psychological wholes. As a result of these developments, the former traditional hospitals are being replaced by modern ones; attempts to treat psychiatric patients within the community are being made; a careful psychiatric evaluation of criminals is made prior to their punishment; those criminals who have mental illnesses are being treated by psychiatrists in special wards of the prisons, and in cases when this is not possible, they are being treated in hospitals under the supervision of guards; the living conditions of the prisons are being improved; psychologists, social workers, and nurses are assigned to work in prisons; and handicraft courses are being conducted in prisons. In the past, psychiatric patients were used to being locked up in wards; nowadays they are sent to stay with their families and are encouraged to participate in social life. The idea that mentally retarded people should be kept in mental hospitals to protect them from outside negative effects is now being replaced by ideas that enable them to be educated and trained just like normal people, but through a special education system. In these institutions they are treated to overcome the consequences of physical and metabolic factors that cause the mental retardation. Likewise, alcoholics are sent first to special detoxification centers and are then treated individually and/or in groups.

Until the year 1980 the Ministry of Health and Social Services, the insurance institutions, and the Ministry of Defense developed programs that were in line with the Five-Year Development Plans in order to establish new mental hospitals and to improve the present conditions of the hospitals to treat mentally ill patients in the best way possible. In those years not much thought was devoted to prevention. The main emphasis was on increasing the number of beds and, therefore, hospitals. In the years 1969–70, for example, there were 6,900 to 7,000 beds for mentally ill patients, and almost all of such patients (92.8 percent) were being treated together, regardless of their being children, adults, drug addicts, criminals, or alcoholics. Only a small portion (7.2 percent) of them could be kept in special wards and could receive special treatment. Sixty-six percent of the health institutions where psychiatric treatment was possible had fewer than 20 beds; 23 percent had 20–50 beds; 9 percent had 51–100 beds; and 2 percent had 101–200 beds. The number of hospitals and other institutions for psychiatric patients gradually increased, and in 1978 there were nine such hospitals and institutions; 37.5 percent of these hospitals and institutions had a capacity of 100–500 beds, and 12.8 percent had more than 1,000 beds.

The statistics given here and the present situation make it clear that the effort made for treatment of psychiatric patients is not sufficient, and that merely increasing the number of hospitals, bed capacities, and physicians will not be a remedy for the problem. It has been realized that besides short-term, intensive psychiatric treatment in hospitals, serious psychiatric cases should also receive ambulatory treatment. This kind of treatment is sure to be more effective and economic.

POLICY, ORGANIZATION, AND SERVICES IN THE 1980s
AND 1990s

Current Policy Developments

Findings in 1980 strengthened the opinion that special mental hospitals for long-term treatment, clinics and welfare centers for outpatients, and counselling services for children were necessary. The principle behind this mental health policy was the idea that most of the psychiatric patients receiving treatment in hospitals would need ambulatory treatment in the future and that outpatient treatment centers and counselling services would therefore be needed. The change made in 1980 in policy was very advantageous and introduced the concept of keeping the patient in unenclosed sections of the hospitals instead of indoors; initiated the diagnosis and treatment of psychiatric diseases at early stages, if possible without isolating the patients from their families and the society; and placed emphasis on first-, second-, and third-step prevention applications. The coordination and cooperation of mental health personnel and enlightening the public through the mass media are now considered very important.

Mentally retarded people were previously isolated from the society and were locked up in wards in hospitals, but they are now given the opportunity to be trained and educated in special institutions, the number of which is increasing every year. Alcohol and drug addicts are being treated not only in mental hospitals but also in special clinics and are provided with the opportunity of participating in aftercare and self-help group therapies. Programs involving four categories— preventive measures, therapy and rehabilitation, international control and co-operation, and legal measures—are being put into application. Addiction-forming drugs such as tranquilizers and hypnotics, for example, are sold only by prescription by authorized physicians.

The main principles of the present Turkish mental health policy are as follows:

1. The promotion of a mental health concept that also includes healthy living conditions
2. The integration of mental health with physical health
3. The decentralization of services
4. The maintenance of coordination between other sectors and disciplines
5. The strengthening of the Mental Health Department of the Ministry of Health and the mental health divisions of the provincial health directorates and increasing their efficiency

Current Organization

One of the first laws passed on the issue of health in Turkey was the General Hygiene Law of 1930, which especially defined the preventive medicine services and the responsibilities and duties of the Ministry of Health and Social Services.

The Ministry of Health and Social Services and the Employees Law went into effect in 1936. Another very important law involving the socialization of health services was put in force in 1961 and was aimed at bringing health services to the smallest villages in Turkey. A more recent law on the same issue to enable carrying out health services more efficiently was passed in 1981 and required compulsory service for the health personnel in certain branches of the health services. This can be considered an important step in bringing the health services to the desired level. Article 56 of the 1982 constitution states that every Turkish citizen has equal rights for living in healthy circumstances. It is the state's and the individual's duty to protect the environment from pollution and to improve the present conditions. The state organizes the health services of every kind to establish coordination and cooperation among the various branches in order to save on effort and resources and to maintain the physical and psychological health of its citizens. Besides organizing these institutions, the state controls and inspects their effectiveness and efficiency. A general health insurance program is also planned and can be put to use almost immediately. The Ministry of Health and Social Services is the branch of the government authorized to carry out all of these services and duties. Nevertheless, other ministries such as Public Economic Organizations, Faculties of Medicine, and certain other institutions also contribute to the needs of the Ministry of Health and Social Services.

Two different laws on the issue of protecting children in need were put in force in 1949 and 1957. In addition, the semiofficial Society for the Protection of Children, which was established June 30, 1921, in Ankara, is still functional (under another name). A law passed in 1959 enabled the state to have control over all these official and semiofficial institutions. A more recent law (May 24, 1983; reference number 2828) replaced all the former laws and enabled the establishment of the General Directorate of Social Services and the Society for the Protection of Children. This organization is a branch of the Ministry of Health and Social Services based on its budget and is of a corporate body nature. Its main duty is to provide social and health services to needy people, and it gives priority to children in need of care, handicapped people, and the old. In order to bring adequate services to these people it establishes nurseries, care centers, old people's homes, orphanages, and rehabilitation centers (*General Directorate of Press and Information*, 1988).

The Mental Health Department now functions in coordination with the General Directorate of Primary Health Care, which is also attached to the Ministry of Health. The aim is the integration of psychiatric and general health services. The Mental Health Department is considered to be a vital branch of the Ministry of Health and is given importance. Although the Mental Health Department is connected to the General Directorate of Physical Health Services, most mental institutions, such as mental hospitals and the psychiatric clinics of other hospitals, function in line with the General Directorate of Curative Services (Coskun, 1989). In addition, there are mental health divisions in the provincial health directorates.

Current Services

Psychiatric treatment is now available mostly in hospitals. The Ministry of Health has five hospitals with psychiatric clinics. These hospitals are in different geographic regions of Turkey and serve mainly the people living in those regions. These hospitals are in the Marmara region (Istanbul), the west (Manisa), the south (Adana), the north (Samsun), and the east (Elazığ). The provincial health directorates present in every city have mental health divisions that are established to carry out the mental health policies of the government. The number of psychiatric patients and the limited services offered, which are insufficient to meet the needs, have revealed the importance of preventive aspects of mental health and have initiated the attempts to prevent mental health problems in the society. It is stated that peripheral preventive mental health services will be functional in the very near future. Chronic psychiatric patients who have already received treatment in hospitals, mentally retarded people and their families, and children who are in need of counselling are sure to greatly benefit from these services.

In Turkey five of the seven mental hospitals belong to the Ministry of Health, and the total bed capacity in these five hospitals is 6,040; the other two hospitals have a total bed capacity of 376. As for ambulatory treatment, besides the psychiatric clinics, the mental health dispensaries, located especially in two big provincial cities, do their best to be of help to psychiatric patients. The aim is to establish such institutions in all the other cities as well.

Mental Health Personnel and Treatment

The fact that most psychiatrists live in certain cities has led many people to support the idea of carrying out the mental health services through other practitioners. There are more than 3,000 local health offices all over Turkey. If these could be equipped to bring mental health services to people living nearby, they would certainly have a major role in diagnosing and treating psychiatric patients at very early stages and in directing the serious and complex cases to the main hospitals. In order to achieve this, practitioners are going to take certain courses to be well informed on the issue.

The services in mental health institutions are carried out through psychiatrists and nurses, similar to other branches of medicine. In principle, teamwork is preferred; however, the lack of psychologists and social workers who are trained in psychiatry makes this impossible. According to 1989 statistics, the total number of psychiatrists in Turkey was 304: 118 of these psychiatrists worked for the Ministry of Health, 53 worked for the social insurance institutions, 116 worked in university hospitals, and 17 worked in various other health organizations. On the other hand, most of the 189 psychologists working for the Ministry of Health are not trained in psychiatry, and the number of social workers who are trained in psychiatry is not more than 94. Certain in-service training courses are planned for these personnel. For the present, there are no nurses trained in either psychiatry or public mental health services. An immediate remedy for this problem can be in-service courses, but for a long-term solution, vocational faculties for nurses are now starting programs to train the nurses in specific branches; moreover, psychologists are offered master's programs in clinical psychiatry.

PUBLIC POLICY PROCESS

Mental health policy in Turkey is in line with the general health policy and is defined by the state. General Health Council meetings held at certain times enable professors, specialists, and the representatives of the ministry and the social services institutions to come together and discuss the current situation and possible solutions to problems, drawing the outline of the health policy.

The Ministry of Health and Social Services considers the decisions of this council as the basis of policy and functions accordingly. Another council that is influential on the Ministry of Health and Social Services is the State Planning Council, which defines the aims to be achieved in five years and prepares investment and application programs to reach the defined goals. The 1982 constitution assigned the state to organize and control all the health institutions in order to maintain the physical and mental health of the citizens. The coordinated functioning of these institutions would also serve to save on effort and material resources and to gain efficiency and effectiveness. A general health insurance system will eventually be very effective in bringing health services to citizens all over Turkey. The constitution further states that measures should be taken by the state to protect especially the young generation from drug abuse and alcohol dependency, crime, gambling, and other destructive habits. Likewise, it stresses the major role the state should play in providing equal right on the issue of health by protecting the handicapped, children, the old, and others in need. All these services will be carried out by making the best use of the limited economic resources.

These duties are carried out by the related ministries and state institutions. The state itself is responsible for the organization of the health services and fulfills this role through state and private institutions of health. This makes it clear that the state has a voice in the functioning of every institution, whether it is a branch of the state or not. The laws put in force by the Grand National Assembly determine the state's authority and dominance over these organizations. While the Basic Health Policies are planned in line with the constitution, certain ministries, such as the Ministry of Health and Social Services, the Ministry of Defense, the Ministry of Justice, and the Ministry of Education, and some professional groups also represented in the General Health Council meetings are asked to contribute their ideas and experiences as well. Political party representatives do not generally attend these General Health Council meetings. The

Ministry of Health and Social Services carries out its duties through commissions it forms and by considering the opinions of the related branches.

In order to prepare the regulations dealing with mental health, the legislative council members consult every related organization and institution. A similar procedure is applied in commissions of the ministries. The opinions of other related ministries are considered important in trying to overcome the shortcomings encountered in practice. For example, if a law is being prepared on the socialization of the health services, not only the Ministry of Health and Social Services, but also the Ministry of Defense, the Ministry of Education, the Ministry of Finance, some other ministries, the universities, social services institutions, and various specialists and organizations are consulted, and only after a cooperative study would the law be considered ready.

A continuous coordination and coalition is required at every level of mental health programming. Societies and organizations dealing with mentally retarded and mentally ill patients function according to their own regulations. Each society or organization has specific aims and objectives, and its council of managers can decide to cooperate with another society or organization to achieve the aims and objectives defined in the regulation. In Turkey there are many such societies and organizations for the physically handicapped (blind, deaf, dumb) and mentally retarded people. Among these are the Society to Protect Teachable Children and the Society to Protect Children in Need.

There are various factors that can hinder mental health policies from being applied effectively, the most important being the education level of the citizens in general. As stated before, 22.5 percent of the population over six years of age are illiterate. A great majority of this group lives in rural areas and can only be informed through radio and television. It is crucial to eliminate certain misconceptions about psychological and psychiatric diseases. Some people still believe that certain patients will recover if married, if taken to religious people to be blessed, or if given special things blessed by religious people. Marrying close relatives is another tradition in some villages that has to be stopped. Unless these beliefs can be changed by educating people through audiovisual mass media, Turkey will have to await the coming generation, which, of course, will take some time. Primary education is now compulsory, and, therefore, the percentage of the illiterate will soon drop, as intended.

Although all the required plans and programs on the issue of mental health are ready, the lack of sufficiently educated and trained personnel slows the pace down and hinders Turkey from reaching the desired level. It will be possible to bring mental health services to people all over the country only when educational and economic levels of the population in general reach the desired standards. In the rapid industrialization process, another major problem is protection of the physical and mental health of people and the cure and rehabilitation of patients as soon as possible. The Social Services Institution established to serve this aim is sometimes unable to cope with the general and mental health of workers in various sectors of industry. Besides the workers with social insurance, there are millions of people living in rural areas without social insurance of any kind who also require general and mental health services. The government is working on a law on general health insurance that will demand additional funds.

It is apparent that the solution of all these indicated problems will require some time in which officials and the public can be informed about the dimensions and the importance of the problems. The cooperation of people from every sector will facilitate the solution. Conferences and seminars to enlighten the public (organized by university professors), establishing model centers that provide ambulatory and inpatient treatment, treating and rehabilitating chronic patients without isolating them from their families and the community, providing counselling services, and enabling health personnel to enter in-service programs are some of the activities being carried out in order to bring the mental health services to the desired level.

SPECIAL POLICY ISSUES

The Mentally Ill and the Mentally Retarded

Until the 1970s mentally retarded people were taken care of either by their families or at mental hospitals of the Ministry of Health and Social Services. Several factors, including the recognition of certain etiologic factors such as phenylketonuria, Down's syndrome, and other chromosomal defects; the recognition of certain maternal and infant illnesses resulting in mental retardation; the habilitation and sometimes prevention of mental retardation, if diagnosed at early stages; the recognition of the effects of smoking and drinking during pregnancy; and the recognition of prenatal and postnatal problems have led to distinguishing mental retardation from chronic mental diseases, which in turn makes it possible to use different approaches in their treatment and to provide special training, education, and rehabilitation opportunities for mentally retarded persons. At present, there are different hospitals and institutions for patients who are mentally retarded and for those who are chronically mentally ill. Mental hospitals are no longer places where patients are kept forever, but places where they receive intensive but temporary treatment before they can enter rehabilitation programs that do not isolate them from their families and the community. Mentally retarded people, on the other hand, are sent to other institutions that provide special training and rehabilitation programs. In addition to existing ones, the establishment of four new training centers with a total bed capacity of 1,500 is planned for mentally retarded children aged three to twelve. Despite the acceptance of the fact that mentally retarded people should be treated and trained in different institutions, there are still some mentally retarded people, abandoned by their families, in separate wards of mental hospitals.

The 1982 constitution states that it is the state's duty to care for mentally retarded, handicapped, and parentless children and to help them integrate with the community. The Society for the Protection of Children, which is connected to the Ministry of Health, is responsible for the effective and efficient functioning of the educational and rehabilitation centers for children with mental retardation and physical handicaps. There are two centers for the blind aged eighteen to thirty-five, one of which is in Saray, Ankara, and the other in Emigran, Istanbul. There is a center for spastic children in Istanbul that is functional only during the day and cannot receive inpatients. However, in Saray, Ankara, there is a 288-bed educational and rehabilitation center where 350 mentally retarded children now receive the required educational and rehabilitative services. In Yarmica and Unye there are two centers for mentally retarded children, one with a bed capacity of 30 and the other with a bed capacity of 66; four other educational and rehabilitation centers, each with a bed capacity of 1,500, are planned for those aged three to twelve and will soon be constructed in Istanbul, Mersin, Eskisehir, and Denizli. In the present centers the educational and rehabilitation programs are carried out successfully, and all kinds of special materials are available. In Arifiye, Sakarya, there is a 206-bed institution for handicapped people over the age of eighteen. For the same age group there is a 120-bed institution in Bor and a 50-bed institution in Konya, making a total number of 376 beds.

The total bed capacity of the thirty-two Old People's Homes for people over sixty is 4,121. In these homes 876 men and 756 women pay for their stay, and another 913 men and 342 women stay without paying anything. Chronic mentally ill patients and severely handicapped patients are not accepted in these homes. The expenditures of these homes are paid partly by the patients, partly by the state, and partly by social funds. There is a lack of personnel specially trained to help patients with mental-motor retardation. Although the psychologists, social workers, and child development specialists working there are devoted to their jobs, their training is not sufficient to carry out the education, rehabilitative, and recreational activities as efficiently as is required. Occasionally, women volunteer to help these personnel; therefore, the institutions in provincial cities are luckier than those in smaller cities and town (Ustunoğlu, 1991).

There are many items about psychiatric patients in Turkish criminal and civic laws. For instance, article 355 of the Turkish Civic Law states that people who are unable to take care of themselves due to their psychiatric diseases should be appointed a guardian to stand up for their rights. Article 46 of the Turkish Criminal Law expresses that criminals who cannot consciously control their behaviors due to severe psychiatric diseases are not to be punished. These articles are valid for mentally retarded people as well. Turkish Republic laws, as exemplified by these articles, protect psychiatric patients and mentally retarded persons in just the same way (*Turkish Republic's Constitution*, 1982).

The Mentally Ill and Substance Abuse

Until recently, mentally ill patients and drug and alcohol abusers were treated together in mental hospitals. However, the latest developments in the field of medicine and different treatment techniques have made it essential to treat and rehabilitate them in different departments of the same institutions. At present, in major mental hospitals and in most psychiatric clinics of universities, these two groups of patients are kept in different buildings where different approaches and treatment methods are applied. Alcoholics and drug abusers, for example, are not taken to group therapies for psychiatric patients. They do not want to be considered psychiatric cases and state that they do not have psychiatric diseases.

These two groups of patients are indeed very different and require different treatments. The criminal law, as well, differentiates alcoholics and drug abusers from psychiatric patients. Article 46 frees psychiatric patients from punishment. Article 48 states that alcohol and drug addicts are subject to punishment if they committed a crime. Nevertheless, if their addiction can be proved by psychiatric reports, their sentence can be reduced. When these people do not take drugs or alcohol, they object to being in the same ward or to receiving the same treatment as psychiatric patients and are therefore happy to be differentiated. They receive more support and encouragement from their families and the community than the psychiatric patients do, the reason being their easier adaptation to the society and their return to their former status and jobs after their recovery.

Occasionally a psychiatric patient can also be a drug addict. In such cases it is necessary to decide which is the primary diagnosis. If a chronic psychiatric patient, for example, is taking drugs, the underlying or the present psychotic symptoms should be treated first. Also, however, the reason for a mental disorder may be severe addiction. In such cases (for example, a Korsakoff psychosis), while the dosage of the drugs taken is controlled, antipsychotic treatments are also employed.

The Mentally Disordered Offender

The legal procedure for the psychiatric patients in Turkey functions similarly to those in other countries. Article 46 states that if it is proved that a person was unable to consciously control his or her behaviors due to mental diseases or defects, he or she may be committed and is not subject to punishment. The police court magistrate at the preliminary criminal proceeding, the examining magistrate at the first trial, and the court at the final trial have the right to decide about the protection and treatment of the patient. The duration of the protection and treatment depends on the recovery of the person. However, if the crime the patient has committed requires imprisonment with hard labor, the protection and treatment duration cannot be less than a year. The patient can be dismissed from the institution where he or she received treatment after the report of a health commission. In this report, whether the person should receive further treatment or medical examination and the duration he or she should be periodically examined must be stated, taking the crime he or she has committed, the seriousness of the disease, and the safety and welfare of society into consideration. In periodic examinations, if the person displays symptoms of the disease again, he or she goes through the same treatment and therapies once more until complete recovery. The members of the committees that give such psychiatric reports should fit the qualifications defined by another law. According to the Forensic Medicine Law (no. 6119), only authorized people from forensic medicine institutes and psychiatry and neurology clinics of university and official mental hospitals can be members of psychiatric committees (Cifter, 1990).

When a person commits a crime and the court decides to send him or her to the hospital for psychiatric examinations, a file of documents stating his or her crime and the way the crime was committed is also sent to the hospital, where the person is put through psychiatric tests for six weeks. The results of these tests are then added to the file and returned to the court. If a person has committed a serious crime and is a psychiatric patient, he or she is sentenced to stay in specially guarded sections of mental hospitals and treated for at least one year.

Deinstitutionalization

When deinstitutionalization started and mentally ill patients began to leave the limits of hospitals to receive therapy and treatment without being isolated from their families and the community, there was much criticism. The families had difficulty getting used to sharing part of the responsibility with the mental hospitals. Similarly, the citizens in general felt uneasy to know that these people could now live freely among them. During this critical period authorized officials of mental hospitals and psychiatric clinics tried to convince the society through the mass media that these patients should not be left alone, but would recover sooner if their families and the community joined in their treatment by providing the necessary support. These officials were quite successful in making the public understand that the desocialization of these patients delayed their recovery and made it harder.

There has not been a significant increase in the number of hospitals and other institutions of health during the last few years. For the last five years there has been no addition to the seven mental hospitals and their bed capacity of 6,416. Deinstitutionalization has not resulted in a decrease in the number of beds for psychiatric patients, because for every 100,000 people there were only 1.9 beds and 0.05 ambulatory psychiatric centers for psychiatric patients. These figures make it clear that the number of beds was not sufficient in the first place, and, therefore, the principle of treating the patients outside the hospitals has not reduced the number of beds, but has helped the psychiatric patients who needed urgent treatment to receive this immediately. Likewise, it has made it easier for psychiatrists, who were too few to meet the needs (1.5 psychiatrists for every 100,000 people), to have enough time for their patients. Deinstitutionalization has caused a great change in the type of inpatients and the length of stay. Previously, most of the inpatients were chronic mentally ill cases, but now a majority of the psychiatric beds are occupied by patients who receive short-term therapy and treatment. Moreover, the concept of not necessarily treating these patients in hospitals has led to the establishment of more institutions that can provide ambulatory treatment, making it cheaper and more efficient for the patients. This application also helps the patients to be with their families and the society and enjoy their support. Outpatient clinics have become more effective and functional in comparison to institutions. It is now easier to find places and the required financial resources for such clinics. The funds for maintenance of mental health and for hospitals and the application of deinstitutionalization have improved the conditions for inpatients and allowed the purchase of necessary modern equipment. Some of the money is also spent on emergency psychiatric clinics and dispensaries.

It can be said that the deinstitutionalization process has been successful in Turkey. This approach has enabled the inpatients to receive better treatment, and many psychiatric patients continue their therapies as outpatients without being isolated from their families and the society.

Funding Issues

People who are unable to be productive either because they are chronic mentally ill patients, mentally retarded people, or physically handicapped present problems for their families and the community in which they live. Their long-term and expensive treatment requires a lot of money, and for some psychiatric patients, such as those suffering from schizophrenia and some mentally retarded persons, lifelong treatment is necessary, which, of course, is a great financial burden for the family and the community. Nevertheless, they should have equal rights with healthy people in sharing the national income and in receiving medical treatment, as in other countries. In Turkey, too, efforts are being made to improve the living conditions of physically and psychologically handicapped people. However, only 2.7 percent of the total budget goes to health, and only a small part of this goes to psychiatric services.

Consumer Rights

There are many regulations dealing with the mentally retarded, psychiatric patients, mentally disabled who have committed crimes, and alcohol and drug addicts. Articles 13, 14, and 15 of the Turkish Civic Law state that people who cannot employ reasonable behavior due to factors such as age (too young), psychiatric diseases, mental retardation, drunkenness, and so on are not able to appreciate their civic rights. According to article 8 of the Turkish Civic Law, every citizen has equal civic rights defined by law. However, psychiatric patients, mentally retarded people, children, legally incompetent people, and alcohol and drug addicts who cannot control their behavior cannot practice these rights. Article 89 of the same law announced that only people with reason can have the right to get married. Article 112 states that if the husband or wife was suffering from psychiatric diseases, mental retardation, or addiction at the time of marriage, the marriage is not considered valid. As can be seen, the law has brought some restrictions to the rights of these groups and has therefore saved them from probable material and moral risks. Articles 404, 561, and 562 of the Turkish Criminal Law state that a person who provides drugs for psychiatric patients and drug addicts and who lets the patient or addict under his or her control free will be punished. Furthermore, if this person is the manager of a mental hospital or a physician, the punishment is accompanied by prohibition of the profession. Articles 459 and 471 of the Turkish Criminal Law indicate that "whoever does anything, either accidentally or because of inexperience, that causes a physical or psychological defect to anyone else is to be punished" and "people who employ certain operations to demolish a woman's or a man's fertility, even with the consent of the person are to be punished as well as the person who asks them to actualize the operation" (*Turkish Civic Law*, 1967; *Turkish Criminal Law*, 1986).

Besides these articles of the Turkish Civic Law and the Turkish Criminal Law, there are a number of articles in the Penal Proceedings Law on procedures to be followed. Mentally retarded and psychiatric criminals should be treated in circumstances that are not contrary to human rights and that avoid as much restriction as possible; however, if they have been found guilty by the court, they will be guarded by people appointed by the attorney generalship. It is forbidden to keep them working like slaves, but some of them are given duties in open prisons and are paid according to their efficiency. In Turkey there are closed, semiopen, and open prisons. The Ministry of Justice has the right to send a criminal from a closed prison to a semiopen or open prison if considerable improvement is witnessed in his or her behavior. Nevertheless, a deterioration in behavior might result in a person being sent from an open prison to a semiopen or closed one. In cases like severe illness, fire, earthquakes, floods, and so on, the Ministry of Justice may decide to let the prisoners go home for up to ten days (plus the time required for the journey), and this period of release is excluded from their total sentence. All public institutions must employ a certain number of prisoners who have been cooperative and obedient at least for one-fourth of their sentence. Managers of prisons are responsible for the education, training, and organizing of personal and workshop activities of the prisoners.

Moreover, Article 31 of the Turkish Criminal Law states that people who are sentenced to more than five years of imprisonment with hard labor are deprived of their civic rights, such as electing and being elected, forever, and a sentence of three to five years of imprisonment with hard labor requires deprivation of these civic rights for the same period as the sentence. Prisoners can have access to all mass media, and their communication with the outside is, although controlled, permitted. Letters, magazines, books, and other materials either sent by them or to them are first checked and then delivered.

CONCLUSIONS AND DISCUSSION

In understanding Turkish mental health policy, one should consider the country's population, migration to provincial cities, the level of education, rapid economic improvement and industrialization, ever-increasing health problems, the lack of medical treatment and rehabilitation centers and qualified personnel, the sudden social changes that bring about changes in the concept of the family, the newly arising demands created by the influence of improvements in other countries made publicly known through mass media, and the inability of limited budgets to met all these needs.

The population in Turkey has increased almost fourfold over the past fifty years. The improvement of health services and the decrease in death rate have had an important role in this rise in population. The problems caused by overpopulation have led to birth-control campaigns. The integration of physical and psychological health services has not yet been successful due to the rapid increase in population. The amount of money provided to the Ministry of Health makes up 2.7 percent of the total budget, and psychiatric services receive only a share that is not sufficient to meet the present needs. There has been improvement of preventive medical services, and more outpatient centers are planned. Moreover, practitioners working in about 3,000 health offices all over Turkey can be trained to help with psychiatry also. Likewise, adding psychiatric sections to the provincial health directorates in every town and city is believed to help bring mental health services to individuals. In addition, teachers, religious people, lawyers, policemen, and other professionals are accepted by mental health personnel and are trained to help others regarding these issues. As a result of all these efforts, deinstitutionalization can be said to have been successful in Turkey. Some negative influences of mass media are being overcome by using the mass media themselves to protect the mental health of the community. Both the state and some private companies prepare educational programs to be broadcast on radio and television on mental disorders, their reasons, and avoiding addiction. Establishing a mental health concept, integrating physical and mental health services, decentralizing the psychiatric services and their planning process, providing for the coordination of sectors and disciplines, improving the mental health departments of provincial health directorates and the preventive mental health services, broadening the education and training activities, bringing better service to chronic mentally ill ex-patients and mentally retarded people, and, finally, training the practitioners working in about 3,000 health offices all over the country to bring mental health services as well as physical health services are the main principles of the mental health policy in Turkey.

REFERENCES

Bayat, A. H. (1979), September, October. Kurulusunun 400 yilinda Manisa Durussifasi. *Dirim*, 9(10) 290–296.

Cifter, I. (1990). *Psikiyatri*. Ankara: Gazi University Press.

Coskun, B. (1989, November). *Mental health services in Turkey*. Paper presented at the Working Group on the Development of Mental Health Care in Primary Health Care Settings in the European Region, Lisbon, Portugal.

General directorate of press and information of the Republic of Turkey. (1988). Ankara: Kurtulus Yayincilik.

Gokay, F. K. (1975, September). Turk Tababet-i Ruhiye Tarihi. *Tip Dunyasi*, pp. 368–369.

Ministry of Health. (1989). *Health statistics, yearbook of Turkey*. Ankara: Prime Ministry Printing Office.

Ministry of Health. (1990). *Statistics of ministry of health hospitals (1989)*. Publication Number 539. Ankara: Ministry Printing Office.

Olgac, S. (1967). Turk Medeni Kanunu. *Ismail Akgun Matbaacilik ve Kitapcilik*. Istanbul.

State Institute of Statistics, Prime Ministry, Republic of Turkey. (1989a). *Judicial statistics 1987*. Ankara: State Institute of Statistics Printing Division.

State Institute of Statistics, Prime Ministry, Republic of Turkey. (1989b). *The statistical yearbook of Turkey*. Ankara: State Institute of Statistics Printing Division.

State Institute of Statistics, Prime Ministry, Republic of Turkey. (1990). *Suicide statistics 1989*. Ankara: State Institute of Statistics Printing Division.

State Institute of Statistics, Prime Ministry, Republic of Turkey. (1991). *Statistical pocketbook of Turkey 1990*. Ankara: State Institute of Statistics Printing Division.

Turkish Civic Law. (1967). Ministry of Justice. Ankara: Yaoriaçik Cezaevi Press.

Turkish Criminal Law. (1986). Ministry of Justice Publications Number 71. Ankara: Yaoriaçik Cezaevi Press.

Turkish Republic's Constitution. (1982). Ankara-Istanbul: Alkim Yayinevi.

Ustunoğlu, E. (1991). *Situation analysis of mother and children in Turkey*. Ankara: Government of Turkey–UNICEF Cooperation Program.

19

The United Kingdom

Nigel Goldie and Liz Sayce

OVERVIEW

The United Kingdom in northwest Europe consists of one large island (Britain), a small part of a second island (Northern Ireland), and a number of lesser islands scattered around the coasts. It comprises four constituent countries or regions: England, Wales, Scotland, and Northern Ireland. The total land covered is 94,500 square miles.

The population is 57,200,000, concentrated heavily in urban centers in England. Wales, Scotland, and Northern Ireland are predominantly rural. Women outnumber men: 29,300,000 women as compared to 27,900,000 men. People under eighteen account for 13 million and those over sixty-five for 10.5 million. The elderly population is rising steadily and is expected to peak at 14.5 million in the year 2034 (Office of Population and Census, 1989).

The United Kingdom is historically a multiethnic area and has experienced successive waves of immigration of groups including Normans (eleventh century), Huguenots (sixteenth century), Jewish people (nineteenth century), and Eastern Europeans (twentieth century). In the second half of the twentieth century significant immigration occurred from newly independent ex-British colonies, notably countries in the West Indies and the Indian subcontinent, to fill a postwar labor shortage. Since 1971 immigration policy has become increasingly restrictive and effectively discriminates against black people, although white immigration from British Commonwealth countries such as Australia and Canada continues. Present-day Britain includes approximately 2.5 million people from black and ethnic minority communities, including sizeable Afro-Caribbean, Asian, and Irish groups and smaller populations such as Chinese, Vietnamese, Greek and Turkish Cypriot, Polish, and Somali. Wales, Scotland, Northern Ireland,

and England also have distinct cultural identities. From 1992 free movement of labor will occur within the European Community, of which the United Kingdom is a member, which is likely to add further to the cultural mix.

The United Kingdom's system of government is based largely on parliamentary democracy, with remnants of a system of government through hereditary privilege. The first chamber of the legislature, the House of Commons, is democratically elected. The second chamber, the House of Lords, consists of both hereditary peers and peers appointed, from all political parties and other sources, by the prime minister. The prime minister is democratically elected through her or his political party; yet there is also still a monarchy, albeit with limited powers. Despite pressure for devolution of power to Scotland and Wales and for unification of Northern Ireland with the Republic of Ireland, the government remains unitary rather than federal (although Scotland passes legislation through the Scottish Assembly as well as electing members of Parliament to the House of Commons in Westminster).

The main political parties—the only two to have been in power since 1945—are the Labour Party and the currently ruling Conservative Party, in power since 1979. Other smaller parties include the Liberal Democrats, an emerging Green Party, and a declining Communist Party.

Recent U.K. history can be understood in terms of the country's rapid decline as an imperial power during the twentieth century (previous colonies such as Jamaica and India had almost all achieved independence by the 1960s) and difficulties in competing industrially and economically with powerfully emerging economies with as those of Germany and Japan. Since 1979 the Conservative government has attempted to ward off decline by three main means. First, it has continued to assert a place in world politics and has fostered a spirit of nationalism: for instance, by retaking the Falklands/Malvinas Islands from Argentina in 1983 and taking quick action with the United States against Iraq in 1991. However, it cannot in reality achieve this status alone and is torn as to whether to make primary allegiance with the United States or Europe. Second, it has adopted free-market policies, encouraging individual and business enterprise and presiding over the denationalization of many state-run industries and a reduction in the manufacturing base in favor of the finance and service sectors. Third, it has introduced large-scale reductions in state support for public services such as health, welfare, education, and transport. This was a direct reversal of previous multiparty commitment to the British postwar welfare state, which aimed to improve health and welfare through public services such as the National Health Service.

Welfare cutbacks and the philosophy of individual self-reliance that accompanies them have a major impact on mental health provision. While services provided by publicly funded services in the statutory and not-for-profit independent sector face budgetary cuts, a relatively unregulated for-profit private sector is expanding, and the expectations placed on informal carers, usually women in families, are rising. In addition, major changes have been introduced to the overall funding and organization of the health services, leading to the introduction of an internal market, in which hospitals and other units of service providers compete with one another for contracts from the purchasers of services.

EXTENT OF THE PROBLEM

In the United Kingdom any discussion about the prevalence of mental health problems is complicated by a lively current debate concerning the concepts that explain mental health and the language that best describes people's experience. A growing user movement, made up of people who use or have used mental health services, tends to prefer the term *distress* to *illness* on two grounds. First, a medical conceptualization locates the problem in the individual rather than in the personal or social context. Second, it may predispose professionals to offer medical rather than more popular psychosocial forms of help. Distress tends to be more broadly defined than illness, within a discourse that views health and distress as two points on a continuum.

Nonetheless, research-based statistics tend to use internationally standardized diagnostic categories such as *International Classification of Diseases 10*. Official government statistics concentrate on service usage, which underestimates prevalence. Research conducted in 1980 found that of 1,000 people in the general population, 250 experience some form of psychiatric symptom each year. Of these, 230 visit their general practitioner (GP), who diagnoses an emotional or mental health problem in 140. Seventeen are referred on to a psychiatrist, and 6 are admitted for inpatient psychiatric treatment (Goldberg & Huxley, 1980).

In England the rate of admission to mental hospitals is 417 per 100,000. Since the mid-1950s, when the resident population of psychiatric hospitals peaked at 150,000, there has been a steady decline, to 60,000 in the mid-1980s. Nonetheless, both the admission rate and the discharge rate have risen over the same period, a reflection of the fact that individuals have become more likely to have several short hospital stays than a single long one. In 1986 there were 15,932 admissions to English psychiatric hospitals or units under specific sections of the Mental Health Act (i.e., compulsory admissions). Total admissions in 1986 were 197,251.

High-security "special hospitals" house 1,700 patients, and regional secure units 650. In the prison population it is estimated that 20 percent of the 47,000 people in English prisons are mentally disordered (Gunn, 1991). Approximately 5,000 people commit suicide in the United Kingdom each year. The ratio between male and female suicides is 2:1.

In 1989, 14,785 people were notified as addicts of opiates or cocaine to the Home Office. Real prevalence of drug abuse is doubtless higher. The 1981 British Crime Survey found that one in twenty adults—and one in eight people under twenty—had used an illegal drug. The 1987 General Household Drinking Survey found that 1.5 million people had reported that they were drinking at levels that would seriously damage their health. Again, real prevalence is likely to be higher, since respondents in such surveys notoriously underreport consumption.

There are clear gender and ethnic differences in patterns of usage of mental health services. Women are overrepresented as users of both general practitioner and hospital services. Women are 2.5 times as likely as men to be prescribed minor tranquilizers. For every two men admitted to psychiatric hospitals, three women are admitted. This is only partly explained by higher numbers of older women admitted as a consequence of a longer female life span; indeed, it is also worth noting that among children under fifteen admission rates are higher for boys than girls. For certain diagnoses the disparity is especially great: Twice as many women as men are admitted with depression each year (23,469 women and 11,740 men in 1986 in England).

Data on ethnicity are available only through research studies, as official statistics do not record ethnic origin. Existing research data consistently suggest that certain ethnic groups—notably Afro-Caribbean and Irish people—are overerrepresented in psychiatric hospitals (Littlewood & Lipsedge, 1982). Afro-Caribbean people are also especially likely to be compulsorily detained under the Mental Health Act 1983 and to be treated with major tranquilizers, often at higher dosages than their white counterparts (Davies, 1989). Meanwhile, they are underrepresented in less coercive, community-based facilities (MIND, 1990).

Explanations for the disproportionate presence of women and certain ethnic groups in the British psychiatric system center on three hypotheses:

1. Women may experience higher levels of distress than men, and black people than white, as a result of social and economic discrimination.

2. Women and ethnic minorities may be more easily labelled as deviant as a consequence of cultural stereotyping, racism, and sexism. Black people may be readily seen as highly disturbed or dangerous, rather than as depressive or sensitive, and be treated coercively as a result. Evidence from special hospitals suggests that women can acquire a label of psychopathy on the basis of much less violent or disruptive behavior than men: for instance, through promiscuity, minor delinquency, or other slight infringements of the traditional female role.

3. Help-seeking behavior may vary by gender and ethnicity. Women may be culturally conditioned to express emotional difficulty easily. Afro-Caribbean people may be deterred from seeking help because of a mistrust of statutory authorities, rooted in previous bad experiences with agencies such as the police or child protection bodies. This can prevent early help-seeking, with the result that contact with mental health services occurs only at the point of crisis.

Many commentators draw on a combination of these hypotheses to explain differential service usage.

MENTAL HEALTH HISTORY

In Britain it is possible to trace the origins of mental health services to the fourteenth century. The history of mental health services is both highly developed and complex. In recent years there has been a considerable outpouring of scholarly work on the history of mental health services from historians of medicine and social scientists (Bynum, Porter, & Shepherd, 1985–1988). Some clearly articulated and conflicting perspectives have developed as to not only how the subject should be studied, but also the nature of the subject itself. Stated briefly, the Whiggish tradition adopted by many psychiatric historians of seeing unfolding progress has been severely challenged by a view that contends that the history of madness reflects little in the way of increasing understanding of madness itself. Alongside this debate there have been others regarding the role of institutions of control within an evolving capitalist society, and controversy as to the nature of the experience of being a mental patient in different historical epochs (Miller & Rose, 1986).

In the early medieval period the involvement of religious orders with medicine and healing meant that madness was regarded mainly as a form of possession. Madness subsequently featured as an important element in both literature and drama, for example, the grief-related madness of both Lear and Ophelia in Shakepeare's work. In the eighteenth century madness became a source of income for some medical practitioners (Parry-Jones, 1972). The nineteenth century saw increasing state regulation and the growth of the large public asylum, to be followed in this century by an increasing differentiation of provision as the century progressed.

An event of particular significance in the emergence of psychiatry as a specialism within medicine was the madness of King George III at the turn of the nineteenth century (Hunter & MaCalpine, 1969). The emergence of "alienists" as doctors specializing in the treatment of madness marked the beginning of a controversy that continues to the present day as to the legitimacy of medicine as the dominant profession in this area. Since that time there have been phases when medicine has clearly been ascendant. However, at other times, such as the late nineteenth century, following scandals over false detention, the legal profession and courts usurped the position of medicine. Since the early part of this century medicalization of madness has been consolidated: linguistically through change in nomenclature from asylum to hospital and from lunatic to patient, and in the integration of psychiatry into general hospitals. But recent concerns with the civil liberties of mental patients, following a series of scandals in psychiatric hospitals, have led to an increased role for social workers and the courts to provide checks on the power of medicine.

An important feature of the history of the mental health services in Britain was the growth of the large public asylums, still to be found on the outskirts of large cities. In part their significance lies in the fact that they were the first example of the central state enabling and later requiring local government (the county councils) to make specialist provision. This separation of madness from both the provision for the poor and the physically ill led to the segregation of mental health services that has continued until recent times (Busfield, 1986). It also meant that psychiatry became separated from other developments in both medicine and neurology and also in psychoanalysis and the emerging social sciences. Given the international significance of much of the pioneering work in psychoanalysis undertaken in Britain, foreign observers are often surprised at how little impact this has had on mainstream psychiatry (Ramon, 1985).

The issue of mental retardation or handicap or, as it is increasingly known, learning difficulties also has a complex history. Until the 1970s mental subnormality, as it was then called, was subsumed as a branch of psychiatry, and people with this condition were contained in large isolated institutions. Over the last twenty years the problem has come to be regarded as primarily an educational one, with the aim being to provide social care in the community rather than nursing care in a hospital.

The services for people who abuse alcohol and drugs also have an uneasy relationship with the mental health services. In recent years such people have not generally been treated by mainstream mental health services. Instead, specialist facilities have developed, frequently run by the private and voluntary sector, to meet this need.

POLICY, ORGANIZATION, AND SERVICES IN THE 1980s AND 1990s

Current Policy Developments

In 1983 Parliament passed the Mental Health Act. This was the culmination of a sustained campaign by mental health pressure groups to change the previous laws governing mental health. This act in part reflected parallel concerns in the United States regarding the civil liberties of mental patients, and it changed the procedures for compulsory detention and treatment, as well as introducing other developments such as a Mental Health Act Commission to oversee the treatment of people detained under the act. It is widely recognized that funding is inadequate for services for mental health, for learning difficulties, for older people, and for people with long-term disabilities. One solution has been the separation of what are euphemistically called "priority care" services from the acute services. Thus mental health services may coexist with acute physical illness services, yet be managed and funded separately. The aim of this separate treatment is to ensure that such services do not simply remain the "Cinderella services" that many government reports and inquiries suggested they were in the 1960s and 1970s.

The provision of long-term care and support in the community is increasingly being seen to be the responsibility of local authorities, rather than the National Health Services (NHS). Local authorities already provide social care services for people with mental health problems such as home support, day centers, hostels, and supported housing. These services are funded by a mixture of locally raised taxes, central government grants, and, increasingly, charges for some services. The NHS and Community Care Act 1990 requires Local Authority Social Services Departments to take the lead in both planning for and providing the social care required by a range of client groups, including mental health. Delays over the transfer of central government funding to local government have meant that this policy as of 1992 had not yet been implemented, although in some areas local authorities have developed a variety of services for people with both mental health and learning difficulties. Some of these developments have occurred through partnerships with health authorities, and mechanisms do exist for both joint planning and funding of services.

Current Organization

Mental health services in Britain are an integral part of the NHS. This means that treatment provided by GPs, by outpatient clinics, and to inpatients is provided free, although some charges may be made for medication. The NHS is funded through taxes raised by the central government, and funds are allocated by the Department of Health to Regional Health Authorities. These RHAs in turn allocate funds to District Health Authorities. The size of these districts varies from around 100,000 population for small inner-city districts to around 500,000 for ones covering large rural areas. Each district should be providing a comprehensive range of mental health services. In addition, certain regional specialties are provided, such as forensic psychiatry and medium-secure units, drugs and alcohol services, and specialist units for adolescents.

Alongside the so-called statutory or public sector there exists an increasingly important independent sector. Voluntary agencies provide a considerable range of mental health services. The largest of them, MIND (National Association for Mental Health), has over 230 local associations in England and Wales that offer supported housing, employment projects, advocacy and befriending schemes, counselling, carers' projects, and social support. The private, for-profit sector is expanding rapidly in the United Kingdom. In the provision of nursing homes, residential care, and hospital services, large companies, both British and foreign (for instance, American), appear to be attracting markets most successfully. The for-profit sector is also expanding—but in this case through a multiplicity of small providers—in the field of psychotherapy, which is of limited availability from the NHS. Most available private insurance schemes give limited or even no coverage for psychiatric problems. Concern is therefore widespread in the United Kingdom that the growth of the private sector will lead to a two-tier system: private care for those with high income and a less well resourced service for those without.

Current Services

The service delivery structure can best be described by considering the means of access a person experiencing mental health difficulties might encounter. First, it is important in the British context to point to the existence of an extensive primary health care system provided in the main by general practitioners. Evidence suggests that on average people visit their GPs four times a year. GPs both provide substantial help for people with mental health difficulties (primarily with medication) and act as key gatekeepers to the specialist services. Referral routes include voluntary hospital admission, compulsory admission (requiring agreement by an approved social worker), or referral to a psychiatric outpatient clinic at a general hospital. Possible outcomes of referral include access to further specialists such as a clinical psychologist, a community psychiatric nurse, or referral back to the GP.

There are other routes through which a person may enter the mental health system. The police have powers to remove someone to a place of "safety" for up to thirty-six hours. There is also the possibility of self-referral through accident and emergency services or to such facilities as community mental health centers, where they exist. Social services departments are also a point of access for many people with mental distress.

The largest numerical group of residents in mental hospital beds are older people, in particular those affected by senile dementia. The demographic aging of the population is leading to increasing demands on the services and also on informal carers in the community. Government policy is to develop services to enable such people to live as long as possible in their own homes: community psychiatric nursing, home helps, meals-on-wheels, day centers, and in some instances respite services for carers. The availability of such services is very uneven. Much depends on the priority given to mental health by both health and local authorities. In 1987 one local authority spent £22,000 in total on mental health, while another spent over £2,000,000.

The government is now requiring both health authorities and social services to move to being purchasers of services rather than exclusive providers (Home Office, 1990). The aim is to stimulate the growth of a larger independent sector through the contracting out of service provision to either voluntary (not-for-profit) agencies or to the private sector. Both health and social services are being subjected to major reorganizational change, the outcomes of which are yet uncertain.

Mental Health Personnel and Treatment

Within hospitals, registered mental nurses (RMNs) play an important part in the provision of services, for unlike some other countries there has been a tradition in Britain of having trained specialist nurses for mental patients. One by-product of this development is the growth in recent years of community psychiatric nurses (CPNs). Such nurses are among the most experienced mental health professionals and are increasingly operating as semi-independent practitioners. Many have attachments to GP surgeries and health centers where they not only provide support and drug treatments to the long-term users of services, but also counselling and other means of intervention with people with milder conditions.

An important development within the United Kingdom is the emergence of social work mental health specialists. Until 1971, when generic social work departments were created following the Seebohm Report (1969), the psychiatric social workers had been regarded as an elite within social work. Such staff often have the longest periods of training and occupy a dominant position on social work training courses. After twenty years of generic social work, distinct specializations are now reappearing. This process was galvanized by the Children's Act 1989 and the NHS and Community Care Act 1990. Many social service departments are being reorganized into children's and adults' divisions. Within the adults' divisions a clear mental health specialization is also developing. The prior development of the approved social worker qualification (ASW) in mental health is furthering this process. ASWs are a creation of the 1983 Mental Health Act, for this act gave them distinct powers to service disturbed people. These powers have been granted as a counterweight to the powers of the medical profession.

PUBLIC POLICY PROCESS

In the United Kingdom the broad outline of mental health policy is determined by the central government, which is responsible for passing and amending relevant legislation, setting resource allocations for health and social services, and issuing guidance to local health authorities and social services departments. The guidance specifies the parameters within which they must develop detailed local policies: It states, for instance, that community care is to be offered in preference to institutional care where possible, but it does not specify what level of community services should be developed for a given population size, nor what range of different types of services should be available.

The administration of health and social services is conducted by the Department of Health (England), the Welsh Office, the Scottish Office, and the Northern Ireland Office. While policy in the four countries/regions follows broadly similar patterns established by the UK government, implementation of policy can occur in different ways and at different speeds. This scope for variation has allowed Scotland and Northern Ireland to observe the results of English deinstitutionalization before taking exactly the same steps.

At the local level, district health authorities are responsible to an appointed board, whereas local authorities are elected bodies that form local policy on issues such as education, transport, the environment, and housing. While there are some relevant statutory obligations placed on both health and local authorities—for instance, to provide assessments of people being considered for compulsory detention in hospital by specially trained approved social workers—in general it is up to each authority to decide what percentage of its budget it spends on mental health and what form of mental health services it provides.

Unlike some countries, for example, Italy, where psychiatry has been highly politicized, in Britain mental health policy is the result of a complex interplay between the forces of large institutions such as government and a range of specialist agencies: professional bodies (such as the Royal College of Psychiatrists), voluntary-sector pressure groups like MIND, user groups, relatives' groups, political parties, and trade unions. A brief examination of recent developments in community care policy will demonstrate how this process occurs.

During the 1960s and early 1970s, when welfare expenditure was expanding and reformist optimism was high, debate on mental health policy was dominated by a concern for individual rights and dignity. A movement to replace excessively coercive and degrading institutions with more humane alternatives gained momentum. However, from the late 1970s this progressive consensus began to be undermined by a contraction in welfare spending. Closures of local general hospitals, reduced social security benefits, and cuts to social services budgets were carried out under the banner of increasing self-reliance. The welfare state, in which all parties had previously taken pride, was scorned as a "nanny state" that stifled individual enterprise and dignity.

The defenders of the welfare state decided to support its existing institutions, including psychiatric hospitals. These included trade unions, whose members were concerned about their job prospects if hospitals were to close, and relatives' groups, who were concerned at the increased expectations that could be placed on families by a decline in institutional services. These lobbies were joined by certain professional groups, notably psychiatrists whose preeminent position was threatened by a shift to community mental health services, where working styles tended to be more interdisciplinary.

The result was a set of arguments that tended to stress the need of people with mental health problems to be looked after by medical experts. By the late 1980s these groups formulated the view that psychiatric hospitals should not be closed unless community services were already in place. This was a problematic position in that, with 85 percent of the mental health spending by health and social services combined going to hospital care in 1988, it was necessary to close some hospitals to release funding for community alternatives (Social Services Select Committee, 1990). Nonetheless, it gained some credence with the general public, whose preexisting fears of mentally ill people were being whipped up by the media at the behest of relatives' groups. Numerous scandals concerning the purported dangerousness of ex-patients were covered by the media, and in some cases the public responded by trying to obstruct local projects to rehouse people being discharged.

Both major political parties were influenced by these developments. In the late 1980s the government began to say in policy documents and statements that it was government policy not to close hospitals until community services were in place. The Labour Party made a number of attempts to embarrass the government about the purported failure of community care.

However, there were and are opposing currents. The 1980s witnessed a huge growth in the user movement: patients' councils and self-advocacy and other user groups grew up rapidly and became increasingly nationally coordinated. Users consistently state that they dislike the medically dominated hospital service that has constituted about their only choice to date. Those discharged from hospital to community care have no wish to return, and new users are gaining confidence to demand something better than what was available to their predecessors. In many parts of the United Kingdom users are involved in local planning committees and are influencing the shape of services being planned. They also have allies among some professional groups—for instance, social workers, who tend to a psychosocial rather than medical conception of mental distress and who have a vested interest in challenging the power of psychiatrists in the context of multidisciplinary mental health work. Voluntary agencies such as MIND are also allies, as are organizations concerned with the needs of elderly and physically disabled people, where community care has not come into quite such supposed discredit.

Debate between the two lobbies described was quite polarized in the mid-1980s, but in the late 1980s and early 1990s they began to influence each other. Key trade unions became convinced that community care was preferable to institutions and made their position clear in publications and conferences. Conflict between users' and carers' groups was replaced by some common commitment to providing high-quality community care services. The media began to cover stories about scandals in institutions and about user satisfaction with community services to balance the scandals of community care.

One result was the passing of the NHS and Community Care Act 1990, which should give increasing impetus to community care developments and could signal a shift from medical to more psychosocial provision. In these respects the lobby that wanted to halt deinstitutionalization and community care development appeared, for the moment, to have been silenced. However, one month after the act was passed, the government announced that most of its provisions were to be delayed in effect until after the next general election. This decision had nothing to do with the community care debate, but was motivated by cost-cutting considerations combined with a political reluctance to give local authorities any further power. This is a classic example of the ad hoc, short-term policy making that repeatedly characterizes mental health planning. Mental health is not a high-enough governmental priority to attract proper long-term planning.

The new alliances are fragile because certain issues have been confounded rather than successfully separated out. In 1983 MIND asserted its commitment to community care, but explicitly without using this as an excuse to withdraw services. Yet many people have seen deinstitutionalization as synonymous with service cuts. This confusion has created some improbable alliances between seemingly progressive and conservative forces (for instance, trade unionists and psychiatrists). It had also meant that the only choices available seem to be between a culture of self-reliance that equals neglect, on the one hand, and access to paternalistic services offering no choice or empowerment, on the other. The solution to this impasse being actively pursued by the ever-stronger user movement and its allies is to define self-reliance in collective as well as individual terms and to understand that independence can be combined with using respectful and empowering services. The involvement of users of services in planning groups in health and local authorities and the increasing commitment among health and local authorities to purchasing only those services that users want and need suggest that new alliances, based around the user movement, can succeed in changing the terms of mental health debates and the emphasis of the services.

SPECIAL POLICY ISSUES

The Mentally Ill and the Mentally Retarded

Policies of deinstitutionalization and community care apply equally in both the field of mental health and the field of learning difficulties (a recent substitute for the term *mental handicap*, adopted in response to the wishes of the people affected, who find *learning difficulties* less stigmatizing). In practice, policy has proceeded further for people with learning difficulties: Slightly more large mental handicap than mental illness hospitals have closed, and in England in 1986 there were 27,000 residents in mental handicap hospitals, as compared to 60,000 in mental illness hospitals. Community facilities for people with learning difficulties are also more advanced.

People with learning difficulties and their advocates were more successful than people with mental health problems in arguing against the need for institutional care provided by experts, especially medical experts. Principles of normalization, adopted from the original American work by Wolfensberger, were adopted as consensual values by professionals in the learning difficulties field by the early 1980s. Following the influential publication of the King's Fund's *An Ordinary Life* in 1980, it was virtually unanimously agreed the people with learning difficulties could lead socially valued lives in ordinary community facilities, with specialist support provided where necessary by social and educational services rather than by the medical establishment. It followed logically that services should be provided in the community, not in hospital, and that budgets should be held by social services departments rather than health authorities.

In the mental health field this shift is still a matter of great controversy, with a powerful medical lobby continuing to argue the need for a medical response to "illness" and for health authority budgetary control. Although the principles of normalization have been translated from the learning difficulties field to the mental health field, for instance, through "PASS" normalization workshops for professionals, there is no consensus on the values of normalization, notably because some commentators see adherence to principles of community integration as an avoidance of the reality of mental illness and disturbance (Clifford, 1988).

Organizations representing the two user groups have on occasion collaborated on common concerns relating to community care—for instance, to lobby on relevant legislation—but there has been no special allegiance that exceeds working relationships across the whole disability field. Nor, however, have relationships been characterized by major competitiveness or hostility. Although people with mental distress can wish to distance themselves from people thought "unintelligent," and conversely, people with learning difficulties can wish to distance themselves from the stereotypes of dangerousness and disturbance that surround mental illness, these tendencies do not erupt into open conflict.

Mental health services and learning difficulties services are generally organized separately; and in theory, people with learning difficulties are not placed in mental illness hospitals unless they have a dual diagnosis. In practice, certain long-stay psychiatric institutions, especially the high-security "special hospitals," do contain a number of people with learning difficulties, usually placed there many years previously when practice differed from the current pattern.

There is a lack of comprehensive evidence on the number of people who have both a mental health problem and learning difficulties in the United Kingdom. Corbett (1979) found that 46 percent of people with learning difficulties in the Camberwell Health District also had psychiatric problems, if one included "behavior problems" (present in a quarter of this group). Government policy tends to advocate the use of generic psychiatric facilities for people with a "dual diagnosis" (Jay, 1979), although where specialist services do exist in the psychiatry of mental handicap, it is claimed that they can prevent people from slipping between two services (which may each attempt to refer to the other). Specialist skills are also sometimes necessary to reach a psychiatric diagnosis of people who are severely handicapped (Bouras et al., 1988). The availability of such specialist services, comparable to the multidisciplinary community-based approach described by Bouras et al. (1988), is, however, patchy.

The Mentally Ill and Substance Abuse

Issues of substance abuse sit uneasily within any consideration of mental health services. While psychiatry has played a part in the treatment of people who abuse drugs and alcohol, there is an ongoing controversy as to how appropriate medical models of treatment are for these conditions. What is not in doubt, though, is the scale of the problem and the increasing demands that people who abuse drugs and alcohol place upon health and social services and the numerous voluntary agencies providing services in this area. *General Household Drinking Survey* (1987) conducted by the Office of Population and Census estimated that for a population of 250,000 there will be 4,500 men and 2,500 women experiencing two or more physical or psychological symptoms of dependence on alcohol and a further 9,850 men and 5,000 women who will have thought that they should reduce their consumption. Estimates of the extent of drug abuse are even harder to establish.

The government's main approach to tackling these problems is to promote special drug prevention initiatives in inner-city areas, while looking to the voluntary sector to be the main provider of services. New grants have been made available for the development of services under the overall coordination of local authorities, while policy making for future drug and alcohol services will be developed within community care plans that all social service and health authorities are now required to produce.

The Mentally Disordered Offender

The Mental Health Act 1983 lays out a number of ways in which a person's mental health status can be taken into account within criminal justice procedures. First, at the point of trial a court may decide to remand someone to hospital rather than to prison. The remand may be for purposes of a psychiatric report or for treatment. Second, at the point of sentencing the court may, as an alternative to a prison sentence, make a hospital order, with or without restriction on subsequent discharge (restriction being designed to prevent the public from serious harm), or a probation order with a condition of psychiatric treatment. Third, after a person is imprisoned, he or she may be transferred to hospital, again with or without restrictions being placed on subsequent discharge.

It is also possible for a person to be found unfit to plead under the Criminal Procedure (Insanity) Act 1964, in which case the judge is obliged to make a hospital order with restrictions on discharge, without limit of time. This obligation has led to notorious cases such as that of Glen Pearson, described as a deaf-mute of limited intelligence, who in 1986 appeared in court charged with stealing three light bulbs and a five-pound note, but was found unfit to plead. He was sent to special hospital, via prison, where he could have stayed indefinitely under a hospital order with no limit of time. In fact, due to the efforts of his lawyer he was released after his case came before a Mental Health Review Tribunal (see the section on "Consumer Rights" for explanation of tribunals).

In 1991 a new act was introduced that allows courts to decide if a person who was unfit to plead had committed an offense, and subsequently to decide between a variety of options, including a complete discharge where appropriate. Finally, a person charged with murder can claim diminished responsibility on grounds of abnormality of mind, in which case the charge of murder may be reduced to the lesser charge of manslaughter.

Despite the provisions of the Mental Health Act 1983, concern has risen steeply in the late 1980s and early 1990s about the fate of mentally disordered offenders. It is estimated that 20 percent of the prison population is mentally disturbed (Gunn, 1991). Moreover, the proportion appears to be rising, as 38 percent more prisoners were referred to a psychiatrist in 1989 than in 1988. A high suicide rate in prison and a major riot at the Strangeways prison fueled further concern, which led to two official inquiries, both of which reported in 1990 (Tumin, 1990; Woolf, 1991). One result of escalating concern has been a Home Office Circular, *Provision for Mentally Disordered Offenders*, circulated to courts, the police, probation services, and prison medical services in 1990. This encourages police to consider whether charging is necessary and to liaise with health and social services at the point of arrest; it encourages courts to consider making noncustodial disposals of cases; and it also asks the probation service to act as part of a network of agencies providing accommodation, care, and treatment in the community for offenders.

While this policy should in theory divert mentally disordered offenders out of the prison service, the problem is that resource constraints mean that there are few alternative facilities to which to divert them. In England there are only 650 places in regional secure units (these are reasonably local, health service–run secure facilities). Although there are 1,700 places in the high-security special hospitals, these facilities are huge, remote, and arguably so severe and institutional that they are hardly more appropriate than prison. Moreover, the Special Hospital Services Authority that runs them admits that the majority of people in them do not need to be there: It is only a lack of community alternatives that is preventing them moving on. Ordinary psychiatric hospitals, which between them have about 2,000 locked or partially locked wards as well as numerous nonsecure places, are also often filled with people who cannot move into the community because of a lack of appropriate supported facilities. The result is that hospitals often will not take people from prison or secure hospital provision, and mentally disordered people continue to accumulate in the prison system.

The same resource problem affects the likelihood of diversion at an early stage after the offense has been committed. In a handful of areas in the United Kingdom—for instance, Peterborough and two areas of London—special schemes are in place to assist the courts in disposing effectively of cases involving mentally disordered offenders. In these schemes either a psychiatrist or a special advisory panel is present in court to help identify people with mental disorders and to advise on noncustodial options for disposal. Results in these areas seem promising; but in most parts of the country such systems are not in place, for reasons of resource constraints.

Diversion from custody will only operate effectively in the United Kingdom when adequate resources are made available. Until then, large numbers of mentally disordered offenders will continue to be held in prisons, where the health and social care available to them falls far below the standards available in the hospital system. The prison medical service is run quite separately from the mainstream health service and is not covered by the Code of Practice covering psychiatric patients in the health service. This means a generally lower quality of staffing, environment, and operational practices.

At the end of 1990 the government announced a review of the health and social services for mentally disordered offenders. It remains to be seen whether this further evidence of official attention to the problems in this sphere will result in improved practice or only in further policy statements that are not backed by the resources needed to implement them.

Deinstitutionalization

As in many other countries, the policy of closing large isolated mental hospitals is a controversial one in the United Kingdom. The debate has become more sharply focused in recent years, although the decline of these institutions began in the 1950s. The high point of mental hospitalization was 1954, when there were 150,000 beds in specialist mental hospitals. There are differing explanations as to the reasons for the subsequent decline of beds to the point where in the mid-1980s there were 60,000. Hospital decline preceded the introduction of psychotropic medication, despite the claim to the contrary (Warner, 1985). Humanitarian values and the demand for labor in the economy provided opportunities for people with marginal skills to exist outside the hospital. The shortage of labor pulled people into the economy who would have otherwise remained unemployed. An important factor in the debate over the role of large hospitals was the emergence of the therapeutic community movement in the 1950s (Jones, 1952, 1968). Much of the pioneering work of this movement occurred in Britain, and while it has ceased to have much impact on mental hospitals themselves, it continues to flourish in smaller units and various community-based services (Bloor, McKeganey, & Fonkert, 1988).

In 1962 the government stated its intention of developing services for acute mental patients in the emerging district general hospitals, with the vague hope that local authorities and health authorities would develop other services for those with long-term needs. Over the subsequent twenty years an increasing diversity of service provision has developed. However, as a government Audit Commission report in 1986 pointed out, the rate of development of new services has nowhere near matched the decline of provision in the large mental hospitals. Further, there is a great problem of uneven development of services, for much has depended on the commitment of local politicians, health and social service managers, mental health professionals, and, not least, an active local voluntary sector.

In an earlier section the range of residential provision that has been provided was outlined. In addition, there is the major question of how adequate the daytime (and evening and weekend) provision has been. Again it is possible to point to a diversity of developments over the last twenty to thirty years, including sheltered employment schemes, day hospitals and day centers, and various forms of drop-in and club-type arrangements. As with all other services, great variability exists across the country, with considerable innovation occurring in some places, where there are well-developed schemes catering for the specialist needs of ethnic minorities, women, and people with particular mental health diagnoses. In particular, the voluntary sector has often been the only provider of services that have actively encouraged the involvement of users in the running and provision of their own services. In other parts of the country only minimal provision exists.

In addition to the provision of places for long-term users to go to, there is the issue of developing services that go to them and that support them in their often-isolated housing. Previous mention has been made of the developing role of community psychiatric nurses, who often play a key role in visiting people in their homes. In addition, in several parts of the country schemes are emerging that employ generic mental health workers undertaking the task of providing practical and continuing support to people with long-term needs. While being generic across disciplines, this role is a specialist one insofar as it represents commitment to working with a particular client group. This reflects a change occurring in British social services departments, where there are signs of increasing specialization, and a move away from the officially espoused genericism that has dominated the provision of social work for the last twenty years, to the detriment of such groups as the mentally distressed.

As in many other countries, one of the most controversial issues surrounding the closure of mental hospitals has been the apparent increase in the numbers of homeless people requiring mental health services. London and other major cities have witnessed a dramatic increase in the numbers of people sleeping rough in cardboard cities and under railway arches. In many respects the problem is not one of lack of specialist provision, but one of inadequate levels of housing provision and income support for people who have experienced mental health problems.

Similarly, as noted earlier, there has been a significant increase in the numbers of mentally disturbed people detained in prison. The causes for both these phenomena go well beyond that of the closure of hospital beds, and the answer would not appear to be one of retaining such inappropriate provision. What is evident, however, is that the levels of government funding to replace old facilities and develop new facilities for all users of mental health services have been and continue to be inadequate.

The government has provided some special funding for the reprovision of mental hospital beds out of its capital allocation grants to Regional Health Authorities and through various loan schemes. The responsibility for funding such closures lies primarily with RHAs, who have been banking on the profits to be realized from the sale of mental hospital land and sites to pay for new developments. Again, what this points to is considerable inequity across the country, depending on where the old hospitals were sited. For the districts that have to provide services, there has also been a major problem of how to cope with the double running costs of both an existing hospital, large and costly to maintain and run, and new services. One method developed in some parts of the country to provide funding for new services has been to transfer a dowry payment with each long-term patient leaving hospital. This has often amounted to the equivalent sum it costs to keep that person in hospital. It has not taken long for the discovery to be made that such sums are woefully inadequate to cover the costs of care in the community. A recent initiative by the central government is that of providing a mental illness grant to local authorities to provide social care services to people with long-term mental health needs. The total sum of money available in 1991/92 across the whole country was only £30 million, of which local authorities had to provide one-third.

Funding Issues

To focus attention on deinstitutionalization is to suggest that mental health services are increasingly provided outside of hospitals. This is certainly the case with regard to the move away from specialist mental hospitals; however, the pattern of expenditure on mental health services still points to the dominance of inpatient expenditure. Indeed, what is striking, in light of the earlier discussion on the move to community care, is how little the pattern of expenditure has changed in almost ten years. Total hospital, community health, and personal social services expenditure in 1987/88 was £2,354.2 million, which represents in real terms an increase of 13 percent from 1978/79.

It was noted previously how mental health services are provided free through the NHS. Over the last ten years the Conservative government has sought to encourage the growth of private health insurance schemes and private hospitals. Such developments, while significant for general medical services, have had negligible impact on the mental health services. Private health insurance schemes provide only limited coverage for mental ill health, while the only significant growth in facilities has been for the treatment of alcohol and drug users. The private sector, though, continues to flourish with regard to the provision of psychotherapy and other therapies dealing with problems in relationships and with living generally. A multiplicity of voluntary agencies, often subsidized by the statutory sector, provide counselling and therapeutic support. Access to and use of such services tend to be dominated by the middle classes.

Consumer Rights

Both the 1959 Mental Health Act and the 1983 Mental Health Act introduced safeguards for the rights of consumers. The 1959 act, in changing the basis of deciding whether someone should be compulsorily detained from a judicial to an administrative process, rendered most admissions to hospital voluntary rather than compulsory. The 1983 act strengthened consumer rights, for instance, by placing an obligation on the newly created approved social workers to assess opportunities for alternatives to inpatient care when compulsory admission is under consideration.

Under the 1983 act compulsorily detained patients have periodic access to a Mental Health Review Tribunal, made up of legal, medical, and lay members, which is empowered to discharge the patient and is obliged to do so if certain statutory requirements are met. The act also introduced a Mental Health Act Commission, whose functions include review of the exercise of the act's compulsory powers. Further safeguards in the 1983 act include provisions on "consent to treatment" for people compulsorily detained. The following safeguards apply to people detained under specified sections of the Mental Health Act 1983: In effect, the most commonly used sections are for assessment and treatment, other than detention for seventy-two hours or less. For potentially highly damaging treatments, notably psychosurgery, it is required both that the patient consent and that a second medical opinion agree. For a second category of treatment—electroconvulsive therapy, and medication after three months—treatment cannot be given unless either consent or a second opinion is obtained.

These protections have not been sufficient to prevent continuing abuse of rights, and there have been frequent reports since the passage of the act of such abuse. Sometimes this is because of failure to comply with the law. For example, the MIND/Roehampton Institute (1990) survey of over 500 people who had used psychiatric services found that of those prescribed major tranquilizers, 73 percent had not been asked for their consent. Considering that most of these people were voluntary patients, they should have been informed of the treatments proposed and asked for their consent under common law. Sometimes the problem concerns the limits inherent in what the law prescribes.

In 1989 the government eventually responded to continuing evidence of scandals, inadequate protections, and insufficient guidance on the details of implementing the law by issuing the Code of Practice relating to the Mental Health Act 1983. This contains many useful provisions, including that physical restraint should be used as little as possible and only as a last resort; that consent for treatment should always be sought, even if—as in the case of medication given in the first three months following compulsory admission—it is legally possible for the responsible medical officer to administer treatment without consent; that all patients should be given as much information as possible about their care and treatment throughout their stay in hospital; and that decisions on compulsory admission should take account of the individual's cultural background.

CONCLUSIONS AND DISCUSSION

The development of mental health services in the United Kingdom has had an impact beyond the shores of the islands that constitute this country. There have been many pioneering developments that have been followed elsewhere in the world. In the early nineteenth century there was the rise of moral treatment and the optimism that led to the growth of asylums. There was the early emergence of a specialist branch of medicine concerned with madness, as well as legislation requiring the provision of asylums by public authorities. Later in the century concerns over the legal rights of detained patients led to measures to strengthen their civil rights. This century has seen many influential developments. The therapeutic community movement of the 1950s and 1960s started in the United Kingdom, and the country has been in the forefront of the moves to close mental hospitals and move to community-based services.

There has, of course, been an underside to these achievements. As this chapter has pointed out, there continue to be major concerns over the adequacy of service provision; over the reality of legal rights for mental patients; over the excessive use of psychotropic medication; and over the continuing reluctance of the general public to be accepting of mental distress. Some mental hospitals have been closed, but large numbers remain, although with greatly diminished numbers of patients. The development of facilities in the community remains very uneven. There are exemplary schemes in some local areas, with negligible provision in others. Mental health and learning difficulties continue to be "Cinderella" services in terms of the amount of funding they receive compared with other service areas. The quality of life of the many thousands of people with long-term mental health difficulties living in the community continues to be a major cause for concern.

This chapter has also highlighted many of the continuing concerns over the legal rights of mental patients, and in particular the plight of those people with mental health needs incarcerated in prisons. Fortunately, this matter is now receiving the attention of the government, and new initiatives are being developed to divert people with mental health difficulties away from the courts.

This chapter has also given attention to people with learning difficulties. In some respects this area of service provision is no longer subsumed under mental health in the United Kingdom. Learning difficulties are now largely regarded as social and educational concerns with only marginal medical involvement. A major problem remains, though, the adequacy of provision, especially all the backup care that carers require if they are to support a person with learning difficulties in their own home.

In conclusion, the mental health services in the United Kingdom are still very uneven in terms of their quality and quantity. Indeed, they contain many contradictions and conflicts over their provision. Given the purpose for which they exist, this is neither surprising nor undesirable.

REFERENCES

Audit Commission. (1986). *Making a reality of community care*. London: HMSO.

Bloor, M., McKeganey, N., & Fonkert, D. (1988). *One foot in Eden*. London: Routledge.

Bouras, N., et al. (1988). *Mental handicap and mental health: A community service*. London: NUPRD.

British crime survey. (1981). Home Office. London: HMSO.

Busfield, J. (1986). *Managing madness*. London: Hutchinson.

Bynum, W. F., Porter, R., & Shepherd, M. (1985–1988). *Anatomy of madness* (3 Vols.). London: Tavistock.

Clifford, P. (1988). *Why I haven't joined the normies: Some doubts about normalisation*. London: NUPRD.

Davies, R. (1989). *Afro-Caribbean people and the psychiatric system*. London: MIND.

General Household Drinking Survey. (1987). Office of Population and Census. London: HMSO.

Goldberg, D., & Huxley, P. (1980). *Mental illness in the community*. London: Tavistock.

Gunn, J. (1991). *Mentally disordered offenders*. Home Office. London: HMSO.

Home Office. (1990). *Provision for mentally disordered offenders*. London: HMSO.

Jay, J. (1979). *Report of inquiry into mental handicap nursing and care*. Department of Health and Social Security. London: HMSO.

Jones, K. (1972). *The history of mental health services*. London: Routledge & Kegan Paul.

Jones, K. (1989). *Experiences in mental health: Community care and social policy*. London: Tavistock.

Jones, M. (1952). *Social psychiatry*. London: Tavistock.

Jones, M. (1968). *Beyond the therapeutic community*. New Haven: Yale University Press.

King's Fund. (1980). *An Ordinary life*. London: King's Fund.

Littlewood, R., & Lipsedge. (1982). *Aliens and alienists*. London: Penguin.

Macalpine, R., & Hunter, I. (1969). *George III and the mad-business*. London: Penguin.

Martin, J. P. (1984). *Hospitals in trouble*. London: Blackwell.

Miller, P., & Rose, N. (1986). *The power of psychiatry*. Oxford: Polity Press.

MIND/Roehampton Institute. (1990). *People first: Special report*. London: Author.

National Health Service and Community Care Act. (1990). London: HMSO.

Office of Population and Census (OPCS). (1989). London: Author.

Parry-Jones, W. L. (1972). *The trade in lunacy*. London: Routledge & Kegan Paul.

Ramon, S. (1985). *Psychiatry in Britain*. Beckenham: Croom Helm.

Social Services Select Committee. (1990). *Seventh report: Community care: Quality*. London: HMSO.

Tumin, M. (1990). *Suicide and self harm in prison service establishments in England and Wales*. Her Majesty's Chief Inspector of Prisons for England and Wales. London: HMSO.

Unsworth, C. (1987). *The politics of mental health legislation*. Oxford: Clarendon Press.

Warner, R. (1985). *Recovery from schizophrenia: Psychiatry and Political Economy*. London: Routledge & Kegan Paul.

Woolf, J. (1991). *Prison disturbances, April 1990: Report of an inquiry by the Rt. Hon. Lord Justice Woolf (Parts 1 & 2) and his Honour Judge Stephen Tumin (Part 2)* London: HMSO.

20

The United States

Christopher G. Hudson

OVERVIEW

Mental health policy in the United States has been an arduous and ambivalent struggle of Americans to care for those who experience the anguish of mental illness. It has been marked by periods of idealistic policy development aimed at the widespread prevention and cure of mental illness, as well as by periodic retreats to containment, control, and avoidance of mutual responsibility.

The ambivalence of the U.S. response has been complicated by several key political and socioeconomic features of this nation. Its population of 250 million and its extensive ethnic and racial heterogeneity pose formidable barriers for independent-minded Americans in assuming responsibility for those in need. The ideal that the United States should be a "melting pot" of diverse immigrant groups has taxed Americans' tolerance for diversity, especially when those who are different suffer the pain and stigma of psychosis. The United States also is struggling to address itself to the special problems of two key subpopulations. The "baby-boom" generation, a large population cohort that came about as a result of GIs returning from World War II, has been progressing through the stages of the life cycle, highlighting and often experiencing unique mental health problems. Most recently, this generation has contributed to a swelling of the ranks of "young chronics," often-hostile, hard-to-engage, and severely mentally ill persons (Bachrach, 1982, p. 189). In addition, the growing population of older adults, as in many industrialized nations, has also posed an ongoing challenge in adapting services to the multiple economic, health, and psychosocial problems of this population.

Mental health policy making in the United States has been further complicated by the country's political structure. Its Constitution and subsequent legal precedents have been vague as to which levels of government are to assume various social welfare functions. Thus the federal government, with its independent judicial, legislative, and executive branches, has alternatively competed and cooperated with fifty state governments, each with their three branches of government, as well as about thirty-nine thousand other country, municipal, and town governments. This system has resulted in the provision of some demanded services, but it has too often meant the avoidance of responsibility for those groups who are in need and who are inadequately represented.

Two critical issues form the backdrop to current efforts in mental health policy development in the United States. Significant fiscal cutbacks at both the federal and state levels have been brought about in recent years by the nation's extensive commitments, especially the enormous expenditures associated with the Cold War and the resulting military buildup of the 1980s. These are now forcing the downsizing of many of the nation's public mental health programs. Skyrocketing health care costs have also contributed to the diminishing availability of resources for public mental health.

For a number of years a central theme in health and mental health policy development has been cost containment. Numerous devices have been experimented with, most recently the concept of managed care. The continuing struggle to contain the costs of mental health care has been both a cause and consequence of the trend toward the privatized delivery of mental health services, a trend that has also been reinforced through the efforts of the recent Reagan administration to decentralize social welfare and mental health policy. Finally, the consumer rights movement has fueled a growing advocacy movement on the part of mental health patients, their families, and providers. These groups have often allied themselves with cost-conscious state governments to target services to the seriously and long-term mentally ill.

EXTENT OF THE PROBLEM

Almost one-fifth (18.7 percent) or 29.4 million adult Americans have a diagnosable mental illness at some point during a given six-month period (National Institute of Mental Health [NIMH], 1986, p. 4). About one-third (28.9 percent to 38.0 percent) have been mentally ill sometime during their life (Robins et al., 1984, p. 952). These estimates are based on the definitions of mental illness contained in the American Psychiatric Association's *Diagnostic and Statistical Manual of Mental Disorders* (1987) and the methodologies employed in the Epidemiological Catchment Area (ECA) surveys conducted during the 1980s (Regier et al., 1984, pp. 934–941). These estimates were obtained through community interviews with 11,520 randomly selected persons. They exclude children, as well as most personality diagnoses other than antisocial personality disorder (Regier et al., 1984, pp. 934–941).

The most prevalent conditions in the United States are anxiety and somatoform disorders, which include phobias, panic disorders, and obsessive-compulsive disorders. These are experienced by 8.3 percent of all adults. The next most prevalent problems are affective disorders, which include depression and manic episodes, representing 6 percent of the adult population. Another critical problem is substance abuse, which includes the 5 percent of adults who have problems with either alcohol abuse or dependence and the 2 percent who have difficulties with drug abuse or dependence. Finally, almost one out of every hundred adults (0.9 percent) suffer from the devastating effects of schizophrenia (NIMH, 1986, p. 4).

The prevalence of the various mental illnesses varies significantly in the United States when personal characteristics such as sex, age, social class, and urban-rural status are considered. The most prevalent mental health problems of men are alcohol abuse and dependence, with phobias and drug abuse ranking second and third. For men over sixty-five severe cognitive impairment is the most pervasive problem. For women of all ages phobias are the most common difficulty, with major depression and dysthymia (neurotic depression) ranking second and third. However, the second most common problem of women in the eighteen to twenty-four age range is drug abuse, and in the group over sixty-five it is severe cognitive impairment (NIMH, 1986, p. 5). The ECA studies also revealed that urban Americans are more at risk of mental illness, as these people experience a lifetime prevalence rate of 32.2 percent, compared with 27.5 percent of those who live in small towns and rural areas (Robins et al., 1984, p. 957). A wide range of studies in recent years have revealed a consistently negative association between rates of virtually every type of mental illness, including the organically based psychoses, and social class. There is evidence to suggest that the difference in these rates may be more acute in urban than in rural areas (Hudson, 1988).

Thus, it is evident that the various forms of mental illness constitute one of the more pervasive health problems American face. This is consistent with the reported statistic that about one-quarter (25 percent) of all hospital inpatient days in the United States are for diagnosed mental disorders, even though this figure had fallen from 50 percent during the preceding thirty-five years (Kiesler & Sibulkin, 1987, p. 272).

MENTAL HEALTH HISTORY

During the colonial period of American history responsibility for the mentally ill, often referred to as the ''distracted,'' was assumed by the family and community, specifically by the local parish. Along with paupers and other indigent and disabled citizens, the mentally ill were provided for mainly through the Elizabethan poor relief laws. Theological theories of mental illness predominated, especially those that emphasized demonic possession. However, there was a gradual shift during this period to naturalistic explanations, in part due to the work of Philippe Pinel in France (Miller, 1991, pp. 19–39).

In the late eighteenth century there was also a movement away from the mere detention of the mentally ill and an emerging interest in their cure. The first general hospital was founded in Philadelphia, Pennsylvania, the services of which included care for the mentally ill. Shortly after this, the first hospital designed exclusively for the insane was established in Williamsburg, Virginia, in 1776 (Miller, 1991).

During the 1820s and 1830s the states began establishing mental hospitals, hoping to recreate the earlier successes of Pinel and William Tuke. The philosophy of "moral treatment" permeated these early institutions and brought with it a new optimism concerning the elimination of mental illness. A "cult of curability" developed in which superintendents of these early institutions sometimes claimed cure rates as high as 90 percent.

The early optimism inherent in the era of moral treatment, as well as the slow growth of the state mental hospital system, formed the backdrop to Dorothea Dix's efforts on behalf of the mentally ill during the middle of the nineteenth century. Dix, a frail, retired schoolteacher in her forties, was so moved by the plight of the mentally ill that she undertook one of the most dynamic campaigns involving extensive investigation and legislative advocacy in the history of American mental health. Her work led to the dramatic expansion in the system of state mental hospitals and almost succeeded in creating a federal program involving land grants to the states for mental hospitals.

During the last half of the nineteenth century the state hospital system continued to expand in spite of periodic efforts to contain the rising patient rolls and associated costs. These were due to a confluence of the forces of rapid urbanization, industrialization, and immigration from Europe. Patient populations were also swelled by those suffering various organically based dementias that are symptomatic of syphilis and what is now recognized as Alzheimer's disease. There was a lack of more appropriate long-term care settings for these people. Because of this expansion, the state insane asylums quickly became extremely crowded, defeating the earlier optimism that a sufficiently benign environment would be provided to enable the cures that were not happening.

The next major policy development occurred in the early years of the twentieth century. Clifford Beers, a young businessman who attempted suicide and was later hospitalized in mental institutions for several years, published in 1908 the classic *A Mind That Found Itself*. This initiated the mental hygiene movement, foreshadowing the recent era of community mental health. Beers, with the help of Adolf Meyer and William James, organized the National Committee for Mental Hygiene and at first advocated the reform of state mental hospitals. This goal, however, was eventually abandoned in favor of the establishment of community mental hygiene clinics. The movement was associated with not only the creation of some of the first psychopathic hospitals, but many of the psychiatric outpatient and child guidance clinics that are now considered traditional (see Grob, 1983).

The preoccupation of Americans with the two world wars and the Great Depression of the 1930s contributed to the further neglect of patients in state hospitals. However, during each of these wars, many draftees were rejected from wartime service due to various mental illnesses, revealing to the general public the extensiveness of mental illness in the community. This newfound concern enabled the passage of the National Mental Health Act of 1946 (Pub. L. 79-487). This landmark legislation gave the federal government some nominal responsibility in overseeing the nation's mental health systems. It established the National Institute of Mental Health (NIMH) to conduct research, provide for training of mental health professionals, and, in very limited cases, fund some demonstration programs (see Morrissey & Goldman, 1986).

Several further developments during the late 1940s and 1950s set the stage for the community mental health and deinstitutionalization movement. There were numerous exposés of the atrocious conditions of the state mental hospitals, most noteworthy of which were those of Albert Deutsche, who characterized these institutions as "snake pits" (1948). Other influential works focused on the pernicious effects of psychiatric labelling as well as the disabling consequences of custodialism. During the early 1950s the first psychotropic medications were introduced into the country. The costs of upgrading mental hospitals, new philosophies of mental health care, and the availability of psychotropic medications all contributed to the decline in resident populations in public mental hospitals that began in 1955. During that same year President Eisenhower established the Joint Commission on Mental Illness and Health, which articulated the need for a national community mental health program.

Once the study commission produced its final report, *Action for Mental Health* (1961), President Kennedy introduced and Congress later enacted the Community Mental Health Centers Act of 1963 (Pub. L. 88-164). The intent of this act was for the federal government to provide seed money to establish a system of 1,500 private, multiservice community mental health centers (CMHCs) blanketing the nation, each responsible for a catchment area of 75,000 to 200,000 persons. Each of these centers initially was mandated to provide outpatient, day-program, inpatient, emergency, and consultation and education services that were adapted to the particular needs of its community. Although part of the plan called for these centers to follow up on the newly discharged patients from state mental hospitals, the other part, which found considerably more support from professional staff, involved a philosophy emphasizing primary prevention and early intervention. Unfortunately, these centers failed to follow up on most of the patients discharged from the state hospitals during the era of deinstitutionalization, a topic to be explored in a later section of this chapter.

The history of mental health policy in the United States has been marked by several recurrent themes. Too often, one level of government has attempted to evade responsibility for the seriously mentally ill by passing it along to other levels. There have been periodic fluctuations in the conception of mental illness, alternating between one focusing on the psychoses and their biological and genetic features to one concerned with a broad range of problems in living and their psychosocial dimensions. This cyclic pattern may be in part cause, and in part consequence, of changes in the level of public tolerance for the mentally ill, as well as the intensity of economic insecurities weighing on the collective consciousness (see Rochefort, 1988). Whichever mood has predominated, the preferred mix of institutional and community services has no doubt been significantly affected. At present the expansionary phase of the recent community mental health movement has reached its apex, and most efforts now involve the solution of the many unanticipated side effects of deinstitutionalization. These include service system fragmentation, homelessness, and criminalization of the mentally ill, as well as the preservation of significant gains already made.

POLICY, ORGANIZATION, AND SERVICES IN THE 1980s AND 1990s

Current Policy Developments

The central transition in the 1980s in U.S. mental health policy was that from a federally driven mental health system to state-driven systems. The passage of the Mental Health Systems Act of 1980s promised the states an enhanced role in planning mental health services and distributing mental health dollars if specific conditions were met. The act, however, was short-lived and was supplanted in 1981 by the block-grant program. This grant program was one of the central devices used by the Reagan administration in its goal to decentralize and deregulate decision making to state government. The mental health and substance abuse categorical grants, which the federal government formerly had provided directly to local agencies, were consolidated and given to the state governments to distribute to their mental health agencies according to their own policies and procedures. Some protections for the former federally funded community mental health agencies were included at the last minute; however, many of these funds were shifted from the CMHCs to those community mental health services that some states had developed under their policy guidance and that were more sympathetic with the needs of the long-term mentally ill (Hudson, 1987). Although the Alcohol, Drug Abuse, and Mental Health Administration (ADAMHA) block grant was a financially small program, it functioned to shift the target of much of mental health advocacy to state government.

Perhaps the single greatest development of the 1980s, unleashed by the devolution of leadership to the states, was the targeting of state services to the seriously mentally ill. Many states, such as Massachusetts, have rewritten key pieces of legislation to specify services to this population as a priority. Throughout the nation this trend has been accompanied by a retreat from the ideals of prevention and early intervention. It has, however, reinforced the need for a broader range of services for the seriously mentally ill than most state mental health authorities formerly assumed responsibility for, such as assisted housing, psychosocial and vocational rehabilitation services, and social clubs. It has also led to the widespread adoption of case management services,[1] though in too many instances this has been used to circumvent the need for expensive professionals as well as to avoid the need for systemic organizational changes and direly needed services and resources for the seriously mentally ill. Each of these developments, nevertheless, represents an evolving response to the shortcomings of deinstitutionalization.

In 1986 the U.S. Congress passed the State Comprehensive Mental Health Services Plan Act (Pub. L. 99-660), which requires the states to provide case management as a condition of federal funding and also mandates the development of state mental health plans. During the 1960s there was widespread support for mental health planning. Since then there has been pervasive cynicism about the efficacy of such undertakings, with their presumed futility often attributed to "politics." This act, however, supports planning in somewhat consolidated state mental health authorities, ones that have been continuing to upgrade their planning capabilities.

A critical trend in the 1980s was the rapid expansion of the mental health advocacy movement. Numerous groups of patients, families, and service providers have been organized and have recruited large and articulate memberships, the most prominent of which is the National Alliance for the Mentally Ill (NAMI). Mental health administrators on all levels are acutely aware of the need to be responsive to and form alliances with these groups. These organizations have sponsored significant pieces of legislation supporting patient rights and have entered into several court consent decrees mandating enhanced community services.

NIMH has largely withdrawn from the funding of direct services and has focused its efforts on training and research. In recent years the focus of research has shifted away from psychosocial explanations of mental illness to biological theories. This has been partly in response to important developments in biological psychiatry. The mental health advocacy movement, and particularly groups consisting of families of the mentally ill, have often felt blamed by a narrow psychosocial focus of many mental health professionals, especially those who precipitously attempt to deflect focus from the mentally ill family member—the "scapegoat"—to instead examine dysfunctional family dynamics that may contribute to (and be caused by) the illness of the identified patient. Thus it is not surprising that Lewis Judd, director of NIMH in 1990, proposed that the 1990s be considered as the Decade of the Brain, establishing research in biological psychiatry as a key priority of NIMH.

Some of the most critical policies in mental health are embodied in the psychiatric commitment statutes of each of the fifty states. During much of the nineteenth century and the first half of the current century these laws were vaguely formulated, permitting considerable latitude on the part of physicians and others to commit persons suspected to be mentally ill. The abuses of these laws are well known and were a major force in expansion of patient populations during this time. During the period of deinstitutionalization most states revised their commitment statutes, restricting commitment typically to those who are imminently dangerous to self or others by reason of mental illness. In the aftermath of dein-stitutionalization, anger at the perceived "dumping" of patients from state mental hospitals has led to further revisions in these laws. The statutes of some states such as Washington now include the possibility of civil commitment due to "grave disabil-ity" (Mills, Commins, & Gracey, 1983, pp. 39–55). Because of these revisions em-phasizing degree of mental illness, grave disability, and functional capacity, greater discretionary authority in the commitment process has been delegated to mental health professionals (Durham & Pierce, 1986, pp. 42–55).

The specter of homeless and psychotic individuals wandering the streets of the major cities has also fueled interest in such devices as outpatient commitment, legal guardianship, and durable power of attorney. Many severely mentally ill persons refuse treatment, including psychotropic medications, yet are not dan-gerous and do not require institutional care. During the 1980s several states such as North Carolina and Hawaii adopted outpatient commitment statutes in which a patient may be "committed" to a community treatment program or even a mental health board (Korr, 1991, pp. 58–63). The use of coercive measures such as outpatient commitment was an important, though problematic, policy development in the 1980s. It will probably remain a strategy appropriate for only a small minority of the more severely disabled patients. American mental health professionals are learning that many more can be reached through strategies emphasizing empowerment, self-determination, and participatory programs such as the social clubhouse exemplified by Fountain House in New York City.

Current Organization

The organizational structure of mental health services in the United States is complex and is best understood in the context of the multiple layers of government involved. At the national level, the president, as the head of the executive department, directs politically appointed department heads, who in turn oversee a range of mammoth federal agencies. The largest is the Department of Health and Human Services (DHHS), which was responsible for a budget of $340.4 billion in FY 1991, a budget large than that of all but a few nations. Besides administering the Social Security program, DHHS contains several divisions, including the Public Health Service (PHS). This unit administered the Alcohol, Drug Abuse, and Mental Health Administration (ADAMHA), which had a budget of $2.6 billion in FY 1991. This agency oversaw the National Institute of Alcohol and Alcohol Abuse (NIAAA), the National Institute of Drug Abuse (NIDA), and the National Institute of Mental Health (NIMH). NIMH was mandated to engage in mental health planning, fund research, train mental health profes-sionals, and conduct some demonstration programs.

Legislation was passed in 1992 to reorganize the mental health programs in the Department of Health and Human Services. In October 1992 ADAMHA was eliminated. The service programs that were formerly part of NIMH, NIDA, and NIAAA remain under the Public Health Service and are now directed by a newly formed subunit called the Substance Abuse and Mental Health Services Administration (SAMHSA), which consists of three centers: the Center for Mental Health Services, the Center for Substance Abuse Prevention, and the Center for Treatment Improvement. The three institutes—NIMH, NIDA, and NIAAA—were moved to the National Institutes of Health, which is under a different arm of DHHS, and these now focus exclusively on the promotion of research in mental health and substance abuse.

Mental retardation and developmental disabilities programs also receive support from the Human Development Service (HDS), parallel to DHHS' Public Health Service. Funding for many health and some mental health services is also provided through two public health insurance programs—Medicare, for the aged, blind, and disabled; and Medicaid, for the indigent. Standards and overall direction for these programs are provided through DHHS' Health Care Financing Authority (HCFA), also parallel to the PHS. Direct payments to individuals are made through Supplemental Security Income (SSI) and Social Security Disability Insurance (SSDI).

The federal government directly provides mental health services to special populations through the Veterans Administration (VA), the Department of Defense (DOD), and the Bureau of Indian Affairs (BIA). The largest of these systems is the VA, which operates 139 psychiatric programs through its hospital system, almost all of which include both outpatient and inpatient programs for mentally ill and substance-abusing veterans (NIMH, 1990, p. 21).

All fifty states, the District of Columbia, and some territories (Guam and the Virgin Islands) have designated mental health authorities under the direction of the governor. These departments almost always operate the state's mental hospitals as well as many of its community mental health programs either directly, through local boards, through private agencies, or some combination. These departments have budgets of anywhere from $15.7 million in Wyoming to $2.1 billion in New York state (NIMH, 1992, pp. 172–173) and are directed by an executive officer, often referred to as a commissioner, who reports either directly to the governor, to another official, or to a state mental health board. Close to one-third (fifteen) of these authorities in 1989 were independent, freestanding departments, established by state legal codes, typically referred to as departments of mental health. Another third (fifteen) of these authorities are divisions or other subunits of an umbrella department of human services, health, and welfare, or some combination. About one-fourth of the state mental health authorities (thirteen) are under the auspices of a department of human resources. A small number of state mental health programs come under a health agency (four), department of institutions (three), or a welfare agency (one). However, the number using these last three models diminished between 1982 and 1989 in favor of umbrella and human resource departmental auspices (Wolf, 1991, p. 88). Examples of states with integrated, umbrella arrangements are Alaska, Rhode Island, and Florida, and those with independent departments include Alabama, Maine, and West Virginia.

Within each state there are usually substate areas, each with its own office. Often these are subunits of the state mental health agency, as is the case in Connecticut, which has a strong regional system. In several states, such as North Carolina, New Jersey, California, and Wisconsin, there are county board systems in which designated county mental health authorities receive their funding from some combination of local taxes and state allotments. These local boards may be subunits of either country or municipal governments, or occasionally they may operate as independent mental health authorities. In states such as Illinois mental health services may be funded in the same community by the state, by a township or country mental health board, and by a municipal government health department. In other states, such as Wisconsin or California, the county mental health program is mandated to provide mental health services and has a more clearly defined authority over the agencies falling within its jurisdiction. However the mental health authorities are defined in a given state, it is typical for them to purchase most services from private, not-for-profit agencies with voluntary boards of directors.

During the 1980s and early 1990s there have been continuing efforts to create more unified mental health authorities. These efforts have meant either reducing the number of overlapping authorities or more clearly defining their respective responsibilities. The most noteworthy such undertaking has been that of the Robert Wood Johnson Foundation (RWJ), the philanthropic arm of the Johnson and Johnson Corporation. The RWJ Foundation has provided seed money to nine cities, including Philadelphia, Pennsylvania, Columbus, Ohio, and Denver, Colorado, to develop integrated mental health authorities (Goldman et al., 1990, pp. 1217–1221).

Current Services

The structure of governmental mental health authorities represents a distinct level of analysis from an examination of the structure of mental health services themselves, many of which are private or fall outside the rubric of "mental health." NIMH reports typically categorize these services into four sectors. The first and largest is the speciality mental health sector, which includes state and county mental hospitals, general hospitals with psychiatric units, private psychiatric hospitals, VA services, community mental health centers, halfway houses, and residential treatment centers for children, as well as private-office practices of mental health professionals. Second, the human services sector provides many mental health services through such programs as special education in public schools, forensic programs in the criminal justice system, and family service agencies. Third, the general medical sector is a rapidly expanding provider, and these services are delivered in general hospital medical units, in nursing homes, and by physicians who lack psychiatric training. The last and smallest is the nonhealth sector, which includes transportation services and pastoral counselors (NIMH, 1986, p. 95).

In 1988 there were 3,251 organizations providing psychiatric inpatient services in the United States. Of these only 285 (8.8 percent) were state and county hospitals and these contained 39.4 percent of the total available beds. Hospitalization is also provided in 1,425 (44.1 percent) psychiatric units in general private hospitals, 440 (13.6 percent) residential treatment centers for children, 444 (13.7 percent) private psychiatric hospitals, 125 VA hospitals (3.9 percent), and other institutions (NIMH, 1992, pp. 21–24). Almost two-thirds (64.5 percent) of all psychiatric beds are in public facilities that accommodate a much smaller proportion of all episodes (31.5 percent) (NIMH, 1990, pp. 28, 31, 33). An increasing number of persons with psychiatric diagnoses are also being hospitalized in general hospitals on medical units (see Kiesler & Sibulkin, 1987).

Community mental health services include some 2,965 organizations that provide services to 3.0 million clients, representing 1.22 percent of the population (NIMH, 1992, p. 68). The most prominent model in recent years has been the community mental health center (CMHC), initially mandated to provide a minimum of outpatient, inpatient, crisis, day-programming, and consultation and education services. Outpatient services typically consist of various counselling modalities—individual, group, family—as well as medication monitoring and information and referral. Inpatient services are often provided under contract with a private psychiatric hospital unit for short-term inpatient services for stabilization and assessment, so as to forestall a longer episode in a regular psychiatric hospital. Crisis intervention services provide assessment and acute management of psychiatric emergencies in the community, and some also provide brief therapeutic services.

Of the 2,161 day programs in the nation in 1988, some were designed for maintaining the severely mentally ill in the community, and others, referred to as day hospitals, provided short-term treatment of somewhat higher-functioning patients. About two-thirds (1,309) of these are operated by other organizations such as freestanding psychiatric clinics and multiservice mental health organizations (NIMH, 1992, p. 23). An emerging variant is the social club that deemphasizes any kind of formal treatment and instead aims at providing an ongoing community support system and rehabilitative services for the seriously mentally ill.

An important trend in community mental health has been the diversification of agency models in recent years, and a move away from the multiservice community mental health center toward greater specialization. This has resulted from the demise of the federal CMHC program as well as an increase in Medicaid funding for mental health clinics. Medicaid standards are considerably more flexible than those that established the community mental health program. As a result, many child welfare and other social service agencies are now organizing systems of mental health clinics that resemble the traditional single-service psychiatric outpatient clinic of a general hospital. As of 1988 there were 1,751 freestanding psychiatric clinics in the nation and another 2,215 clinics associated with public and private hospitals, residential treatment centers, and multi-service mental health organizations (NIMH, 1992, p. 22).

Residential services are increasingly provided through group homes, assisted housing, foster care, and halfway, quarter-way, and three-quarter-way houses. While most of these models have been used for many years now, they continue to represent one of the greatest deficits in U.S. mental health services. Many state mental health authorities did not consider residential services to be their responsibility until recently. Other residential services are provided in nursing homes, typically funded by Medicaid. Many states have relied on Medicaid-funded intensive care facilities for the mentally ill (ICF-MI); however, these are coming under greater scrutiny. It has been estimated that about 29 percent of discharged mental patients have been placed in nursing homes (Kruzich, 1986, p. 6). Out of a total of 1.7 million residents, nursing homes care for 750,000 chronically mentally ill, or 44 percent of their residents (Gronfein, 1985, p. 201).

Mental Health Personnel and Treatment

A key feature of the American mental health system is the professionals who manage the programs and deliver the services. Social work, psychology, and psychiatry are the three most prominent mental health professions, with nursing, occupational therapy, and pastoral counselling also making important contributions. In 1988 there were about 531,072 full-time workers staffing the nation's mental health programs. Of these, over two-thirds (71.8 percent) were patient care staff, while the remainder served as administrative, clerical, and maintenance workers. About two-thirds of the patient care staff (46.8 percent of the total) were professionals with a B.A. degree or above; the other third (25.0 percent of the total) were paraprofessional and nonprofessional caretakers. The two largest professional groups were nurses (13.8 percent) and social workers (8.7 percent), while there were considerably fewer psychologists (4.4 percent) and psychiatrists (3.4 percent) (NIMH, 1992, p. 30). American mental health professionals tend to be quite well educated in university-based academic programs that make active use of clinical internships. For instance, over two-thirds of social workers (70 percent) hold the master's or higher degrees.

The clinical approaches of mental health professionals in the United States most frequently are psychoanalysis, behavioral and cognitive psychology, and biological psychiatry. Humanistic and family systems approaches have also gained widespread popularity. Although the psychoanalytic orientation is prominent in the major urban centers, particularly the East Coast, behavioral approaches are more common in the Midwest and West and in many inpatient and residential treatment centers. Most mental health professionals consider themselves as either eclectic or as generalists who use a psychosocial or ecosystems approach, particularly in clinical social work. Some eschew any kind of formal theoretical orientation.

Treatment modalities used in the nation's mental hospitals vary significantly depending on auspices. In 1980 public mental hospitals tended to provide the least treatment, with 63.9 percent of the patients receiving individual therapy; 49.9 percent, group therapy; 65.2 percent, drug therapy; 48.3 percent, activity therapy; 25.8 percent, social skills training; and 7.2 percent, family therapy. The private hospitals provide individual therapy to about 90 percent of their patients and also provide significantly higher levels of family and activity therapy than other hospitals (NIMH, 1986, p. 49). Many private hospitals continue to provide electroconvulsive therapies (ECT) and some psychosurgery, more so than public mental hospitals. Two of the more systematic local studies reported rates of 21 and 25 percent usage of ECT (see Brown, 1985, p. 160).

As the exigencies of fiscal retrenchment have taken hold, certification issues have played a more prominent role than previously in mental health policy, especially in the public sector. Most states are struggling to upgrade their institutions to meet the certification standards of the federal Health Care Financing Administration (HCFA) so that they may be eligible for Medicaid and Medicare reimbursement, as well as those of the Joint Commission on the Accreditation of Health Care Organizations (JCAHCO) so that they may collect private insurance reimbursements. One strategy has been for states to guarantee payment for indigent psychiatric patients in private hospitals to maximize the use of third-party payments, which these hospitals are able to more effectively collect due to their certification and accreditation.

Closely linked with institutional accreditation is the licensing of professional staff. Several professional groups have moved to secure licensing for their better-trained and educated members. None in recent years has done this more effectively than social work. Such licensing has usually enabled the subsequent mandating of private insurance coverage for these professionals. For example, in Massachusetts, Illinois, and several other states, the state insurance laws now require those insurance companies that provide also for payment for therapy from psychiatrists and psychologists to provide for similar payments for services rendered by licensed clinical social workers.

Mental health policy in the United States is now being refined to confront key problems in the deinstitutionalization of public mental hospitals, transinstitutionalization, privatization, and fragmentation of service delivery, as well as ballooning costs. Policy leadership has passed from the federal government to the states, which have become a rich source of experimentation in their efforts to address the needs of the seriously mentally ill. Some of the most critical challenges in policy development involve the integration of public and private mental health services, not only among themselves, but with the larger social welfare systems, including health, education, income maintenance, and criminal justice. A key part of this challenge involves coordinating the various accreditation and licensing systems, as well as professional education and mental health career ladders. The following section will discuss some of the public policy processes that may be critical to this undertaking.

PUBLIC POLICY PROCESS

It has often been observed that policy making in the United States is largely an incremental process of "muddling through," otherwise referred to as an incremental-disjointed process (Lindblom, 1968). Policies are introduced often in Congress or in state legislatures but are adopted only after partisan political negotiations have modified them so that they deviate only slightly from existing arrangements. These processes are characteristic of much policy making in mental health. However, policy making in this field can also be understood in terms of the dynamic interplay between efforts of local, state, and federal administrators and the larger partisan political process. On the one hand, governmental officials engage in their own decision making, which involves both a "bureaucratic enterpreneurialism" and attempts at rational planning, often to protect vested interests. On the other hand, the political process takes place in the interactions between the legislative, executive, and judicial branches, as well as a range of constituencies.

It has been observed that "iron triangles" involving coalitions between bureaucrats, legislators, and special interests once dominated mental health policy making (Rochefort, 1987, p. 97). Now a more useful model may be Heclo's notion of "issue networks" comprising an expanded number of participants acting in a highly politicized environment (Rochefort, 1987, p. 97). These participants include most mental health agencies, which are usually represented by both state- and national-level associations concerned with advocacy, public education, and some research. The more prominent include the National Council of Community Mental Health Centers and the National Association of State Mental Health Program Directors. Representing patients and families are such groups as the National Alliance for the Mentally Ill (NAMI) and the Mental Patients Liberation Front. Associations of professionals, such as the American Psychiatric Association (APA) and the National Association of Social Workers (NASW) are also key players. Other organizations, such as the National Association of Mental Health, represent a wider range of constituencies.

The proliferation of advocacy associations has contributed to a growing politicization of mental health decision making. Other forces influencing this have been an increasing level of competition between state agencies now that the older categorical funding for mental health services has been replaced by the block grants. One of the manifestations of this trend has been the efforts of governors and legislators to become more involved in the operational decisions of their mental health departments. Historically, most of the critical policies of state mental health authorities (SMHAs) have been made by small groups of administrators, and these are often codified through administrative rule-making procedures with scant community input. This increasing politicization has threatened the autonomy of departmental professionals, especially those in SMHAs (sometimes for better, sometimes for worse). A key strategy that many of these officials have used to attempt to preserve their autonomy vis-à-vis both generalist politicians and a range of constituency groups has been the upgrading of formal planning procedures utilizing needs assessments, program evaluation, and program budgeting procedures, among others.

A series of case studies of SMHAs conducted in the early 1980s by Hudson and Dubey (1986) suggested that the rationalization of decision making appeared to be the dominant trend, largely in reaction to the increasing politicization. Analysis of more recent 1988 survey data of forty state departments of mental health has supported this hypothesis. This correlational study presented significant but not conclusive evidence supporting two key propositions: (1) SMHAs are markedly upgrading their provisions for rational planning and decision making, and (2) the more frequently they use methods of rational decision making, the more likely it is that they will develop quality community mental health systems (Hudson, Salloway, & Vissing, forthcoming).

The study's finding that there is a negative impact of state delivery of services on rated service quality suggests that direct, public delivery of services may be counterproductive. One interpretation of this finding is that state planners may find it considerably more difficult to implement their plans when dealing with entrenched interests, state regulations, and unions than when they are managing contracts with private agencies. Thus the most appropriate role for SMHAs may lie in planning, licensing, funding, coordinating, and evaluating services, rather than actually delivering them.

In recent years there has been some debate as to the most effective strategies for community groups interested in improving mental health services. There have been several court cases in which community groups and others have sued on behalf of a class of mental patients for direly needed community services; most noteworthy among these efforts are *Wyatt v. Stickney* (1971) in Alabama and *Brewster v. Dukakis* (1978) in Massachusetts. In Alabama the judicial branch proved to be ill suited to supervise a complex service system, especially when the legislature refused to appropriate needed funds. In other cases, such as *Brewster v. Dukakis*, which resulted in the Northampton Consent Decree, which mandated generous funding levels for a wide range of community mental health services in an area of western Massachusetts. Such suits have proven to be effective devices for change. There seems to be growing interest on the part of advocacy groups in working with the designated mental health authority to resolve the intricate problems of policy implementation. But when problems in policy and financial support cannot be resolved on that level, it then becomes vital that community groups consider first establishing new administrative rules, turning to the legislature for revised or new legislation, or, as a last resort, working through the court system to mandate the enforcement of existing constitutional rights and laws.

American mental health policy usually has represented the outcome of the policy-making efforts of a wide range of private and public organizations and has been implemented by parties who may have had little part in the inception of the policy. For this reason, the official or de jure policies of various governmental bodies often do not correspond to the de facto policies, or the way they are actually implemented. The most dramatic example is the policy of deinstitutionalization, which will be discussed in a later section of this chapter.

Some of the failures and successes of state mental health programs have been rated and described by Torrey and his coworkers in their biennial study of the programs of the fifty states and the District of Columbia. In their most recent survey (1990), they identified several of the New England states—Vermont, New Hampshire, Rhode Island, and Connecticut—as well as Ohio, Colorado, and Wisconsin, as having the highest-quality mental health systems in the nation. Hawaii, Wyoming, Idaho, Montana, and Mississippi were considered to have some of the worst. The authors observed that most (forty-four) of the states failed to get even half of the total possible points, clearly pointing out the failure of most states to provide for people with serious mental illnesses (p. ii).

A secondary analysis of the results of the 1989 version of these ratings was conducted by the author to identify factors that are predictive of high-quality community mental health systems. This study concluded that states with (1) highly reputed administrators who (2) work in an integrated organizational structure of state human services, (3) utilize rational decision-making procedures, (4) adopt policies supportive of comprehensive community mental health services, and (5) have access to a sufficient number of professionals and agencies to implement these policies are most successful in developing highly rated community mental health systems. The statistical path model based on these factors explained over half (54 percent) of the variation in quality ratings. A preliminary analysis revealed that these factors have their greatest impact in environments in which there is a relatively higher level of socioeconomic development, racial homogeneity, and citizen participation in governmental affairs (Hudson, 1990, p. 115).

SPECIAL POLICY ISSUES

The Mentally Ill and the Mentally Retarded

During much of American history, mentally retarded persons have often been cared for in the same institutions as the mentally ill. However, by 1990 the states had clearly separated these services. Some SMHAs, such as that in Illinois, may have oversight responsibilities for parallel divisions of mental retardation and mental illness, but in many cases the units are by law separate departments.

In the United States mental retardation is usually included under developmental disabilities, which the federal government defines as severe, chronic disabilities that are attributable to either severe physical or mental conditions, are manifested before a person attains age twenty-two, are likely to continue indefinitely, and result in substantial functional limitations in several areas of activity (42 U.S.C.

§ 6102). This definition most typically covers mental retardation, epilepsy, cerebral palsy, and autism; however, a number of groups, such as those representing persons with learning disabilities, have argued for an even broader interpretation. Noteworthy in the definition is the deemphasis on intellectual criteria or particular diagnostic groups, the focus on functional limitations, and the clear attempt to reduce stigma (see Summers, 1981, pp. 259–265). The prevalence of mental retardation has most commonly been placed at 3 percent. In recent years there have been arguments for a lower percentage.

This definition is consistent with a greater emphasis on functional assessment, habilitation, training, and lifetime support issues in the developmental disabilities field than is found in mental health. There is also widespread use of case management and the development of individualized habilitation, training, and treatment plans in this field.

There has been much publicity in recent years about the development of small group homes for mentally retarded persons. However, recent research of Braddock, Hemp, and Fujiura indicate that these reports may be exaggerated (1987). Services for persons with developmental disabilities are predominantly provided in large congregate care settings funded through the federal Medicaid program. Eighty-seven percent of all reimbursement budgeted under the Medicaid Intermediate Care Facility/Mental Retardation (ICF/MR) program in 1986 was for large congregate care settings with sixteen or more beds, many with several hundred residents. Because these facilities are often mistakenly categorized as community care, the level of deinstitutionalization in this field has been consistently exaggerated. In 1982 there were only 9,714 residents of small fifteen-bed or smaller group homes in the United States, or about 7 percent of all ICF/MR residents (Braddock, Hemp, & Fujiura, 1987, p. 129). Nevertheless, the development of community services is continuing, and the period 1977 to 1986 saw a dramatic growth in state expenditures for community services.

The developmental disabilities constituencies have a longer history of active advocacy than do those concerned with mental illness. For this reason, it is commonly believed that this constituency has been more effective than that of mental health in garnering increased allocations from the state and federal governments. A pivotal group has been the Association for Retarded Citizens, an organization of families of mentally retarded persons. A comparison of changes in state allocations for developmental disabilities and mental health from 1977 to 1983 supports this impression. Developmental disabilities spending, controlling for inflation, grew 8.3 percent from $18.83 per capita in 1977 to $20.39 in 1983, whereas mental health per capita state expenditures dropped 7.2 percent from $28.41 in 1977 to $26.37 in 1983.[2]

There has been a continuing need for more treatment services for mental illness among the developmentally disabled. Mental disorder can either be a contributing cause to or a consequence of mental retardation, or a separate issue altogether. While SMHAs are usually legally mandated to provide appropriate treatment for the mental illnesses of individuals diagnosed as mentally retarded, they are reputed to assiduously avoid doing so; thus there is a serious deficit in mental hospitalization resources for the mentally retarded. This may be partly a reaction to long-standing criticisms of mental hospitals in past eras for not providing specialized services to mentally retarded persons in their treatment units. Unfortunately, most staff in retardation programs are not mental health professionals, and extremely few have expertise in diagnosing and treating mental illness among their clients. The developmental disabilities field has moved away from a medical model toward a social services and disabilities approach.

The Mentally Ill and Substance Abuse

The trend toward greater specialization in the mental health field has occurred in substance abuse also. Alcohol and drug programs are gradually being removed from state mental health authorities. Directors of these programs often prefer to have more direct access to gubernatorial and legislative decision makers than they have when they are part of a larger mental health bureaucracy. Only half (twenty-four) of the states' alcohol and drug agencies were part of the SMHAs as of 1983. In about one-third of the states (sixteen) both the substance abuse and mental health programs were in parallel units in a larger umbrella department. In the remaining fifth of the states (ten) the substance abuse programs were in unit(s) administratively separate from mental health (Council of State Governments, 1983). These agencies make extensive use of purchase of service contracts with private agencies, perhaps even more so than in mental health.

It has often been easier for community advocates to mobilize around a narrowly defined need and program, such as alcoholism, than a broader area such as mental health. Perhaps for this reason, alcoholism and drug abuse programs, like those in developmental disabilities, have been more effective in their competition for funding than public mental health. During the same period of 1977 to 1983 in which state mental health programs lost 7.2 percent of their funding, alcoholism programs saw a 48 percent increase in per capita funding levels, while funding for drug abuse programs increased 5.5 percent.

As substance abuse and mental health programs have become separated, there has been less effective coordination between these systems. Substance abuse professionals often report difficulty in arranging hospitalization for those with dual diagnoses. Mental health officials insist that they do not have the facilities or expertise to detoxify addicts, and until the addicts are detoxified, they can not adequately assess whether or not a psychiatric problem exists. Mental health professionals historically have little training or interest in substance abuse and chronically fail to diagnose and treat substance abuse problems, which are extremely prevalent among mental patients.

Some reports suggest that as many as 60 percent to 80 percent of the seriously mentally ill have substance abuse problems (Rose, Peabody, & Stratigeas, 1990). In contrast, NIMH reported that in 1986, 3 percent of all persons admitted to mental hospitals in the United States had drug-related disorders as a primary diagnosis, with the lowest rates in state hospitals (1.6 percent) and the highest in general hospitals with psychiatric units (5.9 percent). In contrast, 6.2 percent of all patients had a principal diagnosis of alcohol-related disorders, again with the lowest rates in state hospitals (3.1 percent) and the highest in VA centers (18.8 percent) (NIMH, 1992, p. 287).

One of the forces driving the effort to confront the problems of the dually diagnosed, as well as the increasing specialization of service delivery systems to the point of fragmentation, has been public attention generated from the federal government's War on Drugs. During the 1980s the explosive rise in the use of cocaine and its various derivatives such as crack stimulated massive federal efforts directed primarily toward interdiction and law enforcement. Some new funds have been allocated for education and treatment; however, these have been grossly inadequate. The explosive growth of AIDS among intravenous drug users also has highlighted the need for prevention and treatment services for drug users. Recent statistics released by the federal government suggest that in the later part of the 1980s there was a significant reduction in the abuse of a range of drugs, including cocaine (Shenon, 1990).

The Mentally Disordered Offender

The care and detention of mentally disordered offenders is now a critical issue in the United States. The mentally ill in the community, especially those among the homeless, are becoming more visible, and as a result, long-standing public fears about the dangerousness of the mentally ill have been inflamed. Furthermore, as the formal community mental health system fails to support these individuals, they have often been jailed. It has been observed that the Los Angeles County Jail is the largest de facto mental institution in the nation, with an estimated 3,600 mentally disordered inmates. Second, the growing crime rate and incarceration levels (1,042,136 prisoners in 1989) (Torrey et al., 1990, p. 6) gives the United States the highest incarceration level in the world. This also highlights the problems of the mentally disordered offender.

For many years mental health professionals and the public have held diverging views as to the degree of dangerousness of the mentally ill. Professionals routinely dismiss public fears, as they claim that the mentally ill are no more dangerous than the general population, not realizing that these views originated in studies from the 1930s and 1940s that have not been replicated. In fact, a review of recent studies indicates disproportionately high levels of crime among the seriously mentally ill (Brown, 1985, pp. 133–141). This may not be entirely unexpected, considering the degree of deinstitutionalization in the public sector and the scarcity of community support systems.

Traditionally included under the rubric of "mentally disordered offenders" are defendants found not guilty by reason of insanity; defendants found incompetent to stand trial; persons adjudicated under special statutes, for instance, sexual psychopath or defective delinquent; persons adjudicated guilty but mentally ill; convicted offenders who display symptoms of serious mental illness while serving a sentence, some of whom are transferred to a hospital for treatment of mental illness; juveniles who are convicted of, or found involved in, crimes and are committed for treatment of mental illness; defendants being evaluated for competency to stand trial; and defendants being examined for criminal responsibility (Kerr & Roth, 1986, p. 128).

The system of 150 institutions for mentally disordered offenders is primarily state operated. A 1986 survey of these indicated that 62 percent were state mental health facilities, 24 percent were operated by corrections departments, and 14 percent came under auspices of agencies such as social services or youth services. About 70 percent of all residents were found in the mental health facilities. Only 4 of these institutions were specifically designed for women, while 17 were dedicated to juveniles. These centers typically held 100 to 250 residents, with 8 holding over 500 persons. Collectively, they housed a total of 16,289 residents. It is estimated that at least 10 percent of the total incarcerated population of the United States, which recently surpassed a million, may have a severe mental illness such as a psychosis (Jemelka, Trupin, & Chiles, 1989). Thus these facilities serve only about one-sixth of an estimated 100,000 in need. An additional 31,746 persons were committed on a criminal basis to public and private psychiatric hospitals, with 26,941 of these in state and county mental hospitals (NIMH, 1986, p. 45).

The single most common reason for a resident being in a forensic institution is his or her transfer from regular jails because of mental illness, as 22 percent of residents are in this category. Other major groups include the civilly committed (15.7 percent), those not guilty by reason of insanity (13.6 percent), sex offenders (12 percent), and those found incompetent to stand trial (11 percent). The least common are those adjudicated "guilty but mentally ill," a relatively new innovation in a few states; these represent only 0.7 percent of the resident population (Kerr & Roth, 1986, p. 135).

Individualized treatment planning is routinely provided in these institutions, but in some it is in name only. The most common form of treatment is psychotropic medication, which is administered to a median of 61 percent of the residents in virtually all of the facilities. Also, almost 90 percent of the institutions offer group and individual therapy at least weekly, to medians of 60 percent and 34 percent of the residents, respectively. Some of the problems these facilities face are a relatively low level of education and training on the part of staff and the recurrent expectation that the same personnel perform guard and treatment functions. While the typical center has two psychiatrists and seven graduate-level therapists, it employs close to fifty technicians and paraprofessionals on its treatment staff (Kerr & Roth, 1986, p. 138).

Issues concerning the mentally ill offender should not obscure attention to the broader criminalization of the mentally ill. There have been numerous reports that the mentally ill in the community are more and more being diverted from the mental health to the criminal justice system. A recent survey of 260 families of persons with schizophrenia and bipolar conditions found that the majority had been arrested, and that one-fifth had been convicted of a crime. The two most significant correlates of arrest were substance abuse and noncompliance with psychotropic medication. Their families overwhelmingly attributed the arrests to psychiatric crises, reporting that in about half of the cases arrest follows a failed attempt at psychiatric commitment (McFarland, Faulkner, Bloom, Hallaux, & Bray, 1989, p. 718).

While the United States has been deinstitutionalizing its public mental health facilities, it has been dramatically expanding its prisons. Similarly, while it has become more difficult for the indigent mentally ill to qualify for hospital care, growing numbers commit crimes and find themselves in penal institutions where they are unlikely to receive adequate mental health services.

Deinstitutionalization

Deinstitutionalization is most popularly characterized as the policy of discharging mental hospital patients to the community, diverting potential patients from admission or readmission, and the development of community services to support this shift in locus of care. Such a view, however, fails to reflect the de facto policy of deinstitutionalization in the United States as specifically a policy of depopulating public state and county hospitals and transinstitutionalizing a portion of these patients in nursing homes, jails, or, occasionally, private hospitals.

The development of the federally funded system of community mental health centers during the 1960s and 1970s fell considerably short of the original goals; less than half the nation was to eventually be served by these agencies. The initial slow decline of state hospital censuses between 1955 and 1965 became precipitous during the decade between 1965 and 1975. Perhaps the single greatest contributor to the deinstitutionalization of state and county mental hospitals during this period was the passage of Medicare and Medicaid in 1965 and 1966 (see Rose, 1979; Gronfein, 1985). These are two federal health insurance programs, the first designed for the aged, blind, and disabled, and the second for the indigent. The Medicaid program, in particular, provided massive funding for the nursing home industry. At the same time nursing homes were proliferating, many of the aged in mental hospitals, as well as some of the younger severely disabled, were being transferred to these facilities, resulting in what has been termed *transinstitutionalization*. State governments, which fund their hospitals predominantly from tax revenues, were thus given considerable financial incentives to discharge patients to the community and to nursing homes where the federal government would assume a substantial share of the expense. This trend was propelled by legal developments during the late 1960s and early 1970s that narrowed the ground on which psychiatric commitments could be made. These new statutes, in general, restricted commitment to those persons who are imminently dangerous by reason of mental illness. This simultaneously made it very difficult to hospitalize a person and, if the person was hospitalized, shortened the stay, resulting often in premature discharge.

Despite the increase from 1970 to 1986 in the number of outpatient programs from 2,156 to 2,946 (36.6 percent), the number of inpatient facilities proliferated from 1,734 to 3,039 (75.3 percent). Although there was a slight decline in state and county hospitals from 310 to 285 (8.1 percent), the number of private psychiatric hospitals rose from 150 to 314 (109.3 percent), and general hospitals with psychiatric units grew from 664 to 1,287 (93.8 percent) (NIMH, 1990, pp. 27–29).

An analysis of changes in the numbers of residents and psychiatric episodes in hospitals reveals a similar pattern to the foregoing. The average daily census in state and county hospitals stood at a height of 662,000 in 1955; however, by 1983 it dropped to 139,000, a 79 percent decline (Kiesler & Sibulkin, 1987, pp. 48–49). The disparity in these numbers is partly attributable to the declining length of stay of patients in public hospitals, from a mean of 421 days in 1969 to 143 days in 1982. In contrast, lengths of stays in private hospitals have been stable since the early 1970s (Kiesler & Sibulkin, 1987, pp. 86, 93).

Most analyses of deinstitutionalization only consider NIMH statistics on hospitalizations in state and county hospitals and sometimes those in private psychiatric hospitals and general hospitals with psychiatric units. These analyses reveal only a slight decline in the total rate of psychiatric hospital episodes, which declined from 843 per 100,000 in 1969 to 756 in 1981, or 10.3 percent. However, Kiesler and Sibulkin took a broader view, considering also hospitalizations for psychiatric episodes in private hospital and VA medical units. The most dramatic increase in hospitalizations for psychiatric diagnoses occurred in general hospital medical units, and these increased over fivefold, from 184,000 in 1965 to 1,069,000 in 1980 (Kiesler & Sibulkin, 1987, p. 63). When all episodes of psychiatric hospitalization in both private and public facilities were tallied, the total rate of psychiatric hospital episodes rose from 950 to 1,323, or 39.3 percent (pp. 74–75).

The estimated 3.3 million chronically mentally ill persons in the community (NIMH, 1992, p. 256) were served by 2,965 outpatient services and 2,161 day treatment programs (NIMH, 1992, pp. 22–23). The largest single category of outpatient services, accounting for 40.8 percent of these agencies, were multiservice mental health organizations. The second-largest group were the freestanding psychiatric outpatient clinics that offer a traditional mix of therapies and accounted for 751 or 25.3 percent of the agencies. Since 1970 day treatment services more than doubled, their numbers increasing from 778 to 2,161 by 1988 (p. 23). Systemic interorganizational problems have delayed developing effective links with inpatient services, especially with the state systems. Inadequate funding, skewed financial incentives, and a professional culture that overemphasizes psychotherapeutic approaches have all seriously delayed the development of community support systems that address the needs of the seriously mentally ill.

By the middle 1970s the shortcomings of deinstitutionalization had become public knowledge. Congress responded in 1975 by amending the 1963 act to additionally mandate prescreening and aftercare services and programs for children, the aged, and drug abusers and alcoholics, as well as for minorities. Some centers were given additional time before they were expected to be self-supporting. However, few extra dollars were allocated to implement these amendments, and no changes were made to address the overall systemic problems of coordinating disjointed federal, state, and local services. In the late 1970s NIMH did fund demonstration programs in seventeen communities around the country in which community service system (CSSs) were established to create more unified mental health authorities, ones based on an ''accountability model.'' This program involved the concept of linking client-level coordination, through case management, with program-level coordination, through a designated ''lead agency'' (Grusky, et al., 1986, pp. 160–164). Little was done, however, to address problems of policy-level coordination in the CSS projects. The program did target the severely mentally ill and began to address some of the interorganizational problems, and for this reason it formed an important backdrop to current efforts at systemic integration, as well as introducing case management as a key strategy for client-level coordination of services.

A range of forces have driven the deinstitutionalization of public mental health services. The overwhelming costs of renovating and operating massive state hospitals (a few with over 10,000 patients), the introduction of psychotropic medications, the ideology and promise of community mental health, the introduction of such programs as Medicare and Medicaid, and the patients' rights movement leading to restrictive commitment laws have been some of the major driving forces. Both conservatives concerned about cost cutting and downsizing government and liberals enthusiastic about getting patients out of the hospital snake pits and into idealized communities have contributed to what many recognize as a precipitously fast and unplanned process. The movement thus took more of a negative focus on getting patients out of hospitals than a positive one of locating them in needed community support systems. Despite its failures, few seriously question the ideals and objectives of deinstitutionalization, but most consider its unplanned implementation to be profoundly flawed. The states that have developed noteworthy systems are those that have considerably lower rates of poverty and mental illness, as well as more politically integrated service systems (Hudson, 1990). The accomplishments in developing community support systems have unfortunately been overshadowed by the many unanticipated consequences of this movement: marginal care for the seriously mentally ill, contributing to their rising homelessness and criminalization.

Funding Issues

Health care costs in the United States doubled during the 1970s and again during the 1980s (Maloy, 1990, p. 1). Thus there has been considerable pressure on all types of health care providers to contain costs. Perhaps one of the greatest barriers to the conflicting tasks of controlling expenditures and developing more effective mental health policies is the complex and often-hidden nature of the various funding systems. Not only is there a wide range of public and private funding sources, but each source typically channels its dollars through one or more funding streams, passing often through several layers of government. By the time these dollars reach the actual implementers, the policy directives may be conflicted or unknown. It is not unusual for local agencies to be receiving funding from fifteen to twenty sources, sometimes with no single governmental or private source providing a substantial portion of the budget. This complicates the life of agency administrators; however, it provides them with a fair degree of autonomy, as no single funder can exercise substantial control over the agency. But most important, it undercuts any effective means of interorganizational coordination.

It has been estimated that in 1980 the United States spent $19.9 billion on mental health care, about 0.76 percent of the gross national product that year. Of this, just over half (53.6 percent) was spent by the speciality mental health sector, while close to one-third (30.6 percent) was spent in the general medical sector. The remainder was spent in the human services (14.7 percent) and non-health (1.2 percent) sectors (NIMH, 1986, p. 101). Close to half (44 percent) of this expense in 1980 was assumed by individuals through direct payment and private insurance, while almost one-fourth (23.4 percent) was paid by the federal government. Between 1980 and 1986 total expenditures on inpatient care more than doubled, increasing from $10.2 billion to $21.4 billion (NIMH, 1990, p. 224).

About one-third (32.6 percent) of the total expenditures are those of state governments; in 1981 the fifty states collectively spent $6.1 billion for mental illness, or 1.9 percent of their total revenues (Hudson, 1983).[3] This compares with $5.6 billion for developmental disabilities, $413 million for alcoholism, and $333 million for drug abuse. The total of $12.4 billion spent by state governments in these three fields of mental health included $900 million in federal dollars from such sources as the ADAMHA block grant, general revenue sharing, Medicaid, and Medicare, leaving $11.5 billion that states generated mostly from tax revenues (Hudson, 1983). There are few categorizations of expenditures by either age or diagnostic categories. However, it has been esti-mated that in 1985 state mental health agencies spent an average of 8 percent of their budgets on programs specifically for children, a disproportionately small amount (Dougherty, 1988, p. 808).

At the same time states spent close to $4.1 billion on institutional care (66.5 percent of budgets), they spent $1.8 billion on community-based programs (29.7 percent). In addition, they allocated 2.8 percent for central administrative ex-penses and 1 percent for research and training (NIMH, 1986, pp. 105–106). Of the states' total revenues for mental health, 79.6 percent were obtained from state sources, while 12.9 percent came from the federal government, 3.5 percent from local governments, 3.5 percent from first- and third-party payments, and 0.5 percent from other sources (p. 113). The four major federal sources include Medicaid, which accounted for 68.1 percent of federal receipts; Medicare, 12.8 percent; Title XX, 8.9 percent; and the ADAMHA block grant, 4.4 percent (pp. 117–118). The de facto federal policy has been to support institutional care, and this is reflected by the observation that 83.3 percent of all federal dollars to state mental health authorities went for institutional care, and 92.2 percent of Medicaid and 98.4 percent of Medicare funds (calculated from pp. 117–118, 123–124).

A major development in the late 1980s involved the Medicaid program. Although some Medicaid dollars are allocated directly to SMHAs, substantial amounts are allocated through the state Medicaid program, almost always operated under a separate administrative unit than the mental health department. States now have the option to provide various mental health services through the Medicaid program to the indigent, as well as those with marginal incomes who do not qualify for public assistance but are "medically needy." The costs of Medicaid are shared between the federal and state governments on a formula basis, with each state typically contributing 30 to 60 percent of the cost. The optional mental health services under Medicaid consist of clinical services in nonhospital facilities, nonphysician services, inpatient care for those under twenty-one and over sixty-four, prescription drugs, rehabilitation services in day programs, targeted case management, and waivers for home and community-based care. This last option—the Medicaid waiver program—involves the planned diversion of funds from institutional care to community services such as homemakers, home health aides, respite care, personal care, and day treatment. Substantial numbers of the states in 1990 provided prescription drugs (68 percent), clinical services (60 percent), and inpatient care for those under twenty-two (50 percent) to both the indigent and the medically needy. Also provided by a significant minority of states were inpatient care for the elderly (48 percent), skilled nursing care for those under twenty-two (48 percent), and nonphysician services (36 percent). Few states have chosen to use the rehabilitation option (24 percent) or the Medicaid waiver programs (14 percent) (Marvelle, 1990, p. 5). The lack of more frequent use of the rehabilitation and the waiver programs has been attributed to turf struggles between state mental health and Medicaid departments.

State mental health programs have been gradually shifting their own funding from institutions to community mental health programs. While the mean per capita expenditures by the states for institutional services declined nominally from $17.05 in 1977 to $16.85 in 1983, or 1.2 percent, at the same time, expenditures for community care services grew steadily from $7.75 in 1977 to $8.71 in 1983, or 12.4 percent. During these six years the average ratio of community to institutional expenditures grew from 0.31 to 0.34—evidence of a continuing shift of dollars from institutional to community services. These shifts took place most dramatically in the Northeast and Midwest, where the growth rates in the community/institutional ratio were 10.5 percent and 7 percent, respectively, compared with 3.5 percent and 1.4 percent in the Southeast and West. The shift was greatest in states with regressive taxation systems, Democratic governors, departments of welfare or comprehensive human service departments, and right-to-treatment statutes (Hudson, 1987, p. 9).

Due to the increasing visibility and power of state departments of mental health during the 1980s, they often struggled to gain greater control over the system of private providers. Traditionally, the federal government has funded many of these agencies through advance payment grants, while the states have most commonly used contracts. These contracts have often not been effectively managed, with negligible program evaluation. Recently, however, there has been a trend toward performance contracting, in which contract renewal is dependent on specific performance indicators, such as the percentage of rehospitalizations or community tenure of seriously mentally ill persons in the area. Other trends have involved experiments in capitation funding, in which a provider is given advance payment for each enrollee to provide whatever services may be needed. Health maintenance organizations (HMOs) use prospective funding systems and are widely available; however, their mental health benefits are quite limited. There have been experiments with specialized HMOs for the seriously mentally ill (see Dickey & Cohen, 1991).

When states fund services through private agencies, most of them (89.3 percent) provide these funds through contracts, and almost two-thirds (65.4 percent) of them make use of performance contracts. Just over half (52 percent) of the states use categorical grants, and close to a third (30 percent) use fee-for-service plans (Hudson, Salloway, & Vissing, forthcoming).

Most of the population in the United States is covered by one of a wide variety of private health insurance plans, usually given as a fringe benefit by a private or public employer. The employee typically contributes, through salary deductions, some part of this cost, usually between 10 percent and 50 percent. Depending on the size of the employee pool, the employers negotiate group plans with insurance companies, each of which contains a unique mix of covered conditions, deductibles, copayments, and maximum permitted fees for providers. The larger corporations are usually able to offer considerably better benefits with smaller employee contributions because of their massive pools of employees. The mentally ill have historically been discriminated against by insurance companies, and thus coverage has been extremely limited. This has been partly due to fear on the part of insurers that mental health represents a financial "black hole" and because of the perceived availability of public mental hospitals. However, these benefits have been improved in recent years, accounting for the increased use of private psychiatric facilities.

Group insurance policies typically pay for services on a fee-for-service basis, and these have historically created considerable incentives for psychiatrists to use inpatient and other expensive treatments, such as electroshock. Also, in private psychiatric facilities there has been a dramatic increase in adolescent psychiatric units. Insurance coverage is good for what is legally and effectively a "captive" audience. Furthermore, the profit margins on these units are some of the highest in the psychiatric industry.

Due to the expansion in all types of health care costs, there have been numerous efforts to control these costs. In addition to the widespread availability of HMOs, another development has been managed care. Insurance companies are increasingly developing a range of devices to decrease hospitalization such as employee assistance programs and requirements for preauthorization for hospitalization from the insurance company, utilization review, and, sometimes, use of specialized case management systems.

Although deinstitutionalization and the development of community services have been the most visible policy thrusts in recent years, the various funding systems have created considerable incentives to institutionalize the mentally ill. This has especially been the case in respect to the federal Medicaid and Medicare programs, which mostly support institutional services, as well as private insurance, which operates mostly on a fee-for-service basis. These two systems have been the major forces in the privatization of service delivery and the transinstitutionalization of patients into private hospitals and nursing homes. Because of the labyrinthine complexity of these systems, these developments have been largely hidden from public view until recently. This privatization, in turn, has contributed to skyrocketing health care costs that have seriously depleted the availability of revenues for public mental health services.

Consumer Rights

The consumer rights movement in the United States has played a decisive role in the adoption of a wide range of laws that define the rights of mental patients. New commitment laws have restricted both the criteria and procedures by which a person can be forced to enter a mental hospital. Although laws vary in each of the fifty states, in most, psychiatric commitment requires evidence that the person is imminently dangerous to himself or herself or others by reason of mental illness. He or she has a right to due process, to representation by counsel, to call and interrogate witnesses, and to a decision based on the existence of "clear and convincing" evidence. If detained on an emergency basis, patients have the right to examination by a psychiatrist typically within twenty-four hours and, at all times, the right to confidential communication with an attorney or court officials. Patients have rights to visitors and other communications; however, these can be modified based on clinical considerations. Voluntary patients can sign a request for discharge, which must be honored typically within five days, or commitment proceedings must be initiated. Most states have strict laws and regulations governing the use of restraints, seclusion rooms, and invasive treatments such as psychosurgery and ECT.

Legally committed patients have a right to treatment. If this is not provided, they must be discharged. Unfortunately, this right has not been established for voluntary patients or for outpatients. Several legal cases in the late 1970s and early 1980s, in particular the *Mills v. Rogers* (1981) case, established the right to refuse treatment. Before many states reformed their commitment laws in the late 1960s and early 1970s, it was assumed that committed patients had no such rights since psychiatric commitment was based on the presumed need for treatment. However, when the laws were changed to instead emphasize dangerousness, it became reasonable to question whether commitment meant the loss of other constitutional rights (Applebaum, 1988, p. 414). Although the Supreme Court has declined to rule on the matter, most state courts have established the right to refuse treatment, though this has various interpretations. For instance, in Massachusetts, if either a voluntary or involuntary patient refuses medication, the physician may seek a court hearing to have the patient adjudicated incompetent. The judge will then review testimony concerning the appropriateness of medication, the patient's competency, and the patient's best interest or substituted judgment (pp. 416–417). Treatment will then be ordered only if all three criteria are satisfied.

Most states employ a combination of mechanisms to protect patient rights. Some have guardianship and advocacy commissions, but unfortunately these tend not to have sufficient autonomy or resources for effective performance of these functions. There has been a trend toward the establishment of human rights committees. In many states agencies are required to organize committees to investigate abuses of patient rights. In several states advocacy groups have made arrangements with the SMHA to regularly send visitors to state hospitals and other programs to inspect conditions. It is becoming a more common practice for quality-assurance committees to include members of citizen groups when they evaluate a program. Patient advocates, state attorney's offices, and private legal aid services will also investigate abuses of human rights.

There has been a fair degree of unanimity among mental health constituencies in respect to many patient rights. However, professionals have often disagreed with patient groups about two issues. One has been the restrictiveness of the criteria for commitment, and the other, the right to refuse treatment. This second issue has been particularly divisive. Many professionals, especially psychiatrists, argue for greater control over the treatment process, while civil libertarians and patient groups have sought restrictions on such prerogatives (see Brown, 1985, pp. 167–208).

Even committed patients normally retain voting rights and right to a minimum wage while working in a mental hospital, among other rights. When a long-term mentally ill patient is adjudicated as incompetent, voting rights, among others, man be lost. A guardian is then appointed, usually a relative but possibly a mental health or legal professional. In recent years guardianship laws have been refined to permit limited guardianships, in which a person only loses the specific rights that he or she is judged as incompetent to exercise, such as management of finances or control over treatment decisions. Both guardianship and outpatient commitment statues represent efforts to protect mentally ill and marginally dangerous individuals in community settings. Increasingly, case management and other programs are utilizing representative payee status, in which a legally competent patient agrees to have a family member, case manager, or residential program manager manage his or her welfare checks, paying rent and food bills and providing periodic allowances for incidentals.

Several legal cases such as *Wyatt v. Stickney* (1971) have established the right to treatment in the least restrictive setting necessary for the purposes of the commitment. Although this right technically only applies to committed patients, the principle is popularly accepted as applying to all patients. This principle, thus, has been one of the driving forces behind the deinstitutionalization of public mental hospitals as well as facilities for the mentally retarded.

Both the consumer rights and the larger antipsychiatry movements have been decisive forces in defining mental health policy in the United States, specifically in propelling the deinstitutionalization of public mental health facilities. Their many interactions with the courts as well as professionals, service providers, and the larger community have gradually led to some refinement of the criteria and procedures through which the rights of individuals to their freedom, privacy, treatment, and protection are counterbalanced with societal interests, both in respect to public protection and in the successful care of the mentally ill. Unfortunately, as the public mental health system has restricted itself, its treatment, and social control efforts to the most severely mentally ill and dangerous, many of the social control functions relative to other patients have been assumed by other systems such as criminal justice.

CONCLUSIONS AND DISCUSSION

The ambivalence of Americans concerning the care of the mentally ill has resulted in the periodic shifting of responsibility from one level of government to another. This has led to a labyrinthine, fragmented service system consisting of a range of programmatic models, each originating in a particular era of mental health policy development such as the mental hygiene or community mental health movement.

Fragmented service systems, as well as the lack of any consensus on the origins, nature, and treatment of the various mental illnesses, all undercut attempts at rational and systematic planning. Because of this, policy implementers rarely carry out policies as initially conceived; de facto programs fail to match de jure policies. The prime example has been the failure of deinstitutionalization to be implemented as envisioned.

The myth of deinstitutionalization has camouflaged the specific policies of depopulating public mental hospitals, the displacement of many of the seriously mentally ill into nursing homes, jails, shelters, and the streets, and the privatization of psychiatric hospital care for other groups. Thus the American mental health system, which has historically been a two-class system, has become increasingly lopsided due to the contraction of some services to only some of the seriously mentally ill in the public sector, and the expansion of other services for less disturbed populations, such as some adolescents and the elderly, in the private sector.

During the last decade the nation has made major strides in identifying and responding to the repercussions of a precipitous process of depopulating public mental hospitals and the privatization of services. Much of this response has been unleashed by the devolution of authority to the states. This newfound leadership in state mental health authorities has often acted in concert with the burgeoning advocacy movement to target the seriously mentally ill and to provide many of the neglected services such as rehabilitation, assisted housing, social clubs, and case management, among others.

The targeting of the seriously mentally ill, however, has had a downside, as it has complicated problems of interorganizational coordination required for the many clients with multiple disabilities. It has also meant a movement away from primary prevention and early intervention in those areas where such strategies have proven effective, such as those involving children. While the new priority given to the seriously mentally ill promises to redress many of the problems of the deinstitutionalization of public mental hospitals, the ideal of a balanced service remains elusive. It is, therefore, critical that governmental mental health authorities continue to upgrade their abilities to rationally plan comprehensive services.

There is growing support in the United States for a universal health insurance plan, perhaps one similar to that of Canada's. With the expansion of both private insurance and Medicaid and Medicare, such a prospect is becoming increasingly likely. A key task for mental health advocates and policy makers is to plan for the mental health component of such a system. It would need to be carefully crafted so as to preserve the planning, monitoring, licensing, and other oversight functions of the state mental health authorities, which would operate within a clearly articulated national mental health policy promulgated by the federal government.

NOTES

1. Case management is a service approach intended to mobilize and coordinate service delivery at the client level so as to enable the recipient to live successfully in the community. It typically involves the provision of some combination of the following direct and indirect services, depending on the particular model used: outreach, client assessment, case planning, referral, advocacy, direct casework, developing natural support systems, reassessment, resource development, monitoring quality, public education, and/or crisis intervention.

2. These data were collected as a preparatory step in the author's research on the ADAMHA block grant. Methodology for the collection of these data is reported in Hudson and Dubey (1984/1985).

3. Expenditure data from the author's previous budgetary research are used here instead of the NIMH data since they contain parallel breakdowns for developmental disabilities

and substance abuse. Totals from the two studies are substantially the same, with Hudson's estimates $422,000 less than those from NIMH, 1986. While Hudson estimated $1.854 billion for community care, NIMH estimated $1.812 billion.

REFERENCES

American Psychiatric Association. (1987). *Diagnostic and statistical manual of mental disorders* (rev. 3rd ed.). Washington, DC: Author.

Appelbaum, P. A. (1988). The right to refuse treatment with antipsychotic medications: Retrospect and prospect. *American Journal of Psychiatry, 145*(4), 413–419.

Bachrach, L. A. (1982). Young adult chronic patients: An analytical review of the literature. *Hospital and Community Psychiatry, 33*, 189–196.

Beers, Clifford. (1960). *A mind that found itself: An autobiography*. Garden City, NY: Doubleday.

Braddock, D., Hemp, R., & Fujiura, G. (1987). National study of public spending for mental retardation and developmental disabilities. *American Journal of Mental Deficiency, 92*(2), 121–133.

Brewster v. Dukakis, No. 76–4423 (D. Mass., December 6, 1978, final consent decree).

Brown, P. (1985). *The transfer of care*. London: Routledge & Kegan Paul.

Council of State Governments. (1983). *State administrative officials classified by functions*. Lexington, KY: Author.

Deutsche, A. (1948). *The shame of the states*. New York: Harcourt, Brace.

Dickey, B., & Cohen, M. D. (1991). Financing state mental health programs: Issues and options. In C. G. Hudson & A. J. Cox (Eds.), *Dimensions of state mental health policy* (pp. 211–229). New York: Praeger.

Dougherty, D. (1988). Children's mental health problems and services: Current federal efforts and policy implications. *American Psychologist, 43*(10), 808–812.

Durham, M. L., & Pierce, G. L. (1986). Legal intervention in civil commitment: The impact of broadened commitment criteria. *Annals of the American Academy of Political and Social Science, 484*, 42–55.

Goldman, H. H., Lehman, A. F., Morrissey, J. P., Newman, S. J., Frank, R. G., & Steinwachs, D. M. (1990). Design for the national evaluation of the Robert Wood Johnson Foundation program on chronic mental illness. *Hospital and Community Psychiatry, 41*, 1217–1221.

Grob, G. (1983). *Mental illness and American society, 1875–1940*. Princeton, NJ: Princeton University Press.

Gronfein, W. (1985). Incentives and intentions in mental health policy: A comparison of the Medicaid and community mental health programs. *Journal of Health and Social Behavior, 26*, 192–206.

Grusky, O., et al. (1986). Models of local mental health delivery systems. In W. R. Scott & B. L. Black (Eds.), *The organization of mental health services* (pp. 159–195). Beverly Hills, CA: Sage.

Hudson, C. G. (1983). *The impact of a block grant on decision making in state departments of mental health*. Ph.D. dissertation, University of Illinois at Chicago.

Hudson, C. G. (1987). An empirical model of state mental health spending. *Social Work Research and Abstracts, 23*, 3–12.

Hudson, C. G. (1988). Socioeconomic status and mental illness: Implications of the research for policy and practice. *Journal of Sociology and Social Welfare, 15*, 27–54.

Hudson, C. G. (1990). The performance of state community mental health systems: A path model. *Social Service Review, 64*(1), 94–120.

Hudson, C. G., & Cox, A. J. (Eds.). (1991). *Dimensions of state mental health policy.* New York: Praeger.

Hudson, C. G., & Dubey, S. N. (1984/1985). State mental health spending under the ADAMHA block grant: An empirical study. *Journal of Social Service Research, 8*, 1–24.

Hudson, C. G., & Dubey, S. N. (1986). Decision making under the ADAMHA block grant: Four case studies. *Administration in Mental Health, 14*, 97–116.

Hudson, C. G., Salloway, J., & Vissing, Y. (1992). The impact of state administrative practices on community mental health. *Administration and Policy in Mental Health, 19*, 417–436.

Jemelka, R., Trubin, E., & Chiles, J. A. (1989). The mentally ill in prisons: A review. *Hospital and Community Psychiatry, 40*, 481–490.

Joint Commission on Mental Illness and Health. (1961). *Action for mental health.* New York: Basic Books.

Kerr, C. A., & Roth, J. A. (1986). Populations, practices, and problems in forensic psychiatric facilities. *Annals of the American Academy of Political and Social Science, 484*, 127–43.

Kiesler, C. A., & Sibulkin, A. E. (1987). *Mental hospitalization: Myths and facts about a national crisis.* Beverly Hills, CA: Sage.

Korr, W. S. (1991). The current legal environment. In C. G. Hudson & A. J. Cox (Eds.), *Dimensions of state mental health policy* (pp. 58–63). New York: Praeger.

Kruzich, J. M. (1986). The chronically mentally ill in nursing homes: Issues in policy and practice. *Health and Social Work, 11*(1), 6–14.

Lindblom, C. (1968). *The policy-making process.* Englewood Cliffs, NJ: Prentice-Hall.

Maloy, K. A. (1990, November). Medicaid financing for mental health services: Intertwined in the health care policy Gordian knot. In *Policy in perspective.* Washington, D.C.: Mental Health Policy Resource Center.

Marvelle, K. (1990, November). A new way to examine Medicaid mental health services. In *Policy in perspective.* Washington, D.C.: Mental Health Policy Resource Center.

McFarland, B. H., Faulkner, L. R., Bloom, J. D., Hallaux, R., & Bray, J. D. (1989). Chronic mental illness and the criminal justice system. *Hospital and Community Psychiatry, 40*, 718–723.

Miller, S. O. (1991). Historical perspectives on state mental health policy. In C. G. Hudson & A. J. Cox (Eds.), *Dimensions of state mental health policy.* New York: Praeger.

Mills v. Rogers, 478 F. Supp. 1342 (D.C. Mass. 1979), 634 F2d 650 (1st Cir. 1980), *cert. granted,* 49 U.S.L.W. 3788 (1981).

Mills, M. J., Cummins, B. D., & Gracey, J. S. (1983). Legal issues in mental health administration. *International Journal of Law and Psychiatry, 6*, 39–55.

Morrissey, J. P., & Goldman, H. H. (1986). Care and treatment of the mentally ill in the United States: Historical developments and reforms. *Annals of the American Academy of Political and Social Science, 484*, 12–17.

National Institute of Mental Health (NIMH). (1986). *Mental health, United States, 1985.*

C. A. Taube & S. A. Barrett (Eds.). DHHS Pub. No. (ADM) 86–1378. Washington, DC: Superintendent of Documents, U.S. Government Printing Office.

National Institute of Mental Health (NIMH). (1992). *Mental Health, United States, 1992*. R. N. Manderscheid & M. A. Sonnenschein (Eds.). DHHS Pub. No. (ADM) 92–1942. Washington, DC: Superintendent of Documents, U.S. Government Printing Office.

National Institute of Mental Health (NIMH). (1990). *Mental health, United States, 1990*. R. W. Manderscheid & M. A. Sonnenschein (Eds.). DHHS Pub. No. (ADM) 90–1708. Washington, DC: Superintendent of Documents, U.S. Government Printing Office.

Regier, D. A., Myers, J. K., Kramer, M., Robins, L. N., Blazer, D. G., Hough, R. L., Eaton, W. W., & Locke, B. Z. (1984). The NIMH Epidemiologic Catchment Area Program: Historical context, major objectives, and study population characteristics. *Archives of General Psychiatry, 41*, 934–941.

Robins, L. N., et al. (1984). Lifetime prevalence of specific psychiatric disorders in three sites. *Archives of General Psychiatry, 41*, 949–958.

Rochefort, D. A. (1987). The political context of mental health care. In D. Mechanic (Eds.), *Improving mental health services: What the social sciences can tell us* (New Directions for Mental Health Services, No. 36). San Francisco: Jossey-Bass.

Rochefort, D. A. (1988). Policy-making cycles in mental health: A critical examination of a conceptual model. *Journal of Health Politics, Policy, and Law, 13*(1), 129.

Rose, S. M. (1979).Deciphering deinstitutionalization: Complexities in policy and program analysis. *Milbank Quarterly, 57*, 429–460.

Rose, S. M., Peabody, C. G., & Stratigeas, B. (1990). *Surviving abuse and its neglect: Towards increasing responsiveness of mental health systems*. Unpublished paper, State University of New York at Stony Brook.

Shenon, P. (1990, September 2). Cocaine epidemic may have peaked: Emergency hospital visits by users of drugs continue to drop, U.S. data show. *New York Times*, sec. 1, p. 32.

Summers, J. A. (1981). The definition of developmental disabilities: A concept in transition. *Mental Retardation, 19*(6), 259–265.

Torrey, E. F., Erdman, K., Wolfe, S. M., & Flynn, L. M. (1990). *Care of the seriously mentally ill: A rating of state programs* (3rd ed.). Washington, DC: Public Citizens Health Research Group and the National Alliance for the Mentally Ill.

Torrey, E. F., Wolfe, S. M., & Flynn, L. M. (1989). *Care of the seriously mentally ill: A rating of state programs* (2nd ed.). Washington, DC: Public Citizen Health Research Group and the National Alliance for the Mentally Ill.

Wolf, J. (1991). Organization of state mental health systems. In C. G. Hudson & A. J. Cox (Eds.), *Dimensions of state mental health policy* (pp. 84–96). New York: Praeger.

Wyatt v. Stickney. (1971). 325 F. Supp. 781 (M.D. Ala.).

21

Zambia

Alan Haworth

OVERVIEW

Geography and demography are important factors in determining the nature of mental health care in Zambia, and more so than in some other developing countries, with which, however, it also shares important characteristics. Zambia, known as Northern Rhodesia until its independence in 1964, is situated in south central Africa and is completely landlocked, being surrounded by Zaire, Tanzania, Malawi, Mozambique, Zimbabwe, Botswana, Namibia, and Angola. Situated within the tropics, with a highly seasonal rainfall, it has recently experienced severe drought in its southern half. Although relatively large in area (752,614 square kilometers), its total population, based upon the 1990 census, is just over 7,818,500, but many parts are sparsely populated (density varying between 4 and 40 per square kilometer, with an average of 10.4—as compared with an average density of about 74 per square kilometer in Malawi and about 26 in Zimbabwe). Forty-two percent of the population is now resident in urban areas, a much higher proportion than in most African countries (in Tanzania, for example, the proportion is about 19 percent, and in Zimbabwe 25 percent). The low density of population and the inadequate road network contribute to the high cost of provision of services. As in most developing countries, there is a large child population, and 48.8 percent are below the age of fifteen years. The life expectancy at birth is 55.4 for males and 57.5 for females. The current population growth rate is 3.2 percent per annum overall, but the cities have shown spectacular growth. Thus Lusaka, the capital city, had an African population of only about 50,000 in 1954; ten years later it had about 150,000, when Zambia gained independence; the population was 400,000 at the time of a sample census in 1974; and it is currently estimated to be over 1.2 million.

Zambia is divided for administrative purposes into nine provinces and, within the provincial structure, 636 districts. These include both conurbations and rural districts, and each has a structure of services that may be controlled and to some extent financed at district level, although up to the present, health services have largely been under central administration.

There are about seventy ethnic groups, although giving an exact number would depend upon the actual criteria used in determining "ethnicity," with seven major language groups (all classed as Bantu languages) in addition to English; the latter is also an official language and is the main one used in government and, for example, health service records. None of the ethnic groups is predominant, and only two have enough people to constitute about 20 percent of the population. Although the ethnic groups, or "tribes" in an older terminology, have a common basic culture, there are also many differences between them with regard, for instance, to belief in specific aspects of sorcery or spirit possession and in terms of bringing up children, marriage customs, mutual obligations in marriage, inheritance, and so forth, while for villagers, whether the economy is primarily pastoral or not can be extremely important. There are now proportionately fewer persons of European or Asian origin in the country.

The constituent peoples of Zambia (such as the Lunda, Bemba, Ngoni, Chewa, Lozi, and Tonga) had established their territories long before the colonial scramble for Africa in the final two decades of the last century. Zambia began to take its present shape with the amalgamation of territories. Those under the control of the British South Africa Company were joined with the eastern areas, under direct British colonial office control, and the western part, ruled by a traditional dynasty. Its potential for commercial development became apparent when minerals were found (a lead mine was opened in 1902), and a railway was built from the south, reaching the Zambezi River in 1904 and through to Katanga in what was then called the Belgian Congo in 1910. The main mining developments, however, were not to take place until about thirty years later.

Zambia was formerly known as Northern Rhodesia, and it remained a British colony until 1953. Its capital, Lusaka, was only established as such in 1935. Northern Rhodesia was incorporated (against the wishes of the people) into the Federation of Rhodesia and Nyasaland in 1953. Of the three countries forming the federation, Northern Rhodesia was at that time the strongest economically, with a relatively high income from its extensive deposits of nonferrous metals (principally copper), but with hardly any other developed revenue-earning potential. Since the colony of Southern Rhodesia had a much larger white population and power, at this time, was concentrated in their hands, there was a considerable draining of resources from Northern Rhodesia to finance development in the southern partner; for example, no university was established in the northern territory, the development of health services was strictly limited, and there were at this time, for example, no schools for the training of professional nurses. Zambia gained its independence in October 1964 and within two years had its own university. A massive expansion of educational and health services followed independence, but development was much curtailed by mounting economic problems beginning in the early 1970s.

Zambia recently became a multiparty democracy after twenty-seven years of rule by a single party, the United National Independence Party, which had been responsible for leading the fight for political freedom. From June 1990 it had become increasingly clear that the people of Zambia wanted to have political change with greater freedom of expression and the opportunity to vote for a party of their choice. A revision of the constitution allowed for multiparty elections to the one-chamber parliament and the election of a new president, with fairly well defined powers. There is now a marked reduction in the overlapping of the functions of party and government that had characterized the previous administration, which had established ascendancy of the party in decision making and a top-heavy party hierarchy. A new party named the Movement for Multiparty Democracy (MMD) gained an overwhelming victory in elections held at the end of October 1991, and the new government is currently engaged in a radical restructuring of all sectors, including health care provision.

Despite major efforts to develop services, based upon socialist principles, the rapid increase of population and the continuing economic deterioration have combined to curtail the further development of services, and the present government is now considering a policy of decentralization in which major health institutions will be in a position to raise their own funding, communities will be encouraged to have greater responsibility for the functioning and financing of the services they use, and an increased reliance will also be placed on the private sector. The implications of these policy changes will be discussed again in more detail later.

A new and important element must now be taken into account, both from the point of view of provision of mental health care and because of the potential economic cost. The first case of acquired immune deficiency syndrome (AIDS) was recognized in 1985, although sporadic cases had probably occurred before this date. Zambia is now one of the most seriously affected countries, and sentinel surveillance during 1990 revealed a prevalence of just under 25 percent seropositivity for human immunodeficiency virus (HIV) among women attending a number of antenatal clinics in Lusaka, the capital city. The current report of a total of over 20,000 symptomatic HIV-infected persons is a gross underestimate. The economic impact of HIV/AIDS will increase, and there will also be an increase in the number of children seriously affected by the distress of living in families where the parents are infected with HIV or ill, and those who have become orphans.

EXTENT OF THE PROBLEM

As in most countries in Africa, it is almost impossible to give an accurate picture of the extent of the problem in Zambia. Because Zambia has a service built upon the network of provincial and district government hospitals, some

Table 21.1
Admissions in Three Main Centers in Zambia, 1982

	Total adm.	Readm.	M/F ratio	Total OPs	M/F ratio
Lusaka	2,247	51.9	2.7	9,583	2.16
Ndola	1,427	47.9	2.8	2,722	3.0
Country	7,032	46.6	2.6	27,406	2.11

Source: Zambian government statistics, 1982.

statistics are available of admissions to these institutions and to certain general and central hospitals, as well as to the only psychiatric hospital, but these represent only patients needing admission according to local criteria and with access to a unit. Many patients who ought to have been admitted for investigation and care have not had access because a facility was too far away (Haworth, 1980), while others have been taken for care to traditional healers. No adequate reporting system is in place for those patients cared for at smaller units or by mental and general health workers operating from the extensive network of urban and rural clinics, although one is being developed. As will become apparent, much mental health care is delivered via small units, and hence inability to collect these data is a serious deficiency in the service. One of the reasons why even acute psychotic episodes can be treated in a local facility is that a high proportion of them are of brief duration—one day to three weeks, with the majority showing remission of salient symptomatology within forty-eight hours. They can thus be treated within the local community but outside the present reporting system.

It is convenient to start statistical comparisons with total admissions country-wide as they were known between 1965 and 1973. During this period admissions rose from 1,401 to 5,789. There was an initial rise in prison admissions when it became known that treatment could at last be offered to the mentally ill, and the number rose from 584 in 1965 to 1,054 in 1967, but had dropped to 268 by 1973; the current admission rate of "civil mental patients" is not known. Many units were offering outpatient services, and the total attendances throughout Zambia rose from 2,800 to 14,318 in the period 1965 to 1973. An analysis of the figures reported for 1982 is typical of the situation up to the present time, so far as is known. Figures are given for the only mental hospital (in Lusaka), for a major unit at Ndola (essentially serving the whole of the Cooper Belt—the main mining area in Zambia), and for the country as a whole (table 21.1).

No up-to-date figures are available for the country as a whole, but the total admissions for the Lusaka Hospital were 1,924 in 1990, with 54.6 percent readmissions and a male/female ratio of 2.83. Some comment is needed first on the male/female ratio, which, it will be noted, is more or less the same throughout the country. This is typical of the pattern found in many countries in Africa, where one of the main reasons for being brought for care is violent or disruptive behavior (the stereotype of the "madman") and not, often, more subtle symptomatology; a woman who is depressed but causing no special disturbance is less likely to be admitted, and hence the preponderance of males.

The figures for Lusaka show an important trend, for, as has been pointed out earlier, the capital city has shown a remarkable growth rate, and its population is currently estimated to be 1,207,980, including the periurban areas (which is also serviced by the mental hospital in Lusaka). Yet the number of admissions is currently reported to be less than it was in 1982, with a slight increase in the readmission rate. This reflects (at least partially) the success of the community mental health program, for mental health workers operate in all the urban health centers, which provide the bulk of outpatient medical care. In 1988, for example, the health center that is used for the training of general clinical officers (described later) reported a total attendance of 1,674, including 375 new patients. The rising readmission rate could well reflect the fact that, while the community service can cope with patients suffering from short-term psychotic illness (the brief psychotic episodes already referred to), a relatively higher proportion of patients with actual schizophrenia will need readmission, and this will be reflected in returns from the mental hospital (see Guiness, 1992, for a useful discussion of this phenomenon).

There is no specific forensic psychiatric service, but the courts may order the medical or psychiatric examination of accused persons. As will be described in more detail later, the British M'Naghten rules have been incorporated into statute law, and these are invoked in the examination of those who have committed serious offenses; other types of forensic problems are rarely referred for psychiatric examination. Those who are found "not guilty by reason of insanity" are confined in either a special psychiatric hospital or in a designated prison; the hospital accommodation is adjacent to Zambia's only civil mental hospital, while the prison accommodation is some 525 kilometers away and has the services of a visiting psychiatrist only. There is no special accommodation of any kind for women. The special hospital had a "bed state" of 120 per day during 1990; 35 patients were admitted; 21 were readmitted (usually after trial, on being ordered to be detained); there were 25 transferred into prison accommodation and none released from judicial detention; and there were 3 deaths.

The main substance of abuse in Zambia is alcohol. Cannabis grows readily and is easy to obtain; it is usually taken by smoking the dried flowering tops and leaves. Although cannabis is not taken to be a major substance abuse problem, it is possible that it contributes to some of the brief psychotic episodes seen in various facilities. Patients are only rarely brought for treatment on account of dependence upon benzodiazepines, and these drugs are not available in Zambia in large quantities because of the economic situation. Zambia has been a transit country for methaqualone (Mandrax) for some years, but because of the cost of the drug and vigilant drug enforcement officers, very little has become available for local use. Some three or four years ago Zambia became a transit country for the importation of heroin to the United States and Europe from Southeast Asia, and a small number of well-off expatriates and Zambians became dependent; no intravenous injection of heroin has been reported. Some opium use a small amount of cocaine use have been reported, but no abusers have been admitted for medical or psychiatric treatment. The number of admissions for heroin abuse has also been small, totaling less than fifteen over a three-year period. Both because of the economic situation and because of the orphaning of an increasing number of children due to AIDS, street children are rapidly increasing in numbers, and they are specially vulnerable. The use of petrol and various solvents has been reported, as well as Mandrax, benzodiazepines, alcohol in the form of both legal and illicit beverages, and cannabis. There have, however, been no reports of the use of the so-called hard drugs.

Since there is insufficient space to discuss all variations in psychopathology, it is not possible to enter into the reasons for the apparent comparative rarity of both attempted and completed suicide. However, no reliable statistics are available on either.

MENTAL HEALTH HISTORY

Prior to the arrival of the missionaries and those engaged in the slave trade, the part of Africa that was to become Zambia had no contact with cosmopolitan medicine, and it must be assumed that the mentally ill, and particularly those with minor psychiatric illnesses, were usually cared for by traditional healers. As colonization began, cosmopolitan or Western medical care generally was provided only for Europeans and some of their employees and to a limited number of local people living within reach of mission stations where medical facilities were being set up. In 1928 there were only fifteen official (colonial) medical officers in the country, yet it was estimated that there was a 50 percent mortality rate among infants, and 25 percent of the population in one area was said to be suffering from yaws. However, a Lunacy Ordinance (based upon the Indian model) had been enacted in December 1927, making the High Court responsible for jurisdiction with regard to the mentally ill (lunatics were defined as "idiots" or persons of unsound mind). Provision was made for magistrates to order the detention of such persons after having received a report from two doctors, except that in the case of "natives" one medical certificate (report) would suffice. No special institutional care was provided, there was no specially trained doctor, and the policy was essentially to send a patient back to his village as soon as he was deemed not to be dangerous. Such patients were, in any case, usually looked after in prison and not in hospital, and the mission hospitals were noteworthy for refusing admission to those with mental illnesses. In 1935 a prominent member of the country's Legislative Council, Sir Stewart Gore-Brown, asked during a debate: "I wonder if Hon. Members realize—certainly the country does not—that we still, in this enlightened country adopt the medieval practice of putting lunatics in prison and, when necessary, chaining them up.''

At that time the country had a population of about 1,366,000 Africans and 13,000 non-Africans, and there were six official notifications of mental illness. From this time onwards, however, there was a steady but slow expansion in the provision of medical care, with, for example, only 15 rural health centers in the whole of Zambia in 1935 expanding to 106 in 1953. It had been appreciated that some form of provision for the mentally ill was necessary, and the Ministry of Health reported in 1946: ''As for mental hospitals, Northern Rhodesia has none and badly needs one and probably two.''

A year later the provision of a mental hospital was said to be still under consideration, but as a temporary measure a small mental annex was being constructed in Ndola, the administrative center for the main mining area of the country. The following year, four psychiatric nurses were recruited to join a staff for the whole country of only 230 (European) health workers. During its first year of operation the Ndola annex admitted 26 patients: 17 male Africans, 3 female Africans, and 6 Europeans, 3 male and 3 female. The experiment was considered to be so successful that it was decided to build similar annexes at all major centers. A typical one, that at the African Hospital in Lusaka, was known as ''the wire'' since patients were incarcerated in a prisonlike structure surrounded by barbed wire.

The Lunacy Ordinance had in the meantime been amended on a number of occasions, notably in 1930, 1933, and 1936, in order to allow temporary detention prior to official adjudication that a person was mentally ill. On adjudication, patients were sent to a large mental hospital in Bulawayo, in Southern Rhodesia, as far as 2,500 kilometers or more from their homes, where they could only hope to find the occasional staff member or fellow patient who spoke their language. Rather than follow the official and cumbersome process of discharging patients legally and returning them to Zambia, many were released on leave of absence in the expectation that they would find their way back to their homes. Their names were removed from the books after one year in Bulawayo, but they officially remained adjudicated persons and subject to various legal disabilities within Zambia. The anomaly of requiring two medical certificates for one class of person and one certificate for another was removed—all would now require two. This was recommended so as to protect the ''rights'' of the individual but ignored the fact that there were so few doctors that some patients had to be detained for many months or sent many hundreds of kilometers before they could be declared sane. The case for setting up better facilities for mental health care was increasingly self-evident. Yet there was a form of unwritten policy in operation—namely, that provided a person did not appear to be dangerous, he or she was returned to his or her relatives or the village headman or chief; only ''special'' (the word was not defined in reports) patients were sent to Bulawayo.

In the year 1953 the country known as Northern Rhodesia became a party of the Federation of Rhodesia and Nyasaland, and health care became a federal responsibility. The same policy was continued by the federal authorities, and their attitude can be gleaned from the following quotations from the Federal Ministry of Health Annual Report for 1960:

Lunatics have rained about our ears from all sides, some of them for the second time (or more) in a year. It is felt that the present system of certification, adjudication and transfer to Bulawayo is very cumbersome and the long wait between adjudication and the receipt of a warrant of removal is very tedious to all concerned. Many of the patients are returned to villages for supervision by the headman. They are the ones who have really no mental disease and are eccentrics with a "Government must help me" complex. A large boot directed to the appropriate party of the anatomy would be very helpful for some of these and save a lot of time and trouble, however politically undesirable. . . . Should we not restrict ourselves to the really curative services? . . . there was again an increase in the daily average number of patients. . . . What, however, contributed more to our difficulty than the increase in patients, was the consequent increase in relatives. The nuisance and frustration these people cause must be experienced to be believed. (Federal Ministry of Health, 1960)

With this kind of thinking there was little chance of promoting a community-based approach, relying upon relatives to care for patients, with the active assistance of health professionals. Rather, the building of a mental hospital became a main imperative. Conditions in Bulawayo had in any case become intolerable, and a Commission of Inquiry examining the operation of the health service in 1959 reported that the hospital, built to accommodate 690 patients, had 1,391 on the day of its visit. No actual beds were provided for African patients (except for a few suffering from physical ailments), and because there was no special forensic unit, long-stay patients were accommodated with the criminal patients in grossly overcrowded conditions. According to the federal government's 1959 Annual Report on the Public Health, there was an increase of from 747 to 1,595 patients admitted with mental illnesses between 1955 and 1959, and many theories were propounded to explain this increase. In spite of the very negative attitude to the mentally ill shown in the quotation given earlier, the Federal Ministry of health proposed that patients should be treated in a mental hospital with a proper respect for human rights, that some patients could be treated at general hospitals, that the mental annex system be expanded to all provinces, that teaching on mental health be incorporated into the curricula of general health workers, and that "African doctors" and nursing staff be trained to replace the Europeans because they would have a better cultural understanding and be able to establish a strong bond of sympathy with their patients.

A mental hospital was opened in June 1962 in Lusaka, and immediately more than half its 260 beds were filled by patients returned from Bulawayo. The country's first (necessarily expatriate) psychiatrist was soon appointed, and better care for patients countrywide was anticipated. Fortunately, there was no thought of building more hospitals; the one psychiatrist would, however, be expected to travel to main centers from time to time, advising on the care of patients in the various mental annexes.

This was the situation at independence on October 24, 1964. With an additional psychiatrist, more regular visits were made countrywide, and as a result patients who had previously been held, sometimes in wooden manacles, sometimes in scarring bicycle chains, were brought for treatment; and neither was there enough room, nor did the staff exist to provide the care. The psychiatrists found most of their patients incarcerated in prison cells, fed reluctantly by fearful prison warders. The first task was to train sufficient staff, and since there was no registered nurse training at this time in Zambia, it was decided to train assistants, or clinical officers as they are now known.

In order to understand the place of clinical officers in health care, it is necessary to turn back to the history of health services in Zambia once more. As soon as any form of health care was being offered, it became apparent that some local people would need to assist. Initially, some had been chosen to visit villages and provide very elementary treatment; they were called indigenous medical orderlies. As they walked from village to village, they could be thought of as the forerunners of the famous Chinese "barefoot doctors." It is not known if they ever dealt with the mentally ill, but this is doubtful. In 1935 a two-year dispensary assistant course had been instituted with an entry requirement of six to eight years of primary education. In 1942 the two-year course was phased out and replaced by a three-year hospital assistant course that admitted candidates with eight years and sometimes ten years of schooling; there was much emphasis upon nursing care since no actual nurse training was being given. Over the next few years graduates of these courses were given different names, but all were eventually called "medical assistants," and the length of training was established at three years, with entry after obtaining a secondary education leaving certificate. A final change occurred when the medical assistants were redesignated "clinical officers"—their current title. This has particular significance, however, for at this time, clinical officers became registrable by the Medical Council of Zambia (which had formerly licensed only physicians), and so they were given recognition as professionals.

As it happened, at the time when medical assistants were being given a two-year training, it was decided to train a group of workers to meet the needs of the mentally ill—they were to become psychiatric medical assistants, now called clinical officers (psychiatry). These workers were given special training focusing upon psychiatry and mental health, but their course began with a solid introduction to basic sciences and then to general clinical sciences. They were trained at the same institution as the general clinical officers who still provide the bulk of health care from the many health centers catered around Zambia. There was no formal nurse training, and registered nurses were imported either from Europe or from neighboring African countries; medical assistants both provided nursing care and also acted as "minidoctors"—a role that they were to increasingly assume. It was only in 1965, when Zambia had gained its independence, that both registered (three-year, professional) and enrolled (two-year, practical) nursing training programs were established. Although a psychiatric enrolled nurse training program was established after 1968 in parallel with the clinical officer training, a course for registered psychiatric nurses was only established in 1991. The expansion of mental health care depended largely upon having a steady output of clinical officers who would be willing to work in remote rural areas and who would be increasingly integrated into the total health system.

POLICY, ORGANIZATION, AND SERVICES IN THE 1980s AND 1990s

Current Policy Developments

Zambia prepared a key document in 1978, entitled ''Priorities in Mental Health Care.'' This came both from our own initiative and from the advice of the World Health Organization (WHO), which advocated a policy of establishing a multisectorial advisory group that would essentially keep the program on course. The development of services at this time and this policy document in particular came at a critical time in the determination of policy on health on the world scale. The WHO/UNICEF conference on Primary Health Care held at Alma Ata in 1978, with its theme of Health for All by the Year 2000, has had a major impact on health service planning in third-world countries, including Zambia; and in Zambia we had even anticipated the recommendations of this meeting with regard to mental health. On the publication of the Alma Ata report and recommendations the Zambian government decided to embark upon a policy of putting the recommendations into effect on a countrywide scale, eschewing any pilot projects carried out in limited geographic areas. A series of intersectorial meetings was held countrywide, and these culminated in the holding of a national conference at which the reports and recommendations from all parts of Zambia and from all sectors would be amalgamated into a final and authoritative policy document.

It was noted that the people of countries in which rapid social and economic changes are taking place are especially vulnerable to stresses caused by conflict with traditional values, the results of rapid urban migration (with stress in rural as well as urban areas), the extremely high proportion of women who are bearing children, and the large number of children under the age of fifteen, with a high dependency ratio. Note was taken of the disruption of family and community life in both urban and rural populations related to the abuse of alcohol and other drugs among youths. (This was essentially a political statement and not based upon adequate data; the political masters are more likely to accede to recommendations when a statement that is congruent with their beliefs is made.) It was also noted that particular difficulties arise with regard to preventing and coping when problems of mental ill health derive from an often-multifactorial etiology in which often more than one member of a family would experience some degree of psychiatric disability.

The definition of primary health care adopted in Zambia is that it is essentially health care made universally accessible to individuals and families in the community by means acceptable to them, through their full participation, and at a cost that the community and the country can afford. It therefore aims to tackle the main health problems in the community with particular emphasis on the undeserved, high-risk, and vulnerable groups—which must include the mentally ill and handicapped.

Current Organization

The overall health plan as determined by the national conference started by looking at the village or community level and provided for the training of village or community health workers (CHWs) who would normally be respected persons living in that community with sufficient education to undergo a six-week course of training focusing upon prevention of common diseases, but with some training in simple treatment and rehabilitation, who would have been selected by the community members, and who would receive no remuneration but would be supported by the community in carrying out their tasks, with the guidance of a community health committee and technical advice and support from professional health workers. It was proposed that there should be a mental health component based upon the following job description: The community health workers will

- encourage active participation and cooperation of all the members of the community by providing simple mental health education and dissemination of information about the availability of services;
- be able to identify and refer persons who might have emotional problems, serious mental illness, or epilepsy and children with learning and/or behavioral disorders;
- ensure that those persons who are on long-term treatment take their medicines as prescribed—but without having the authority to initiate or modify treatment with psychoactive drugs—and encourage acceptance of the patient within the community; and
- collect and compile simple data about the mentally ill in that community.

Since it was proposed that rural health centers would serve populations of up to about 10,000 and some of them would have a staff of up to five persons with a small inpatient unit of fifteen to twenty beds, their team of general medical workers would be responsible for delivery of mental health care at this basic level. Tasks would include education and guidance of village health committees (and CHWs) on matters pertaining to activities as described in the duties of CHWs; the assessment of all patients with suspected psychiatric problems with a view to deciding whether the patient could be managed locally or should be referred; dealing with patients presenting in an acutely disturbed state or with epilepsy; maintenance of treatment regimes and rehabilitation; and being aware at all times of the mental health (psychosocial) component in all patients presenting with apparent physical illnesses. Training for these workers (general clinical officers and enrolled nurses) would take account of these duties. Correspondingly, higher-level units would be better staffed, including mental health workers, and would be responsible both for assisting and supervising lower-level activities and also for providing short- or long-term care (depending upon the type of facility) for patients with psychiatric illnesses, only referring those needing specialized investigation or management to higher-level or specialized units. The policy of training specialized clinical officers and nurses for work in the mental health field meant that staff would be available to begin implementing this program.

This schema, worked out in 1981, was meant to fit into the already-existing structure of mental health care and to also be compatible with the overall development of health services. It was acknowledged that provision of mental health care should have both a vertical and a horizontal component. The former refers to the professional support system for mental health services within the health service and the latter to the local organization of care, with full integration with all other components of care. The operation of these components will be discussed later in terms of policy process. The implementation of this program was but a continuation, with slight modifications, of previous policies. The one mental hospital and the main mental health units (a term preferable to "mental annexes") have continued to function with psychiatrists operating only in Lusaka and Ndola and sometimes, when they were available, in other locations. The bulk of the work has been carried out by the clinical officers (including the promotion grades of "senior" and "principal" clinical officer) and enrolled nurses within the framework of health care and the laws pertaining to the mentally ill.

Mention has already been made of the initiation of multiparty democracy in Zambia. The new government, in contending with major economic problems, has proposed radical restructuring of the health service, with an inevitable consequence for mental health care. Thus although health care was formerly provided free to the individual, user fees and cost sharing have been introduced, but there is provision that no one will be denied health care because of the inability to pay, and note has been taken of the necessity of providing help to those suffering from chronic illnesses. The fact that there will be encouragement of private-sector provision of health care is hardly likely to affect the mental health sector at present; in any case many minor disorders are treated by the traditional healers on a fee-for-service basis. As a preliminary working paper puts it, "In the final analysis Zambia has put in place mixed systems of financing health care which has resulted in stratification whereby the state would continue providing for those who could not otherwise have access (e.g., the poor and those with chronic health problems)."

The policy document restresses the importance of the primary health care (PHC) approach. It remarks that in its initial implementation "enthusiasm and haste have often triumphed over coordinated planning and management." Decentralization is a key concept and especially that of the District Health Management Team since "the district can play a vital role in matching local needs and priorities with national policy guidelines and resources.'' The plan also envisages restructuring at the central (ministry) level, and a Public Health Department will encompass a PHC Coordinating Unit, an Epidemiology Unit, and CMH Unit, and an Environmental Health Unit. Special programs supervised by the PHC unit will include mental health, oral health, traditional medicine, and primary health care. It is thus seen that while mental health is to be found in the right place, in some regards, as an important element in PHC, it has neither the centrality nor prominence that it would appear to deserve. Its place has recently been established by statute in a neighboring country (Kenya), and it is intended to make a similar proposal to the Zambian government; in the meantime the current law on mental illness has limited applicability.

The present Mental Disorders Act (Chapter 538 of the Laws of Zambia) is essentially the same as the first one brought into force over fifty years ago; the modifications have been relatively minor. The definitions of mental illness need to be brought up to date, but in addition, it is noteworthy that mentally subnormal persons are classed with the mentally ill and in the remainder of the act are nowhere differentiated in terms of their examination, care, custody, and other treatment. The act, which allows for a two-week period of detention during which two doctors may submit reports on whether the person should be judged (adjudicated) to be mentally ill, has a number of anomalies. The detention is ordered by a magistrate upon receiving written affidavits concerning the behavior of the alleged patient, which refer only to certain forms of behavior—often in effect dictated to a deponent by a clerk of the court. An Order of Detention having been issued, it may in effect be renewed indefinitely, once every fortnight. Although it is effective for only two weeks, no mechanism for discharge exists should the doctors not submit certificates, even if no request for extension has been made. Once a person has been adjudicated, there is no mechanism for regular review, and indefinite adjudication (but not necessarily detention) may result. Fortunately, the act is becoming superfluous. Until 1965 there was no legal means of admitting a patient to a designated institution except by means of a Detention Order. In that year a Ministerial Statutory Instrument was issued that allowed ''voluntary'' or ''informal'' admission. This allowed a person to enter hospital and submit himself or herself to the same disabilities as though he or she had been detained, but it did allow of discharge on demand unless the hospital staff, relatives, or other persons swore an affidavit in due form. From this time patients were encouraged to enter the psychiatric units as ordinary patients, and the use of the power of adjudication became extremely rare. Furthermore, no list of designated hospitals was issued, while, outside Lusaka and Ndola, most of the care of the mentally ill was in the hands of clinical officers (nominally working under the supervision of medical practitioners) who had no powers under the act. Taking these various aspects and the anomalies listed, as well as others, into account, it has been decided to review the law and to draft a new act, which will also more firmly establish the place of mental health care within the total health care system. The process of admission and discharge will be placed more firmly in the hands of health and social welfare personnel while continuing to afford legal protection of patients' rights, and it is intended that the important role of clinical officers (who are licensed by the Medical Council) will be recognized, and that they will be allowed to sign certain documents. The question of the mentally disordered offender will be dealt with in detail later.

Current Services

Although much reference has been made to primary health care, no account has yet been given of the health care delivery system in Zambia. The original health system depended upon the activities of traditional healers (who could be divided into various categories such as herbalists, diviners, and so forth) who were often in "private practice," especially as the conurbations grew. Three main services then grew up in parallel. A government service provides the public health and specialist hospital components as well as the general countrywide system of hospitals, health centers, and health posts. This overlaps with a service provided in the rural areas by church (formerly mission) hospitals and that remains very important. As the mines grew, they provided their own medical services with hospitals that tended to be better equipped than those of either churches or government. There is also some care provided by other industries and in the commercial sector, and there is a relatively small but expanding private sector. At the time of Zambia's independence there were only two or three Western-trained indigenous doctors, and a limited private sector existed, with foreign doctors from many countries. When they were barred from access to government hospitals and private nursing homes were closed, the service they could provide consisted of office practice only. Only now are plans being made for the opening up of the private sector. Mission (or church) hospitals have never been willing to admit the mentally ill, although this seems somewhat curious. The mine medical service has dealt with the mentally ill in essentially two ways—either by shifting the patient (if an expatriate) out of Zambia as quickly as possible, or by making use of the government service. This is still the case. A treatment center for alcoholics existed on the Zambian Cooper Belt before independence, but this catered only to white expatriates and did not admit indigenous miners; it was sold in order to raise funds for an outreach campaign on prevention of drinking when the Zambian Council on Alcoholism and Addictions came into existence and took over control. There have been only a few attempts to provide psychiatric care through private office practice, but none has really taken root, partly because there have been too few psychiatrists and it has not been possible to earn enough in private psychiatric practice alone. Clinical officers are not allowed to engage in private medical practice. This means that all mental health care has been in the hands of either the indigenous traditional healers or of the government health service, including that provided by the single university department of psychiatry.

Mental Health Personnel and Treatment

It is evident that most formal psychiatric care is provided by paramedical personnel, and their contribution will be described in more detail later. Zambia has few psychiatrists, and the maximum (at a time when funds were available to pay expatriates) reached one per half-million population. There are currently seven in the country, five of whom work in Lusaka and one each in Ndola and Livingstone. Cuba has been supplying doctors to Zambia, and psychiatrists are occasionally sent, who then work in provincial centers but rarely have any contact with their other colleagues; it is not known if any are currently working in Zambia. The School of Medicine in Lusaka turns out about forty doctors per year, and of these, three who elected initially to remain in Zambia have so far qualified as psychiatrists. One is now working in Botswana, one works as an industrial doctor (where the terms of service are better), and only one works full-time in the mental health service. Two others are currently in training in the United Kingdom, and others are preparing to leave. Because of Zambia's poor economic situation many young doctors leave the country early, and it is understood that several others have trained as psychiatrists and are working in other countries.

Since Zambia has only just established a training program for registered mental health nurses, the only ones currently working in Zambia are either expatriates or Zambians whom we have been able to send to other countries for training. There are 505 other mental health workers in the grades of clinical officer or enrolled psychiatric nurse spread throughout the country. Lusaka, with its mental hospital (used also for teaching, as a referral center, and for research), has 165— a ratio of 1 mental health worker per 7,352 population, or about 14 workers per 100,000 population. This compares with an average of 6 workers per 100,000 population in the remainder of the country. Although many of them work in provincial or district hospital units, many have also been posted to work at the basic level in health centers, but even so we have attained only a 10 to 20 percent coverage of the 557 health centers, except in Lusaka, where mental health workers are found in 51 percent. Depending upon the local density of population and other factors, it is not necessary to have a mental health worker at every health center, and many of those currently working at these centers give a good part of their time to general duties; we expect general workers in other centers to give a proportionate part of their time to mental health work, with assistance from mental health workers visiting from the nearest hospital mental health unit. The whole of the health service in Zambia has currently only 18 medical social workers and there are no fully trained psychiatric social workers. Three psychiatric clinical officers are trained in social work; one is acting as a tutor training clinical officers and nurses, and the two others are not working in the mental health field. Although we have one psychologist working at the mental hospital, she still awaits an opportunity to train as a clinical psychologist; another works in Ndola. Of two trained clinical psychologists in the country, one is a tutor at the Health Sciences College and the other teaches at the university and does not engage in clinical practice. Zambia evidently has to manage to care for the mentally ill with a minimum of human resources, and it will take some time to build up the numbers in the various cadres to acceptable levels. How this will be done, with more emphasis upon giving clinical officer and psychiatric enrolled nurse training at the postbasic level (that is, after general training and experience in the field), with an inevitably lower output, and with a possible disinclination on the part of some graduates to accept work in remote health centers, has still to be established.

PUBLIC POLICY PROCESS

In this small country policy tends to be determined or evolve at the central governmental level. Each of the three main sources of medical care (apart from the small private sector) consists of a highly centralized and hierarchical system, including that provided by the churches, where policy is determined both by the individual funding church body and by the Churches Medical Association of Zambia. In any case, both church hospitals and industrial medical services have hardly been involved within the mental health sphere and have had little interest in policy matters. The situation is changing with regard to the care of patients with AIDS, where church members are increasingly being asked to help with home-based care, including psychosocial counselling, and industry is waking up to the fact that there must be a positive response; but it has been almost impossible to establish psychosocial counselling on the scale required in the mine medical service. Although critiques of some aspects of mental health policy have been made by final-year law students in special assignments, these often-excellent pieces of work have usually been confined to the library shelves; there is no formal mechanism for using them to open up debate.

As mental health workers were sent to work in the original mental annexes, they were instructed that they should become integral members of the hospital staff team and that they would be fully responsible in terms of their work to the person in charge of the hospital. They were told, furthermore, that they would rely for professional advice on the workers in Lusaka who would visit them regularly to sort out both clinical and administrative problems. This was still too close to the time when services were looked upon as essentially curative for anything approaching the primary health care model to have been considered. Yet, psychiatry being what it is and with the example of close collaboration with relatives already experienced in their training in Lusaka, these workers were soon establishing links with the local communities. Here we have the core concept of the interaction of the vertical and horizontal approaches, coupled with a community approach.

In 1969 questions of policy were considered at a special high-level meeting convened in the Ministry of Health and chaired by the permanent secretary. The meeting was attended by senior staff from the ministry, from the health field generally, from the university, and also from the Department of Social Welfare. The policy of having only one actual mental hospital in the country with units attached to other hospitals was affirmed, and funds were requested for the construction of purpose-built units. It was reported that an institution (based upon a village model) was being established for long-stay patients who could have little expectation of discharge, and this was approved. It was recommended that the training of clinical officers be expanded and integrated with the training of general clinical officers, while the content of the training on psychiatry and mental health for the latter should be increased. Emphasis was to be put on the teaching of psychosocial aspects of disease in all parts of the training of health workers generally. It was also recommended that the School of Medicine should establish a department and chair in psychiatry. Finally, it was recommended that there should be at least a special liaison person within the Ministry of Health who could consolidate links between mental health and all other aspects of health care at a high level. This meeting was memorable because of the eloquent plea made by a British psychiatrist, Christopher Nunn (1969), who could perhaps look at service developments more dispassionately, for the strengthening of the training of the clinical officers, who, as he put it, ''are working in most of the main centers of population. The fact of their presence means that Zambia is in the forefront of African psychiatry; but what they are able to do falls very far short of what would be desirable because of lack of facilities . . . and the nature of their own training. . . . The service will therefore come to be based on the skill and dedication of the psychiatric clinical officer. . . . They are required to be their own psychiatrists, doctors, nurses and social workers.'' This was a key meeting, and many of the recommendations were put into effect, except that no funds could be found for setting up special units, even in the larger provincial hospitals.

It will be apparent that much of the policy on the development of mental health care since Zambia gained its independence has come from the mental health workers themselves, collaborating with administrators in the Ministry of Health and with their colleagues in the peripheral units and in related fields. There were also, however, inputs from various external agencies such as the World Health Organization (both the Geneva and African offices) and the Organization of African Unity (OAU), and these sources must be discussed since they have been of special importance in many developing countries. For example, a further input on policy came in 1975 when a Scientific Advisory Panel of the Organization of African Unity met in Addis Ababa to examine mental health and mental diseases in Africa. A psychiatrist from Zambia acted as a rapporteur to the meeting. The delegates were unanimous that the training of mental health personnel was a top priority and that all other recommendations could not be realized without this being tackled urgently. Other priorities included revision of mental health legislation and research, but there was no mention of the priority of community mental health activities. These were discussed in the section on objectives and priorities in development of mental health services, where the first objective mentioned was an emphasis on treating the patient within his or her own environment with decentralization of services and the use of small-scale psychiatric units as opposed to large mental hospitals and, in view of the meager resources available, the delegation of work to nurses and other paramedical personnel. With regard to chronic patients, it was recommended that community facilities should be set up as halfway houses toward eventual discharge, for example, community farms or villages. In the discussion of legal aspects, much emphasis was put upon human rights aspects.

It would appear that Zambia was moving in the right direction in the development of its service when comparison is made with these recommendations. In the late 1970s the Division of Mental Health of the World Health Organization was promoting the idea of setting up high-level interministerial coordinating groups, and the idea was readily taken up in Lusaka. The group was intended to be truly intersectorial and interministerial, and hence psychologists, social workers, other health workers, and representatives from the Ministries of Education, Social Development, Labor, and others were invited; full-time mental health workers were in a significant minority. The majority of the members attending the meeting had little knowledge of mental health problems or of psychiatry, and when it was proposed that papers be written on priorities in mental health services, most (including one on psychiatry and leprosy) were written by the psychiatrist member, with one notable exception: a key paper from a psychologist on community services for assisting families with handicapped children. Unfortunately, the Mental Health Coordinating Group was given little priority by the permanent secretary (the civil servant head of the ministry), and there was no executive unit to carry out policy within the ministry of Health; one of the main recommendations—that an executive unit should be connected with a national resource center linked to provincial resource centers—was ignored. Although no executive unit was established, a national mental health resource center (MHRC) that had already been set up was further strengthened, but without establishing the provincial network. The concept of the resource center is probably unique and hence requires some description. Because of the nature of the preventive, curative, and rehabilitative aspects of mental health service provision, a variety of resources need to be provided in a way that is flexible and caters for the transmission of information regarding needs and responses as well as help in coping with technical demands. A MHRC fulfills these functions through collection of statistics and other mental health service information; organization of training, including especially in-service and further educational courses and the organization of workshops and seminars, for example, on the law and mental illness or on mental illness and employment; publication of materials and maintenance of a library and stocks of informational and teaching materials; establishing special departments such as community mental health, AIDS counselling, epilepsy, and so forth; and promoting and carrying out research. This is the structure of the National Mental Health Resource Center in Zambia, which has departments or personnel dealing with all these topics. Because of its responsibility for gathering information and carrying out research as well as organizing seminars, it has a special role to play in helping formulate policy as well as promoting the practical application of these formulations. Thus it has organized workshops involving representatives of other ministries or departments (including members of the judiciary) in formulating recommendations on the law and mental illness, problems of children and adolescents, and the rights and obligations of employers, among other topics. The unit has increasingly gained the respect and confidence of senior administrators and professionals in the Ministry of Health, which is why it was accorded the responsibility for organizing all aspects of counselling for HIV/AIDS in the national program; yet while the counselling unit does have executive functions in its sphere, the unit as a whole has none in administering the mental health service.

The Mental Health Association of Zambia, a voluntary, lay body affiliated with the World Federation for Mental Health, has played a key role in examining issues and acting both as a pressure group and in the role of innovator. It was represented since its inception on the now-defunct National Mental Health Coordinating Group, described briefly earlier. But although the Mental Health Association continues to help in public education at the national level and in education and mobilization of resources at the local level, it has not had power to effect any significant changes in policy.

It may be said that the process of policy change in Zambia has mainly been by evolution rather than revolution, and there have been no dramatic crises or public outcries or protests. Yet even evolution has not always been without its problems or struggles. Sometimes this was because it was felt that an innovation or management decision (we might sometimes dignify it by the term *policy*) would not be readily accepted and partial implementation had to come first. An example lies in having mental health workers posted to urban health centers in the capital city. The idea had been opposed by some physicians at the mental hospital who did not wish to work beyond the walls. The postings were done almost in secret, certainly without fanfare. It later became possible to set up a regular meeting of these workers under the chairmanship of a physician who had expressed an interest in extending the principles of community care. Meetings were held regularly and to the outsider seemed impressive, but they resulted hardly at all in the required development of integration between care in the hospital and in the community, for the chairman remained unwilling to move beyond his familiar environment, and there was a constant pull, as it were, toward the center, rather than a push outward into the community. There is still no formal link between hospital and community, even with the division of Lusaka into three zones with physicians and other staff members visiting key zonal health centers.

It is possible that some crisis in mental health care or a related field might have persuaded the Ministry of Health to provide greater material resources, including the building of small units and the establishment of resource centers. Thus the government has recently been convinced that drug abuse is on the increase because of the actual increase in trafficking and has provided resources that are probably disproportionate to the need, while the related area of mental health (in terms of treatment and rehabilitation) has been neglected. If a service is provided that is recognized as being reasonably adequate, which is currently the situation with regard to mental health, it is difficult to develop powerful arguments for demanding change, especially in times of economic stringency. But formulating policy in accordance with evolutionary change in service provision does demand mechanisms for administration and integration from the central level, even at times of devolution of responsibilities to the periphery, and we have not so far been able to establish these in as formal a way as is desirable. An interministerial/intersectoral advisory group established at a high level needs to be revived, but it will need an executive mechanism that will fully link it into the various networks of service provision.

SPECIAL POLICY ISSUES

The Mentally Ill and the Mentally Retarded

As has already been mentioned, the mentally retarded are not distinguished as a special group in the Mental Disorders Act. While there was some provision for the blind and the deaf in the colonial and federal periods, no special provision was made for those with learning disabilities. When a number of severely handicapped children were referred to the mental hospital, it was decided to open a ward for their care, together with an associated day center/school. In 1977 the government produced a major policy statement on education in which it was proposed that children with learning disabilities and other handicaps should be educated so far as possible in an ordinary school environment, but that in addition, some special schools should be set up. In a detailed proposal made in the document on priorities in mental health care a psychologist suggested that even severely handicapped children should be brought up at home and might often go for normal schooling, provided that the parents were trained and given help and supervision in their difficult task and taking into account that in extended families (often with six or more sibs), older children would be assisting in household work. He proposed that training manuals be produced and that three workers from the fields, respectively, of health, education, and social welfare from each district be trained together to implement the necessary training and supervision. The program was initiated on a countrywide scale in 1981–83. Much work was put into the exercise, but the initiative was never adopted as official policy, agreed jointly by all three ministries, and because of the fact that the three members of each team were responsible to different supervising authorities, the teams soon began to break up, while there was no clear locus of responsibility for sustaining the program.

The proposals that had been made in the 1977 recommendations were also not given any legal status, and developments in the last ten years have been on an ad hoc basis, relying upon the initiative of the Special Education Unit of the

Ministry of Education, with no effective input from the Ministry of Health. The establishment of a program offering a certificate for teachers of the handicapped has proved to be important, and it is now proposed to link the program with the university and award a degree. The most recent (1991) figures record 11,072 handicapped children registered with the Ministry of Education, of whom 16.2 percent are classed as having a "mental" handicap (others' handicaps being visual, physical, and hearing), with 683 special teachers, 21.4 percent being for the mentally handicapped, but including only three diplomates and one graduate. Of a total of 120 special schools and units, there are 3 special schools and 33 special education units within ordinary schools for those requiring special education. A few severely handicapped are admitted to the mental hospital, and the day center/school continues to operate under the aegis of the Ministry of Education, but there has been no further advance in policy.

The Mentally Ill and Substance Abuse

A description of the nature and extent of substance abuse has been given earlier. It needs to be stressed that most cannabis use is of brief duration, and psychological dependency is almost unknown; there are very few persons dependent upon other drugs; and the pattern of alcohol use does not lead to what might be termed "classical" alcohol dependence, except in a small proportion of drinkers. The manifestations of alcohol abuse most often seen in psychiatric practice are alcoholic hallucinosis and pellagra, and patients with both these conditions are admitted to ordinary hospital wards or to mental health units. Some persons who have become dependent upon alcohol are admitted to these units also, since there are no special facilities, and some patients are occasionally sent to other countries.

Because of the increased amount of trafficking of methaqualone and the occurrence of sporadic but very few cases of abuse of opium, Mandrax, and heroin, the previous government set up a Drug Enforcement Commission with a relatively large staff (about 100) engaged in enforcement operations and a unit concerned with education; it has been stated that the policy includes setting up facilities for detoxification and rehabilitation operating under the aegis of the commission. Since the Drug Enforcement Commission was set up by statute and hence is an official body, operating within the Ministry of Home Affairs (interior ministry), this must be taken as official policy, although there is increasing doubt as to whether supply reduction and demand reduction should be so closely linked. Most resources go into supply reduction, that is, enforcement activities. While the few addicts (dependent upon heroin, for example) belonging to the upper, economically very well off stratum of society rarely accept treatment in any mental health facility and may instead travel outside the country for treatment, there is no evidence of there having been sufficient need for any private detoxification unit to be set up. From the official point of view there is some doubt as to whether scarce resources should be invested in building special units at the present time, when the problem is so far not numerically a specially serious one. However, the action is setting up a commission at all contrasts with the earlier rejection of a cabinet paper proposing that a statutory commission on alcohol and drug abuse be set up, with the emphasis essentially upon alcohol abuse, which was seen at the time as a major problem in Zambia. Although drug abuse is by far the lesser problem, it attracts more concern from policy makers, while the needs of problem drinkers (say in industry) have so far been largely neglected. But alcohol-related problems and disabilities are seen more often in emergency rooms than in mental health units, and it is here that further attention will be directed, linked to workplace programs aimed at early detection of problem drinkers and swift action to guard against the establishment of more severe disabilities requiring intensive and extensive rehabilitative measures.

The Mentally Disordered Offender

There is no comprehensive forensic psychiatric service in Zambia. Although occasionally offenders who have committed less serious crimes such as causing malicious damage—say to a foreign diplomat's car—or special offenses such as defaming the president of the country, or more serious offenses such as committing violent sexual acts against small children are referred, the majority of those referred for examination are charged with murder. In the case of less serious offenses any medically qualified person may be asked to report on an offender in terms of the Criminal Procedure Code, and this examination may be ordered by a magistrate sitting in a lower court but is not ordered by assessors in the "traditional courts" that still operate in parallel with the system established in the colonial period. A separate section of this code allows an examination in order to determine an accused person's fitness to stand trial or make a defense. There were initially defects in this statutory law in that no provision was initially made for the trial to proceed in cases where rapid assumption of ability to stand trial was unlikely, and it was only when psychiatrists visiting prisons noted the presence of some persons who had been detained for very long periods without any determination of whether the accused had committed the crime that a change was made; the policy decision on this category of offender was initiated by the psychiatrist. The English M'Naghten rules have been incorporated in large part into statute law (in the Penal Code), and hence a defense on account of insanity exists and may be initiated by the defense or by the court itself, often when a question has arisen as to the accused's ability to stand trial.

Trials are usually conducted by a High Court judge sitting alone with no jury (although Zambia uses the British adversarial system), and the psychiatrist (usually only one) who has been ordered to examine the accused person, having submitted a report, made available to both defense and prosecution, may be called upon to give evidence. Since there are so few psychiatrists and since court hearings are held at main centers in all parts of Zambia, bringing a psychiatrist to court can cause actual disruption of provision of medical services, and hence the practice has arisen, when both defense and prosecution counsel agree, for the report to be accepted in absentia. Since most members of the public are unaware of the niceties of legal process, and in any case the admission of a medical report without cross-examination is usually of benefit to the accused, there has been no protest regarding a practice that is essentially undesirable. On a finding of "not guilty by reason of insanity" the patient is ordered to be detained during the president's pleasure, but may be released upon a medical recommendation, usually after a considerable period of detention.

While all those ordered to be examined may be accommodated at the special psychiatric hospital (males only), there is not space there for all who are being detained after trial, and these are usually accommodated in an ordinary prison, but specially designated for the purpose. Women are held in the ordinary ward of the Lusaka psychiatric hospital. Although Zambia's population has increased very greatly since independence, there has been hardly any increase in prison accommodation, and hence prisons are very overcrowded; but building such facilities in times of financial stringency tends to be of low priority. In like measure, there are no funds for extending forensic accommodation at the only psychiatric hospital or for building special units elsewhere.

Deinstitutionalization

Having had the advantage of developing its mental health service almost from scratch, Zambia has had the opportunity of not having to cope with the problem of institutionalization on any large scale. Since the psychiatrists resisted the idea of building more than the one moderate-sized national mental hospital and could say that they had no input into decisions regarding its design—indeed the poor design had led them to ask for an increase in size in order to have built open villa-type wards as well as the prisonlike building they initially found—the question of institutionalization could not arise except on a very small scale. The need for providing asylum for a small number of patients who could not otherwise care for themselves was dealt with by converting two former leprosaria that had formerly been built by church hospitals in remote parts of the country. Several small institutions (in effect, small villages) would have been best, so that patients could have been able to live not too far from their (linguistic and cultural) home areas; having only two of these villages so far has imposed some limitations either on who could be sent there, or on the degree of reintegration into the local community of patients who in many regards were foreigners. For the most severely incapacitated patients, however, this was not a major factor since they were in any case incapable of this degree of integration.

The organization of Zambia's highly community-oriented service has already been described, but far too little is known of its success or not from the point of view of formal studies. There have been no reports of changes in the prison populations, with a larger number of persons with psychiatric disorders being admitted. This is perhaps because there is already a tradition for the policy to bring anyone suspected to be mentally ill, or whom they know to be suffering from such an illness, to be nearest mental health facility rather than charging the person with an offense. Unfortunately, this often means that the patient has to be kept at the police station for a while, due to lack of transport. There has been an increase in the number of "vagrants" on the streets of major cities, but the speed of growth of the cities has to be remembered; in a recent survey in Lusaka, only 10 percent appeared to have any severe psychiatric disability. The survey was carried out by a church group in cooperation with members of the Mental Health Association of Zambia.

While the Mental Health Association, which has branches in most of Zambia's districts, has set up some community-based projects for helping the mentally ill, there is hardly any other specific service outside the sparse sprinkling of mental health workers operating at the community level from clinics and health centers. The question of the need for halfway houses, sheltered employment, and day hospitals has been examined. It is not possible to simply transplant Western institutions into third-world countries. Day hospitals are feasible when patients do not have to travel too far and public transport is adequate and inexpensive, or alternative transport can be provided. Unfortunately, these conditions largely do not apply even in Zambia's major towns, while the question of such care is not feasible in rural areas where basic services are widely spaced and the aim of government, for example, is to have no patient live more than 12 kilometers from the nearest health center. While sheltered employment may be possible in countries with advanced economies and nearly full employment, it becomes very difficult to justify (or finance) employment for the disabled in countries where there are no employment opportunities for the majority of the population. In rapidly expanding cities such as Lusaka, where so many have to live in substandard accommodation, the person finding himself in a halfway house that is at all decent is reluctant to move, and members of the extended family, already living in overcrowded conditions (this is one negative aspect of the extended family that is too little talked about), are unwilling to find a place for their fortunate relative. So far, in practice, we have found that fostering extended family links is the best strategy. But extended families are coming increasingly under pressure. The advent of AIDS and HIV infection has brought a new dimension to care, since so many families are being overstretched, both as they attempt to care for sick relatives at home and because they have to take on more and more orphaned children. The presence of AIDS, which in Zambia is beginning to strike at every family, is really beginning to test the theory of primary health care, as communities are faced with new challenges. Mental health aspects are not insignificant, and psychosocial counselling is proving to be an important component of care, especially that of patients with advanced disease living at home with their families. As will be discussed in more detail later, this type of care, using also community volunteers, brings into focus the question of having specially trained personnel in a vertical approach as compared with using generalists in a horizontal approach—a question as relevant for AIDS care as for mental health care.

Funding Issues

The question of funding for mental health care has already been indirectly alluded to in discussions of the policies for health care of the new government that came into power on November 1, 1991, after twenty-seven years of rule by the previous government under a one-party system. In the former system mental health care was entirely the responsibility of the central government in the guise of the Ministry of Health, and apart from provision for the one psychiatric hospital, other funding came from votes given to institutions where facilities were provided, to primary health care, and to staff as separate items. It is not possible, therefore, to give a comprehensive picture of expenditure on mental health care generally, let alone on specific groups such as the mentally ill, the mentally retarded, and so forth. The funds for financing the health services come largely from general revenues plus contributions from donors for specific projects, and the amount spent on health care provision amounts to less than five dollars per annum per capita.

Consumer Rights

It is not generally realized in Zambia how restrictive the laws are regarding those who have been adjudicated to be mentally ill. However, the most severe restrictions rarely apply in these days simply because hardly any patient is adjudicated under this law; the number is a mere handful compared with the thousands who are being brought for treatment. The law is less definite when it applies to a person who is detained, suspected of suffering from mental disorder. For example, there is no reference in the Mental Disorders Act to whether treatment may be given, and what form it might or might not take, but it is assumed that it may be given since the approved form of medical certificate required under the act inquires if any treatment has been given. This leaves open the question as to whether treatment may be given against the patient's will, and it has been assumed by some psychiatrists and other mental health workers that this is the case. Electroconvulsive therapy is given, for example, but usually after the patient's or a relative's informed consent. But large doses of phenothiazines and related drugs may be given to sedate a dangerous or destructive patient, and patients may be placed in ''seclusion'' rooms without seeking special consent.

There can be no doubt that human rights are better respected in the one mental hospital and major units than elsewhere because the staff are better aware of these rights and try to maintain an acceptable standard of practice. The mental hospital has a hospital advisory committee that is charged with looking after the welfare of all patients and listening in confidence to any complaints. In fact, all hospitals in Zambia are supposed to have similar committees, but few are really active, and even when they are, few give attention to the needs of the mental health unit and its patients at that particular hospital.

The situation is even worse for those detained in prison cells prior to being brought to a hospital or other health facility. An examination of police regulations showed that while funding was officially provided for feeding those held in detention and suspected of committing some offense, no funds were provided for suspected mentally ill persons; in consequence, some police officers refused to feed their charges. In theory, the period of detention should have been minimal, but transport problems sometimes made it otherwise. It may also be noted that where patients are held by the police, no separate accommodation is provided for them, and they have frequently been reported to have been beaten or otherwise abused by fellow inmates.

CONCLUSIONS AND DISCUSSION

In a sense the developmental path of the mental health service in Zambia was inevitable. With thinking in psychiatry moving toward community care and later with the promotion of the Alma Ata concept of primary health care, it was not difficult to convince health service administrators of what should and should not be done. There was in any case no other complex system already in place. The use of clinical officers was also in a sense inevitable in that no other form of training could have been easily offered; there was no nurse training when the program began, for the school system was producing few candidates for training as nurses outside Zambia. General clinical officers had already proved their worth, and something urgent needed to be done. The development of the service was initially largely in the hands of one man, the author of this chapter, who returned to Zambia after psychiatric training in 1963, just fifteen months after the mental hospital was opened, and has been involved in planning, development, and administration since then. In practice, the margins between policy, development, and administration were blurred, and I believe that this is often the case. Actions taken on the basis of long-term or even short-term necessity acquire the status of a policy and may be rationalized retrospectively. Yet this is not to say that definite policies, developed on the basis of an assessment of needs, did not exist, as has been illustrated in the preceding narrative.

A major problem has been that of both the conceptualization and practical application of the principle of the integration of mental health care (including prevention and rehabilitation) in a model of primary health care. Some publications on this process seem to suggest that general health workers can learn enough about psychiatry to make a major difference in three or four days of study (World Health Organization [WHO], 1984), yet at the same time it is often suggested that the reason for the success of traditional healers in many societies is their long apprenticeship into and understanding of the cultural milieu in which they practice. While it is admitted that the authors differentiate between serious mental illness ("easy to learn about") and subtle psychosocial problems, such conflicting statements do not help in developing services when the expertise of the mental health worker is at least by implication devalued. There is always a need for the underpinning of any service by more or less expert and highly experienced workers who feel that they belong to a continuum of learning and practice, who communicate easily with each other, and who establish and maintain standards of care. This core group will operate facilities that respond to the special needs of the mentally ill and provide not only practical care, but also an example of such care and guidance on how it can be implemented. In Zambia this component was developed first (rather like the leprosy or tuberculosis service), with some degree of separation from other components of health care; it was a vertical approach in which professional service provision was separated off to a greater or lesser extent from general health service provision. Even when mental health workers began to establish a more community-oriented approach, this still did not operate through the general health service, which initially had not in any case begun to think in these terms—those of primary health care. The PHC approach has a hierarchical structure that is supposed to be firmly rooted within the community. The degree of involvement of the community and of other sectors (such as social welfare and education) in health matters is a measure of the horizontal component; ideally, there should be an intermeshing in such a way as to meet various types of need. There can be many variants, depending upon factors as diverse as density of population and the prevalence of particular diseases; AIDS is a current and important example. Thus in planning the provision of mental health care it is necessary to ask, for instance, to what extent outpatient care should be an extension of hospital care and to what extent it should be transferred to the local general health workers; and how a further intermediary, say the local area trained mental health worker, might fit in.

The last question asked is important in the Zambian situation. While mental health care provided its own network with outreach into the community, without meshing with the general health care system it was evident that it would be inefficient. Yet introducing mental health care workers into the general system has exposed them to the danger of being swallowed by apparently more pressing needs. A schoolboy with the "brain-fag syndrome" is not presenting a life-and-death problem; a child with meningitis is. The mental health worker is often called to give more time to such urgent problems to the neglect of his proper function. It has been remarked that "nearly 26 years [after the inception of a mental health service it] has only achieved 15 percent coverage of the at-risk population in the country. Mental health workers have not been able to visit all the patients, police cells, prisons, schools, colleges, community leaders and service organizations in their community to follow up patients and to give mental health education respectively. . . . one explanation . . . is that mental health workers are working in general medical work"(Banda, 1988). This author goes on to recommend the training and utilization of polyvalent health workers as a solution to the problems he mentions. But are these real problems? It is unrealistic to think of mental health service provision in terms of the total coverage described, while the fact that mental health workers devote some part of their time to general work could be converted into an advantage if they can include a training and supportive function and demonstrate that all health problems include psychological and social components. The policy issue is that of establishing the range of duties to be expected of various workers and the means of ensuring that this policy is carried out by suitable supervision and other means of monitoring.

A final question: Has the input from the major international organizations been of value? The answer must be equivocal in the sense that many of the proposals made by visiting consultants appear to have been based more on current theory than on practical experience of implementation and evaluation. The World Health Organization might claim that it does try out its ideas practically, but an examination of the resources given to these experiments almost always demonstrates a quite unrealistic level of funding and personnel; how often have the experiments been followed up, some five or ten years later, when the research teams have left long before? WHO must be prepared to face this challenge. In Zambia's case we have had to implement our programs with minimal resources, looking occasionally with envy at neighboring countries where several million dollars have been made available from donor countries, and we have been pleased to see many of our ideas adopted elsewhere. This is not to say that we will not be happy to collaborate in further experiments, should some kind donor wish to join us, but we will insist upon our own ideas being given due consideration.

ACKNOWLEDGMENTS

Grateful acknowledgment is made for the help given by S. K. Chileshe, J. Mukupo, and P. Chita, members of the staff of the National Mental Health Resource Center, Lusaka.

REFERENCES

Banda, W. W. (1988). *Constraints affecting the administration of mental health services in Zambia*. Unpublished M.P.A. thesis, University of Zambia.

Federal Ministry of Health. (1960). *Federal Ministry of Health Annual Report*. Lusaka: Author.

Guiness, E. A. (1992). Patterns of mental illness in the early stages of urbanization. *British Journal of Psychiatry, 160*(suppl. 16), 4–72.

Haworth, A. (1980). Geography, demography, and mental health services. In A. Kiev, W. J. Muya, & N. Sartorius (Eds.), *The future of mental health services* (pp. 51–65). Amsterdam: Excerpta Medica.

Nunn, C. (1969). *Comments*. Lusaka: Ministry of Health.

Republic of Zambia. (1992). *National health policies and strategies*. Lusaka: Government of the Republic of Zambia, Planning Unit.

United Nations. (1978). *Primary health care: A joint report by the directors general of WHO and UNICEF*. Geneva: WHO.

World Health Organization. (1975). *Organization of mental health services in developing countries* (Technical Report Series 564). Geneva: WHO.

World Health Organization. (1984). *Mental health care in developing countries: A critical appraisal of research findings* (Technical Report Series 698). Geneva: WHO.

World Health Organization. (1990). *The introduction of a mental health component into primary health care*. Geneva: WHO.

Index

About the Contributors

MAX W. ABBOTT is Dean of the Faculty of Health Studies, Auckland Institute of Technology, and President of the World Federation for Mental Health. From 1981 to 1991 he was Director of the Mental Health Foundation of New Zealand. He is a ministerial appointee to the New Zealand Victims Task Force and has served on a variety of governmental, quasigovernmental, and national voluntary-sector organizations and advisory bodies. He has over eighty publications in various fields, including neuropsychology, addictions, health services, mental health, clinical and community psychology, and family sociology.

KUNIHIKO ASAI is Vice-Director, Psychiatrist, Medical Doctor, and Designated Physician of Mental Health of the Asai Hospital, Togane City, Chiba Prefecture, and Vice-President, World Federation for Mental Health (WFMH), Western Pacific Region. He is Councillor of the Japanese Society of Psychiatry and Neurology; Chairman of the Committee on Public Relations and Information of the Japanese Association of Psychiatric Hospitals; Councillor of the Japanese Association of Mental Health; Director of the Japanese Society of Mental Health; Member of the Psychiatric Review Board (Chiba Prefecture); and Secretary General, 1993 World Congress of the World Federation for Mental Health (Japan).

ROB V. BIJL is a sociologist with the research department of the Netherlands Institute of Mental Health (NcGv), Utrecht, the Netherlands. His scientific work concentrates on occupational incapacity due to mental disorders and psychiatric epidemiology. His dissertation subject was policy-oriented scenario research, applied to the field of mental health and mental health care.

MONICA BROWN is pursuing a doctoral program in clinical psychology at the University of Ottawa. Her present research interests are focused on the psychophysiological and structural correlates of adolescent schizophrenia. Her clinical interests include neuropsychological assessment and rehabilitation and family therapy.

ISMAIL CIFTER is Professor and Chairman of the Department of Psychiatry of the Medical School of Gazi University and correspondent member of the World Federation for Mental Health. He has many publications both in Turkish and English and is a member of many Turkish and international mental health associations. At present he is the Vice President of Gazi University.

CEZAR I. CÎMPEANU is with the VAMC at Brockton/West Roxbury, Massachusetts, a Harvard-affiliated program, where he has a four-year training residency in psychiatry. He has had numerous clinical clerkships in Romania and has worked as a general practitioner in Pantelimon near Bucharest. He was resident of psychiatry at the Clinical Hospital, Ghesrghe Marinescu, in Bucharest.

SERGIU DIACICOV is a psychiatrist in Bucharest.

SILVIA EVERS is working as a research worker at the department of Health Care Economics, University of Limburg, Masstricht, the Netherlands, where she is convening a cost-effectiveness study of the use of medication with schizophrenic patients. She has worked with the department of Epidemiology/Health Care Research of the same university.

MARTIN FAKIEL is a Resident in Psychiatry at the Albert Einstein College of medicine/Montefiore Medical Center, Bronx, New York.

ANGEL FIASCHE was appointed National Director of Mental Health of Argentina during President Carlos Menem's administration. He has also been Chairman of the Department of Psychiatry, Institute of Medical Research, University of Buenos Aires; and Director of Residency Training in Psychiatry and Inservice Training Education at Maimonides Medical Center, Brooklyn, New York. His many academic appointments include Associate Clinical Professor of Psychiatry at the State University of New York–Downstate Medical Center; Professor of Psychiatry of the School of Humanities at the University of La Plata, Buenos Aires, Argentina; Associate Professor of Psychiatry, University of Buenos Aires, School of Medicine; Professor Emeritus of the School of Humanities of the University of Parana, Entre Ríos, Argentina; and Professor of Psychiatry at the Department of Psychology and Psychopedagogy at the University of Gothenburg, Sweden. He has published extensively and has an international reputation as a lecturer.

ABRAHAM FISZBEIN is Chief Fellow in the Child and Adolescent Clinical Fellowship in Psychiatry at the Albert Einstein College of Medicine/Montefiore Medical Center, Bronx, New York, and a part-time Attending Psychiatrist at the Outpatient Mental Health Substance Abuse Services of the North Central Bronx Hospital. Until 1983 he was Coordinator of the Division of Adolescents of the Outpatient Department of Psychiatry of the Ezrah Jewish Hospital, Buenos Aires. He was Chief Resident at Albert Einstein College of Medicine, New York, and Head of Research and Training and Attending Psychiatrist at the Montefiore Medical Center, North Central Bronx Hospital Psychiatric Emergency Services. His academic appointments were Clinical Instructor of Pathologic Anatomy at the School of Medicine, University of Buenos Aires, and Assistant Professor of Psychiatry at the Albert Einstein College of Medicine. He has published and presented extensively in the area of schizophrenia and coauthored the PANSS (the Positive and Negative Syndrome Scale and Manual), a tool for the assessment of schizophrenic symptoms. This has been translated into fifteen languages and includes several training videotapes.

ROBERTO GHIRARDELLI is a specialist in psychiatry and clinical criminology and is the Director of the Community Health Center in Genova, Servizio di Salute Mentale of the Unita Sanitaria Locale XII.

NIGEL GOLDIE is Head of Strategic Planning, Development, and Inspectorate for the London Borough of Lambeth's Directorate of Social Services. He has taught and researched issues concerned with mental health, social policy, and health and illness at South Bank University in London.

AMY GORELICK is currently a Clinical Fellow in Geriatric Psychiatry at the Albert Einstein College of Medicine, Bronx, New York, where she was also Chief Resident. She has worked in both the private and public sectors of psychiatry in the United States as the Medical Director of the Anne Arundel County Mental Health Clinic at Annapolis, Maryland, and as an attending psychiatrist at both the Bronx Municipal Hospital Center and Our Lady of Mercy Medical Center in the Bronx. Her academic appointment was Instructor in Psychiatry at the Department of Psychiatry of the Albert Einstein College of Medicine. She is a Diplomate of the American Board of Psychiatry and Neurology in Psychiatry and has published work in the area of positive and negative symptoms in schizophrenia.

MEINDERT J. HAVEMAN is an Associate Professor at the Department of Epidemiology/Health Care Research at the University of Limburg, Maastricht, the Netherlands. From 1981 to 1986 he worked at the Chief Inspectorate for Mental Health (Ministry of Social Welfare, Health, and Cultural Affairs).

ALAN HAWORTH is a Professor and Head of the Department of Psychiatry in the University of Zambia School of Medicine. He worked in Zambia as a government psychiatrist from 1974 as a full-time member of the staff of the University of Zambia. Research interests have included work on the epidemiology of mental illness and of drug- and alcohol-related problems. He has visited countries in Africa and Southeast Asia as a WHO consultant on drug abuse and on mental health service development. His most recent consultancies have been in Myanmar, Afghanistan, and Liberia as well as in some of Zambia's neighbors. He is currently working on the development of counselling services for persons with HIV/AIDS.

CHRISTOPHER G. HUDSON is a Professor and Chair of the Master of Social Work Health/Mental Health Concentration at the School of Social Work, Salem State College, Salem, Massachusetts. His research interests include state mental health policy, community mental health administration, decision making, homelessness, and case management. Recent publications have appeared in *Social Work Research and Abstracts*, *Social Thought*, *Journal of Sociology and Social Welfare*, and the *Social Service Review*. Recently he edited *Dimensions of State Mental Health Policy* (Praeger, 1991).

S.T.C. ILECHUKWU is a Senior Lecturer and previous Acting Head of Department, College of Medicine, University of Lagos; Consultant Psychiatrist, Lagos University Teaching Hospital; Research Associate, Division of Social and Transcultural Psychiatry, McGill University; Associate Editor, *Nigeria Medical Journal*; and Editorial Advisor for *Transcultural Research Review*. He is a member of the draft Committee for the National Mental Health Policy for Nigeria and is well published in general and cultural aspects of psychiatry in Nigeria and Africa.

CURD M.V.W. JACOBS is with the research department of the Netherlands Institute of Mental Health (NcGv), Utrecht, the Netherlands. His main research subjects are psychiatric epidemiology and analysis of quantitative data on mental health care, patients as well as personnel, production, and costs.

DONNA R. KEMP is a Professor and Graduate Coordinator of political science and public administration at California State University, Chico. She previously worked as a planner and a program manager in health and other policy areas in the State of Idaho and has practiced marriage and family counselling in Idaho and California. Her research interests include health and mental health policy and public personnel. She was a Fulbright Fellow at the Mental Health Foundation of New Zealand in 1989–90. She has published two books, *Supplemental Compensation and Collective Bargaining* and *Employee Assistance Programs: An Annotated Bibliography*, as well as numerous articles in journals including *Mental Retardation*, *Public Administration Review*, *Public Personnel*, *New England Journal of Human Services*, *Journal of Mental Health Administration*, *California*

Mental Health Counselors Journal, and *Community Mental Health in New Zealand*.

CHEON BONG KIM is a Professor and Dean of Law and Public Administration at Jeon Ju University, Jeon Ju, Korea. His research interests include the management of social services, bureaucracy and comparative administration, Korean government and administration, and development administration for national integration of developing countries. In 1987 he was a visiting scholar at the University of Southern California, and during the summer semester 1988 he was a visiting professor at George Washington University. He has served as a Director of the doctoral program in public administration at the Policy Science Research Institute at Jeon Ju University. He serves on the council of the Korean Association for Public Administration and is a member of the International Institute of Administrative Sciences, the American Society for Public Administration, the International City Management Association, and the Academy of Political Science. He has published *Administrative Culture and Korean Government*.

CARL M. LAKASKI is Senior Consultant on community mental health with Health and Welfare, Canada. He has been a program evaluator at the Royal Ottawa Hospital, an independent research consultant under contract to the Ontario Ministry of Community and Social Services, a statistical analyst with the Canadian Centre for Justice Statistics, Acting Director of the Mental Health Division, Health and Welfare Canada, and concurrently the Editor-in-Chief of *Canada's Mental Health/Santé Mentale au Canada*, the quarterly journal of the department on mental health issues. Besides being a key contributor to *Mental Health for Canadians: Striking a Balance*, he has been a consultant in the development and production of *Mental Health Services in Canada, 1990* and the *Report of the National Task Force on Suicide in Canada*.

YU. I. LIBERMAN is Doctor of Medical Sciences and the leading research worker of the Psychiatric Network Department, Moscow. He studies the epidemiology of mental diseases. His main publications are devoted to the epidemiology of schizophrenia.

THOMAS J. LIPS is a consultant working with the Mental Health Division of Health and Welfare, Canada. Since 1981 he has edited *Canada's Mental Health/Santé Mentale au Canada*, a mutlidisciplinary, peer-reviewed, quarterly journal published by the department. He has a particular interest in psychogeriatric services and the mental health of elderly persons and has edited and/or contributed to several government publications in this area, most recently *Services to Elderly Residents with Mental Health Problems in Long-Term Care Facilities* (1990) and *Designing Facilities for People with Dementia* (1991).

MARCO LUSSETTI is a specialist in psychiatry and in biomedical statistics. He is working in a community mental health service in Genova, a day hospital of the Servizio di Salute Mentale of the Unita Sanitaria Locale XVI, and collaborating in the Psychiatric Case Register of the Liguria Region.

UNAIZA NIAZ is a consultant psychiatrist and Head of the Department of Psychiatry, Pakistan International Airlines. She is a member of the Expert Advisory Committee, College of Physicians and Surgeons Pakistan, a member of the World Federation for Mental Health, and Secretary General of the Pakistan Psychiatric Society. Her research interests include stress in aviation, state mental health policy, postgraduate education facilities, and psychiatric problems in women. She has several publications to her credit. Recent publications include articles in the *Specialist* (Pakistan), *British Journal of Psychiatry*, and *Psychological Medicine* (United Kingdom). She recently authored the book *A Caring Vision: Women and Children*.

OSAMA M. AL-RADI is the Director of the al-Radi Psychiatric Clinic in Taif. He was General Medical Director of the Taif Mental Hospital, 1962–1985, and Director General of Psychiatric Services of all inpatient and outpatient clinics in all general hospitals in Saudi Arabia. He is an organizer of mental health postgraduate and undergraduate education in Saudi Arabia. He is a committee member of the World Psychiatric Association representing the Middle East, a member of the Arab Psychiatric Association, President of the World Islamic Mental Health Association (WIMHA), Vice President of the Gulf Psychiatric Association, and a Life Member of the World Federation for Mental Health. His research has focused on rehabilitation of chronic schizophrenic patients, drug addiction, community therapy policy, pray therapy policy as a part of community therapy policy, Islamic psychiatry, the role of faith in dealing with addiction problems, the proposed Mental Health Act in Saudi Arabia, and Islamic (religious) group therapy. He is the author of numerous publications and professional papers.

V. G. ROTSTEIN is Doctor of Medical Sciences and Chief of the Epidemiologic Section of the Psychiatric Network Department, Moscow. He is engaged in research questions on mental disease epidemiology and psychiatric service organization. His main publications are devoted to clinical issues and epidemiology of paranoid schizophrenia and optimum models of mental health service.

LIZ SAYCE is Policy Director of MIND, the National Association for Mental Health. MIND works throughout England and Wales to promote mental health and to improve the quality of life of people with mental health problems. She has a background in social work and mental health research and has published work on a number of issues in British mental health policy, including community mental health centers, psychiatric case registers, and user involvement.

INDIRA SHARMA is Head of the Department of Psychiatry, Institute of Mental Sciences, Banaras Hindu University. She has twenty years of clinical and teaching experience. She was Vice-President of the Indian Psychiatric Society (IPS)–Central Zone, 1987–88, President of IPS–Central Zone, 1988–89, and Elected Member of the International Brain Research Organization in 1991. She organized the Fortieth Annual Conference of the Indian Psychiatric Society; served as editor of the *Indian Journal of Behavioural Sciences*; has been an Expert Member of the Board of Studies (Psychiatry) of Lucknow University, Gorakhpur University and Banaras Hindu University; and has been an M.D. and Ph.D. examiner of BHU and other universities. She has published over fifty articles in journals and two book chapters and has presented over thirty papers at national conferences.

YU-CUN SHEN is Professor and Director of the Institute of Mental Health, Beijing Medical University. Her professional and research interests are in psychiatry. She holds memberships in numerous professional societies, including Chair of WHO/Beijing Mental Health Collaborating Center for Research and Training and National Coordinator of WHO Mental Health Collaborative Activity with China. Her research includes studying the metabolism of neurotransmitters, related enzymes, and neuroendocrine in the mechanism underlying mental disorders (schizophrenia, depression, and MBD children); and pharmacokinetic study on blood levels of haloperidol and tricyclic antidepressant. She is the author of numerous publications, including six books and ninety-two articles.

L. S. SHEVCHENKO is a research worker at the Psychiatric Network Department, Moscow, and an economist. She studies economic problems of public health. Her main publications are devoted to mental health financing.

T. A. SOLOKHINA is Candidate of Medical Sciences and Chief of the Demography and Aging Section of the Psychiatric Network Department, Moscow. She studies questions of medicosocial consequences of mental diseases. Her main publications are devoted to the analysis of the work of psychiatric settings (hospitals, dispensaries, and so on) and economic and social consequences of mental diseases.

BOGDANA TUDORACHE is a psychiatrist in Bucharest.

M. E. VARTANYAN is an Academician of the Russian Academy of Medical Sciences, Director of the National Mental Health Research Center, member of the American Association of Behavior Genetics, member of Argentina's Psychiatric Society, member of the Czechoslovakian Society after Jan Purkinie, Assistant Chief of the Russian Academy of Medical Sciences' International Committee of the international movement Physicians Against War, and member of the Russian Presidium of the Russian Scientific Psychiatric Society. His main works are in the field of biological psychiatry, fundamental investigations in molecular genetics neuropharmacology, and mental health service organization. He is the author of more than 100 works in these areas.

BENJAMIN VICENTE is Assistant Professor, Department of Psychiatry and Mental Health, University of Concepción, Chile. He is also Head of the Mental Health Unit, Las Higueras Hospital, Talcahuano, Chile, and Vice President for South America of the World Federation for Mental Health.

MABEL VIELMA is Chief Psychiatrist of the Mental Health Unit, Navy Hospital, Talcahuano, Chile, and Psychiatrist, Mental Health Unit, Las Higueras Hospital, Talcahuano.

VALERIE WILMOT is the Consultant on Research for the Mental Health Division of Health and Welfare Canada. She has academic training in physiology, biochemistry, education, and behavioral sciences. She has been a researcher at the Montreal Neurological Institute, a policy analyst in the federal Ministry of State for Science and Technology, a program development officer with the National Health Research and Development Program, and a senior advisor in the Policy, Planning, and Information Branch of Health and Welfare Canada. Besides supervising the production of *Mental Health Services in Canada, 1990*, she performed similar functions for *Epidemiology on Mental Retardation*—the report of a special working group. She was principal organizer of the Canadian-sponsored International Conference on Promoting the Mental Health of Children and Youth and supervised production of its Proceedings. Recently she has served as a member of the Federal Centre for AIDS' Working Group on HIV infection and Mental Health.

V. S. YASTREBOV is Doctor of Medical Sciences and Chief of the Psychiatric Network Department, Moscow. He studies questions of mental health service organization. He is a specialist in the fields of psychiatric law and ethics and social problems in psychiatry and is author of more than fifty articles concerning these problems.

YAEL YISHAI is an Associate Professor at the Department of Political Science in the University of Haifa, Israel. She has published numerous books and articles on Israel's interest-group politics and health care policy.